THE TROUBLES

The Troubles

Ireland's Ordeal 1966–1996
and the Search for Peace

Tim Pat Coogan

ROBERTS RINEHART PUBLISHERS

Published in the United States by Roberts Rinehart Publishers,
5455 Spine Road, Boulder, Colorado 80301

Distributed by Publishers Group West

ISBN 1–57098–092–6

Library of Congress Catalog Card No 96–67091

Typeset in Times by Deltatype Ltd, Ellesmere Port

Printed in the United States of America

To all the peace-makers.

In particular, to President Bill Clinton, Fr Alec Reid, C.SS.R., Gerry Adams, John Hume, Jean Kennedy Smith, Senator Edward M Kennedy, Niall O'Dowd and Albert Reynolds

Strange Meeting

It seemed that out of battle I escaped
Down some profound dull tunnel, long since scooped
Through granites which titanic wars had groined.

Yet also there encumbered sleepers groaned,
Too fast in thought or death to be bestirred.
Then, as I probed them, one sprang up, and stared
With piteous recognition in fixed eyes,
Lifting distressful hands, as if to bless.
And by his smile, I knew that sullen hall, –
By his dead smile I knew we stood in Hell.

With a thousand pains that vision's face was grained;
Yet no blood reached there from the upper ground,
And no guns thumped, or down the flues made moan.
'Strange friend,' I said, 'here is no cause to mourn.'
'None,' said that other, 'save the undone years,
The hopelessness. Whatever hope is yours,
Was my life also; I went hunting wild
After the wildest beauty in the world,
Which lies not calm in eyes, or braided hair,
But mocks the steady running of the hour,
And if it grieves, grieves richlier than here.
For by my glee might many men have laughed,
And of my weeping something had been left,
Which must die now. I mean the truth untold,
The pity of war, the pity war distilled.
Now men will go content with what we spoiled,
Or, discontent, boil bloody, and be spilled.
They will be swift with swiftness of the tigress.
None will break ranks, though nations trek from progress.
Courage was mine, and I had mystery,

Wisdom was mine, and I had mastery:
To miss the march of this retreating world
Into vain citadels that are not walled.
Then, when much blood had clogged their chariot-wheels,
I would go up and wash them from sweet wells,
Even with truths that lie too deep for taint.
I would have poured my spirit without stint
But not through wounds; not on the cess of war.
Foreheads of men have bled where no wounds were.
I am the enemy you killed, my friend.
I knew you in this dark: for so you frowned
Yesterday through me as you jabbed and killed.
I parried; but my hands were loath and cold.
Let us sleep now . . .'

Wilfred Owen, killed in 1918 aged 25

CONTENTS

ILLUSTRATIONS

ACKNOWLEDGEMENTS

I WOULD PARTICULARLY LIKE TO THANK John O'Mahony for his kindness in reading the proofs of this book with his customary knowledgeable thoroughness; my editor, Tony Whittome, an enabling and scholarly man, for his assistance, particularly in the final, frenetic stages of production; and my daughters Jackie and Thomond and my son Tom.

I must also thank several people who gave generously of both their time and insights during the research stage: Albert Reynolds, Jean Kennedy Smith, Niall O'Dowd, John Hume, Austin Currie, Lords Callaghan and Whitelaw, Sir Frank Cooper, Garret FitzGerald, Sir Robert Armstrong, Merlyn Rees, General Glover, Sir Anthony Farrar-Hockley, Charles Haughey, Gerry Adams, Roy Bradford, Dermot Nally, Robert Fisk, Nigel Wade, John Ware, Peter Taylor, Roger Bolton, Rita O'Hare, Jim Gibney, Sean O'hUiginn, Dr Martin Mansergh, Michael Farrell, Brendan Scannell and Martin Dillon, who turned over to me a priceless set of interviews which he had conducted with many of the main players in the drama of Northern Ireland.

To the many others who must remain anonymous because of the duress of the circumstances I also offer my sincere thanks.

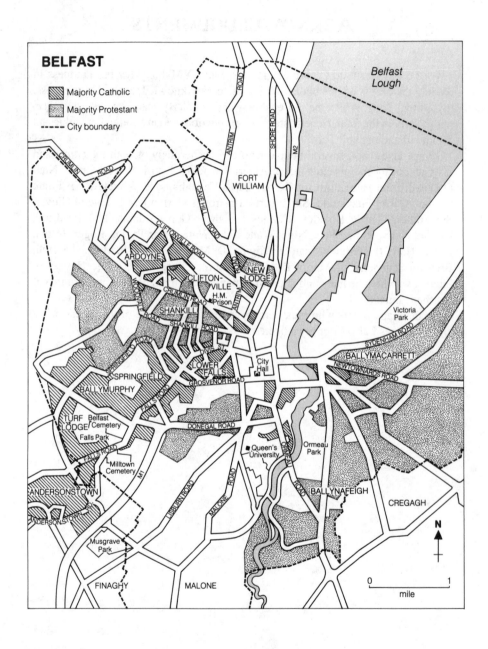

PREFACE

TO WRITE ABOUT such a volatile and complex relationship as the Anglo-Irish one, and especially about its bloody spin-off in Northern Ireland, is by definition a fraught and uncertain business. But the laws of hospitality and of 'off-the-record' briefings also contribute to a writer's frustrations. Would that I were free to reveal such matters as the name of a well-known priest who once went to the IRA Army Council and asked that the IRA assassinate Paisley; or the name of the former British Secretary of State for Northern Ireland who thinks the troops should be withdrawn; to say nothing of the Irish Cabinet Minister who thought that 'had Brighton succeeded, it would have been greater than 1916'. Such revelations go a long way towards illustrating the real attitudes of people concerned with 'the Troubles'.

However that kind of disclosure is but peripheral to what I have been driven by my researches to conclude are the real obstacles to a guaranteed peace in Ireland. Before describing these obstacles, I freely acknowledge that any value judgement is likely to be hailed as prejudice, and any prediction may be overtaken by events. But it appeared undeniable, as this book was gestating in 1993 and early 1994, that new and hopeful thinking was making itself felt in Belfast, Dublin, London, and, significantly, in Washington. The dreamers of dreams, the men and women who substituted the vibrant 'Why not?' in place of the mere dun 'Why?' appeared to have won a far fierce hour and sweet. Following a communiqué of great portent issued from Downing Street by the British and Irish leaders, John Major and Albert Reynolds, on 15 December 1993, the IRA declared a ceasefire on 31 August 1994. The vision of the hopeful appeared to be underpinned when a loyalist paramilitary ceasefire followed.

Throughout Ireland, and in the media of the world, euphoria prevailed. The Berlin Wall was down, Mandela was free, perhaps the unthinkable could be thought: maybe peace was coming to Ireland too. Unprecedented images filled the mind. As the Irish Government relaxed its broadcasting ban, Gerry Adams, Martin McGuinness and other Sinn Fein spokesmen could be seen on television. Albert Reynolds, the Irish Taoiseach, received at Government Buildings two of the peace-brokers, Gerry Adams and John Hume, the leader of the Northern Ireland's Constitutional Nationalist party, the SDLP. For some Republican prisoners the Republic's jail gates flew open. Dublin Castle, long the symbol of oppressive British rule in Ireland, was also thrown open – to a Forum on Peace and Reconciliation. Two of the fairest and most derided Irish gods, Enthusiasm and Optimism, smiled on their devotees.

But in the bowels of the gods' dark counterparts, Expediency and Prejudice, resentment and resistance stirred. One expected, as a given, that the brazen-voiced and the disturbing of Northern Ireland, such as Ian Paisley, would oppose any step towards ending the strife as a 'sell-out', if it involved Dublin. And so indeed it proved. Both communiqué and ceasefire were denounced, loudly and continuously, as a 'dirty deal' by Paisley and his cohorts. As readers will see for themselves in the final chapter of this book, there was in fact no 'deal'. Multi-channelled and often conflicting currents of circumstances and personalities had flowed, or been painstakingly canalised into, a confluence.

But what few expected (apart from those infected with the virus of anti-British feeling, which is inevitably part of Britain's sojourn in Ireland) was that the British Government would also become a major retarding factor in the situation. For, after concluding the Downing Street Declaration, John Major's position worsened so badly that, although his personal commitment to the Irish issue remained high, it is said that fear of the interaction between his 'Euro-sceptic' wing and the Unionist MPs from Northern Ireland, who sit at Westminster, caused him to stall rather than advance the peace process.

The Downing Street Declaration had promised that if the violence ceased, then the way would be open for Sinn Fein to 'join in dialogue in due course between the Governments and the political parties on the way ahead'.[1] The promise was not kept. Instead fresh conditions were imposed, conditions which had never been mentioned either in the formal Downing Street negotiations or in the secret British–Sinn Fein talks described within. 'De-commissioning' for example, the demand that the IRA give up their weapons in advance of talks. In marked contrast with the approach of the Dublin Government, the British did not move to free prisoners, but instead indicated that they were using them as hostages, to gain leverage in the 'de-commissioning' argument.

Instead of regarding the Americans, or Gerry Adams for that matter, as partners in a joint search for peace, the British, through the Foreign Office and the Northern Ireland Office, mounted a ferocious campaign, first to keep Adams out of the US altogether, then to prevent him from being received at the White House. The intensity of this diplomatic offensive may be gauged from the fact that, when it failed, John Major refused to pick up the telephone to answer President Clinton's calls. The decision in July 1995 to release the paratrooper Private Lee Clegg, who was serving a life sentence for the murder of a Belfast teenage joy-rider, within the octave of the traditionally perfervid 'marching season' in Northern Ireland, made this bad situation worse. Clegg's release was occasioned not by any considerations of justice but by the exigencies of John Major's leadership struggle.

It may be that history will show the release to have had an ultimately beneficial effect, in the sense that it, and other palliative gestures to the Tory Right, may have helped to secure Mr Major in the saddle, and in a position to resume progress towards a lasting peace in Ireland. But by the end of the marching month following 12 July 1995, it had to be acknowledged that the use of both police baton and petrol bomb had made their reappearance in Belfast for the first time since the IRA ceasefire. Talk of ultimata, and setting deadlines for either a commencement of talks or a resumption of war was common. The events of the ceasefire-shattering bombings in London in February 1996 proved that these fears were justified.

Just as a blade of grass can deflect a speeding bullet, so can a fragile peace process be deflected. To succeed, the process needs two things, momentum and reconciliation. So far it has received both from Dublin and Washington. But the peace partner with the greatest amount of initiative in its grasp, the British Government, is proving curmudgeonly and unimaginative. A window of opportunity, unequalled in the history of the Anglo-Irish relationship, is not being opened with anything like the flair, imagination and generosity that is called for. It is my hope that this book will do something to jolt both consciences - and momentum.

Tim Pat Coogan
Glenageary, Co. Dublin
8 March 1996

INTRODUCTION

ISLANDS AT WAR

THE CONDITION OF affairs suggested by the term 'the Irish Troubles' was already some three centuries old when Columbus discovered America. A degree of strife between the inhabitants of the islands of what now constitute Ireland and the United Kingdom existed long before the discovery. For example, St Patrick, whom legend has established as the Irish National Apostle, was a Briton brought to Ireland, supposedly in 432, by Irish pirates after one of their frequent forays against the neighbouring isle. But in our day the 'Irish Troubles' are generally understood to refer to a murderous dispute which, for the past quarter of a century only, has come to involve the English and the Irish in a sectarian quarrel in the north-eastern part of Ireland commonly, but erroneously, referred to as 'Ulster'. Like many stereotypical depictions of the Anglo-Irish relationship, depending for their coloration on considerations such as whether they are Irish or English, Nationalist or Loyalist, the varying calculations as to when and how the Troubles began contain both truth and distortion.

The tragedy of the last twenty-five years did come upon the two islands both gradually and suddenly – like bankruptcy. In fact, as we shall see, in a very real sense there was a bankruptcy, of policy, which led to the Troubles bursting upon an unsuspecting population with appalling suddenness. But the Irish agony had been building up slowly also, rooted in complex factors, one of which, geography, pre-dates the dawn of history: others involve the outworkings of two forms of colonialism, those of Mother Church and Mother England.

Geography has decreed that Ireland's head almost nestles on Scotland's shoulder, being separated by only some twelve miles of water between the Antrim coast and the Mull of Kintyre. And while her buttocks, the south-eastern coasts of Wexford and Waterford, are further removed, they are still no more than eighty miles from the coast of Wales. It was in this area that the first serious Norman penetrations occurred during the late 1160s. To the physical force school of Irish nationalism the Norman coming is generally regarded as the starting point for 'eight hundred years of British oppression'. The Norman invasion, and what preceded and followed it, requires a more complex interpretation than that, but it does provide a most important signpost to the present 'Troubles'.

By the time the Normans arrived, geography had dictated that the two islands had both shared and escaped great events together. The Romans conquered England but, having looked across the turbulent Irish Sea and weighed up the difficulties of subduing the equally tempestuous inhabitants of the then thickly

1

forested isle to the west, decided not to attempt to extend their imperium to Ireland. Insularity therefore ensured that, unlike its neighbour, Ireland did not become influenced by Roman laws and culture or, for some centuries, by significant changes in living patterns such as the development of cities. These only began to sprout after the arrival of the Vikings in the ninth century, long after the Roman legions had vanished. Gaelic society continued to be centred on cattle rearing, rather than on tillage.

But indicators such as the near-Pharaonic knowledge of mathematics and building skills needed to construct huge tombs, like that at Newgrange in Co. Meath, or the survival of skilfully worked golden artefacts suggest that Ireland had achieved high levels of learning and wealth long before the coming of Christianity. It was the subsequent concentration of wealth – generated by the learning – in the monasteries which first attracted the Vikings to the country. The power of the Vikings was broken in 1014 at the battle of Clontarf, in which armies of the provinces of Connacht and Munster, under Brian Boru, defeated those of Leinster, under King Maelmordha, for the high-kingship of Ireland. Viking contingents fought on both sides, but the destruction of Maelmordha's forces also entailed breaking the grip of the Norse King Sitric on Dublin, which because of its fleets and anchorage facilities had effectively grown into the commercial and political capital of the country. Thereafter pockets of Norse influence remained throughout the country, notably at Wexford and Waterford, but the dominant influence became Gaelic once more.

Although Irish cultural achievement was considerable, the achievement lay, and continued to lie, against a different religious backdrop to that occurring in England. As far back as the Synod of Whitby, in the seventh century, Anglo-Saxon monks, inspired by the teachings of Rome, had successfully led the charge against Irish practices which had established themselves not only in Ireland but throughout Northumbria. Unlike the Roman custom of leaving the skull bare, surrounded by a fringe of hair, the Irish monks tonsured themselves at the front. They also calculated Easter as occurring on a different date to that favoured by their Roman-influenced counterparts.

By the time of the Norman invasion of Ireland in 1169 the effect of such controversies had been heightened and added to by reports that Irish Christianity had wandered into barbarity, far from the path aspired to by the Gregorian reformers favoured by Rome. Geography, with its consequential virtually unbroken Celtic tradition in matters social and cultural, had resulted in the growth of marked incompatibilities between the Celtic and Latin churches. These, as the distinguished historian Dr F. X. Martin has noted, 'found expression in attitudes towards marriage, celibacy of the clergy, baptism and the sacramental system, control of church lands'.[1] Where the question of control was concerned it should be noted that Celtic usage had resulted in great abbeys frequently passing into the hands of powerful families whose appointees exercised far greater 'clout' than did the bishops appointed by Rome.

It did not matter that the Irish also possessed a distinctive and highly developed religious tradition renowned for both its scholarship and its missionary zeal, to a

2

degree that caused Thomas Cahill to claim that the Irish 'saved civilisation'. As Cahill points out:

> Without the zeal of the Irish Monks, who single-handedly refounded civilisation throughout the continent in the bays and valleys of their exile, the world that came after them would have been an entirely different one – a world without books. And our own world would never have come to be.[2]

Cahill is supported in his evaluation of the Irish contribution by another independent authority who judged that:

> The travels and settlement of Irish monks and scholars on the Continent of Europe, that complex movement of expansion . . . is one of the most important cultural phenomena of the early Middle Ages. There is nothing in pre-Carolingian Europe that could match it in either extent or lasting effect. In Northern France and Burgundy, in the territories of modern Switzerland, Northern Italy, in the Rhine Valley, in Franconia, in Bavaria and in the Salzburg area, the Scotti, as the Irish were called until the eleventh century, have left their traces. They were as famous for their learning as they were for their religious zeal and for the rigour of their monastic rules, no less known was their wrangling spirit, which involved them in many a controversy. Even in the Carolingian Empire they played an important role, which was not always to the liking of their continental colleagues.[3]

It was certainly not to the liking of their neighbouring colleagues. When the time became opportune, Anglo-Norman statecraft and Vatican geopolitics would act in concert to further Anglo-Norman imperialism at the expense of the Irish. As a result of direct anti-Irish lobbying with Pope Adrian IV, an Englishman, by his compatriot, the celebrated philosopher and clerical diplomat John of Salisbury, Salisbury was later able to write with accuracy: 'In response to my petition the Pope granted and donated Ireland to the illustrious king of England, Henry . . .'[4]

Thus was papal policy towards Ireland set. Adrian's plans for the Irish were carried forward by his successor, Pope Alexander III. Despite the fact that Henry II was out of favour with the papacy, because of the murder of Thomas à Becket, the Pope issued the King with letters ordering the Irish to be subject to him. But this confabulation between Christ and Caesar required one more ingredient for success. It was to be forthcoming from Ireland. One of the ironies of history is that Salisbury's initiative on behalf of Anglo-Norman imperialism was given its final successful impetus by an Irishman, Diarmuid MacMurchada, King of Leinster, who invited the help of Henry II in putting down his local enemies. After much parleying and delay a party of Norman knights and their followers arrived on the Wexford coast in 1169, capturing the major cites in the area, Waterford and Wexford, and eventually gaining control of Dublin. In return for his support of MacMurchada, the Norman knight Richard FitzGilbert – or Strongbow, as he is better remembered in Ireland – was given MacMurchada's daughter, Aoife, in marriage and succeeded him as King of Leinster.

MacMurchada to this day is execrated by some in Ireland for thus initiating both the 'eight hundred years of British oppression' and its corollary, 'The Full National Demand' of later generations of Irish nationalists. The Demand, which the IRA are still making as this is being written, is that the British presence be removed and Ireland be ruled by the Irish. MacMurchada was in fact probably not a great deal bloodier, nor more treacherous, than other leaders of the period, merely more innovative and far-seeing. For example, he secured the position of abbess of a great convent in Co. Kildare for a female relative by having his soldiers abduct and rape the existing abbess. As the post could only be held by a virgin, the rape debarred her from continuing. In one sense there was ample precedent for MacMurchada's Norman initiative: previous Irish kings had made copious use of Viking mercenaries in their incessant wars.

The difference was that the Normans would not so much assist Irish kings as supplant them. Henceforth the King of England considered himself the King of Ireland. Norman methods of warfare, involving chain mail, the use of cavalry and the building of castles, devastated the lightly armed Irish foot soldiers. There was not only a clash of culture, but of agriculture. Norman expertise furthered tillage to the disadvantage of the semi-nomadic, cattle-herding natives. And, more lastingly, the Normans' arrival henceforth meant that what happened in, or to, England affected Ireland, and vice versa. However, though Ireland lay too close to England for independence, unlike the other Celtic regions of Wales and Scotland, she lay just too far away for complete conquest. Though successive British kings and generals arrived in Ireland imbued with the same attitude towards the natives as that displayed by the whites towards the aborigines of both Australia and North America, insurgency – be it of native origin, or in concert with some enemy of hers, Spain or France – continued throughout the centuries to be a problem for England. Off her western approaches there now lay a green Cuba.

The underlying military policy used to address that problem is concealed in a famous, deceptively innocent, couplet commemorating an incident which occurred at a creek near Waterford the year after the first Norman party landed at Wexford:

> At the creek of Baginbun
> Ireland was lost and won.

Here some hundred Anglo-Normans defeated roughly ten times that number of Norse and Irish, taking seventy of them prisoner. By way of terrorising those who would oppose the invaders and their ally, MacMurchada, these had their limbs broken and were then beheaded and their bodies thrown over the cliffs. And so it continued through the ages and the monarchies: the Tudors, Stuarts, Cromwell, William of Orange. The English throne continued with varying degrees of success to exert its influence in Ireland, through making invasions and settlements, the difficulties posed by geography and terrain being partially compensated for by the Irish tendency to either feud amongst themselves, or follow Diarmuid MacMurchada's example of entering into alliance with the outsiders. While all this meant that it was generally the native Irish who went over the cliffs, there were a number of other consequences.

To begin with, as the Irish normally came off second best in set-piece military encounters, and did far better when they used the tactic of employing the bogs and forests to harry and hide, a tradition of guerrilla warfare entered Irish folklore to emerge finally with a degree of success in the early part of the twentieth century. Secondly, the Reformation gave a new religious coloration to the pursuit of imperial aims, the Irish, including the 'old Irish', as the descendants of the original settlers became known, continuing faithful to Rome, whereas the Crown forces were Protestant. This distinction became particularly significant for our day during the rule of James I. He added to the pro-Protestant policies of the Tudors, and their resultant slaughter, by 'planting' six of the north-eastern counties of Ulster, in the process creating the new county of Londonderry around the hinterland of the ancient settlement of Derry. The plantation involved settling both English colonists and Scottish Presbyterians and Episcopalians on confiscated Irish lands. The planters with the biggest holdings, known as Undertakers, were forbidden to have Irish tenants. Smaller estate holders, known as Servitors, were permitted to take Irish tenants but, if they did so, their rents were increased. The planters' descendants still live in the area, some of them as keenly aware of the dangers, real or imagined, posed by their Catholic neighbours as were their ancestors during the periods of ferocious warfare involving Protestants and Catholics which ensued throughout the seventeenth century.

The massacres by Catholics of Protestants, which occurred in the religious wars of the 1640s, were magnified for propagandist purposes to justify Cromwell's subsequent genocide. In a very Irish fashion the Williamite wars – and one battle in particular, that of the Boyne, in 1690 – which followed the butcheries of Cromwell and his generals have been thoroughly misrepresented subsequently for contemporary political purposes. The leitmotif of today's Orangeman, emblazoned on banner and gable end, is the image of his icon, William of Orange, armoured, mounted on a white charger, sword aloft, as he leads the Protestant forces to victory. In the words of a famous Orange song, he 'fought for the freedom of religion . . . on the green grassy slopes of the Boyne'.

In fact William was fighting for the English crown against his rival James II as part of a far wider European campaign in which the Pope was opposed to Louis XIV and his allies and supported a coalition which included William of Orange. The papacy was thus on the side of the Protestant William, not the Catholic James. On learning of William's victory the Pope was so delighted that he arranged for the celebration of a Pontifical High Mass in Rome and ordered a Te Deum and the ringing of church bells.

Despite the Pope's exultation, William's victory meant that Irish Catholics had cause to mourn, not celebrate. A factor which frequently bedevilled Irish affairs, and which, as we shall see, re-entered the scene yet again in the post-1968 period in manner both decisive and malign, now re-emerged: the attitude of the dominant Protestants. An enlightened ruler, William had successfully concluded his campaign at Limerick by negotiating a reasonable treaty – by the standards of the time – and sailed off to his wider European theatre leaving the treaty's administration in the hands of the victorious Protestant settlers who had fought alongside him. To them the term 'Catholic' equalled 'treacherous', and they interpreted the treaty not in terms of equity, but as a means of ensuring Protestant ascendancy.

The effects of the penal laws further depressed Catholics, making it nearly impossible for them to own property, receive an education, or enter the professions without renouncing their religion. The penal laws bore severely on English Catholics also, but the difference between the Irish and the English Catholics was that in Ireland the laws were used as a means of subjugating a race as much as a religion.

Edmund Burke described the penal code as a

> machine of wise and elaborate contrivance and as well fitted for the oppression, impoverishment and degradation of a people, and the debasement in them of human nature itself, as ever proceeded from the perverted ingenuity of man.

The effect of these laws on the swelling Irish underclass was brought home to me by two chance conversations conducted many years apart and on different sides of the globe, in Seoul and in London. The London encounter was between myself and an Irish professor of history who was describing a recent tour of old English farmhouses. 'You know,' he said, 'I have always thought of myself as an Anglophile, but it came home to me, looking at ordinary artefacts, I'm not talking about grand stuff that you'd see in castles, but dishes, knives, forks, jugs, plates, things like that that have survived from as far back as the sixteenth century, how little of that sort of thing exists in Ireland – and the reason. Just when people would be getting a little prosperity, every fifty years or so there'd be some new devastation and they'd be pounded back into the slime.'

The other observation came from a Korean presidential adviser who had been Korean ambassador to Washington. I commented on his impressive knowledge of the poet Yeats and he told me that his initial interest in Irish culture had come about because the Japanese used English colonial practice in Ireland as a headline for their own policy in Korea: extirpation of native culture, systems of land-holding, and inculcation of feelings of inferiority where things like language and traditional dress were concerned. It was an unexpected and telling illustration of the reasons why a nineteenth-century Irish school text instructed the learner to be thankful because he or she was a 'happy English child'.

London regarded the Protestant settlers in Ireland not merely as members of the favoured Church but as bulwarks of the Crown. For example, during the 1770s forces raised amongst northern Protestants were used to put down Catholic peasant agitation in the south. Against this backdrop, in 1762 the English Government intervened to abort a scheme, promoted by a Colonel Alexander McNutt, to populate Nova Scotia with Ulster Protestants. Hardy, self-reliant, and, unlike their dispossessed Catholic counterparts, generally possessed of a trade, money, and a woman kinswoman, be it sister or spouse, the Ulster planters were ideally suitable for dealing with the challenges of Canada's lonely opportunities. Accordingly the scheme was at first given official backing, but on further investigation a government committee vetoed it in fright at the prospect that it might lead to 'depopulation of Protestant communities in Ireland'.[5] It is idle, but nevertheless beguiling, to speculate that, had it not done so, there might be no 'Ulster Troubles' today.

However, arguably, as the century closed, it was the Protestants who had given London most pause for thought. As the flag of revolution was unfurled in America and France, the Protestant ruling class set up their volunteer force, in 1782, ostensibly to defend Ireland from any foe. The strength of the Irish Volunteers forced the British to agree to the setting-up of a parliament in Dublin the following year. It was of course subservient to the House of Commons and, like the Volunteers, dominated by the landowning Protestant Ascendancy, chiefly Anglicans or Church of Ireland. The Anglicans looked with disfavour on one section of Protestantism, almost with as much disfavour as they did Catholics. These were the Presbyterian Dissenters in the north of Ireland, who also suffered a certain amount of disability under the law, thereby encouraging some of them to make common cause with the Catholics. However, the concerns the Dublin parliament addressed, with varying degrees of success, were the concerns of Ireland: the destruction of the Irish woollen trade in favour of Britain's; edicts forcing Irish merchants to sell their produce to England, not its colonies; the evils of absentee landlordism; and, significantly, defence. Moreover, the mere existence of a parliament in Dublin served to concentrate the wealthy, decision-taking echelon of the country in the capital so that the arts, commerce, and social life flourished. A Catholic middle class emerged.

In a sense the British rulers were back where Henry II had found himself when his knights invaded Ireland in the first place, back in 1169. The knights had speedily grown so powerful that the King had to come to Ireland at the head of an army to take personal control of the developing situation. Now, five hundred years on, the government in London felt an equal compulsion to take control of events in Ireland, but by different methods. For at the same time the Catholics, their eyes also fixed on what was happening abroad, came to be organised into a secret, oath-bound society, the United Irishmen, founded by middle-class Protestants. The aim of the United Irishmen was to unite Catholics, Protestants and Dissenters in setting up an Irish republic which would separate from England.

In the same year, 1795, following a sanguinary skirmish between Catholics and Protestants at Loughgall in Co. Armagh, another important society was founded in the ranks of the Catholics' opponents. The Orange Society, which swiftly became the Orange Order, held its first Twelfth of July demonstration the following year, 1796. To this day the Order is a powerful political and economic force in Northern Ireland. Also in that year, one of the United Irishmen's principal leaders, Theobald Wolfe Tone, a Protestant, generally regarded as the father of Irish republicanism, made contact with the Directory in Paris with a view to acquiring arms and soldiers with which to put teeth into the United Irishmen's doctrines.

The country was in such a state of turmoil that one peer, Lord Moira, told the House of Lords that Ireland existed in 'the most disgusting tyranny that any nation ever groaned under . . . creating universal discontent and hatred of the English name'. A principal source of the opprobrium attaching to things English was the behaviour of the British Army, whose members were frequently forcibly billeted on unwilling Catholics. Its commander-in-chief, General Abercrombie, issued a famous general order which described the army as being 'in a state of licentiousness which must render it formidable to everyone but the enemy'. Not surprisingly, Abercrombie subsequently resigned. He was replaced by General Gerard Lake, whose prescription for dealing with the state of rebellion which broke out, or was provoked, in that blood-drenched year of 1798 was: 'take no prisoners'.

Suffice it to say that between the enforcement of Lake's order, by both regular troops and Protestant militia, and the sometimes savage reaction to it by Catholic insurgents, the 1798 rebellion fully lived up to the traditions of frightfulness established with such frequency over the previous centuries. It is the aftermath of the rebellion which concerns us. The rebellion itself, and in particular the capture of Wolfe Tone and a part of the French fleet which he was bringing to Ireland, gave the British a pretext for proroguing the Irish parliament. By the Act of Union of 1800, it was amalgamated with the British parliament. Gladstone later said of the bribery and intimidation which secured the Irish votes necessary for the passing of the Act that there was 'no blacker or fouler transaction in the history of man'. The parliament had represented the interests of some half a million Anglo-Irish Protestants, the Ascendancy as they were known, not the other three million who inhabited the island. The latter were Catholics whose voice counted for little or nothing. Nevertheless, the Anglo-Irish representation did have Irish interests at heart, and it took a massive exercise in bribery and coercion to secure the 162 votes (out of a total of 303) by which the Union passed. Instead of representing their constituents and legislating for themselves in Dublin, Irish parliamentarians, some one hundred in all, henceforth had to travel to London where they were in effect rendered impotent through being subsumed into an assembly approximately 650 strong. The seventeen MPs who are today returned from Northern Ireland owe their positions to the Act of 1800.

But before we come to the events which reduced the Irish representation at Westminster by over 80 per cent, it is necessary to examine briefly what happened in Ireland after the Union. Economically Dublin began to decay as the centre of power shifted to London and society went with it. Bereft of their patrons, both arts and crafts entered upon a period of prolonged decline. Throughout the country the scourge of absentee landlordism grew more pronounced. Too often London lifestyles came to be maintained by the subdivision of holdings into ever more numerous, and therefore smaller, rent-producing units. One consequence of the attempt to maximise yields from smallholdings was the reliance on the potato which created the great famine of the 1840s. I say 'great famine' advisedly, because in fact fertile Ireland had been afflicted by some ten other serious famines, accompanied by war, pestilence and starvation to the death, in the previous five hundred years.[6] One of the landmarks of Ireland is the Obelisk standing atop of Killiney Hill, overlooking Dublin Bay. It was erected as a relief work during a famine which occurred one hundred years before the major nineteenth-century famine.

Unlike many of its predecessors this famine was not attributable to war, or invasion, but to crop failure. It was clearly foreseeable as there had been lesser potato crop failures on fourteen occasions between 1816 and 1842. But the system of administration was so inefficient and so geared to the interests of the Protestant Ascendancy that nothing was done.

An assimilative, energetic race like the Irish could not be completely subjugated, of course. Catholics found loopholes in the penal laws to slip into positions of some prosperity in trade and commerce. A certain leniency in the entry regulations to the legal profession, combined with the availability of education on the Continent for those who could afford it, produced a number of successful Catholic lawyers, of whom the most eminent was Daniel O'Connell. To paraphrase Joyce, it became possible for some Irish Catholics to achieve a relatively prosperous domicile by silence and cunning. But, particularly in the west and north-west, the general position of the Irish peasants was one of near helotry, living out their lives in conditions of poverty and disease which objective English observers adjudged unfit even for the rearing of animals. Fear of famine was the great underlying political reality of peasant Ireland.

Sex being one of the few outlets from their wretchedness, the Catholic peasantry produced children in such numbers that not even the virulent fevers of the time could prevent a population explosion which the failure of the potato crop in the 1840s turned into a nightmare.

However, while the Act of Union stunted the political and economic growth of Irish Catholics, it had the opposite effect on their Church and its clergy. Rome was not unmindful of the merits of being brought more closely into the orbit of a great imperial power and at the same time gaining a powerful bulwark against the spread of godless French republicanism. Symbolically enough, the year which saw the formation of both the United Irishmen and the Orange Order also saw the opening of the great Catholic seminary, St Patrick's, at Maynooth, Co. Kildare. The British allowed this substantial relaxation of the penal laws largely on the basis that it was cheaper to fund Maynooth professorships than to pay Crown prosecutors. They got value for their money, with the natural conservatism of the Church and its abhorrence of secret societies being continuously deployed against Irish revolutionary forces.

The greatest mass movement to emerge in the country following the Union was Daniel O'Connell's campaign for Catholic emancipation. Emancipation was finally conceded in 1829. This was followed in 1837 by the Tithe Commutation Act which put an end to a major source both of Catholic grievance and of sectarian conflict. The Catholics had been forced by law to contribute a tithe of their income to the upkeep of a church which was not theirs. But, as one historian has noted, in some cases the tithe 'had been racked up by lay impropriators, and in other ways, until it often reached nearer to a quarter of the produce than one-tenth'.[7] The injustices of the system eventually led to a 'tithe war' in which the tradition of underground secret agrarian societies came alive once again in Ireland. The 'tithe war' culminated in the 'Rathcormack massacre' in Co. Cork during May 1834. A score of peasants were killed and several more injured during fighting which broke out over the collection of forty shillings in tithe arrears from a Catholic widow. The resultant adverse publicity led to a blunting of Tory opposition to the passing of the Commutation Act.

By that time O'Connell had built up what deserves to be regarded as the first successful non-violent civil rights organisation in history, the Catholic Association. Its strength was based on organisation, moral force and the influence of the clergy, who, because of their education and respected place in Irish society, occupied positions of authority throughout the Association. O'Connell's success therefore carried with it the demerit of creating a bogeyman figure for either anti-clerical Nationalists, or Protestant propagandists: the Priest in Politics. O'Connell's other great cause, repeal of the Union, was not a success. The repeal movement lost momentum in 1843 after the British proclaimed illegal a huge meeting which he had intended to address at Clontarf. Fearing a slaughter if he went ahead, O'Connell called it off and his authority suffered something of the same diminution as did that of the Danes because of the earlier, bloodier, battle of Clontarf. The famine provided an apocalyptic eclipse of O'Connell's career. He died during its worst year, 'black forty-seven'.

The following year, 1848, the Young Irelanders' Revolution, which was in effect nothing more than a burst of outraged idealism on the part of a group of O'Connell's more radical young opponents and disillusioned former followers, petered out in a fracas in the widow McCormack's cabbage garden. However, the Young Irelanders are respected by separatists of the physical force tradition for ensuring there was a rising in every generation, even in the appalling aftermath of the famine.

In all, the famine years consigned some one million people to the grave, a further million to emigration and probably condemned a further million to a half-life of poverty and near-starvation. Previously there had been heavy emigration from Ireland, particularly after the Napoleonic wars when agricultural prices fell steeply. But this swelling tide of human misery carried with it, to America in particular, a lasting characteristic of anti-British feeling that forms part of the tradition of continuing support for physical force which, to a degree, continues to assist the IRA today.

In his novel *Paddy's Lament* the novelist Thomas Gallagher quotes statements from Gladstone, and by the London *Times*, prophesying the effects of the famine on the Irish diaspora, principally in America.

Gladstone wrote to his wife referring to 'that cloud in the west, the coming storm, the minister of God's retribution upon cruel and inveterate and but half atoned injustice'. The *Times* said:

> We must gird our loins to encounter the nemesis of seven hundred centuries' of misgovernment. To the end of time spread over the largest inhabitable area in the world, and confronting us everywhere by sea and land, they will remember that their forefathers paid tithe to the Protestant clergy, rent to absentee landlords and a forced obedience to the laws which these had made.

Significantly, the passage from Gallagher's work using the quotations was reprinted in the newsletter[8] of an Irish-American ginger group which also recorded the success of the Irish-American lobby in defeating an anti-IRA move in the Senate. The right-wing Senator Jesse Helms, a friend of Ian Paisley, was forced to drop a planned amendment to the Senate Appropriations Bill which would have cut off all aid to Ireland until the IRA surrendered its weaponry.

Another outcome of the famine which had a lasting impact was the formulation of the Irish Republican Brotherhood. The IRB – or Fenian movement, as it became popularly known after the legendary Irish version of the Samurai – was founded in 1858 in Dublin, and the following year spread to New York, where the movement became known as Clann na Gael (Family of Gaels). Like the United Irishmen, of which it was a lineal descendant, it was an oath-bound secret society whose revolutionary objectives were as much anathematised by the Church as by the British. Bishop Moriarty of Kerry produced one of the more celebrated denunciations, saying of the Fenians that: 'Eternity is not long enough nor hell hot enough to punish such miscreants.'[9]

But despite being greatly feared and hated, the Fenians' significance, like that of the Young Irelanders, lay less in the field of actual revolution than in the impetus which it gave to a body of revolutionary ideas concerning republicanism, separatism, identity and a consciousness of being Irish whose historical hour did not strike until the following century. The British infiltrated the movement with informers, and a planned uprising in 1867 fizzled out with nothing much in the way of military activity beyond some dynamite explosions in London and other cities which were the precursors of the contemporary IRA bombing campaign. Hangings, floggings, jailings and transportations added new martyrs to the Irish physical force tradition, and constitutional Ireland turned to other movements.

The O'Connellite demand for repeal became adapted to a call for Home Rule. Under Charles Stewart Parnell, the leader of the Irish parliamentary party at Westminster, this call came close to success. He did succeed in exerting sufficient pressure on Gladstone to commit the Liberals to supporting Home Rule. But in 1890 Parnell was cited as co-respondent in a divorce case. In the ensuing controversy the party split, and Parnell died prematurely the following year. He had managed to unite the three major streams of Irish self-assertion under his leadership: firstly the parliamentary party itself, which he had made into a formidable force through a strategy of giving or withdrawing his support to either the Liberals or the Conservatives according to the circumstances of the moment; secondly the Fenians, who agreed to put their energies at his disposal; and lastly the Irish Land League, founded by an ex-Fenian, Michael Davitt, with the objective of rectifying the crisis on the land.

A combination of the Land League's activities and the adoption by the Conservatives of a policy known in Ireland as 'killing Home Rule by kindness' ultimately did lead to a solution of the land issue. Throughout the later part of the nineteenth century and the first years of the twentieth, a series of reforming Acts facilitated the buying-out of the landlords and the creation of a peasant proprietorship. But politically Parnell's fall meant that the life force of the people began to express itself through cultural and sporting channels.

It was the era of the so-called Celtic Dawn. An Irish literary renaissance, spearheaded by Protestant intellectuals like Yeats, Synge, and Lady Gregory, centred on the Abbey Theatre. Another Protestant, Douglas Hyde, founded the

Gaelic League, which generated widespread enthusiasm for the idea of restoring the Irish language. The Gaelic Athletic Association, founded by a Catholic, Michael Cusack, attracted even more widespread support for the ancient Irish sport of hurling, and for a hybrid version of rugby and soccer, Gaelic football, which also gave rise to Australian Rules 'footie'. All this energy, coupled with a corresponding enervation on the part of the Protestant Ascendancy, inevitably had a political effect also.

At Westminster John Redmond accomplished the herculean task of both uniting the pro- and anti-Parnellite wings of the Irish party and persuading Herbert Asquith's government to once more bring forward a Home Rule proposal for Ireland. By now the contours of the present Irish Troubles had established themselves both in north-eastern Ireland and at Westminster. Dependent for his continuation in government on the support of Parnell and his Irish votes, Gladstone had put forward a Home Rule Bill in 1886. Introducing it he had said:

> I cannot conceal the conviction that the voice of Ireland as a whole is at this moment clearly and constitutionally spoken. I cannot say otherwise when five sixths of the lawfully chosen representatives are of one mind on this matter . . . certainly I cannot allow it to be said that a Protestant minority in Ulster, or elsewhere, is to rule the question at large for Ireland. I am aware of no constitutional doctrine tolerable on which such a conclusion could be adopted or justified.[10]

Gladstone had described the situation regarding Home Rule with both eloquence and accuracy. However, he was about to be presented with a 'constitutional doctrine' which made nonsense of his efforts, and the efforts of many who came after him, to apply democratic principles to the Irish situation. That doctrine was summed up by Randolph Churchill, the man who coined the phrase, before a Belfast audience: 'Ulster will fight and Ulster will be right.' Churchill is also generally credited with being the man who introduced into British politics the tactic of 'playing the Orange card', that is, using the situation in northern Ireland for English electoral advancement. As Gladstone was making up his mind about Home Rule, Churchill wrote to a friend: 'I have decided some time ago that if the GOM [Gladstone] went for Home Rule, the Orange card would be the one to play.'[11] The emotion generated by the Tory/Unionist alliance defeated Gladstone's proposal and his government fell. His assessment of the support in Ireland for Home Rule was borne out: eighty-six Home Rulers were returned, as against seventeen opposed. However, the election also returned a Conservative government, thus rendering the Irish Home Rule representation impotent.

From the time of the plantations by Scottish settlers, the province of Ulster as a whole had developed differently from the rest of Ireland, and particularly so during the nineteenth century. Politically, the experiences of the Presbyterians – who, because they too were discriminated against by the Anglicans, though to a lesser extent than the Catholics, had thrown in their lot with the Catholics during the 1798 rebellion – had been so traumatic that Anglicans and Presbyterians now formed a united front on the Union against their Nationalist and Catholic neighbours on the Home Rule issue.

The system of land-holding for the planters had traditionally been more liberal than in other parts of the country; the land issue was not the source of discontent it was in the south and south-west. Moreover, as in other countries, the north had become more industrialised than the south. Linen, ship-building and heavy engineering generated wealth, employment – and friction. By the time of the First World War, Belfast had an only too well founded reputation for bigotry and sectarian strife. Catholics, attracted by the jobs, frequently came into conflict with Protestants. The Protestants got most of the jobs, certainly the more skilled, craft-worker positions, but there was sufficient work about for a thriving Catholic community to have established itself in and around the main west Belfast artery of the Falls Road, where it existed in resentful proximity to its Protestant counterpart, the Shankill Road.

Visually Belfast differed in appearance from other Irish cities like Dublin or Cork. It was a red-bricked Mancunian look-alike set down in the Irish countryside. That countryside also looked different to what one would have seen around Cork or Dublin. Instead of the unkempt lusciousness of the south there was the neat fertility of the Scottish lowlands. Opposition to Home Rule was thus the external, political manifestation of a series of fundamental differences between the Catholic and Protestant traditions. The Tory espousal of the Unionist cause also introduced a different approach by the Conservatives to that normally associated with parliamentary democracy.

The 'playing the Orange card' strategy had the twin results of enshrining a fundamentally anti-democratic strain in Conservative thinking on Ulster and giving to the Unionist cause the incalculable benefit of the support of one of the great political parties of England in their efforts to negate the returns from ballot boxes in Ireland. The outcome was to be amply demonstrated in 1912 during the third major effort to introduce a Home Rule measure for Ireland. The Liberals, under Herbert Asquith, were once again dependent on the Irish parliamentary party. Introducing the Bill, Asquith echoed Gladstone's arguments and pointed out that over the previous twenty-five years four-fifths of the Irish electorate had consistently returned Home Rule candidates. To no avail: the near treasonous behaviour of the Conservatives overpowered all rational political argument on the issue. As the distinguished historian Nicholas Mansergh has stated:

> No stranger episode is to be found in the history of Conservatism than in the abandonment of pretensions in the three years before the First World War to be the party of law and order.

The principal actors in the drama of Tory/Unionist resistance to Home Rule were the Conservative Party leader, Andrew Bonar Law, and the Unionists' leader, Edward Carson, a Dublin-born lawyer. Apart from a desire to return the Tories to power via the Orange card, the Scots-Canadian Bonar Law had strong Ulster connections. His father had been a Presbyterian minister in the province. In addition, his London hostess was the doyenne of Unionism, Lady Londonderry, whose house in London was also Carson's second home. Carson had been an indefatigable Crown prosecutor in Ireland. Operating in a world of 'packed' juries and coercive legislation, he had implemented the 'stick' portion of Chief Secretary

Arthur Balfour's policy of 'the carrot and stick', as it was known to Nationalists. The slow pace of reform on the land issue, 'the carrot', with its consequential widespread agrarian outrage was balanced by an equally widespread application of coercion. One of the great 'remember' cries of the period was 'remember Mitchelstown'. It was the Mitchelstown incident in Co. Cork which really launched Carson. He was the Crown prosecutor in a case against William O'Brien, one of the leaders of the land agitation, which became a *cause célèbre* in 1887 after police had fired on a crowd of stone-throwing demonstrators, killing three of them and wounding many more.

Carson went on to become one of the leading barristers in English legal history. An 'ugly hatchet-faced man', he had a type of mind not uncommonly met with at the bar: 'Ruthless, defiant, with thinly veiled contempt for democracy', he made no bones about his methodology, saying flatly that he 'intended to break every law that is possible'. Bonar Law's rhetoric was even more extreme. At the Balmoral show grounds in Belfast, standing under the largest Union Jack in the world (48 feet by 25), on 9 April 1912 he solemnised the 'wedding of Protestant Ulster with the Conservative and Unionist Party', in the presence of some 100,000 spectators, and a platform that included seventy MPs. His speech included emotive comparisons between the siege of Derry during the Williamite war and the contemporary situation:

> Once again you hold the pass, the pass for the empire. The timid have left you; your Lundys have betrayed you; but you have closed your gates. The government have erected, by their Parliament Act, a boom against you to shut you off from the British people. You will burst that boom. That help will come, and when the crisis is over men will say to you in words not unlike those used by Pitt – you have saved yourselves by your exertions, and you have saved the empire by your example.

This could have been defended on the grounds of being delivered merely for local consumption, but speaking later in the summer, at Blenheim Palace on 24 July, after several incidents of sectarian violence had already occurred in northern Ireland in the wake of his April speech, Bonar Law made it clear that he was consciously lending his position to violent resistance to Home Rule. Reading his remarks, even at this remove, it appears incredible that they could have been uttered by a man who was not only leader of the Conservative Party, but also a potential prime minister of England. He said:

> We regard the government as a revolutionary committee which has seized upon despotic power by fraud. In our opposition to them we shall not be guided by the considerations or bound by the restraints which would influence us in a normal constitutional struggle. We shall take the means, whatever means seems to us most effective, to deprive them of the despotic power which they have usurped and compel them to appeal to the people whom they have deceived. They may, perhaps they will, carry their Home Rule Bill through the House of Commons but what then? I said the other day in the House of Commons, and I repeat here that there are things stronger than parliamentary majorities ... Before I occupied the position I now fill in the party I said that, in my belief, if an attempt were made to deprive these men of their birthright – as part of a corrupt political bargain – they would

be justified in resisting such an attempt by all means in their power, including force. I said it then, and I repeat now with a full sense of the responsibility which attaches to my position, that, in my opinion, if such an attempt is made, I can imagine no length of resistance to which Ulster can go in which I should not be prepared to support them, and in which, in my belief, they would not be supported by the overwhelming majority of the British people.

The foregoing was, as Asquith said, a 'declaration of war against constitutional government'. But Bonar Law and Carson continued unimpeded as they made it clear that they intended to back up their words with deeds. Later in 1912, on 19 September, Carson called a press conference at Craigavon, the mansion near Belfast owned by Sir James Craig, the heir to a whiskey-distilling fortune, at which he revealed that the Unionists had drawn up an Ulster Covenant, based on the old Scottish Covenant. It contained the following:

Being convinced in our consciences that home rule would be disastrous to the material well-being of Ulster as well as the whole of Ireland, subversive of our civil and religious freedom, destructive of our citizenship, and perilous to the empire, we . . . loyal subjects of His Gracious Majesty King George V . . . do hereby pledge ourselves in solemn covenant . . . to stand by one another in defending for ourselves and our children our cherished position of equal citizenship in the United Kingdom, and in using all means which may be found necessary to defeat the present conspiracy to set up a home rule parliament in Ireland . . . and mutually pledge ourselves to refuse to recognise its authority.

This was no empty formula. Some 470,000 people signed the Covenant and 100,000 more were enrolled into an Ulster Volunteer Force. A senior English officer, General Sir George Richardson, was placed at the head of these 'loyal subjects of His Gracious Majesty'. As an indication of how the UVF was looked upon by the British 'officers and gentlemen' class, it should be noted that Richardson was suggested for the post by one of England's most eminent soldiers, Field Marshal Sir George Roberts, on the grounds that Richardson 'knew men and war from fighting the Pathans and the Afghans on the North-West Frontier'. Richardson did not have to depend solely on his NWF experiences; there were frontiers of influence readily open to him a great deal closer to home. Supporters of the Orange card strategy included members of the Establishment such as Waldorf Astor, Lord Rothschild, Lord Milner, Lord Iveagh, Sir Edward Elgar and the Duke of Bedford. Considerations of the indivisibility of empire, or affection for Irish Unionists, were not uppermost in these gentlemen's minds, convulsing their dinner parties, and those of society London generally, with heated controversy over the 'Ulster crisis'. As a historian of Unionism, Patrick Buckland, has pointed out:

Not only was the unionist leadership more responsive to Ulster unionism. The party at large was more inclined to endorse the vehemence of Ulster unionists . . . Unionists [i.e. Conservatives], furious with frustration at their continued exclusion from power, were . . . willing to adopt almost any means to defeat the Liberals and return to office.

The Duchess of Somerset articulated the feelings of Tory grandees when she wrote to Carson in January 1914 that 'this country will follow you now and we shall all help you to see this thing through and this vile government will go out'.

But in their public support for the Unionists Conservative apologists concentrated their fire not on party advantage but on large questions of empire and of religious freedom, summarised by Rudyard Kipling in lines from a poem he wrote for the Tory *Morning Post*:

> We know the hells declared
> For such as serve not Rome –
>
> One law, one land one throne.
> If England drive us forth
> We shall not stand alone.

Lest anyone labour under the illusion that their activities stopped short at poetry readings, the Unionists also formed a provisional government ready to take over the province should Home Rule be applied. The Curragh Mutiny drama played out during March 1914 ensured that it would not. The Curragh incident began when a majority amongst the British officers stationed at the principal Irish base, the Curragh Camp in Co. Kildare, let it be known that they did not wish to be involved in forcing Home Rule on their fellow Conservatives in the north. They were confronted neither by enforced resignations, nor courts martial. In fact they were not confronted at all. Having been summoned to London, their leader, Brigadier H. P. Gough, came back to the Curragh from the War Office with a document, the last paragraph of which, written in his own handwriting, read as follows: 'I understand the last paragraph to mean that the Troops under our command will not be called upon to enforce Home Rule and we can so assure our officers.'

What this assurance meant in practice was spelled out a month later, on 24 April, when police and customs officials stood idly by as 300 tons of rifles and ammunition were landed illegally from Germany for the UVF at three separate locations, Bangor, Donaghdee and Larne. Whoever was going to enforce Home Rule, it would not be the British Army. In the event there was no pretence at enforcement. Shortly after the Great War broke out, and on 18 September 1914, Asquith sidelined the Home Rule issue by formally introducing Home Rule to law but accompanying the measure by an Amending Bill which suspended its operation until after the war.

Though the crisis thus appeared to pass inconclusively, it had in fact thrown up the formula which the British would later use in what for many years appeared to be a successful attempt to solve the Irish question: partition. Partition had been formally proposed by Bonar Law at a conference convened by the King at Buckingham Palace on 21 July 1914. He suggested the exclusion of six of Ulster's nine counties from the working of the Home Rule Bill. This was opposed by both Redmond and Carson, Redmond on the grounds that the six excluded counties – Armagh, Antrim, Down, Derry, Fermanagh and Tyrone – contained sizeable Catholic minorities. Instead he sought a system of option whereby counties could opt for or against Home Rule depending on their religious coloration.

Carson objected on the cunningly chosen grounds that nine counties would be the best solution, because the increased Catholic representation from the remaining three Ulster counties, Donegal, Cavan and Monaghan, would be a force for the eventual coming-together of the two parts of the island! The sincerity of this argument need not detain us long; Carson was opposed to Home Rule for any part of Ireland but he was keenly aware that the Liberals, and many Conservatives, supported the county option idea, and did not wish to leave himself open to charges of obduracy. Later the Unionists would abandon the pretext of favouring ultimate unification, but before looking at how and why this was done it is necessary to examine how nationalism reacted to the Home Rule crisis, because it was this reaction which led to the establishment of today's republic.

Throughout most of the controversy the vast bulk of Nationalist opinion supported John Redmond. People expected England to keep faith. The Unionists could huff and puff all they liked, but the ineluctable fact appeared to be that the majority in favour of Home Rule in the House of Commons was over 100 votes. That was the significant statistic, not how many people signed a strange-sounding covenant in Belfast. Moreover, in the middle of the controversy, during 1913–14, people's attention became focused on the great industrial dispute between the Irish Transport and General Workers' Union, led by Jim Larkin and James Connolly, and the Dublin employers, led by William Martin Murphy. After Murphy dismissed workers who refused to resign from the IT&GWU, Larkin declared a general strike of his members. Murphy and the other employers responded by declaring a general lock-out. Connolly and Larkin were both arrested. Clashes between strikers and police became commonplace in Dublin. In November of 1913 a citizens' army was founded to protect the workers from police brutality. This tiny but significant unit was shortly to be subsumed into another, larger grouping.

For, unknown to the public, the IRB had secretly become reorganised. Imbued with the conviction that Home Rule was a sham – and indeed a fact overlooked in the welter of controversy was that the financial provisions of the Bill were so limited that Ireland would have had less independence than Britain's other colonies – the IRB had decided that the time was approaching for an implementation of Wolfe Tone's dictum that England's difficulty was Ireland's opportunity. The formation of the UVF gave the IRB the chance it had been waiting for. Eoin MacNeill, a respected scholar, was persuaded by colleagues in the Gaelic League, who unknown to him were members of the IRB, to write an article in the League's newspaper, *An Claideamh Soluis* (*The Sword of Light*), proposing that the Green tradition should have a corps to match that of the Orange in order to withstand any effort to frustrate the introduction of Home Rule by force. The article appeared on 1 November 1913. The response to it, an overflowing public meeting in the Rotunda, Dublin, on the 25th, showed how the behaviour of the Conservatives and Unionists had begun to affect Nationalists. The meeting unanimously adopted the Volunteer Manifesto which proposed the setting-up of an Irish volunteer corps all over the country in order to frustrate the plan

> . . . deliberately adopted by one of the great English political parties . . . to make a display of military force and the menace of armed violence the determining factor in the future relations between this country and Great Britain.

The government, which of course had made no response to the formation of the UVF, reacted by issuing an order banning the importation of arms into Ireland. This was the order which the UVF openly flouted a few months later. The hatred of the Unionists for Home Rule was genuine enough and understandable against a background of centuries of sectarian warfare. In fact, in view of this background it was a major blunder on the part of the framers of the first Home Rule proposals not to have incorporated in the Bill safeguards for those of the Protestant tradition. Failure to do so gave a patina of reality to the 'Home Rule is Rome rule' argument which became embedded in the Unionists' resistance. Nevertheless it was not the genuineness of the Unionists' resistance which gave it its strength. That came from Conservative backing in press, parliament, and security forces.

The numbers who signed the Covenant were certainly impressive. But in assessing them, British governmental reaction to similar, earlier, manifestations of Catholic feeling has to be borne in mind. O'Connell, for example, had addressed a peaceful meeting of 750,000 people at Tara in Co. Meath in favour of repeal of the Union. It was the largest gathering seen in Ireland until the Eucharistic Congress of 1932. But the reaction of the British was to threaten bloodshed if he went ahead with his planned meeting at Clontarf, and to arrest O'Connell. In 1860 The O'Donoghue brought a petition to London seeking an Irish plebiscite on self-determination. The petition contained 423,026 signatures, but it was ignored. In a rural country with a strong oral tradition, where politics was the staple diet of fireside conversation, it appeared to Nationalists that history was not so much unfolding before their eyes as merely repeating itself.

This impression was heavily underscored when the Rotunda Volunteers staged a mini-version of the UVF gun-running (1,500 rifles as opposed to 35,000) at Howth on 14 July 1914. In contrast to the proceedings at Bangor, Donaghdee and Larne, which had been overseen by British officers, the army made a bungled attempt to seize the Howth weaponry. As a result a riot developed at Bachelors' Walk and frightened soldiers fired on a stone-throwing mob, killing four people and wounding dozens more. 'Remember Bachelors' Walk' joined Mitchelstown in the litany of Ireland's Stations of the Cross.

However, mainstream Nationalist sentiment still supported John Redmond. It did not matter that he did not join the wartime coalition cabinet, although both Bonar Law and Carson did. Nor that Irish Nationalists, including his own son, were refused commissions. Even though he made a recruiting speech two days after the Home Rule Bill was adjourned, thereby causing a split in the Volunteers, the largest segment of the movement followed his leadership, becoming known as the National Volunteers. As a result tens of thousand of young Irish Nationalists went to their deaths wearing British uniforms, believing that they were fighting for the freedom of small nations. A tradition, built up over centuries, of 'listing for the Crown' and 'taking the King's shilling' was not easily eradicated. Nevertheless a small section of the Volunteers did remain opposed to recruiting. These, still nominally led by Eoin MacNeill, but in fact controlled by the IRB, became known as the Irish Volunteers. Through manipulation of the Irish Volunteers the IRB now stood on the threshold of the greatest alterations in the relationship between Ireland and England since the coming of the Normans in 1169.

To the accompaniment of much undercover negotiation involving Clann na Gael leaders in New York and the German foreign service, the IRB leadership had decided that the Great War offered an ideal opportunity to implement Wolfe Tone's teaching about taking advantage of England's difficulties. Unknown to MacNeill, who still believed the Irish Volunteers' mission to be wholly defensive, an uprising was planned for Easter 1916. Though no German aid reached the rebels, and MacNeill destroyed whatever slim prospect they had of success when he did hear of the plot, by countermanding it, so that only some six hundred Volunteers, backed by the tiny Citizens' Army, actually went out to fight, chiefly in Dublin, Ireland, in the words of Yeats, was 'changed utterly' by the rising of Easter Week, April 1916.

The people of Dublin at first execrated the rebels: the business community because of the destruction caused, chiefly by British shelling, during the week-long fighting; while the working class were stirred to wrath by the 'separation women', who were receiving separation allowances because their husbands were fighting in the war, and who viewed the proceedings as stabbing the lads abroad in the back. Prisoners were booed as they were led to the dock for transhipment to prisons in England. However, British policy soon had the effect of swinging the popularity pendulum in the opposite direction. Sixteen of the rising's leaders were executed, including all seven signatories of the Proclamation of a Republic for all Ireland. The rising had begun with the reading of it on the steps of the General Post Office in Dublin. Amongst those shot were James Connolly and Padraig Pearse. Pearse was a well-known writer, orator, and educationalist, whose writings became after his death the inspiration of revolutionary Ireland. Connolly had been so badly wounded during the fighting that he had to be propped up in a chair to face the firing squad.

Apart from creating martyrs, the British compounded their error by a nationwide round-up of suspects. So many innocent people were arrested and incarcerated in England that not only was wrath swiftly converted to sympathy, but the IRB's infectious doctrines, inculcated in camp and prison, were later carried to the four corners of the land on their release. The prisoners provided a fertile source of propaganda in America too, where the feelings of famine-recalling Irish-Americans were of considerable concern to the pro-British Woodrow Wilson in his efforts to win support for America's entry into the war on Britain's side. The chorus of 'remembers' became ever more damning and more insistent, both in Ireland and throughout the Irish diaspora, as the contrast between the treatment of Orange and Green dissidents began to sink in. Realising their mistake, the government ordered the prisoners released within months. It was too late: they returned home, metamorphosed in the public imagination from murderous vandals into revolutionary heroes, to be cheered back on to the streets they had been booed off from.

As by now news of the horrors of trench warfare was also circulating, recruiting fell off, which, coupled with the limitation of opportunities for emigration, created a potentially explosive pool of manpower for nationalist radicals to draw on. And draw on it they did. There is no need to go into the intricacies of the struggle which eventuated. Suffice it to say that the lack of response to honourable John Redmond's painful toil at Westminster destroyed his and his party's credibility.

'Remember John Redmond' joined the litany. This particular incantation, carrying with it damaging implications of contempt for moderation in politics, and for parliamentary methods generally, bedevilled Irish political life for decades afterwards, and still affects Northern Ireland.

Politically, Nationalist Ireland turned to Sinn Fein (We Ourselves), which before the rising had been little more than an opinion group. The party had been formed by a gifted journalist, Arthur Griffith, who preached separatism, self-sufficiency and a dual monarchy for Ireland and England on the lines of the Austrian-Hungarian example. He saw this as the formula for resolving the claims of Loyalists and Nationalists. However, sections of the British media had mistakenly described the rising as a 'Sinn Fein rebellion' because of the success of Griffith's book, *The Resurrection of Hungary*. The newspaper assessment of Sinn Fein became a self-fulfilling prophecy. Having successfully frustrated an attempt to introduce conscription to Ireland the party won seventy-three seats in the 1918 general election. The Unionists won their customary one-fifth of the poll, 315,394 votes out of a total of 1,526,910. However, the Irish parliamentary party retained a mere seven of their former eighty seats. Home Rule was a dead letter.

Following the election Sinn Fein withdrew from Westminster, set up its own parliament, known as the Dail, in Dublin, and, in reiteration of the demand made in the proclamation of 1916, declared an all-Ireland republic. From then on the Volunteers became known generally as the Irish Republican Army (IRA). Spearheaded by the genius at the head of the IRB, Michael Collins, regarded as the father of modern urban guerrilla warfare for his work in building up an underground intelligence network which defeated the British secret service, the IRA ultimately brought the British to the conference table.

The course of the war need not concern us here. Sufficient to say that if a historical template were cut out and superimposed over the North's troubled counties today, it would fit all too well. Ireland became used to the techniques of ambush, justification of civilian casualties, elimination of spies, demoralisation of police forces, propaganda, and the consequential retaliation: the formation of special forces, the Black and Tans, ex-service men so called because of their black and khaki uniforms, and the Auxiliary Police Cadets. These last were so christened in order to give the impression that this was a 'police war' aimed only at putting down a handful of unrepresentative criminals. The 'auxies' were ex-officers who, like the IRA, were brave men, elected their own officers – and made their own rules: repression, murder, retaliatory destruction of property, torture, unacknowledged shoot-to-kill policies, the use of the judicial system as part of the counterinsurgency methodology, propaganda. In guerrilla warfare, as in other spheres of human activity, there is little new under either the sun or the Irish rain.

However these activities did produce two new developments. Under pressure from both the IRA and public opinion, particularly American public opinion, the British moved to meet the conflicting claims of Orange and Green by partitioning Ireland. Firstly, under the terms of the Government of Ireland Act, 1920, the Unionists were given a parliament in Belfast to rule over their portion, the six counties in which they predominated, that part of northern Ireland that is today erroneously known as 'Ulster'. The opening of the northern parliament facilitated the establishment of a truce and an invitation to the Nationalists to come to London later in the year for negotiations. As a result of these, the south and south-western parts of the country were ultimately hived off into a Roman Catholic-dominated Irish Free State with the same constitutional status as either Australia or Canada. This state evolved into today's Republic of Ireland.

The irony about partition is that it worked in the area which most bitterly resented it, the Catholic zone. The enforced acceptance came about as follows. The treaty which Michael Collins brought home from London at the end of the tortuous negotiations was rejected by his great rival, Eamon de Valera. In July 1921, before the negotiations began, de Valera, who was then the leader of Sinn Fein, had seen Lloyd George alone in London for a number of tête-à-tête meetings. However, having been fully informed of what was on offer, he managed to evade going back to London for the treaty negotiations, which were conducted by plenipotentiaries led by Michael Collins and Arthur Griffith.

Collins had warned even before the truce was declared that once it came into operation his principal weapon, secrecy, was gone. He and his underground army would be like rabbits coming out of their holes. His intelligence network had left him in no doubt as to the extent of the forces in men and money which the British were deploying to bolster the Unionists' resistance to any encroachment on the six-county state. If he did not seize the opportunity of setting up an imperfect twenty-six-county state, the British might not withdraw from the south either. There was precedent for such missed opportunities for Ireland in Parnell's career and what had happened to Home Rule. Conservative Party members and senior figures in the army, like Sir Henry Wilson, who had been one of the architects of the Curragh Mutiny saga, were strongly opposed to such withdrawal, arguing that it was 'giving in to terrorism'. Collins did not regard the treaty as a perfect solution but as a 'stepping stone', as he put it, to full and final freedom. Eventually, after one of the most sterile and rancorous debates in Irish political history, the 'stepping stone' argument carried the day and the treaty was accepted by a majority of the southern electorate.

The sizeable Catholic minority in the northern state viewed the treaty with considerable apprehension because of the prospect of being handed over to the tender mercies of the Unionist and Protestant majority. But their fears found little resonance in the Dail debates. Knowing that he could do little or nothing about the reality of partition – the northern parliament had been in existence before Lloyd George sent for him in the first place – de Valera and his cohorts concentrated their fire on the Oath of Allegiance to the Crown which dominion status entailed. Incredible as it might appear today, partition was almost overlooked in the endless arguments about the Oath, and forms of government. The result was one of the most pointless civil wars recorded since Swift, in *Gulliver's Travels*, described how a conflict broke out between two factions over which end of an egg should be topped. Many sincere young men in the IRA believed that they had taken an oath to an Irish republic and that it was wrong to stop short of this goal. The machiavellian de Valera appears however to have been motivated, at least in part, by rivalry with

Collins and pique at the fact that the treaty was signed without his consent. Certainly in subsequent years he did more to validate Collins's 'stepping stone' theory than anyone else in the manner in which he jettisoned the IRA and used the Free State apparatus to work towards dispensing with the link with the Crown.

But his change of approach affected only the twenty-six counties. The civil war which he did so much to foment had copper-fastened partition by the time it ended in 1923. It claimed the life of the charismatic Michael Collins with a bullet and that of the overworked Arthur Griffith through a brain haemorrhage. The importance of Collins's death to the partition issue only became generally known long afterwards as a result of research I conducted while writing his biography. I discovered that Collins, in his capacity as head of government, commander-in-chief of the Free State Army, and, possibly more importantly, head of the IRB, had used the 'stepping stone' as a base for undeclared military actions against the north. Apart from the fact that he abhorred partition and intended using the treaty to end it either by fair means or foul, Collins's seemingly indefensible behaviour has to be understood against the backdrop of the fact that the Catholic population were under severe pressure from the authorities of the Six Counties. In the disorder of the time, undercover squads drawn from the B-Specials (the north's armed, Protestant militia), the Royal Ulster Constabulary, and the British Army seemed to be able to murder Catholics at will. Those deaths in the early 1920s formed part of the litany of 'remembers' which accompanied the coming to life again of the IRA in the 1960s. But in the 1920s Collins was the only leader in the Free State cabinet who showed himself willing to respond by assisting the Catholics militarily.

Following his death, his colleagues, none of whom possessed his drive or initiative, had their hands full in merely trying to keep alive the newly formed twenty-six-county state. The aftermath of the death and destruction of the civil war, the waste, and above all the disillusionment – that this was what the independence struggle, 'that delirium of the brave', had led to – drained the infant Free State of vision, political energy and financial resources. Trying to maintain an Irish currency in the face of, at best, unsympathetic, and at worst, unfriendly, British treasury officials assumed a far higher priority than events north of the border in another jurisdiction.

It is to the credit of the first Free State administration that democracy survived in such conditions. But so did the border. When, in 1925, the British, in effect, reneged on one of the provisions of the treaty, there was nothing the Dublin Government could or would do about it. One of the arguments in favour of the treaty had been that it allowed for the setting-up of a boundary commission. This, it was hoped by the Nationalists, would redraw the boundary in accordance with the wishes of the inhabitants. Had this been done, the most the Unionists could have hoped to control of their six counties would have been an unworkable three and a half. The city of Derry, most of the country around it, and the bulk of Counties Tyrone and Fermanagh would probably have gone to the Nationalists and been ceded to the Free State.

It was intended that the commission be composed of a British, a Nationalist and a Unionist representative. However, the Unionists refused to nominate anyone, while the British concurred in the refusal and appointed a South African instead. The man who originally suggested the commission, Sir James Craig, the Six Counties prime minister, who had succeeded Carson as Unionist leader, said he was prepared for war if 'one inch of the loved soil of Ulster' was removed by the commission. No one in authority in London pointed out that this constituted a violation of the treaty. In the circumstances, neither Dublin nor the Nationalist representative on the commission, Eoin MacNeill, had any power to 'deliver'. Amidst much sabre-rattling in the north and disappointment in the south, MacNeill resigned, and the commission left the border unchanged.

The only subsequent changes to the southern state which need concern us were internal. Prior to the treaty the laws of England were the laws of Ireland. Now, in the south, they were altered to take a Catholic complexion. The legal system was changed to allow for prohibitions on abortion, contraception, divorce and the introduction of censorship. While there was no official policy of discrimination against Protestants, the ethos of the south became unwelcoming to aspects of Protestantism. Ethos, economics, emigration, a lower birth rate, the change in administration all played their part in making the south's small Protestant population become smaller still.

It fell from 327,171 in 1911 to roughly 130,000 fifty years later. When James Craig declared that the Belfast parliament was a 'protestant parliament for a protestant people', his hearers understood that custom and usage meant that the Protestants got and would continue to get the jobs and the houses at the expense of their Catholic neighbours. The southern state was much more benign and democratic than that. But it was nevertheless a benign, democratic Roman Catholic state.

The Free State Government, led by William T. Cosgrave, proved itself more committed to democracy than the pursuit of power when in 1927 it encouraged de Valera back into the parliamentary arena from the wilderness to which his war spasm of 1922–3 had consigned him. Five years later he succeeded Cosgrave and began making the southern state appear more republican. The office of governor-general was removed, and so was the Oath. But while thus attempting to placate the republican rump, which had supported him since the civil war, he also sought to assure right-wing elements of his basic conservatism. In 1937 he introduced his own constitution, which was an attempt to marry these conflicting currents. It was a theocratic, frankly sectarian document which recognised God in its preamble and the 'special position' of the Roman Catholic Church in its text. In Articles 2 and 3 it reiterated the republican ideal by making a specific claim to Northern Ireland. All of these things aroused, and continue to arouse, northern hackles, but did absolutely nothing to tackle the problem of partition. They were nothing but cosmetic window-dressing designed to impress the population of the Twenty-Six Counties.

During World War II Northern Ireland formed a valuable staging ground for the Allies, in particular for flying sorties to protect convoys, and during the Normandy landings. By contrast, de Valera having renegotiated the return of a number of ports deeded to Britain in the treaty which would have been valuable in convoy protection, the south decided to remain neutral. Therefore, to all the historical baggage inclining London towards Belfast's side of the argument, there was added a great weight of wartime obligation. But this fact was ignored by the south a few years after the war ended – with consequences which persist today. In 1949, a coalition government which had managed to oust de Valera decided to steal his republican clothes by declaring the Twenty-Six Counties a republic.

The Unionists riposted by cashing in some of their wartime gratitude chips to secure from the Attlee government a guarantee that there would be no change in the constitutional position of Northern Ireland without the consent of the assembly at Stormont. Even though Stormont was later dissolved by London, that guarantee still exists: the veto which the Unionists continue to employ on moves towards a united Ireland. And now, before turning to examine how Stormont came to be dissolved, a number of points have to be made about the northern state: firstly, its extent.

Carson, as we have seen, during the Buckingham Palace conference claimed that if partition were to come it should be on the basis of nine counties, not six. However, after the war, when the setting-up of the northern state was becoming imminent, this argument was inverted. Craig informed Lloyd George that the Unionists wished the new unit to be based not on the nine counties of Ulster, but on six only. As Lloyd George subsequently explained to his surprised cabinet colleagues, the vastly greater Unionist area which would have resulted, were Donegal, Cavan and Monaghan included, seemed logical, but what Craig wanted was control. The extra land would have brought with it extra Catholics and would, as Carson had said, have made for assimilation into a united Ireland. Accordingly, the Unionists got not a state of nine counties, but a statelet of six. But they also took control. The Catholics under their domination would get not the protections of the law, but its sanctions, forcing them into either subjection or emigration. Control, however, would remain.

Two other provisions which the British and the Nationalists agreed with initially were dropped because of the control philosophy. One was an upper house for the new parliament which would have been weighted to provide a redress for Catholic concerns. Carson vetoed this, flatly saying he was as prepared to take to the streets against the proposal as he had been against Home Rule itself. The other proposal was that the electoral system be by proportional representation as it was in the south. However, the very reason that it was introduced by Collins and Griffith to the south, because it protected minorities, was anathema to the Unionists. The last altercation Collins had before his death with Winston Churchill, who was responsible for Irish affairs, concerned Churchill's caving-in to the Unionists' demands that PR be dropped. Churchill, like Lloyd George, wanted the six-county state set up at whatever cost, in whatever shape, for one overriding reason – to get Ireland off the British agenda.

It might have stayed off if the three points concerning extent, structure of government, and the nature of the voting system had been persisted with. Perhaps peaceful assimilation could have taken place. In the event, however, what was created was a fundamentally undemocratic state specifically designed to prevent power changing hands, or to allow reform to take place from within by the normal democratic processes of education, organisation, and the ballot box. In many ways the hard-working, God-fearing fundamentalists of the Six Counties resembled the Boers of South Africa. They developed the same laager mentality and a system of administration very similar to apartheid, albeit based on religion rather than colour. But, unlike the South Africans, no British prime minister warned the Unionists that they must heed the winds of change. London took exactly the opposite approach, hands off, not hands on. The cheques were written, but no effort was made to ensure that the money was spent on maintaining a state that conformed even remotely to British standards. A gathering storm of Catholic grievance burst during the 1960s and a new generation of British decision-takers found that it must return to the old question of Ireland.

ONE

BICYCLING TO BUSBY

This country, with its institutions, belongs to the people who inhabit it. Whenever they shall grow weary of the existing government, they can exercise their constitutional right of amending it, or their revolutionary right to dismember or overthrow it.

Abraham Lincoln, First Inaugural Address, 4 March 1861

THERE WERE A number of sparks blowing about the Six Counties in the 1960s, any one of which might have ignited a conflagration. In the event the one that did was the housing question. We will examine later the statistics of the electoral system which helped to shape the housing issue, but let us for a moment eschew the statistical approach for the human one. We will begin our journey through the labyrinth of the north of Ireland's troubles by following in the footsteps, or more accurately the cycle path, of one Co. Tyrone man and his family as, through the generations, they moved towards the most significant confrontation on the housing problem by Catholics since the state was set up.

John Currie had not realised that he was cycling towards Northern Ireland's destiny that evening in 1945. All he was aware of was that his family was growing. He already had four children and he correctly anticipated that he could expect many more. (He eventually had eight boys and three girls.) He knew he needed a new house urgently. The man to see about the provision of this necessity was Moses Busby, a properous Protestant farmer, who was also chairman of the local rural district council. Although Busby was not only a Unionist and an Orangeman, but was even rumoured to be a Freemason, he had the reputation amongst Currie's fellow Catholics of being a 'decent enough old sort'.[1] Perhaps he would prove helpful. Amongst the other changes which the ending of World War II had brought to Coalisland, Co. Tyrone, had been a slight but noticeable increase in the provision of public housing. Also, Currie knew that some houses were becoming vacant on an existing estate. Perhaps one of these might be given to him. On the face of it he had an irrefutable case. As he cycled along, Currie rehearsed the arguments he intended to deploy: the size of his family; the length of time for which he had been waiting to be rehoused, since before the war; the unsuitability of his present two-bedroomed home. Those facts did not constitute a problem. The fact of his religion did. Were he a Protestant he would have been rehoused long ago.

Currie was not normally resentful about being discriminated against. That was simply the way things were, like the fact that although he had given some of his children Irish names like Sean and Seamus, these would only be accepted for registration by the authorities in their English forms of John and James. There was no point in railing against such matters. One might as well feel aggrieved at the way that, approaching the July marching season, his Orange neighbours not only paraded ostentatiously with banner, fife and drum in commemoration of King William's victory over the Catholics of yore, they also became distant and withdrawn from the Catholics of the day. They ceased to either speak or mingle with them until after the 'twalfth', when normal Irish friendly relationships would re-establish themselves for another year as though nothing had happened. If one elected to live in the Six Counties, rather than emigrate as so many were forced to, then one accepted the system. He earned a reasonable income from his job as a lorry driver. It at least enabled him to live in the land of his forebears, a pleasant land, free of crime, where traditional family values flourished and he and his wife, Mary, could bring up their children in the fear and love of God and of His Blessed Mother.

As befitted a man on an important occasion, Currie had worn his Sunday suit for the interview with Busby, who indeed turned out to be decent enough. They got on together as Christians should. Then, having explained his mission, Currie, as the liturgy demanded, discreetly produced a five-pound note, 'to make up for any trouble' that his request might cause. Busby graciously accepted the large white English banknote, folded it carefully, put it away, and, assuring his Catholic caller that he was 'a dacent man', delivered his verdict on Currie's request: 'The next time one of your own leaves a house vacant I'll see that you get the first offer.'

Currie cycled home, more slowly than he had set out. He made no complaint about Busby's reaction, but, as he was hanging up his Sunday suit, he said to Mary: 'Next time I'll find a better use for my good five-pound note than giving it to Moses Busby.' Five pounds was, after all, a week's wages in those days. But somehow Currie saved up £400 with which he one day bought a house standing on an eight-acre farm. His eldest child, a boy, Austin, took full advantage of another change brought about by the war, the Butler Education Act of 1944. He studied, became eligible for a free university education at Queen's University, Belfast, and in 1964 won a by-election in East Tyrone as a Nationalist candidate, which made him at twenty-five the youngest MP ever to enter Stormont.[2]

Dungannon was an important town in his constituency. Apart from the historical significance of being the starting point for both the Irish Volunteers in the eighteenth century and the Irish Republican Brotherhood's rebirth in the twentieth,[3] it had the contemporary relevance of being the home of Dr Conn McCluskey and his wife Patricia, both Catholics. In January of 1964, the year in which Currie entered Parliament, the McCluskeys had founded the Campaign for Social Justice. The aims of the CSJ were to collect and disseminate accurate statistical data on how discrimination in all its various forms worked in the Six Counties: in electoral practices, such as the existence of a property vote, or the redrawing of electoral boundaries so that Catholic voting power was nullified; in employment, in public appointments, and, in what as we will shortly see was the keystone of the arch, in housing. Here is Dr McCluskey's description of the results of discrimination in Dungannon, in the year of the CSJ's foundation:

... most of the good shops were owned by Protestants. There were two factories in which the lower echelons were Catholic, but they had no managerial representations in the factories. There were two secondary schools: St Patrick's, the Catholic institution, and the Protestant Royal, a fine school. But the difference between the Royal and St Pat's was that the people there knew that its pupils were going to get the jobs when they were educated ... because of what had happened before, the worst farms were in the mountainy parts and they were the Catholic farms. The good lowland farms were mostly Protestant because they had owned them since the sixteenth or seventeenth century. The picture was one of Catholic workmen looking after the roads under a Protestant supervisor or foreman ... among solicitors and doctors there was a fair allowance on each side, because people could choose their school and they could choose their doctors. This was one of the few areas where there was equal treatment. It was a middle-class thing, the golf links, there wasn't the opportunity to discriminate and the community got on well together.

We can see by looking at the career of Michael Farrell that McCluskey's description applied not merely to Dungannon but all over the Six Counties. Farrell, whose destiny was to intertwine with that of Austin Currie and the McCluskeys, played a significant role in the northern upheavals at a crucial stage. Like the McCluskeys and the Curries he no longer lives in Northern Ireland, but in Dublin, where, at the time of writing, he is a prominent lawyer and historian.[4] Growing up in south Co. Derry, he had a somewhat untypical childhood, in that both of his parents came from the south and therefore had no inherited knowledge of the northern situation. He learned about Six County life 'from the other kids' and says that:

The two things that came across very clearly were one, the almost apartheid nature of society. Though people, Protestant and Catholic, lived side by side literally, there was very little contact between them. Secondly you learned very quickly from the other children at school that Catholics couldn't get jobs in a whole range of occupations. There was no point in applying for jobs under the local authorities or within the Northern Ireland civil service for instance. Nor in a whole lot of private employments, the shipyard and the aircraft factory [Short Brothers, and Harland and Wolff in Belfast] and so forth. That was just the inherited folklore of all the children around, they didn't bother applying for these jobs, they were just closed to them.

An important part of Farrell's childhood folklore concerns the B-Specials, an official, armed Protestant militia, which during his formative years was an all-pervasive feature of the Six County scene:

I was a teenager during the IRA campaign of the 1950s. There was a very heavy B-Special presence in our area and I remember the oppressive nature of their patrolling. My father had no political involvement whatsoever. He was a very peaceable individual. But I remember him getting very annoyed at the aggressive behaviour of the B-Special patrols who would stop people [i.e. Catholics] and question them. Even when they were neighbours and knew their names well, they would demand their names and addresses and identification and so on. It just gave an impression that the Catholic community were an oppressed and suppressed group to whom all sorts of avenues were blocked and who had no redress against that.

'No redress'? Leaving aside the question of the responsibility and jurisdiction of the two parliaments involved, those in London and Belfast, to which we shall advert in the relevant context, what about the ordinary structures of democracy? Could a Catholic like Currie Senior not have gone along for example to a local representative, a Nationalist, rather than someone like Moses Busby, and had his problems addressed at county council level? The answer is that he could perhaps have had his problems raised, but not solved. Farrell explains why:

> Our area had a small Catholic majority which voted Nationalist. Prior to partition the local rural council, under the system of proportional representation, had been Nationalist-controlled. But the abolition of PR after the state was set up, and the practice of gerrymandering and discrimination, which went hand in hand with the abolition, meant that for all of my youth it was a Unionist-dominated council. No Catholics were employed by the local council and the bulk of council housing was allocated to Protestants. Gerrymandering meant that electoral boundaries were drawn in such a way that an area with a Nationalist majority would be hived off to form a single electoral unit. Then two areas with very small Unionist majorities would be set up as separate electoral units.

How this system worked in practice can best be seen in Derry City, the capital of the county Farrell grew up in. It was also the storm centre where, in a real sense, the gerrymandering system blew up in the Unionists' faces, bringing British troops on to the streets in 1969 and thus inaugurating the contemporary Irish Troubles. The population of Derry was roughly two-thirds Catholic to one-third Protestant, and the Catholic population kept growing. Nevertheless, the population increase did not mean that the Catholics could ever overtake the Protestants. Successive gerrymanders repeatedly redrew the electoral boundaries, so that the Unionist one-third were able to control the city. The results were that Catholics could not get municipal jobs or houses. Unemployment was rife and Farrell recalls:

> ... appalling slum conditions in Derry and yet people just couldn't get houses. They had to live in converted army huts. They had to live a couple of families to a house and so on.

The enforcement of these conditions was not due to an inherent cruelty on the Unionists' part. Inefficiency played a role, because they did not build enough houses anyway for either Catholic or Protestant, but, overall, housing policy had a basic political goal. It could be summed up in the same word that governed Sir James Craig's action in turning down the recommendation of a British cabinet committee in 1919[5] which offered not a six- but a nine-county Ulster. The word is: control. The principle of adult suffrage – that is, one man, one vote – was severely distorted in Six County elections. The electoral methodology employed will shortly be described, but here it should be noted that, bearing in mind the fact that most business and property was owned by Protestants, although long abolished in England both business and property votes still counted in local elections when Austin Currie entered Parliament. The general vote was confined to the occupier of a house and his wife. Occupiers' children over twenty-one, and any servants or subtenants in a house, were excluded from the local franchise. Austin Currie explained how the system worked and how it affected him as a young MP:

Housing was the key to the vote. The vote at local government elections was restricted to property owners and their spouses. Or to tenants of public authority houses and their spouses. I was an MP at Stormont. I could just as well have been an MP at Westminster. I had a vote in general elections to either Stormont or Westminster. But I did not have a vote in local elections to elect councillors because I wasn't married and lived at home with my mother and father. My mother and father were the only two in our large household who had a vote in council elections.

The purpose of the exercise was to ensure that Unionists had continued supremacy in the areas where in fact they were in the minority. Places like Derry, Armagh, Dungannon, Enniskillen and so on. This was the only way in which the Unionists could remain in control. That's why housing was such a fundamental matter. The allocation of a public authority house was not just the allocation of a house. It was the allocation of two votes. Therefore, in marginal areas, he who controlled the allocation of public authority housing effectively controlled the voting in that area.

For four years after his election Austin Currie struggled within the confines of the parliamentary system to improve the housing system in particular and the lot of Catholics in general. Like other young Catholics of his background whose names we will become familiar with throughout this book, such as John Hume, and Bernadette Devlin, he had presentational skills and a confidence acquired through his Butler Act education. The confidence was often more apparent than real. 'I was shaking,' he recalls, 'when I stood up to ask my first question in Stormont.' It was about discrimination and was addressed to the imposing figure of Lord Brooke-borough, the then Six County prime minister. However, the fact that Currie was wearing a new suit gave him the extra impetus he needed to master his fears and speak out clearly. After that, he said, 'I felt that if I could confront Lord Brookeborough I could confront anyone.' Confront the system he did, as, bolstered by the McCluskeys' research, he went on to build up a justifiable reputation for being courageously articulate. However, he achieved little in the way of tangible reform. In his own way he was traversing the same fruitless political cycle path which his father had travelled to see Moses Busby twenty years earlier.

Then, in June 1968, he stepped outside the confines of Parliament to make his protest. There was talk of civil rights in the air. The activities of students on the continent of Europe, and of Martin Luther King and his followers in America, were beginning to work their alchemy in Northern Ireland also. A specific civil rights issue came to hand in the improbably picturesque setting of Caledon, a tiny, stone-built Co. Tyrone town that looks as though it was transported to Ireland from the estate of some great English landowner. In and around Caledon there were as usual many Catholics waiting patiently and uselessly for a council house. The housing list contained a total of 269 names; many of them had been on the list for ten years and more. Some of the families had as many as fourteen children. All of them were outraged when the eighteen-year-old Protestant secretary of a nearby Unionist politician was awarded a house when she became engaged – to a local B-Special.

It was decided that, for once, something positive should be done about this injustice. Inspired by the new ideas of protest emanating from the civil rights movements abroad, two aggrieved local families, the Goodfellows and the McKennas, staged squats in vacant council houses. The squats, promptly and brusquely dealt with by the Royal Ulster Constabulary, raised ripples of local interest only. But then Austin Currie decided that the time had come for such a protest and personally led a third sit-in. This one caught the headlines because Currie was an MP. It is generally regarded as the first significant direct action initiative of what was to grow into a historic civil rights movement. For the Catholics in the Six Counties of north-eastern Ireland, the era of Bicycling to Busbys was drawing to a close. The Curries and their like had decided to sit down and be counted.

By now readers should have a reasonable grasp of the 'feel' of Catholic grievance and what it focused on. But the Unionist and British Establishment is not without its apologists. Even at the time of writing, subtle attempts continue to be made to suggest that these injustices were somehow exaggerated and unreal. A professor of sociology at the University of Aberdeen, Steve Bruce, who has become something of a media figure through his writings about loyalism and Unionists, has stated that:

> The civil-rights slogan 'One Man – One Vote' was aimed not at domestic audiences but at London, Paris and Washington, and it was successful in mobilising international support for the movement.[6]

Here is the precise statistical background to the system at which the slogan 'One Man – One Vote' was addressed. The 1961 Census Report for Northern Ireland gives the population as 1,425,462. Computed by the normal standards of adult suffrage, i.e. 'one man – one vote', the electorate for Westminster in 1964, the year Currie entered Stormont, was 891,107. However, if one consults the electoral register for that year (published on 15 February), a different statistical picture emerges for what might be termed the 'domestic' electorate. This retained the business and property votes which 'the UK mainland' had abolished and broke down as follows:

Stormont Electors

Adult suffrage	885,514
University second vote	13,763
Business second vote	12,663
Total	911,940

Local Government Electors

Residents and spouses	648,417
Business second vote	6,467
Company votes	3,894
Total	658,778

One can see at a glance how the inbuilt unfairness of the system distorted both sets of statistics to a greater or lesser degree. In the case of Stormont, the university votes, overwhelmingly Protestant, favoured the Unionists. They obtained a vote both in the perpetuation of a hold on the four university seats and in their local constituencies. In local government they secured a property vote, for both husbands and spouses, on premises valued at £10 and over. They thus legally obtained more votes than there were voters on the electoral lists. (Illegal methods, for instance the widespread custom of personation, not confined to Unionists by any means, served to create the impression that in Northern Ireland the dead somehow reached beyond the grave at election time.) As a former Stormont minister has written, no one in the Unionist Party 'considered it incongruous that 80,000 people in Belfast should be denied a Local Government vote while 12,091 graduates at the University could claim a sizeable parliamentary representation'.[7] The Queen's University franchise gave it four seats out of fifty-two. At least two of the four were invariably Unionist. By redrawing constituency boundaries, or by giving equal parliamentary representation to widely disparate population and geographical areas, it was possible to obliterate the Catholic vote. For example, Co. Antrim had a population of 273,905. Of these, 66,929 were Catholics. Yet all seven Stormont seats went to Unionists. Mid-Down had 41,402 electors but was given equal representation with Belfast's Dock division, which had only 7,612. The discrimination was even greater in the case of local government where, as can be seen in the table above, some 220,000 voters were disenfranchised from the number shown on the Westminster lists. How this worked in practice is best seen in Derry, important to the Unionists in both psychological and political terms. Derry, the Maiden City, was the scene of that historic gesture of 'conditional loyalty', the shutting of the gates in the faces of King James's troops by apprentice boys who defied the governor of the city, Lundy. Lundy is today burnt annually in effigy by the Protestants of Derry, while the apprentice boys' memory is correspondingly venerated. Deep in the Unionists' psyche there still lurks a hope that some contemporary apprentice boys will arise to make a similar gesture in the faces of oncoming liberalism, Dublin, Irish-America, the media, and betrayal from London.

However, in the 1960s Derry's ruling Unionists had more tangible reason to believe in the continuing supremacy of their cause than ancestral yearnings. The 1961 census gives the population of Derry City as 53,744. Of these 36,049 were Catholic and 17,695 Protestant. The franchise stipulations cut this two-to-one Catholic ratio so heavily that only 14,325 Catholics were entitled to vote. However, this still represented a sizeable majority over the 9,235 Protestants who had the suffrage. But incredibly enough, this numerical superiority was turned into a minority on the council by an exercise in gerrymandering. The town was divided into three wards: North, Waterside and South.

North contained 6,711 voters, divided in the Protestants' favour in a ratio of two to one. It returned eight representatives, all of them Unionists. Waterside had 5,459 voters, again roughly divided in the Protestants' favour by a majority of two to one. It returned four representatives, all Unionist. This left some 11,390 voters penned into the South Ward, which returned eight representatives. Of these voters, 10,130 were Catholics. Understandably, this ten-to-one majority returned a clean sweep of Catholic representatives. But when the Catholic South Ward's eight seats were placed against North and Waterside's combined return of twelve seats, the majority population of Catholic Derry was outvoted 12–8 and housing policy remained in Unionist hands. What this meant in practice was that in 1965 – while there were only a handful of unhoused Protestants – there were 2,000 Catholic families on the city's waiting lists. Of the 177 employees of Londonderry Corporation, 145 were Protestants, earning a total of £124,424. Thirty-two were Catholics, earning £20,424. Derry is the microcosm which enables the reader to understand why the Catholic one-third of the north's population furnished 58 per cent of the north's emigration between 1937 and 1961. Emigration was the reason why the ratio of Protestant to Catholic remained at the same two-thirds:one-third ratio which had obtained when the Government of Ireland Act was passed forty years earlier in 1920 – despite the high Catholic birth rate.

At this stage the question which logically arises – and which has to be answered before we can hope to proceed towards understanding what subsequently befell in both Ireland and England – is: how did England allow a political slum like the Six Counties, whose public housing system and much else besides embodied such marked departures from British practice, to develop into what London claimed to regard as as much a part of the UK as either Scotland or Wales? The short answer is given in the historical introduction to this book. Partition was viewed as a device for getting Ireland off Britain's agenda. Ireland, north or south, was a notoriously thorny issue, a graveyard of political reputations. Getting involved in the internal affairs of the six-county state meant facing the high risk of fetching up in that graveyard.

The longer answer would involve producing a thick book documenting the number of occasions on which London was informed of injustices in Northern Ireland, either by Six County Nationalists or others, and did nothing about them. The reason why this was done was spelled out at a top-level, off-the-record seminar[8] in London by the former British prime minister, James Callaghan. The seminar was one of a series run by the Institute of Contemporary British History. It attracted former decision-takers on Northern Ireland, who included British and Irish prime ministers, generals and senior civil servants. Callaghan was addressing the question: 'Did the Government miss an opportunity to take policy initiatives that could have prevented the breakdown of law and order in August 1969?' He said:

> I think it was like so many things in politics. It took a crisis to enable us to take the action that was necessary. It is like so many things that you cannot really act [on] even though you know it is logical to act and you ought to be able to act, until circumstances are right that permit you to do so. This is why, probably, we shall enter the European currency, because it will be seen that is inevitable and must be done, and this happens all the time in politics. So I think yes, theoretically and logically we should have taken action to press the Stormont government to do things. In practice it was not, given the surrounding circumstances, politically possible to do it. That's the answer.

Put bluntly, what Callaghan was saying was that it took a crisis, not to 'enable', but to force Britain to do something about the political slum which it had allowed to fester under its jurisdiction for half a century. The 'surrounding circumstances' to which Callaghan was referring were not merely those of the Wilson–Callaghan era. They relate back to the state's inception. For, as the seminar was also informed,[9] since 1922 there had been a Speaker's ruling that Northern Ireland matters could not be raised in the House of Commons. Peter Rose has commented that: 'So successful was this muzzle that during the 1960s the amount of time spent on Ulster at Westminster averaged less than two hours a year.'[10] The original ruling, which quickly became settled policy, was to prevent discussion of sectarian assassinations, which at the time were mostly of Catholics. However, as a result of pressure on London by Michael Collins to hold a public inquiry into the murders, Colonel Stephen Tallents was ordered to produce a report.[11] He found the behaviour of the B-Specials to be 'disgusting'[12] and said privately that the northern Government had 'failed to perform the elementary duty of guaranteeing life and property'. Nevertheless, the report was suppressed and Tallents was bribed into silence by being appointed the British Government's permanent representative in Belfast.

Neither Tallents nor anyone else attempted to prevent the Unionists from abolishing proportional representation in local government elections the following year (1923), thus facilitating the introduction of the system of discrimination and gerrymandering described earlier. The British Government connived at the abortion of the Boundary Commission in 1925, leaving the Unionist Party, secure within the state's existing boundaries, to carry on as it wished, unhindered by London. As the storm clouds gathered in the latter half of the 1960s, the level of awareness in the House of Commons concerning Northern Ireland was, according to Callaghan, that 'Most members of Parliament knew less about it than we knew about our distant colonies on the far side of the earth.'[13]

The subject seldom, if ever, came up at Cabinet, and Northern Ireland's concerns had '. . . fallen into a settled routine at the Home Office . . .'[14] When Callaghan took over at the Home Office in 1967 he found, on his first day, that there was not one word in his dispatch box about what was shortly to become Britain's worst headache.[15] Some pains had been experienced: the first riots and car burnings of the era had occurred in Belfast, in 1964, and the re-created UVF had been responsible for sectarian murders in 1966. But as Callaghan opened his Home Office dispatch box it was still impossible to foresee the migraine that was to come. In fact, if one were of an optimistic cast of mind, the political situation in the Six Counties, viewed from London, and in particular from Dublin, could be, and was, perceived as taking a turn for the better.

True, the Unionist Party was firmly in power, as it had effectively been since the passing of the Government of Ireland Act in 1920. Indeed, the party had but recently given a demonstration of its effectiveness in the manner in which it had seen off a growing challenge from the Labour Party during the 1965 Stormont elections. Under the leadership of the Prime Minister, Captain Terence O'Neill, the party had simply wrapped the Orange flag round itself and declared that a vote for Labour would weaken the Union. Election literature of the period spoke of the Labour Party being more of a threat to 'Ulster' than the IRA, the communists, or all the parties in the Republic put together. The growth of a broad-based Labour movement, embodying a commitment to civil rights and, remarkably, embracing both Catholic and Protestant, came to an abrupt stop with a swing to the Unionists of some 7 per cent. The handful of Nationalist MPs at Stormont, outnumbered as usual by the order of three to one, had neither the clout nor, on average, the calibre to force reform.

Nevertheless, O'Neill was widely regarded as a reformer. He had surrounded himself with liberal-minded advisers, made gestures to the minority, such as visiting a Catholic convent, unprecedented in the history of the northern statelet, and, above all, had received the Republic's Prime Minister, Sean Lemass, at Stormont Castle, the first time a southern prime minister had crossed the threshold since the inception of the state. Later that year, ironically, the same 1965 in which he decimated the NILP by playing the Orange card, he again made history by visiting Lemass in Dublin. But above all O'Neill's main attraction to what might be termed optimistic political opinion was that he was not Lord Brookeborough.

But this was both his strength and his weakness. In the interviews I conducted with him I found that, while O'Neill was no seminal intellect, he was an open, fair-minded man who, within the limits of his conditioning, genuinely sought to move his state forward. This was precisely his demerit in the eyes of his opponents within the ranks of Unionism. The Unionist Party which he inherited from Brookeborough was not the monolith it seemed to outsiders. It was united on upholding the Union and maintaining the border; any drift of Protestants to more exotic shores such as the NILP could speedily be checked, as we have seen, by a rattle on the Orange drum. But within the laager there was a great gulf fixed between the working-class Protestant in, say, the Shankill Road district of Belfast, and the Anglican mill-owner, landlord, or textile baron who reigned on the upper reaches of the party. The grandees of Unionism were able to so ordain matters that meetings were often held midweek, when workers would not normally be free. But social tensions were contained and diluted through membership of the all-pervasive Orange Order. The Order was the keystone of the arch of Unionist patronage and political advancement, its role in the Six County Government and ethos described in the classic summation of the state's first prime minister, James Craig: 'I have always said that I am an Orangeman first and politician afterwards, all I boast is that we are a Protestant Parliament for a Protestant State.'[16]

When O'Neill took over, every member of the Northern Ireland Government was also a member of the Orange Order, as was every Westminster MP. He had to become one himself, joining the Ahogill, Co. Antrim, branch, which was considered so staunch that it gave rise to the parable of the apocryphal Sammy McFetridge. Sammy had been a fine, upstanding bigot all his life, but on his deathbed the dreadful rumour swept the village that he was turning pape. Fearing that Ahogill was in danger of losing its place amidst the Nations of the Earth, a delegation of elders visited the dying man to enquire how the rumour had spread. With his dying breath, Sammy gasped out: 'It's no rumour. It's the truth – it's better that one of them goes than one of us.'

However, most Catholics saw little humour in the Orange Order's activities. With very few exceptions, Unionist local government representatives, such as county councillors, were also members of the Order, which had the right to nominate some 130 members to the Ulster Unionist Council.

Writing around this period, Andrew Boyd estimated that:

> . . . nearly every other member of the Unionist Council, apart altogether from the direct nominees of the Orange Order, is also an Orangeman or an Orangewoman . . . the local lodges of the Orange Order have the right to nominate delegates to every local Unionist Association . . .[17]

Another characteristic of Unionism, particularly strong in the Presbyterian Dissenting tradition, was, and is, the concept of conditional loyalty. This strain, deriving in part from the Scottish covenanters, had, and has, a certain view of what one should be loyal to. So long as the Crown, or Parliament, did as one wished then one was unswervingly loyal. If not, one reserved the right to take action as one saw fit in defence of the state or constitution. The concept of being British did and does not imply a fidelity to British standards of parity of esteem, respect for Parliament or civil and religious liberties. This was made clear by the leadership of the Orange Order not long before O'Neill became prime minister. From an enlightened wing of Unionism there had come a proposal that Catholics should be admitted to the Unionist Party. It was even suggested that some day they might stand for Parliament.[18] The Orange Order was outraged. Sir George Clark, Grand Master of the Grand Orange Lodge of Ireland, issued a statement to the papers saying that 'under no circumstances would such a suggestion be countenanced by our institution'. He went on:

> I would like to draw your attention to the words 'civil and religious liberty'. This liberty, as we know it, is the liberty of the Protestant religion, fought for and given to us by King William who at the time secured the Protestant succession to the Throne and gave us our watchword: The Protestant religion and liberties of the nation I will maintain. In view of this it is difficult to see how a Roman Catholic, with the vast differences in our religious outlook, could either be acceptable within the Unionist Party as a member or for that matter bring himself unconditionally to support its ideals.[19]

Sir George's words of course carried the implication that if Catholics were not suitable for membership of the party which ruled the state, they were not kosher where the state was concerned either. Many Unionists would have accepted this corollary without question. Sir Basil Brooke is on record as having told a Twelfth of July gathering in 1933 that because Roman Catholics were disloyal they should not be employed. He said that he took care to ensure that not one was employed about his estate. Pleased with the reaction this statement elicited (from Unionists), he repeated it several times, ultimately becoming the object of a censure motion put down by Nationalists at Stormont in 1934. The then prime minister, Lord Craigavon, responded by moving an amendment which said that the employment of 'disloyalists' was prejudicial to the state and took jobs away from loyalists.[20] Sir Basil went on to become Viscount Brookeborough and to rule as prime minister for twenty years until O'Neill succeeded him in 1963.

O'Neill described his predecessor as follows:

He was good company and a good raconteur and those who met him imagined that he was relaxing away from his desk. What they didn't realise was that there was no desk. A man of limited intelligence, his strong suits were shooting and fishing in Fermanagh and when he came up on Monday night or Tuesday morning it was difficult to shake him from some of his more idiotic ideas. In short, it would have been quite impossible, even with his immense charm, for him to have been a minister in London.[21]

Within Nationalist circles Brookeborough was depicted in more sombre hue. He was regarded as epitomising both the control which the security forces exerted in Northern Ireland and the essential lawlessness of the statelet. Brookeborough was the man who had first conceived the idea of the B-Specials, actively assisted in their setting-up, and connived at the turning of a blind eye to their murders and widespread illegalities. He was also rumoured to be the biggest smuggler in Northern Ireland.

Another, authenticated, cattle smuggler tells a tale of woe concerning what is alleged to have befallen when, as a young man, he once flouted 'the Lord's' authority in this area. The smuggler had come to an agreement that he would pay £1 a head for every beast he took across the border to a prominent RUC inspector. As a result he was not stopped on his nocturnal crossings of unapproved border roads. For some years he observed the arrangement faithfully, but as his business grew so did his resentment at the levy. Finally, having built up a herd of 700 cattle, he decided to save the £700 involved, and crossed the border by a normally deserted road – into the arms of a patrol of B-Specials and RUC.

Following his trial, which involved a fine and forfeiture of the cattle, he was disconsolately emerging from the courthouse when he was accosted by his former business associate, the district inspector, who bought him a commiseratory drink over which he said to him: 'Weren't you the foolish man. That pound did a lot more than give you the clear run. Two and six went to the lads on the patrol, two and six went to the sergeant, five bob went to the DI and ten shillings went to the Lord.' All I can say with certainty about this and other stories is that 'the Lord' did have an agent in Dundalk who discreetly bought cattle for him. Whether these Fenian Friesians found themselves, in their subsequent careers, transported back and forth across the border so as to avail him of the various subsidies and tariffs which the presence of borders inevitably create, I simply do not know. But it is certainly curious that a man in Brookeborough's position would have tolerated Catholic cattle about his place while making a virtue of excluding Catholic herders. Loyalty to the half-crown, rather than the Crown, has long been a Nationalist taunt hurled at Unionists.

Like many things in the Six Counties it is not the details of such stories that really matter but the perception they give. The image conveyed by the foregoing was that held of Lord Brookeborough by many Catholics, particularly in the farming community.

At all events, O'Neill states that when the Governor-General asked Brookeborough who should be his successor, mentioning O'Neill's name, Brookeborough made no comment. Seemingly he intended that his son, Captain John Brooke, should succeed him. The problem was that the son did not even have a seat in

Parliament at the time. In the Unionist Party, 'hands were laid on' when it came to the selection of a prime minister. In other words, there was a convention that the outgoing prime minister informed the Governor-General whom he thought should succeed him, and the Governor-General rubber-stamped the choice. But before John's career had had a chance to blossom to a point where he became an MP (in fact he did not become one for another five years), two unforeseen events occurred. One was an unprecedented call for Lord Brookeborough's resignation, signed by ten Unionist backbenchers worried by rising unemployment levels. The other was a duodenal ulcer which made Brookeborough fear he was developing cancer. The twin pressures caused him to take the unusual step of submitting three names to the Governor-General; Brian Faulkner, Sir John Andrews and Terence O'Neill.

There may have been a third pressure. Faulkner, heir to a sizeable shirt-manufacturing concern – which incidentally did a thriving business in the south – was not a member of Unionism's ruling ascendancy, which was both Anglican and landowning. He was out of the prosperous Presbyterian trader class, who were not altogether chic in the eyes of the squirearchy. Moreover, Lucy Faulkner, his wife, had been Brookeborough's secretary, and it has been suggested that the strong-minded Lady Brookeborough, who exerted considerable influence on her husband, did not wish to see the former secretary elevated to the status of prime minister's wife in her stead. At all events, when the Governor-General consulted the chief whip of the Unionist Party, William Craig, as to who would be the most acceptable, Craig informed him that an exhaustive canvass of the party had revealed that O'Neill had overwhelming support. Faulkner was in America at the time, and hands were duly laid on. However, it is said that Brookeborough adopted the triple nomination approach to block Faulkner, whom he thought would make a success of the job and thereby seal off John's chances of ever becoming prime minister. Andrews, whose main claim to the post was that his father had also been prime minister of Northern Ireland, had no chance of being appointed. This left O'Neill, who was Minister for Finance and who, it is alleged, Brookeborough reckoned would inevitably make a mess of things and be forced into resignation, thereby perhaps giving John his opportunity. *Peut-être* as the French say, for as finance minister O'Neill certainly held the senior posting after Brookeborough.

But three things may be said with certainty about the foregoing. One is that a senior Unionist minister of the time, Harry West, Minister for Agriculture, is on record as saying that he never encountered any member of the Unionist Party who was canvassed by Craig as to O'Neill's suitability. Secondly, O'Neill came to the premiership not only with no following amongst the working-class and evangelical elements within the party, but with the undying enmity of Brian Faulkner. As the former Stormont minister David Bleakley would write later, O'Neill and Faulkner were always 'on a collision course'.[22] Thirdly, there was such dissatisfaction within the party amongst Faulkner's supporters that new rules were drawn up for the selection of future prime ministers. These factors combined to make O'Neill a sitting duck for attack by Ian Paisley's fundamentalist opportunism once his reformist colours began to peep through his Orange straitjacket. Unionism was not about reform. It was, and is, about control. David Trimble, of the Official Unionist Party, has articulated this feeling perfectly:

> ... the Apprentice Boys myth is very deeply embedded within the consciousness of the Ulster British community ... a community that had then been abandoned or misled by the natural leaders of society ... if they feel their leaders are taking them down a road they do not wish to go or are in any way abandoning them then they are prepared to act themselves ... the banding together element has always been present within rural Ulster at times of unrest ... Terence O'Neill never really sounded or behaved as if he was one of us. Not like Brookeborough, not like Craigavon, not like Faulkner ... really until he arrived here to as it were inherit one of the family seats he had no connection with Ulster ...

O'Neill's career epitomised the twilight of the Big House, as the homes which formed the centrepieces of the great Anglo-Irish estates were known. The light had already gone out in the Republic, to be lit only in remembrance by writers such as Elizabeth Bowen and Molly Keane. But in the north there was still a plethora of majors and captains to be found commuting between their country residences and the upper slopes of the Stormont political establishment. Colonels were scarcely met with and sightings of generals were almost unknown until the British began sending them over from England at the close of the decade to patch up what the captains and the majors had wrought. O'Neill was a direct descendant of Sir Arthur Chichester, the Lord of the Plantation in Ulster under James I. His father, again a captain, had been Westminster MP for Mid-Antrim, and was the first MP to be killed during the 1914–18 war. Both O'Neill's brothers were killed in the Second World War, in which he served in the Irish Guards. His uncle, Sir Hugh O'Neill, had also represented Antrim at Westminster, from 1915 to 1949, and was a founder member of the Conservative 1922 Club. His aunt, Dame Dehra Parker, represented South Derry from 1920 to 1931 and then passed the seat on to her son, Major Chichester-Clark. However, he died only two years later and, things being as they were in Unionism, the Dame repossessed the seat, and, having become a minister in the interim, passed it on in 1959 to her grandson, James Chichester-Clark. When O'Neill became prime minister the chief whip at Stormont was a cousin, as was the Stormont MP for North Antrim. Two other cousins represented Derry County and North Antrim at Westminster.

It was an impressive superstructure, but the foundations were susceptible not only to an erosion of mistrust as indicated by Trimble, but to a form of economic erosion which had already begun when O'Neill succeeded Brookeborough. The economic situation was now about to trigger explosive political and religious consequences. Prior to O'Neill's taking over, unemployment had risen at a steady rate which traditional Unionism showed neither the will nor the capacity to arrest. A development council, set up under Lord Chandos in 1955, 'did little more than wine and dine visiting industrialists and had little success'.[23] The Hall Committee, a conglomeration of British and Northern Ireland civil servants, issued a report in 1963 suggesting that an economic advisory council be set up – and that the unemployed be encouraged to emigrate to Britain.[24] In 1963 unemployment was running at 9.5 per cent of the workforce (45,000). The Six Counties' principal industries were those most exposed to world trends: agriculture, engineering, and textiles. During the period 1951–61 the decline in agricultural and textile employment was of the order of 40 per cent. In the deep heart of militant loyalism, the Belfast shipyards, it was nearer to 60 per cent. Moreover, it was not merely in the realm of civil rights that the area had been allowed to depart from British standards – average weekly earnings were only 78 per cent of those in Britain. While the significance of the possession of a house has already been adverted to, it should also be noted that the quality of the housing which the captains and the majors – who of course lived in the Big Houses – had made available to the 'other ranks' was a further source of discontent, and one which bore heavily on Protestants. Some 32 per cent of all the houses in the statelet either had no piped water or no flush toilets. The rate of house building, some 6,000 a year, was woefully inadequate either to deal with new demand or improve existing conditions.[25] Ten years after the decade covered by the foregoing figures, an authoritative report, speaking of the proportions of aged to newer housing stock, said that '. . . the housing stock in Northern Ireland is worse balanced than any region of the United Kingdom'.[26]

By that time, however, an appalling tide of violence had already broken over Northern Ireland. The traditional Unionist response towards meeting social needs was articulated by two Unionists shortly before O'Neill took over. One, Professor Corkery, a Unionist senator, opined that 'The parents of large families should be fined for having so many children.'[27] This was no isolated view. In 1956 the Catholic birth rate had caused the Unionists to attempt a derogation from the established policy of moving in step with Britain to introduce to the north any social welfare improvements effected in the 'UK mainland'. The initial enabling Bill sought to give fourth and subsequent children less than the British benefits. But liberal Protestant opinion forced Brookeborough to announce on 12 June 1956 that he was dropping the proposal. History does not record the views of the other Unionist, Robert Babington, a barrister, on the question of birth control, but we do have his opinions on unemployment policy. He suggested that:

Registers of unemployed Loyalists should be kept by the Unionist Party and employers invited to pick employees from them. The Unionist Party should make it quite clear that the Loyalists have the first choice of jobs.[28]

This was vintage Brookeborough philosophy and its articulation helped Babington to succeed in his ambition of becoming a Unionist MP. However, O'Neill was no traditionalist. He set out to introduce such modern theories as economic planning, and co-operation with trade unions, to the Six Counties, and achieved a measure of success. Brookeborough had had an aversion to both. Accepting that the traditional north of Ireland industries were in terminal decline, O'Neill encouraged a number of industrial giants involved in twentieth-century technology to come to the province. These included Courtauld's, Du Pont, Enkalon, Goodyear and ICI. Unlike Brookeborough, who had refused to recognise the Irish Congress of Trade Unions (ICTU) because it was an all-Ireland body, he opened a link with ICTU through a Northern Committee of Congress, which paved the way for the formation of an economic council based on government, employers and labour.

O'Neill's blueprint for these and other innovations was provided by a number of academics: chiefly Professor Thomas Wilson of Glasgow University who, in October 1963, was appointed economic consultant to the Government; and Sir Robert Matthews who had been commissioned to produce a report on regional development before O'Neill became prime minister. Following the Wilsonian prescription really meant no more than attracting multinationals to the Six Counties, with the consequential drawback of profit repatriation elsewhere. However, while they led to the successes outlined above, they also led O'Neill to espouse policy initiatives involving both Northern Ireland and the Republic which would eventually bring him down. His drive for new outside investment meant that the economic and political dominance of the old Unionist industrialists diminished, albeit very slightly. Both the Unionist rulers and the Protestant working class saw danger signals in the fact that the institutionalised discrimination practised in the older firms could not easily be translated to the newer businesses. Discrimination apart, the old industrial élite's resentment rose as the newer industries begin to dominate the economic landscape, while their own financial and political clout diminished. The workers found that the tradition of the discreet word in Orange or Freemason lodge was not given its customary due by young personnel managers in Courtauld's or Du Pont. The latter were not greatly concerned whether fingers were Catholic or Protestant. All they asked was that they be deft. As a result there was a noticeable increase in female Catholic employment, especially around Derry. Here there was a tradition, described in a famous song by Phil Coulter, that the Catholic '. . . men on the dole played the women's role', while the women worked in the mills.[29]

These tensions, which had been growing during O'Neill's sojourn at Finance, crystallised around Brian Faulkner early on in O'Neill's reign as prime minister. A stalking-horse of Faulkner's, William Warnock, a hard-line former Attorney-General, sponsored an ineffectual backbench challenge to O'Neill in October 1963. Warnock's stated *casus belli* was the manner in which O'Neill had been appointed. He suggested that Faulkner was the man for the job. This threat soon petered out, but other aspects of the new Matthews-Wilson approach, or rather the attempt to adapt it to the old-guard Unionists' concerns, began to open up a second front for O'Neill, bringing him into conflict with the Catholics and undermining the value of his ecumenical approach to them.

Apart from the ongoing complaints about housing, there were four principal issues which aroused strong Catholic protest during 1964–5. All were concerned with another aspect of Unionist policy, the strengthening of the Protestant east as against the Catholic west of the province. In 1963 the position was as follows. Belfast held half the north's population and half of its industry. The triangle formed by the eastern countries Antrim (which contains Belfast), Armagh and Down contained the bulk of the rest of the Six Counties' industry and population. Two official employment statistics of the period record the gross imbalance thus created between east and west.

In the east the number of people employed in manufacturing by firms with twenty-five workers or more, classified by counties and county boroughs, was 160,392. In the west, embracing the counties Derry, Fermanagh and Tyrone, the figure was 28,773. In the Republic of Ireland to the south there was, and is, a constant complaint against the imbalance of the power and wealth of Dublin and its environs in the east compared with that of the west. But in the Republic no one thought the imbalance was based on religious grounds; everyone believed the problem to be political and economic. Some government action, however faltering and ineffectual, could be forthcoming through normal parliamentary pressures. In the Six Counties the position was reversed. Everyone believed the discrepancies arose for religious reasons. No one seriously thought Parliament would do anything to improve matters.

This belief was strengthened when in 1964 the Government cut one of the two rail links serving Derry City and county. The severance left most of the county, and those of Fermanagh and Tyrone, with no railways. The strongly Catholic Newry was also affected by a rail closure and in addition Derry suffered the loss of a shipping link with Glasgow. On top of the railway issue there came the Copcutt controversy. Geoffrey Copcutt was an English town-planner appointed by the Government to design a new town in Co. Armagh. On 13 August 1964 he resigned his post and issued a statement to the press, saying: 'I think there are better regions, environmentally and strategically.'[30] He cited the development of Derry City as a 'priority'. However, the Government went ahead with the building of the new city of Craigavon, called after the man who had declared Stormont to be a 'Protestant parliament for a Protestant people'. Apart from the choice of site and name, chosen to commemorate Sir James Craig, later Lord Craigavon, the founding father of the six-county state, Catholics had other reasons for believing that the new venture was less an exercise in town planning than in fortress Unionism. For example, despite the fact that Catholics made up only a third of the overall population of the north, their higher birth rate meant that 48 per cent of the Six Counties' primary school children were Catholic. But the new town plans only provided for the building of five Catholic schools, thereby practically guaranteeing that many young Catholic parents would be discouraged from taking jobs in the town, no matter what new industries were sited there.

The following year, 1965, while the echoes of the Craigavon controversy were still rumbling through the correspondence columns, the Government adopted a development plan drawn up by Professor Wilson, incorporating Sir Robert Matthews' ideas,[31] which proposed to create 65,000 new jobs by making a total investment of some £900 million in all sectors of the economy, including housing, for which a target of 64,000 was set. However, the implications of these very desirable goals were offset for Catholics by the publication of the list of growth centres wherein most of the employment and development was to take place. Of the ten specified in the report, eight[32] were clustered within a thirty-mile radius to the east. Only one, the last mentioned, Derry, was in the west. It would have appeared to have been a logical area for development as it possessed a port, an airport and some existing industry. But its placing in the list indicated to Catholics that its inclusion was cosmetic and there was no real intention to develop it.

The feeling was intensified beyond anything seen in the state for many years by the publication the same year (in February) of the Lockwood Report on Higher Education. The terms of reference of this committee were: 'To review the facilities for university and higher technical education in Northern Ireland having regard to the report to the Robbins Committee, and to make recommendations.' There was nothing in that remit about also making recommendations as to the site or sites of any proposed new educational institutions. However, this is what the committee did. Its recommendation, Coleraine, in the east, was accepted by the Government.

Derry, which had hoped to be the beneficiary of any extension of university facilities, was outraged. Firstly, it already had a university college, Magee, a constituent college of Queen's University, Belfast. Being the only university unit outside Belfast, Magee had appeared the logical base for expansion. Secondly, Coleraine only had a population of 12,000, less than a quarter of Derry's 54,000. Thirdly, and the third was more than equal to the first, there had not been a single Catholic on the committee. The resultant protest movement was unprecedented. The same sort of liberal Unionist sentiment which had prompted the suggestion that Catholics be admitted to the party surfaced and made common cause with the Catholics of Derry and with the opposition parties at Stormont. A University for Derry Campaign was founded, under the chairmanship of a young Derry schoolteacher, John Hume, who had built a reputation for himself through his pioneering work in establishing the Credit Union movement throughout Ireland. On 18 February 1965 the city of Derry virtually closed down; shops, schools, businesses of all kinds. A motorised cavalcade containing 1,500 vehicles drove the ninety miles to Stormont to protest the Coleraine decision.

It was to no avail. The Government carried the proposal by a majority of 32–20. This, though substantial, was one of the smallest in the history of the state. Two Unionists voted with the opposition and two more abstained. The university agitation led to the expulsion from the parliamentary party of a prominent Unionist, Dr Robert Nixon, Stormont MP for North Down. His crime was to reveal publicly that prominent Derry Unionists had colluded with the Government against the interests of their own area in favour of Coleraine in order to preserve overall Protestant hegemony. More educated Catholics were the last thing the Unionist hierarchy wished to see coming out of Derry. A petition containing 15,000 signatures was collected, asking in vain that his allegations be investigated. However, although defeated on the university issue, for John Hume, and many other educated young Catholics, the seeds of a civil rights street protest movement had been planted by the Magee controversy. They would shortly sprout.

But in Ireland overall these tensions between the newer, technocratic policies which O'Neill strove to introduce and the visceral 'them and us' nature of northern politics were obscured, for the moment, by another watershed event in which he was involved. On 14 January 1965 he received at Stormont his opposite number from the Republic, the Taoiseach, Sean Lemass. It was a meeting of seismic importance in Irish terms, the first time in the history of the two states that there had been a prime ministerial meeting.[33] Lemass, like O'Neill, was also a moderniser. As with O'Neill from Brookeborough, he had inherited a situation in which his predecessor had stayed on well beyond the point of usefulness. It is one of the tragedies of contemporary Ireland that the aged de Valera did not yield the reins earlier. The Republic, which, unlike the Six Counties, had no subsidies, had almost collapsed economically by the time he did so in 1959. By then he was seventy-eight, blind and incapable of innovation.

As the fifties drew to a close, income in the Republic overall was only some 55 per cent of that in the UK. But as it was nearer 65 per cent in the eastern province of Leinster where Dublin is situated, the sort of imbalances we have seen in the Six Counties were if anything worse in the impoverished western province of Connacht. The population was falling, but the Catholic birth rate meant that births were greatly in excess of deaths. As an outspoken economist, Professor C. F. Carter, said, it was a situation:

> . . . dangerous both to the Republic and to her neighbours. Faced by it, the universal resort of politicians is to seek refuge in fantasy, and usually in the dreary fantasy that prosperity must await the re-union of Ireland.[34]

Lemass was not a man to indulge in fantasy. As a youthful idealist he had fought in the 1916 rising at the age of sixteen. Of Huguenot stock, he was nevertheless a pragmatic politician who understood clearly the co-relation between the growth, or demise, of democracy and economic prosperity. Once, while I was interviewing him about the economic changes he was making in the Republic, he broke off to discuss the fall of the Weimar Republic and urged me to study how economic conditions had helped the rise of Nazism. 'Oh, read about it, you must read about it,' he said. Long sat upon by de Valera, who refused to act on his ideas while he was Minister for Industry and Commerce, as Taoiseach he cut through the old dogmas of protection, tariffs, self-sufficiency and sloganising about the fourth lost green field which had passed for policy. New men were appointed to the Cabinet. The Secretary of the Department of Finance, Dr T. K. Whitaker, produced a Programme for Economic Development which became government policy which Lemass seized upon. Together he and Whitaker revolutionised Irish society. International capital was sought, the country began to look outward.

As in other parts of the western world the sixties were a time of optimism in Ireland. As a new generation took over, new ideas began to permeate the Catholic Republic from a variety of sources: the liberalising influence of Pope John XXIII and his Vatican Council; the coming of television; increased travel; and the relaxation of literary and cinema censorship. The travel was made possible by increased prosperity, the invigorating side effect of new industries. Buoyed by all this, Lemass, in his sixty-fifth year, decided to drive north and meet O'Neill, who reciprocated by coming to Dublin a month later (on 9 February 1965), nine days before the Derry cavalcade set off for Stormont to protest about the Coleraine decision.

The visits had the effect of both adding to the forces ranging against O'Neill, and bringing to centre stage in the swelling northern drama an actor who had hitherto played relatively minor roles: Ian Kyle Paisley. I have heard him defend the term bigot on the grounds that it stems from the last protestations of the Protestant martyrs, who, during the Spanish Inquisition, proclaimed their faith, as they were led to the stake, 'by God'. Paisley's eruption before the footlights of twentieth-century western European politics made him appear a ludicrous figure to some observers. He seemed an aberration from the Thirty Years War who had somehow survived in a theological version of Plato's cave, only to appear, appalling and bawling, into the light of an ecumenical setting in which he was totally miscast.

Paisley in fact was rooted in a historical line of fundamentalist political evangelists like Henry Cooke and Hugh 'Roaring' Hannah, who in times of economic, political or sectarian tension arose in stentorian fashion to make a bad situation worse. Of them all Paisley deserves to be regarded as Stentorius Maximus, the loudest political voice in Northern Ireland. He cannot be fully exculpated for his own contribution. For most of the period of the Troubles under review he was a dominant figure, bestriding the political landscape of Northern Ireland with the Bible in one hand and both eyes on the ballot box. Apart from the mesmeric effect of his husky oratory, raw sex appeal, and powerful personality and physique, he articulated key elements of some forms of Northern Irish Protestantism.

Conditional loyalty, for example. He stated that: 'If the Crown in Parliament decreed to put Ulster into a United Ireland, we would be disloyal to her Majesty if we did not resist such a surrender to her enemies.'[35] His anti-Catholicism was the purest and most virulent available: 'Through Popery the Devil has shut up the way to our inheritance. Priestcraft, superstition and papalism with all their attendant voices of murder, theft, immorality, lust and incest blocked the way to the land of gospel liberty.'[36] Using such language in press (he founded his own newspaper, *The Protestant Telegraph*, in February 1966), platform and pulpit, Paisley and his 'attendant voices' did more than anyone else in Ireland over the entire period of the troubles to 'block the way' to a constitutional solution of the problems.

Paisley was born in 1926 in Armagh. Conditional loyalty was the leitmotif of his early life. His father had been 'loyal' in the classical Unionist sense through having been a member of Carson's original defiant volunteer corps. He was also deeply steeped in the north's Bible culture and became a Baptist minister – an Independent Baptist minister who founded his own church. At twenty-five, after being a preacher since his middle teens, Paisley too formed his own church, the violently anti-Catholic Free Presbyterian Church of Ulster, with himself as its moderator. A few years later he made headlines through being mixed up in the proselytising of a fifteen-year-old Catholic girl, Maura Lyons, who was kidnapped from her home in 1956. Paisley was ordered by a Belfast court to stay away from her.

He was in the news again in 1959 for throwing a Bible at the liberal-minded Methodist minister Dr Donald Soper, during a visit to Ballymena. He derived more valuable publicity amongst the north's anti-Catholics through getting himself arrested in Rome for protesting at the opening of the Second Vatican Council in 1962. In 1966 he organised a march to the General Assembly of the Presbyterian Church in Belfast to protest against its 'Rome-ward trend' at which the Governor of the province, Lord Erskine, as well as the various church dignitaries present, were heckled and abused. This was one of Paisley's more beneficial pieces of hooligan street theatre. He refused to be bound to the peace in subsequent court proceedings and earned for himself the martyr's crown of a three-month jail sentence, whose value could probably be translated into votes at the rate of a thousand a week. The following year Paisley's influence had grown to a stage where he was able to force the cancellation of a planned visit to the north by the ecumenical-minded Bishop of Ripon, Dr John Moorman.

Part of Paisley's anti-Catholicism has sexual overtones. Bob Cooper, the head of the north's Fair Employment Agency, a body which strives to undo everything Paisley stands for, has described him as 'the great pornographer'. Certainly Paisley can mix sexual imagery with incitement to hatred and fear of eternity in the most extraordinarily potent fashion. The night after Pope John XXIII died, Cooper attended a sermon preached by Paisley in Belfast's Ulster Hall. He recalled hearing Paisley describe 'the flames of hell at that moment licking around the dead Pope. It was so graphic and colourful that the audience could almost feel the flames and feel the heat. I will remember the horror till the day I die.'[37] Cooper went on:

It is certainly extraordinary the close relationship there appears to be between the effects of pornography and the anti-Catholicism preached by Paisley. It is not just that the vast majority of his images are sexual. Rome is always described as the painted woman out to seduce the innocent Ulster Protestant youth. His sermons are full of sexual innuendoes about priests and nuns. Following the visit of the Moderator of the Presbyterian Church in Scotland to the Pope, Paisley produced the extraordinary front-page headline in *The Protestant Telegraph* – 'The Church of Scotland drunk with the wine of the fornication with the Roman whore'.

Cooper has undoubtedly correctly diagnosed pornography as an essential component of Paisleyism. But there is nothing particularly new about Paisley's form of anti-Catholicism. He may have marched visibly with the Bible clutched in his hand. As one of his opponents in the Unionist Party remarked to me during 1969 when the full horror of what the man had helped to excite could be seen in the form of burned-out streets and nightly rioting in Belfast: 'And the trouble is, no one can say a word to him. He does all this with the Bible in his hand.' But in this history of the debased philosophy he articulated there lay another book: *The Awful Disclosures of Maria Monk*. Along with his Bob Jones University degree, Paisley imported into Ireland the language and the hate creation that filled this ghost-written work which first appeared in America in 1836. The work, the fictionalised ramblings of a deranged woman who ultimately died in prison, was one of the foundation texts of the anti-Irish, anti-Catholic nativist movement that convulsed America *circa* 1835–60. Maria described how she ran away from her convent because the reverend mother forced her to 'live in the practice of criminal intercourse with priests'. Nuns who did not were murdered. The children born of such couplings were baptised and strangled. Maria enjoyed a brief period of respectability after her story appeared, being taken up by a committee of Protestant clergymen. But both respectability and credibility vanished when her mother revealed that Maria had never been in the convent she spoke of. She had been in a home for delinquent girls from which she had run away with a boyfriend by whom she apparently did have a child. However, this Catholic version of the anti-Semitic tract, the Protocols of the Elders of Zion, has remained in circulation; an attempt was made to make use of it during the Kennedy presidential campaign of 1960.

In his early years as a preacher, Paisley produced 'nuns' at his church meetings, who, the congregations were informed, had also run away from convents rather than submit to unspeakable happenings. *The Protestant Telegraph* specialised in articles with headlines such as 'The Love Affairs of the Vatican',[38] 'Priestly Murders Exposed'[39] and 'Children Tortured – Monks Turned Out as Sadists'.[40] But there is another overtone to Paisleyism: a patina of violence which tinges his presentation of popery and the bogus connection he forges between the papacy and the IRA. *The Protestant Telegraph* also claimed, in April 1967, that the following is the Sinn Fein Oath:

> These Protestant robbers and brutes, these unbelievers of our faith, will be driven like the swine they are into the sea by fire, the knife or the poison cup until we of the Catholic Faith and avowed supporters of all Sinn Fein action and principles clear these heretics from our land . . .
>
> At any cost we must work and seek, using any method of deception to gain our ends, towards the destruction of all Protestants and the advancement of the priesthood and the Catholic Faith until the Pope is complete ruler of the whole world . . .
>
> We must strike at every opportunity, using all methods of causing ill-feeling within the Protestant ranks and in their business. The employment of any means will be blessed by our earthly Fathers, the priests, and thrice blessed by his Holiness the Pope.
>
> So shall we of the Roman Catholic Church and Faith destroy with smiles of thanksgiving to our Holy Father the Pope all who shall not join us and accept our beliefs.

It is not surprising, after Paisley's promulgation of such doctrines, that a former supporter of his who took part in an effort to kill a prominent Republican, and instead ended up shooting an apolitical Catholic barman, should have been quoted at his trial as saying: 'I am terribly sorry I ever heard of that man Paisley or decided to follow him. I am definitely ashamed of myself to be in such a position.'[41] Nor is it surprising, having successfully translated his particular brand of sectarianism into the religious life of the Six Counties, that Paisley should have done the same in politics. As his church grew throughout the fifties so did another creation of his, the Ulster Protestant Action group. The object of the group was the familiar one of keeping 'Protestant and loyal workers in employment in times of deep depression in preference to their Catholic fellow workers'.[42] The UPA also campaigned against the allocation of public housing to Catholics.

One of the earliest recorded mob actions associated with the Great Disturber occurred on the Shankill Road in 1959. After Paisley had concluded a passionate address to a UPA meeting the crowd attacked a fish and chip shop owned by Catholics. A far more serious breach of the peace occurred in 1964 during the Westminster election campaign. Paisley discovered that the Sinn Fein candidate, Liam McMillan, had displayed a tricolour, the Irish national flag, in the window of his election headquarters in Divis Street, off the Falls Road. One of the arrows in

Unionism's quiver of defence against Nationalism was the Flags and Emblems Act which prohibited the showing in public of the tricolour. No one troubled too much about its provisions when it came to displaying the flag in Nationalist areas only, particularly in a dingy, inconspicuous little back street like Divis. However, Paisley told a packed and perfervid meeting at the Ulster Hall on 27 September that if the flag were not removed within two days he would lead a march to do so himself.

Next day scores of RUC men were sent to break down the door of the Sinn Fein office and remove the flag. Accordingly, instead of holding the march, Paisley staged a meeting outside City Hall, well away from the Falls Road. But a crowd, several thousand strong, which had gathered on the Falls in the expectation of confronting Paisley's marchers, vented its dissatisfaction at his non-arrival by burning buses, the first such activity of the period under review. Belfast's temperature continued to go up throughout the week. The night after the bus burnings a Sinn Fein meeting broke up in rioting and baton charges. Two days later the tricolour was again displayed and the RUC smashed their way into the building with pickaxes to remove it.

The removal was the signal for the worst rioting in Belfast for thirty years. Petrol bombs began making their appearance as the RUC deployed armoured cars and water cannons. Next night, Friday, the RUC 'pacified' the Falls. Hundreds of helmeted police backed up by armoured cars drove protestors off the streets and some fifty of them into hospital. The tension spread to Dublin where a crowd marched on the British Embassy and stoned the Gardai. In Belfast, Nationalist leaders appealed for peace. A compromise was worked out whereby the rioting stopped and the RUC did not interfere when the tricolour was carried openly on the Sunday at a Republican parade. The increase in Orange fervour, however, benefited the Unionist candidate, Jim Kilfedder. There had been fears that the notoriously volatile West Belfast seat might have gone to an opposition candidate. But at 21,337 votes Kilfedder came in some 7,000 votes ahead of his nearest rival and with nearly seven times the total achieved by McMillan (3,256). However, the display of Paisleyite power forced Terence O'Neill to temporarily forsake liberal paths, and he was driven, not to condemn Paisley's incitement, but to comment for the benefit of his Unionist audience: 'Today certain Republican candidates, many with backgrounds in the IRA . . . appear to be using a British election to provoke disorder in Northern Ireland.'[43]

Paisley suffered from no such constraints in targeting his enemy – O'Neill himself. The Lemass visit to Stormont gave him an opportunity he seized with both hands. O'Neill had not dared to tell any of his colleagues in cabinet about Lemass' coming until the morning of the visit, and Paisley evoked many resonances both within and outside the Government as he stumped the province, demanding that 'O'Neill must go'. The month after the visit, he and his supporters staged a huge demonstration outside the Unionist headquarters in Glengall Street that forced O'Neill to call off a function there. Paisley's rhetoric was particularly directed at the Protestant working class. Again the wretched state of Northern Ireland's housing stock was a potent political issue. He made capital out of the fact that

O'Neill and his like lived in 'Big Houses', while many poorer Protestants lived in 'kitchen houses' with no flush toilets. The repetition of the term 'dry closets' became something of an antiphon with 'The Big Man', giving rise to jokes about Paisley's 'turd world'.

But his populist appeal was no joke. He was able to pull the Pope, O'Neill, the communists, and later the IRA, out of those closets like a conjurer plucking electoral rabbits from a hat. 1966 was a big year for Paisley, and a bad one for Northern Ireland. He went to jail and a number of people went to their graves. This was the year which saw the first deaths of the Troubles. It was the fiftieth anniversary of the 1916 rising, an event widely commemorated in the Republic, and in some Catholic areas of Northern Ireland also. This gave Paisley a chance to stage further rallies and protests at which he fulminated against celebrations of disloyalty and treachery. It was also the year he founded *The Protestant Telegraph*; an organisation called the Ulster Constitution Defence Committee which oversaw his supporters' activities, including those of the UPA; and a grouping called the Ulster Protestant Volunteers (UPV), which was organised throughout the province by one Noel Doherty, a printer who worked on *The Protestant Telegraph*. Doherty was also the secretary of the UCDC and a member of another Protestant organisation which emerged from the shadows of history in that year, the Ulster Volunteer Force (UVF).

The man who helped to reactivate the UVF was 'Gusty' Spence, an associate of Paisley's in the UPA. Spence came of a strongly Unionist family; his brother was the Unionist election agent for West Belfast. He was a shipyard worker who had some military training, having been in the British Army and served as a military policeman in Cyprus. The new UVF was a long way from the force which in Carson's day was supported by earl, general and mill-owner. Its predominantly working-class membership consisted, in Michael Farrell's description, of '. . . a small group of Paisley supporters who, alarmed by his denunciations of the Unionist sell-out, had set up an armed organisation'.[44]

It was an inefficient, confused, but deadly organisation which, apart from the fears of the sell-out trumpeted by Paisley, wanted to strike in some way at Republicans in the year of the rising's commemoration. The UVF did this by mounting a series of petrol bomb attacks on Catholic homes, schools and shops throughout the spring of 1966. On 7 May the UVF claimed the first life to be lost in the Troubles, that of an elderly Protestant, a Mrs Gould, who had the misfortune to live beside a Catholic pub which the UVF attacked with petrol bombs. The first fatal shooting occurred that month also, in Clonard Street, an area which was to prove one of the most significant trouble spots in the entire statelet. The attack followed the issuing of a statement on 22 May which said: 'From this day on we declare war against the IRA, and its splinter groups. Known IRA men will be executed mercilessly and without hesitation.'[45]

On 27 May a UVF gang set forth after this declaration to find and kill a well-known Belfast Republican, Leo Martin. Failing to find him, they shot the nearest convenient Catholic, John Scullion, who died of his wounds on 11 June. By 23 June stories about both the UVF and the UPV had become so commonplace in Loyalist areas that a Labour MP, Tom Boyd, publicly urged the Government to take action. Three days later, however, Spence and Co. set off again in pursuit of Martin. Again they missed him and retired in disgust to their local pub in Malvern Street, off the Shankill Road. Here they discovered a group of off-duty Catholic barmen having a drink. They ambushed them leaving the pub; one, Peter Ward, died of his wounds.

Ironically, 1966 was also the fiftieth anniversary of the slaughter of the original UVF membership at the Somme. Terence O'Neill attended the commemoration on behalf of the northern Government. He had to interrupt his trip to France to return to Ireland to ban the UVF under the Special Powers Act, a grave shock to the Protestant psyche, which regarded this piece of legislation as being for use against Catholics only. O'Neill also made public the fact of Doherty's role in Paisley's UCDC. Doherty was picked up in the police swoop that netted the Malvern Street killers. He subsequently received two years on explosive charges. Spence was one of those who were sentenced to a minimum of twenty years.

On 21 April, Paisley, who was going to Armagh, had dropped Doherty off at Loughall, where Doherty met the local UPV to discuss the procurement of arms and explosives. Paisley collected him on the way back from Armagh (there is nothing to indicate that Paisley was aware of his mission). The following month Doherty introduced the UVF to the Loughall men, who gave them gelignite. Paisley denied knowledge of the UVF, although he had publicly thanked the UVF for taking part in a march on 7 April, four days before he left Doherty in Loughall. He also claimed that he had dismissed Doherty from both the UPV and the UCDC prior to the Malvern Street round-up.

But the main focus of attention in that fatal year of 1966 was not what those associated with Paisley were doing, but what he was doing himself. The most lasting TV image of the year was of the Big Man with the blazing eyes, wearing a Roman collar and a white raincoat, leading protestors into various street confrontations. He brought Carson's son Edward to Belfast in March. Carson said that O'Neill was leading the statelet to the 'destruction of Ulster's hard-won constitution and liberties'.[46] The following month Paisley forced the Government to mobilise the B-Specials for the whole of April because of the Easter 1916 commemorations. He wanted the commemoration parades banned, but though he failed in this objective he succeeded in having a prohibition issued against allowing trains from the Republic to transport people to the Six Counties for commemoration ceremonies.

Then, on 6 June he led a highly provocative march through the Catholic Cromac Square area of Belfast, which provoked a riot between the RUC and local residents who tried to block his parade. The Paisleyites wound up outside the Presbyterian General Assembly where their behaviour caused the wife of the Governor to collapse and enabled Stentorius Maximus to win his jail sentence. Brian Faulkner supported Paisley's behaviour in the teeth of demands from the Moderator of the General Assembly, Dr Martin, that his violent demonstrations be stopped. Protestants, said Faulkner, had the right to protest. Dr Martin's request was 'an unwarrantable interference with the right of free speech and free assembly'.[47]

Paisley reciprocated by telling his supporters at a meeting in Castlewellan, Co. Down: 'Thank God for Brian Faulkner.'[48]

That year's Twelfth of July celebration was a Paisley 'twalfth'. His followers shouted down members of O'Neill's cabinet, and resolutions were passed at the various gatherings condemning the statelet's 'Romeward trend'. Brought to court on 18 July, when marching season fervour was still in full swing, he refused to be bound to the peace for two years and was duly deposited in 'The Crum', Belfast's Crumlin Road jail, in the heart of Loyalist Belfast. It now became a target for rioting. On 22 July vicious clashes occurred outside the jail between Paisleyites and the RUC. The following day there was further rioting as Protestant mobs, several thousand strong, rampaged through the city, smashing windows and trying to damage businesses owned by Catholics. The violence culminated in an orgy of baton-charging and mob thuggery outside the prison that night which precipitated a government crack-down. The RUC were empowered to ban all meetings involving more than three people, and all Belfast meetings and marches were banned for three months.

Not only was O'Neill under attack from Paisleyism in the streets, he was also assailed within the Unionist parliamentary party by Paisley's ally, Desmond Boal. Boal, a barrister whose victory in a Stormont by-election in 1961 was due to Paisleyite support, took up a petition amongst Unionist backbenchers demanding that O'Neill go. His conspiracy interacted with Faulkner's ambitions, and a number of prominent Unionists were invited to Faulkner's house. When this became known, Faulkner refused to back O'Neill, but made the brazen assertion that he had left the room while Boal and the other dissidents were talking![49] However, when the crucial Unionist Party meeting was held on 27 September, Faulkner was in America. He had reckoned, correctly, that O'Neill would survive Boal's onslaught. Boal himself was one of those who left before the vote was taken.

O'Neill staged something of a counteroffensive the following year when he sacked one of his opponents, Harry West, the Minister for Agriculture, over a somewhat malodorous land deal in Co. Fermanagh where West farmed extensively. On 26 April 1967 O'Neill told Stormont that the dismissal had occurred because he did not feel it right that a minister should acquire land in the knowledge that it might 'in the reasonably near future be acquired for a public purpose'. This unfamiliar intrusion of principle into Unionist politics caused Brian Faulkner to remark on the BBC that the deal was '. . . a situation in which Mr West is certainly absolutely blameless'.[50]

Apart from the Unionist Party itself there were two other sets of observers vitally concerned with Northern Ireland to whom Faulkner's machinations and the mounting tide of Paisleyism were matters of great significance. These were the British Government and the opposition parties of the Six Counties. At this stage these could roughly be divided into two groupings, Nationalists and Labour. We shall return to the Nationalists shortly. Let us, however, first examine the British reaction since it was, potentially at least, the more significant, and had implications for the Labour movement in both Britain and Northern Ireland. James Callaghan spelled out the Wilson Government's attitude, at the Witness Seminar in London on British policy in Northern Ireland to which I have already referred:

> ... the government very sensibly said we are not going to get involved in this when we are not welcomed by the Northern Ireland government. We would have to override the Northern Ireland government if we did. We're not going to do that. We want to use them as far as we can – that is what I understood the position was – in order to introduce the reforms. I think that was the attitude and for the very good reason that's been given. Nobody anticipated ... everybody knew what would happen if we did intervene and nobody wanted to get into the situation that if we once got in there we would never get out. That was certainly my policy when I got there, which wasn't until '67, to use O'Neill to put the reforms through and not in any circumstances to get our own fingers burned as indeed we have done when we eventually had to go in. And if we had gone in earlier we would have just got our fingers burned two years earlier that's all.[51]

In British politics the Unionists of course took the Tory whip. But for historical reasons there was a tradition within the Labour Party of taking an interest in Ireland. Harold Wilson used to boast to Irish prime ministers that he had more Irish in his Liverpool constituency than they had in theirs in Ireland. In 1954, Callaghan, Arthur Bottomley and Alf Robens visited Derry at the instigation of north of Ireland Labour figures like David Bleakley and Sir Charles Brett. They in turn visited London and succeeded in interesting Hugh Gaitskell in the Northern Ireland question. But there were a number of limitations on the efficacy of the Northern Ireland Labour Party's link with the British Labour Party. On the one hand the party was sufficiently affiliated for a Bleakley or a Brett to be invited to attend British Labour Party conferences and to sit on platforms. However, they could not take part in debates. On the other hand, at least until O'Neill effectively destroyed the party in the 1965 Stormont election, the NILP for a period entertained the hope that it could either one day form the Government of Northern Ireland, or become an effective opposition. Therefore the NILP was not overly keen on promoting measures which might have had the effect of whittling away the powers of the Northern Ireland Government and Parliament.

In fact, the hopes of the NILP were never well grounded in reality. The party was always susceptible to being squeezed between Orange and Green extremism. In 1949 all of its nine candidates were swept away in a tide of Orange fervour after the south declared a republic. It fared little better in 1953, but in 1958 it picked up four seats. To a rising generation of young Catholics, reaping the benefits of the Butler Acts, the NILP seemed to offer a vehicle for change. But mindful of the need to attract fundamentalist support, the party voted with extreme Unionists in 1964 against a proposal that corporation swings should be opened to children on Sundays. Young radicals like Michael Farrell, Bernadette Devlin, and in Derry the socialist Eamonn McCann were given food for thought about the NILP's commitment to change. The following year O'Neill gave them less to think about. His onslaught on the NILP cost the party two of its four seats, including David Bleakley and a Labour stalwart, William Boyd. Frank Hannah, a prominent lawyer and an independent Labour MP, did not contest the election.

Nevertheless, at Westminster prominent British Labour members like Geoffrey

Bing, Lords Longford and Fenner Brockway, Stan Orme, Paul Rose, Kevin McNamara – all of whom had lobbied for reform both before and after Labour came to power in 1964 – continued their activities. After he won the West Belfast seat in 1966, their efforts were considerably added to by Gerry Fitt, a former seaman who had formed his own Republican Labour Party.

In one of his earliest parliamentary skirmishes Fitt asked Harold Wilson the question which successive British governments should have addressed, but did not. His question was to ask Wilson to agree that:

> . . . under Section 75 of the Government of Ireland Act, 1920, the ultimate responsibility for everything which happens and good government in Northern Ireland is with the United Kingdom Government? Would he further agree that in the 46 years which have elapsed since this Act was put on the Statute Book it has been made increasingly obvious that democracy does not exist in Northern Ireland?[52]

Wilson's reply in turn was a distillation of all the Westminster equivocation and evasion that led to twenty-five bloody years in British–Irish history:

> The question raises some very difficult issues because of the division of functions between the United Kingdom parliament and government and the Northern Ireland parliament and government. We are all aware that Hon. Members in more than one part of the House are very disturbed about certain things which go on. I am not taking sides in this because there are allegations and counter-allegations by one side or another within Northern Ireland.
>
> I do not believe that this is a matter to be dealt with in the manner suggested [setting up a Royal Commission to enquire into the workings of the Government of Ireland Act]. I think that the right thing would be for my Hon. friend the Home Secretary and myself to have informal talks with the Prime Minister of Northern Ireland to see whether some of the difficulties which all of us recognise exist might be overcome in an informal way.

The admission that it was realised that 'difficulties' – i.e. injustices – existed did not mean they would be rectified. The ginger group within the Labour Party which came to form the vehicle for those seeking Northern Ireland reform was the Campaign for Democracy in Ulster. It had the support of perhaps a hundred Labour MPs. But Callaghan has summed up the influence of the CDU dismissively and accurately: 'That group was always interested just as there is always a group interested in relations with Namibia, or with South Africa or with any other part of the Commonwealth at the time. That was the basis of it and I think there was as much interest and as much detachment as that.'[53] As Callaghan was the Home Secretary who Wilson intimated would be joining in the 'informal' tête à trois with the Northern Ireland Prime Minister, that 'detachment' has a significant ring to it. It was that same 'detachment' which, as we shall see, resulted in a historic decision being taken to bring the civil rights issue on to the streets of Northern Ireland.

But before the situation matured to the point where this could happen, a great number of organised Nationalists had had to be convinced that the issue was civil rights and not the border and the existence of the northern state. This process may be said to have begun in October 1959 after Lemass made a speech to the Oxford Union which proposed a non-violent, federal solution to partition. Although unacceptable to Unionists it represented something new to northern Nationalists, who at this stage almost invariably took their cue from the 'Free State', as it was still spoken of, indicating that the south contained a degree of flexibility they did not possess in Northern Ireland. In December of that year a group of Catholic graduates, styling themselves National Unity, set up as a kind of Nationalist think-tank to work for unification through 'the consent of the people of Northern Ireland'. The principle of consent was important because there was a *de facto* arrangement within the ranks of nationalism whereby constitutional-minded Nationalists colluded to a certain degree with Sinn Fein. Sinn Fein was left unchallenged to contest Westminster elections, whereas the Nationalists contested Stormont.

The impulse towards new thinking continued in Nationalist circles, although National Unity itself had little impact on the Nationalist MPs at Stormont, half of whom were unconvinced that they should give the place legitimacy by remaining there and continuously toyed with the idea of abstention. The Nationalist Party was in reality a largely uncoordinated protest grouping of rural representatives and some businessmen, few of them of outstanding calibre. Dissatisfaction with this set-up led to the holding of an important Nationalist conference in Maghery, Co. Armagh, on 18 April 1964, attended by Nationalist supporters and representatives. A Nationalist representative, James O'Reilly, had been outclassed on a TV programme by Brian Faulkner on what should have been the unassailable ground of discrimination. But in those days inexperienced countrymen, with little formal education and unused to the type of statistical approach which the McCluskeys were pioneering, could still be overawed, in the daunting confines of a TV studio, by opponents armed with nothing more than the weapons of condescension and imitation British upper-class accents.

There was much vehement criticism of old-guard attitudes which could be summed up as: 'Go home, learn Irish and the Catholic birth rate will eventually take care of the problem.' A Nationalist Political Front was formed, involving National Unity, rural Nationalists and Belfast representatives such as Harry Diamond, Frank Hannah and Gerry Fitt. The Front only survived for some months before a split developed over lack of consultation on the issue of contesting a seat in Fermanagh–South Tyrone. From this split there evolved the National Democratic Party. This consisted largely of teachers and helped to contribute ideas and organisational talent to the Nationalist movement, but had little success in its own right. On 2 June a new leader of the Nationalist Party was chosen: Eddie McAteer, who represented Derry at Stormont and whose brother Hugh was a former chief of staff of the IRA. The Front had its mandatory split shortly afterwards but the Nationalists published a policy document in November 1964.

This pledged the party to working within the constitution to achieve various goals, including a democratisation of party structures, action on unemployment, an end to discrimination and gerrymandering, and the initiation of training schemes. It was in effect a recognition of the state, and a move away from concentration on the partition issue and towards civil rights. The demand now was basically that of the McCluskeys and their Campaign for Social Justice. Northern Ireland was a part of the United Kingdom, therefore it should have United Kingdom standards. This was a major shift within Nationalism; no longer was the problem seen as inextricably bound up with the necessity of removing the border. After Lemass met O'Neill he advised McAteer to accept the role of official opposition leader at Stormont, which he did on 2 February 1965. The following year I found the position on the ground amongst the Northern Ireland Catholics to be as follows:

> The plain truth about the North today is that the secret wish of most Northern Catholics is not for union with the South (entailing a fall-off in social benefits) but for an end to discrimination and for a fairer share of the Northern spoils. This truth may be unpalatable to us in the South, but it has to be faced.[54]

I researched two books consecutively in the years 1964–70[55] and for most of that time was assured on all sides that a new day was dawning throughout Northern Ireland. As we know now it was, but not in the sense that people spoke of. However, one area definitely did appear to have taken a turn for the better: there was no IRA activity. And for a very good reason: there was no IRA. The IRA's last border campaign had officially concluded in 1962. In fact it had been virtually finished since 1957. It was, as I have described it, largely a border campaign. Groups of young southern Republicans attacked targets along the border. They were motivated by the old tradition of 'a rising in every generation' which had inspired the men of 1916.

Like the 1916 insurgents they were execrated on all sides. Unlike the Easter rebellion, however, no dragon's teeth were sown by their martyrdom. Internment was introduced north and south of the border, by de Valera in the Republic and by Brian Faulkner as Minister for Home Affairs in the Six Countries. There was very little protest at this and no mass movement of support. The campaign was subsequently referred to in the north as 'the incidents'. That is what it was, a series of incidents along the border which aroused no significant supportive chord either in Nationalist rural areas or in major centres like Belfast and Derry. In fact the IRA had in a sense recognised their lack of support in one vital area, the Republic, as far back as 1954. In that year the organisation introduced Standing Order Number Eight as official IRA policy. It said:

> Volunteers are strictly forbidden to take any militant action against 26–Co. Forces under any circumstances whatsoever. The importance of this Order in present circumstances, especially in Border areas, cannot be overemphasised . . . Volunteers arrested during training or in possession of arms will point out that the arms were for use against the British Forces of Occupation only.[56]

This order had been prompted by a recognition of the fact that the years since the civil war, particularly those of World War II, when de Valera ruthlessly made use of emergency powers to cripple the organisation, had demonstrated that the south would not tolerate a physical force policy against the state. Partition had worked in that part of Ireland anyhow. The failure of the 'incidents' seemed to indicate that it had worked north of the border also. After the inevitable splits and internal upheavals – occupying more of the movement's time and energy than the occasional raid on a customs post or RUC barracks, which was about all the visible activity that occurred between 1957 and 1962 – the then IRA leadership decided to recognise the inevitable. On 26 February 1962 the Irish Republican Publicity Bureau announced that:

> The leadership of the Resistance Movement has ordered the termination of 'The Campaign of Resistance to British Occupation' . . . all arms and other materials have been dumped and all full-time active service volunteers have been withdrawn.[57]

From that date onward, Republican militarism ceased, except for a series of some seventeen funding bank robberies carried out in the name of front organisations, such as Saor Eire.[58] The movement began to devote itself increasingly to political activities. The then chief of staff, Cathal Goulding, was influenced by two Trinity College lecturers of left-wing inclination, Roy Johnston and Anthony Coughlan. Sit-ins to further housing protests, agitations over mineral or riparian rights, the gaining of influence within trade unions – these became the targets of the former physical force movement. The Wolfe Tone Society, a Republican-minded debating club, which attracted a membership outside the ranks of the IRA, became an increasingly favoured vehicle for IRA activity in both Dublin and Belfast. The Dublin Housing Action Committee, which campaigned on behalf of Dublin's homeless, was also commended to Republican activists. Generally speaking, it would be true to say that, despite the evidence before their eyes of what had befallen Labour in Northern Ireland, the Marxist theoreticians who now influenced republicanism steered towards the grail of a brotherhood of the Orange and Green proletariat. The 1916 rising anniversary in 1966 helped Sinn Fein to pick up membership in the Republic. It did so also in the north, but less openly, under the guise of republican clubs.

The most important landfall in the charting of this new course occurred in August 1966 when a meeting was held in Maghera, Co. Derry, at the home of a prominent Derry Republican, Kevin Agnew, a solicitor. It was decided to take advantage of the new currents stirring in Ireland, north and south, by setting up a broad-based north of Ireland civil rights movement. Goulding is on record as stating unequivocally that: 'The IRA set up NICRA [Northern Ireland Civil Rights Association]. The Army Council of the IRA set up NICRA, it and the Communist Party together.' This is an oversimplification, however. The meeting was treated to a lecture by one Eoghan Harris on the desirability of infiltrating the northern trade unions – a lecture which was in fact written by Roy Johnston. This, it was argued, would bring Protestants and Catholics together. The reaction to this suggestion on the part of the northerners at the meeting was that it showed very little understanding of Northern Ireland. A senior academic present, Professor Michael Dolley, of Queen's University, found the paper 'embarrassing'.[59] Ciaran Mac an Ali, a prominent Dublin solicitor well versed in Republican history, was aware that this 'new departure' had in fact already been tried and abandoned as a failure by the IRA of the 1930s.

Mac an Ali suggested on the second day of the think-in that a better approach would be to launch a broad-based civil rights movement. The National Democratic Party, mentioned earlier, had also been advocating this course, but the Maghera meeting decided to go it alone without the NDP because it was deemed too Catholic. Mac an Ali's suggestion bore fruit the following January in Belfast when the Northern Ireland Civil Rights Association was formed publicly. Its constitution was based on that of the British National Council for Civil Liberties, and NICRA's inaugural meeting was attended by the NCCL's secretary, Tony Smythe.

Only two of those who had taken part in the meeting at Agnew's house were on the first NICRA committee: Agnew himself, and Professor Dolley, who was a civil libertarian, not a Republican. Noel Harris, a prominent trade unionist, was elected chairman, Dr Con McCluskey was the vice-chairman. Two prominent Wolfe Tone Society members, Fred Heatley and Jack Bennett, became treasurer and information officer respectively (Bennett was a prominent journalist with the *Belfast Telegraph*). The other members of the committee were: Ken Banks, a member of Harris's union, the Draughtsmen and Allied Trades Association; Betty Sinclair, a communist and member of the Belfast Trades Council; Joe Sherry, of the Republican Labour Party; Paddy Devlin, of the NILP; John Quinn, of the Ulster Liberal Party; Terence O'Brien, unattached; and Robin Cole, who was co-opted because of his position as chairman of the Queen's Young Unionist Group.

The standing of the foregoing in the Six County community lent weight to NICRA's demands, which were: the ending of the plural voting system in council elections, simplified into a call for 'one man, one vote'; an end to discrimination and gerrymandering; machinery to deal with complaints against public authorities; the disbandment of the B-Specials; fair play in public housing allocation; and an end to the Special Powers Act, which basically permitted the Stormont authorities to do whatever they wished in opposing dissent. However, in view of what has already been written, it is not necessary to labour the point that the NICRA shopping list was like a red rag to a bull in the eyes of Unionist fundamentalists, constituting a root-and-branch attack on the whole idea of a Unionist state. Rumours that NICRA had a hidden agenda began to spread almost as soon as the organisation was formed. And not merely within the Unionist community: in Derry the cautious John Hume refused to join, fearing a left-wing hand in the puppet's glove of civil rights.

By now Hume was emerging as a figure of some stature in the Nationalist community. His instinctive caution had made him resist strong pressure to go forward as a Nationalist candidate in opposition to McAteer in the 1965 election. Yet he was also showing a contradictory aptitude for new thinking. Apart from his work in the Credit Union movement, he had written two noteworthy articles for the *Irish Times* in May 1964 which had aroused discussion north and south of the border. In one of these he had argued, after criticising both Nationalists and Unionists, that:

> One of the greatest contributions, therefore, that the Catholic in Northern Ireland can make to a liberalising of the political atmosphere would be the removal of the equation between nationalist and Catholic.[60]

He had also been one of the moving spirits behind efforts to bring new ideas to bear on the housing problem in Derry. For example, the Derry Housing Association's innovations included buying large premises which were then converted into flats and let to young couples at a high rent. At the end of two years or so, half the rent was returned to the couple as a deposit for a mortgage. A former Maynooth seminarian, Hume was at this stage married, and was a French teacher in Derry's St Columb's School, respected both for the exam results he achieved and for his skill in public debate with the Columcille Debating Society.

One of those he debated with was another rising star from Derry's working-class Bogside district, Eamonn McCann, who would become the author of one of the best books of the coming conflict, *War and an Irish Town*.[61] Humorous, with a passionate compassion for the underdog, the mercurial McCann, like his supporters, was the antithesis of the dour, cautious Hume and the forces he attracted. McCann was the political exemplar of the slogan on the portraits of the Sacred Heart which once hung in every Irish Catholic home: 'Where two or three are gathered together in my Name, there will I also be.' McCann's creed seemed to be: 'Where two or three are gathered together in the name of revolutionary socialism, therein lies the possibility of a split.' In 1968, McCann, who would have been a psychology graduate had he not been expelled from Queen's three years earlier, was a leading light in the Derry Housing Action Committee. The HAC was to be the motor force in one of the seminal events in Northern Ireland, the 5 October 1968 civil rights march in Derry. McCann himself has accurately described, in terms of both mood and historical fact, who and what organised the march:

> The march had been organised by a loose group of radicals who had been trying for months, with some success, to create general political mayhem in the city. Those involved were drawn mainly from the local Labour Party and James Connolly Republican Club. In March they and others had organised themselves, if that is not too strong a word, into the Derry Housing Action Committee, which set out with the conscious intention of disrupting public life in the city to draw attention to the housing problem.[62]

However, though the HAC did organise the march, the idea of taking to the streets to protest Catholic grievances did not originate with the Derry group. Once again the catalyst for this type of protest was Austin Currie – or probably more accurately, British indifference to the need for reform in Northern Ireland and/or the impossibility of Terence O'Neill's being able to bring it about. O'Neill himself has said of this period:

> As the Party would never stand for change, I was really reduced to trying to improve relations between North and South; and in the North itself between the two sections of the community. In this regard I think I can truthfully say that I succeeded. During this period between 1965 and 1968 the Catholics came to realise that I was interested in their welfare.[63]

The real point was that while some Catholics, not all, accepted O'Neill's interest, very few were confident that he could translate it into action against the wishes of his party. The only hope was vigorous action from London. And by the summer of 1968 Austin Currie for one did not believe that this would be forthcoming. He had spent the years since his election deploying the arguments provided by the McCluskeys' pamphlets at Stormont, on TV, to sympathetic Labour audiences in

England, all to no avail. Stormont was hostile, resistant, Westminster took refuge behind the Speaker's ruling which batted the ball back to Stormont. An incident at Westminster made up Currie's mind.[64] A Gerry Fitt initiative about discrimination had run into the customary brick wall. Currie happened to be in the House at the time, in the company of Paul Rose, one of the staunchest supporters of the Campaign for Social Justice. Rose turned to Currie and said: 'You're making no impact. You'll never get anywhere over here until you force this government to take action.' Over a quarter of a century later Currie told me: 'That was a significant occasion. I went back home and started organising. The first civil rights march took place the following August.'[65]

Two

Marching Feet and Angry Voices

Principiis obsta; sero medicina paratur
Cum mala per longas convaluere moras.

(Stop it at the start, it's late for medicine to be prepared when disease has grown strong through long delays)

Ovid, *Remedia Amoris*, 91

FOUR THOUSAND PEOPLE took part in the march on 24 August 1968. It was the first time in the Six Counties that the civil rights song 'We Shall Overcome' was heard. The route was from Coalisland to Dungannon where it had been intended to conclude with a rally in the market place. Police prevented this, because, in what was to become a familiar tactic, the Paisleyites had organised a counterdemonstration. Nevertheless, unlike the repeat performance at Derry in October, the march passed off peacefully. Here it should be explained that it was not merely the idea of marching for civil rights that was new, it was the idea of Catholics marching. Marching in the Six Counties was something that the Orangemen did of right and the Catholics on sufferance, and in designated areas. Faulkner's rise to fame, for example, had been aided by his role in the 'Long Stone Road affair'. The Long Stone Road is in a Catholic area of South Down, near Kilkeel. In 1955 a proposal to hold an Orange march through it for the 'twalfth' aroused major controversy. Two days before the march, locals blew craters in the road. But, on 12 July, protected by six hundred armed police, augmented by dogs and armoured cars, the Orangemen duly marched, led by Brian Faulkner. A few days after the Long Stone incident Faulkner banned an Irish cultural demonstration at Newtownbutler in Co. Fermanagh.

Around the same time Orangemen disrupted a Gaelic week in Castlewellan, Co. Down, by organising Orange parades through the town. Faulkner was again deeply embroiled in the politics of marching during 1960. His predecessor as Minister for Home Affairs, W. B. Topping, had refused Orangemen permission to parade through Dungiven, Co. Derry, because the police had advised that it would create trouble in this strongly Nationalist area. However, Faulkner sanctioned a large demonstration involving lodges from several different parts of the Six Counties. After the march, one of its leaders, the Revd John Brown, a B-Special commandant, said that the object of the march was to show that Orangemen could march anywhere they liked in the Six Counties. There was, he said, 'No such thing as a Nationalist district . . . Dungiven has been restored to the Queen's Dominions.'[1]

To those of Brown's way of thinking – and there were many, including the hard-line Minister for Home Affairs, William Craig – it now began to appear that the march planned for 5 October 1968 was designed to remove Derry City from 'the Queen's Dominions'. McCann and company wanted to encourage them in that belief so as to ensure the maximum confrontation and publicity. A march held in July to commemorate James Connolly had been banned, but a rally in Guildhall Square had attracted about a thousand people. It was, as McCann said, 'a significant success'.[2] He and his supporters had developed a routine of disrupting Derry Corporation meetings. Their followers at the corporation meeting following the demonstration, who had numbered only some thirty in March, were so numerous that they 'overflowed the council chamber out into the foyer of the Guildhall building and into the street'.[3] Derry's pulse was quickening. On leaving the Guildhall, one of McCann's associates, Eamon Melaugh, phoned NICRA and invited them to hold a civil rights march in Derry.

NICRA agreed, both to the holding of a march, and, not knowing anything about Derry, to McCann and company's inflammatory choice of route. This was from Duke Street in the Waterside area, across Craigavon Bridge, through the ancient city walls, and into the Diamond. In Derry terms it was as if Hamas had paraded through Jerusalem's Holy Places and concluded with a rally at the Wailing Wall. Hitherto only Unionists had marched along that predominantly Loyalist route. John Hume was one of those who refused when asked to sign the necessary application form for permission to march, under the Public Order Act. Currie's August civil rights march followed. Melaugh and McCann confidently expected 5 October to be a considerable occasion, perhaps even the day that would bring Stormont down. It was anticipated that the attendance would be bigger than at the Dungannon march. The date had been chosen in the mistaken impression that the Derry soccer team was playing away. Two days before the march, William Craig issued an order banning it on the grounds that an Apprentice Boys march was scheduled for the same route at the same time. Moderate opinion within Derry and NICRA, two of whose members had eventually signed the application to march, urged that either the ban be obeyed or that the march be postponed.

The conflicting calls of moderation and football eventually resulted in only some four hundred marchers turning up. Had they been allowed to proceed, the history of Northern Ireland would have been entirely different. But a police cordon halted the march before it had cleared Duke Street. Another group of police then formed up behind the marchers, thus trapping them. Two days earlier Gerry Fitt had attended the British Labour Party Conference where he had warned that there would be trouble from the RUC. He brought over three Labour Party MPs with a brief to report back to Callaghan and Wilson.

What they saw was approximately five minutes of speeches from Fitt, McCann and Betty Sinclair, followed by a simultaneous police baton charge from either end of Duke Street. Men, women and children were batoned to the ground, the marchers adding to the confusion by colliding with each other as they fled in panic from either end of the street. Those who succeeded in running the gauntlet of the batoning, and breaking through to Craigavon Bridge, faced another hazard. A water cannon, the first to be deployed in Derry, hosed them back across the bridge.

John Hume was one of those hosed. McCann and his colleagues had set the pace so much that he and other moderate figures, like Eddie McAteer, felt compelled to march, though they disagreed with the organisers' provocative tactics. Hume said afterwards that 'all hell broke loose' and that he would never forget the hate he saw in the faces of the police. What gave the events of 5 October their significance was the fact that millions of other people also saw that hate. An RTE cameraman, Gay O'Brien, filmed the whole thing, and his images went around the world. One of the most potent was that of Gerry Fitt, with blood streaming from his head. The Irish being so notoriously fair-minded that they never speak well of each other, it is probably not surprising that Bernadette McAliskey (née Devlin), who also took part in the march, would later say:

> Gerry Fitt made a very astute political decision that if the press were to be interested in it, there would have to be an interesting head, so Gerry stuck his in the way and got sliced – proceeded to bandage it very ostentatiously and gave interviews outside the City Hotel. In between interviews he would come into the bar and take the bandage off and have a few drinks and go out again when he was called upon.[4]

Fitt subsequently lent some coloration to McAliskey's assessment in a newspaper interview (*Irish Times*, 3 October 1988), in which he said: 'I knew long before that they were going to beat me up . . . I felt the blood running down. I thought to myself, I'm going to let that blood run because the cameras are there.' But Austin Currie and Eddie McAteer were batoned also; a prominent Tyrone businessman, Paddy Douglas, was cudgelled in the groin as he interceded with an RUC man; a police officer, his face contorted in rage, was caught by O'Brien running after a fleeing demonstrator, striking him savagely to the ground, and then, pausing to glance around to see whether he had been observed, adjusting his cap. He was later promoted.

That night the Catholic Bogside area had its first riots. The destructiveness, with which Derry was to become all too familiar, manifested itself in stoning police cars, petrol-bombings and smashing shop windows. For the first time, too, a few short-lived barricades went up. There would be more and they would not come down so easily. The aftermath of the batonings falls into three categories: reaction in England, in the north generally, and in Derry itself. British public opinion was shaken, but not stirred into action. In the House of Commons (on 22 October 1968) Harold Wilson made it clear where his sympathies lay. In the course of a reply to a question arising from the march, put by the Grand Master of the Ulster Orange Order, Captain William Orr, he said: 'Up to now we have perhaps had to rely on the statements of himself and others on these matters. Since then we have had British TV.' However, he did not take any British action.

In the case of the North and Derry, McCann has summed up the position accurately: '. . . a howl of elemental rage was unleashed across Northern Ireland, and it was clear that things were going to be the same again. We had indeed set out to make the police overreact. But we hadn't expected the animal brutality of the RUC.'[5]

However, Craig praised the police for their handling of the affair. McCann and Co. were arrested next day and charged with contravention of the Public Order Act. They reacted by calling a meeting in the City Hotel the following Tuesday which agreed, all fifteen of them, to hold another march the following Saturday. Next day another meeting, of more than a hundred people, took place in the hotel. McCann denounced them as 'middle-aged, middle class and middle of the road' and walked out. The group consisted of representatives of clergy, Nationalists, liberal Unionists, the professions and trade unionists. They proceeded to form a new organisation, the Citizens' Action Committee, as an umbrella organisation for all the existing protest organisations in the city. Its character may be gauged from the fact that its chairman was Ivan Cooper, a prominent member of the Labour Party and a Protestant, its vice-chairman was John Hume, and Campbell Austin, a liberal Unionist and the owner of what was then the largest department store in the city, became its press officer. The CAC's first action was to cancel the planned Saturday march as being too dangerous in the perfervid atmosphere of the time. Its second was to arrange instead a sit-down in Guildhall Square for 19 October. Campbell Austin resigned in protest.

That was how things were in those revolutionary days. The tide of civil rights was running so strongly that it swept up all sorts of people in one wave, only to drop them off in the next breaker. The original IRA/communist motivators were amongst its earliest casualties. The IRA's only contribution to the movement was in the stewarding services provided by some of its members. Throughout its short life it remained non-violent, non-sectarian, a genuinely cross-party (and creed) mass movement, aimed not at a united Ireland, but at reform within the system. Its song was 'We Shall Overcome', not 'A Nation Once Again'. In fact, this absence of a Nationalist goal disgusted many old-guard Republicans and was a major contributory factor in the emergence of the Provisional IRA just over a year later.

Nevertheless, the Unionists persisted in seeing the civil rights movement as a Republican front. And persisted is the word. More than a quarter of a century after the formation of NICRA a prominent Unionist, David Trimble, at the time of writing the Official Unionists' party spokesman on justice, was asked for his reaction to the emergence of the civil rights movement. He replied:

> Puzzled I must admit. One appreciated after a little thought that yes there were some things. I mean we had the local government franchise on a ratepayer basis, they'd abolished that in England in '48. One could see that that was a hangover. But the behaviour and tactics, of civil rights, the civil rights movement, soon clarified the matter and one felt after seeing the way that they actually behaved on the streets that this was really just the Republican movement in another guise.

Those words were uttered in tranquil recollection. At the time, as O'Neill wrote, 'the activities of the Civil Rights movement appeared to the Party to be nearly treasonable'.[6] Civil rights groupings were springing up all over the province. On the same day the Derry Citizens' Action Committee was set up (9 October) the

People's Democracy movement was formed by a group of radical Queen's University students after a demonstration in Belfast against police brutality. Its aims were one man, one vote, an end to gerrymandering, discrimination, and the Special Powers Act, and the beginning of freedom of speech and of assembly. A large student protest march took place to Belfast City Hall a week later. The Derry Guildhall sit-down also went ahead as planned. It attracted 5,000 people and passed off peacefully. In the midst of the turmoil few people paid attention to an event which had helped to spark the entire protest movement. The New University of Ulster opened in Coleraine on 25 October, with 400 students.

On 2 November, the CAC committee traced the route of the October march through Derry without any more serious incident occurring than a few stones being thrown, and a brief halt being called by police. A full-blooded re-enactment of the October march was carried out on 16 November. A week before it, Paisley and his henchman, Major Ronald Bunting, held an unopposed march to the Diamond. But three days before the CAC march Craig issued an order banning all marches in Derry until 14 December. The world's media descended on the city in the expectation of violence. At the suggestion of the Protestant Bishop of Derry, Dr Charles Tyndall, both he and Dr Robert Farren, the Catholic Bishop of Derry, opened their cathedrals for all-night prayer vigils.

The unprecedented ecumenical gesture set the tone for an impressive and orderly march. Marshalled by an army of stewards, many of them either former members of the IRA or Republican supporters, perhaps as many as 15,000 people confronted the inevitable police barricade. This time good sense prevailed. After a thirty-minute argument during which the stewards contained the anger of the younger and more militant marchers, the CAC committee were allowed to make a token breach of the barriers. A way was left open though the police cordon so that the crowd could filter through to the Diamond. Here, on forbidden ground, the banned meeting also passed off peacefully. Catholic Derry was jubilant. In the following week workers left their jobs to hold impromptu celebratory parades through the centre of the city by way of putting further breaches in the ban. The CAC leaders, Cooper and Hume, whose stars were rising by the hour, became so worn out by endless bouts of negotiation between police and marchers that they called for a moratorium on such spontaneous marches. However, on 20 November there were serious clashes between Protestants and civil rights demonstrators in which dozens of people, twelve of them police, were hurt.

One man whose star was definitely not rising throughout all this was Captain the Right Honourable Terence Marne O'Neill, Prime Minister of Northern Ireland. On the Monday after Gay O'Brien's images of 5 October had seared themselves into the minds of the TV-viewing public, he had the ill luck to be opening an Ulster Week in Leicester. He said afterwards:

On every floor of every shop in Leicester I was overtaken by reporters, some with notebooks, others with tape recorders, who wanted interviews on what I thought of the present situation. The shopkeepers who had thrown so much into this Ulster promotion were not amused, and I have a particular memory of seeing a reporter half hidden by a forest of ladies' underwear who emerged as we finished admiring a display of Ulster's best lingerie![7]

The Leicester vignette epitomises the British reaction, not to Ulster's lingerie, but to her dirty linen being displayed. As O'Neill lunched with the Lord Mayor he was informed that he was to be 'invited' to meet the Prime Minister, Harold Wilson. Helped by the TV, Messrs Fitt, MacNamara, Orme and Rose had at last succeeded in getting their message across; to Wilson, but not the Unionists. Wilson gave O'Neill almost a month's breathing space before seeing him on 4 November. The idea was that passions would have had time to cool, and the Unionists be given a chance to come up with their own proposals. The former did not occur and the latter was not availed of. The two ministers who were to accompany O'Neill to the meeting, Craig and Faulkner, flew to London separately. O'Neill went through his notes with them before seeing Wilson, but the ministers remained uncooperative. He afterwards described the occasion in rueful terms:

> By their joint decision we went naked into the Cabinet Room. In the end, of course, they were forced to agree to a package of reforms. It would, however, have been more dignified if we had been able to make our own proposals.[8]

More dignified and more far-seeing. It would also have been more effective for the British Cabinet to have been seen to firmly support O'Neill in pushing through reform. Either that, or take control of the situation directly. British intelligence must have been aware of what was happening in the region. But the 'hands off' policy described by Callaghan prevailed. In the event O'Neill had to struggle with his cabinet and parliamentary party until 22 November before he could even announce publicly what had been forced on him in London. On him, but not on the diehards. Craig made speeches denouncing the civil rights movement as a creature of the IRA and the Trotskyites, while further to the right Paisley turned up the decibels in the chant 'O'Neill must go'.

The O'Neill reform package contained five points: the abolition of Derry Corporation; the appointment of an ombudsman; a new system of housing allocation; a promise that the Special Powers Act would be abolished when it was safe to do so; and an end to the company vote. On this last, a notable omission from the package was any commitment to enfranchise non-ratepayers.

Nevertheless, before the civil rights movement got going, the package would probably have appeased the Catholics. As the *Belfast Telegraph* writer Barry White correctly judged: 'In just forty-eight days since the first Derry march, the Catholic community had obtained more political gains than it had in forty-seven years.'[9] Now it proved to be too little, too late to appease all sections of Catholic opinion; and at the same time it inflamed and frightened the Protestants. By way of heightening the inflammation, Paisley staged one of the most dangerous confrontations of the year shortly after the package was unveiled. A civil rights march had been scheduled for Armagh on 30 November. He and Bunting arrived in the town before the march at the head of a cavalcade of cars from which emerged men armed with cudgels whose efficacy had been improved by having large nails protrude from them. Further aids to the democratic process were provided by the contents of the car boots – these had been filled with stones. The Paisleyites then proceeded to take over the centre of the town. In order to prevent trouble the RUC halted not the Paisleyites but the civil rights march. The counterdemonstration tactic was a favourite Paisleyite ploy. By staging a counterdemonstration to a planned civil rights march it proved possible to get the civil rights march cancelled.

Craig, the man in charge of law and order, made it clear where his sympathies lay. On 3 December the newspapers carried a statement saying: 'One of these days one of these marches is going to get a massive reaction from the population. Ordinary decent people have been at boiling point for some time. It's not just Mr Paisley.' The Armagh incident later added more gems to Paisley's diadem of martyrdom. The following January, he and Bunting were sentenced to three months' imprisonment for unlawful assembly, but only served six weeks. Meanwhile, after another, more violent, confrontation between Loyalist and civil rights marchers, at Dungannon on 4 December, O'Neill made a notable effort to both cool the situation and win public support for his policies over the heads of his enemies in Stormont.

On 9 December he made what became known as his 'Ulster at the Crossroads' speech live on both the BBC and the then ITA. Although his rather slight version of a Churchillian delivery jarred on some Nationalist-minded viewers, it was a historic and generally well-received broadcast. The strain in his face, his evident sincerity, and the seriousness of the situation struck a chord, north and south of the border. He said:

> Ulster stands at the crossroads . . . our conduct over the coming days will decide our future . . . These issues are far too serious to be determined behind closed doors or left to noisy minorities . . . For more than five years now I have tried to heal some of the deep divisions in our community. I did so because I could not see how an Ulster divided against itself could hope to stand . . .
>
> There are, I know, today some so-called loyalists who talk of independence from Britain – who seem to want a kind of Protestant Sinn Fein. These people will not listen when they are told that Ulster's income is £200 million a year but that we can spend £3000 million a year only because Britain pays the balance . . . Rhodesia, in defying Britain from thousands of miles away, at least has an airforce and an army of her own. Where are the Ulster armoured divisions and the Ulster jet planes?
>
> . . . Unionism armed with justice will be a stronger cause than Unionism armed merely with strength . . . What kind of Ulster do you want? A happy and respected province in good standing with the rest of the United Kingdom? Or a place continually torn apart by riots and demonstrations and regarded by the rest of Britain as a political outcast?[10]

He concluded by making it clear that if he could not get support for his policies he would resign, and asked 'all our Christian people, whatever their denomination' to go to church the following Sunday to pray for 'the peace and harmony of our country'. For a moment it appeared that the broadcast had worked. Craig was one of the few in Cabinet to put his head over the parapet to venture a criticism. Borne up by a tide of goodwill, O'Neill promptly sacked him. The parliamentary Unionist Party supported O'Neill on the issue by a majority of 29–0, with four abstentions.

In Belfast, the *Belfast Telegraph*, then the most influential paper in the province, ran an 'I'm backing O'Neill' coupon which was eventually signed by 150,000 people. This, in percentage terms, would have represented more than five million people in Britain. In Dublin, the *Sunday Independent* voted O'Neill 'Man of the Year'. More importantly, the civil rights leadership in both Belfast and Derry agreed to call a halt to marches for the time being. For a moment a pie crust of optimism formed over the bubbling, poisonous northern stew.

It soon crumbled under the marching feet of the student activist group, the People's Democracy. When a society is content, a small group, like those who took over the GPO in Dublin during Easter 1916, or the People's Democracy in Belfast in 1969, can march, commandeer buildings, or whistle jigs to milestones without provoking any significant reaction. But when a community is angrily debating issues such as 'Whose law?' and 'Whose order?' such gestures can spark an uprising. So it proved in the Six Counties in January 1969.

The People's Democracy was partly inspired by the student demonstrations in Paris in May 1968 and by those in Czechoslovakia which led to the brief Prague Spring. And partly by frustration at not being allowed to march through Belfast to demonstrate against the behaviour of the police in Derry on 5 October. After a sit-down protest near City Hall, the students had marched back to Queen's University and set up an organisation modelled on the Paris assemblies. It was to be leaderless, a form of mass democracy. Michael Farrell, who helped to found the PD, was one of those who had been batoned on 5 October. Afterwards he said:

> . . . my reaction was . . . we're not going to get anywhere with these people. The ban was imposed by the Northern Ireland Government, the baton charge was ordered, or was certainly under the direction of a County Inspector, one of the top officers of the RUC. Clearly the State was fully behind this type of repression, of civil rights protests. I felt we're not going to get anywhere by protests in Stormont or people putting motions in Parliament about this sort of thing. My reaction was we should do two things. One, mobilise protest as widely as possible within Northern Ireland and two, demonstrate to the outside world that this is what Northern Ireland was like.

He was still strongly of that view after watching the O'Neill broadcast:

> The crucial demand at the time of the civil rights movement was one person, one vote. I listened carefully to the speech to see when he would mention that they were going to grant one person, one vote and he didn't . . . I thought the speech was a sham. I thought there was going to be no change until there was one person, one vote and therefore the civil rights movement should continue . . . We decided to go ahead with the march we'd already been discussing from Belfast to Derry in the New Year . . . we felt that nothing had changed and that in fact O'Neill was trying to defuse this movement which had gained tremendous momentum . . . we were trying to force the British government to intervene and we felt the momentum should be continuing to do that.

Farrell and his companions modelled their march on the American civil rights march from Selma to Montgomery, Alabama. The PD felt that they would achieve the same effect in the Six Counties as had the blacks in Alabama. By highlighting the repressive nature of the state they would force an intervention by the federal government, in this case Westminster. As the students were officially leaderless and operated on the principle that democracy meant what the membership said it meant, even what a very small segment of the membership said, the fact that NICRA had officially decided on a marching moratorium presented no obstacle to the PD's resolution not to observe the decision. Several of the prominent figures in the civil rights movement, including Cooper, Currie and Hume, criticised the PD for being deliberately provocative and indulging in a dangerous coat-trailing exercise by setting out to walk through Loyalist towns. To this day many people feel that the situation would somehow have settled down had the students not marched. It might have done, but would Paisley and company? The PD march has to be regarded as one of the catalytic moments of the tragedy. But had the conditions not existed to generate tragedy the march either would not have taken place, or else would have produced nothing more than blisters and a few head colds.

At all events a group of about forty Queen's University students, accompanied by Eamonn McCann and half a dozen or so Derry supporters, set off from City Hall, Belfast, to walk to Derry on New Year's Day 1969. One point about the group deserves to be made. It contained some of the brightest young people in Northern Ireland – some of them Protestant – many of whom subsequently made considerable careers for themselves.[11] I afterwards worked with some of them, and, through journalism, came to know others. They certainly made, and are making, a contribution to society that few would have guessed at as they set off in a blizzard of arguments, criticism and threats. The argument and criticism came from moderate opinion on all sides; the threats from the Paisleyites. Major Bunting and a group of followers turned up to see the students off with promises that they would be 'harassed and hindered'. The promises were kept, along what Eamonn McCann has described as a '. . . horrific seventy-three-mile trek which dredged to the surface all the accumulated political filth of fifty Unionist years'. There was very little hostility from ordinary people along the way. But there was organised harassment. The students were frequently ambushed by groups of men armed with stones and clubs. The RUC only intervened to prevent the marchers from entering towns they wished to walk through, 'for their own protection'. Otherwise the police offered no protection and were often observed chatting cordially with the attackers. One prominent northern personality who had a daughter on the march contacted some former colleagues in the IRA to ask them to keep an eye on the students. The first intimation the marchers had of this unasked-for protection came when a marcher got up to relieve himself outside a barn one night and bumped into a man with a shotgun. The incident gives an accurate insight into the state both of policing and of the IRA's armament at the time.

On the fourth day of the march, with the pendulum of public sympathy already swinging massively towards the bloodied but unbowed students, two further major ambushes took place. One occurred at Burntollet Bridge a few miles outside Derry. Several hundred B-Specials had gathered here, wearing identifying armbands to prevent embarrassing mistakes in the utilisation of the clubs, stones, iron bars and bicycle chains which they carried. The marchers were halted for half an hour or so by the police, less than a mile from the bridge. By now, hundreds of sympathisers had joined the marchers, who were accompanied by around eighty policemen. Farrell, the principal organiser, was given the impression by the police that there would be some stoning ahead, but that '. . . it was only going to be a very minor sort of a skirmish'. He says now: 'I've always wondered since then whether the hold-up . . . was so that the attackers could get better organised before we arrived because we were definitely led into an ambush by the police.' Bernadette Devlin has painted a vivid picture of what happened:

> . . . from lanes at each side of the road a curtain of bricks and boulders and bottles brought the march to a halt. From the lanes burst hordes of screaming people wielding planks of wood, bottles, laths, iron bars, crowbars, cudgels studded with nails, and they waded into the march beating hell out of everybody . . .[12]

Farrell and his helpers managed to manhandle and marshal the marchers at the front of the procession to safety when the stoning began, but those at the rear, particularly young women, were singled out for especial attack. Apart from being stoned and beaten, sometimes with cudgels with nails driven into them, a number were driven into the freezing waters of the River Fahan. When things quietened down Farrell made his way back to the ambush site to see if there were any injured stragglers. This is what he saw:

> . . . the ambushers, who were wearing little armbands, and the police were standing around chatting and smoking quite happily. There was no attempt by the police to disperse them, arrest them or anything like that. They were just literally standing around having a chat and a smoke. I sort of observed this for a minute or two until some policeman said to me, 'For God's sake get out of here, they'll kill you.' I got out of it as fast as I could . . . the collusion was complete.

Just outside Derry, at Irish Street, a Protestant district, there was another ambush. Again the marchers had to run a gauntlet of some hundred yards while stones and a new invention, petrol bombs, were hurled at them. Again the attackers, some 150 strong, had obviously been stockpiling the stones, petrol bombs and other weapons for some time, but the police had made no effort to interfere. Here Farrell's luck ran out and he was knocked unconscious and taken to hospital. But in Derry the battered marchers were given a heroes' welcome at a reception organised by their former critics, Hume and his colleagues. All argument fades before a gallant deed. Anger, unfortunately, does not. After the bloodstained marchers had described their experiences to a large crowd in Guildhall Square, serious rioting broke out.

When this had died away, and the city had gone to sleep, a crowd of policemen entered the Bogside at about 2 a.m., shouting and singing.[13] They smashed windows and demanded that 'the Fenian bastards' come out and fight. Even if they did not come out to fight, unwary householders who came to doors or windows were either beaten up or stoned. In one street, St Columb's Well, John McMenamin owned the only phone. Never very fond of pop music at the best of times, McMenamin was particularly underwhelmed by a version of the Monkees' hit which the forces of law and order had adopted as their theme song for the occasion:

Hey, hey, we're the Monkees,
And we're going to monkey around
Till we see your blood flowing
All along the ground.

He picked up his phone, dialled 999 and had been put through to the RUC's Victoria Barracks before he realised the absurdity of his action. The drunken mob, bawling and brawling outside his door, were the police. He hung up. His example, metaphorically speaking, would be followed by many of Northern Ireland's working-class Catholics before the year was out. The next day the slogan 'You are now entering Free Derry' appeared at the entrance to St Columb's Well. The first barricades of the Troubles went up, and stayed up, for a week, until Hume and Cooper managed to talk them down again.

Under pressure from London, O'Neill moved to set up the Cameron Commission,[14] which would:

enquire into and report on the course of events leading to, and the immediate causes and nature of the violence and civil disturbances in Northern Ireland on and since 5 October 1968; and to assess the composition and aims of those bodies involved in the current agitation and in any incident arising out of it.

Faulkner and a henchman, William Morgan, the Minister for Health, reacted by resigning on 28 January. Others within the Unionist fold took a more liberal view. The New Ulster Movement came into being to combat sectarianism by demanding the setting-up of a Central Housing Executive and a Community Relations Commission. It also demanded the abolition of the B-Specials. It was chiefly supported by professionals and business people. While it had no immediate impact in those heady days of January 1969, the NUM was to prove its importance, not only by the fact that its proposals were ultimately largely adopted, but by being the seedbed from which sprouted the liberal Alliance Party in the following year.

A somewhat less liberal grouping took place that month also. Twelve Unionist backbenchers met in Portadown in the wake of Faulkner's departure, and issued a call for O'Neill's resignation. He had already told Wilson and Callaghan that he wanted to resign, but they had refused to hear of the idea.[15] Even a wobbling prime minister who could not get much done was better than the prospect of no prime minister and having to do something themselves. However, watching the arrogant demeanour of the 'Portadown Parliament', as it became known, on television on 30 January, O'Neill decided to go for confrontation rather than resignation. He met the Portadown Parliament head-on by dissolving the Stormont Parliament and calling for a general election on 3 February.

It was a confused affair, in which men of goodwill encountered that much talked-of but elusive middle-of-the-road meeting place only during interludes of fleeing sniper fire from one side to the other. O'Neill was under fire from Craig, Lord Brookeborough, Paisley, the PD and a new influx of opposition candidates who had cut their teeth in the civil rights movement. He stood for reform; his opponents within Unionism accused him of taking the Six Counties towards a united Ireland.

He was opposed in his own Bannside constituency by both Paisley and Michael Farrell. Farrell argued that if he could diminish O'Neill's vote sufficiently to allow Paisley into Stormont, the result would be to bring Harold Wilson into Belfast. Paisley did poll well, but O'Neill held his seat by a majority of 1,400 votes. However, the 'crossroads election', as he termed it – which, incidentally, also revealed something significant about the Six Counties by returning only one woman member to Stormont, a Unionist, Mrs A. Dickson – created what were in effect two Unionist parties and a new-look opposition.

While overall the Unionists won a substantial majority of the fifty-two seats, they were fractured into pro- and anti-O'Neill Unionists. Some twenty-four out of a total of thirty-nine were reckoned to be pro-O'Neill. Ten were officially opposed to him, and there were five others poised to make that crucial dash from one side to the other depending on how the wind blew. The new-look opposition included, for the first time, John Hume, Ivan Cooper and Paddy O'Hanlon, all of whom had stood as independents on a civil rights ticket, and Paddy Devlin, NILP. Hume had defeated Eddie McAteer, the former Nationalist leader, by 3,600 votes in his own Foyle constituency. The new men, along with Austin Currie, Gerry Fitt and another Republican Labour colleague, Paddy Kennedy (see p. 110), constituted the most formidable opposition in the history of the state.

They gave early indication of their mettle when, on 20 March, the Unionists voted to close a discussion on the Public Order Debate while Hume was still speaking. They promptly sat on the floor and sang 'We Shall Overcome'. But O'Neill had more dangerous opposition to contend with in his own ranks than in the opposition. He had in fact only one more month in office ahead of him. After a series of those infallible guides to the existence of implacable political hostility, votes of confidence, he was, in his own words, 'blown out of office by the Protestants'.[16]

In March and April there were a number of explosions which destroyed a large electricity substation outside Belfast and blew up pipes bringing water from the Silent Valley reservoir in the Mourne Mountains to Belfast, causing serious water shortages. O'Neill himself was never in any doubt that these were the work of Protestant extremists. But Loyalists attempted, for a time, to pretend they were the work of the then quiescent IRA, so as to smear O'Neill's 'Republican' policies. Paisley did not know the identity of the bombers.

The *Protestant Telegraph* hailed the explosions as proof of the IRA's potential and intent.'[17] What the *Protestant Telegraph* said (on 5 April 1960) was: 'This is the first act of sabotage perpetrated by the IRA since the murderous campaign of 1956 . . . the sheer professionalism of the act indicates the work of a well-equipped IRA . . . this latest act of terrorism is an ominous indication of what lies ahead for Ulster.'

The last lines were certainly correct. But the various explosions were the work not of the IRA, but of the UPV, whose connections have already been described. The UPV connection became undeniable on 19 October 1968, when Thomas McDowell, a Free Presbyterian and a member of the UPV, died as a result of a premature explosion while he was trying to blow up an electricity substation at Ballyshannon, Co. Donegal, in the Republic.

On 22 April, O'Neill had finally announced unequivocally that the Stormont Government would bring in one man, one vote in local government elections. Next day the Minister for Agriculture, Major James Chichester-Clark, who had his eye on the premiership, resigned on the ostensible grounds that he felt the timing of the announcement was wrong. On 24 and 25 April the waterpipe bombings occurred. O'Neill resigned on 28 April 1969. David Bleakley has painted a not unfriendly portrait of his tenure in office:

> ... he was in many ways a prisoner of the aristocratic remoteness associated with the O'Neill line. It was at once his greatest asset and his heaviest liability – good for foreign consumption, but difficult to retail at home . . . It was right for O'Neill to make the attempt and a great pity that more of his party had not made the move earlier . . . But O'Neill laboured under the difficulty of his clan: he moved among the Roman Catholic population like some ancient lord, anxious to do the decent thing by his tenants, but he could not really make contact . . .[18]

Within a few days of resigning, O'Neill, with that devastating instinct for knowing how to say the wrong thing that one associates with the English public school tradition, had validated Bleakley's assessment. In the course of an interview with the *Belfast Telegraph* (10 May 1969) he said:

> It is frightfully hard to explain to Protestants that if you give Roman Catholics a good job and a good house, they will live like Protestants, because they will see neighbours with cars and television sets. They will refuse to have eighteen children; but if a Roman Catholic is jobless, and lives in the most ghastly hovel, he will rear eighteen children on national assistance. If you treat Roman Catholics with due consideration and kindness, they will live like Protestants in spite of the authoritative nature of their Church.

Without pausing overly long to dwell on the sense of empathy and gratitude that that aroused amongst the denizens of the Falls Road and the Bogside, let us move on to record the fact that O'Neill was replaced by another scion of the Big House, he of the strategically timed resignation, Major James Chichester-Clark. In order to keep Faulkner out, O'Neill joined in the 'laying-on of hands' that ensured that Chichester-Clark got the nod from the Governor-General. Paisley greeted the appointment with the observation that he had 'brought down a captain and could bring down a major as well'.[19] Apart from the bombs which had facilitated his succession, Chichester-Clark had to contend with another explosive force, detonated appropriately enough on 22 April, the date that O'Neill had given him the pretext for resigning by introducing one man, one vote. On that day, Bernadette Devlin, who had been elected for Mid-Ulster in a Westminster by-election, delivered her maiden speech in the House of Commons. Standing as an Independent Unity candidate, she had defeated the widow of the former Unionist holder of the seat, George Forrest, and so at twenty-one became the youngest woman ever elected to Westminster, and the youngest MP for half a century.

Paul Rose had cited the bombings in making use of a procedural device

(Standing Order No. 9 of the House rules) to persuade the Speaker to allow an Adjournment Debate on the Irish issue so that Devlin's first speech could have maximum impact. Normally new members did not make their maiden speech on taking their seat. Rose and Fitt agreed that they would sponsor her. The next problem was to contact her to inform her of the debate. Fitt retired to the Irish Club and began making phone calls. Eventually, he says, later that evening he located her in the bar of the Stormont Hotel, Belfast.[20] At that stage she was not all that enamoured at the thought of travel. More importantly, she had no money. Fitt got the manageress on the phone and arranged that she would loan the Hon. Member for Mid-Ulster £50, for which he would be responsible.

Thus Bernadette Devlin arrived in London. She and Fitt set off for the House of Commons from the Irish Club through a thicket of photographers, some of whom aroused Fitt's wrath by attempting to get the new MP to perform with a hula-hoop. At the House he and Rose introduced her to John Silkin, the Labour chief whip, who explained to her the protocol for a new member and took her to lunch. Another offer of hospitality gave rise to an incident which, as Fitt describes it, helps to illustrate why Bernadette and Fitt soon found themselves at odds. After her speech, which created a sensation, she was surrounded in the Members' lobby, which normally does not admit strangers, by what Fitt termed a 'crowd of lefties and loonies'. Lord Longford enquired of Fitt whether 'Miss Devlin would be available to have dinner at my house'.

Paul Rose breasted Devlin's throng of well-wishers to find out. One of them, according to Fitt, turned to the veteran friend of Ireland and exclaimed: 'Who the fuck are you, trying to jump on Bernadette's bandwagon? Fuck off!' Fitt says that 'the blood drained from Paul Rose's face' and that he turned 'as white as a sheet'. According to Fitt, he said: 'That's me finished' and dropped out of Irish affairs subsequently.[21] Nor did Fitt develop any relationship with Devlin. Rose's later departure from politics generally probably had more to do with his disappointment at not receiving a well-merited cabinet post from Harold Wilson than any insult, however gross, from a supporter of Bernadette Devlin, who did in fact dine with Lord Longford that night. And Devlin herself was probably accurate in her analysis of her association with Fitt:

> I never had much to do with him at Westminster, simply because I was too young to be sensitive to the fact that Gerry Fitt had ploughed that furrow and I had bounced in as some kind of new invention that had stolen his thunder . . . It affected Gerry . . . his nose was out of joint.[22]

Not only did Fitt's nose have to contend with Ms Devlin's eruption; it would also have to compete with the emergence of the galaxy of new talent thrown up by the 1968 Stormont election, from the ranks of the Six County minority. As we shall see, discomfiture of the political proboscis was going to be a feature of Fitt's politics in the coming years. But unquestionably Devlin was accurate in her judgement on another area, the state of Northern Ireland society. In one of the most brilliant maiden speeches ever heard at Westminster[23] she suggested that:

... since there can be no justice while there is a Unionist Party, because while there is a Unionist Party they will by their gerrymandering control Northern Ireland and be the government of Northern Ireland ... consider the possibility of abolishing Stormont and ruling from Westminster ...[24]

In stark terms she encapsulated the problem facing Northern Ireland, the challenge facing the House and the fate around the corner for many an unfortunate British soldier – service in Northern Ireland. She said:

The question before the House, in view of the apathy, neglect and lack of understanding which this House has shown to these people in Ulster whom it claims to represent, is how in the shortest space it can make up for fifty years of neglect, apathy and lack of understanding. Short of producing miracles such as factories overnight in Derry and homes overnight in practically every area of Northern Ireland, what can we do? If British troops are sent in I should not like to be either the mother or sister of an unfortunate soldier stationed there.[25]

The hour of the widow-makers was at hand. When Devlin again appeared on the world stage later that summer she did so amidst the mists of CS gas and the smoke from exploding petrol-bombs. Derry had been in a state of suppressed ebullition all summer. There had been fierce rioting on 19 April. It arose after police banned a planned civil rights march from Burntollet to Derry, following the use of the familiar Paisleyite ploy of threatening to stage a counterdemonstration. While chasing a group of stone-throwing youths, police burst into a house they mistakenly thought the youths were sheltering in, and batoned the occupants. The house owner, Samuel Devenney, a forty-two-year-old taxi-driver, received severe internal injuries from which he died on 16 July. The CAC decided after the riots that it was time to call a halt to demonstrations.

But by then the unemployed Catholic youth of the city had got a taste of 'aggro', as it came to be known. Because of the civil rights demonstrations they had been able to take their frustrations out on the system to some degree. Indeed, their volatile, aggressive energy had been a principal strength of the movement in Derry. Now they had been given an appetite for protest, but deprived of a movement through which it might be canalised. A combination of this factor, the Devenney case, and the approach of the marching season, particularly the Apprentice Boys march on 12 August, convinced many people in Derry that they would have to prepare for serious trouble. At the best of times there was a level of resentment against the Apprentice Boys march, which was seen in Derry as a calculated gesture of Protestant supremacy. These were the worst of times. Accordingly, a group of old Republicans, led by Sean Keenan, set up the Derry Citizens' Defence Committee towards the end of July.

The Committee acquired a sudden, terrifying relevance following an outburst of sectarian rioting around the Catholic Unity Flats area of Belfast on 2 August. Lurid reports of collusion between the RUC and Orange mobs, which lost nothing in the telling, filled the Bogside with expectation that its people would get the Unity Flats treatment on 12 August. The materials for making barricades were stored at each of the area's forty-one entrances. Some were erected pre-emptively on the night of the 11th. All had gone up by the following day. Opinions differ as to whether the riots were begun by the Protestants throwing down pennies on the Catholics, a traditional gesture of contempt, from the city's old walls, or by the Catholics stoning the marchers as they passed the end of William Street, where Devenney had lived. They are agreed, however, on the first victim to be felled: one of the Catholics' representatives, Ivan Cooper, who with John Hume and others had been trying to keep the two sides apart.

The stoning increased and a mob consisting of both Apprentice Boys marchers and police made an attempt to force its way into the Bogside. They were beaten back by a hail of missiles. The barricades went up and a rerun of the siege of Derry commenced, with the Catholics playing the defensive role of the original apprentice boys. In Ireland, history repeats itself first as tragedy, and then as tragedy. Not immediately, over the next forty-eight hours, but as a result of them. To preserve the gerrymander and prevent the Catholics overflowing into another ward, the Unionists had built a block of high-rise flats at the main entrance to the Bogside, Rossville Street. The flats, a potent symbol of discrimination, were literally to bring fire down on the Unionists. A group of teenagers got on to the roof and pelted the police with petrol bombs. Impromptu factories were set up all over the Bogside to ensure that the bombs kept falling.

Permission to use CS gas, 'tear smoke', as it was euphemistically termed, was given by London, the first time it had been used in the UK. The gas never got near the rooftop petrol-bombers, but its use heightened the sense of siege. It hung in the air like smog, saturating the narrow streets, invading the tightly packed homes, racking lungs, damaging eyes, wreaking havoc on the old and those with respiratory complaints. Only Bernadette Devlin seemed impervious to its effects. She kept telling people that 'it's OK once you get a taste of it', as she led the Bogsiders' resistance in the main war-zone area of Rossville Street. Pictures taken of her breaking bricks to throw at the police later helped to earn her a six-month jail sentence. In the forty-eight hours that the battle lasted, Dr Raymond McClean, who had established a field hospital in the Candy Corner sweet shop, is reckoned to have treated over a thousand casualties. More seriously injured cases were ferried across the border to Letterkenny Hospital. Few people accepted the authorities' assurance that no action would be taken against those who sought treatment at Altnagelvin Hospital nearby.

John Hume was shot in the chest with a gas cartridge at point-blank range as he walked up the path to Rosemount police station, by a policeman standing at the door. Hume was attempting to mediate between the police and a mob who wanted to stone and, if possible, petrol-bomb the barracks. As soon as he recovered he continued his efforts, eventually persuading the mob to stop stoning in return for the police ceasing to fire gas canisters. The mob did not know that the police had almost run out of gas. After the riots someone remarked to a sergeant that Hume had saved the barracks. 'No he did not,' said the RUC man, pointing at an arms rack on the wall. 'We always had these.' The rack contained sub-machine-guns.

Incredibly, no guns were used by anyone during the fighting. The young Martin McGuinness, who later emerged as the IRA chieftain of Derry, and subsequently vice-chairman of Sinn Fein, is remembered only for being an active stone-thrower throughout. During the rioting prompted by Burntollet a radio transmitter had found its way to the Bogside, apparently 'borrowed' from Athlone army barracks in the Republic. This came into the hands of McCann and those working with him in Derry, who used it to broadcast rebel songs and exhortations such as 'Keep the murderers out. Don't weaken now. Make every stone and petrol bomb count.' They made appeals to 'every able-bodied man in Ireland, who believes in freedom' to come to Derry. How able-bodied all those who arrived were is a matter of conjecture, but it is a matter of record that a high percentage of the practising revolutionaries and anarchists of Europe did descend on Derry like moths drawn to a light. In order to draw off police strength from Derry, phone calls went out from the DCD to other centres in the north. The result was an outburst of ferocious rioting across the Six Counties, in Coalisland, Armagh, Dungannon and Belfast. In Belfast, as we shall see shortly, the upheavals were far more serious than in Derry.

But it was Dublin that really put up the temperature. Mild-mannered Jack Lynch, the Republic's prime minister, went on television and announced that the Irish Government was sending army field hospitals to the border to treat people who did not want to go to Northern Ireland hospitals. He continued:

> It is evident that the Stormont Government is no longer in control of the situation. Indeed the present situation is the inevitable outcome of the policies pursued for decades by successive Stormont Governments. It is clear, also, that the Irish Government can no longer stand by and see innocent people injured and perhaps worse.

He went on to say that the deployment of British troops would be 'unacceptable', that the RUC was no longer accepted as an impartial force, that London was being asked to apply immediately for a UN force, and that he also intended to ask London to enter into negotiation on the North's constitutional position. A united Ireland was the only permanent solution. That served to concentrate minds wonderfully in Stormont. It also put up the hopes and fears of ordinary people in Northern Ireland, both Catholic and Protestant, by many, many percentage points. In Derry and Belfast, Catholics rushed around excitedly telling each other that the Irish Army was on its way. Their Protestant counterparts reacted with fear and hatred and prepared for war. Left to himself the dovish Lynch would not have made such a speech, but he was under pressure from hawks within his cabinet like Neil Blaney, who represented a border constituency. Also, he had to do something to quell the rising passion which was manifesting itself in every town in the Republic as the rioting progressed. From my office in Burgh Quay I could hear the loudspeakers which nightly blared forth pleas on behalf of the beleaguered Nationalists from outside the GPO in O'Connell Street, the headquarters of the insurgents during the 1916 rising. People got carried away at these meetings. Paddy Devlin, the Stormont MP, has described in his autobiography how, having come to Dublin to seek aid for his Belfast constituents, he was recognised by an organiser of one of these impromptu GPO demonstrations and asked to speak. In that setting, microphone-itis set in rapidly. Devlin made a fiery speech demanding guns that he was never subsequently allowed to forget.[26]

Had Lynch not made the gestures he did, there could have been serious trouble in the Republic. But in real terms Lynch's speech was for the optics. The amount of respect which London held for Dublin's views was shown two days later when, apparently unexpectedly, the Irish Foreign Minister Dr Patrick Hillery turned up at the Foreign and Commonwealth Office. 'He was reminded,' says Richard Crossman, in a footnote to p. 610 of his diaries, which was all he apparently thought Hillery's intervention merited, that the 'Northern Irish troubles were an internal affair of the United Kingdom, of no concern to the Republic or the United Nations'. For several years, the reality behind the Dublin-speak rhetoric prepared for Lynch and his successors by civil servants would be that the Republic would in fact stand idly[27] by. However, in August 1968, London at long last found that it could no longer do so.

On 14 August the battle of the Bogside had reached a crucial stage. The exhausted police were being pushed back when suddenly the advancing Bogsiders caught sight of a force of B-Specials moving forward. There was consternation. McCann writes:

> Undoubtedly they would use guns. The possibility that there was going to be a massacre struck hundreds of people simultaneously. 'Have we guns?' people shouted to one another, hoping that someone would know . . . suddenly fearful of what was about to happen.[28]

It was at that moment that the troops were first sighted. The initial response of the people was one of delight – the appearance of the troops meant that the Bogsiders had beaten the RUC – but as McCann observed there was confusion too: 'It was not in our history to make British soldiers welcome.'[29] Harold Wilson was fully aware of this, as Ben Pimlott has noted in his excellent biography.[30] Joe Haines warned Wilson that 'The troops will have to be there for months.' Wilson replied: 'They're going to be there for seven years at least.' He had been on holiday on the Scillies when the news of the rioting broke. He flew to Culdrose, near Penzance, where on the morning of 15 August 1969 he was joined by Callaghan, who also arrived by air. They agreed that troops would be sent, if Stormont asked for them, stipulating that a number of reforms would be demanded in return. Callaghan had only been airborne for five minutes on the return flight to London when the request was radioed to him and assented to.

He and Crossman dined together that night at Pruniers. Callaghan was upbeat and buoyant over the decision:

> Jim was big and burly and happy. 'By God,' he said, 'it is enjoyable being Minister. It's much more fun being Home Secretary than the Chancellor. This is what I like doing, taking decisions, and I had to take the decision to put the troops in while I was in the plane on the way back from Cornwall.'[31]

James Callaghan must have been one of the few people in the world to have managed to derive any enjoyment out of the situation in Northern Ireland. The atmosphere in Belfast in particular was very far from that of Pruniers. The scale of the rioting and destruction was much greater there than in Derry. There was more use of guns, and the fighting was not largely confined to a battle between citizenry and police. Where there had been occasional sectarian incidents in Derry – for example, Catholics staged the midnight petrol-bombing of a Methodist-run hostel for down-and-outs, causing the inhabitants, mostly Catholics, to flee for their lives – there were continuous bouts of warfare between Catholic and Protestant mobs in Belfast throughout August. Readers will be able to study for themselves the impact of these events, and their influence in the subsequent emergence of the Provisional IRA.

Here it is sufficient to say that disturbances were on such a scale that another reputable eyewitness, Paddy Devlin, has estimated that 650 Catholic families were burned out in one night.[32] In all, the three months of July, August and September 1969 are said to have caused 1,505 Catholic families and 315 Protestant to flee their homes. The Protestants generally fled to the east of the city; many of the Catholics across the border to the Republic. The Irish Army set up camps to cope with the flood of refugees, catering for some 6,000 at one camp alone, Gormanstown in Co. Meath, off the main Belfast–Dublin road. One of those who urged the Dublin Government to set up the camps was Austin Currie. Later his wife and children were amongst those who were forced by events to avail themselves of the facilities. Eventually the dislocation would become so great that a Community Relations Commission report established that some 60,000 people were forced to leave their homes between the summer of 1969 and February 1973.[33] It was 'considered Europe's largest enforced population movement since 1945'.[34]

With reports of riot and insurrection coming in from all sides, the Stormont Government authorised a number of steps which had the effect of making a bad situation worse. In Belfast, Shorland armoured personnel carriers mounted with heavy Browning machine guns were deployed by the RUC. The sound of these weapons, magnified in built-up areas, spread panic. The bullets tore through walls as if they were cardboard. A nine-year-old boy, Patrick Rooney, was killed as he lay asleep, leaving his distraught father to scrape his brains off the wall with a spoon and a saucer.[35] At Stormont the deputy Home Affairs minister, John Taylor, caused a walk-out from the chamber by the Opposition when he announced that he was mobilising 11,000 members of the exclusively Protestant B-Specials.

But before the Opposition actually left the building they were halted by word of another announcement, this time from the Minister for Home Affairs, Robert Porter. He revealed that the Unionists had appealed to the Home Office to send in the army. The appeal, which bore the signature of the Inspector-General of the RUC, Anthony Peacocke, was couched in terms which made it appear that a large-scale IRA attack was imminent. Having stated that the police could no longer contain the situation and were falling back to defend their barracks, Peacocke said:

Information is to hand from a reliable source that an infiltration of members of the Irish Republican Army is about to commence from Eire into Northern Ireland. It is the intention to escalate the degree of control over inward bound traffic and to this end assistance in the form of patrols by armoured cars is also requested. The information indicates that the infiltrators will be armed and the support of mobile armoured units, which I cannot supply, would be of material assistance in countering these subversive activities against the Government and people of Northern Ireland.

The British Cabinet, having acceded to the foregoing, was fully aware of the dangers of the situation but, remarkable as it appears now in retrospect, thought that the Government could derive benefit from Northern Ireland's miseries. Writing in anticipation of the important cabinet meeting on 19 August, which ratified the decision to send in the troops, Crossman sadly contrasted the situation in Northern Ireland with that of Czechoslovakia a year earlier:

> . . . no sense of tragedy or principle involved. It is so mucky, untidy; it really is street rioting, with boys and girls chucking beastly petrol bombs at each other and potting each other with old guns. It is the most messy kind of civil war one has ever seen and it doesn't give a sense of stirring, epic tragedy but is just awful and depressing.[36]

However, 'awful and depressing' as the Irish mess was, Crossman judged that:

> . . . from the point of view of the Government it has its advantages. It has deflected attention from our own deficiencies and the mess of the pound. We have now got into something which we can hardly mismanage. The Tories are with us on this . . . I don't see any issue on which Cabinet is likely to be deeply divided.[37]

Crossman proved to be fundamentally accurate, and monumentally wrong. For the remainder of Labour's stay in office (until June of the following year), it proved possible to represent the Cabinet's Irish policy as a success story. And the Tories did show bi-partisanship. But one can't help feeling that there was more than a touch of symbolism about the manner in which Ted Heath, the Tory leader, came to the problem. He was taking part in the Fastnet yacht race, off the coast of Cork, when he was contacted by radio to discuss the statement which Reginald Maudling, the Tories' Northern Ireland spokesman, intended to issue on the sending-in of the troops. The toing and froing over the wording of the statement used up so much power that the batteries of the yacht's engines went dead. Because of the siting of the mast it proved impossible to get at the engine to recharge the batteries. Then the wind dropped, leaving the Conservative leader helplessly adrift in Irish waters.

The policy decisions arrived at during the fateful cabinet meeting of 19 August ensured that successive Tory and Labour governments would find themselves equally adrift on many other occasions. Instead of accepting that the Stormont experiment had failed, and opting for direct rule in the wake of sending in the troops, the Cabinet decided to prop up Chichester-Clark and work for reform through him. The Cabinet had seen in O'Neill's fall the impossibility of getting Unionist agreement to the kind of root-and-branch improvement that the situation demanded, but the need, in Callaghan's phrase, to avoid getting fingers burned governed all. In Crossman's words: 'It wasn't so much deciding what policy to have as being able to excuse it.'[38] The man directly responsible for the troops, Denis Healey, Minister for Defence, argued against a takeover. His view, which was generally accepted, was that they could 'only push Chichester-Clark as far as he wanted to go'.[39] It was felt that direct rule 'would put the British soldiers under pressure from the Republicans and the Catholics'. Both Healey and Callaghan, the two ministers most affected, argued that the Cabinet's interest lay in working:

... through the Protestant Government. The Protestants are the majority and we can't afford to alienate them as well as the Catholics and find ourselves ruling Northern Ireland directly as a colony. We have also to be on the side of the Catholic minority and try to help and protect them against their persecutors.[40]

Direct rule was only contemplated as an option in the event of Chichester-Clark objecting to the transfer of power from the RUC to the military. And so the second great turning point into disaster was reached. In the event Chichester-Clark agreed to all the reforms which the British sought. Apart from a general commitment to reform and the military takeover, the substantive changes were to include: disbandment of the B-Specials, though it was intended to keep this secret for the time being; an inquiry into the RUC with the object of securing leadership changes; and the appointment of a senior civil servant, Oliver Wright, the British Ambassador to Denmark and a former private secretary at Number 10, Downing Street, as the British Government's representative in Northern Ireland with direct access to Harold Wilson. The communiqué which was issued on 19 August following the meeting between Wilson, Callaghan and Chichester-Clark reflected the Cabinet's effort at a circle-squaring policy. Known as the Downing Street Declaration, it sought to calm Unionist fears and at the same time reassure Catholics, saying that:

nothing which has happened in recent weeks in Northern Ireland derogates from the clear pledges made by successive United Kingdom governments that Northern Ireland should not cease to be a part of the United Kingdom without the consent of the people in Northern Ireland . . . The Border is not an issue . . .

The Declaration welcomed the announcement of reforms which the Northern Ireland Government had already made as indicating the

determination of the Northern Ireland Government that there shall be full equality of treatment for all citizens. Both governments have agreed that the momentum of internal reform should be maintained . . . every citizen of Northern Ireland is entitled to the same equality of treatment and freedom from discrimination as obtains in the rest of the United Kingdom, irrespective of political views or religion.

The Declaration had a certain credibility problem on both sides of the Northern Ireland divide. The promise that the affairs of Northern Ireland were an entirely domestic matter for the UK did little either to reassure Protestants about Dublin's intentions, or to quell resentment that the whole civil rights movement was a bogus IRA–communist front. Indeed, Wilson inadvertently added to the Protestant resentment. While announcing the terms of the Declaration, the Prime Minister, to Callaghan's annoyance, remarked that the B-Specials would be 'phased out'. The British were setting in train an inquiry under Lord Hunt, the Everest climber, into the touchy subject of policing, and for the moment wished it to appear merely that the Specials were being withdrawn from places like Belfast and Derry. Having helped to unhorse the moderate O'Neill, the Chichester-Clark–Faulkner leadership, ground between the immoderate forces of Paisleyism on the one hand and

London on the other, now, to change the metaphor, had some circle-squaring of its own to do. The ineffable Faulkner proved himself more than equal to the task. Two days after Wilson's gaffe, the Irish papers carried a statement from the Stormont Minister for Home Affairs saying: 'There is absolutely no suggestion the USC will be disbanded. Let me make that crystal clear.'

Where some sections of Catholic opinion were concerned, the Northern Ireland Government had given such clear proofs of being unreconstructed supremacists that nothing but the abolition of Stormont and a green field restart would have convinced them that there was any sincere movement towards reform. The nearer one got to the Catholic ghetto areas of Derry and Belfast, particularly Belfast, the more pronounced this distrust became. The nearer the ghettos lay to Protestant districts, the more fear intermingled with distrust. In the wake of the burnings, evacuations, and riotings, with their consequential injuries and deaths, an ancient formula began to have an application once more: fear + distrust = IRA. Let us now turn to examine how this formula operated in one Belfast ghetto which can serve as a microcosm of the province as a whole.

THREE

LETTING SLIP THE DOGS OF WAR

> Stop up the access and passage to remorse,
> That no compunctious visitings of nature
> Shake my fell purpose, nor keep peace between
> The effect and it!
>
> Shakespeare, *Macbeth*, Act V

SEVERAL VIVID DESCRIPTIONS have been published concerning the burning and rioting that swept different parts of Belfast on the nights of 14 and 15 August.[1] However, one account, hitherto unpublished, and delivered from the unlikely setting of the pulpit of a Redemptorist church in the Clonard district of Belfast, both provides an unrivalled insight into what the Catholics of the area lived through on those nights, and allows us to gain some understanding of the role of the Church in the average Catholic's life. Both factors, taken against the backdrop of the Clonard area itself, help to illustrate how, in frequent flagrant disregard of church teaching, these experiences could provide a seedbed for the emergence of the most ruthlessly efficient guerrilla force to appear in western Europe since the ending of World War II.

The Redemptorist church is part of the large red-bricked monastery complex that dominates the interface between the militantly Republican Clonard area and the equally militant Protestant Sandy Row district. It is situated at the top of a gentle incline that slopes up Clonard Road from the Falls Road about four hundred yards away. If one stands at the church door, looking down this incline, Sandy Row is immediately over the monastery boundary wall to the left. Protestant Belfast curls away behind one to both left and right. About two hundred yards down Clonard Road, Cupar Street, on the right-hand side, connects with what was in 1969 a Protestant area. To the immediate right, and projecting behind the length of the church for a few yards, is the complex of little red-brick terraced 'kitchen houses' that earned the Clonard area the nickname 'little India'. Bombay Street, Cawnpore Street, Kashmir Road, Lucknow Street, are the sort of names one sees on the street signs, ghosts from an imperial past that returned to haunt those London decision-takers, and their satraps, who found themselves dealing with the detritus of empire. For 'little India' is also one of the Belfast IRA's heartlands. There can be few families in the district who have not had one or more relatives involved. A casual check in a pub, or with a family, will generally turn up someone who has been jailed, beaten up, interned, or shot for Republican activity.

In August 1969 the district was the home of the numerous Hannaway family, Gerry Adams' mother's people. Liam Hannaway would emerge as a principal figure after the burnings. Liam's son, Kevin, would later become second-in-command of the Belfast IRA, and be one of the 'hooded men', who were tortured after internment. Proinsias MacAirt, Frank Card, also to emerge as one of Belfast's principal Republican leaders, lived there. The people of the area will show you a house where in the 1940s a group of six young IRA men were captured after a shooting in which a policeman died. All six were sentenced to be hanged. Eventually, largely as a result of Irish-American pressure, only one, Tom Williams, went to the gallows. On the eve of his execution he wrote a letter to the then IRA chief of staff, Hugh McAteer, a brother of Eddie, the Nationalist Party leader. Having expressed his sorrow, and that of his comrade 'Joe', at not being able to attack the court and the 'Northern Junta' which had sentenced them, he concluded with a message to the IRA:

> . . . carry on, no matter what odds are against you . . . carry on no matter what torments are inflicted on you. The road to freedom is paved with suffering, hardship and torture, carry on my gallant and brave comrades until that certain day.[2]

Hugh McAteer died in 1970. The following year the 'Joe' Tom Williams had referred to, Joe Cahill, one of the five who were reprieved, would emerge as a principal leader of the IRA to 'carry on' Clonard's Republican tradition. Clonard's other tradition, that of association with the Redemptorist order, would also be maintained throughout the Troubles. Maintained and interwined. Clonard was where Gerry Adams went to Sunday Mass (when at liberty) all through the Troubles. The father of his colleague Tom Hartley, later vice-president of Sinn Fein, was a prominent member of the Men's Confraternity.

The Redemptorists are part of the warp and woof of Irish Catholicism. The order reflects the independence, hospitality and alms-giving tradition of the monasteries and the all-pervasive influence of the Roman Catholic Church. Pre-Vatican II the order would have been regarded as drawing an obedient flock. It belonged to the more conservative strand of Catholicism, that of the hellfire preacher, made famous by Joyce in his *Portrait of the Artist*. The Confraternity tradition was one in which men, and, separately, women, met in church weekly, or sometimes monthly, to pray, sing hymns, and be instructed from the pulpit as to how this life should be lived, i.e. largely with one eye on the next and an ear to whatever Mother Church said was to be done. Done it generally was. The changes of the Pope John era brought a more complex pattern. A Redemptorist, Fr Sean O'Riordan, became one of the Church's more liberal and influential theologians. In Washington, as the troubles progressed, a Redemptorist priest, Fr Sean MacManus, would set up a sophisticated organisation to lobby on behalf of the Nationalist agenda. Another Redemptorist, Fr Brendan Meagher, would come to be spoken of as 'an Sagart mait', the good priest, for his mediation efforts during the great hunger strikes of the 1980–1 period. And appropriately enough, for an area in which so much of the Troubles originated, it would be another Redemptorist, Fr Alec Reid, who became the unsung hero, in doing more than practically anyone else involved, in helping to bring about the IRA ceasefire of August 1994. The time span involved in that date, so far into the future of our story, helps to underline the strength of the forces unleashed in August 1969.

In that year the monastery was a focal point, as it had been since it was built in the 1830s, of a great deal of religious and charitable activity. Prior to August 1969, the early Protestant resentment at having such a bastion of Catholicism erected alongside a Protestant stronghold seemed to have evaporated. During World War II both Protestants and Catholics had huddled together in the monastery cellars to avoid German bombs (Belfast suffered far more, for example, than Coventry from German attacks). Many a food parcel found its way from the monastery discreetly to needy Protestant families, even though the young braves of both Catholicism and Protestantism were prone to periodic outbursts of fisticuffs.

Northern Irish Catholicism was more deferential to clergy and nuns than had become the norm in the south, where, in the absence of such a pronounced 'them and us' syndrome, time had moved on somewhat. The official attitude of the Church towards Protestantism was still of the arm's-length variety. Ecumenicalism was not a widely sown crop. There was church–state disagreement over separate education, which the Roman Catholic hierarchy insisted on, and the presence of Catholics in Protestant churches, even for weddings or funerals, was still discouraged by some older members of the hierarchy. But, the activities of Ian Paisley notwithstanding, these attitudes were crumbling. Again, as in politics, education was playing a part in altering the texture of the Church Deferential. But it would be true to say that the great majority of those who attended Mass at Clonard would have received their education in Catholic schools, learned Irish history, considered themselves Irish and would not have had a great deal to do with Protestant children at the school-going stage. Such contact more commonly occurred later, if it occurred at all, at university. Their Protestant counterparts would have acquired their education at Protestant schools, learned English history, and considered themselves British.

Clonard church was unusually well filled for the regular meeting of the Men's Confraternity in the week after the burnings of 14 and 15 August. There was a sprinkling of business and professional people in the congregation, but most would have been tradesmen, or unemployed, as much because of discrimination as economic conditions. Like the homes they came from, they would have appeared neat and tidy, displaying more of a concern for maintaining 'a good appearance' than the dictates of fashion. The practice of their faith involved things like pilgrimages to Knock Shrine in Co. Mayo, where Our Lady was said to have appeared, regular Mass-going, saying the rosary, and novenas for 'special intentions'. In general, for them and their womenfolk, the Church, in anatomical terms, could be thought of less as the cerebral than as broad Shoulders of Consolation. Above all, one Respected the Priest.

No priest was more respected in the area than Fr P. J. Egan, the superior of the monastery, and spiritual director of the Men's Arch-Confraternity. A measured, restrained man in his late forties, of medium height, red-haired, square-jawed, Egan was a noted preacher, clear in diction, simple in language, assured in delivery.

Theologically he would have been placed somewhere between the old hellfire 'reds' and Fr O'Riordan. Politically he was a staunch Nationalist. Courteous in manner, he carried an aura of authority. When 'Paudge' Egan spoke, you listened. And never was he listened to more attentively than that evening in Clonard. Coughing died away, eyes came fixedly to attention as he began in the conventional way: blessing himself, invoking the name of the Father, Son and Holy Spirit, and addressing the congregation as 'My dearest men'. He went on:

My dear men of the Arch-Confraternity, only one thought is in the minds of most of us and were I to speak to you about any subject other than the one that fills your minds you wouldn't listen to me. I think it would be a little bit unrealistic to speak of anything else except the great tragedy that has befallen our city within the last couple of weeks. You men, I am sure you have heard very many rumours floating about, I certainly have. I would ask you to discount most of them. Some of these rumours are quite dangerous. So I would ask you to discount them, pay no attention to them. But tonight what I will tell you is not rumour. Tonight I will tell you about Clonard, the attempt that was made on Clonard, because I know that Clonard is very dear to you, to the hearts of every man present here tonight.

We remember, my dearest men, I don't suppose we forget it easily, the night of Thursday, the 14th of August. We remember this night when the Falls Road area was devastated by gunfire and by petrol bombs. In the early hours of the morning I was standing at a fourth storey window of Clonard, looking out at a scene of desolation. And when I saw the leaping flames reddening the sky and the machine gun fire breaking the silence of the night I found myself asking this question: Is it possible that only three or four days ago we were assured by Stormont spokesmen that the forces of law and order had everything completely under control?

Like many others in the locality I did not retire to bed that night. I stayed up the whole night. I said the half past six o'clock mass. And immediately after mass, I was just taking off the vestments in the sacristy, a distress call came, a message saying that 'they' were dragging people from their homes in a nearby street. This was seven o'clock in the morning of August 15th. So I went to the spot to find two police vehicles drawn up on the street. One of them was, so far as I know, a tender, I'm not an expert on these things, the other I don't know what it was, it was some sort of armoured vehicle with a large gun mounted on it. As I approached there was a middle aged man dressed in his shirt and trousers standing on the pavement with his arms raised and he was being searched or questioned by the the police. Whether they were regular police or B-Specials don't ask me, I can't distinguish between them. But there was a man being questioned anyhow and when I approached the questioning, or searching, discontinued. I stood watching, closely, and when I stood there, beside the tenders, passersby, some on their way to mass and some on their way to work, hastened their step when they saw the police vehicles.

I saluted some of them but they were obviously frightened to enter into conversation with me. But there was one exception, a lady stood chatting with me and she deplored the violence that was taking place and expressed a fervent hope that peace would soon be restored, the hope that a spirit of neighbourliness would prevail. Now this lady was a Protestant from nearby Cupar Street.

While I was there the police took two men into custody, they ordered them in to tenders. I did not see any evidence of violence. While I was there there was no force and there was no violence. I did not see any violence. When the police vehicles moved off, the doors of the houses opened one by one and the people came on the streets. A group of women remonstrated with me for having exposed myself to danger. They said I could have been shot. 'You know,' they insisted, 'these B-Specials would shoot you.' Well, my dearest men,

I don't believe that there was the slightest danger of my being shot but when I thought about that remark I felt that it was typical of the lack of confidence so many of our people have in the forces of law and order.

Later that morning, that Friday morning, a voice on the telephone warned the Community of Clonard they had better clear out or they'd be burned out. Well, we didn't clear out and we're still here. Well anyway, the message came across, and the priests in the monastery that you know only too well, not myself, brought this message to the local police station, phoned the message to them. They promised protection, but no help came. At three o'clock that Friday afternoon the trouble really started. A large mob, there is no other word to describe them, a large mob, advanced from the Cupar Street area. I do not say for a moment that they were residents of Cupar Street. I do say that they came from that area, armed with stones, sticks and petrol bombs. At that time I didn't see any other instrument, but they advanced on the Catholic area.

At this particular time of the day, three o'clock approximately, the men of the area were at work, as you would expect. So the defence of the area was left to a handful of teenagers. And they did a great job. We were proud of them. They hurled every missile they could lay hands on into the faces of the advancing assailants. They did a good job. An urgent phone message went out from Clonard monastery to the local police station asking for protection for the threatened area. The call was received politely but no help came.

After making a vain attempt to stop the fighting down there at the junction of Cupar Street, I heard a number of women and girls panicking, they were crying and shrieking all over the place. So I brought them to the monastery, brought them into the kitchen, into the monastery where a large number of people had already gathered. They were all over the place, in rooms where I certainly never saw a female in my life. It was open house. It was a time of emergency. It was at this stage that I heard the first shots ringing out. And moments later, looking through a window in the monastery, I saw a prostrate figure on the pavement below. The exact spot is at the lamp post which is directly opposite the old credit union offices in Waterville Street. The body was lying there in Waterville Street on the pavement just across the road from the credit union offices. I dashed down the stairs immediately. Once on to the street, a man had arrived there before me I think, I can't be sure of that.

I looked into the face of the boy, I didn't recognise him at the time. It was Gerard McAuley. And Gerard was still conscious. He opened his eyes and I did think that he showed signs of recognition as he looked at me. I gave him absolution. I anointed him. We helped to put him on to a lorry. Just at this stage an ambulance arrived and we got him on to the ambulance. I heard afterwards that he died on the way to the hospital. It was now between four and five o'clock in the evening.

At this time a Father, from the monastery, accompanied by a local man, went to visit the local police station appealing for help. There were a number of police officers sitting around. They said that their orders were to remain in barracks. The news of the attack spread like wild fire, the attack on the Clonard area, and men came speeding from their work, to protect their homes, to protect their families, to protect their church. And goodness knows they had very very little with which to protect themselves. Comparatively speaking you could say that the men in this district were defenceless. Within the space of one hour I anointed five people, on the road out there. Fearing a real massacre I got on the phone, and I had to go across the roadway to do it because our phone was out of order. I got on to the offices of the GOC of the British forces in Lisburn. The GOC was not available, but the officer who took the call said he would do his best to help. At about seven in the evening the first group of soldiers arrived. They marched through Clonard Street, Clonard Gardens, and they took up their positions on the Falls Road. Now you will understand that soldiers on the Falls Road are pretty useless as far as protecting Clonard is concerned, when you are being attacked from the rear as we were from the Cupar Street area.

So I sped down and I met the officer in charge of the soldiers. I tried to explain the position to him. But he said he had his orders, and, being a military man, he had to take them I am sure. But I must admit, when you see a boy being murdered, when you see people, defenceless people, being shot down, and the houses burned over their heads . . . Well, little bits of rules and regulations and orders do not appear very important. They did not seem very important to me that evening. While I was talking the officer of more senior rank came along and he listened sympathetically and he said he would try to help. At nine o'clock approximately (about two hours later), another group of soldiers arrived and they took up their position outside the church to protect the area. They got into military formation and they charged down the street, charged the attackers. And the man in command shouted out an order to the assailants: 'Come out,' he said, 'with your hands up, and we'll not shoot.'

But the command was answered with a litany of obscenities, punctuated with uncomplimentary references to the Pope and Fenians and to the British Tommies. Instead of coming out with their hands up they shortly came out with guns blazing and petrol bombs being fired all over the place. More houses were set on fire and at their approach the soldiers turned and ran away. Well I have not heard, despite all this gun play coming from the area, I certainly have not heard that on the following morning police tenders pulled up at the houses of well-known leaders of the extreme Protestants, pulling them out of their beds and taking them into custody on the suspicion of their being illegally in possession, I haven't heard that, of arms. And if you have heard it, I'd be very interested if you'd come and tell me, because, so far as I know, during fifty years of British rule in the Six Counties of Ireland that has never happened.

Again we are tempted to ask ourselves, was it perhaps people who were the possessors of legally held firearms that did the shooting on this occasion? But the supposition is too dreadful to pursue it. After retreating, the military soon reformed their ranks and they came down along these streets again and they took up their positions, some in Kashmir Road, and some in Waterville Street. But, undaunted by their presence, the attackers came along again with their petrol bombs and systematically, they went from door to door in Bombay Street, kicking in some doors and breaking in some windows, and throwing petrol bombs into the houses.

They stood outside the school, and in full view of the military, they broke the windows, and threw bombs, fire bombs into the premises, into the school. Now, men, do not for one minute blame them. They had orders and their orders on this particular night were: 'Don't fire.' So they told me afterwards, because I was amazed at the performance and I asked them, and they told me their orders were not to fire. I do not blame these men who must act on their orders. But I certainly do blame the people who gave the information which resulted in the military getting that type of order. The people who supplied that type of information are responsible for most of the destruction in Bombay Street and in the Clonard area.

Obviously the soldiers didn't know the area. They certainly didn't know they were dealing with ruthless men who had no regard for human life or for property, as they showed on this particular night, under my very eyes. Three times the school beside our monastery was set on fire. And three times our local boys went into that school, went into that blazing school and bullets whistling all over the place, I was with them once in the school and I didn't feel a bit brave with bullets whistling all over the place. These lads went in there, and three times they fought the fire with extinguishers which they got from the monastery. They fought the fire and they put it out. And I must say I marvelled at their bravery. Again and again these attackers came during the night, and during the early hours of the morning, and outside the monastery and outside the school, they chanted and encouraged each other: 'Let's get the so-and-so school and let's get the so-and-so monastery.' That was the cry during the night.

Well they failed. They did not completely destroy the school, although they did extensive damage to it. And they did not damage the monastery at all, although they did succeed in getting one fire bomb into our backyard, within two feet of the back door. They did succeed in getting up on a shed, with evil intent of course. But they were repulsed. They failed in their evil design that night. But their failure, my dearest men, was not due to any protection given by the forces of law and order. Let that be recorded. Let it also be recorded that they failed because of the bravery of the local lads who, totally unprepared and ill equipped, and comparatively speaking defenceless, fought against terrible odds, and saved this district from complete destruction.

For, let there be no doubt about it, that was the objective that night, complete destruction. Well, my dearest men, there's the story of the attack, savage, murderous attack made on the Clonard area during these days of madness. I gave you the story as I saw it because I knew you'd be interested. Now a few more points before I finish. These were terrible days, my dearest men, but some good has already come from these attacks on our communities.

For one thing I have noticed that the various communities that were under attack are much more closely knit than ever before. You have young people, and elderly people, all closely knit. That's a grand thing, just like any good Christian community should be. Now there is one danger and I want you Confraternity men to avoid this danger. Don't fall into that trap. Already I have heard people say: 'Father, I can never again act in a normal way with Protestants.' That's understandable. That's just emotional. Now let's think the thing out. The vast majority of Protestants are thoroughly ashamed of what has happened. They would not have had hand, act or part in what has happened. Now that is true and we must realise that and we must accept that. They are thoroughly ashamed of what has happened. So we mustn't allow hatred to spring up in our hearts for our Protestant brethren. There is of course the lunatic fringe amongst them.

You have the extremists and you have their leaders, and you have the so-called leaders of this little state who have done nothing at all to deal with those people. That is an abuse which we hope will be remedied. What we are aiming at now, my dearest men, is justice. Justice, no more and certainly no less, certainly no less, my dearest men. So I suggest that is one lesson that we must learn from what has happened. We demand justice, we're not just begging it. We demand it. It's our right. We demand it and we'll keep on demanding it until we get it. We don't ask for any more. Just a fair deal. No discrimination in housing, or voting power, or jobs, or anything else. So I suggest that you pray, my dearest men, that soon we will have a community where everybody, irrespective of his religious belief, or irrespective of his political ideology, will be able to lead a normal life and will not be unjustly discriminated against, as has happened so often in the last fifty years. So pray, my dearest men, all of us pray, that we will have a society, that Catholic and Protestant will have a society where they will live, as they should live, helping each other out. We must live together. It is a mixed society, but that does not mean that we will not demand justice. We pray tonight that God will give us that justice which is our due.[3]

There is no need to labour the obvious point that, while Fr Egan clearly intended that the pursuit of justice should be by constitutional means which would respect Protestants' rights, the Clonard congregation also got a message that the pulpit shared their sense that they lived under an unjust regime which should be pressed to mend its ways. There were those in that church that night, and in the district outside it, who would adapt that sense to their own methodology: a resurrection of the physical force tradition. Elsewhere in the city the troops' arrival had been greeted with delight and relief, as in the Bogside, but already there was one district wherein the manner of the arrival had spoiled the welcome. A number of other points should be borne in mind concerning Fr Egan's sermon. The young lad, Gerard McAuley, to whom the priest referred, was fifteen years old and a member of the IRA's Na

Fianna, or youth wing. He was helping Catholics to evacuate their homes when he was shot by a Protestant sniper. The Provisional IRA regard him as the first martyr of the troubles. The street he was killed in was renamed after him. Crossman, in faraway London, understandably derived no feeling of 'epic tragedy' from what was happening in Northern Ireland, but Fr Egan's hearers certainly would have from his description of McAuley's death. As the Irish poet Patrick Kavanagh said, 'from such a local row was the *Iliad* made'. Of additional historical significance is the fact that it was during the fighting in Cupar Street on the 14th mentioned by Fr Egan that the first IRA shots fired in anger during the Troubles were heard. The shooting occurred when the RUC moved in to break up Protestant–Catholic fighting by baton-charging the Catholic side only.[4]

In fact the IRA posed very little threat to anyone during those days. So little that the disgusted inhabitants of the area, used to regarding the IRA in the traditional role of 'the Defenders', wrote up the letters IRA on gable walls as Irish Ran Away. Cathal Goulding had become so obsessed with ideas of furthering the brotherhood of the proletariat that the IRA had become almost demilitarised. Liam Hannaway, who took me on a tour of the district, re-creating what had happened, told me that he reckoned the IRA only had ten weapons in the area when the rioting broke out. A remark he made concerning the calibre of the armament has recurred to me subsequently when pictures of an IRA arms seizure flash on the TV screen, or the effects of Semtex explosive are displayed: 'One of the guns was an old-fashioned .45 Wild West-type Colt with a defective chamber that had to be turned manually after each shot was fired.' This was what Fr Egan was referring to when he described the youth of the area as being comparatively defenceless. In fact it was only some of the older IRA men from the forties period who managed to dig up a few weapons and deploy their nearly forgotten skills to keep Protestant mobs at bay until their ammunition ran out. It was the absence of weaponry that led to Bombay Street being totally burned out. Fr Egan's reference to the middle-aged man being arrested, in contrast to the lack of such arrests on the Protestant side, probably relates to Proinsias MacAirt, who was one of a number of older Republicans picked up. At this stage the sort of alarmist IRA thinking which dominated the Unionists' official request to Callaghan for troops still influenced events.

It was this mind-set which caused Fr Egan's reference to information being given which led to troops taking up positions along the Falls Road, approximately a quarter of a mile from where the monastery was being attacked with impunity behind their backs. The army had been led to believe that the Falls Road would be the main centre of attack. In addition, army procedure was very inflexible and unsuited to the situation. Paddy Devlin has described watching the soldiers take up their positions along the Falls Road:

> . . . to my horror they pointed their guns at the Catholic families who had been attacked the day before. We got on to Callaghan's office again to protest, but it made no difference. The military had a drill for this sort of thing, already well practised in Cyprus, Hong Kong and other outposts of empire . . . Bombay Street, near the Clonard Monastery, was under attack by the loyalists. The sky was red from the burning houses, torched while the military stood by, not raising a finger.[5]

Within a year army inflexibility would lead to the third and possibly most significant turning point to disaster, the Falls Road curfew, but for the moment the police provided the greatest source of anger for Catholics. Not only did the RUC make no effort to prevent the Clonard onslaught, or other similar attacks elsewhere in the city, notably the Ardoyne area, but some members of the force may have joined in. Certainly the B-Specials did. There are reports of police, in uniforms covered in civilian overcoats, being recognised amongst Loyalist mobs.[6] There are also strong suggestions of prior knowledge of the attacks, and of collusion with them, in the sense that the police seemed to have disappeared from some Catholic areas as if by prior arrangement shortly before the mobs arrived. Hatred of the police was one of the factors which would enable an emerging IRA to extend its influence by setting up 'no-go-areas'.

It would not be true to say that every member of the RUC, or even a majority, colluded with the Loyalist mobs. Individual police officers and men acted with great bravery. So did occasional members of the B-Specials. I have heard reports of some members of the force helping old people with their belongings as they fled their homes. But overall the events of August 1969 fell heaviest on the Catholics. Of the homes and buildings either destroyed or requiring rebuilding, 83 per cent were occupied by Catholics. In all, some 750 people were reported injured. Miraculously, in view of the scale of fighting, only seven were killed. Of these casualties, seventy-two Catholics and sixty-one Protestants suffered gunshot wounds. But it is accepted that the reluctance of Catholics to go to hospitals in the Six Counties for treatment means that far more Catholics must have been injured.

In a nutshell, August 1969 saw two crude notions of liberty come into conflict. One side, the Protestant, was admittedly open to the definition of being every bit as supremacist as the South African Boers of the period, the comparison being heightened by similarities in attitude and religion. Nevertheless, there was a sense of defending a heritage of Britishness and of freedom of religion. The other side, the Catholic, from which came the Provisional IRA, could be said to have emerged from the mists of history and the burnings of August, but at base, they too were moved, not by hatred, but by an instinct for freedom. Two sets of Irish Christians, overseen by an arm's-length British Government, and observed by a reluctant but increasingly involved Irish Government, were about to engage in a war which would prove yet again that one man's terrorist is another man's freedom-fighter.

Events now moved on two planes, the outward and the hidden. The hidden centred principally around an internal power struggle within the Republican movement and some *sub rosa* activities by Irish government figures. The major player in the visible drama was James Callaghan, although other actors drew attention to their importance, or lack of it, in various ways. The impotence of the Dublin Government was underlined in New York on the day after the issuing of the Downing Street Declaration. An attempt by the Irish Foreign Minister, Patrick Hillery, to have a UN peacekeeping force sent to the Six Counties was adjourned by the Security Council on 20 August. The British had little difficulty in mounting a diplomatic counter to the proposal. For, being permanent members of the Security Council, they could invoke the proviso in the UN charter that no matter could be considered by the Council which a member deemed 'domestic'.

Dublin of course had been fully aware of this ruling; the Hillery visit to New York was purely an optical exercise designed to calm the hawks in Lynch's cabinet by being seen to take action of some sort. Another New York visit of the period was calculated to ruffle rather than adjust feathers. On 22 August Bernadette Devlin flew in to collect money for NICRA. Her initiative so disturbed Stormont that a large Unionist delegation was sent toiling after her in a vain effort to counter her mini-skirted media impact. In Belfast, in the wake of the Declaration, Craig and Paisley vied with each other in the indignation stakes, Craig demanding Chichester-Clark's resignation, Paisley leading a demonstration to Stormont to protest at 'military dictatorship'.

Callaghan elicited a memorable Paisleyism when he visited Belfast on 27 August. He unwisely attempted to convince the fundamentalist that 'we are all children of God'. The reply was: 'No, we are not, Mr Callaghan. We are all the children of Wrath.'[7] Callaghan's 'all' might have been taken to include Catholics! But Callaghan had better luck in his dealings with Catholics and with the media. He held a huge press conference in the Conway Hotel in Belfast, and both it and his subsequent peregrinations around the province dominated headlines and screen for the subsequent forty-eight hours. The impression conveyed was that he had come over to see to it that the Stormont regime toed the line in the matter of reform. Another inquiry was set in motion alongside Cameron and Hunt, a tribunal under Mr Justice Scarman to enquire into what had led to the riots.[8] And, after a well-publicised meeting with Callaghan, the British Government issued yet another communiqué saying how devoted it was to the cause of reform.

The reaction to all this may be gauged by the reception Callaghan received when he addressed a crowd in the Bogside from the upstairs window of a small house. The physical barricades guarding the enclave had been taken down, but the army, by agreement, still did not cross a set of white lines painted on the road where they had stood. It was quite a brave act on Callaghan's part to step over the lines, accompanied by John Hume. He was 'swept along by a surging crowd of thousands'.[9] Having met a delegation from the Defence Committee which included Sean Keenan, a Republican, Michael Canavan, a close associate of Hume's who had painted the white lines, and Eamonn McCann, Callaghan, who by now, under the impact of crowd pressure, was beginning to feel his years,[10] delivered an address which the inimitable McCann described in these terms:

> It had been said, he began, that the London government was impartial. That was not true. The government was firmly on the side of justice. There was loud cheering. Mr Callaghan left and went to the Protestant Fountain area, where, it was reported, he had a distinctly more subdued welcome.[11]

To the Protestants, 'reform' meant 'erosion'. One erosion which Callaghan did seek was that of the no-go areas. 'Free Derry' was a problem inasmuch as the wall slogans telling the world's media that they were 'now entering Free Derry' were a constant reminder that the Queen's writ ran into trouble when and if it got there. But Belfast's barricades of burned-out vehicles, paving stones and rubbish of all sorts were literally an ugly reminder of what could be going on behind them. The solution decided on was a 'peace line'. As the barricades' principal motivation was protection, Callaghan argued that better protection would be afforded by having a galvanised fence erected between Catholic and Protestant districts. This of course also meant that the security forces could patrol the fence on either side. Accordingly, Chichester-Clark announced this innovation on 9 September 1969. There would be a physical manifestation of the divisions in the hearts and minds of Belfast's citizens. Twenty-five years later the barricade still stands, by now taller, and made not of galvanised sheeting, which eventually rusted away, but replaced by steel and concrete. However it did not solve the no-go issue which, as we will see, flickered on and off for the next few years, with Protestants sometimes following the Catholics' example by putting up barricades at moments of excitation.

One of the most excited of these moments occurred in October 1969, following the publication of two important reports of the period. The first was the Cameron Report (12 September), which found that the civil rights protestors had had right on their side in a number of key areas: housing, discrimination in local government appointments, the absence of one man, one vote, and gerrymandering. The report was a thoroughgoing indictment of Unionist government which, it said, had been 'hidebound' and 'complacent'. It recorded the frustration of the Catholics at the Government's refusal to do anything about minority grievances. And it highlighted the resentments caused by the existence of the B-Specials and by the operations of the Special Powers Act. The report also spoke of how the fears of the Unionists, that the Catholic birth rate might end their domination, had been inflamed by the activities of Paisley's organisations, the UCDC and the UPV. These organisations had helped to create a climate which was: 'readily translated into physical violence against civil rights demonstrators'.[12] The report said that its findings were 'confirmed by decisions already taken by the Northern Ireland government since these disturbances began'.

This last was something of a circular judgement because it is generally accepted that Callaghan had had sight of Cameron before his first visit to the North. The reforms which he demanded from Chichester-Clark were in fact based on the report's findings. The second report was to give rise to more disturbances. Callaghan paid another visit to Northern Ireland on 9 October 1969. After two days of arm-twisting and persuasion there were further protestations of impending reform. A communiqué was issued promising improvements in the area of policing, the legal system, local government and administration. A new housing authority was to be set up, incitement to hatred laws were to be examined. None of this mattered very much in Protestant eyes. They had heard it all, or something like it all, before. What mattered a great deal was the fact that the communiqué also accepted the findings of the Hunt Report which was published on the same day. Hunt recommended that the B-Specials be abolished.

To make matters worse, he recommended that the RUC become an unarmed police force. The fact that he advocated replacing the B-Specials with the setting-up of a special RUC reserve and a new part-time military force under the command of the British Army did nothing to quell a fierce outburst of Protestant anger. There was heavy rioting in the Shankill Road area on both 10 and 11 October. This was noteworthy for two reasons, apart from its intrinsic ferocity. One was the fact that the British Army openly and impartially took on Loyalist mobs. Belfast was treated to the unfamiliar sight of Protestants waving Union Jacks while attacking the forces of the Crown, to the accompaniment of slogans such as 'Englishmen go home, we want the B-Specials' and 'Paisley is our Leader'.

The second was that a Protestant sniper shot and fatally wounded a policeman, Constable Arbuckle, who thus became the first policeman to die in the Troubles. He was killed as he and his RUC colleagues attempted to prevent a Protestant mob, some thousands strong, led by a lambeg drummer, from marching on the Catholic Unity Flats. Eventually the police had to be augmented by troops who returned the Protestant fire, dispersing the crowds and killing two demonstrators. Scores of Protestants were later treated for wounds inflicted by the army either with bullet, boot, or baton. But a far more horrible form of retribution for Protestant violence was coiling around the corner. In the five years which had passed since Paisley had initiated the first rioting of the period by his reaction to the display of the tricolour in Divis Street, the Protestants had had a monopoly of grisly 'firsts'.

The first killings of the period had been carried out by the UVF through the use of petrol bomb and bullet. The first explosions, which had blown Terence O'Neill from power, had been the work of Protestants. Protestants had shot the first Republican and killed the first policeman. As a result reforms were in the pipeline which would deprive their community of some of their most prized instruments of power, the B-Specials, housing policies and so on. But the reaction would not stop there. The Protestants had also, as we saw, provoked another 'first', the first sanctioned IRA gunfire of the period. There was more firing in store, much more. Also in the pipeline was the formation of the Provisional IRA.

The August burnings had had the effect of quickening a perennial debate within the ranks of the Irish physical force tradition: force v. constitutional action. Major political parties in the Republic, including the ruling Fianna Fail and its principal opposition, Fine Gael, owed their inception to that debate.[13] At various junctures in the past the founding fathers of those parties had decided to eschew the gun and enter politics. Now the debate within the IRA was to swing the other way; the proponents of force would triumph over the constitutionalists, or, more accurately, the infiltrators. Initially it was the infiltrators who seized the initiative. Billy McMillen, the commander of the Belfast IRA, had been one of those picked up by the police during the riots. His second-in-command, Jim Sullivan, was responsible for setting up the Central Citizens' Defence Committee, on 16 August, to organise defence and welfare for Catholics who were throwing up barricades all over Belfast. Paddy Devlin has described life behind these barricades at this stage:

> ... good cars, which local people had worked strenuously to borrow for or buy, had been commandeered and thrown into the debris of the barricades. Local traders and businessmen who provided employment also found their vans and implements hijacked ... young vigilantes had taken over my house. They sat around the floors demanding meals, tea and coffee, sleeping, plotting revolution and revenge, until in a temper, when more tried to get in the already overfilled house, she [his wife, Theresa] chased them all ... Criminal elements

were gradually emerging, charging 'royalties' to tradesmen for using the roadways and robbing vans of their contents if they did not pay . . .[14]

The IRA would also emerge, teaching 'defensive' techniques such as bomb-making and the use of firearms. But, like NICRA, the CCDC, although Republican-inspired, was not a Republican organisation. Sullivan, and his associates from around the city, held positions of influence in the movement, but so did the clergy, the most prominent of whom was Canon Padraig Murphy, a parish priest, Paddy Devlin himself, and Tom Conaty, a businessman. The bulk of its activists were ordinary citizens. Apart from welfare and defence, the CCDC patrolled the ghetto areas at night, as much to curtail the activities of Catholic drunks as those of Protestant assassins, and published a newsletter; and Sullivan organised broadcasts over an illicit radio station, Radio Belfast. In addition the CCDC provided a handy source of interviews for the media of the world which had descended on Belfast. The cement holding all these disparate elements together was fear of further Protestant incursion.

That cement did not work within the Republican movement itself, however. Within days of the CCDC's foundation, on 24 August, a group which had been sparked into angry activity by the IRA's Irish Ran Away performance during 14 and 15 August met to discuss Goulding's overthrow. The group included Gerry Adams, Joe Cahill, Billy and John Kelly, Leo Martin, Billy McKee, Jimmy Drumm, Jimmy Steele, Seamus Twomey, and Daithi O'Conaill. With the exception of Adams, the youngest, all had been prominent in the IRA in the forties or fifties. They decided to get rid of the Belfast leadership of McMillen and Sullivan at the earliest possible opportunity and then move on to topple Goulding and his associates in Dublin. Their strategy was to force the British to remove Stormont and introduce direct rule, which, they reasoned, would inevitably lead to a united Ireland. McMillen was released from jail the following month and arranged a meeting to pick up the threads of his command. Instead he found it invaded by an armed group led by McKee who said they were taking over from him because of the IRA's failure to protect the Catholics.

As most of the older members of the group had dropped out of the movement in the previous five or six years, because of the Marxist drift, McMillen was on good ground when he refused to hand over control to men who had left the IRA. A compromise was worked out whereby he stayed on but was forced to accept McKee and a group of his supporters on his largely nonexistent staff. He was forbidden to communicate with Goulding and plans for a northern command independent of Dublin were agreed. Such money as was available, through Sullivan, for CCDC purposes would not be devoted to relieving distress, but to causing it – by using it to buy guns.

However, the pretexts for using guns refused to present themselves. For a time the Catholics proved to be dismayingly appreciative of the British Army's presence. Joe Cahill would later be quoted as saying that it brought tears to his eyes to see how the British, whom he considered to be responsible for the entire mess, were received by the populace.[15] Pictures of Tommies accepting cups of tea and playing football with street kids appeared in the newspapers. Even more remarkable photo-opportunities went unnoticed: for example, soldiers' rifles lying untouched in a pub patronised by Republicans while the squaddies answered a call of nature.

Callaghan shrewdly encouraged this mood. As part of the police reform package he brought over the former City of London Police commissioner, Sir Arthur Young, as the new RUC Commissioner to replace Anthony Peacocke, who resigned on publication of the Hunt Report. Paddy Devlin records a breakfast at which Callaghan introduced him to Young:

> Callaghan gripped my arm and called Sir Arthur Young over. This is my man. I want you to look after Arthur. He should be in retirement but is staying on to sort out Ulster for me. He cannot do it without your help.[16]

As a young man, Devlin had done his almost mandatory Falls Road stint in the IRA and as a result was not unused to being in the hands of the police. To find a police chief being entrusted to his hands, however, was a new experience. Filled with emotion, his reaction was: 'I decided to give this request of Jim's my best shot.'[17] The same sort of thing happened in Derry. Callaghan introduced Young to a cheering crowd in the Bogside, saying:

> 'This is Sir Arthur Young. He's going to look after you.' 'Oh no,' said Sir Arthur, all London bobby and affability, 'they're going to look after me.' There were more cheers.[18]

The barricades came down in both Bogside and Belfast to the echoes of those cheers, the Roman Catholic Bishop, Dr Philbin, being driven through the Falls in an army vehicle in his full purple regalia to indicate that the dismantling had his imprimatur. It was also taken to bear that of Jim Sullivan, who had taken part in the CCDC negotiations with the army, a further black mark in the eyes of the McKee faction. But the tide of Callaghan reform was running too strongly for any IRA opposition to be mounted against it. Fears of Protestant incursion remained high but military police patrolled the Falls and the Bogside with impunity. A new Minister for Community Relations was appointed on 29 October, a Unionist, Dr Robert Simpson, who resigned his membership of both the Orange and Masonic orders on taking up the post. On 24 November the Electoral Law Act (NI) foreshadowed the removal of the ratepayer qualification and the introduction of one man, one vote in local government elections.

Nevertheless, underground, the split within the IRA deepened. In December the IRA leadership met in secret and ratified two proposals sponsored by Goulding and inspired by Johnston which, though the logical outcome of their policies, had as much relevance to what was happening in Northern Ireland as did space travel. One proposed to established a National Liberation Front between Sinn Fein, the Irish Communist Party and other left-wing groups. The other to drop the traditional Republican policy of abstention so that Sinn Fein representatives, if elected, could take their seats in either the Dail, Stormont or Westminster. The only concession to reality in the two resolutions was contained in the words 'if elected'. Both decisions ran counter to traditionalist Republican thinking, which was anti-socialist and anti the 'usurping' parliaments legitimised by the 1921 treaty which had partitioned Ireland. At any time such departures would have caused controversy; to bring them forward after the events of August was to invite a split. The resentment within the movement crystallised around Sean MacStiofain, who had once been jailed with Cathal Goulding in 1953 for a raid on an arms depot in Felstead, Essex.

MacStiofain had been born in England of an Irish mother. A love of Ireland caused him to change his name from John Stephenson, by which he had been known during a spell of service in the RAF. By August 1969 he was responsible for IRA intelligence and noted for being an uncompromising Republican of the old school to whom all constitutional activity was anathema. I had figures like MacStiofain in mind when designing the cover for the first edition of my book on the IRA: it showed the stock of a rifle draped with rosary beads. As soon as the meeting which voted through the National Liberation Front proposal was finished he drove straight to Belfast, where he knew another meeting, of Republican traditionalists, was in progress. This gathering decided to set up a new Provisional IRA Army Council, with MacStiofain as chief of staff. Also on the council were Ruairi O'Bradaigh, Daithi O'Conaill, Patrick Mulcahy, Joe Cahill and Leo Martin. This army council was dominated by southerners. Only Cahill and Martin were from the north. By the end of a year the new IRA had consolidated itself and dropped the word Provisional. (The term had been chosen to make a connection with the 1916 rising leaders, who had declared a provisional government.) However, it stuck, as did the term 'Sticky', or 'Stickies', to denote a member of Goulding's organisation, which regarded itself as the 'Official' IRA. Both wings wore Easter lily emblems at Easter, to commemorate the 1916 rising. The Provisionals, also known as 'Provos', 'Provies', and, sometimes, 'Pinheads', used to affix their labels to their lapels with pins. The Officials used gum, hence the term 'Stickies'.

The secret rift in the IRA became a public split in Sinn Fein on 11 January 1970 when the party met in open session at the Intercontinental Hotel in Dublin to ratify the December decisions on abstention and the formation of a National Liberation Front. Ruairi O'Bradaigh, Daithi O'Conaill, Sean MacStiofain and their followers, at that stage numbering less than half the delegates, walked out, and convened another meeting at a hall in Parnell Square named after Kevin Barry, who had been executed by the British in 1920. This meeting set up a provisional caretaker executive of Sinn Fein, which would function from premises in Kevin Street, Dublin, close to Kevin Street Station, one of the Republic's largest police barracks. The Gouldingites continued to occupy the Official headquarters in Gardiner Place, near Belvedere College, the Jesuit institution where James Joyce went to school. All things considered, the Provisionals' proximity to the police was probably the more appropriate location.

From January until midsummer, when the defeat of Labour by the Conservatives created a new situation in Belfast, was something of a marking-time period for the Provisionals. The bulk of the IRA's grass-roots membership was unaware of the changes at the top, but during the six months after the split the Provos gradually became the stronger of the two factions in both Belfast and Derry. Initially the

Provos did not seek confrontation with the security forces. Their first concern was to prepare the organisation for what was regarded as an inevitable recrudescence of Protestant violence and only subsequently, as opportunity offered, to take on the British. Sean MacStiofain has written:

> ... it was agreed that the most urgent priority would be area defence ... as soon as it became feasible and practical the IRA would move from a purely defensive position into a phase of combined defence and retaliation. Should British troops ill-treat or kill civilians, counter operations would be undertaken when the Republican troops had the capability. After a sufficient period of preparation ... it would go into the third phase, launching an all-out offensive action against the British occupation system. It was also agreed that selective sabotage operations would be carried out ... [19]

The issue of 'area defence' brings us to one of the strangest incidents to occur as a result of the events of the summer of 1969: the drama which is usually referred to in Ireland as the Arms Trial. The trial, which involved former members of Jack Lynch's government, came about as the end result of the frantic scurryings between Belfast and Dublin that followed the Falls Road burnings. However, a more sinister interpretation of what happened in those perfervid days is put about by various parties. The Goulding IRA faction seeks to maximise its own pre-1969 importance by suggesting that the Fianna Fail Government was so worried about its progress that it sought to split the movement by supporting the formation of the Provisionals. Others, with the skin-deep knowledge of Dublin's drawing-room left concerning Northern Ireland in general and the IRA in particular, shown by the paper which Eoghan Harris delivered at the meeting that ultimately led to the foundation of NICRA, argue that Fianna Fail elements set up the Provisionals so as to secure a guarantee from the Republicans that henceforth they would confine their attentions solely to the Six Counties. Dr Conor Cruise O'Brien, for example, has written:

> The deal that launched the Provos was essentially this: certain members of the Lynch government approached those leading members of the IRA who were known to be disgusted with the Marxist leadership, on both nationalist and Catholic grounds, and also on operational grounds. These leaders – who were to become the leaders of the Provisionals – were offered money, arms and general support if they would abjure operations against the Republic, and concentrate on operations inside Northern Ireland. The Provisional leaders-to-be agreed. The policy, in exchange for which the emerging Provos received support from the then Dublin government, is enshrined in the IRA's General Order No. 8. [20]

Dr O'Brien then quotes General Order No. 8 and concludes: 'Thus the Provos were born, and the dirty war began.' I have interviewed a senior British general, an impressive man, who served in Northern Ireland and who, like his colleagues, also believed this conspiracy theory of the Provos' origins. But as I have already explained (see p. 55), General Order No. 8 pre-dates the birth of the Provisionals by more than fifteen years. It owed its creation not to conditions in Northern Ireland, but to the fact that the south was so hostile to the IRA that it was necessary to reassure the Republic that the IRA meant it no harm. Moreover, in 1969 the IRA was still observing the ceasefire which it had declared in 1962. The Provos did not come into being as a result of a promise to 'abjure' operations in the Republic, but because the existing IRA had shown itself unable to conduct them, either in the Republic or in the Six Counties.

The British general I mentioned above thought that the greatest service I could perform for humanity in the writing of this book would be to unearth the story of how southern businessmen founded and funded the Provos. However, long before meeting the general, the nature of Irish society, and of the research I have conducted on various facets of the northern conflict since the mid-sixties, had given me a pretty fair grasp of what went on. Within the constraints of the laws of libel, the following, necessarily abbreviated, account is, I think, as accurate a resumé as can be furnished at the time of writing. Firstly, it has to be borne in mind that the prime aim of Fianna Fail since its foundation in 1962 has been the ending of partition. De Valera laid it down that Fianna Fail's first priority was: 'Securing the political independence of a united Ireland as a Republic.'[21]

A great deal of the party's commitment to this aim was of the public house or Guinness school of Republicanism. And there were in addition many men in mohair suits who had no national aspirations and had merely joined Fianna Fail, as the ruling party, in pursuit of power, commercial or professional advancement. Nevertheless, there was at the party's core an influential segment of opinion which took the partition issue seriously. No one more so than the forceful Minister for Agriculture, Neil T. Blaney, from Co. Donegal, whose strongly Republican father had been one of the founders of Fianna Fail. Donegal, in the Republic, is the most northerly of the nine Ulster counties and the one whose economy and infrastructure is most badly affected by partition. Apart from being a legendarily effective director of the Fianna Fail election machine, Blaney was well known for his outspoken views on the division of the country. Consequently, for this reason, in addition to being a deputy for a border county and a member of the Cabinet, Blaney's advice was increasingly sought throughout the sixties by differing sections of Six County opinion.

In the wake of the Lemass–O'Neill initiative, professional and commercial interests in border areas – including Protestants, chiefly, though not exclusively, from the Newry area – consulted him on matters such as how northern professional qualifications, or business enterprises, would be likely to fare in the event of a united Ireland. As the situation worsened he received visits of a different character from people warning him of the gathering storm. These included figures like Hugh McAteer, the former IRA chief of staff, and John Kelly, who, as we have seen, later became one of the founders of the Provisionals. Blaney is known to have briefed his cabinet colleagues as to how matters were shaping.

On the night and early morning of 12/13 August 1969, Blaney was a principal, possibly the principal, link between Dublin, London, Derry and Stormont. His private phone was almost continually in use, receiving reports of what was happening in all four centres and passing the news from one point to another. He was in touch in Dublin with the Minister for Defence, James Gibbons, who in turn was conferring with the army chief of staff and his senior officers, and with civil servants in the Departments of Foreign Affairs and of the Taoiseach. Blaney could not raise the Taoiseach, Jack Lynch, either by phone or by sending emissaries to his home. Lynch later told me that he had taken a sleeping tablet that night.

Next day, in a move scarcely paralleled in the Republic's history, the Cabinet, after a review of all that had happened and was likely to happen in Derry and elsewhere in Northern Ireland, drafted a collective speech for Lynch to deliver. Several different members of the Government contributed to the speech, in which Lynch announced the sending of 'field hospitals' to the border, and said that the Irish Government could not stand by in the face of what was happening. The speech should have read 'stand idly by', but the word 'idly' was omitted from the RTE teleprompter. One can still meet with senior Fianna Fail figures who believed that the British at the time were hanging back to allow the Irish Army, not to in fact stand idly by, but to cross the border. Had this been done, these sources argue, the Troubles would have come to a head and partition would have been over in a matter of weeks. Others will also tell you that to their certain knowledge around a score of Dail deputies and senators from all parties gave their own guns to northerners 'for defence'.

What is certain is that after the Bogside and Belfast eruptions Blaney was descended upon by representatives of all shades of Nationalist opinion seeking assistance. These included people looking for help for refugees driven from their homes, members of the CCDC and future members of the Provisional IRA. He facilitated many of these contacts, including the last category, with introductions to his colleagues.

Later, one of these men, John Kelly, declared:

> I want to be very emphatic here, that we were coming from all parts of the Six Counties not to indulge in tea parties, not to be entertained, but to elicit in so far as we could what was the opinion of the Government in relation to the Six Counties. We did not ask for blankets or feeding bottles. We asked for guns and no one from Taoiseach Lynch down refused that request or told us that this was contrary to Government policy.[22]

Another Fianna Fail minister who was also descended upon was Charles J. Haughey, the Minister for Finance. Hitherto he had appeared to be the epitome of the Men in the Mohair Suits with little interest in anything beyond power and the making of money. However, he was also the son of a strongly Republican father, from Co. Derry, who, in his day, had assisted Michael Collins in smuggling guns across the border to help the beleaguered Catholics. When a priest and a lawyer from Belfast visited Haughey in the wake of the burnings, seeking help for families afflicted by the Troubles, he immediately wrote a cheque for £20,000. The money was duly administered by a Catholic charity for the purpose for which it was subscribed. Haughey, whose eye on the leadership of Fianna Fail never faltered, even in the most unpromising of circumstances, certainly would not have wished it to appear that Blaney was the only member of the Cabinet who had an interest in Northern Ireland.

Other interested spectators in what was happening north of the border included members of the staff of Irish Military Intelligence, particularly a Captain James

Kelly. Kelly, who believed that at all times he was acting on behalf of the Irish Government, was authorised to convene a meeting of CCDC personnel at Bailieboro, Co. Cavan, on the weekend of 4 and 5 October 1969. The fact that Kelly, a victim of the situation, was acting on orders was underlined when he was given money by his superiors to stand a dinner to those present. The guest list, drawn from each of the Six Counties, included the senior Derry Republican, Sean Keenan, Jim Sullivan, and Billy Kelly from Belfast. There was only one item on the diners' agenda: the provision of guns. Captain Kelly was satisfied that the guns were needed for defensive purposes only to protect the Catholics when, as was generally expected they would, the Protestants returned to the fray. He reported accordingly to his superiors and was subsequently authorised to become involved in efforts to supply weapons from the Continent.

A £100,000 fund, which was supposed to be administered by the Red Cross, had been set up by the Government on 21 August 1969, for the alleviation of distress. Some £24,000 was given to Cardinal Conway for use at his discretion and another portion of the fund went to the CCDC. But some government money would also appear to have been spent on the *sub rosa* purchase of arms. At this stage there was a cabinet subcommittee dealing with the north, and contingency plans for a cross-border invasion in a doomsday situation had also been drawn up. The impracticality of these led to their being dropped almost as soon as they were proposed. By the time even the border town of Newry had been secured by the Irish Army, the Catholics of Belfast could have been massacred. Also dropped was a plan to train Six County citizens in weapons at Fort Dunree in Co. Donegal. After a handful of volunteers, mainly from Derry, received some initial training the scheme was abandoned the day before the Bailieboro meeting. Lynch was moving steadily away from the tone and import of the 'standing idly by' speech forced on him by his colleagues.

A former hurling star, the quiet, unobtrusive, pipe-smoking Lynch was not on the Republican wing of Fianna Fail. In fact, when he was head-hunted by the party as a Dail candidate, he could as easily have stood for the more conservative Fine Gael party. A widow's son, his early career was that of a promising Cork Christian Brothers' boy. The civil service, a call to the bar indicated a dutiful willingness on his part to apply himself 'to the books', not to becoming a future taoiseach. However, when Lemass retired in 1966 he was an acceptable compromise candidate between Lemass' son-in-law, Haughey, and Haughey's main rival, George Colley (Blaney would probably have come third had he entered the race). On 20 September 1969 Lynch made a speech of his own at Tralee in which he said he was not seeking the violent overthrow of Stormont. Unity by consent was his objective.

However, other people moved in a different trajectory to Lynch. Cathal Goulding is on record as saying he was contacted by a priest, who was related by marriage to the brother of an Irish public figure, and invited to meet this person at an Irish centre in Kilburn to discuss the provision of funds for the IRA. He told him that it would take some £50,000 to buy the necessary arms. He was given only approximately £3,000. No other money changed hands but there were several other meetings.

Both the hawk and the dove wings of Fianna Fail had a shared interest in trying to assess what was going to happen in the Six Counties. Were the IRA in a position to defend the Catholics? Who in the IRA could be trusted? Were the Catholics really in such great danger? To what degree could or should the Republic become involved?

Increasingly, the doves' answer to the last question was along the lines of Lynch's Tralee speech. The hawks continued to make their soundings, but became progressively dubious about the Gouldingites' commitment to arms. For example, according to Goulding, a meeting was arranged between a prominent Derry IRA man and some Fianna Fail supporters, who included a cabinet minister, in the Intercontinental Hotel, Dublin. The purpose of the meeting was said to be to put a proposal to the Derry IRA man to organise a more militant branch of the IRA in the Six Counties. Goulding advised the IRA man, who said he was promised a car and money, to get the car registered in his name, so that it could not be taken back from him. No car or money were forthcoming.

However, I am told that, arising out of the welter of contacts with decision-taking people in Dublin, one shipment of arms did pass through Dublin Airport and into the hands of the IRA in October 1969. That was the last time anything of that nature came the way of the Gouldingites. But Captain Kelly continued his activities. With the assistance of Albert Luyks, a Belgian friend of Blaney's, he made contact with a Hamburg arms dealer. Kelly had access to the bank accounts which were opened as a result of the fund set up by the Government on 21 August. On 19 February 1970, in Dortmund, Kelly gave the dealer £10,000 for arms which were to be shipped to Dublin from Antwerp. However, British intelligence intervened to abort this shipment. All that arrived were some bulletproof vests. Kelly then arranged for a private plane to fly the arms to Dublin Airport on 19 April. A document was obtained from the Department of Finance requesting the airport authorities to pass the arms through customs.

Somehow, throughout the welter of meetings and skulduggery which had gone on practically since August 1969, Lynch managed to remain oblivious to what was happening. However, at this stage the efforts of British intelligence went into overdrive. Peter Berry, the strongman Secretary of the Irish Department of Justice, received information which enabled him to arrange that a Garda cordon, which included a section of the Irish Special Branch responsive directly to him, was thrown around Dublin Airport on 18 April. But the hawks had their sources of intelligence also and John Kelly, of the Belfast Provisionals, flew to Vienna in time to warn Captain Kelly (no relation) to cancel the mission. The guns never arrived, but the sands were running out for the hawks.

A government meeting scheduled some mornings later was unaccountably delayed for over half an hour. Such a delay was unprecedented in Irish cabinet history. Later it emerged that Lynch had had a visitor, the British Ambassador. He had another some time afterwards, Liam Cosgrave, the Leader of the Opposition. Cosgrave had a document which was supposed to have emanated from the Gardai.

A version of this document had already been supplied to the *Sunday Independent*, which had refused to print it, and it then found its way to Cosgrave. The real source of the information in both documents is thought to have been the same: British intelligence. Cosgrave's contained seven names, five of whom were subsequently unsuccessfully prosecuted on gun-running charges: Blaney, Charles Haughey, Jock Haughey, Luyks and Captain Kelly. John Kelly was later given six months for IRA membership. It was during his trial that he made the statement quoted on p. 99 about not asking for feeding bottles.

Such, in essence, was the 'Arms Trial' affair. The sackings, and subsequent arrests, of figures like Blaney and Haughey needless to say sent shock waves through Irish society during most of 1970. Between sackings, resignations, and reshuffles, the Fianna Fail parliamentary party underwent the greatest upheaval in its history. One of the figures who resigned from the Cabinet, Kevin Boland, subsequently founded his own party, Aontacht Eireann (Republican Unity Party), which achieved little beyond keeping the 'Arms Trial' alive in the public mind for a few years. Effectively speaking, Lynch's Tralee approach became settled Fianna Fail policy. The actual court proceedings commenced on 28 May. Blaney was acquitted on 2 July and the others on 23 October. But did the disturbing arms trial saga also have a lasting booster effect on the Provisional IRA? Obviously the use, or misuse, of Irish taxpayers' money must have given the emerging Provisional movement some impetus. For this reason alone, the anger and suspicion of figures like the general I mentioned earlier is understandable. But neither the amount of money nor the arms involved were of continuing significance. The first British soldier to be killed (in February 1971) was not shot until over a year after the solitary consignment was smuggled through Dublin as a result of Fianna Fail/IRA contact. And those guns went to the Officials, not the Provisionals. Other events of a militaristic character which also occurred in 1970 had a more marked and lasting impact on the Provisionals' fortunes.

But before detailing these, it is necessary to remind ourselves of the constitutional developments of the period. Though the events of the 'Arms Trial' obviously occupied a high proportion of the year's headlines, two sets of elections were more important for most people in Northern Ireland. The first were two by-elections, significant for the light they cast on the public warfare being waged in the Unionist camp over the issue of reform. (The planning for warfare by the Provisionals was of course carried on in secret.) One of these had the added importance of returning Ian Paisley to Parliament for the first time. He won Terence O'Neill's old seat, Bannside, in a by-election held on 16 April, standing as a Protestant Unionist. His associate, William Beattie, also won in South Antrim.

Other facets of the reform programme which facilitated the victories of Paisley and Beattie concerned the police and the B-Specials. The Specials' disbandment date occurred at the end of the month in which the by-elections were held. The Ulster Defence Regiment (UDR) was commissioned that month also, but its duties pointedly did not include crowd or riot control. The month before the election (on 26 March), the Police Act came into effect. This set up a civilianised, unarmed force and established a police authority. These were highly unwelcome intrusions into traditional Unionist concepts of 'their' law and 'their' order.

At the time, also, the Macrory Committee on local government reform had yet to deliver its report (it came on 29 May). But the committee, under the chairmanship of Sir Patrick Macrory, a leading northern industrialist, was viewed with considerable suspicion by Unionists. I happened to meet Sir Patrick during the committee's deliberations in a restaurant in Dun Laoghaire where I was having dinner with Tommy Roberts, the likeable PR man for the Northern Ireland Government. In his jesting introduction, Roberts echoed the view of many Unionists concerning Macrory's work: 'This is Paddy Macrory, he's carving up the place for you.' Reforming the Six Counties local government structures was regarded as a prelude to a Dublin takeover.

What Macrory in fact recommended was a streamlining of the existing county council system into twenty-six new district councils, and the creation of area boards to administer the health, education and library services. Membership of these boards was by government appointment, which meant they were taken out of Unionist Party control. Later, through no fault of Macrory's, these democratic reforms unintentionally became part of the north's democratic deficit. In the absence of a local parliament, the introduction of direct rule meant that such appointments were removed from local representatives altogether and placed in the hands of London politicians.

The arrival of Paisley in Stormont was a most significant event. From now on, whenever moderation showed its hideous fangs in the camps of either Unionism or Protestantism, the presence of Paisley in the mainstream, coupled with the 'conditional loyalty' principle, meant that there was a politico-evangelical shelter for the traditionalists to flee to. Only one week after Paisley was elected, on 24 April, the Unionist Party held a meeting at which a vote was taken that showed what the party felt about reform. The vote was 281 to 216 against the changes in housing policy. Whatever reforms London might urge on the Unionist Government at Stormont, the spirit of Moses Busby was still strong amongst the party rank and file. Housing was still seen as the keystone of the arch of control. Moderates were thus greatly encouraged to keep their mouths shut and their actions circumspect.

Unfortunately, the result of the second election was to ensure that circumspection was to be removed from the British Army's lexicon for a critical period. On 18 June 1970, a British general election toppled Labour and returned a Conservative government under Edward Heath. Instead of the hands-on Callaghan, there was installed the hands-off Reginald Maudling. The Unionist Party vote on housing indicates the difficulties that lay in the path of even the most vigorous London overseer in obtaining reform. Maudling displayed a lack of vigour to the point of indolence. But above all, in place of the considerable restraint to which the army was subjected under Labour, a quite brutal search-and-ransack operation of the Falls Road area was sanctioned within days of the Tories taking over. This action confirmed moderate Nationalist opinion in the belief that the Conservative and Unionist Party was resuming the traditional alliance which had led to the setting-up of the statelet in the first place. Where the Provisional IRA was concerned, a tidal wave of recruitment was released which transformed the movement from a conspiracy to a guerrilla army.

And conspiring the Provisionals certainly were. The reason O'Bradaigh, O'Conaill, MacStiofain and the others had founded the Provisionals in the first place was so that they could go to war. But initially, apart from the obvious difficulty of laying hands on guns and explosives, they faced the problem of not having a base in public opinion from which to proceed. Morale was high and there had been a certain amount of reorganisation in which three Provisional IRA battalion areas had been formed. The First Battalion took in Andersonstown, Ballymurphy and the Upper Falls district. The Second, Clonard, the Divis Flats area and the Lower Falls. These two battalion areas were in solidly Catholic districts, in the general vicinity of the Falls Road. The Third, however, took in three Catholic enclaves surrounded by Protestant districts, the Ardoyne, the Bone and the Short Strand. In all of these working-class streets, there of course existed a strong sense of 'them and us' and a concomitant fear that the 'them' would be returning to stage a Clonard-style repeat performance. But there was no widespread hostility to the British Army.

Outside of the Republican cadres, ordinary people regarded the troops with a residual gratitude for several months after their arrival. The soldiers had saved them from the Protestants. The IRA were the Irish Ran Away. In fact when they first arrived, to be greeted with cups of tea and welcoming smiles, the soldiers' reception contrasted markedly with the abuse which some IRA men received when they appeared in Catholic districts after the August burnings. Joe Cahill is on record as saying that he was chased out of Ballymurphy, where Gerry Adams grew up, when he first appeared to organise defensive measures after the rioting, and that it took him several days to talk his way back into the district.[23]

Despite Britain's record in the country, the ordinary British soldier was not normally a hate object in Ireland. Loathing was generally reserved for corps raised expressly to provoke that emotion, for example, the Black and Tans. During the Black and Tan war the Tommies were never regarded in the same hostile light as the Tans. That attitude would not have changed in the Catholic ghettos of Belfast in 1970 just because the Provisionals were trying to goad the troops into first reaction and then overreaction. The mere fact of having troops on the streets in such a highly charged atmosphere would have brought the honeymoon period to an end one way or another. The nature of the state which the British Army had underpinned meant that their initial favourable reception was going to be fretted away, even in the absence of Provisionals, if reform did not come quickly. An armed soldier on a west European city street is a fairly stark indication that something is radically wrong in that society. The use of Scottish regiments also made for an inevitable and specific type of culture clash. Traditionally the Orange bands from Scotland were the most unpopular, because in demeanour and gesture they were provocative to Catholics during the traditional Orange marches on the Twelfth of July. On top of this, the ever-present 'Whitby' factor in Anglo-Irish relations manifested itself. The average young soldier got a very strange picture of the sort of society he was being sent to from the manual dealing with Ireland which the army gave him. It contained the bogus Sinn Fein Oath which I have quoted. The manual was withdrawn after I published its contents in the *Irish Press*.

The clash between the army and Republican elements took about six months to erupt, from the time of the Provisionals' founding meetings in September. In the meantime the Provisionals were probably responsible for setting off some dozens of small, unclaimed home-made bombs, petrol bombs and ugly variants on both in the shape of nail bombs, which used gelignite and nails taped together to create a shrapnel effect. The underdog bites at the testicles. The more obvious source of hostilities in the interim was the rivalry between the two wings of the IRA. This led to a number of shooting incidents and many fights. Enmity between the two IRAs, and Protestants and Catholics, plus the increasing frustration of the army with both sides made Easter 1970 an unpleasant time on the Falls Road. Fighting broke out around Ballymurphy on 31 March after what the army said was Provisional-inspired rioting and what some locals still claim was insulting behaviour on the part of soldiers of the Royal Scots Regiment towards Catholic girls. The set-piece occasion for hostilities to commence was that familiar *casus belli* in Northern Ireland: a march.

An Orange parade which had unwisely been allowed to march through a Catholic area was set upon by Catholics. A Royal Scots riot squad with batons attacked the Catholics, using snatch squads to rush into the rioters and haul out stone-throwers. Sometimes doors were torn off hinges as the soldiers also rushed into houses, not always the right houses, on the same mission. The fighting was some of the most intense seen in Belfast and the most significant confrontation between Catholics and the army since the arrival of the soldiers. Over the next couple of days some thirty-eight soldiers were injured by brick, bottle, hurling stick, fist or head butt. No one knows how many Catholics were hurt, because of the traditional reticence about notifying injuries to hospitals. But CS gas was used, plentifully, for the first time in Belfast, alienating the majority of the inhabitants. One of those who developed a stammer as a result of the canisters of gas being fired into his home was Dominic Adams, Gerry's younger brother. Subsequently the Adams family would prove itself to be more moved by this fact than by a stern warning issued by the British GOC, General Sir Ian Freeland. On 3 April, he announced a new 'get tough' policy by the army. He said that anyone caught making or using a petrol bomb was liable to be 'shot dead in the street' if after a warning they persisted. The penalty in lieu of shooting was to be ten years in jail.

Understandably, few people in Ballymurphy voted for Oliver Napier and Bob Cooper's newly formed Alliance Party (founded on 21 April) in the general election the following June. Its appeal was to moderate middle-of-the-road support in favour of reform within the system. After three days of riot Joe Cahill's welcome in Ballymurphy was no longer in doubt, his policies more appealing than those not only of Alliance, but of the official IRA, or anyone else for that matter. An ugly follow-up to the riots was the fact that Protestant families were intimidated out of their homes in the New Barnsley estate nearby. One can only speculate as to what effect these expulsions may have had on the political development of a former New Barnsley resident, Andrew Tyrie, a machine operator, who later became supreme commander of what was to be the Loyalists' mirror organisation of the IRA, the Ulster Defence Association (UDA). What can be said with certainty is that the spirit of rising inflammation was one well calculated to collide head-on with an incoming Tory administration. And it was not only rising in Ballymurphy, but all over the province. In the election the Unionist Party won only eight of the twelve Westminster seats. Paisley took North Antrim, Frank MacManus, a Nationalist standing as a Unity candidate, won Fermanagh/South Tyrone, Gerry Fitt held West Belfast and Bernadette Devlin was returned for Mid-Ulster and a jail term.

Her appeal against her six-month sentence for her Bogside activities was dismissed on 22 April and she was arrested at a roadblock four days later. She had intended to address a meeting, after which, her supporters say, she was going to give herself up. The news of her arrest in these circumstances sparked off a riot in Derry which had appalling collateral casualties. The riot took the usual form of stones and petrol bombs being hurled at troops, who replied with CS gas. But in a house in the Creggan, what was in effect the local Provisional unit attempted to provide the Catholic side with something more lethal, a home-made bomb. It went off prematurely, killing three men, Joseph Coyle, Thomas Carlin and Thomas McCool – and two of McCool's daughters.

As in the previous August's rioting the troubles spread to Belfast, and, in the three days ending 27 June, the army is estimated to have fired 1,600 cartridges of CS gas in the enclosed streets.[24] Most of these were in Catholic areas. However, there were no British troops in evidence in the Catholic Short Strand enclave as Protestant mobs began an incursion on the night of the 27th, a Sunday. Armed with a Thompson gun, Billy McKee, the Provisional leader, and four or five of his men took up a position in the grounds of St Matthew's Church on the Lower Newtownards Road. Through the night, under heavy rifle and small-arms fire, McKee and his men defended the area. Five Protestants and one member of the group, Henry McIlhone, were killed. But despite the fact that the army never arrived, the mobs were repulsed and St Matthew's was saved. McKee received a wound that bled so much that a comrade of his, Kevin Hannaway, told me: 'You'd think he was after washing his overcoat in blood.' The engagement, which subsequently entered the folklore of Republican Belfast, was the emerging Provisional IRA's most significant operation to date. No Irish Ran Away this time. Instead, a classic piece of defenderism that saved a church, provided a martyr, McIlhone, and a hero in the neat, slight, unobtrusive figure of McKee, who looked more like a church sacristan than a gunman. Kevin Hannaway said of him: 'That man would never ask you to do anything he wasn't prepared to do himself.'

The Protestants riposted next day by expelling the 500 Catholics (less than a tenth of the Protestant workforce) known to be working in Harland and Wolff's shipyard. General Freeland responded with an announcement that anyone carrying a gun was liable to be shot. This was the backdrop against which Reginald Maudling arrived in the Six Counties on 1 July. It could be said of James Callaghan that he talked Green and acted Orange. But of Maudling it could hardly be said that he acted at all. The scene was set for his tenure in office by his performance on his first day in Ulster. The intensity of the situation, and of those he met, so overcame him that at the end of the day the new Home Secretary collapsed into his plane seat, exclaiming: 'For God's sake, bring me a large Scotch. What a bloody awful country!' Two days later it got a lot bloodier.

At this stage a word should be said about the British Army, albeit from an Irish perspective. From any perspective its position in Northern Ireland in July 1970 was not an enviable one. There was a crumbling administration at Stormont vainly trying to introduce reform against the wishes of a majority of the party which had placed it in government. The RUC was in a state which Sir Frank Cooper, a former head of the Northern Ireland civil service, had described as '. . . total collapse. It was not merely dismembered. It was a shambles . . . it meant inevitably that the Army had to go on for much longer playing the lead role.'[25] Thus, in a real sense, the force of law and order was the army.

But, even apart from the fact that to Irish Nationalists a British uniform in Ireland is an irritant in the political oyster around which no pearl will ever form, the army was an army, not a police force. Moreover, it was an army which had come to Ireland against an operational background that included Aden, Cyprus, Kenya, Malaya, all 'foreign', post-colonial, counterinsurgency theatres. The techniques which it had acquired along the way could be, and were, profitably deployed on behalf of Sultans friendly to Britain, away from the cameras, in places like Brunei and Oman. But they were counterproductive in a white, English-speaking, Irish city which was supposed to be treated as a part of the United Kingdom. A strain of frankly racist condescension, influenced by colonial experience elsewhere, was encapsulated in a term frequently used in military circles to describe the Irish: bog-wog. The fact that the Irish responded with equally derogatory nomenclature did nothing to improve community relationships. Nor did the regimental system. The entire character of the contact between the Catholic civilian population and the army became adversely affected when certain units arrived in the north for a tour of duty. This was particularly true of some Scots regiments and of the paratroopers. Also, the culture of the British Army was different from anything in Irish Nationalist experience. A former Irish prime minister who had spent many hours in negotiations with London over complaints concerning British Army behaviour told me:

> Their tradition is totally different. The Army is a kind of sacred thing in British society. If the Army says something is an operational necessity, then that's it. Whether it's an installation they want built, or the introduction of internment. We have much tighter political control on our Army. But it's an accepted thing over there that Army officers can brief the leader of the Opposition, and make representations at all sorts of political levels. It's partly the old boy network, partly the club thing, the interaction of the officer and gentleman class. They all look after each other.

My English friends might disagree with that assessment. It obviously leaves out the difference in the size and background of the two armies, and the substantive point which weighed with the 'officer and gentleman' class, the exigencies of the arms industry. But it was made by a former Irish prime minister. One can imagine the bafflement of Nationalist politicians working on the ground in Northern Ireland, trying to maintain a constitutionalist stance against the growing popularity of the IRA and yet finding themselves undercut time and again during the conflict by army actions which seemed divorced from any form of political rationale. Paddy Devlin titled the chapter in his autobiography which dealt with his unavailing attempts, and those of his colleagues, to get Westminster to rein in the army 'Our Boys – right or wrong'.[26] On top of these factors there was the manner in which the army was controlled while Stormont stood. General Sir Harry Tuzo, who replaced General Freeland as GOC, said of his tenure:

> It was a complicated situation because I was in effect a sort of Minister of Defence and Chief of Staff to two people, so far as Northern Ireland was concerned, and I worked to the Prime Minister of Northern Ireland . . . and I had to report back to Westminster and, of course, I gained all my sustenance from Westminster and was entirely dependent on Westminster for the forces I had, so there were no indigenous forces. My relationship with the Stormont government I like to think [was] entirely cordial, but it was totally advisory and subject to the imprimatur or call it what you will, the permission of Westminster, except of course in day-to-day minutiae.[27]

One could interpret Tuzo's remarks another way. The distinguishing characteristic of a government, as opposed to say a county council, is that it has the ability to enforce its own laws. Although the British initially shrank from direct rule, from the moment the army arrived, Stormont, in fact, did not have a law and order capability. That responsibility passed to Britain, whose hand it was in the puppet's glove which Stormont became. Sir Kenneth Bloomfield, one of the most knowledgeable civil servants of the period, was Under-Secretary to the Cabinet at the period Tuzo spoke of, and took part in many of the 'cordial' meetings with him. His view of the period differs sharply from that of the general:

> . . . it was a peculiarly uncomfortable period, because the citizenry in Northern Ireland, understandably enough, continued to look to the government of Northern Ireland to discharge those responsibilities which they still felt were the responsibilities of the government of Northern Ireland, but the ability and practice to discharge them was extremely limited, so I would certainly describe that as an extremely uncomfortable and difficult integration.[28]

Tuzo had the reputation of being more 'political' than most army men who came to the Six Counties. His political skills may have been called on because of Freeland's exercise of his autonomy in a spectacular piece of 'day-to-day minutiae': the Falls Road curfew, or 'The Rape of the Lower Falls', as Republicans prefer to call it. The incident began on the afternoon of Friday 3 July, ironically enough the day after Stormont passed the Prevention of Incitement to Hatred Act, and concluded around nine o'clock the following Sunday morning. Rioting had broken out after the army had discovered an arms cache belonging to the Officials in Balkan Street on the Lower Falls. Freeland decided to crack down hard and sent in approximately 3,000 troops, supported by helicopters which hovered overhead using loudspeakers to warn the inmates of an area of approximately fifty small streets to stay indoors. The curfew was only lifted for a two-hour break to allow a procession of women into the area with prams loaded with bread, milk and other groceries. It is said that when they wheeled them out again they contained many of the weapons the soldiers were looking for.

But arms were not the only objectives of the search. It was intended as a rough-handed ransack operation which would pacify the natives. By chance the curfew trapped an Italian film crew inside the cordons. Its producer, Franco Biancicci, a veteran of the Algerian war, had also been in the Kasbah immediately after General Massu had ransacked it. 'It was the same thing exactly,' he told me. Doors were kicked in, furniture smashed, floorboards pulled up, wall plaster ripped off, holy pictures stamped underfoot or thrust down lavatories, mainly by members of the Scots Black Watch regiment. Above and beyond all this, there was some of the most savage fighting of the period to date. The army used their rifles and CS gas. The two IRAs fought back with guns, petrol bombs and nail bombs. Civilians used stones or their bare hands. In all, five civilians were killed, one through being run over by an army vehicle. Forty-five were injured, as were fifteen soldiers.

The total arms haul secured by the army came to some 100 weapons (including the original Balkan Street cache), a similar number of home-made bombs, about 250lb of explosive waiting to be made into bombs, 21,000 rounds of ammunition and eight two-way radios. It looked impressive enough when displayed for the cameras, but it was as nothing compared with the scale of recoil from the army by the Catholic working-class community of Belfast. For the foregoing bald account does nor, and cannot, recapture the sense of alienation engendered by commands, in an English accent, pouring from the sky, ordering people to remain in homes which were shortly to be burst in upon and wrecked by their official protectors. Moreover most of the weapons seized had been stockpiled by the Officials, whose area it was, for defensive purposes only. The restraint which McMillen and Sullivan had somehow managed to enjoin on their followers in the face of the Provos' growing militancy meant that the Provisionals were the main beneficiaries of the huge swing towards Republicanism that now took place.

I attended a big IRA funeral at Milltown Cemetery in Belfast the following September (of a Provisional who had blown himself up) and conducted such an intensive personal survey into allegiances that one polite young man came up to me to enquire if I was from the Special Branch! The overwhelming majority of men present were Provisionals and they all gave the Falls Road curfew as their reason for joining. To make matters worse, after the curfew concluded, the army brought two Unionist ministers into the 'pacified' area in army vehicles to inspect their handiwork, so as to prove that the army was tough on Catholics. One was William Long, the other Captain John Brooke, Lord Brookeborough's son. The choice of Brooke was grossly insensitive, an insensitivity underlined when, in response to a cascade of outrage from Nationalists, a minister from the Republic, Dr Patrick Hillery, visited the area on their heels. The Unionists were outraged. Chichester-Clark said the visit was 'deplorable' at a time of such tension. At Westminster, Sir Alec Douglas-Home, the Foreign Secretary, echoed the Unionist reaction, saying the visit was an act of grave 'diplomatic discourtesy'. In fact, the visit was a minimalist response by Dublin, given the severe pressure on Lynch at the time to take strong action. He gave a reassurance to the northern Nationalists, and at the same time fended off his critics in Fianna Fail, by making a broadcast on 11 July. In it he said that the Dublin Government was the 'second guarantor', after London, in securing the Catholics' rights. This annoyed the Unionists still further.

Apart from the Falls residents themselves, Sir Alec may not have been the only one to feel that a lack of courtesy was involved. The month after the curfew, the minister in charge of law and order, Robert Porter, of Home Affairs, resigned for 'health reasons'. However, he later said[29] that he was not consulted about the operation beforehand and the first he knew of it was when he heard about it on the radio. His departure was used to instal as Minister of State at Home Affairs John Taylor, a trenchant critic of the reform programme, in an effort to placate the right wing of Unionism.

The month ended with fierce rioting in Belfast, during which a Catholic youth was shot by the army. Paddy Devlin summed up much of Catholic Belfast's post-curfew reaction when he issued a statement on the boy's death, saying:

> The army are deliberately provoking trouble in certain selected areas where Catholics live to justify saturation of these areas by troops. The British Army are now behaving like a conquering army of medieval times. With the restraining hand of Mr James Callaghan gone from the Home Office, General Freeland is reverting to the type of general that Irish people read about in their history books.[30]

Devlin was to take part in a more considered attempt to articulate Catholic grievances a few weeks later. On 21 August, the Social Democratic and Labour Party was founded. On grounds of intellectual prowess, John Hume would have been the natural leader of the party, but because he represented a Belfast constituency, and had the important publicity adjunct of a Westminster seat, the longer-established Gerry Fitt was chosen. Hume became deputy leader. Austin Currie also joined the new grouping, as did Devlin, Ivan Cooper and another civil rights MP, Paddy O'Hanlon. Paddy Wilson, a Republican Labour associate of Fitt's, was another founder member. He was later murdered by Loyalists. The party had a radical programme of wealth distribution, civil rights, friendship between Catholic and Protestant and cross-border co-operation, leading to eventual unity. It effectively took over from all the existing Nationalist groupings, became a member of the Socialist International and made inroads into the NILP. The party's rather cumbersome name had its origins in Hume's desire to be regarded as a Social Democrat, Fitt's to retain the name Labour, and a characteristic intervention by Paddy Devlin. When the name Labour and Social Democratic Party was proposed, Devlin exclaimed: 'Fuck no! Not the LSD Party!'

However, this attempt at constitutional advance, deep-rooted though it would ultimately prove itself, was not paralleled elsewhere in the divided community. As Sir Frank Cooper said, chaos reigned among the police. Sir Arthur Young resigned in September. Belfast was no place for a London bobby. On the Catholic front he was faced with an increasing propensity towards murder by those whom he had said would look after him. Two of his men had been blown up in a booby-trapped car in Crossmaglen on 12 August. On the Protestant side he and his men were being excoriated for not stopping the riots, taking down barricades in Catholic areas and generally not acting as 'their' police force. Worse, some members of the RUC had been known to so forget their role as to break up Protestant riots and arrest the rioters. This could have been overlooked as an aberration had it not been for the fact that the flood of legislation pouring on to the statute books included, from 1 July 1970, a provision whereby rioting carried a mandatory sentence.

On the British side the military commanders who had come in 'in aid of the civil power' were increasingly in effect becoming the civil power. They did not want a London bobby. They wanted the sort of tough-cop counterinsurgent who would emerge later in the conflict. There was a good deal of internecine fighting of all sorts going on. The old hands in the Northern Ireland civil service resented the new arrivals from London. The British marked sensitive documents 'for UK eyes only', to prevent the Unionist civil servants reading them.[31] A more sensitive choice of wording might have been employed in a situation whose intensity derived from the fact that those excluded, and their community, wanted to be considered 'UK only'. But there was a good deal of rank ignorance about. I have already quoted the bogus 'Sinn Fein Oath' (p.47). That was solemnly reproduced as fact by the army spin-doctors in the official manual which was issued to the incoming squaddies and later withdrawn. In sum, a demoralised and understrength police force, riven by Freemasonry, fear, prejudice, outmoded training and briefing, was performing a Canute-like role in attempting to stem a rising tide of violence from both communities.

The Sir Arthur Young approach surfaced briefly, pathetically almost, on 15 September, when the RUC voted in favour of being unarmed. Sir Arthur himself resigned a week later. That was not the sort of wimp-like behaviour the army wanted to hear about. It was of course fine in theory, precisely the sort of value judgement the army was there to uphold. But they were being asked to uphold it with rubber bullets. These were six-inch-long, five-ounce projectiles with a range of fifty yards, lethal if they were fired at the upper body at close range, but intended (it was said) to be aimed at the legs and, if possible, to ricochet off the ground. In fact they caused several fatalities through being fired into people's faces at point-blank range. On one level, Ireland was being used, as it had been traditionally, as a laboratory for military techniques.

One of the senior British generals in Ireland at this period, Brigadier Frank Kitson, wrote:

> There are other potential trouble spots within the United Kingdom which might involve the Army in operations of a sort against political extremists who are prepared to resort to a considerable degree of violence to achieve their political ends.
>
> If a genuine and serious grievance arose, such as might result from a significant drop in the standard of living, all those who now dissipate their protest over a wide variety of causes might concentrate their effort and produce a situation which was beyond the power of the police to handle. Should this happen the Army would be required to restore the position rapidly. Fumbling at this juncture might have grave consequences even to the extent of undermining confidence in the whole system of government.

Some people say that Kitson was the *deus ex machina* of the entire British Army operation. One of his principal adversaries, Sean MacStiofain, refers to him a dozen times in his memoirs. The American writer J. Bowyer Bell, however, avers that 'his views were not significant within the British Army'.[32]

The squeezing of Catholics might be said to have begun with the Falls Road curfew in July 1970, but curiously it did not result in any army fatality until February 1971. Symbolically, in view of what had happened in August 1969, it was precipitated by events in the Clonard area. Throughout 1970 and into early 1971 the army had been in contact with IRA leaders, all names familiar in Clonard: Liam Hannaway, Kevin Hannaway (his son), Proinsias MacAirt, Billy McKee, and Leo Martin, the bungled attempt on whom had led to the first fatal shootings (by the UVF) of the Troubles, in 1966. However, the talks had not produced any inroads for the army either in the Clonard area or elsewhere. In fact, the Provisionals were getting stronger, riots so common that it was said in Belfast that 'Friday night is gelly night'. On 3 February 1971 there was particularly vicious rioting in the Clonard area. The soldiers used rubber bullets and their protective shields; the rioters everything from steel darts to hand grenades, from acid bombs to petrol bombs. A machine gun was briefly brought into play.

The army had had enough. General Anthony Farrar-Hockley went on television to name the Republican leaders he had been dealing with, and blamed them for the rise in violence. The genial Sir Anthony has been known in Clonard ever since as Sir Horror-Fuckley. On the same day the hard-line junior Home Affairs minister, John Taylor, signalled a rise in stakes. He told the London *Times*: 'We are going to shoot it out with them, it is as simple as that.' The next night the army shot a young Catholic during a riot in the Ardoyne area. An IRA man, Billy Reid, was appealed to for assistance. He borrowed a machine gun, which he did not know how to use, from a unit outside his area, and emptied the magazine more or less blindly.

One bullet killed twenty-year-old Ensign Robert Curtis of the Royal Artillery regiment. He thus became the first British soldier to be killed in Ireland since the 1920s and the treaty that was meant to take Ireland off the British agenda. By an eerie coincidence, Reid himself was killed three months later – in Curtis Street. The night of the unfortunate Curtis' death was marked by some of the worst rioting the Six Counties had seen, in both Protestant and Catholic areas of Belfast and in Derry. In a night of heavy firing, two more deaths occurred. Next day a haggard Chichester-Clark went on television to announce: 'Northern Ireland is at war with the Irish Republican Army Provisionals.'

Four

A Job for the Army

Between the acting of a dreadful thing
And the first motion, all the interim is
Like a phantasma, or a hideous dream.

Shakespeare, *Julius Caesar*, Act II

THE IRA THAT Chichester-Clark declared war on could be described in two ways, either in terms of statistics and materiel, or in the sense of the Irish phrase *uisce fe talamh*, literally, 'water under the ground'. In practice it means secret doings, matters not to be discussed publicly. A consciousness of race and place, formed by history and circumstance, whereby one grows up knowing things without realising where one learnt them. Knowing how to fight, how to kill. Inclining instinctively to guerrilla warfare, because in the Irish physical force tradition the Catholic and Gaelic side of the conflict hid in, and struck from, fog and bog. They might not be able to spell the term 'status of belligerents'. But they understood what not having it meant. If caught, they were more likely to face a rope than a cell. This tradition, its legacies of infliction and endurance, was probably the IRA's greatest weapon on the day Chichester-Clark spoke.

Numerically the IRA probably did not have more than 300 active soldiers at the time he made the announcement, although it could have had the services of innumerable recruits had it been able to arm them. Behind it there probably stood as many as a thousand auxiliaries, and a network of safe houses and sympathetic medical personnel. This last category gives an indication of the level of constant, hidden support for the IRA, as opposed to, say, voting figures for Sinn Fein, or the equally constant public condemnation which the movement has attracted. Very few examples can be cited of IRA personnel being arrested in hospital, or surgery, after being treated for gunshot or shrapnel wounds. Yet the law stipulates, both north and south of the border, that such injuries must be reported to the authorities. In addition to this sort of help, guns were trickling in from the US. Explosive was falling off some quarry lorries, and not getting put on to others. Nevertheless, the strength of the IRA could only be likened to that of some deadly form of yeast which caused expansion and swelling when mixed with other ingredients. The northern term 'racking' is one such example.

This derived from the conflicts arising from marches. By local agreement a Protestant band might march through a Catholic district in the morning quite peacefully. The drums wouild fall silent passing through a flashpoint town or

113

village and no provocation would be offered. But then in the evening, on the way back, after the drink had circulated, the flutes would play and the drums roar out the 'Protestant Boys' or some other anthem of defiance and supremacy. The Catholics would attack the marchers and a riot would develop. This was very likely to be followed up a week or so later by a return raid by the Protestants on the offending village, which would be lucky to escape with only having windows smashed and a few heads broken.

The techniques learned in such encounters might have been seen in action had one witnessed a Belfast riot in, say, the Clonard district during the early 1970s. The scene would have been one of swirling confusion, seemingly uncoordinated chaos: stone-throwing youths shouting insults at troops or police; the sight and sound of exploding petrol bombs or the detonation of coffee jars stuffed with explosive; the sound of the army riot squads beating their batons on their shields, or the cries and curses of struggling men and exhorting women. But if one looked more closely one would have become aware of older men standing along the street, or outside the door of a pub, signalling inconspicuously to the younger men. Then one would subsequently notice a bomb hurled here, a sudden surge by the rioters there. Or maybe, if one happened to be in certain houses, the crackle of a walkie-talkie transmitting a message along the lines of: 'Another patrol coming up Dunville Street. Open up a second front on the Kashmir Road . . .' There would be more crackling bursts on the walkie-talkie and suddenly a group of lads, who had quite possibly been at school with Gerard McAuley, would be rampaging down the Kashmir Road, creating a new focus of attention for the army.

But initially, very few people outside the Provisionals understood what was happening. I remember, one Sunday afternoon, driving halfway across Ireland with my children, in my innocence, to explain to Ruairi O'Bradaigh that the media of the world was on the Catholics' side. Reform, a new Ireland, would assuredly come if the IRA would exert itself against the spread of violence so as to prevent a loss of sympathy for the Nationalists. As O'Bradaigh, a former schoolteacher, is a most courteous man the drive at least produced a pleasant, if somewhat one-sided, conversation. Southern thinking was simply not attuned to what was happening in the north. The Republic was concerned with its own day-to-day political life into which the Arms Trial had been an unwelcome intrusion. Partition had worked, insofar as very few people in the Republic ever thought about the North before the troubles erupted. Few went there, unless for business reasons. Northerners came south much more readily. The events of the Arms Trial had generated considerable heat and rekindled traditional fervour within the ruling Fianna Fail Party, but had done little to provide light in the way of new policies.

In an effort to open up the debate, the Taoiseach, Jack Lynch, made a speech addressing the effect of the Republic's constitution and legislation (i.e. on divorce and contraception) on northern thinking, at the first Ard Fheis (annual party conference) to be held after the Arms Trial affair, on 20 February 1971. The speech went down well in London and so impressed Jim Callaghan that he quoted from it approvingly in his memoirs. It contained the following:

Where it can be shown that attitudes embodied in our laws and Constitution give offence to liberty of conscience, then we are prepared to see what can be done to harmonise our views so that . . . a new kind of Irish society may be created agreeable to North and South. We wish to extend an olive branch to the North and we wish the North to accept it. If this means that we must grasp some nettles which sting our pride then we will readily do so if the result be a just and lasting peace throughout our island.

As I had suggested this approach to Lynch, and had written the foregoing, I went along to the Ard Fheis to gauge reaction. I very much doubt whether fifty people in the huge hall even heard what Lynch was saying. Claques representing the various personalities in the Arms Trial were attempting to shout him down, while Lynch's equally vociferous supporters attempted to drown out the dissidents. While this was going on, early editions of the following day's *Sunday Press* were brought to the platform. They contained a very large bunch of stinging nettles indeed – an onslaught from the Archbishop of Dublin, Dr John Charles McQuaid, on any notion of alteration to the Republic's laws. I don't know how the Archbishop learned of the speech's content, but he followed up his newspaper comment with a letter read at every church in his archdiocese the following month. It said, amongst other things:

One can conceive no worse fate for Ireland than that it should, by the legislation of our elected representatives, be now made to conform to the patterns of sexual conduct in other countries. It is also being suggested that such uniformity of sexual outlook and practice can, in some obscure way, assist the reunification of our country . . . it would indeed be a foul basis on which to attempt to conduct the unity of our country . . . it would be, and would remain, a curse upon our country.[1]

That took care of any move on legislative change for many a long day. Meanwhile, the reality on the ground in the North was that the British Army was the IRA's best recruiting agent. The saturation was such that at one stage there were 2,000 soldiers billeted in Paddy Devlin's Belfast constituency alone, one to every ten voters. On a specimen Saturday night Devlin counted thirty army vehicles in the district. Soldiers moved along in groups of twenty or more, dispersed on both sides of the streets, guns at the ready. There were no police to be seen. He describes the effect of the army methodology with characteristic vigour:

I was downright angry at the mindless harassment, degrading obstruction and casual brutality the soldiers meted out to all who came in their path. I spent hours boiling over in anger and frustration, incoherent with rage, complaining to arrogant, overbearing British officers who failed to see the damage they were doing, the way they were walking into the trap the ruthless Provos had laid for them and how they were only acting as recruiting sergeants for the Provos.[2]

Devlin also singles out a factor which was to be of crucial importance in tipping the Six Counties into anarchy later in 1971: the quality of military intelligence. Devlin terms this 'appalling'. He says:

They failed to understand that many families shared common surnames, but were not related in any way . . . they arrested fathers when they wanted the sons and the sons when they were after the fathers. Innocent teenage boys and old men thus found themselves held at the point of a British rifle, and many people I dealt with then were so alienated by the experience that they joined the Provos and later became notorious terrorists.

The Provisionals became the motor force in the situation after a vicious feud with the Officials, which left the latter with little territory in Belfast outside the Lower Falls area. Ironically, matters came to a head because the Officials attacked the British Army! Unfortunately the site of the attack was in the Provo stronghold of Ballymurphy. After the Officials conducted a raid on 5 March 1971 on troops billeted in the Henry Taggart Memorial Hall, the Provisionals demonstrated their displeasure at this intrusion on their turf by pistol-whipping the local Official leader. This triggered a spate of shootings and hostage-takings. There was a major encounter on 8 March in which the two wings shot it out while the army stood by watching delightedly. By coincidence Paddy Devlin got caught up in the excitement. He had brought an Officials' leader, Jim Sullivan, and his wife Mary for a birthday drink. The Provos turned up and burned the pub down. Then, after Paddy had taken the couple back to their house from the scene of this decidedly un-happy birthday party, they encountered another group of armed Provos. In deference to Mary's presence they decided not to assassinate Sullivan and contented themselves with machine-gunning Paddy's car.

Another group of Provos then shot up a pub where Billy McMillen, the Officials' leader, was drinking. An attack on one pub might be regarded as a misfortune. To shoot up a second looked suspiciously like enemy action. McMillen ordered the killing of a number of Provo leaders in response. Revolution devours its children; by ill chance the only Provisional leader to be killed was Charles Hughes, a widely respected young man who had deployed the members of his unit in defence of the Officials during the Falls Road curfew. Another prominent Provisional to be shot was Tom Cahill, a brother of Joe's. He was a milk roundsman and had separated his pistol and its magazine in the belief that if he were stopped by police he would not be arrested because his gun was disarmed. However, in a panic as an Official hit squad approached, he mislaid the magazine and got badly shot up as he scrabbled amongst his milk bottles. Later the police found the magazine and, when he recovered from his wounds, he was jailed for possession of firearms.

A truce was arranged between the two IRAs through the mediation of the clergy. But the general carnage was not so susceptible to settlement. Throughout 1971 the Six Counties degenerated into chaos. Apart from countless incidents of intimida-tion, robbery and extortion, and the split within the IRA, the first seven months of the year contained a number of events which are lodged in my memory, either for the indication they gave of what was occurring, or because of their intrinsic horror or significance.

Mid-January to mid-February was characterised by a ferocious series of riots in Belfast. In Ballymurphy they continuously fought the army with brick and stone and hurling stick. Every family learned to have a basin of vinegar and towels handy to cope with the tear gas. Never a shot was fired, but any British soldier who lost his comrades in a dark alley had more to fear from the women than the men. In the middle of January the Ardoyne went up in smoke in sympathy with Ballymurphy. By the end of the month the Protestant Shankill was seething with disorder in protest at both. In early February screeching hordes of women literally tore into soldiers searching for arms in the Crumlin Road and Ardoyne areas. And the bin lids! People in the south, and in England, saw the women on the television and wondered at them. Crouching, legs asprawl, hair in curlers. Medea-like creatures, in an unlikely setting, fighting with what they had: hate, hysteria and bin lids.

When they were little girls they would have heard their grandmothers reminisce about 'the pogroms', the early twenties, when the six-county state was founded. At Christmas, or christenings, they would have heard snatches of ballads like:

> Oh, she got up and rattled her bin,
> For the Specials they were a-comin' in.

They would have heard of the communal 'M-u-u-r-dher' howl, used when the 'auxies', or the Tans, or the Specials, dressed in civvies, their faces blackened, shod in tennis shoes, slipped into the Catholic ghetto areas at night with feral intent. These torrential women could be good lovers, good mothers, but terrible adversaries. I remember some of them expressing the deep, bitter grief of womb and tomb on television after a five-year-old girl had been killed by an army vehicle on 8 February. The following day, though there was no direct connection between the two tragedies, the television system itself was made an object of death. On Brougher Mountain, five people were blown up. They should been 'the army'. In fact they were three local construction workers and a couple of BBC engineers who wanted to have a look at the transmitter. In terms of historical significance their deaths probably rate below those of the RUC men who were shot in an off-licence on Alliance Avenue, Belfast, on 26 February.

They had intended to buy a few bottles of wine before going to dinner with the family of the older of the two. He was born near where I live and went to school, Blackrock, Co. Dublin. But, having failed to get accepted by either the Gardai, the Irish Army, or the RAF, he had taken the one 'yes' response to his myriad job applications and joined the RUC. I remember discussing these and related matters some time later with a Sinn Fein leader, who explained to me that: 'We're shootin' the uniform, not the man.' So that was all right. Anyway, the deaths caused the RUC to be rearmed and issued with flak jackets. Not long afterwards there occurred another deed of blood, which even as I write is still remembered. Three young off-duty Scottish soldiers made a forcible down-payment on the memories of 'racking', the excesses of the Falls Road curfew and all the rest of it: their lives. They were taken on a drinking spree by three members of the Provisional IRA. At a place called Ligoniel, outside Belfast, as they urinated, glasses in hand, they were swiftly shot in the head by their drinking buddies. Two of them were teenagers, and brothers. Like the RUC man born near me who died in the wine shop, they too had found other work hard to come by. Later, one of their killers asked me to his wedding reception. Who was it said that we're all the children our mothers warned us against . . . ?

The unfortunate young soldiers' deaths resulted in my getting a nasty warning that also helps to illustrate the level of official thinking at the time. My book on the IRA had appeared the previous year and I found myself sought after in British Embassy circles. I had resisted the overtures but after Ligoniel felt caution was no longer appropriate and accepted an invitation to lunch with the Ambassador, Sir John Peck. He suggested that when in London I should see his superiors at the Foreign Office and pass on my views. 'My management,' he said, 'think I'm going native.' Accordingly, I turned up a few weeks later at the Foreign Office, intending to give first-hand examples of the dangers of the heavy-handed security policy, and the need for more political initiative and progress on reform.

After some conversation with a senior official, the official got to the real point of my visit – in his eyes. 'There are two colleagues of mine from MOD, down the hall, who want to talk to you.' The penny dropped. I was not there to give a briefing. I was expected to act as an informant. It was a standard colonial response: 'Get the editor of the local rag and milk him. He knows all the terrorists.' I terminated the conversation rather abruptly and it was a long, long time before I allowed myself to come within range of any British diplomat again.

The situation on the ground continued to deteriorate. Rioting, killing, more rioting. There was one deed of British Army heroism I still remember as I drive by the Springfield Road Barracks, off the Falls Road. On 25 May, an IRA volunteer deposited a suitcase containing gelignite, and emitting smoke, in the hallway of the barracks. Sergeant Michael Willets of the Parachute Regiment held the door open and ushered those present to safety. They included at least two children. He was blown to bits after the children escaped. His posthumously awarded George Cross later fetched £20,250 (in March 1985), the highest amount ever paid for such a medal.

Two other deaths were to have profound consequences in propelling the province into its final lurch to disaster that year. Two youths, Seamus Cusack and Desmond Beattie, were shot by the army on 8 July in Derry. The shootings caused violent rioting in the city. John Hume called for an impartial inquiry into the deaths. He failed to get it, and, against the wishes of Fitt and Devlin, organised the withdrawal of the SDLP from Stormont. Hume gave a press conference on the 12th at which he explained why he was withdrawing support from the parliament: 'There comes a point where to continue to do so is to appear to condone the present system. That point, in our view, has now been reached.' The SDLP then proceeded to set up what it called 'an Assembly of the Northern People'. The party issued a call for a campaign for civil disobedience which it suggested should include a rent and rates strike and the withdrawal of all Catholics from public bodies. Why did the party act in such a seemingly irresponsible fashion?

I had been given a small insight into the reality of political life in Derry some time before this. I had called on Hume, who introduced me to a middle-aged woman whom he was visiting on constituency business. She was a friendly, motherly, open person, the sort of constituent that any MP would be glad to help with her application for a house, or to get the bins collected, or a new streetlamp installed or somesuch. But John was not helping her with any of these things. He was giving her the latest progress report, or lack of it, on the RUC inquiry into the death of her husband, Samuel Devenney. One of Sir Arthur Young's last public comments before he left the province was that there was a 'conspiracy of silence' amongst the police concerning her husband's fatal beating.[3] Later we drove to Donegal where I wanted Hume to meet a Republican whom I thought might help to cool things down a bit. Hume grumbled characteristically: 'Every time I talk to someone in the IRA I find there's a harder man further up.' But, also characteristically, he went, after I used the clinching argument that the man I wanted him to see, Frank Morris, had received the cat-o'-nine-tails during the Second World War, and therefore had to be regarded as a person of some consequence in the movement. We ended up sleeping in the same bed, after a night that was long on hospitality but short on results. Next day in Derry we called at the home of Hume's colleague, Ivan Cooper. Outside Cooper's house, his car was a heap of tangled wreckage. While we were in Donegal he had got a phone call telling him that one of his principal election workers had been injured in an accident and taken to hospital. He was rushing out to the car when it struck him that the caller had not specified which hospital, so he turned back into the house and rang to check. While he was doing so a bomb went off under his car. Had he driven straight to the local hospital, as he had intended, he would have been killed.

A specimen twenty-four hours of constituency work in Derry under Stormont. I left the two MPs posing beside the bombed-out car for BBC television and drove off, pondering on a remark of Hume's which I felt held ominous implications for the future. He had said: 'Of course we can reach accommodation with the Unionists, and we will. Once the Unionist understands that he has to take his foot off the Catholic's neck.' Hesitating to argue with Hume, it nevertheless seemed to me that he was underestimating the problem. The *raison d'être* of Unionism was to keep its foot on the Catholic's neck. Logical argument in forum or TV studio was irrelevant to that central fact. Any attempt to remove it would be resisted. By July 1971 the SDLP had made the attempt and politically the result had been to carry the party back to the position of the Burntollet marchers. There had been a harder IRA man at every level and, along with the army's behaviour, the Unionist had helped to justify the hardness in the eyes of increasing numbers of Nationalists by refusing to remove his foot.

For throughout this period, powerful elements within the Unionist family had met the challenge of the situation in two ways. One was to block or delay reform in any way they could. The other was to deal with the growing security problem by calling for internment. On the reform front, the delays meant that though genuine progress was made, it first tended to be obscured in the fog of rioting and bitterness, and was then later swamped by developments on the security front. We have seen how the RUC was first disarmed and then had to be rearmed. The housing system was also reformed, but the Unionists staged rearguard actions wherever they could. For example, in Austin Currie's stamping ground of Dungannon, seven years after he had led the first sit-in, the activities of Unionist county councillors led to a High Court action on 21 January 1971. In December 1970 the council had allocated forty-three houses to Protestants and only five to Catholics. The High Court granted a Catholic who had been passed over an injunction to prevent the council giving houses to Protestants. Brian Faulkner, who was in charge of local government reform, had dismissed SDLP complaints about housing as being 'all part of a plot to discredit the established local authorities'.[4]

One of these 'established local authorities' was Fermanagh County Council. At the time of the publication of the Macrory Report it had thirty-five Unionist councillors, while the Catholic majority was represented by only seventeen. The chairman of the council, Captain John Brooke, Faulkner's partner in government, whom the army had taken on a tour of the 'pacified' Lower Falls, was on record as saying that the council would only be reformed 'over my dead body'.[5] Brooke, be it noted, was on the 'moderate' wing of unionism. Some five months after the Macrory Report was published, and nearly twenty after he had been put in charge of local government reform, Faulkner was attacked in a January edition of the *Belfast Sunday News* for his performance:

> For all his talk of supporting local government reform the Minister of Development, Mr Brian Faulkner, has a strange way of going about it. Last week he said it would be a considerable time before proportional representation would be introduced into council elections, despite earlier government assurances on this point. Hardly a good way of silencing critics within the minority who feel that Stormont is stalling and giving way to right-wing Unionists on reform.

The right-wing Unionists referred to might be thought of as the Paisley–Boal faction on one side and the followers of Craig and West on the other. Both wings grew increasingly stentorian on the issue of security and the need for internment as the violence escalated. By now the IRA were attacking 'economic targets', burning and blowing up shops and business premises of all kinds. After the murder of the three young Scottish soldiers at Ligoniel, four thousand shipyard workers poured on to the streets of Belfast to demand internment. The Catholics wanted reform; the Unionists tougher security, which to some meant anything from the introduction of the death penalty to internment. Others would have settled for an end to the no-go areas in Belfast and Derry, and a saturation-level increase in troops. Everyone wanted an end to the IRA campaign. However, Paddy Devlin's description of existing troop levels indicates the effect that granting any or all of these requests would have had on Catholic opinion.

Chichester-Clark flew to London on 16 March and presented a security shopping list. The only item on it which Heath was prepared to concede was a request for more troops, and then only 1,300 more, bringing the total in the province at this stage to 9,700. Chichester-Clark threatened to resign, and despite being pressurised by Heath to stay on, carried out his threat four days later, in the teeth of entreaties from Heath, Lord Carrington (the Minister for Defence), and a brace of British generals, Sir Geoffrey Baker, Chief of Staff, and Sir Harry Tuzo. He was succeeded by Brian Faulkner on 23 March 1971. Faulkner was elected by twenty-three votes to four for William Craig. Paisley was amongst those who voted against him.

Faulkner's election meant that the Stormont Parliament had become the political equivalent of the Last-Chance Saloon. The pace of change was accelerating inexorably. Brookeborough had ruled unbrokenly for twenty years, O'Neill for six,

Chichester-Clark for two. Faulkner would get a few days short of one. He had come to power with the reputation of being the Six-County expert on security, the man who had broken the 1956–62 IRA campaign by introducing internment when he was Minister for Home Affairs. Now, privately, he urged the same nostrum on London. The month in which he was appointed saw changes in the army also. General Freeland had been replaced as GOC in February by Lieutenant-General Vernon Erskine Crum. He, however, suffered a massive heart attack and died on 17 March, St Patrick's Day. His replacement was the redoubtable Lieutenant-General Sir Harry Tuzo, who came to Belfast via Borneo. By now Kitson had been in place for six months. He and Farrar-Hockley were *ad idem* on the need for good PR to keep British public opinion onside, and henceforward the army information services at Lisburn Army HQ paid considerable attention to the dissemination of 'information' which many Nationalists would dismiss as disinformation.

Apart from being involved in stepping up propaganda, Kitson is credited with giving an impetus to theories which were already in circulation concerning information-gathering, and interrogation of IRA suspects. Two concepts have been associated with him in particular: 'de-escalation' and 'attrition'.[6] The former meant removing the water of civilian support in which the IRA swam by using propaganda and spending money on community projects. 'Attrition', directed against the IRA, meant what it said. But how to employ attrition effectively against the IRA leadership, rather than the rank-and-file stone-throwers and bomb carriers? Kitson was acutely conscious that the sort of methods needed to crush the IRA were not possible under the law as it stood. Army nomenclature can be made to sound very impressive, especially if accompanied by wall charts, fluent lecture techniques, and the use of slides and projectors at briefing sessions. But what about the real world? The problem for General Tuzo and his colleagues was that techniques which might have been employed effectively against the Wild Man of Borneo were apt to end up on page one if deployed against the even wilder men of Clonard and Ballymurphy.

Kitson, Tuzo and the new Chief of the General Staff, General Sir Michael Carver, later Field Marshal Carver, were all aware, intelligent, modern professional soldiers. But here I would make two points. Firstly, most of their experience had been in colonial campaigns which generally had one thing in common – they failed. Secondly, and the obvious cannot be overstated, they were not politicians, they were soldiers, schooled to render the other side incapable of continuing warfare. To achieve the objective in the six north-eastern counties of Ireland in the spring and summer of 1971 was not possible, militarily, morally or politically. My information on the feeling of the army leadership at the time was that Carver and Tuzo thought that they could contain the IRA without internment, thus leaving the politicians free to find a political solution. Tuzo's inclination was to get stuck into the Catholic ghetto areas, seize the guns and the IRA leadership, and render them amenable to due process. It was a formula which apparently overlooked the lessons of the Falls Road curfew. I would certainly not have sought, with or without wall charts, to commend it to Gerard McAuley's schoolmates. Tuzo had another problem. The RUC were not co-operating with him. He wanted the force to free up his troops by performing duties such as guarding police stations and patrolling the border. Here, however, the police turned, not so much Unionist, as trade unionist. They said to the army, in effect: 'You are in charge of security. You patrol, guard, etc.' Given the state of demoralisation in the force, it was about the only response which could have been expected. However, at the same time, Unionism being Unionism, the local concept of 'security' being what it was – i.e. 'their' law and 'their' order, etc. – another problem, affecting Catholic disaffection, was manifesting itself.

The new UDR was rapidly becoming the old B-Specials; the same personnel in different uniforms. As Loyalist paramilitarism spread it became a fact of life that in addition to the recruitment of former B-Specials, the UDR also took on, and trained, members of the Unionist community anxious to emulate the IRA. British intelligence did not discourage this development. It provided handy sources of information, and, later, surrogates who carried out missions, which the British did not wish to be associated with. British intelligence itself also became engaged in faction fights: MI5 did not co-operate with MI6; the Scotland Yard anti-terrorist squad complained bitterly about both. It is difficult to know how much all this rivalry aided the IRA. But in subsequent years, as the onion skins peeled off and I became aware of the layers involved in the British counterinsurgency effort, I began to see why at that early stage the Foreign Office would have wanted to avail itself of my poor insights, or those of anyone else, for that matter. The basic truth was that for all the assurance of the plummy accents and the officer and gentleman class network, the British were not informed about what was going on in the province.

Heath's government adopted the methodology of other British governments at various moments of crisis earlier in the century. A cabinet committee was set up to deal with the Irish question. This one was called GEN 42.[7] It consisted mainly of the Prime Minister, the Home Secretary, the Foreign Secretary and the Chancellor. Other interested parties attended when necessary, for example the Secretary for Defence and senior officers such as the Chief of the General Staff and the GOC, Northern Ireland. Insofar as he had any fixed ideas about Northern Ireland, Maudling, from what I have been able to glean, appeared to think that direct rule was a distasteful inevitability. Until it arrived, any political activity was useless and in the interim a military approach was the only one possible. During his celebrated visit to the north, which concluded with the heartfelt *cri de* Scotch, he indicated this to the army. He is quoted as saying bluntly: 'It's your job to sort out those bloody people.'[8]

Brian Faulkner shared Maudling's view that 'Ulster' was a job for the army. He was invited to a GEN 42 meeting after becoming prime minister. The meeting, which took place in April, was also attended by Generals Carver and Tuzo, who entered Downing Street through the back door to avoid publicity. Faulkner was keen to repeat his success of the fifties and strongly pressed for internment. Apart from other practical objections to internment, which will shortly present themselves very forcefully, it should be noted here that there was a fatal flaw in his analysis. Internment was not the factor which destroyed the 1956–62 IRA campaign. What principally defeated the IRA was the lack of support from the Catholic population of Northern Ireland. In 1956–62 the Catholics were far more cowed than they were in 1971. Then they were fearful of the RUC and the B-Specials, in awe of the British Army. Now, in 1971, he faced a risen people, stirred by the civil rights movement and angry at the Unionists' stalling on reform. While in the main critical of IRA violence, the Nationalists were no longer prepared to accept a wholescale policy of repression.

Faulkner ignored this fact and urged a security programme on the British which, had it been adopted in full, would have created even worse havoc than that which did occur. Apart from seeking the introduction of internment, he wanted the border sealed off and raids into the Republic to seize known members of the IRA. This suggestion, had it been acted on, would have extended the effects of the Falls Road curfew into the Republic. As a minimum response Dublin would have been forced to break off diplomatic relationships with London. More through the natural inclination of politicians to avoid taking decisions than anything else, Faulkner's suggestions were not taken up at that meeting. Some of those present agreed with his ideas, but the generals were opposed, either on operational grounds or because Tuzo favoured the implementation of his own theories already outlined: 'disruptive' arms searches of Catholic areas and an increase in random personnel searches in the street. In other words, the 'toothpaste' policy: squeeze the Catholics until they vomit out the IRA.

However, though he did not get his way at that meeting, Faulkner continued to work steadily towards his goals. By 25 May he felt confident enough to signal a new hard-line policy on the part of the army. Speaking at Stormont he said:

> Any soldier seeing any person with a weapon or acting suspiciously may, depending on the circumstances, fire to warn or with effect without waiting for orders.

It was the implementation of this policy which caused the shootings of Cusack and Beattie and the consequent withdrawal of the SDLP from Stormont. But at the same time as orchestrating a security crackdown directed at the Nationalists, Faulkner had been attempting to woo the Nationalists' representatives, the SDLP. He succeeded with some of them. Paddy Devlin has written that: 'From our point of view Faulkner made a brisk and encouraging start.'[9] Faulkner made history by appointing a non-Unionist to his cabinet, David Bleakley of the NILP, who became Minister for Community Relations. He also made a number of speeches promising fair play to the Catholics. Devlin was so impressed that he judged that had Faulkner, not O'Neill, succeeded Brookeborough, he had the political skills needed both to have introduced reform and headed off the crisis which broke over the Six Counties.[10]

Faulkner was undoubtedly an able politician, but, against Devlin's judgement, one is bound to set other episodes in his career, such as the fact that, under O'Neill, this born-again reformer resigned from the Cabinet in protest at the setting-up of the Cameron Commission into discrimination and gerrymandering. His most imaginative gesture was the establishment of parliamentary committees which were to include Catholics. These were touted as a form of power-sharing, even though they were consultative and review, rather than representative, bodies. However, they did give an increased outlet to the opposition, who were otherwise automatically outvoted at Stormont. Moreover, of the four salaried posts of chairmen, two were reserved for the opposition. In his memoirs Faulkner said of the Orange Order that it was:

> Not the Ku Klux Klan, but a reasonable organisation which, by and large, sought to restrain the wilder element of the Protestant Community and taught justice and respect for the beliefs of our neighbours.[11]

However, his faith in the efficacy of the Order's teachings of justice and respect was not apparently sufficient to prevent him from indulging in an exercise that took much of the credibility from the committee's gesture. Four days after he announced them it was discovered that he and some of his senior cabinet colleagues had touched their forelocks to the Order in a very revealing fashion.[12] The Prime Minister and his ministers had driven to Lurgan to the headquarters of the Royal Black Institution, the seniors of the Order, to explain away these concessions.

While introducing the committees, on 22 June, in Stormont, Faulkner made a comment, the significance of which escaped the opposition. He said:

> It must be recognised that any concept of participation will be hollow which does not recognise the duty to participate in bearing the burdens of the State as well as enjoying its advantages, and that no duty is more important than to mount a sustained opposition to terrorism.

A 'sustained opposition to terrorism' was code for internment. However, the SDLP did not get much time for decoding. Three weeks after the announcement of the committees, the shooting of Beattie and Cusack drove the party out of Stormont. Faulkner continued to urge internment by every means at his disposal. There were apparently full-blown meetings of GEN 42 held on at least three occasions after the shootings. Faulkner felt himself to be in a strong position. He told the cabinet committee that if he did not get internment he would be forced to resign. In that event either Ian Paisley would become prime minister or the British would have to introduce direct rule.

He also refused to consider rerouteing the Apprentice Boys march in Derry which had caused the original explosion in August 1969. Nor would he agree to a crackdown on the spread of 'rifle clubs'. These were a device which the Orangemen had first used prior to the First World War. Emulating the 1913 strategy, Justices of the Peace had granted legal gun licences to members of rifle clubs, with such enthusiasm that it was calculated by the *Sunday Times*, on 28 March 1971, that there were 73,000 licensed weapons in the Six Counties. Faulkner's resistance to curbs on these gun licences helped to ensure that by the following November the number had risen to 110,000 licensed weapons, the vast bulk of them in Loyalist hands. Thus were the fruits of Paisleyism seen. Brian Faulkner was not going to allow Ian Paisley to steal his right-wing clothes while he bathed in the waters of moderation.

On 5 August the crucial GEN 42 meeting took place. Faulkner was flanked by Kenneth Bloomfield and Howard Smith, who was then stationed at Stormont, described as a Foreign Office adviser, and who later became head of MI5. When Faulkner struck up his familiar refrain, Bloomfield and Howard joined him in singing the internment tune. Carver and Tuzo were then asked to join the meeting. Tuzo repeated the Kitson thesis about the inadequacies of the law in dealing with the IRA at officer level, i.e. the planners who were really responsible for what was going on. The conventional wisdom is that this support for Faulkner's earlier arguments decided Heath in coming down in favour of internment.

Unfortunately Mr Heath, apparently wounded by disclosures concerning his advocacy of very drastic activity on the part of the army made in the documentary *The Last Colony* shown on Channel Four in July 1994,[13] has temporarily at least shut down on interviews about this period, over which, of course, a thirty-year rule still obtains. But I do not accept that the British simply decided to go for internment on the basis of Brian Faulkner's arguments which finally struck a chord on 5 August 1971.

Granted, there was a very serious security problem in existence in 1971. For example, General Tuzo has calculated[14] that the IRA had managed to set off some two tons of explosive in a three-week period prior to the introduction of internment. Therefore, he said, 'There was no doubt in anybody's mind that something different had to be done . . . you had to do something a bit more dramatic in order to . . . lance the boil.'

However, quite deep-laid preparations for internment and some well-rehearsed ancillary procedures were already in place by 5 August, and, by their very nature, must have been in place for some time. There were a number of set-piece co-operations already under way which of themselves were not so much sinister as obviously practical. For example, the provision of lists of those who would be subject to internment, and places in which to intern them. Three of the latter locations were prepared. One, the major centre, was a World War II airfield at Long Kesh, near Lisburn, about ten miles from Belfast; the others were Magilligan Prison, near Derry, and an old prison ship, the *Maidstone*, moored in Belfast Lough. But there were other plans, plans for the systematic employment of torture against detainees. This policy had its origins in earlier British experience, in theatres such as Aden, Cyprus, Kenya, and in the brainwashing techniques employed against American and British servicemen in Korea. These were subsequently adopted by the British Army against EOKA during the Cyprus campaign.

This kind of expertise was unknown in the RUC and the British had to set up a special team of instructors to train the RUC Special Branch. The nature and extent of these preparations were both fully understood and sanctioned by the proper authorities within the Ministry of Defence, British intelligence and the upper echelons of Stormont. The training of the RUC personnel in interrogation techniques, for example, began in April at the British Intelligence Centre in Maresfield, Sussex, and continued throughout the summer. However, the British are past masters of the art of denial. A member of GEN 42 was able to look me in the eye and tell me that neither he nor any member of the committee knew of the techniques in advance. They were informed on strategy, but not detail! There is no evidence that anyone – be it Lord Carrington, the minister responsible, Heath, or Lord Carver – sought to inform themselves on the potentially explosive nature of the proposed strategy. On at least two subsequent occasions, both during the filming of *The Last Colony*, and in his autobiography, Lord Carver stated that he was not consulted, and regrets that he did not pursue the issue of 'special treatment' with vigour.

Although ruinous in PR terms, the use of torture was, in a sense, only the poisoned icing on the internment cake. For Operation Demetrius, as the internment drive was termed, was botched in practically every respect one can think of. It was preceded by what in boxing terms is known as a telegraphed punch. On 23 July a trial run operation was conducted throughout the province in a series of dawn raids which netted a total of forty-eight suspects. Then, when the fully fledged operation did begin, at 4 a.m. on 9 August, it relied on lists drawn up by the RUC Special Branch. There were 450 names on the lists, but only 350 of these rendered themselves available for internment. Key figures on the lists, and many who never appeared on them, were warned before the swoop began. The lists were weighted towards the Officials, who, despite being the more pacific of the two IRA wings, were regarded by MI5 as the more dangerous adversaries because of their Marxist orientation. Hence their potential was assessed in cold-war terms, rather than in an Irish context. The names included people who had been interned previously, or had been active in the IRA decades earlier, but who, despite Republican sympathies, were no longer active. They also included people who had never been in the IRA, including Ivan Barr, chairman of the NICRA executive, and Michael Farrell. What they did not include was a single Loyalist. Although the UVF had begun the killing and bombing, this organisation was left untouched, as were other violent Loyalist satellite organisations such as Tara, the Shankill Defenders Association and the Ulster Protestant Volunteers. It is known that Faulkner was urged by the British to include a few Protestants in the trawl but he refused.

The lists were so out of date that 104 people had to be released within forty-eight hours. A contributory factor in the number of releases was that mentioned earlier by Paddy Devlin, concerning other army swoops. The army quite often simply picked up the wrong people, a son for a father, the wrong 'man with a beard living at no. 47' and so on. But by the time they were released, a number had suffered quite brutal treatment, as had those still detained – apart from the 'five techniques' meted out to a select group, of which more anon. Internees were beaten with batons, kicked and forced to run the gauntlet between lines of club-wielding soldiers. Some, like Michael Farrell, were forced to stand in a tea chest and sing 'God Save the Queen' in circumstances which added a new definition to the term 'conductor's baton'. Others were subjected to the 'five techniques' mentioned above, and reserved for those who were considered to need special treatment.

The five techniques consisted of hooding, sleep deprivation, white noise, a starvation diet, and standing for hours spreadeagled against a wall, '. . . leaning on their fingertips like the hypotenuse of a right-angled triangle. The only sound that

126

filled the room was a high-pitched throb, which the detainees liken to an air compressor. The noise literally drove them out of their minds.'[15] These techniques were accompanied by continual harassment, blows, insults, questioning. This treatment usually went on for six or seven days. It produced acute anxiety states, personality changes, depression and, sometimes, an early death. I spoke to a psychiatrist who had the thankless task of trying to rehabilitate some of the interrogation victims (at the behest of the British Government), and he told me that they were 'broken men', most of whom did not survive into their fifties.

One such was Patrick Shivers, a thirty-seven-year-old plasterer from Toomebridge, Co. Antrim. He was later awarded £15,000 damages by Belfast's High Court.[16] His experiences included being hooded, handcuffed and deprived of sleep for long periods so as to produce disorientation. In evidence Shivers said that, during the week of his torture, 'I heard men crying out for death and I still hear those men crying today.'[17] The court found that Shivers had been subjected to 'unbearable' noises, stripped naked, and photographed. Shivers was one of those whose name should not have appeared on the RUC lists. After undergoing his ordeal, it was accepted that he was innocent and he was released, uncharged, in October 1971.

Kevin Hannaway is a Republican who also received damages for what was done to him. The reason he gave me for being able to withstand the treatment he received is instructive for an understanding of an essential component in Republicanism, the will to resist. He told me:

> After they arrested me, I was thrown into a lorry where I got a kicking. Then I was taken to another barracks where I got another kicking. They took me up in a helicopter and told me they were going to throw me out. I thought we were hundreds of feet up, but were only up a few feet. They set Alsatians on me. My thigh was all torn, and they made me run in bare feet over broken glass.[18]

Hannaway was then subjected to the 'five techniques'. Afterwards, he told me, lowering his voice because his wife was in the room, 'My privates were the size of a football from the kicking.' When I asked him how he managed to survive he replied: 'I kept thinking of *The Last Words*, and I thought of what those men went through and I said to myself, sure what am I getting – nothing. So I stuck it out.' *The Last Words* is a compendium of the last words and speeches of the executed 1916 leaders, which would no doubt be treated as simplistic propaganda by a majority of the academics who have contributed to the flood of profundity which the northern tragedy has elicited.[19] Nevertheless, the resolution engendered by such material, in a largely working-class movement, is why Hannaway was still alive at the time of writing, and the Provisionals benefited rather than were crushed by internment.

Later in the day of the internment swoop Faulkner issued an oft-quoted statement in which he said, amongst other things, that: '. . . the security forces and the government feel that internment is working out remarkably well. It has exposed the gunmen.' He justified his action by saying: 'I have taken this serious step solely for the protection of life and security of property. We are, quite simply, at war with the terrorists and in a state of war many sacrifices have to be made, and made in a co-operative spirit.'

Within a few hours of his making the statement it became obvious that internment was not working out well and that there was a complete absence of a 'co-operative spirit' throughout the Six Counties. Suffice it to say that in the eight months prior to internment, thirty-four people had been killed. In the four months following it 140 died, twenty-two of them in the three days after internment was introduced. They included a Catholic priest, Fr Hugh Mullan, shot dead as he administered the last rites, and the first member of the UDR to be killed, Winston Donnell, shot at a roadblock. Some of the worst Protestant–Catholic rioting of the century broke out in the wake of internment. Catholic incursions in the Ardoyne area forced Protestants to flee, burning some 200 homes as they left rather than have them fall into Catholic hands. Elsewhere Catholic homes were burned also, so that in all 7,000 people, the bulk of them Catholic, were rendered homeless. Again the people sought the safety of their co-religionists. A fresh wave of some 2,500 Catholic refugees poured south and new refugee camps were set up. The Protestants retreated to Loyalist districts like Ballysillan, Dundonald and Glencairn. In a renewed bombing campaign the IRA blew up a series of targets across the Six Counties which included the Unionist Party headquarters in Belfast. Another casualty of the chaos was impartiality in reporting. Carrington fired the first shots in what was to be an ongoing campaign to control not only the BBC but the media generally. The BBC's reporting, he said on 19 August, was '. . . below the standards of fairness and accuracy which we are entitled to expect'.

The BBC coverage had been reflecting the fact that contrary to what Faulkner claimed, and the British hoped, internment had increased rather than diminished the violence. One of the most wounding reports had been of a press conference, given by Joe Cahill, who had succeeded Billy McKee as OC of Belfast after the latter's arrest some months earlier. In the midst of the chaos engendered by the supposed crushing of the IRA, Cahill told the world's media that only some thirty IRA men had been picked up and that the Provisionals' capacity to wage war had not been affected by the swoop. The sound of gunfire all over the city as he spoke underlined his point. Stormont, the Last-Chance Saloon, was emptying rapidly, direct rule was obviously no longer a matter of 'if', but 'when'. For, as the Saloon emptied, the ranks of the Provisionals were filling up. The stories about the brutality which accompanied the internment process saw to that. These were augmented as the reports of the 'deep interrogation' method began to filter out a few days later. Recruits came forward in huge numbers to join both the Provisionals and the Officials, not only in Belfast and Derry, but in many rural areas where hitherto there had been little or no IRA support. McMillen and Sullivan had to abandon their attempts to restrict the Officials to a purely defensive role. The Provisional IRA had received an accession of strength which, though it sometimes ebbed, would never die out again throughout the next twenty-four years, despite an ever-lengthening list of atrocities.

By 31 August the level of public outrage was such that the British were forced to set up a committee of inquiry, under Sir Edward Compton, into the treatment of detainees. Compton accepted that the 'five techniques' had been used.[20] However, the inquiry decided that these amounted only to 'ill-treatment' not 'brutality'. Internees were so mistrustful of the British and of Compton that only one detainee consented to give evidence. In a foreword to the ensuing report Maudling wrote:

> . . . it is clear from the report that there were very few complaints, and those there were had, in the Committee's view, very little substance. The record of events reflects great credit on the security forces . . . the Committee have found no evidence of physical brutality, still less of torture or brain-washing . . .

The name Compton became a synonym for 'whitewash' in the minds of many Irish people – so many, in fact, that the Irish Government were forced to refer what became known as 'the torture case' to the European Court of Human Rights. The case dragged on for several years, becoming a source of considerable tension between Dublin and London. The European Commission on Human Rights found, on 2 September 1976, that the interrogation techniques did constitute a breach of the Convention of Human Rights: '. . . in the form, not alone of inhuman and degrading treatment, but also of torture'. However, on 18 January 1978, the European Court of Human Rights, ruling on this finding, rejected the Commission's use of the word 'torture'. But the court did accept that the suspects had suffered 'inhuman and degrading treatment'.

Throughout the period of military escalation, the Provisionals, with the aid of sympathetic advisers, had also been drawing up a political programme. This was unveiled to the public in the wake of internment, on 5 September 1971. The central proposal in the document was aimed at calming the Northern Protestants' fears of being subsumed into the all-Ireland Republic which remained the Provisionals' prime objective. It envisaged four regional parliaments based on the four provinces of Ireland. The northern one, Dail Uladh (Ulster Dail), was designed to meet the requirement that:

> . . . the Protestant and Unionist fears of being swamped in an all-Ireland Republic must be considered. Their fears could be adequately satisfied if they formed a large part, possibly a majority, in an Ulster regional parliament.[21]

However, the Protestants had their own ideas as to how their interests might be safeguarded. Paisley and Craig, who throughout this period were conducting discussions on the possibility of founding a new party, held a rally at Victoria Park, Belfast, the day after the Provisionals unveiled their proposal. Here, in the presence of a crowd which the newspapers estimated to be 20,000 strong, they called for something Paisley would return to again in his career: a 'third force' to defend their 'Ulster'. This force did not emerge at Victoria Park. But by the end of the month another highly significant grouping had surfaced from within the ranks of loyalism – the Ulster Defence Association (UDA). The UDA had its origins in the Protestant equivalent of the conditions which led to the formation of the Catholic Citizens' Defence Committee. Barricades were going up and Protestants were fleeing, or being driven, from their homes in Catholic districts in the wake of internment.

Volunteer vigilante groups were mushrooming amidst a general sense that since the abolition of the B-Specials a vital defensive wall had come down. It was time to look to their own defences. Many of the existing Loyalist paramilitary groups formed links with the new grouping, which at peak may have had a membership of 50,000. Its activities ranged from public marching, in a uniform which combined dark glasses with masks, bush hats, combat jackets or balaclavas, to welfare, to extortion, thuggery, murder, and, as we shall see, helping to bring down a government.

As the UDA emerged in the turbulent later part of 1971, Paisley and Desmond Boal also formed a new Protestant grouping, the Democratic Unionist Party (DUP). The DUP informed the media, at a press conference on 30 October, that it would be 'On the right on constitutional issues and on the left on social issues.' It certainly lived up to the first part of that declaration. The DUP was based on evangelicalism and social radicalism. A combination of Paisley's Bible-thumping, fulminations against 'dry closets' and the 'enemies of Ulster', his charisma, and the DUP's close links with the Free Presbyterian Church, gave the party a distinctive appeal both in working-class Protestant Belfast and amongst rural Protestants. It was, to paraphrase Padraig Pearse, not Unionist merely, but Paisley as well. Not Paisley merely, but Unionist as well.

The general post-internment discordancy prompted one notable effect at rapport. Heath descended somewhat from the Olympian height of disdain concerning Dublin's role in the crisis, which manifested itself at the time of the Falls Road curfew, to invite Lynch to a two-day 'summit' involving himself and Faulkner at Chequers on 27 and 28 September. Both sides were concerned with the deteriorating security situation. But there were divergent views as to who was responsible for it. Lynch was preoccupied by the effects of internment in inflaming 'Arms Trial'-type sentiment within both his party and the Republic generally. Along with internment, other British tactics, such as cratering cross-border roads, were generating considerable tension for Dublin in the already sensitive border areas. For their part, Heath and Faulkner wanted a crackdown on the Officials' and Provisionals' headquarters in Dublin, and other public manifestations of militant Republican strength. There was a sense on the British side that Lynch should curb RTE and the newspapers in the same way as Heath was beginning to do with the British media. Moreover, there were those in the Unionist camp who were disposed to argue that internment would work only if the Republic would introduce it also. Understandably, the meeting of itself achieved little, but it was at least a tacit indication on London's part that Dublin did have some role to play, even if visualised as being merely that of Britain's policeman.

As direct rule began to loom over the horizon, the Provos sought to hasten its approach with a series of detestable actions to which the Loyalist paramilitaries responded in kind. The mind tends to swim when one looks back at the footprints left on Irish history by the Uncouth Beast that slouched off to Belfast in internment's aftermath.

Two days after Lynch and Heath met, the Provisionals let off a bomb in a Shankill Road bar. Two people were killed, many maimed for life. Trigger-happy soldiers shot two women in a car on the Falls Road a few days later. Next day, other soldiers in Newry dealt with three teenage would-be muggers by shooting them dead. Hatred of the army in Catholic ghettos reached such a pitch that girls who 'fraternised' with soldiers had their heads shorn and were tied to railings or lampposts, covered in ink, and adorned with placards proclaiming their crime. Faulkner despairingly appointed a Catholic to his cabinet, G. B. Newe, a distinguished ecumenicalist. Newe was the first Catholic ever to hold a ministerial position since the state was founded. A sane, rational Nationalist, whose reaction to the appointment I sought, replied that: 'It was like a Jew taking a job in Hitler's cabinet.' Even had the party wanted to, it would have been impossible for the SDLP to call off the rent and rates strike.

In the madness and hatred of the hour, the UVF replied to the IRA's Shankill bombing with the worst slaughter of the period. A no-warning bomb in a Catholic bar, McGurk's of North Queen Street, Belfast, claimed sixteen lives on 4 December. The plastic bags and the shovels were needed again a week later when another bomb went off in a Protestant-owned shop on the Shankill. Amongst the four dead was a seven-month-old boy. When the Official IRA murdered a Unionist senator, Jack Barnhill, in his home in Strabane the following day, he became the twenty-third person to die in eight days. Rather than contemplate the human misery triggered by any one of those deeds, it is easier to take refuge in statistics and say that at the end of 1970 there had been twenty-five deaths; by the end of 1971 there were 174. In 1970 there were 213 bombs planted; in 1971 the number had reached 1,756.

Harold Wilson was one of those who could see clearly where the situation was heading. He had not acted on the logic of his thought whilst in power, partly because of the opposition he encountered to what Denis Healey termed his 'crazy desire' for 'active intervention early on'.[22] That 'active intervention' could very easily have kept the genie of the IRA in the bottle by seeing to it that civil rights were introduced and followed through. However, towards the end of November Wilson made a prophetic speech in the House of Commons which is usually referred to as his 'fifteen points' speech, central to which was his statement that the long-term settlement lay in '. . . finding a means of achieving the aspirations envisaged half a century ago, of progressing towards a United Ireland'.[23] This of course confirmed the Unionists in their view that they had been right to demonstrate their mistrust of Labour by staging a workers' strike when Callaghan had revisited the province at the beginning of the month.

But there were other things in Wilson's speech. Looking down the arches of the years he recalled to the House a Will Dyson cartoon in the *Daily Herald* of 1919. It showed the statesmen of Versailles and a child labelled 'Class of 1940'. The caption had one of the statesmen saying: 'Curious, I seem to hear a child weeping.' Wilson went on:

We are Versailles fifty years later – that is Belfast and Derry today, and we have to pause in our own conflicts and ponder what it means. That child crying today wears the insignia of the class of 1980, the class of 1990, the class of all the years that are to come.[24]

Then, unveiling his fifteen-point plan, on the grounds that internment had so changed the situation that a radical new response was called for he proposed that the settlement envisaged at the time of the treaty – i.e. a united Ireland – be brought forward, saying: 'If men of moderation have nothing to hope for, men of violence will have something to shoot for.' Ironically the men of violence standing around the corner, preparing to shoot in the New Year, were British soldiers. Bloody Sunday was about to dawn.

FIVE

'THEY SHOT WELL, DIDN'T THEY!'

No man has a right to fix the boundary of the march of a nation; no man has a right to say to his country – thus far shalt thou go and no further.

Charles Stewart Parnell, speaking at Cork, 21 January 1885

CASSANDRA, THE FIGURE who had the gift of prophecy, without being believed, was a character whom I increasingly came to identify with as the struggle developed. On 1 January 1972 I wrote an editorial in the *Irish Press* which said:

In the North the Catholics have said: we have had enough . . . the IRA are the hard cutting edge of their grievances and, horrible though many of the deeds which have been done in the North are, the IRA continue to draw support . . . indeed attempting a settlement without the IRA would be like America ending the Vietnam War without reference to the Vietcong.

Two days later the IRA gave evidence of their capacity for horror by letting off a bomb in Callender Street, Belfast, which injured over sixty people, mostly women and children. A few days later, on 17 January, they showed how, despite such deeds, their hold on the Catholic population of Belfast was in no way diminished. Seven internees managed to escape from the *Maidstone* prison ship in Belfast Lough by studying the movements of a seal which had managed to breach the barbed wire entanglements in which the ship was festooned. Once into the Markets area, the seven were simply swallowed up and became known thereafter, as the subject of ballads and song, as the 'Maidstone Seven'.

This type of support and sympathy manifested itself in another gesture of solidarity which set the scene for an event that was to generate far more sympathy for the IRA than the *Maidstone*. On 22 January 1972, a march took place to Magilligan Prison Camp in Derry in protest against internment. It was a peaceful march supported by the sort of people who had come out in favour of civil rights, and by relatives of those interned. Amongst the large contingent of journalists who covered the march was Nigel Wade of the *Daily Telegraph*. Wade,[1] now a senior editorial executive with the paper, was at the time a junior reporter. He was operating in a culture of journalism, particularly strong at the *Telegraph*, in which the pervading belief was: 'Our boys would not do anything like that' – i.e. anything brutal or untoward, as in the case of internment.

The *Telegraph* at the time was particularly supportive of the Unionist position. Wade illustrated the feeling by telling an anecdote about the late T. E. Uttley, a blind man of considerable intelligence who, as the paper's principal expert on Northern Ireland, had great influence over what went into the *Telegraph* concerning the Six Counties. One day Uttley came into the newsroom and placed a letter on the noticeboard. It was from Brian Faulkner, thanking the staff for their assistance in a recent election. Imbued with this culture and background, Wade went along to cover the Magilligan march.

He was horrified at what he saw. The march proceeded without incident until it drew near the camp. Then, from behind sand dunes emerged a squad from the First Paratroop Regiment armed with batons and rubber bullet guns. They began shooting these at the marchers, driving many of them into the sea, the temperature of which, in January, off the northern coast of Ireland, can well be imagined. Some of the paras used their batons with a ferocity that appalled Wade. Eventually it also appalled their NCOs, who tried unavailingly to call off the Dogs of War. The paratroopers' initial reaction was to ignore their superiors and continue their onslaught. They were only brought back to a sense of discipline when the NCOs began wielding their batons fiercely on their own men.

The atmosphere at the time was of course extremely tense. The Magilligan march, for example, was technically illegal because of a general prohibition on marching in operation at the time. And a few days after it, there was an open gun battle between the army and the IRA, who fired from the Republican side of the border at the town of Forkhill in Co. Armagh on the army, who responded with some 1,000 rounds of ammunition. Nevertheless in view of what had happened at Magilligan, the use of the paratroopers in Derry a week later, on Sunday 30 January, copper-fastened the inevitability of tragedy.

Again, the occasion, a rally to protest against internment, could have been technically classed as 'illegal'. It was discussed at a meeting of the Joint Security Committee held prior to the march. Tuzo thought that a low-key strategy to avoid confrontation was the advisable course. However, according to Martin Dillon,[2] Tuzo received a frosty response and was told by Faulkner that it was the duty of the army to take a hard line with troublemakers. Faulkner forecast that the march would lead to violence. It was one of the few prophecies he made at this time with which one could concur wholeheartedly.

Initially the protest passed off in a peaceful fashion, but, as it concluded, the inevitable 'Derry Fusiliers' began throwing stones. The army replied with water cannon and rubber bullets and the crowd were forced back. Suddenly Wade observed 'PIGS', armed personnel carriers, approaching. Doors were flung open and, Alsatian-like, as they had unleashed themselves a week earlier on the Magilligan marchers, the paratroopers hurled themselves forward. The difference was that this time they carried SLR rifles capable of piercing a tree at a range of a hundred metres and still having enough velocity to kill a man. These men began firing on the crowd and killed a total of fourteen people (thirteen died on the spot, one later). Seventeen others were wounded to a greater or lesser degree.

Nigel Wade was understandably in a state of shock after the shootings. He had been struck by a jet from the water cannon and had stood his ground, in wet clothes, to see what would happen next. After he found out and the shooting subsided, he made his way back to the City Hotel, where one of the first people he encountered was one Brigadier Thompson, then the military correspondent of the *Daily Telegraph*, who incidentally had missed the shooting through going off to park his car. However, when Wade met him, Thompson was in ebullient form, sporting a wall-to-wall grin. His greeting to his junior colleague was: 'They shot well, didn't they?'

This was by no means an uncommon reaction. I have a Loyalist friend who remembers sitting in his family home at teatime when the news came that 'thirteen Catholics were shot dead in Derry.' His father, a quiet, God-fearing man, broke the shocked silence: 'There should have been a nought after that.'

I well remember watching General Ford on BBC television that night as he defended what had happened. Looking and sounding every inch the epitome of an officer and a gentleman, he said:

> Paratroopers did not go in there shooting. In fact they did not fire until they were fired upon and my information at the moment . . . is that the 3rd Battalion fired three rounds altogether, after they'd had something between ten and twenty fired at them.

Ford in fact claimed that 'the dead may not have been killed by our soldiers'. The force of this assertion was somewhat lessened by a report a day later from Brian Cashinella of *The Times* in which he reported hearing Ford call out: 'Go on, the paras. Go and get them.' Cashinella said that the paratroopers appeared

> to relish their work, and their eagerness manifested itself, to me, mainly in their shouting, cursing, and ribald language. Most of them seemed to regard the Bogsiders and people who took part in the parade as legitimate targets.[3]

But a day later was a long time in the propaganda war. On the night of Bloody Sunday the army issued an official statement, approved by Tuzo. It was carried on all the news media and said that the paras

> came under nail-bomb attack and a fusillade of fifty to eighty rounds from the area of Rossville Flats and Glenfada Flats.
> Fire was returned at seen gunmen and nail-bombers. Subsequently, as troops deployed to get at the gunmen, the latter continued to fire. In all a total of well over 200 rounds was fired indiscriminately in the general direction of the soldiers. Fire continued to be returned only at identified targets.

This statement has to be viewed in the light not only of the Magilligan episode but of a revelation made by Field Marshal Lord Carver many years later. In the course of his interview for *The Last Colony* TV film mentioned earlier, Carver read the following passage from his memoirs:

> It was being suggested that it was perfectly legal for the army to shoot somebody whether or not they thought they were being shot at because anybody who obstructed or got in the way of the armed forces of the Queen was, by that very act, the Queen's enemy, and this was being put forward by a legal luminary in the Cabinet. I said to the Prime Minister that I could

135

not under any circumstances order or allow a British soldier to be ordered to do such a thing because it would not be lawful. He did say his legal adviser suggested it was all right but I said, 'You are not bound by what they say. What I am bound by is my own judgement of whether or not the act of the soldier concerned would be legal because in the end it is the courts that decide.'

The point about that quotation is that Carver dates the Heath incident from the midsummer of 1972. Around that time also he referred to the GEN 42 Committee a request from Brigadier Frank Kitson to conduct undercover operations. Whether Carver was attempting to establish accountability for such activities, or acting out of disinterested high-mindedness, the fact remains that six months after Bloody Sunday, an atmosphere still prevailed in the higher echelons of British decision-taking which makes what happened on Bloody Sunday entirely explicable.

Explicable, but not excusable, as one of the best reports of Bloody Sunday makes clear. It came from Simon Winchester of the *Guardian* the next day and corroborates Wade's account. He described how, as the march ended, a meeting began at Free Derry Corner. Suddenly:

four or five armoured cars appeared at William St, and raced into the Rossville Street square, and several thousand people began to run away . . . Paratroopers piled out of their vehicles, many ran forward to make arrests, but others rushed to the street corners. It was these men, perhaps 20 in all, who opened the fire with their rifles. I saw three men fall to the ground. One was still obviously alive with blood pumping from his leg. The others, both apparently in their teens, seemed dead.

The meeting at Free Derry Corner broke up in hysteria as thousands of people either ran or dived for the ground.

Army snipers could be seen firing continuously towards the central Bogside streets and at one stage a lone army sniper fired two shots at me as I peered around a corner. One shot chipped a large chunk of masonry from a wall behind me.

Then people could be seen moving forward in Fahan St, their hands above their heads. One man was carrying a white handkerchief. Gunfire was directed even at them and they fled or fell to the ground.

In Dublin reaction to this sort of report, which was borne out by the dispatches of Irish journalists, was so intense that, after two days of siege, crowds finally succeeded in burning down the British Embassy. The Gardai scarcely made a token effort to resist. Had they attempted to intervene, the violence of Derry could easily have erupted on the streets of Dublin, with incalculable consequences. The destruction of the embassy proved to be a sort of national safety valve which drew off a good deal of the poisonous after-effect of the Derry shootings.

John Hume was buffeted from his normal political course to the extent that in the wake of the shootings, he said that: 'Many people down there [the Bogside] feel now that it is a united Ireland or nothing.' Bernadette Devlin took her protest further in the House of Commons. She replied to the Home Secretary, Maudling, who had attempted to defend the paratroopers on the grounds that they only fired after somebody fired on them, by saying: 'The Minister has stood up and lied to the House. Nobody shot at the Paratroopers but somebody will shortly . . . I have a right as the only representative in this House who is an eyewitness to ask a question of that murdering hypocrite.'[4]

However, she decided that the right did not provide sufficient outlet for her feelings, and ran across the floor of the House to slap Maudling in the face and pull his hair. She justified her action subsequently by saying: 'I did not shoot him in the back, which is what they did to our people.'

In New York, Patrick Hillery, the Irish Foreign Minister, expressed Nationalist outrage in a more temperate fashion: 'From now on my aim is to get Britain out of Ireland.'[5] Of course Hillery's gesture was purely for the optics. The Irish Cabinet did not wish to appear to be standing idly by. Dublin was well aware, before Hillery set off for the UN, that Britain's position as a permanent member of the Security Council meant that, under the UN Charter, she had a veto on the discussion of any matter which she termed a 'Vital National Interest'. There was never the slightest possibility of any UN action on the Irish situation.

The effect of Bloody Sunday, however, was not to get Britain out of Ireland but to enmire her ever more firmly in the muddy byways of Fermanagh and Tyrone, as Churchill referred to them during the Home Rule crisis. Violence continued at such a pace that it became clear to Heath that the Last-Chance Saloon had to be closed down rapidly. He moved to limit the damage by setting up an inquiry under Lord Chief Justice Widgery.

However, right-wing Unionists, ever eager to ignore the writing on the wall, pressed ahead as though Bloody Sunday had not occurred. Just over a week after the killings William Craig founded the Ulster Vanguard movement. The object of the movement was to unite the rightist elements of Unionism in a programme of general discontent at the lack of progress on two fronts: the security front and what was seen as the erosion of the constitutional position. Apart from Loyalist paramilitary elements, it attracted the support of rising young Unionists like David Trimble. The rallies organised by Vanguard, with Craig driving around in an open touring car attended by outriders, gave many people uncomfortable memories of Nuremberg. But the Six Counties being the Six Counties, the movement initially at least attracted a very strong following. One rally held on 18 March is estimated to have been attended by a crowd of approximately 60,000. Appropriately enough, 9 February, the day of Vanguard's foundation, was also the day on which the Parker Committee chose to make its ambivalent report on the nature of the 'five techniques'.

However, though disturbing, Craig's response was generally peaceful. The same could not be said for the Republican paramilitaries. By way of retribution, the Official IRA had planned a bomb attack on the 16th Parachute Regiment's headquarters at Aldershot. Bungling or cowardice resulted in the bomb not being placed near a military target but outside a kitchen, where it blew up killing five women, a gardener and a Catholic chaplain. The Officials issued a statement claiming the attack and saying it was in response to Bloody Sunday. The Aldershot attack marked a downward spiral in the Officials' campaign, in terms of both brutality and effectiveness. On 25 February, the junior Minister of State, John

Taylor, was shot in the head by the Officials but later recovered. (The Belfast gallows-humour joke was that he survived because he was not hit in a vital organ.)

The Officials' campaign reached its nadir in early summer of 1972. On 25 May a local Derry boy, nineteen-year-old William Best, who was in the British Army, came home on leave. He was known to have taken part in stone-throwing incidents earlier in his life when out with the Derry Fusiliers attacking the troops. Nevertheless, after an order issued on Bloody Sunday that every British soldier was to be regarded as a legitimate target, he was 'arrested' and then 'tried' and shot. The man responsible for his death told Eamonn McCann: 'Our military orders after Bloody Sunday were to kill every British soldier we could. They didn't say anything about local soldiers.'[6]

But the people of Derry, particularly the women, had a great deal to say about locals. The day after Best's shooting, some 400 mothers marched on the Officials' Derry headquarters and told those present in no uncertain terms what they thought of them. The incident forced the Officials to call a halt, and a ceasefire was declared by one wing of the Republican movement. However, the Officials' ceasefire, brought about as much by a desire on the part of the leadership to get back to the policy of uniting Protestant and Catholic worker on a class basis, as by the Derry incident, was an isolated oasis of peace in a very, very arid desert of disaster.

On 4 March, the Provisionals equalled the Officials in horror with a bomb explosion in the Abercorn Restaurant in Belfast which injured 130 people, including two sisters who lost their legs while on a shopping spree for a wedding dress. The Provisionals also caused an appalling catalogue of destruction and death on 20 March when six people were killed and more than 100 injured in a no-warning car bomb in Donegal Street in Belfast. It was alleged at the time that a hoax call led people towards, not away from, the blast.

Yet Bloody Sunday continued to be the benchmark act of violence for the province. Immediately after it, delegations from Northern Ireland had begun descending on London to question the entire basis of the state. One of these, led by Oliver Napier of the Alliance Party, put it to Heath that he should move in such a way as to remove Stormont and put the blame, if possible, on the Unionist establishment, in other words make demands which would cause Faulkner to resign rather than be fired.[7] The suggested issue was security. Napier recommended that London take over security. This of course ran entirely counter to British policy. The inevitable end to what had been begun in 1920 and 1921, a reliance on the partition solution to keep Ireland off the agenda. However, proof, if proof were needed, that this solution no longer held good came promptly and unwelcomely to Heath's attention. The matter was precipitated by a court case involving John Hume, Ivan Cooper and a group of other men who had been fined for taking part in an anti-army demonstration the previous August. They appealed against their £20 fine and the Northern Ireland High Court upheld their action and ruled that under Section 38 (1) of the Civil Authorities (Special Powers) Act, Northern Ireland, Section 4 of the 1920 Government of Ireland Act had been contravened. This prohibited the Parliament of Northern Ireland from legislating on matters affecting the army, navy and other armed forces of the Crown.

It emerged during the trial that Regulation 38 had been added to the Special Powers Act by Stormont in 1970 in order to give the soldiers right of control over the citizenry. The net result of the decision was to render all acts of the British Army illegal during their operations – on the orders of Faulkner's Joint Security Council – in searching people, entering their homes and arresting them during internment. To say nothing, of course, of a whole range of other ancillary activities of a more or less brutal nature indulged in at the same time. The consternation which this decision aroused may be gathered from a contribution from the long-time Labour spokesman on Northern Affairs, Kevin McNamara, to the Oral History seminar run by the Institute of Contemporary British History:

> . . . the first time it has ever happened in my experience in the House, we had a manuscript, handwritten, one-line whip on a Monday [23 February 1972], so very few of us were there, the handwritten bill legalising the action of the British Government [the House of Lords had also upheld Hume's appeal]. It went through in one day, the speaker would only accept one amendment to it, which was one done by Jeremy Thorpe, that they would actually only remain in operation for six months so that we could in fact have a division on it.

The panic of the British Government was understandable. In a nutshell, the army had been acting illegally during its operations in Northern Ireland, but the effect of the new legislation was to entrust security to Brian Faulkner, as the *Sunday Times* pointed out on 27 February 1972: 'Large extra powers were conferred on Stormont which may now pass any law it pleases to increase the powers and indemnity of the army.'

Heath, although preoccupied with other issues such as the miners and EEC entry, had been increasingly taking a hands-on approach to the Northern Ireland problem. In January he had had another meeting with Jack Lynch, and Faulkner was also repeatedly summoned to meetings. Early in February it appeared that he was tending towards a solution which involved more Catholic representation in Stormont. There were reports to this effect in both the *Sunday Times* and the *Sunday Press* on 13 February. However, as the potential for violence increased, particularly the threat from Vanguard and other Loyalist groupings, Heath veered over to a more radical approach.

On 4 February, Faulkner was flown to London from Aldergrove Airport by the Royal Air Force and taken to Downing Street to meet a top-level cabinet grouping which included: Maudling, the Home Secretary; Carrington, Secretary of Defence; Sir Alec Douglas-Home, the Foreign Secretary; and the man who was to prove himself the most important player, William Whitelaw, Lord President of the Council.

Faulkner was informed at this meeting that unless the Six Counties were brought under control quickly London would assume direct rule, suspending Stormont.[8] It was almost as this meeting was being held that the Vanguard leaders met to launch their movement. At this juncture, at least, the attempt to replay the Orange Card was to backfire. Disorder continued, and finally, on 21 March, after a further spate of inconclusive meetings, Heath again brought Faulkner to London. At this meeting Faulkner was informed that internment was to be phased out, with

Whitehall not Stormont examining the cases of each internee. The entire law-and-order apparatus of Northern Ireland – the police, prosecution, the courts, judges and prisons – was to be transferred to Whitehall. Faulkner, as Napier had suggested, had been made an offer he could not accept. He consulted with his colleagues in Belfast and returned to London on 23 March to say that if Heath continued with his plan, he and his cabinet would resign.

Heath was not intimidated. The following day he arose in the House of Commons to deliver what was in fact an adverse judgement on the history of British rule in Northern Ireland since the Anglo-Irish Treaty had been concluded in 1921:

> We were concerned about the present provision of responsibility for law and order between Belfast and Westminster whereby control remains largely with the Northern Ireland government while operational responsibility rests mainly with the British army, and therefore, with the United Kingdom government. This responsibility is not merely domestic; it is a matter of international concern as well ... The United Kingdom government remained of the view that the transfer of this responsibility to Westminster was an indispensable condition for progress in finding a political solution to Northern Ireland.
>
> The Northern Ireland government's position therefore leaves them [the UK government] with no alternative to assuming full and direct responsibility for the administration of Northern Ireland until a political solution to the problems of the province can be worked out in consultation with all those concerned. Parliament will therefore be invited to pass before Easter a measure transferring all legislative and executive powers now vested in the Northern Ireland parliament and government to the United Kingdom parliament and a United Kingdom minister.[9]

Heath's announcement was received with predictable dismay by the Unionist community. A huge rally was held outside Stormont with Craig at the head of the Vanguard movement. But even though there were an estimated 100,000 people present, Faulkner easily outmanoeuvred Craig. Instead of a series of fiery speeches being delivered by the Vanguard leaders, Faulkner managed to ensure that only one Vanguard leader, Craig himself, appeared with him on the platform on the balcony of Stormont, by the simple expedient of announcing that the parliament buildings were closed to all except elected MPs. Craig was the only one who qualified for the balcony under this limitation.

Craig flinched from declaring UDI and the most memorable line of the day (28 March) was left to Faulkner, who, commenting on a proposal that an advisory commission should be set up to govern Northern Ireland, said: 'Northern Ireland is not a coconut colony and nobody and no coconut commission will be able to muster any credibility or standing.' It was in its way an obituary for Unionist philosophy. Decoded it said: 'We are superior to our neighbours in the Republic, and of course to the Catholics in our midst. We are British, but you British are incapable of understanding us. Very well, you may not be able to live with us, but you will find you cannot live without us.'

Vanguard and other Loyalist organisations led by Billy Hull, a veteran Orange trade unionist, did manage to stage a successful forty-eight-hour strike which shut off public transport and power supplies and closed most major industries. But the underlying private sentiment of most Unionists guaranteed that the public expression of the disquiet was kept within bounds. In a word, the Loyalists were brought face to face with the contradiction of Loyalism: how to proclaim oneself loyal to the Crown and maintain that posture without coming into conflict with decisions by the Crown or its agents with which the Ulster Loyalist profoundly disagreed. The private dilemma was well put, at the level of reproach, by Sir Ken Bloomfield at the Oral History conference.

> . . . at the human level it was really rather disagreeable and upsetting. One felt like someone whose family house, in which the family had lived for umpteen generations, was being taken over and I was actually the caretaker because my boss was ill. I was both the estate agent and the last remaining member of the family and people went around saying here's the room in which the secretary of the cabinet and his predecessor have sat since 1921 and the Minister of State is going to be in there and there's a cupboard for you upstairs . . . it was not the most agreeable time in one's life . . .
>
> People had conflicting emotions. A lot of them were very disturbed by the situation, nevertheless, there wasn't a trace of UDI feeling, there wasn't the slightest doubt that all of us at the end of the day were going to answer to the Lord or the Queen in parliament and that was that and we would plug into the new machinery and we would do our best under it. Institutionally and constitutionally, we did know that it was our duty to do so and I think we did it.

Bloomfield did know what he had to do to survive and prosper under the 'new machinery'. Gifted with a friendly personality, he succeeded so well that apart from his knighthood, a governorship of the BBC followed. The machinery consisted of William Whitelaw, who was appointed the first Secretary of State for Northern Ireland and, assisted by a group of junior ministers, carried out the functions previously exercised by Stormont. That is the system by which the Six Counties are governed as this is being written.

Whitelaw's first ministers were Lord Windlesham and Paul Channon, ministers of state, and David Howell, under-secretary. Legislative effect was given to these appointments by the Northern Ireland Temporary Provisions Bill which was introduced to the House of Commons on 27 March, receiving its second reading the following day and being passed into law by the House of Commons after an all-night sitting on 30 March.

The word used in the Bill was not suspension but prorogation and Whitelaw from the outset made it clear that he regarded the suspension of Stormont as an opportunity for a new beginning from which peace and reconciliation might flow. This was not how the action was regarded in Northern Ireland. The Catholics by and large took the suspension of Stormont as a triumph. I found in talking to SDLP leaders and members of the Provisional IRA at the time that both sections, constitutional and unconstitutional Nationalists, sought to claim the abolition of Stormont as their victory. The Protestants of course regarded it as their corresponding defeat and initially the Protestant reaction was the one with which London had most visibly to contend.

To recap: at this stage Craig and his Vanguard movement were in a shadowy form of loose association with the Loyalist Association of Workers (LAW), led by

Billy Hull. Hull and the Revd Martin Smyth, head of the Orange order, had backed Craig in the formation of Vanguard on 9 February 1972. In less obvious association with them, there stood in the wings the UDA, which set up no-go areas paralleling the Catholic ones in Belfast and Derry and indulged in undercover activities that led to the deaths of several Catholics. Professor Buckland has pointed out that some seventy Catholics were murdered between 1 April 1972 and 31 January 1973. Buckland states that these assassinations included '. . . some very grisly and ritual ones involving the use of pitchforks and blow lamps'.[10]

The 'pitchfork killings', which shocked Co. Fermanagh in 1972, were not in fact committed by Loyalist paramilitaries, but by members of the 1st Argyll and Sutherland Highlanders. A dagger was used, not a pitchfork as was at first assumed. The matter came to light when a former member of the platoon involved called into a police station on 'the UK mainland', because he thought that the injuries inflicted by the 'Yorkshire Ripper' murderer, who was still on the loose at the time, bore remarkable similarities to those inflicted by his former colleagues. Two members of the platoon were sentenced to life imprisonment in 1981, another received four years for manslaughter, and a captain of the regiment received a one-year suspended sentence for withholding information.

The two victims were a Catholic farmer, Michael Naan, and his workman, Andrew Murray. Apparently they were suspected of being members of the IRA, which they were not. Another murder in Fermanagh that year claimed the life of Louis Leonard. His mutilated body was found in his own fridge. He had been shot and stabbed several times. Leonard had been a Provisional volunteer.

As early as February 1972 the UDA paper had said of Loyalist groups, which were not taking sufficiently strong actions against Catholics: 'Why have they not started to hit back in the only way these Nationalist bastards understand? That is, ruthless, indiscriminate killing . . . if I had a flamethrower I would roast the slimy excreta that pass for human beings.'[11] Rhetoric was not limited to the paramilitaries. For example, on 5 March Craig told a Radio Eireann interviewer who asked him whether a Loyalist backlash would target all the Catholics in Ulster:

> It might not go so far as that but it could go so far as killing. It would be similar to the situation in the 1920s where Roman Catholics identified in Republican rebellion could find themselves unwelcome in their places of work and under pressure to leave their homes.

As I have indicated earlier, 'under pressure' had been a euphemism for widespread assassination and pogrom during the early 1920s. Speaking at a huge rally in Ormeau Park in Belfast on 18 March, which was reported in all the media, Craig advised his followers:

> We must build up dossiers on those men and women in this country who are a menace to this country. Because one of these days, if and when the politicians fail us, it may be our job to liquidate the enemy.

Not surprisingly, the fall of Stormont in the week of these utterances served to heighten Catholic fears of assassination. After the Ormeau speech, for example, in the Ardoyne area, the Catholics laid in stocks of tinned food, powdered milk, fuel and other necessities in preparation for an expected siege. First-aid kits and primus stoves became sought-after essentials. Catholic carriers throughout the province offered the use of their vehicles to help Catholics move out in the event of the expected Doomsday situation. However, sporadic assassinations continued . . . or did not, despite Craig's continued eagerness to fight to the last drop of Protestant militants' blood. He made what to me still ranks as one of the most extraordinary statements of the entire period, at the right-wing Conservative Monday Club in London on 27 April. In the course of a rambling and often incoherent, but nevertheless widely reported speech, Craig said that he was prepared 'to shoot to kill' to keep Ulster British, and went on: 'When we say force, we mean force. We will only assassinate our enemies as a last desperate resort when we are denied our democratic rights.'

The following day he addressed a joint Vanguard/National Front rally. By coincidence, the chairman of the UDA, Charles Harding Smith, and four other men, one of them a member of the RUC, were arrested in London and charged with attempting to illegally purchase arms. The trial was one of the first clear indications of collusion between elements within the RUC and the UDA. An RUC Special Branch list of suspects was found in Smith's house, and Smith himself attempted to influence the jury by producing a character reference from the RUC Chief Constable. Whatever the truth about the jury, it influenced the views of a number of Catholics in Northern Ireland about the impartiality of the RUC.

But while it would be true to say that Craig and others' bloodcurdling utterances failed largely because the bulk of the Unionist population had no real stomach for UDI, or for large-scale acts of treason to the Crown, to which they professed loyalty, there was also an element of intimidation which proved the determining factor in dictating a softly-softly approach by the army.

It seems inescapable from the evidence that in the wake of Stormont's demise, the army decided that it could not afford to open a second front against Protestant paramilitaries and risk turning to be shot in the back by the IRA as they faced a new foe. On 20 May the army attempted to bulldoze the UDA barricades in East Belfast but withdrew when a riot ensued. Loyalist no-go areas were allowed to stay unscathed. Seven days after the aborted effort to bulldoze the barriers, the UDA were allowed to march unimpeded, hooded and uniformed, through the centre of Belfast. The wearing of such uniforms had been banned under the Public Order Act.

The Loyalist friend whose father's reaction after Bloody Sunday I have already described joined the UDA following that memorable evening meal. He was already a member of the UDR. Not only did he continue his membership of this organisation while in the UDA, he was also recruited by the RUC Special Branch to act as an agent for them. Every action he took, within either the UDR or the UDA, was known to the Special Branch. In the course of his duties he met and worked with legendary figures like the undercover SAS officer Robert Nairac, whom the IRA abducted, tortured and eventually killed.

My friend's activities, which included preparing to murder a Republic of Ireland cabinet minister, were all on record. The close undercover relationships between the Loyalist paramilitaries and the army incline one to look a little sceptically at claims that these simply either did not exist or were the activities of rogue elements. For example, one young officer writing in the Monday Club magazine, *Monday World*, said that the army's policy towards the UDA was simply based on fear of opening up a second front:

> In order to combat this threat, the army chose, quite deliberately, to give the UDA tacit support. The UDA virtually ran East and North Belfast . . . almost too late, in the winter of 1972, the army realised it had assisted in the birth of a monster. It sought to act, but was only able to cage the beast; the secret of its destruction had been lost with its birth.[12]

There was more to the army's relationship with the UDA than merely the avoidance of a second front. The UDA throughout the entire period would provide a useful source both of intelligence and of surrogates willing to perform actions for which the army did not wish to see any smoking guns left lying around. Towards the end of June, Whitelaw personally met with UDA leaders attired in their uniforms, masks and so on, and urged them to postpone the creation of separate no-go areas. On 3 July, General Ford, CLF, of Bloody Sunday fame, openly negotiated with the UDA. He met the organisation's leader, Tommy Herron, in an army Saracen at Ainsworth Avenue, Belfast, after an army/UDA confrontation. The two agreed to joint patrols. Efforts by Catholics to set up patrols in their own areas to guard against assassination were prohibited.

Needless to say, these actions were regarded by Catholics as evidences of gross collusion with Loyalist paramilitaries, but it was in fact part of Whitelaw's wider policy of the time. This involved one of the more interesting undercover incidents of the period: flying the Provisional IRA leadership to London under safe conduct to negotiate with the Secretary of State for Northern Ireland. Before describing this dramatic incident, however, it is necessary to go back a little in time.

After Bloody Sunday, Nationalist Ireland was in such a state of outrage that even normal diplomatic relationships between Dublin and London were impossible. The Dublin Government recalled the Irish Ambassador to London. Lynch was forced to declare a day of national mourning on the day the Bloody Sunday victims were buried. During this week a pall of both anger and apprehension as to what might occur next hung over both Belfast and Dublin. What happened on the constitutional side of Nationalist opinion was another huge march through Newry, on 6 February. Although it was banned from the centre of the town, and NICRA tried to dissuade southerners from taking part (I was one of the many who cheerfully disregarded their warnings!), some 50,000 people attended.

The march passed off peacefully enough but it was a clear indication that a widescale revolt was under way on the part of the Nationalists as a whole. The Provisionals grimly underlined this by stepping up their campaign. Using often unstable gelignite which blew their own operatives up almost as regularly as it did the selected victims, they attacked 'economic' targets, as well as security forces. By the time Stormont fell, the Provisionals had killed fifty-six soldiers, and wide

Above: The marchers sang 'we shall overcome'. The reality however was symbolised by the 'stop' sign as the RUC halted the first Civil Rights march held in Northern Ireland, at Dungannon, in August 1968.

Right: Eamonn McCann addresses a Derry civil rights meeting.

Below: On hunger-strike in protest against internment, outside No. 10 Downing Street., in October 1971 from left: John Hume, Austin Currie, Paddy O'Hanlon and Bernadette Devlin.

Above: Ian Paisley at an Ulster Resistance demonstration at the Ulster Hall, Belfast in 1986.

Left: Paisley speaking in opposition to the Anglo-Irish agreement of 1985 at a Belfast rally. Beside him is James Molyneaux the Ulster Unionist Party leader.

Right: Michael Farrell, pictured during August, 1973, with his wife, Orla, after winning his release from internment by remaining on hunger strike for thirty-five days.

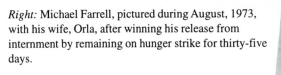

Below: The traditional bin lid protest of Belfast Nationalist women, used in this case to warn of the arrival of troops in their area.

Below: Soldiers of the Scots Guards Regiment forcibly detaining a Nationalist.

Left: The Irish Taoiseach, Liam Cosgrave, left, with the British Prime Minister, Ted Heath, shake hands on the Sunningdale agreement on 9 December, 1973.

Below: Members of the security forces, both Army and RUC, stand by as masked members of the Ulster Defence Association, some carrying cudgels, block roads as part of a protest which smashed the Sunningdale Agreement, to which the British Government was a party, in May 1974.

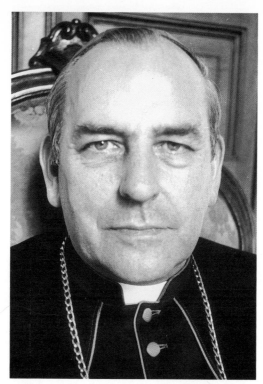

Cardinal Tomas O'Fiaich (d.1990).

Cardinal Cathal Daly, who succeeded
Cardinal O'Fiaich.

Right: Brian Nelson, the British Army's top agent in the UDA.

Below: Some of the classified material, released to the UDA by members of the RUC, which formed the basis of the Stevens Inquiry.

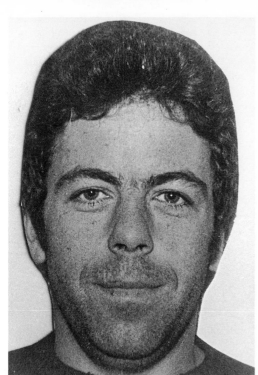

Left: Lenny Murphy, the leader of the 'Shankill Butchers' gang.

Below: A meat cleaver and other implements uncovered by the RUC, during their investigation into the 'Shankill Butchers' murders.

Foot: Robert Knight, one of those charged with the massacre at the Rising Sun bar at Greysteel, Co. Derry, in October 1993, shouts defiance as he is led away from a court hearing.

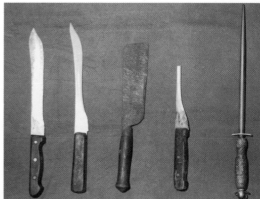

Left: Republican supporters of the hunger strikers, pictured in a social club in Andersonstown, raise their fingers in what can be interpreted either as a victory sign or solidarity with the IRA's Second Belfast Battalion.

Below: Bobby Sands MP, the Provisional prisoner's leader in the H-blocks, and the first of ten hunger strikers to die in 1981.

Left: A picture smuggled out of Armagh Jail during the women prisoners' 'dirty protest' of 1980, showing one of the Republican prisoners Ellen McGuigan in a cell smeared with faeces and menstrual fluid.

areas of the North, including Belfast town centre, were presenting scenes reminiscent of World War II blitzes.

Loyalist paramilitary displays after the proroguing of Stormont did little to make Catholics willing to come together to disown such happenings. Nor did the publication shortly afterwards of two reports into the North's major turning-point events – the Scarman Tribunal into the causes of the 1969 burnings and shootings, and the Widgery Tribunal's report on Bloody Sunday itself. Scarman, for example, found that the RUC had been at fault on a number of occasions but rejected allegations of collusion with Loyalists; and of Paisley's role, the report said:

> Dr Paisley's spoken words were always powerful and must have frequently appeared to some as provocative. His newspaper [the *Protestant Telegraph*] was such that its style and substance were likely to arouse the enthusiasm of his supporters and the fury of his opponents.

Nevertheless, Scarman reported:

> We are satisfied that Dr Paisley's role in the events under review was fundamentally similar to that of the political leadership on the other side of the sectarian divide. While his speeches and writings must have been one of the many factors in increasing tension in 1969, he neither plotted or organised the disorders under review and there is no evidence that he was a party to any of the acts of violence investigated by us.[13]

I will make no comment on the foregoing save to say that there was a most clear-cut dichotomy between the role of Paisley and those of 'the political leadership on the other side of the sectarian divide', such as John Hume and Gerry Fitt, as I think the facts marshalled hitherto will amply demonstrate.

The Widgery Report, published on 18 April, aroused not debate but fury. It concluded that:

> There would have been no deaths in Londonderry on 30th January if those who organised the illegal march had not thereby created a highly dangerous situation in which a clash between demonstrators and the security forces was almost inevitable . . . each soldier was his own judge of whether he had identified a gunman. Their training made them aggressive and quick to decision and some showed more restraint in opening fire than others. At one end of the scale some soldiers showed a high degree of responsibility: at the other . . . firing bordered on the reckless . . . none of the deceased or wounded is proved to have been shot while handling a firearm or a bomb.[14]

As what had happened in Derry had been merely a legal rerun of what the RUC had done in October 1968 to trigger off the entire conflict – i.e. trapping the demonstrators in a confined area and then attacking them – no further comment is necessary. The army continued to maintain its official line that those shot had either been handling weapons or explosives (a member of the Official IRA may have opened up on the army with a handgun after the shooting began, without hitting anyone or being shot in return). The officer in charge of the paras, Lieutenant-Colonel Derek Wilford, was later awarded an OBE for his activities in Derry that day.

Nevertheless, despite these unpromising developments, the suppression of Stormont did offer new opportunities. Dublin, for example, quietly restored diplomatic relationships with London and the SDLP began casting around for methods of getting back into talks. The party issued a statement calling on everyone who had withdrawn from public bodies and entered into a campaign of civil disobedience to abandon this 'as a demonstration of their determination to bring about community reconciliation'.[15] A dramatic opportunity for 'reconciliation' was to hand.

If Whitelaw was to make any impression in his new post, it was essential that he try to reach some agreement with the Provisionals. Following the fall of Stormont, three leading Provisionals, Sean MacStiofain, Daithi O'Conaill and Seamus Twomey, had held a press conference in Derry at which they had offered to extend 'safe conduct' to Whitelaw to enter Free Derry to discuss peace terms with them. Although this offer was rejected, Whitelaw began a series of negotiations in which John Hume and Paddy Devlin played important roles which led to his conceding safe conduct to the Provisionals to come to London to see him.

At the time there was a hunger strike for political status in progress in Crumlin Road jail amongst the Provisional prisoners. Billy McKee was said to be near death's door and there were widespread fears in Belfast as to what would follow in the way of rioting should he die. Hume, who had a relationship with O'Conaill, from their shared Credit Union past, shuttled between the Provos and the British, trying to find a *modus vivendi*. The Foreign Office mandarins operated from Laneside, an imposing residence in Co. Down's 'Gold Coast', various locations in Derry and a pub in Co. Donegal, while the elements of a deal were hammered together.

The Provos wanted two concessions before meeting Whitelaw for negotiations: firstly, an acceptance of the prisoners' political status demands; and secondly, the release of Gerry Adams – who even then, at the age of twenty-five, had become a leading figure in the Provisionals – to take part in the negotiations. Adams knew nothing about these negotiations and he told me himself that he was astounded when the Long Kesh authorities told him he was about to be released. Fearing a trap, he consulted his uncle, Liam Hannaway, who tersely told him to 'get out'. The need to know was ever an important IRA principle. It was not Adams' release but the concession of Special Category status that was to have the most important consequences for both the future conduct of Anglo–Irish relationships and Adams' own emergence as a national, and subsequently an international figure.

Once he was assured that the IRA's preconditions had been met, Hume, as arranged, conferred by telephone with Proinsias MacAirt in Crumlin Road jail. MacAirt gave his imprimatur to the arrangements. Then, watched by Whitelaw and his two principal officials, Frank Steele and Howard Smith, Hume dialled O'Conaill as arranged at a safe house in Derry. When O'Conaill heard that the deal was in place, he responded without equivocation: 'You have got a ceasefire at midnight on 26 June.' Whitelaw 'literally jumped for joy, embracing Hume in a bear hug'.[16]

Whitelaw might not have jumped quite so high had he been able to foresee the future, but he later came to view the concession of Special Category status as a mistake.

However, at the time all was euphoria. For the first time since Michael Collins had negotiated across the table with Lloyd George in Downing Street, the British Government were meeting the IRA. There were, though, a number of important differences between 1921 and 7 July 1972. While Whitelaw was certainly interested in arriving at some form of settlement and had earlier speedily justified his reputation for being a 'quick study', there were very substantial gaps, at that stage unbridgeable gaps, between the Provisional and Conservative stances.

On the one hand, ever since the fall of Stormont, rumours had been circulating in the British press, largely well founded on forthright after-dinner, off-the-record comments by prominent Tories, that the only solution, long-term, for the Irish issue was unity. In practice these same politicians had no intention of attempting anything so drastic. Whitelaw, at that stage, was a newcomer who knew very little about Ireland bar what he had picked up on two golfing trips before becoming Secretary of State. He had a hazy idea of introducing British standards to Northern Ireland and had been horrified at the nature of the evidence on which some of those interned had been incarcerated. He castigated officials that certain people had been interned 'for speaking out against the Government'. 'My God,' he burst out, 'I have been speaking out against the Government for the past six years.' However, what the Provisionals had in mind was rather more than Tory fair play.

The IRA delegation consisted of Sean MacStiofain, Seamus Twomey, Daithi O'Conaill, Ivor Bell, Gerry Adams and Martin McGuinness. Their observer, Myles Shevlin, a Dublin solicitor who kept the minutes of the meeting, travelled separately to London but the IRA delegation were flown in an RAF turbo-prop Andover to Benson in Oxfordshire. From there they were whisked in Special Branch-driven limousines to no. 96 Cheyne Walk. This Chelsea home of the Guinness millionaire Paul Channon is near Thomas Carlyle's birthplace. Carlyle once observed that history is a letter of instruction which has come down to us from the past. The instructions concerning Ireland in England's history did not appear to be of much value to the men who gathered in the library at Cheyne Walk. A vast cultural divide lay between Whitelaw and his aides, Channon, Woodfield and Stephen, and the IRA men.

This was symbolised by two small incidents which occurred on the way to Cheyne Walk. McGuinness was brought from Derry to the Andover in a helicopter which circled near the Glenshane Pass for a time before rendezvousing at the appointed hour. During the circling, RAF personnel thought that McGuinness appeared slightly nervous and attributed this to his being in a helicopter for the first time. McGuinness was not in the least put out by the helicopter. What concerned him was the fact that his colleagues on the ground, not knowing who was in the helicopter, might take advantage of the superb target it presented.

After the delegation had landed at Oxfordshire, Twomey had stopped at Henley to answer a call of nature. He then disappeared, to the consternation of the Special Branch men. When he turned up, it was discovered that he had been impressed by the architecture and taken a brief detour to do a little sightseeing.

The two sides' accounts[17] of the meeting differ as to their tone but not their substance. Whitelaw was later to write loftily that:

> The meeting was a non-event. The IRA's leaders simply made impossible demands which I told them the British government would never concede. They were in fact still in a mood of defiance and determination to carry on until their absurd ultimatums were met.[18]

However, the IRA side told me that Whitelaw appeared to be 'nervous and sweating'. Shevlin said that he wanted to 'adopt an in and out approach. But we weren't having any of it. We had come to let him know how we felt and that is what we did.'

Whitelaw began by saying that he was impressed by the way the IRA had observed the undertakings they had given about the ceasefire, which by that stage had been in place for some ten days. He went on: 'I hope that the trust set between us is reinforced by this meeting. I record that the history of our two countries gives the Irish grounds for suspicion. I hope that in me you will see a British minister you can trust. Look on me as a man who will not make a promise that he will not keep.'

He invited the IRA men to make any point that they wished. He had come there to listen to them. MacStiofain in reply welcomed the opportunity of meeting with a representative of the British Government:

> We hope that the discussions now intended may lead to the settlement of this dispute between our two peoples. The Republican movement views this meeting as an opportunity of participation in devising machinery whereby the will of the whole of the people of Ireland may be ascertained.

MacStiofain then read out the IRA proposals. These included.

1. Britain to make a public declaration that it was for the whole people of Ireland acting and voting as a unit to decide the future of Ireland.
2. The British Government to give an immediate declaration of its intent to withdraw from Irish soil, the withdrawal to be completed before 1 January 1975.
3. British troops to be withdrawn immediately from sensitive areas.
4. A general amnesty for all political prisoners in Irish prisons, all internees and detainees and all persons on the wanted list.
5. A suspension of offensive operations by the British Army and an immediate end to internment.

Not surprisingly, Whitelaw did not find himself 'agreeing entirely' with the IRA's demands. He understood the feelings of the Republicans concerning internment but pointed out that with the marching season upon him any 'moves on my part might bring about a worse situation'. He said: 'Give me the time and the opportunities and I will surprise you, gentlemen, with the rapidity with which I will act.' At this stage an aide produced drinks, which the IRA men took as an indication of perfidious Albion at work and refused. By-play continued between the two sides for some time, with the IRA making the point that the best contribution that Britain could make to long-term peace in Ireland would be a recognition of the right of the Irish people as a unit to decide the future of Ireland. The IRA were prepared to accept that the timing and mechanics of such a declaration were open to negotiation but emphasised that the principle was inviolable. Whitelaw replied by saying that this ran counter to the Government of Ireland Act and not unreasonably said that the matter would have to be 'very carefully discussed' with his cabinet colleagues, in view of the fact that both the Tory and Labour parties had given repeated assurances to the authority that no such declaration would be made.

And the IRA took the view that the Government of Ireland Act was what was rendering the whole political situation sterile and told Whitelaw that this was 'the very root of the trouble'. Whitelaw countered by saying:

> Neither of us is a plenipotentiary. I am an Englishman operating in an Irish situation. The minority in the North have been deprived of their rights. I set myself the task of conquering this. You can give me some help in the matter.

This in fact was the nub of the exchange. Whitelaw was prepared to concede reform within the system and to work sincerely for it, but the Government of Ireland Act was the keystone of the arch. The IRA wanted the arch demolished. They still do at the time of writing. The exchange was notable for a number of vignettes. One involved Daithi O'Conaill telling Whitelaw that there had been too much discussion about a 'Protestant backlash' which had intimidated previous British governments. 'These are our people,' O'Conaill told Whitelaw, 'and we do not desire nor would we welcome a clash with them. But the fact must be faced that they cannot be allowed to intimidate and hold out on the whole people of Ireland.'

Another emotional nerve was touched when the young Martin McGuinness made an impassioned denunciation of the behaviour of the paratroopers who had shot down people he had been to school with, earlier that year on Bloody Sunday. But the member of the delegation who had most cause to remember the exchanges was Gerry Adams. His role at the talks had been that of a watcher: that is, he had instructions not to take part in the direct negotiations but to observe the meaning of what was said as much as listen to words. As the talks broke up he enquired of Whitelaw what the position would be if the ceasefire broke down. Would the IRA be at liberty to make any disclosure to the press that they saw fit? Whitelaw replied, 'That is fair enough. If the truce ends, all bets are off.' The next time Adams was to hear those words he was lying naked in his cell in Castlereagh Interrogation Centre, outside Belfast, being kicked unconscious by an RUC Special Branch man who punctuated his kicks with the antiphon: 'All bets are off now, Gerry.'

In the event the only substantive, if such a word may be used, agreement to emerge from the discussions was a four-point document which stipulated that:

1. A bilateral suspension of offensive operations would continue until 14 July.
2. In the event of a resumption of hostilities, twenty-four hours' notice would be given.
3. On 14 July, a further meeting would take place at which the British

Government's submissions and documents in reply to points 1 and 2 of MacStiofain's submission would be made known.

4. In the event of the documents being unacceptable to the Irish, they would be at liberty to resume offensive operations without notice.

The meeting having thus ended inconclusively, one could take the view that all prospect of agreement had fallen into the social gulf which separated the Scottish land-owner and his aides from the IRA delegation, which included one butcher's assistant (McGuinness), one bookmaker (Twomey), one former barman (Adams), a mechanic (Bell), a teacher (O'Conaill), an Irish-language enthusiast (McStiofain) and a solicitor (Shevlin).

Nevertheless, apart from the fact that the IRA men had at no time shown themselves to be overawed by this gulf, the significance of the Cheyne Walk deliberations was to lie both in their continuing impact on the political prisoner issue and in the illustration they provide of the durability of the IRA movement. The then young Adams and McGuinness would still be conducting serious top-level discussions with the British on behalf of Sinn Fein more than twenty years later, long after Whitelaw and his aides had departed the decision-taking echelons of British politics. And the IRA's goals by that stage would appear considerably less remote than they had in the elegant confines of Paul Channon's library.

The conference took place on a Friday and by the following weekend, the ceasefire was over. The reasons were both complex and simple. It was, as Whitelaw had said, the marching season, and the province was more than ordinarily tense. In fact, so many Catholics were forced out of their homes that the southern authorities recorded 7,000 refugees coming south to seek assistance in this period. Protestants, although to a lesser degree, were also forced out of their homes, some of them from the Lenadoon area on the outskirts of Catholic Andersonstown.

Even while the Cheyne Walk negotiations were in progress, the IRA had been negotiating at a lower level with British Army officers on having some homeless Catholics housed in the former Protestant homes which were now standing idle. The obstacle was that the UDA – some of whose barricade-building and creation of no-go areas had been caused by suspicion and fear arising from the declaration of the IRA ceasefire – had vetoed this proposal, stating that any Catholics who were housed, legally or illegally, would be burned out.

Controversy reached a climax over the Lenadoon issue on Sunday 9 July. Over the weekend O'Conaill had made several efforts to reach Whitelaw by phone to warn him that Lenadoon could bring about the end of the truce. Then, as hostile Protestant and Catholic crowds drew up facing each other, separated only by the British Army, word reached Lenadoon that the army had, against the wishes of the Catholic population of Portadown, insisted on forcing through yet another Orange march over the disputed 'tunnel' route through a bitterly resentful Catholic area. This angered the already wrathful Catholic crowd which moved towards the army lines. Behind these lines a UDA man was seen to level a pistol. Twomey interceded with the officer in charge to disarm the man. While this altercation was taking place, an army Saracen suddenly rammed a truck piled high with the Catholics' furniture. The incident was widely screened all over Ireland and abroad. Meanwhile, O'Conaill was having little joy with Whitelaw, who told him his information was that the IRA were attacking the army. Vainly, O'Conaill tried to argue that the reverse was the case. In the event, the truce broke down amidst recrimination, charge and countercharge.

Who was to blame? Probably the answer is that, at that stage, everyone was and no one was. The simple truth was that the situation had simply not matured to a point where a solution on anything like the IRA terms was even remotely possible. Nor was there any prospect of the IRA accepting that Whitelaw's 'reform within the system' policy came anywhere near their post-internment, post-Bloody Sunday aspirations. The violence which ensued after the ending of the ceasefire was the worst of the Troubles so far. The death toll for the month was ninety-five, including twenty-one members of the security forces. The bulk of those killed, however, were Catholics, victims of sectarian assassination. Any remorse which the Protestant community might have felt at this butchery was dissipated on Bloody Friday, 21 July, when the IRA detonated twenty-two bombs in Belfast within the space of seventy-five minutes. There was no prospect of the security forces being able to deal with the often confusing warning phone calls, which in some cases it was argued were deliberately misleading. In the event, some nine deaths and 130 severe injuries were recorded.

The worst of these incidents occurred at a bus station. The subsequent TV pictures of human remains being shovelled into plastic bags seared into the consciousness of viewers. The shock and horror of Bloody Friday provided the British with the opportunity to crack down finally on the IRA no-go areas in Belfast and Derry. Operation Motorman, as it was known, was the biggest British military operation since Suez. Twelve thousand troops, supported by tanks and bulldozers, smashed their way into the no-go areas but as with internment failed to capture any IRA personnel. The IRA responded viciously with a set of car bombs in the Co. Derry village of Claudy which killed eight people. In addition, two other civilians were shot dead by the British Army in the course of Motorman. Nineteen seventy-two was the worst year of the Troubles. There were 467 deaths, a total of 10,628 shootings, and almost 1,900 bombs were planted.

The British Army were far from being passive participants in all this mayhem. The English sociologist Dr Frank Burton spent a 'period of participant observation' in a working-class Catholic community of Belfast, which he christened 'Anro', between September 1972 and April 1973. This is how he described the impact of the British Army on the civilian population:

> British justice is recognised within Anro not only by the stamp of repressive law, but by brutal enforcement. Soldiers not alone apprehend and detain suspects, they beat them. They interrogate with illegal methods ranging from ill-treatment to torture. They wreak vengeance for their dead comrades. The 'enforcement' can be terrifying, as when the Paratroop Regiment entered Anro.
>
> Reports came in hourly about the latest beating, intimidation or act of destruction. A discotheque was interrupted by a foot-patrol who attacked the teenage dancers, putting one

boy back into the hospital from which he had just been released. He had the stitches from a routine operation on his stomach reopened by the troops.

A baker's hand was broken by the soldiers as he went about his delivery round. A store of furniture, belonging to homeless, intimidated families, was wrecked during a search. Local mill workers were kicked in the genitals as they were searched, twice daily, as they went to and from their workplace. I was hit in the ribs with a rifle as two paratroopers asked me if I was in the IRA.

I said I was not and they replied, 'Well, fucking join so that we can shoot you.' The friend I was living with was beaten up in the back of a Saracen tank by a paratroop sergeant. After being interrogated and cleared he was taken back to Anro by the same soldier, who apologised, 'I am sorry about that, lad, on the way down, we do it to everyone. People soon start talking after we soften them up.' In addition to these and hosts of other examples, four people were shot dead by the regiment in heatedly disputed circumstances.[19]

The 'heatedly disputed' deaths did not merely occur in 'Anro', but all over the province. In their pamphlet 'Death and a Lie' Fathers Denis Faul and Raymond Murray describe the shooting of a twelve-year-old Armagh girl, Majella O'Hare, which aroused countrywide controversy:

On the 14th of August, 1976, just seven minutes before noon, soldiers of the Third Parachute Regiment shot dead a twelve-year-old County Armagh girl while on her way to Confession at the local chapel, St Malachy's, Ballymoyer, near Whitecross. When her father, who was working nearby, ran up and took the girl in his arms he was cursed by the soldiers in the foulest of bad language. A lying statement was issued saying that the girl was killed in crossfire between the IRA and the British Army.

In this brief paragraph are summed up the stories, not alone of Majella O'Hare, but of Leo Norney, of John Pat Cunningham, of Patrick McElhone and of fifty other innocent people who have died by the guns of the British Army in the last four years.[20]

At the time that was written (in 1976) no soldier, or member of the RUC, had served even a day in jail for either killing or ill-treating people in Northern Ireland. When public opinion did succeed in forcing a few prosecutions these were generally unsatisfactory. The device of charging serving soldiers with murder, rather than manslaughter, meant that premeditation was almost invariably argued successfully to have been absent, resulting in acquittal. Even if a charge were sustained, very light prison terms ensued. Private Ian Thain, the first British soldier to be convicted of murder while on duty in the Six Counties, was released to rejoin his regiment on 23 February 1988, after serving only twenty-six months of a life sentence.

The year was not devoid of constitutional and legal initiatives, one of which at least was to have a lasting effect on the area, though hardly a beneficial one. The British realised that, with the coming of direct rule, either a settlement with the IRA or a long war was the choice. The Whitelaw talks were proof, if proof were needed, that settlement was out of the question, and attention turned to counterinsurgency methods. What might be thought of as the first pressing of the button of the conveyor belt system that later swelled the prison populations of Northern Ireland occurred on 20 December 1972 when a report of a committee headed by Lord Diplock into the legal procedures required to deal with terrorist offences was published. The report decided that:

The main obstacle to dealing effectively with terrorist crime in the regular courts of justice is intimidation by terrorist organisations of those persons who would be able to give evidence for the prosecution if they dared.[21]

It recommended therefore that: 'Trials of scheduled offences should be by a judge of the High Court or a County Court judge sitting alone with NO JURY with the usual rights of appeal.' This non-jury proposal was adopted the following year in the 1973 Emergency Powers Act. At the time the report received relatively little attention. There was a ferocious sectarian assassination campaign, and an IRA campaign, in operation on the ground at the time, and it appeared that the political steps being taken by Whitelaw and the British Government commanded the headlines. The political initiatives may be said to have surfaced after the summer holidays of 1972 when the SDLP published a policy document, 'Towards a new Ireland'.

This floated the idea of joint British and Irish sovereignty over Northern Ireland, a thought which is very much in the air at the time of writing, and proposed a new form of treaty between Britain and the Republic, combined with a declaration of intent by the British Government that it intended to work for Irish unity. A few days later, on 25 September, a conference which behind the scenes Whitelaw had been painstakingly manoeuvring for opened in Darlington. For different reasons, both the SDLP and Paisley's DUP boycotted the three-day proceedings: the SDLP because of the continuation of internment and the DUP because Paisley refused to have any truck with anything which bore the taint of a possible *apertura a sinistra* towards Dublin. The Ulster Unionist Party, the Alliance Party and the NILP did attend but even with this diminished representation of the northern parties, no agreement was forthcoming.

Whitelaw tried to advance the political process without agreement and on 30 October authorised the publication by the NIO of a discussion paper, 'The Future of Northern Ireland'. The paper made the appropriate noises about Britain's long-term fidelity to the Union for so long as a majority of the people of Northern Ireland required it. Earlier such pronouncements had referred to the parliament of Northern Ireland but the discussion paper made it clear that even though the parliament had disappeared, the guarantee, or as the Nationalists would see it, 'the veto', remained. However, the paper also contained some new thinking. It hinted broadly that there should be a more generous approach on the part of the Unionists towards the minority: 'There are strong arguments that the object of real participation should be achieved by giving minority interests a share in the exercise of executive power.' The paper also made a reference to 'an Irish dimension', meaning that the Northern Ireland situation could not be viewed in isolation from the south. This was the first time such an idea or phrase had ever emanated from a document originating in the Northern Ireland Office. The result was that the Freudian fears of the Unionist community that anything in the way of benignity towards the minority, or Dublin, would inevitably thrust them towards a united Ireland were kindled afresh. These fears, combined with a lack of political will on the part of the then British Government, and a very marked display of willpower, though of an unhelpful sort, on the part of the British Army, played a significant part in wrecking the remarkable political development to which the discussion paper eventually led.

Unionism, in the first half of the 1970s, had very considerable political and military muscle at its disposal. It would not be practicable to attempt to give a detailed account of the UDA activities during this period, but some illustration of the nature and extent of the organisation is essential for an understanding of what became known as 'the Power-Sharing Executive'. Similarly, the UDA's exemplar, the IRA, also underwent changes but never lost its strength during this time and it too played a role in frustrating any policies which did not factor the IRA into the equation. Therefore, before turning to examine what befell the single most important attempt to replace Stormont, let us take a brief look at the history of both the IRA and the UDA from the middle of 1972 to the run-up to the 'Executive' experiment in the latter part of 1973.

Taking the UDA first: the outline of a concerted Loyalist backlash against what were perceived as Catholic gains could be clearly discerned from the early summer of 1972. In May, four Catholics and a Protestant who had a Catholic girlfriend were murdered. In early June, five Catholics and a Protestant living with a Catholic woman were killed. And there were other sectarian incidents, such as the planting of a bomb outside a Catholic bar in Ballymurphy, following which Loyalist gunmen fired into the rabidly Republican area from the nearby Protestant Springmartin area. The British Army joined in the shooting and when the dead were counted, they were found to include four Catholics, including a fourteen-year-old girl, one Protestant and a British soldier.

The net UDA demand of the time was that the British Army smash the Catholic no-go areas. Failing this, the UDA threatened in May to set up temporary no-go areas in various Protestant districts over a period of approximately a month. These barricades were to be made permanent if the army did not take action against the Catholics. Meanwhile, behind the barricades there was widespread harassment, beatings and intimidation of Catholics aimed at creating some ethnic cleansing. As we have seen, these activities led to a few army–UDA confrontations but in general the authorities turned a blind eye to the UDA's behaviour, even to the extent of issuing UDA leaders with gun licences. Whitelaw continued to attempt to talk to both the IRA and the UDA but the IRA truce inflamed the Protestants into setting up permanent, concrete barricades, both in Protestant areas of Belfast and in Portadown.

Loyalists also murdered Catholics. The Catholics began hitting back on a sectarian basis. Two Protestants, the brothers Malcolm and Peter Orr, had Catholic girlfriends and were killed. Protestants too began to be shot, purely because of their religion. But the brunt of this sectarian warfare fell on the Catholics. A headline in the *Irish Press* of 17 July 1972 reads: 'Refugees still pouring south'.

The British Army were displaying partisanship because of second front fears, to such an extent that in the Springfield Road district, a Catholic area, the UDA were allowed to extend their control by way of patrols and barricades, after the army had first negotiated with the UDA in this area and then retreated. It was in this atmosphere that the Lenadoon crisis which destroyed the IRA truce occurred.

154

Army policy, and the ending of the truce, emboldened the Loyalists to declare open season on the Catholics in a fashion which seems to indicate a desire to demoralise the minority into flight by creating an atmosphere of terror. Sadistic torture began to accompany murder as a matter of routine, and it was in this period that the activities of 'the Shankill Road Butchers' gang began. This group committed well in excess of a dozen murders in which the victims were tortured to death, before being apprehended (see pp. 284).

During the fevered season of the 'Twelfth', four armed Loyalists raped a Catholic widow in the Oldpark area of Belfast several times before shooting her and her mentally retarded son. The widow survived, the boy did not. The following day, on the 12th itself, one of the last Catholics remaining in the UDR was kidnapped in east Belfast, tortured by being branded with a red-hot iron and stabbed before being eventually shot dead. Some days later a well-known Catholic girl singer and her boyfriend were stopped at a UDA barricade. The girl was forced to sing for the UDA men before she and her boyfriend were shot dead. The following August, another Catholic, Thomas Madden, was horrifically murdered, once again in the Oldpark area. His injuries included 150 stab wounds. Death was eventually caused by strangulation.

The Oldpark area was a mixed district, and obviously the deaths, none involving members of the IRA, were aimed at driving Catholics out. By August 1972, Loyalist paramilitaries were killing three Catholics for every Protestant, the same ratio which had occurred during the pogroms of the early 1920s. However, after Operation Motorman, and at the time of the publication of the Northern Ireland Office's Green Paper on what Whitelaw hoped would be the way forward, a tougher attitude on the part of the army began to manifest itself towards the Loyalists. The first manifestation of this was somewhat embarrassing to the authorities. When the paratroopers engaged Loyalists in the Shankill Road area on 7 September, a UDA gunman whom the army shot turned out to be a member of the UDR. By now the UDR had something of the order of 96 per cent Protestant membership, and it was a demonstrable fact that many UDA men were in the UDR. The 11th Battalion of the UDR was set up in the Craigavon area during this period (September 1972). And a few weeks later, the UVF were able to make off unhindered with its entire stock of weaponry.

However, the authorities continued with a crackdown of sorts on the Loyalists and when UDA elements laid siege to a tiny Catholic enclave in Co. Antrim on 16 September, the RUC opened fire. A prominent UVF man was shot dead. The most significant army–UDA clash occurred a month later, on 16 October, when army vehicles killed two rioting Loyalists. Tommy Herron openly declared war on the British Army. The result was two nights of heavy firing between the army and the UDA in which two civilians were killed.

Aghast, local community leaders persuaded Herron to call off his offensive. Even the most obtuse Loyalist politician could see that shooting British uniforms was no way to demonstrate one's loyalty to the Crown. However, the sectarian assassinations continued. The two Catholic farmers were stabbed to death in Fermanagh, by the army, in October (described on p. 142 above) and, in December, a twenty-three-year-old Catholic had his hands and feet practically burned off and his body badly burnt with a blow-lamp. A feature of the killings in the latter part of the year, which in the last four months ran at the rate of thirty-one Catholics to nine Protestants, was that they spread outside Belfast and appeared to have been reprisals for the IRA shootings or bombing of UDR men.

For example, on 20 December, following the shooting of a UDR man outside Derry, Protestant gunmen shot up a Catholic bar in Derry, killing five of the occupants, one of them a Protestant. The south was also attacked. There were bombings and shootings which claimed lives in Co. Cavan on 28 December and in Donegal on New Year's Eve. But it was not the attacks on the south which provoked the final army crackdown on the UDA. At the beginning of 1973, the UDA began shooting Catholic workers in foreign-owned factories such as Rolls Royce and the Hughes Tool Co. The business community began to become alarmed that this might chase industry away from the province. Following a spate of killings which claimed the lives of five Catholics in January, the unprecedented occurred. On 3 February 1973, two Loyalists were arrested and interned, the first Loyalist internees for fifty years. There was a ferocious Loyalist reaction: prolonged gunfights with the army, the assassination of at least seven Catholics and a one-day protest strike called by the combined forces of the UDA, LAW and Vanguard. The strike was accompanied by massive intimidation, combined with looting and the destruction of property which alienated a good deal of middle-class Protestant support.

Describing the UDA at this time, Michael Farrell writes:

> The UDA had become a huge ramshackle organisation heavily infiltrated with gangsters and petty criminals, and involved in protection rackets and extortion, backed by intimidation on a grand scale. Many mysterious beatings, shootings and bombings in Protestant areas were simply the UDA enforcing their levies. Most of the local leaders were taking a substantial cut of the proceeds.[22]

This was the picture which confronted Charles Harding Smith, the previous UDA leader, when he returned to Belfast in December having been acquitted of the arms charges. He apparently tried to clean up the racketeering and at the same time assert his own authority. A feud broke out and another prominent UDA leader, Ernie Elliott, was found shot dead on 7 December. A month later, in January, David Fogel, a henchman of Elliott's, emigrated to London, saying that Smith was attempting a takeover of the UDA with the backing of the UVF. Whatever the truth of this allegation, feuding continued within the UDA as a result of which a prominent leader, Tommy Herron, and his brother-in-law were also murdered in the following year. One of the most prominent Loyalist paramilitaries, John McKeague, a founder member of Tara, a notorious murder gang of the period, was one of those arrested, along with several other militants, and from this time onward the number of Loyalists interned inched upwards, reaching approximately sixty in mid-1974. A mould-breaking operation, but still only one-tenth of the 600 Republicans held by that time.

The fall of Stormont created a new situation for both the Dublin Government and the Provisional IRA. They were to interact with each other, abrasively, as a result. The Green Paper discussion document, issued by the NIO on 30 October 1972, as a result of Darlington contained two paragraphs which summed up the increased importance of Dublin's role in what happened north of the border. One looked to a future which would:

> Provide a firm basis for concerted governmental and community action against those terrorist organisations which represent a threat to freedom and democratic institutions in Ireland as a whole.

The second read:

> It is therefore clearly desirable that any new arrangements for Northern Ireland should, whilst meeting the wishes of Northern Ireland and Great Britain, be, so far as possible, acceptable to and accepted by the Republic of Ireland.

This was indeed 'acceptable' to the Republic. A far cry from the position at the time of internment's introduction when Lynch's call for an ending of the measure was rejected by Heath as an unwarranted interference in the internal affairs of the United Kingdom. The British policy of carrot and stick, a carrot for Dublin and the SDLP, and the stick for the IRA, began to divide the Provisionals from earlier sources of sympathy.

Had the Northern Ireland problem not existed, Britain and Ireland would have had increasingly little cause to be at odds with each other. Both countries were moving steadily towards EEC membership. The Provos' scorning of the abolition of Stormont with a declaration that the IRA would fight on was not well received in Dublin. Nor were aspects of its economic campaign, such as the bombing of the Courtauld's factory at Carrickfergus on 1 May, or the blowing-up of the Belfast Co-Op, the biggest department store in the city, on 10 May. Apart from the ever-rising death toll in Northern Ireland, and the gestation of ever-present fear that this would spread over to the Republic, such spectaculars had the effect of chasing away investment from the Republic as well as the Six Counties.

On 26 May 1972, the Republic announced the establishment of a special criminal court which, under Part 5 of the Offences Against the State Act, 1939, was to consist of three judges and sit without a jury. A certain symmetry between the northern and southern approaches to the IRA was beginning to make itself noticeable. The court began its sittings on 8 June, a few days after a People's Democracy protest march to the Curragh Camp had been met by Irish troops standing with fixed bayonets and loaded sub-machine-guns. Unlike the paras in Derry, however, the troops did not use their weapons. In fact the papers carried pictures of a young officer who stood stoically, unresisting, while paint and muck were hurled at him by demonstrators – further alienating southern support for all things northern. The camp had been opened following an IRA riot in Mountjoy Prison on the part of IRA prisoners. In the wake of the Curragh incident the number of IRA prisoners being picked up increased markedly. Amongst those who fell foul of the general climate of disfavour were Ruairi O'Bradaigh and Joe Cahill, though both were released shortly after, being detained for only two weeks.

Dublin was also in touch with the SDLP and after Operation Motorman, the SDLP were encouraged by Dublin to enter talks with Whitelaw. Accordingly, although internment still stood, the SDLP waived their pledge not to meet the British Government until it was ended and held a meeting with Whitelaw on 7 August. On 11 September, although the climate amongst Six County Nationalists did not allow the SDLP to attend fully fledged talks along the lines of Darlington, the party also saw Heath in London, after Jack Lynch and Heath had met earlier in the month, on 4 September at the Olympic Games in Munich.

Nationalist sentiment in Northern Ireland was breaking down along class lines at this stage: while the middle-class business and professional people were prepared to go along with the SDLP's cautious gradualism, the situation on the ground in Catholic working-class districts militated against such acceptance. Apart from the murderous onslaught of the UDA and its satellite organisations, there was the effect of the British military presence. Following Operation Motorman, for example, Catholic west Belfast became an occupied zone. Public buildings such as schools, recreational halls, even blocks of flats and football grounds including the Casement Park GAA ground, were all occupied by soldiers. This occupancy was gradually transferred to fixed army posts. The Andersonstown area, for example, eventually wound up with sixteen fortified posts, some of the stockades being more reminiscent of something out of *Beau Geste*, with huge iron stockades, than anything recently built in western Europe. And the behaviour of the troops in the saturated areas was heavy-handed in the extreme.

In Catholic areas they showed none of the ambivalence that extended towards the UDA. Writing in the *Guardian* of 13 July 1973, Martin Woollacott quoted an officer in the Parachute Regiment as follows:

> You know when we were in Ballymurphy, we had those people really fed up with us, terrified really. I understand what the refugees must feel like in Vietnam . . . after every shooting incident we would order 1,500 house searches, 1,500. That's hard work and it makes people think.

Another young paratrooper told Woollacott:

> Although you moan about Ireland, you know at least you are going to have a chance to shoot some bastard through the head . . . you are walking around with live rounds, you are there to kill people and see guys get killed, and you are going to get the shit scared out of you.

Not all soldiers had 'the shit' scared out of them. Armies being armies, some of them seemed to enjoy the experience. Another officer claimed that: 'Skiing or mountain climbing has got nothing on a cordon and search when you get old Snodgrass out of bed at four in the morning and go through his house like a dose of salts . . .' Every time the army tipped a 'Snodgrass' out of bed, they also helped to tip the balance back in favour of the Provisionals and away from the horror that the IRA had engendered with atrocities like 'Bloody Friday'. However, with a homogeneous population growing increasingly uneasy with the presence of refugees and the spread of mayhem and death in Northern Ireland, Jack Lynch and his Fianna Fail colleagues operated under no such constraints of divided loyalty in the Republic: 'Arms Trial' fervour was rapidly becoming a thing of the past.

Cooperation with London was the way of the future. Accordingly, in the wake of the setting-up of the special criminal court, Lynch began sanctioning other measures. In October the Provisional Sinn Fein headquarters in Kevin Street, Dublin, was closed down. A few weeks later Maire Drumm, the vice-president of Provisional Sinn Fein, was arrested and jailed because of an inflammatory speech she had made in the Republic. But the most significant arrest occurred on 19 November. Sean MacStiofain, the IRA chief of staff, was given six months in jail by the special criminal court, for IRA membership. Moreover, on the day prior to the start of his sentence, the Government dismissed the entire authority (governing body) of Radio Telefis Eireann because the station had allowed an interview to be broadcast between MacStiofain and one of the station's reporters, Kevin O'Kelly. O'Kelly was sentenced to three months for contempt of court when he refused to identify MacStiofain as his interviewee. However, his sentencing became a *cause célèbre* and he was released after a few days (see Chapter 11).

MacStiofain went on hunger strike and was removed to the Curragh Military Hospital. He eventually ended the strike on 16 January 1973. The O'Kelly incident marked a kind of watershed wherein the campaign against the media, along with security policy, came to operate in Dublin on the same basis as London. It was no accident that the dismissal of the RTE authority occurred on the same day that Lynch and Heath were meeting in London.

The Provisionals continued to feel the effect of the common London/Dublin approach after MacStiofain's arrest. An incident occurred which still generates controversy in Dublin. The Dail was debating an amendment to the Offences Against the State Act whereby the word of a chief superintendent became sufficient evidence to convict a suspect of IRA membership. However, even in the interests of improved Dublin/London relations, this measure proved so distasteful to wide sections of deputies that it began to appear certain that the Government would lose. Even on the government side of the House, Neil Blaney and other dissident Fianna Fail ex-Arms Trial figures were certain to vote against the measure and Fine Gael was unhappy.

Suddenly, two bombs went off in Dublin, killing two and injuring 127. As the echoes of the explosions reverberated through the city, Fine Gael withdrew its opposition to the measure, which passed by 69 votes to 22 with Fine Gael abstaining. These Dublin bombings took on a sinister twist the following July. The Provos had always denied setting them off, which is readily acceptable, as they were manifestly counterproductive to their cause. But no other source admitted to them. However, in July two English brothers, Kenneth and Keith Littlejohn, were convicted in Dublin of a bank robbery. During the trial the Littlejohns claimed to be British agents who had been acting on orders to infiltrate the IRA, and they confessed to a litany of *agent provocateur* activities. The British Government under pressure admitted that the Littlejohns did have an intelligence connection and Dublin public opinion, which had always been inclined to suspect either a Loyalist or a British intelligence hand in the bombings, felt confirmed in this view. The effect was particularly damaging for Jack Lynch, who at first denied all knowledge of the affair but subsequently admitted to 'a lapse of memory' when it became known that the Irish Foreign Affairs Department had briefed him on the Littlejohns' activities. The Department had in turn been briefed by London, which had foreseen that the facts were going to come out in the trial anyhow.

However, the Littlejohn revelations did not break until the summer of 1973, and, in the wake of the amendment to the Offences Against the State Act, the Lynch Government took advantage of its form of legalised internment by picking up not only an increasing number of rank-and-file Provos but also leaders such as Ruairi O'Bradaigh and Martin McGuinness. They were jailed at the end of December 1972. But though the increased attrition, north and south, must have limited the Provisionals' operations somewhat, it did not stop them. Earlier in the summer of 1972, on 9 July, the Libyan leader Colonel Mumar Gaddafi announced publicly at a rally in Tripoli that he had been supplying arms to the 'Irish revolutionaries who are fighting Britain'.

It soon became apparent that this was no idle boast. On 28 March 1973 the MV *Claudia* was intercepted off Waterford with a cargo of arms from Libya. Amongst those arrested aboard was Joe Cahill, who was subsequently jailed for three years by the special criminal court.

In the interim between June and Cahill's arrest the Provisional IRA had stripped itself down into a leaner, and certainly meaner, force than had existed in the early days of mass sympathy and wholesale recruitment. The Provos also became more selective in their operations. For example, on the day the Darlington talks were held, they made a marker for those involved by blowing up Belfast's most luxurious hotel, the Russell Court, at a cost of two million pounds. Later in the year, they proved that their intelligence-gathering had reached a deadly plane of efficiency also. The Provos revealed that a soldier whom they had shot dead in Twinbrook on 2 October was in fact part of a British undercover ring operated by the Military Reaction Force (MRF) which was using fronts such as a laundry and massage parlours to gain information. The MRF disclosures also revealed that the Special Air Services regiment, the shoot-to-kill, counterinsurgency group within the British Army, was also operating in Northern Ireland, and that either the SAS or the MRF had been responsible for a number of unattributed deaths in May and September of 1972.

The *Claudia* shipment was not the only source of IRA armament. Russian RPG7 rocket-launchers came into play, as did newer methods of training and organisation. These cut down civilian casualties and 'own goals', as the British Army termed the deaths of IRA volunteers through the explosion of unstable gelignite in suitcase bombs. The IRA also demonstrated its ability to strike at London, with a series of car bomb explosions on 8 March 1973 which killed one person and injured over 240. Amongst the ten young northerners held for these outrages were two sisters, Marian and Dolours Price, whose prison experiences would subsequently help to change the course of Irish history.

Nevertheless, throughout all this catalogue of destruction and death, the Provisionals maintained General Order No. 8 in place and ensured that no actions were deliberately undertaken against the Republic's security forces. Action was confined solely to the security forces in Northern Ireland. Thus, though the Government continued to view harshly the prospect of a second authority rearing its ugly head within its jurisdiction and the public continued to fear for an overspill of the Northern troubles across the border, the Provisionals managed to retain the affections of their 'sneaking regarders'. In fact the ranks of these received a notable accession of strength on 31 October 1973 when three top IRA prisoners, Kevin Mallon, J. B. O'Hagan and Seamus Twomey, were all helicoptered out of Mountjoy jail in an audacious escape which took place during exercise and in broad daylight. The incident gave rise to a popular ballad, 'The Provie Bird'.

Thus, by the end of 1973, although Dublin, London and a wide swathe of constitutional political opinion in Northern Ireland attempted to arrive at a political solution which would marginalise the Provos and, if possible, the UDA, both organisations continued to show that though they might be curbed, they could not be crushed. In fact the major political initiative of the 1970s, the power-sharing executive, which we shall discuss in the next chapter, was to smash on the rocks of this harsh truth.

SIX

PLAYING THE ORANGE CARD

Video meliora, proboque; Deteriora sequor.
(I see the better way, and approve it; I follow the worse).

Ovid, *Metamorphoses*, vii, 20

THE FALL OF the power-sharing executive told in full would make a book in its own right; in fact there is an excellent work by Robert Fisk.[1] In this short composite it is not possible to do full justice to all the twists and turns involved: changes of government in both Dublin and London; the politicking within both the Unionist parties and the SDLP; to say nothing of the activities of paramilitary groups.

However, I propose to give a short linear account, as it were, of the major events as they could be observed by any outsider, and then, once the reader has a grasp of the broad sweep of what occurred, to give some insights into the thinking of the main actors in the drama as these were revealed to me either by way of interview, or through hitherto unpublished documents. Let us begin, therefore, by detailing the sequence of events.

As we saw, following the failure of the Darlington talks, the British decided to press ahead with initiatives of their own, publishing a Green Paper. It was also announced that a referendum would be held on the border issue in 1973; this was to be followed by local elections under proportional representation and a strict exercise of the principle of one man, one vote. So far as Nationalist Ireland was concerned, the Green Paper discussion document was a combination of carrot and stick. The stick we have already noted in the proposals governing 'terrorist organisations'. The carrot offer could be observed in statements such as: 'There are strong arguments that the objective of real participation should be achieved by giving minority interests a share in the exercise of executive power', which went on:

A settlement also must recognise Northern Ireland's position within Ireland as a whole . . .
it is therefore clearly desirable that any new arrangements for Northern Ireland should,
whilst meeting the wishes of Northern Ireland and Great Britain, be, so far as possible,
acceptable to and accepted by the Republic of Ireland.[2]

The document also made the important point that after 1 January 1973 both London and Dublin would be in the EEC.

The Republic liked the document. The general vague benignity towards

Nationalist aspirations met the unstated Jack Lynch policy concerning Northern Ireland of: 'Oh Lord, make me good, but not yet.' Accordingly, Lynch met Heath in London on 24 November and conveyed his willingness to work with the Green Paper. The Heath/Lynch meeting was timed for the eve of the SDLP conference, which decided to swallow the gnat of internment and voted to strain for negotiations on the camel of the Green Paper. From London's point of view, the document had thus got off to a remarkably good start. Nationalist Ireland seemed to be well on its way to isolating the IRA. But there were serious obstacles in the path of the isolation policy.

The planned border poll was held on 8 March 1973. As internment still stood, the result was a foregone conclusion. The SDLP had no option but to join in a boycott on the referendum called for by both the Provisionals and the People's Democracy. There was a low poll. Only 6,463 people voted for unity, whereas 591,000 voted to remain within the United Kingdom. The Government pressed ahead with its plans for new structures and on 20 March London published a White Paper.[3]

The existing security arrangements were to be maintained – i.e. reserved to Westminster. A central aim of the White Paper was the provision of a firm basis for concerted governmental and community action against terrorist organisations. As a result, special courts and internment were to continue. These provisions sat slightly oddly alongside a suggestion for a charter of human rights and proposals to outlaw discrimination. However, the White Paper also contained some far-reaching ideas. The most contentious of these would prove to be a Council of Ireland. Although this was to be pledged to the securing of 'acceptance of the present status of Northern Ireland', the psychological impact of the Dublin link was to prove fatal to the entire White Paper vision.

The White Paper did not spell out the functions of the proposed council. The mere fact that it involved north and south and that its shape was to be worked out at a conference, not only involving London and the Northern parties but Dublin also, doomed it. The White Paper did spell out the shape it intended the internal Northern Ireland Government to take, under the Secretary of State who was to continue in being at Westminster. There was to be a single-chamber assembly and an executive. The assembly was to have seventy-eight seats and to be elected by proportional representation. The executive was to be drawn from within the assembly but it was 'no longer to be solely based on any single party, if that party draws its support and its elected representation virtually entirely from only one section of a divided community'. In other words, power-sharing was to be imposed on the Six County statelet for the first time in its history.

Leaving the Council of Ireland aside entirely, this fact alone would have been extremely difficult for Northern Unionists to accept and the White Paper conceded as much, noting in conclusion that the Government's proposals '. . . can be frustrated if interests in Northern Ireland refuse to allow them to be tried or if any section of the community is determined to impose its will on another'. There were of course two sections of the Northern community determined to cause frustration and prepared to impose their will on those present – the IRA and the Loyalist paramilitaries. They were shortly to be joined by other forces within the ranks of unionism.

The Orange Order rejected the White Paper, as did Craig. He set up a new party called the Vanguard Unionist Progressive Party, which had the backing of both the UDA and LAW. It proposed to fight the assembly elections in tandem with Paisley and the DUP. Faced with a rebellion on this scale, Faulkner decided to greet the White Paper with a flat maybe: 'we neither reject it totally nor do we accept it totally'.[4] Both the SDLP and the Alliance Party welcomed the document. Not surprisingly, the Provisionals, at whose destruction it was aimed, rejected it totally.

The local government elections which were envisaged as a trial run for the assembly elections proper were held on 30 May 1973. The Provisionals and the People's Democracy suffered something of a setback. Their call for a boycott was largely ignored except in Republican ghetto areas. The local government elections set a pattern of erosion of the centre which was to be continued in the assembly elections. Again the Provos and the People's Democracy tried and failed to organise a boycott, but the SDLP emerged triumphantly as the dominant anti-Unionist party. However, though there were splits and divisions all through the Unionist camp when elected councillors actually met to elect chairmen and vote in the running of their districts, the Unionists found little difficulty in papering over their fissures to combine in order to defeat the SDLP. When the elections were held on 28 June, the SDLP won 159,773 votes and had nineteen candidates elected. The party was unquestionably the recognised vehicle for constitutional Nationalists in Northern Ireland.

No such homogeneity existed on the Unionist side. Craig and Paisley's alliance held. Craig put up twenty-four candidates, Paisley sixteen. Apart from a scattering of independent Loyalists there were twelve Unionists under the shared leadership of Harry West and John Taylor, who took a harder line than did Faulkner, who had forty-four candidates. His support, however, proved to be anything but dependable. Paisley's DUP won 76,254 votes, giving them eight seats. Craig's Vanguard took 69,348 votes and seven seats. The Taylor/West alliance won 61,183 votes and ten seats and there were a variety of other Unionists who managed to collect two seats and 29,088 votes. Thus the anti-Faulknerite Unionists garnered a total of 235,873 votes and twenty-seven seats. The Faulknerites got 211,362 votes and only twenty-two seats.

Thus the forces opposed to the proposals within Unionism to the White Paper were greater than those in favour of power-sharing. Those outside the simply pro- or anti-White Paper arena, the Alliance Party and the NILP, did so poorly as to be almost irrelevant to the result. The Labour Party won only one seat and collected 18,675 votes. Labour was as vulnerable to constitutional rallying calls in 1973 as it had been to O'Neill in 1965. The newer Alliance Party with its appeal to men of goodwill in the centre put up thirty-five candidates but drew only 66,441 votes, not many more than what West and Taylor between them had polled, and won only eight seats.

As the NILP, the Alliance Party and that elusive grouping known as 'moderate

Unionists' had been the cornerstone of the centre on which Westminster proposed building the new assembly, the results were somewhere between a disappointment and a disaster for those optimists still remaining in Whitehall. The very pledge which was intended to break the mould of Northern Ireland politics now proved a barrier to progress in the frenzied negotiations which broke out after the polling results were known. This was the specification that the power-sharing executive could not be formed from only one side of the community.

Faulkner's Unionists had dug themselves into a deeper hole on this front in an attempt to fend off the Paisley/Craig challenge by pledging themselves not to 'share power with anyone whose primary objective is to break the Union with Great Britain'.[5] This made dalliance with the SDLP a difficult task. The Faulkner support was further eroded on 9 July when four of his followers attended an Orange Order meeting of anti-White Paper Unionists. On 15 July another of his supporters was killed in a car crash and Nat Minford, one of his allies, was appointed Speaker of the Assembly. Thus when the assembly met for the first time, on 31 July, Faulkner could only muster twenty members in his parliamentary party, four of them having attended the anti-White Paper rally called by the Orange Order. However, any attempt to test the strength of parliamentary opposition was rendered nugatory by an outburst of hooliganism which resulted in Minford having to adjourn the session. The Loyalists shouted and misbehaved themselves so that finally Faulkner's followers and the SDLP had to withdraw, leaving the Paisleyite anti-Unionists in possession of the chamber.

Outside the chamber similar disruption was taking place. The litany of horrors continued. On 26 June, for example, Senator Paddy Wilson and a woman friend, Irene Andrews, were knifed to death by members of the Ulster Freedom Fighters (UFF), a cover name used by a killer gang operating within the UDA. In an effort to curb dissent the authorities were resorting with increasing desperation to internment of suspects, and the conveyer belt system had ensured that there were an additional 1,000 sentenced political prisoners also in jail. Two of these were members of the People's Democracy, Anthony Canavan and Michael Farrell, who had been sentenced for organising an illegal march. They went on hunger strike for political status. Temperatures rose throughout the Nationalist areas and after thirty-four days on strike both were released. In addition, a hundred other short-term prisoners were set free and the Criminal Justice Act, which carried a mandatory six-month jail sentence, was abolished. Despite these conditions the anniversary of internment provoked huge demonstrations and the feelings elicited by Bloody Sunday continued to fester. On 21 August the Derry City Coroner, Major Hubert O'Neill, said that the paratroopers had been guilty of 'sheer unadulterated murder'.

It seemed as if the assembly experiment was dead in the water, but at the end of August Heath himself took a hand and visited Northern Ireland to knock political heads together. He warned of the dangers of procrastination and asked that an executive be formed as quickly as possible. He also met the new Taoiseach, Liam Cosgrave, at Casement Military Airport in Dublin. Cosgrave had been elected in the general election held the previous February, as a result of which Fianna Fail secured only sixty-nine seats, Fine Gael fifty-four, Labour nineteen and Independents two. Fine Gael was thus in a position to form a coalition under Cosgrave, with the Labour leader Brendan Corish as tanaiste or deputy prime minister.

Heath's visit, the first by a British prime minister since the twenty-six-county state was set up in 1921, was accompanied by enormous security but it acted as a catalyst. Cosgrave agreed to work on the Council of Ireland idea. Nevertheless, what might be termed the pro-White Paper or pro-assembly parties were agreeing on very narrow ground only. For example, although Cosgrave was to prove himself a fiercely anti-IRA prime minister, a few days after he met Heath on 17 September, his Attorney-General, Declan Costello, opened an arraignment by the Irish Government against the British Government at Strasbourg. The Republic was pursuing the British over the torture cases which had occurred at the time of internment. This case was to rumble through the European courts for years, a continuing thorn in Anglo–Irish relations.

In this spirit of strictly limited co-operation the Northern parties who were prepared to give the assembly a trial – the Faulknerite Unionists, the SDLP and the Alliance – agreed on 5 October that they would form an executive. The SDLP conceded that there could be no change in the status of Northern Ireland until another poll was held, some ten years further on, and negotiations between the parties progressed to a stage whereby on 22 November Whitelaw was able to announce that there would shortly be an executive in place consisting of eleven members: six Unionists, four SDLP and one Alliance. It would be led by Brian Faulkner, with Gerry Fitt as his deputy. A London/Dublin/Belfast conference was convened for 6 December to work out the details of the Council of Ireland.

Anti-executive Unionists marked the date by breaking up an assembly session and physically attacking the Faulknerites in a pattern which had become almost the norm during these sessions. Nor was it all plain sailing on the SDLP side. Fitt was pledged to having no talks with the British until internment ended. Now he was in power, or proposed to be in power, with Brian Faulkner, the man who had introduced it. Fitt was forced to assure an SDLP conference on 2 December that the executive would not function if internment continued. The anti-Unionists were even more determined that it would not function. On the day that the Council of Ireland conference began at Sunningdale, the anti-executive Unionists came together. Paisley's group, that of Taylor and West, and the Vanguard under Craig agreed to establish yet another Unionist umbrella organisation, aimed at bringing down the executive. It was known as the United Ulster Unionist Council. None of those involved were participants in the Sunningdale conference. It had been decided not to invite them because on the basis of their behaviour in the assembly, they would have done no more than disrupt the proceedings, and probably leaked them to the media as well.

However, Paisley and Craig were invited to come to Sunningdale to give their views. Paisley rejected his invitation with the typical rejoinder: 'We are simply invited to go and put our point of view and, having received the lunch, to be removed and taken away. We were to have the same privilege as the catering staff, apart from the fact we were going to be allowed to go in and say something before we had this wonderful lunch.'[6] A more serious absentee, however, was William Whitelaw.

The skies had been darkening for Heath's government for several months. War in the Middle East had led to increases in the price of fuel, and the miners were threatening instability. As Whitelaw had achieved much with the Northern Ireland situation, Heath thought he could do the same for the miners. On the very eve of the Sunningdale conference, on 3 December, he brought Whitelaw to London as Secretary of State for Employment, replacing him as Secretary of State for Northern Ireland with Francis Pym, who took almost no part in the Sunningdale discussions.

Whatever gloss Whitelaw or Heath subsequently put on this move, there is no doubt that both Nationalists and, indeed, many Unionists took it as an indication that the interests of Ireland in general and the Six Counties in particular were completely 'subordinate to those of the UK mainland'. In the end, despite all the pressures swirling around the talks, Sunningdale did yield results. After four days it was announced to the media that there would be a two-tier Council of Ireland, a fourteen-man council of ministers, and a sixty-member consultative assembly, half of which would be drawn from the Dail and half from the Northern assembly. All decisions would have to be unanimous and the council's functions were envisaged as lying mainly in the field of economic and social co-operation. The RUC issue was tackled by allowing the council of ministers to be consulted on appointments to both the northern and southern police authorities. The British undertook to review internment and to make some releases before Christmas.

The southern delegates made a commitment which was to haunt them. It was stated that: 'The Irish Government fully accepted and solemnly declared that there could be no change in the status of Northern Ireland until a majority of the people of Northern Ireland decided change in that status.' This guarantee was to form the subject of an action brought before the Dublin High Court by Kevin Boland, who wanted to have it declared unconstitutional in view of the south's constitutional claims to the Six Counties.

The harmful effects of this court case on the Sunningdale agreement will be discussed later. For the moment it is sufficient to say that the other provisions of the agreement included the setting-up of an Anglo-Irish law commission to tackle the thorny problem of extradition from the Republic, and a new executive which took office on 1 January 1974. This consisted of Brian Faulkner (Unionist), chief executive, Gerry Fitt (SDLP), deputy chief executive, Herbert Kirk (Unionist), Minister of Finance, John Hume (SDLP), Minister for Commerce, Basil McIvor (Unionist), Minister for Education, Austin Currie (SDLP), Minister for Housing, Leslie Morrell (Unionist), Minister for Agriculture, Paddy Devlin (SDLP), Minister for Health and Social Services, Roy Bradford (Unionist), Minister for the Environment, Oliver Napier (Alliance), Minister for Law Reform, and John Baxter (Unionist), Minister for Information.

The contradictions within this grouping were very soon apparent. The SDLP's task was to convince its supporters that the Council of Ireland meant more than it actually did; in other words that it did offer the possibility of a united Ireland. The

Unionist component in the executive had the contrary task of telling its constituents that the thing was no more than a figleaf. Both of these claims combined to trip up the members at various junctures, as we shall see. The SDLP, for example, before taking office had to advise its followers to end the rent and rates strike. The SDLP had called for this in the first place, but in government it could hardly strike against itself, even though internment continued.

The IRA campaign also continued. The executive began its sittings against a background of IRA activities which included the hijacking of a helicopter by a group led by Dr Rose Dugdale, whose father was a British airline magnate. This was used to drop milk churns filled with gelignite on an RUC station in Strabane. The following month nine soldiers and three civilians were blown up when a bomb destroyed a coach on the M62 motorway in England. In March the Grand Central Hotel, which the British Army was using as a headquarters in Belfast, was bombed. Other bombings destroyed property in Armagh to the tune of one million pounds in April alone, and there was a continuous onslaught on troops so that by the end of May, 214 British soldiers had been killed. This was the biggest death toll the army had suffered since the Korean War. In addition, fifty-two members of the RUC and forty-five UDR men were shot dead.

The Loyalists also maintained their campaign: assassinations; bombings of churches and pubs; and a campaign to shoot Catholics either at work or on their way to or from their workplace, so as to drive them from jobs in Protestant areas. On the constitutional front, Unionism also maintained an onslaught on the Sunningdale agreement. Faulkner was forced to resign as Unionist leader on 4 January 1974 after a motion rejecting Sunningdale was carried at a meeting of the Ulster Unionist Council.

He remained as chief executive of the assembly and set up new headquarters. Though this gave him a new party, the Unionist Party of Northern Ireland, it left his anti-Sunningdale adversaries in charge of the old Unionist Party headquarters and electoral machine, and the title Unionist Party. Moreover Faulkner's party's numbers were going down. He had seventeen in the assembly to the SDLP's nineteen. But even in this straitened circumstance the executive continued to function. There was an important meeting with members of the Dublin Government at Hillsborough, the old Governor's seat of office, on 1 February which set up an Anglo-Irish legal commission to study the extradition question. Meetings continued between the Garda Commissioner and the Chief Constable, and there was some movement on the setting-up of a Council of Ireland.

However, whatever chance this show of resolution on the part of the beleaguered executive had of succeeding, it was fatally undermined on 28 February by the result of an election called by Heath. In London, Pym had argued against this decision, pointing out its likely harmful effects on the assembly, but to no avail. Ironically, on the day Heath announced the election on 7 February, Kevin Boland's appeal against the throwing-out of his High Court action opened in the Supreme Court, thereby providing further harmful ammunition for the Paisleyites.

The election, coming two months after Faulkner had been forced to leave the Unionist Party, could not have happened at a worse time for him. His followers had no organisation to speak of and only fielded seven candidates. The Alliance and SDLP parties of course also stood separately. The anti-Unionists concluded a pact whereby they only nominated one candidate in each constituency (Harry West had succeeded Faulkner as leader of the Official Unionists), plus the United Ulster Unionist Council (UUUC) succeeded in winning 366,703 votes and eleven seats whereas Faulkner's people polled only 94,331 votes and won no seats. Amongst the fallen was Roy Bradford, the Minister for the Environment in the executive. Gerry Fitt only just scraped back in West Belfast by 2,000 votes; the Republicans had run Albert Price, father of the hunger-striking Price sisters, against him and taken some 5,000 votes. The election of course also returned Harold Wilson as prime minister in place of Heath, a factor which was to prove the ultimate downfall of the Sunningdale experiment.

In the wake of the election Faulkner's group met at Stormont and agreed to oppose a Council of Ireland unless the Republic repealed the claims in Articles 2 and 3 of its constitution to Northern Ireland. Responding to this pressure, Cosgrave gave an assurance in the Dail on 13 March that 'the factual position of Northern Ireland is that it is within the United Kingdom and my government accepts this as a fact'.

However, while Cosgrave thus attempted to put a finger in the dyke at the behest of the pro-Sunningdale Unionists, the SDLP's followers were also getting restless. On 3 April Austin Currie made himself unpopular with a vast swathe of SDLP support by announcing that there was to be no amnesty for those still on the rent and rates strike which he had been instrumental in calling in the first place. He also announced an increase in the amount which was to be deducted from the strikers' social welfare benefits and introduced a 25p-a-week collection charge by way of repayment. Such considerations weighed more heavily with Nationalists than did the visit which Harold Wilson paid to Belfast on 19 April during which he stated that there was no alternative to the Sunningdale package.

One by-product of Sunningdale at this stage was an announcement on 25 April by the Anglo-Irish Law Commission that it was recommending that people whom the British wished to try for offences in the North could be tried in the Republic by 'extra-territorial courts'. It was but a sop to Cerberus. As the Law Commission reported, the UUUC were holding a three-day conference at Portrush, in Co. Antrim, attended not only by representatives of the UDA, but by the redoubtable figure of Enoch Powell. All were determined to work out ways of opposing Sunningdale. Some commentators argue that Powell's presence at the conference gave the UUUC a cachet with the British officer and gentleman class which it otherwise would not have had, and which was of benefit to it in its subsequent dealings with the army. The conference arrived at a number of decisions, all of them to the detriment of Sunningdale.

It called for an immediate scrapping of the executive and for an immediate election. The conference also wanted a return of security powers to whatever northern parliament would emerge from that election, and more spending on the UDR and RUC. There was a hint of steel in these resolutions. Selective sanctions which were to include industrial action were threatened in the event of Westminster failing to agree. The point of the spear thus aimed at London's heart was a new grouping, the Ulster Workers' Council, which had been set up in the wake of the strike which had broken out following the internment of Loyalists in the early part of 1973. It had devoted itself to the quiet recruitment of trade union officials and key workers, particularly in the power stations where the workforce was almost solidly Protestant.

The UUUC showed its teeth on Tuesday 14 May, the immediate *casus belli* a failure to carry a motion at the Stormont assembly opposing Sunningdale. Another Loyalist organisation, the Ulster Army Council, which was really a front grouping for Loyalist paramilitaries, backed the UUUC. It was understood that a stoppage would be continued of essential services, particularly electricity, until Sunningdale was repealed.

The strikers had a number of assets on their side. Apart from their own resolution, organisation and their concentration of influence in the vital electricity sector, they were confronted by a marked lack of resolution on the part of the authorities. Merlyn Rees, who had succeeded Francis Pym as Secretary of State, with his Labour background was not the man willingly to set out to smash a strike. Nor did the army show any inclination to do so. Later, as the years rolled by, it would emerge that there was considerable evidence to suggest that British intelligence agencies, particularly MI5, also supported the Loyalists, to further their own agenda (see Chapter 10). At the time, however, this was not only unknown but unthinkable. The buck was passed to the RUC and as day followed day, the position of the UWC became increasingly like that of a third-division football team which suddenly discovers that its first-division opponents are without either backs or a goalkeeper.

Roadblocks went up all over Belfast. Masked men with clubs intimidated workers out of their jobs. Within a week of the strike's commencement, power cuts were in operation. Len Murray, the general secretary of the British TUC, received paltry support, something under 150 workers, when he attempted to lead a back-to-work march through UDA roadblocks. He and his supporters were jostled and howled at. The day after the march the UWC showed its muscle by banning petrol supplies to all but 'essential users'. The UWC decided who these users were to be and issued passes to them.

As the strike gathered momentum the UUUC leaders threw their weight behind it. That infallible political weathercock, Ian Paisley, who had been in Canada when the strike began, returned to lend his bellowing presence to the proceedings. A pan-Unionist front was set up. A co-ordinating committee included not only Paisley, Craig and West, and leaders of the UUC, but representatives of no fewer than seven Loyalist paramilitary groups.

The strike was also accompanied by some of the worst violence of the Troubles. In fact the worst single day of the entire twenty-five years occurred in the Republic on 17 May. No-warning car bombs went off in Dublin and in Monaghan, killing thirty-three people and wounding hundreds more. Other actions of the time included the killing of two Catholic brothers in Ballymena. They were shot by

UWC 'flying pickets' who at the time were occupying themselves wrecking public houses in Co. Antrim.

On 19 May Merlyn Rees declared a state of emergency and took powers to use troops to maintain essential services. However, the troops showed no signs of moving against the strikers. Soldiers and RUC patrols were observed talking to masked UDA men at barricades. No effort was made to dismantle these. On the day Rees made his announcement Roy Bradford called for negotiations with the UWC. This would in effect have meant capitulation by the executive. Such councils were strongly resisted by John Hume in particular. However, three days later the executive announced that the Council of Ireland was to be watered down somewhat. Firstly what was described as a purely consultative council of ministers was to be established, but its executive powers were to be postponed until after the next assembly elections, some time in either 1977 or 1978. For the UWC and the UUUC it was too little and too late. They rejected the proffered compromise and continued with the stoppage.

All-out war seemed a distinct possibility. People had no light or heat in their homes. The middle class in particular were becoming unnerved by having to queue for passes issued by very dangerous-looking characters who had set up their headquarters in Orange halls throughout the province. From all sides, industry, the professions, and even the churches, Rees was implored to talk to the UWC. Roy Bradford, the Minister for the Environment, broke ranks with his colleagues and issued a statement to the papers, saying: 'The Secretary of State should be encouraged to open lines of communications with the Ulster Workers Council before the province is allowed to slide into chaos.'[7] This caused great anger in the SDLP. Backed by Wilson, however, Rees held out, and after a visit to London on 23 May by the leaders of the parties supporting Sunningdale, Brian Faulkner, Gerry Fitt and Oliver Napier, Wilson went on television and radio, late in the evening of 25 May, to make a remarkable speech. He said the strike was a

deliberate and calculated attempt to use every undemocratic and unparliamentary means for the purpose of bringing down the whole constitution of Northern Ireland, so as to set up a sectarian and undemocratic state, from which one third of the people would be excluded.

The attempt, he said, was being made by 'thugs and bullies'. He went on to talk about the feelings of the people on the UK mainland who had seen

their sons vilified and spat upon and murdered. They have seen the taxes they have poured out almost without regard to cost – over £300 million a year this year with the cost of the army operations on top of that – going into Northern Ireland. They see property destroyed by evil violence and are asked to pick up the bill for rebuilding it.

But it was this passage which struck a nerve:

Yet people who benefit from this now viciously defy Westminster, purporting to act as though they were an elected government, spend their lives sponging on Westminster and British democracy and then systematically assault democratic methods. Who do these people think they are?[8]

171

The effect of the speech was to stiffen Loyalist resolution. Next morning Unionists of every hue appeared sprouting pieces of sponge in their lapels. The strikers had been warned by highly placed contacts in the security forces and at Westminster that after Wilson spoke arrests would follow. Consequently the strike leaders went into hiding. However, as it very soon became clear that no action was to be taken against them, they too donned sponges and showed up next morning, openly triumphant, at their headquarters at Hawthornden Road, in Belfast.

The SDLP wanted deeds not speeches, however ringing. The party threatened to resign on 27 May if troops were not sent in. The troops did move on that day and some twenty-seven petrol stations were occupied. These supplied petrol to essential services. But the Loyalists threatened that if the army was used at the power stations they would be closed down completely, as would water and sewerage plants. The Department of the Environment, headed by Roy Bradford, who of course wanted to appease the strikers, put out a statement, on 28 May, saying: 'The water and sewerage situation is deteriorating . . . Supplies [of water] may now cease almost at once in some areas.' John Hume wanted to fight it out. He told his colleagues that he was prepared to sit in Stormont until 'there is shit flowing up Royal Avenue and then the people will realise what these people [the strikers] are about'.[9] But Faulkner and his supporters gave in. After Rees still refused to talk to the UWC they resigned on 28 May, the same day as the Department of the Environment statement was issued. The UWC called off the stoppage the next day and once more the word 'prorogued' was heard in the Six Counties. Westminster consigned the assembly to the abyss into which Stormont had fallen. After four months the most important constitutional experiment to take place in Northern Ireland since the setting-up of the state had ended in ignominy. Even Conservatives were aghast. Speaking a day after Wilson, Lord Hailsham said:

> It's no good being or calling yourself Loyalist if you don't obey the law, and this [strike] is a conspiracy against the State. There is no doubt about it – in previous times judges would have had no difficulty in describing it as high treason, because it's an attempt to overthrow the authority of the Queen in Parliament.[10]

Could something better have been achieved? In view of the importance of the Sunningdale experiment, the question is worth some examination. The generally met-with view in Nationalist circles is that the Sunningdale experiment collapsed simply because of Loyalist intransigence and the refusal of the British to see that the will of Parliament was maintained through the use of their army. Writing some months after the collapse of the executive, a British army officer said in the Monday Club magazine: 'For the first time the army decided that it was right and that it knew best and that politicians had better toe the line.'[11]

The 'Curragh Mutiny' factor and Loyalist intransigence undoubtedly were present in the May crisis, but so were a number of other complicating circumstances. The effects of the two elections, one in London, one in Dublin; the differing interpretations placed on the meaning of the Council of Ireland by both the SDLP and the Faulknerite Unionists; the impact of the Boland case; the activities of some people within the BBC in Northern Ireland; the weakness of Rees and Wilson's own rather mysterious policy throughout: all of these had some bearing on the outcome. So too had differences of emphasis between Gerry Fitt and other members of the SDLP on the importance of the Council of Ireland and the impact of the Dublin bombings on the Dublin Government's view of Northern Ireland generally.

Attempting to evaluate the army issue first, a former British prime minister told me that in his view: 'The executive thing should have been and could have been seen through.' In other words, the army should have been used and the Loyalists faced down early on. Some of the actual strike leaders were of this view. Glenn Barr has repeatedly said since the strike that had they been confronted in the early stages the thing would have crumbled. Probably the most objective and certainly one of the frankest and best-informed discussions on the vexed question of army intervention in the Loyalist workers' strike took place at the Oral History seminar mentioned earlier. Present at that were former ministers in the Labour Government; Garret FitzGerald, who took part in the Dublin Government's negotiations, and was himself at Sunningdale; the Unionist, Roy Bradford; and civil servants like Sir Kenneth Bloomfield. The army chief of staff of the period, H. E. M. L. Garrett, told the conference that had the army gone in early and broken down the barricades, 'people would have said we had exacerbated the situation, that we had gone in too early with too much and had made the situation far worse'.

He then went on to say that there was in fact no request from the Secretary of State for the army, nor did the RUC ask for army support. However, Garrett did say that the army had a feeling that they 'were still involved in counterterrorism and that they had not enough troops in addition to go in and break down the barricades . . . naturally they were reluctant to go in and indeed at the time the MOD were reluctant for us to get committed on that and to have to rely on further reinforcements.'

Stan Orme, a lifelong civil rights supporter and one of the most knowledgeable men in British politics concerning Northern Ireland, was at the time Merlyn Rees' minister of state. He argued forcefully that he had done 'everything possible with the full support both of the army, the civil servants and of Merlyn. Merlyn did not want to see the strike succeed and collectively I claim, as Junior Minister of State, I accept a substantial role in this, both in negotiations with the SDLP and the army and everybody concerned. But I was not aware of anybody not pulling their weight on this particular issue.'

However, nobody offered any countervailing argument when the normally unemotional Bloomfield interjected to give his recollection of what occurred:

> I can hardly remember a more dispiriting moment in my life in the administration of Northern Ireland than the early days of that strike when I knew outside our office there were men with pickaxes preventing men from going into filling stations to fill up with petrol and there were members of the security forces standing about doing nothing about it. Maybe these things have, at the end of the day, got to be decided on the basis of pragmatism, but I would just say from the point of principle that it was a pretty appalling moment and I have never forgotten it.

Taken in conjunction with Garrett's frank admission that the army saw itself in a counterterrorism role, not as strike-breakers, that is a pretty damning indictment. In plain language, 'counterterrorism' decoded means 'taking on the Catholics only'. Both Merlyn Rees' lack of decision, and the army's contribution to the affair, are shown in an even worse light by a statement Garret FitzGerald made to the conference – which no one even attempted to deny.

He said that he had been told by a British cabinet member that the Cabinet was uneasy about ordering the army into such a situation. They had had difficulties with the army at the time of the Rhodesian declaration of UDI and apparently there were grounds for fears that these problems might be replicated with the version of UDI then being played out on the streets of Northern Ireland. FitzGerald also made two other important points.

One was that the British had been culpable in their slipshod planning for direct rule overall which had failed to protect electricity supplies:

> I can only say that it seems an extraordinary dereliction of duty of a government taking over direct rule in Northern Ireland to leave the power stations in the hands of extremists and do nothing about it. For the government to leave the power supplies of a state outside their effective control was an extraordinary error.

His second point is one I have frequently heard made by Nationalists who lived through the strike. FitzGerald told the conference that: 'The BBC was very much in support of the strike, so much so that Conor Cruise O'Brien finally rang the BBC in London to ask them what the hell was happening! O'Brien was told that the BBC "did not monitor broadcasts in Northern Ireland and they had no idea what was going on". A funny way to run the BBC,' remarked FitzGerald. He said: 'They were running basically a rebel radio station. Day after day propaganda was being turned out and we [Dublin] found that very odd also.' Dr Conor Cruise O'Brien of course would subsequently become notorious in Ireland for his efforts to interfere with the media as a minister in that government, but it is significant that no one at the conference either had anything to say in favour of the BBC or attempted to dispute the fact that there was bias in its broadcasts at the time of the strike.

Irish military and police intelligence also reported to Dublin at the time that the army was on the side of the strikers and would not move. Nothing that emerged from the behind-closed-doors discussion of the Oral History conference serves to dilute that opinion. A factor which I would also advance from my own observation is what I might term that of 'mainland preoccupation'. Throughout all the run-up to the Northern Ireland crisis, 'UK mainland' politicians continuously had their concentration and energies diverted from the Six Counties by the need to devote time to the ordinary business of getting re-elected in their own constituencies.

A contributor to the Oral History conference, Lord Donoughoe, made an interesting observation about, if not the divided attention, then at least the divided councils which seem to have obtained in the Labour Cabinet concerning Ireland at this period. Donoughoe, who worked closely with Wilson in Downing Street, said that he had been surprised at the interest which Wilson took in Northern Ireland. Wilson in fact had demonstrated this interest some years earlier both in his twelve-point speech tending towards the ultimate unification of Ireland and in an extremely unorthodox initiative which he took during March 1972 in the course of a visit to Dublin. He went with the help of a Labour politician, John O'Connell, to meet three Provisional IRA leaders, Daithi O'Conaill, Joe Cahill and John Kelly, and had a discussion with them lasting for several hours. This was of course months before Whitelaw felt emboldened to do likewise.

Donoughoe told the symposium that, following the election which returned eleven Protestants to Westminster, the view of the incoming Wilson administration was that the executive experiment was doomed. Effectively speaking, this was probably true as the election could certainly have been claimed by the anti-Sunningdale forces as a convincing referendum in their favour. However, Wilson was not content to let the Irish issue wither on the vine and he set up a top-secret policy review. At the time Donoughoe, who provided papers to the review body on issues such as dominion status, was appalled at the amount of discussion on Ireland which went on without any consideration of the Republic. When he went to the Foreign Office about this he found that David Owen was particularly helpful, and planning took place along the lines of involving the Republic, Europe and the United States in the situation. This type of approach, which presaged what actually occurred in the 1993–4 period preceding the IRA ceasefire, was of course the way forward and had it been followed up a great deal of bloodshed could have been avoided.

But the policy that the Six County area was 'domestic to the UK', and hence heavily subject to the influence of the Tory backbenches (to say nothing of a reluctant officer and gentleman class in the army) and that of the Ulster Unionists, continued to predominate, with disastrous results. Lord Donoughoe revealed at the symposium that the policy review group, consisting of himself, Wilson, Joe Haines and Robert Armstrong, did think that the British had not taken a 'firm enough line soon enough'. However, the prevailing wisdom in every department or circle of influence consulted outside the policy review body concluded that nothing could be done, and Donoughoe says: 'Wilson was very irritated and washed his hands then.' The net impression conveyed by the symposium exchange was that the army would have moved had it received firm instructions from the Prime Minister to do so. But Wilson was being told on all sides that nothing could be done and therefore nothing was done. General Garrett argued convincingly that if the political will and desire had been made clear, 'the MOD would have provided the extra troops and the army would have acted in the way that people are saying it should have acted'.

In the absence of support from the people he quoted – permanent secretaries from the cabinet office and others – Wilson was not prepared to grasp any nettles himself and so the moment passed. However, the whole executive episode irritated Wilson greatly and it emerges that he took an unusual initiative as a result of his feelings at the time. He had apparently, with some difficulty, obtained from the Treasury the proper costs of running the North. According to Lord Donoughoe, the Treasury at first refused to give the figures. But their ultimate provision, coupled with the prevarication and obstruction which was taking place in Whitehall, apparently drove Wilson to bypass his normal speech writer, Joe Haines, and to compose his 'spongers' speech himself.

Lord Donoughoe told the conference that it was the 'only speech he gave in that whole period where he did not involve his press secretary, Joe Haines, and myself, and we have never understood what happened. It was a bank holiday. We had had some discussions on the speech he might give and then we heard this speech which contained no bearing on what we had discussed.'

Substantively speaking, the mere fact that an election was called when it was by Heath against the advice of Pym, the Secretary of State with an ear nearest the ground, meant that the executive was probably doomed anyhow. Certainly Wilson's decision to set up a secret cabinet committee to look for other ways forward would seem to indicate that he at least believed this. But leaving aside this issue and the factors of army vacillation and Unionist intransigence, the relationship between the Nationalists and the Unionists to Dublin via the Council of Ireland is worth exploring in a little more detail. For if nothing else, the expectation of what each might expect through closer links with Dublin is still at the heart of Protestant–Catholic relationships in Northern Ireland at the time of writing, more than twenty years further on.

It is here that the effects of the Boland court case are of importance. From the point of view of securing an Irish dimension, the Council of Ireland appeared essential in the eyes of elements in the SDLP such as John Hume, who correctly divined that without it the Republicans would soon make inroads into SDLP support. Dublin, becoming increasingly aware of the responsibilities of Northern Ireland in terms of rising security costs and numbers of refugees, and some bombings and shootings, also felt that it should have some authority to go along with the responsibility. But even those determined Nationalists had nothing like the fervour on their side with which the Loyalists opposed the proposal. Gerry Fitt, from his cockpit position in West Belfast dealing regularly with working-class Protestants, was well aware of this feeling and had no particular enthusiasm for the Council of Ireland himself. He said, in his own inimitable way:

> as far as I was concerned we had got an executive composed of Protestants and Catholics representing the unionists and nationalist communities. For me that was the biggest development in Irish politics, certainly in Northern Irish politics, that had happened within my lifetime. I never believed that you would ever have a power sharing executive. As far as I was concerned this was it. I didn't want anything else. But the nationalists outside of Belfast, they said oh no . . . no . . . the Council of Ireland. We have to have this Council of Ireland – article 12.
>
> I said, leave that alone. That's going to drive the Prods mad. It'll drive them up the wall . . . The Prods will accept very reluctantly, but they will accept that the time has come to have a power sharing government but that business of the Council of Ireland, it scared the living daylights out of them. When we went to Sunningdale, that's why we went there to involve the government of the Republic in Sunningdale and this was the government of the Republic – macho getting into the act. You know. Sunningdale came about because of the blood that was spilt on the streets of Northern Ireland, Catholic and Protestant and army. It had nothing to do with the Free State, nothing to do with it.[13]

There was thus an irony at the heart of the debate about Sunningdale. The two leaders of the executive who were supposed to be upholding the Council of Ireland idea – Faulkner, a Unionist, and Fitt, nominally a Nationalist, but certainly the leader of a Catholic SDLP party – had grave reservations about the centrepiece arrangement – the Council of Ireland itself. However, according to Roy Bradford, who was defeated in the assembly election largely on the issue of the Council of Ireland, it was not reluctance on either Fitt or Faulkner's part to process the Council of Ireland which created the most outrage; it was the use Ian Paisley was able to make out of the Kevin Boland case.[14]

Dismissing Boland's action in the Dublin High Court on 16 January 1974, Justice Murnaghan found that the Sunningdale references to the Northern Ireland state were not in conflict with the Irish constitution. He ruled that the statement that 'Northern Ireland could not be reintegrated into the national territory until and unless a majority of the people of Northern Ireland indicated a wish to become part of a united Ireland [was] no more than a statement of policy'.[15] Bradford and the rest of the Unionist element on the executive had been asserting that, despite the constitutional claim, the Sunningdale agreement for the first time gave the northerners a guarantee that there could be no change in their status without their own say-so. The Boland action undermined this claim. Paisley also made much of the fact that the joint arrangement about police authorities gave Dublin a say in a running of the RUC.

On top of these two priceless pieces of ammunition, a heckler at Trinity College, the day after Murnaghan delivered his judgement, also unwittingly provoked Hugh Logue of the SDLP into making further snowballs for Paisley to throw. Accused by a Republican sympathiser of selling out on the national issue, Logue incautiously replied that the Council of Ireland was 'the vehicle which will trundle Unionists into a United Ireland'.

Bradford says that he found on the doorsteps that the pro arguments for the Council of Ireland had turned to ashes while the contra ones had all been strengthened, and he subsequently lost his seat. Explaining to me his attitude to the workers' strike, Bradford says he became disillusioned and, following a visit by two of his constituents, advised his colleagues on the executive that they should talk to the strikers. By that time, he said, it appeared likely that sewage would start flooding parts of east Belfast and the Falls and that there would be dangers to hospitals and the life and health of the province generally if the more gloomy engineers' predictions were borne out. I noted that in his contribution to the Oral History symposium Bradford also referred to the effect on him of the two constituents' visit, saying as he did so that there was 'nothing *sub rosa* about it'. Out of sudden curiosity I asked him the names of the two constituents. One turned out to have been Ken Gibson, the leader of the UVF!

The incident says something for the nearness of Loyalist paramilitaries to the corridors of power. So far as I am aware, even at the height of the arms crisis, no known leader of a paramilitary organisation was able to visit a minister of the Republic openly.

Given all the foregoing, it appears doubtful that Sunningdale could have worked anyway. The doubt unquestionably became a certainty when it became evident early on in the Loyalist strike that the army were not going to put the boot in. Once the first pictures started to appear of UDA men in balaclavas behind barricades chatting amicably to soldiers and their officers, it was game, set and match as far as Loyalist opinion was concerned. Twenty years of bloodshed lay ahead.

Faulkner probably does not deserve any great praise for most of his political life in Northern Ireland but at least he tried to make power-sharing work. Bradford would argue that he did so only because he was afraid of Heath, who wanted to 'Gladstonise' the issue. But he impressed both Fitt and Devlin with his sincerity, Fitt to the extent that he has gone on record to applaud what Faulkner tried to do.[16] And another prominent SDLP figure, Paddy Devlin, made one of his frequent dramatic incursions into a Sunningdale side conference to tear up a list of SDLP demands because they would have resulted in people like Faulkner 'being hanged from lamp posts'. Devlin at least was convinced that it was worth compromising on the basis of the sincerity shown by Faulkner.

I have never found any affection for Unionists in decision-taking London. There is a vague strength of feeling for the idea of the Union, but the Unionists themselves are, I found, disliked generally by both Labour and Tories. One Tory grandee with whom I went through a list of Unionists identified one as 'infernal', another as a 'wrecker', another as 'a trendy who is a secret pal of the Loyalist paramilitaries', another as 'merely stupid', and so on. The one man he was prepared to exempt from this list as having the potential of a De Klerk – that is, of leading his people forward before the tide of history, rather than being swamped by it in Canute-like fashion – was Brian Faulkner.

Some readers may feel I have laboured the point about Faulkner's efforts. But I feel that it is worth making, if for no other reason than that at the time of writing no one has yet come forward in the ranks of Unionism to adopt the role of the South African leader of the former white supremacists. Faulkner did not live long enough to demonstrate his full potential. He died in a hunting accident, at the age of fifty-six, on 3 March 1977.

SEVEN

ACTIVITY WITHOUT MOVEMENT

The ruling passion, be it what it will,
The ruling passion conquers reason still

Alexander Pope, 'To Lord Bathurst', 1731

CONSTITUTIONALLY SPEAKING, THE period 1974–94 was largely one of activity without movement. It was a confusing time, packed with incident, notable for a variety of diverse but interrelating factors. These included the rise of Sinn Fein; a growth in Loyalist paramilitary violence to a point where it eventually exceeded that of the IRA; some very 'dirty tricks', carried out by the British and the various Irish paramilitaries in a very dirty war; and some often bewilderingly rapid Irish governmental changes. Until approximately the last two years of our period Dublin's approaches had one thing in common where the Six Counties were concerned: the familiar cry of 'Oh Lord, Make Me Good, But Not Yet'. For if James Callaghan's policy toward Northern Ireland could fairly be described as talking Green and acting Orange, Dublin's could equally accurately be described as talking Green and acting slowly. Let us turn now to charting the apparent efforts at constitutional change.

The first, after the fall of the power-sharing executive, was a constitutional convention elected in 1975 on the basis of a government White Paper which asked: 'What provision for the government of Northern Ireland is likely to command the most widespread acceptance from the community there?' Readers might well question the practicality of posing such a question at that juncture in the history of Northern Ireland after all that had gone before. The answer in a nutshell was that it helped to take the bare look off things in Washington, where the Irish-Americans had done something to ensure that Sunningdale did not die unnoticed. The convention consisted of seventy-eight members elected by proportional representation.

Its chairman was Sir Robert Lowry, whose task it was to reconcile the views of the forty-seven convention members who belonged to the Unionist groupings within the UUUC with those of their opponents, mainly the SDLP. The Unionists wanted the old Stormont back; the SDLP wanted power-sharing. The Unionists' version of this concept was limited to including the SDLP in special committees along the lines proposed by Brian Faulkner before the old Stormont fell. The SDLP wanted cabinet seats. William Craig emerged as an unlikely peacemaker between the two wings, with a suggestion that a voluntary coalition should be formed along

179

the lines of Westminster's wartime coalition government. This had little effect other than to split his own Vanguard movement. At that stage the Labour Government argued that a Council of Ireland was not a prerequisite to cross-border co-operation with Dublin. It also indicated a reluctance to transfer security powers back to any Northern Ireland assemblage. Labour also pronounced itself opposed to a proposal on which it was to reverse two years later. This was the provision of extra seats for Northern Ireland MPs. In the event the convention was dissolved by Merlyn Rees as Secretary of State for Northern Ireland in March 1976 without achieving anything of substance beyond leaving the idea of extra representation floating in the political air above Belfast.

The resignation of Harold Wilson in 1976, and his succession as Prime Minister by James Callaghan, brought Roy Mason to Northern Ireland in September of that year as Secretary of State for Northern Ireland, Merlyn Rees translating to the UK mainland as Home Secretary. Mason's tenure in office is chiefly remembered for a very tough attitude on security, which included stepping up both the activities of the SAS and the war against those sections of the media which committed such crimes against the people as reporting the ill-treatment of suspects of the RUC. His regime is also associated with an increase in underground 'dirty tricks' operations on the part of the security forces.

Mason and Labour both departed the province after a division in March 1979 in the House of Commons had the opposite effect to that intended by James Callaghan when he increased the representation of Six County MPs in the House to seventeen. The Government fell by only one vote, 311 to 310. Gerry Fitt, along with the Nationalist MP Frank Maguire, abstained from supporting Labour. Had Fitt voted with the Government, as was his wont, there would have been a tie and the Speaker's casting vote would have been in favour of the status quo. But Fitt, like many observers, including the present writer, concluded that the enlargement of the Northern Ireland representation had not been directed at reducing the democratic deficit existing in that area, but at creating more governmental support. It was a remarkable occasion. Fitt told Labour that the Party had 'appeased the blackmailers of the Northern Ireland Unionist minority'. Maguire, who made a practice of not speaking in the House or taking part in its business, gave reporters the memorable line: 'I came over to abstain in person.' Despite the 'sweetener' of the extra representation, eight Unionists had voted with the Conservatives anyhow, thus delivering Labour into the arms of the abstentionists.

The following day, the Conservative Northern Ireland spokesman Airey Neave was blown up by an INLA (Irish National Liberation Army) bomb under his car in the House of Commons car park. Thus an even sterner law and order figure than Mason was denied to the province and Humphrey Atkins became the new Secretary of State.

Atkins' initiatives were completely overshadowed by the effects of the hunger strikes of 1980 and 1981, particularly that of 1981 in which ten hunger-strikers died and Sinn Fein emerged as a political force as a result. As we shall see (Chapter 9) the hunger strike was caused by an effort to impose the 'criminalisation' policy on IRA prisoners in Long Kesh prison. Atkins attempted to stage a constitutional conference which would attract all the Northern parties to Stormont during the months of January and March. However, only the DUP, SDLP and Alliance attended. It was boycotted by the UUP. During 1981, with the North boiling like a political cauldron, he tried to get off the ground a fifty-member advisory council which he intended to consist of nominated members. The question of whether or not this would have worked was rendered otiose by the hunger strikes, and the idea never took off.

James Prior came to the Six Counties in September 1981 as the embodiment of the concept of the Last-Chance Saloon. So far as Margaret Thatcher was concerned he was one of the wettest of the Wets and he was not so much being appointed as Secretary of State for Northern Ireland as exiled there. He arrived while the hunger strike was still in progress, although nearing its end. The Loyalists were exercised both by the strike and by the creation of an Anglo-Irish intergovernmental council at the Dublin 'summit' in December the previous year which had yielded the 'totality of relationship' agreement.

Two months after Prior arrived, the Provisional IRA assassinated the Revd William Bradford, a right-wing Unionist MP known for his demands for a tougher security policy and, according to some in Republican and Nationalist circles, for his links to Loyalist paramilitary associations. The IRA statement on his death said: 'Armchair generals who whip up anti-nationalist murder gangs . . . cannot expect to remain forever immune from the effects of their evil work.'[1] Bradford's death brought further coals of fire on Prior's head. He had the unnerving experience of being booed and jeered at the MP's funeral. Paisley reacted to the killing by establishing what he called a Third Force to defend Ulster. In furtherance of this force's aims Paisley led a number of midnight rallies on mountaintops which, whatever they did for his support amongst Unionists, did nothing to bring political stability to the province. Irish-Americans countered by lobbying successfully to have his US visa withdrawn.

However, in this unpromising atmosphere Prior began experimenting with new political ideas. His first initiative was to see whether it would be feasible to have a local assembly with ministers nominated by himself and in which he would act as a sort of mini US presidential figure. This proved unworkable and he opted instead for what became known as 'rolling devolution'. The idea meant in effect that the assembly would start small and hopefully grow big. Initially it was to have purely consultative and scrutiny powers. As it took hold, the assembly was to enjoy a greater measure of devolution and decision-taking. However, this depended of course on cross-community support, a commodity which above all others was notably lacking in the Six Counties at that juncture.

The SDLP, because of the hunger strikes, were under increasing threat from Sinn Fein and were forced to pursue vigorously the Sinn Fein policy of abstention. Prior's 'rolling devolution' parliament envisaged a seventy-eight-seat assembly in which if 70 per cent or fifty-five of the members backed certain proposals then the assembly could apply to Westminster for devolved powers. The assembly thus embodied the concept of a weighted majority to prevent the Unionists swamping the gathering. Up with this the Unionists would not put and they condemned the weighted majority idea as being the 'hated power-sharing' initiative of Sunningdale in a new guise. The SDLP thought the scheme simply wouldn't work but Sinn Fein, in the wake of the hunger strikes, saw the assembly concept as providing a springboard for future successes.

In the assembly elections on 20 October 1982, the SDLP did lose a number of seats. The party's total of fourteen was three fewer than in the convention and five fewer than in the 1973 power-sharing assembly. Provisional Sinn Fein won five seats, thus adding to Green versus Socialist tensions within the SDLP.

By now the party had suffered a number of notable defections over this issue. Paddy Devlin had been expelled in 1977 because he argued that the party was moving away from socialism. Austin Currie resigned in 1979 to fight the Fermanagh/South Tyrone Westminster seat as an independent SDLP candidate, but lost. He subsequently made his political career in the south. He joined the Fine Gael party, eventually becoming a junior minister in the 'rainbow coalition' Government formed in 1995. Apart from the attention of politics, Currie had other personal reasons for leaving the north. Several attacks on his home included one in which a UVF raiding party missed him and vented their spleen by carving the initials UVF on his wife's breasts. But the party's most notable defection had occurred in 1979 because of Humphrey Atkins' constitutional conference. John Hume, amongst others, regarded the 'Irish dimension' as being unduly minimalist and the entire operation as being too small-scale to produce any settlement. Gerry Fitt regarded this as the last straw in the party's evolution from socialism to nationalism and resigned, being succeeded by Hume.

One outcome of the rolling devolution experiment was that it proved that no system of government could hope to succeed if both Dublin and London were not constructively engaged in its operation. Ironically, it was an attempt to rectify the denial of this truth that led ultimately to the demise of the assembly. The British had firstly attempted to process the assembly independently of Dublin, to an extent whereby the Irish Ambassador was informed in blunt terms that there was no obligation on London to consult Dublin about matters in Northern Ireland. Subsequently the British attempted to undermine a notable Dublin experiment to chart the path of a new Ireland, the New Ireland Forum. This caused such a reaction that London, or at least Mrs Thatcher, was forced to mend her hand by concluding the Anglo-Irish Agreement. In turn this so enraged the Unionists that their protests destroyed the assembly. Catch 22 Northern Irish style.

Briefly, the sequence of events leading to the assembly's fall was as follows. John Hume, acutely aware of the growing power of Provisional Sinn Fein, communicated his fears for the future of the SDLP to Dublin. In an effort to strengthen his position the Dublin Government, then led by Garret FitzGerald of Fine Gael in coalition with Labour, moved to set up the New Ireland Forum at Dublin Castle. This was the equivalent in British terms of the Conservatives, Labour and the Liberal Democrats taking time off from other duties to concentrate for a year on constitutional reform. All the parties in the country, with the exception of the Unionists, who refused to attend, and Sinn Fein, who were excluded, took part in the forum. The result was a report which proposed three options: a confederal Ireland, a united Ireland (unitary state), or joint sovereignty. However, at a celebrated press conference, after an Anglo-Irish summit meeting at Chequers (on 19 November 1984) Mrs Thatcher completely cut the ground from beneath both Garret FitzGerald and Hume by itemising the three findings of the forum and saying after each one, 'that is out'.

The out . . . out . . . out . . . speech, as it was known, produced such a crisis in Anglo–Irish relations that even Mrs Thatcher came to realise the damage she had done. President Reagan had been amongst those who had welcomed the forum's deliberations. Possibly her dismissive attitude was influenced by the fact that the IRA had made a savage attempt on her life and those of her cabinet during the Conservative Party Conference at Brighton a few weeks earlier (on 12 October). Whatever the reason, whatever her motivation, Thatcher's standing in some Irish political circles may be gauged from the attitude that a prominent Fianna Fail politician displayed at lunch with me one day in a fashionable Dublin hotel. We were discussing the Brighton bombing. Glancing around at the gorging glitterati, he stunned me by remarking: 'If it had only gone properly, it would have been greater than 1916 – the whole British Cabinet would have gone up.'

However, to his credit, FitzGerald continued his efforts to find a political settlement. Following a lengthy period of negotiation, the Anglo-Irish Agreement was signed on 15 November 1985 at Hillsborough in Co. Down. The agreement was clearly aimed at the rise in Republican support. It provided in Article 1 that there could be no change in the status of the North without the consent of the majority. Articles 2 and 3 went on to state, however, that 'determined efforts would be made to resolve any differences' under the framework of the intergovernmental conference. In Article 3 it was stipulated that it was expected that the conference would meet regularly at ministerial or official level with a permanent secretariat.

The aims of the agreement were identified as promoting peace, stability and prosperity in Ireland while accommodating both the identities and the rights of both traditions in the North. It stated that British government policy aimed at devolving power on a basis of 'widespread acceptance'. The agreement also covered matters such as cross-border co-operation and furthered the concept of co-operation by stressing again the question of an interparliamentary link between Dublin and London. But it was Articles 5 to 7 which really indicated the upward trajectory of the graph of Dublin influence.

Article 5 stated that the Irish Government could put forward proposals on behalf of the minority and clearly envisaged that these proposals would deal with questions such as human rights and discrimination. Article 6 went on to accept the Irish Government's right to make proposals on the role and the composition of public bodies. These included the Police Authority. Security policy generally was deemed a matter for the conference under Article 7, as was the relationship of the security forces to the community and the question of prison administration.

Taken together, all these matters added up to one of the most significant developments in Anglo–Irish relations since the signing of the Anglo-Irish Treaty in 1921. In personal terms they represented a triumph for both FitzGerald and Thatcher, who had resisted pressure from Paisley and Molyneaux that she should not only not make such concessions, but abandon the talks altogether. In a sense they did no more than recognise the reality of the Republic's relationship with both Northern Ireland and England. But when the contents of the agreement were revealed[2] they had an enormous psychological effect on the Unionists. As one prominent Loyalist paramilitary said to me afterwards: 'I don't have to read the agreement, I *know* what is in it.'

The Irish Foreign Minister and the Taoiseach were in Hillsborough Castle as of right. The Irish flag, the tricolour, which a few years earlier had been banned as an illegal emblem, now flew as of right over Hillsborough Castle. Irish accents, Irish civil servants could be heard at the Anglo-Irish secretariat at Maryfield, as of right. To make matters worse, it was a Conservative government, led by Margaret Thatcher and the Secretary of State for Northern Ireland, Tom King, that had signed this infamous document. Who now could Unionists trust in England?

The Unionists erupted in rage, withdrawing from the assembly and staging every form of riot and demonstration known to political protest in a vain attempt to wreck the agreement. The reaction to the protests was significant, also, because for the first time the Royal Ulster Constabulary as a body was clearly unequivocally seen not to be 'our' police force but to be acting as 'theirs'. In other words upholding the law impartially. Somebody, somewhere, had for once clearly and unambiguously spelled out for the RUC what it should do, and it did it, a commentary, as we shall see, on much else of what the force either got away with or was directed to do. Despite the Unionists' visceral recoil from the notion of anything smacking of a united Ireland, which would appear to have the most depressing implications for any hopes of a political settlement in the future, there were grounds for optimism in the situation. The military appreciation (by both the Irish Army and their foe, the Provisional IRA) of the prospect of a Loyalist backlash has always centred on fears that it would come from elements within the RUC. It is after all a trained force, with local knowledge, and the communications, arms and transport necessary to stage a backlash if they were so minded. That elements within the force are so minded was amply demonstrated during the Stalker–Stevenson controversies discussed in Chapter 10, which made it clear that Catholics were being assassinated as a result of information leaked to the UDA from within the RUC.

But despite widespread intimidation in their homes, causing many RUC families to leave Loyalist districts, the RUC faced down the protesters. However, if the agreement stood, the assembly did not. The Unionists as soon as the terms of the agreement became known withdrew so as to create a multiplicity of protest by-elections. Eventually, as the Northern Ireland Office cut off both staff and access, the British Government dissolved yet another Northern Ireland parliamentary experiment, on 23 June 1986. The RUC provided their last service to the Anglo-Irish Agreement by carrying protesting assembly members from the building.

Before sketching in the violent, non-constitutional backdrop against which the constitutional events of the period occurred, a brief look at the influence of Dublin is warranted. What happened in the Six Counties between 1974 and 1994 was not solely determined by events north of the border or by decisions taken in London. The physical fact that Ireland is one small island inevitably had a practical outcome. Governmental changes in the south had a certain, albeit limited, effect on the course of events. Certainly, overall, one of the significant developments of the period was the gradual growth of the strength of the Dublin input into the situation. Southern public opinion at various junctures of the troubles did have some bearing on what was happening. Each of the taoisig who had to deal with the northern issue imparted a degree of their personality to policy.

Liam Cosgrave, who led the Irish delegation at Sunningdale, was a son of the first Irish prime minister, William T. Cosgrave, who led the Free State to victory over the Republicans in the Irish Civil War of 1922–3. Something of both Cosgrave père's Catholicism and his stern approach to the IRA permeated Liam Cosgrave's tenure in office. On a free vote he voted (on 16 July 1974) against a motion supported by his own government to liberalise the south's contraception laws. This did not do anything to diminish northern Protestant fears that the Republic was a sort of off-shore Vatican State. But he made up for this gesture with his approach to security, which was welcomed by both the British and the Unionists. There was, however, considerable unease in liberal Irish circles about two aspects of this policy: the activities of an anti-IRA Garda 'heavy gang' and efforts to introduce political censorship to the Republic's newspapers. Curiously, the latter was spearheaded by a figure who had hitherto been regarded as liberal, Dr Conor Cruise O'Brien. As Minister for Posts and Telegraphs, O'Brien attempted in effect to introduce to the print media the broadcasting restrictions concerning Sinn Fein and the IRA.

In what would appear to outsiders to be a contradictory attitude, given his anti-republicanism, Cosgrave shared his father's generation's approach to England of sturdy independence. While he continued to harry the IRA, he showed equal toughness in dealing with British cross-border incursions, insisting, for example, on the prosecution of a group of SAS men who were apprehended having crossed the border 'by error'. Eight of them were eventually fined £100 in a Dublin court on 8 March 1977, despite considerable British efforts to have the charges dropped. Although he regarded de Valera's 1937 constitution as a sectarian document, he did not agree with British and Unionist suggestions that it should be changed to take note of the sensibilities of the Unionists. His stated reason was that these changes would not carry against Fianna Fail opposition. In fact he reflected a section of old-school, southern opinion which held that, no matter what changes were made, 'That crowd up there still wouldn't come in!' Through his hunting and show-jumping contacts he had established a friendship with Brian Faulkner and had no difficulty with the Sunningdale provision that there should be no change in the status of Northern Ireland unless a majority in the north so desired.

However, he shared Dublin's general wariness about extradition and was cautious about agreeing to extradition of IRA fugitives to either Britain or Northern Ireland. He did agree to a proposal that arrested persons could be tried on whichever side of the border they were held. However, he developed a mistrust for British policies following the failure to confront the Loyalist threat to the power-sharing executive, and came to think that the less Dublin had to do with the North the better. After Sunningdale fell, he decided that the people in the Republic were 'expressing more and more, and I mention this simply as a matter of record without comment one way or another, the idea that unity or close association with a people so deeply imbued with violence and its effects is not what they want. Violence . . . is killing the desire for unity.'[3]

Two subsequent developments confirmed him in his belief that London could not be trusted. The first was the discovery that Harold Wilson and then James Callaghan's administrations had conducted negotiations with the IRA. The second was the fact that the Labour cabinet member Richard Crossman had decided to publish his diaries. One of his advisers told me that Cosgrave commented to him that 'you couldn't trust those people to keep a secret'.

Cosgrave was defeated in 1977 by Fianna Fail, led by Jack Lynch. The election was fought largely on the economy, but partly also on the Government's handling of the censorship issue, its attitude to the IRA prisoners in Portlaoise, and the Heavy Gang. He had to deal with not only the Northern Ireland problem but the rising strength of Charles J. Haughey, who had by then made a Lazarus-like return from the political nether regions.

The pro-Haugheyites made use of an issue arising from the north to oust Lynch. This was a secret agreement with the British in which Lynch was said to have allowed 'overflights' of the border in order to continue IRA surveillance. The 'overflights' were trumpeted to such an extent as to appear more threatening than any SAS invasion. Following two by-election defeats in his native Cork in 1979, Lynch resigned.

Haughey, whose father had been a prominent northern IRA commander during the Anglo-Irish War of 1919–21, was widely expected to take a tougher line with the British than had Lynch. He could on occasion sound more Republican then Gerry Adams. But in the event, he set off for Downing Street on 21 May 1980 for his first meeting with the Iron Lady armed with nothing more threatening than a Georgian teapot. Thereafter, he frequently sought to portray his relationship with Thatcher as being very satisfactory.[4] The comments made by some of his close associates do not always tend to substantiate this impression. But it is true that Thatcher preferred him to FitzGerald. Civil servants who negotiated with their British counterparts under both say that Thatcher showed a far greater appreciation of Haughey than she did of FitzGerald, whom she regarded as something of a bungler and a waffler, although it was with FitzGerald that she concluded the Anglo-Irish Agreement.

Haughey took office at a time when the viciousness in the H Blocks made for difficulties in relations between Dublin and London. These were not helped by Haughey's assertion, on BBC's *Panorama* of 9 June 1980, shortly after he had met Thatcher, that a British withdrawal was the best solution for the problems of Northern Ireland.

However, despite the hiccoughs, Haughey succeeded in getting Thatcher to bring the most high-powered British delegation seen in Dublin since the treaty to Dublin Castle on 8 December 1980 to conclude a meeting whose precise outcome subsequently suffered due to widely different interpretations. The communiqué did agree to joint studies and recognised the 'totality of relationships' between the two islands. It also set up an Anglo-Irish intergovernmental council which subsequently became the keystone of the arch on which the Anglo-Irish Agreement of 1985 was built. This provided for ministerial, parliamentary, official and advisory committees, all four to be set up in a four-tier structure to improve relationships between the two capitals. What it all meant exactly has rather more to do with Lewis Carroll's definition of words meaning precisely what he chose them to mean. Haughey sold the agreement at every possible opportunity as 'an historic breakthrough', and one could, if one wished, infer that a united Ireland was somewhere around the corner. But the British clearly did not intend 'totality of relationships' to go that far. The phrase in fact emanated from the British, at a dinner given by the British Ambassador, at which Haughey's principal aide, Padraig O'hAnrachain, was a guest.[5] The Ambassador sounded O'hAnrachain on what his boss would think of such a phrase being in an intergovernmental communiqué. It was clearly a Foreign Office concept, possibly intended to point Dublin towards some linkage along the lines of either commonwealth or shared European membership, but hardly towards unity. When Thatcher was running her pencil down the points to be agreed at the Dublin Castle meeting she stopped at the phrase. 'What does this mean?' she exclaimed. Haughey muttered *sotto voce*, 'Here we go', kicked O'hAnrachain under the table, and sat up, expecting fireworks. However, Lord Carrington, the then Foreign Secretary, explained airily: 'Oh, that's all right, Prime Minister, it's taken care of further down.' In fact it was not explained anywhere in the communiqué, but Carrington's intervention got Thatcher over the hurdle and conversation diverted to other aspects of the document.

However, on 22 March 1981, Brian Lenihan, Haughey's Foreign Minister, initiated a period of controversy by indicating that the 'totality' phrase pointed towards a united Ireland in ten years. He was replying to me during a discussion on a BBC Northern Ireland radio programme. Paisley took umbrage at the remark and later, after Lenihan had repeated his interpretation of the agreement to a journalist, so did Mrs Thatcher. I was given a colourful account of what transpired by one of the delegation which accompanied Haughey on the first occasion that the two sides met after Lenihan began giving his interviews. It would appear to have been one of Thatcher's vintage 'handbaggings'.[6] Paisley reacted in more public fashion. He held a rally at Stormont on 28 March which was supposed to have drawn some 30,000 protesters and appropriately enough celebrated 1 April, April Fools' Day, by holding late-night rallies on hillsides at Armagh, Gortin and Newry. The Gortin rally was significant for the fact that DUP supporters clashed violently with the RUC. Paisley's animadversions were one reason for Thatcher cooling on the Dublin summit. She chose to refer to it on television or in public speeches as the 'Dublin bilateral', whereas Haughey continued to refer to it as a 'summit'.

However, as Paisley continued to pursue what he called his 'Ulster Declaration' against the Anglo-Irish talks, more serious strains entered the Dublin–London alliance. Thatcher took an uncompromising stand against another hunger strike which had broken out in Long Kesh (see Chapter 9). This resulted in some of the strikers standing as 'H Block' candidates in a southern election on 11 June 1981.

Overall they took votes from Fianna Fail's Republican rump, and two were actually elected (Kieran Doherty, who subsequently died on the strike, and Patrick Agnew). Following the election, Garret FitzGerald succeeded Haughey as taoiseach at the head of a Fine Gael–Labour coalition.

Like Haughey, FitzGerald came from a prominent Free State family. His father, Desmond FitzGerald, had been a minister in the first Irish Government after independence, and before that had been one of the original Sinn Fein party's most able propagandists. But there the resemblance ended. The approach to politics of the sleek Haughey, whose small stature was compensated for by a Napoleonic air of self-confidence, and a tough, pragmatic approach to life and politics, reflected his training in accountancy and law. I described him in my first book, *Ireland Since the Rising*, as the epitome of 'the men in the mohaired suits' who by then were taking over in public life from the revolutionary generation. Nothing in his subsequent career gave me cause to alter that description.

FitzGerald, an economist and journalist, by contrast looked like an unmade bed, the epitome of the absent-minded professor. He acted (and sounded) like the embodiment of well-meaning, liberal, middle-class Dublin values. However, whereas FitzGerald's father, Desmond, had been the principal IRA apologist of Michael Collins' day, the son was an implacable foe of all things Republican. He said repeatedly that one of his principal political motivations was a desire to crush the IRA. Where Northern Ireland was concerned, he reflected the influence of his Presbyterian, Northern Ireland mother in his continuous attempts to woo the Unionists. However, these, with their northern bluntness, tended to prefer Haughey on the grounds that the devil you know is preferable to one who makes strange, conciliatory noises. FitzGerald's overtures to the Unionists also made Nationalists suspicious of him.

The implications of the shoot-to-kill policy controversy then raging amongst Nationalists in the Six Counties are discussed in Chapter 10. When Thatcher paid a Christmas visit to the area on 24 December 1983, the day after an IRA bomb outside Harrods of London had killed five people, she chose to visit a UDR base in Armagh. The base housed a number of UDR men charged with murdering Catholics. For Cardinal O'Fiaich, who had been repeatedly rebuffed by London in his efforts to defuse the hunger strike, this was the last straw. A few weeks later, on 15 January 1984, he made a deliberate attempt to register the feelings of the Nationalist community, stating that he found the visit 'disgusting'. He went on to say that it was not normally wrong to join Provisional Sinn Fein because of its work on housing and other social issues. The following day, with an eye on the Unionists, rather than the Nationalists, FitzGerald's government said that it could not identify with the Cardinal's statement.

After being elected taoiseach in 1981, FitzGerald announced that he favoured 'a constitutional crusade' to make the Irish constitution more acceptable to the Unionists. Three years earlier (in 1978) he had revealed that in 1974 (the year of the Loyalist strike) he had told Unionists that they would be 'bloody fools' to join the Republic under the existing constitution. One of the few Unionists to take FitzGerald's crusade seriously was William Craig, the former Vanguard leader. He said he found it 'very significant', and had talks with FitzGerald in Dublin in November 1981. However, Craig's electoral star had virtually set by then. He was defeated in the following year's assembly election.

Perhaps his unexpected support for FitzGerald's ideas had something to do with his exposure to European thinking. By some species of divination known only to themselves, the British had nominated him to the Council of Europe in 1977. With this backing, Craig, who had been second only to Paisley in his efforts to deny civil rights to Catholics, was appointed by the council to report on human rights legislation in Europe . . .

Haughey's approach, which he spelled out at the Fianna Fail annual conference in 1980 (the first he addressed as leader after ousting Lynch), was that the six-county state was a 'failed entity', a constant source of strife both on the island of Ireland and between Dublin and London. He saw the solution as lying in a negotiated settlement between Dublin and London. FitzGerald actually achieved some success in negotiation with London.

A month after the ending of the Long Kesh hunger strikes, which had claimed the lives of ten strikers but at the same time had quite obviously strengthened the position of their political supporters in Sinn Fein, FitzGerald and Thatcher met (in London, on 6 November). They agreed to put the Anglo-Irish intergovernmental council into operation. However, it was a period of intense political volatility, brought on by economic as much as Northern Ireland conditions, and FitzGerald went out of office again on 18 February 1982. Haughey returned as taoiseach, holding power with the backing of the splinter party, Sinn Fein, the Workers Party, and a group of independent TDs.

From this unpromising base Haughey appeared at least to take a tough line with London. He had refrained from criticising publicly Thatcher's handling of the hunger strikes, much to Provisional Sinn Fein's disgust. It was, as the party saw it, his failure to lead Nationalist public opinion against the British in the propaganda war over the strike that led to the H Block candidates being injected into the Republic's election. In communications from the jail the prisoners referred to him as 'The Amadán', the fool. On St Patrick's Day he publicly asked the American Government to pressurise Britain to further Irish unity. Reagan, however, replied that a solution would have to be found from within the ranks of Northern Ireland politicians. Haughey followed up his St Patrick's Day initiative by taking an anti-Thatcher line over the Falklands War.

Ireland abstained on the EEC sanctions issue and Haughey authorised the Republic's Minister for Defence, Patrick Power, to make a speech (on 3 May) in which he described Britain as the 'aggressor' in the conflict. British opinion was outraged. David Owen, the former British Labour Foreign Minister, said that 'Ireland has behaved with great impertinence throughout [the Falklands War]',[7] and Gerry Fitt judged that the Irish decision on sanctions had made for a 'greater degree of anti-Irish feeling in Britain than at the time of the Birmingham bombing'.[8] It was against this background that a British government leak (on 27 July) revealed that the British Government had told the Irish Ambassador to the UK that it was under no obligation to consult the Republic about Northern Ireland. A few weeks later (on 16 August), the *Irish Times* reported James Prior as saying that Haughey's relations with the British Government 'are pretty awful at the moment'. An Irish diplomat told me at the time that he thought that Haughey was damaging the country's national interests. This was the position when, on 25 November, power in the Republic changed hands yet again, Fine Gael and Labour being returned once more under Garret FitzGerald as taoiseach.

The incoming government took up John Hume's theme that the assembly envisaged by James Prior 'was unworkable', and at their first meeting in London (on 1 February 1983) the new Irish Foreign Minister, Peter Barry, told Prior that Dublin did not think the assembly had a future. The assembly obligingly underlined its isolation from reality by voting unanimously on 2 March for a halt to the deliberations of a committee which the European Parliament's political committee had set up to see whether the EEC could help with the North's economic problems.

However, though the agreement stood, no parliamentary structure did likewise. As we shall see in the next chapter, when we come to examine the progress of the IRA's campaign over the period, the war continued and politicians could do little save hold talks about talks; until eventually, in the 1990s, a series of initiatives, begun by Sinn Fein with the aid of a Redemptorist priest, Fr Alec Reid, led to the IRA ceasefire of 31 August 1994.

EIGHT

LAW AND DIS–ORDER

Ter sunt conati imponere Pelio Ossam
Scilicet atque Ossae frondosum involvere Olympum;
Ter pater exstructos disiecit fulmine montis.

(Three times they endeavoured to pile Ossa on Pelion, no less, and to roll leafy Olympus on top of Ossa; three times our Father scattered the heaped-up mountains with a thunderbolt.)

Virgil

CONSTITUTIONAL DEVELOPMENTS APART, there were other happenings between 1974 and 1994 which helped to explain the times and the actions of the people who lived through them. These should be noted, however briefly. Certain controversial aspects of the Troubles which will only be touched upon in this catalogue, to indicate where they fitted into the general wash of events, will be dealt with in some detail in succeeding chapters. For example, the evolution of the IRA, the 'shoot-to-kill' and 'dirty tricks' issues, the hunger strikes, and other developments which help to illustrate how the war was really fought, out of sight of the media.

The tale is inevitably a bloody one. As we have seen, the year the power-sharing executive fell, 1974, saw some particularly horrific bombings. The Dublin, Monaghan and M62 atrocities have been adverted to. Later in the year the Provisionals carried out no-warning pub bombings at Guildford, on 5 October, and at Birmingham, on 21 November. In the former, five people were killed and fifty-four injured. In the latter nineteen died and 182 were injured.

The outrage which followed these terrible deeds, and the pressure on police to obtain convictions, resulted in innocent people being sentenced for all three mainland bombings. Their 'unthinkable suffering handed down in the name of justice'[1] has since passed into the lexicon of British injustice in Ireland. Judith Ward, who was afflicted by psychiatric problems, was freed in 1992 after eighteen years, having been falsely imprisoned for the M62 bombing. The Maguire Seven, jailed in 1976 on trumped-up charges of handling explosives used in the bombings, served sentences of between four and fourteen years. One of the Guildford Four, Giuseppe Conlon, died in jail. His son Gerry served fourteen years, after a file which contained evidence that he had been in London on the night of the Guildford bombing was marked by the prosecuting authorities: 'NOT to be shown to the defence.'[2] Conlon said that he signed a confession after being threatened by a police officer that '. . . an accident would be arranged for my mother and sister. He said

191

that if a soldier shot my mother it would be put down to an accident and British soldiers were never convicted in the courts.'³ The Birmingham Six, who were first beaten up by police to obtain a confession, and subsequently by prison warders – to account for their injuries – served seventeen years before being freed in 1991.

The year 1975 was remarkable for the truce negotiated between the Provisional IRA and the British Government (see Chapter 9), which triggered an increase in Loyalist violence. The UVF attacked a Dublin showband (The Miami Showband) on 31 July, killing three and wounding one of them seriously. They also accidentally blew up two of their own men while planting a bomb aboard the band's bus, intending the musicians to ferry it across the border unsuspectingly. The idea was that it would detonate on the Republic's side of the border, thus illustrating that Nationalists were engaged in transporting explosives. This was also the year of a vicious feud between the UVF and the UDA (see Chapter 10) and within the Official IRA, from whose ranks there emerged the Irish National Liberation Army (see also Chapter 10).

Sectarian murder dominated the early part of 1976. On 4 January, two other UVF attacks claimed five Catholic lives. The following day there was a massacre of Protestant workers at Kingsmill, South Armagh. This was claimed not to be the work of the Provisional IRA but of a cover grouping calling itself the Republican Action Force. It had the effect of causing the SAS to be moved into the district.

By way of illustrating the general level of mayhem, it should be noted that the Government announced on 21 January that 25,000 houses had been damaged since the Troubles began. It was against this background that the convention mentioned in the previous chapter broke down in disorder on 3 March, being formally disbanded six days later.

This was the setting in which developed one of the largest peace movements of the entire Troubles. On 12 August of that year, the women's Peace Movement began, after three children of the Maguire family died as a result of the army shooting dead the driver of a stolen car which went out of control. In its early stages, huge processions of Protestant and Catholic women marched together through both Republican and Loyalist parts of Belfast. Its founders, Mairead Corrigan, the dead children's aunt, and Betty Williams, later received the Nobel Peace Prize.

However, there was very little other evidence of peace around either that month or that year. Also, in August Gerry Fitt had had to drive off a group of Republican demonstrators who broke into his home and were only expelled at gunpoint. Maire Drumm, vice-president and the leading woman member of Provisional Sinn Fein, was shot dead while receiving treatment in the Mater Hospital, Belfast. And the year ended with an IRA firebomb blitz causing one million pounds' worth of damage in Derry alone on 9 December.

Three days later, a Loyalist umbrella organisation, the ULCC (Ulster Loyalist Central Co-ordinating Committee) announced that it knew of Loyalist politicians who had taken part in gun-running, selecting bomb targets and promising money for arms and explosives. It was not clear from the statement that the paramilitaries issued to the papers which of these activities were regarded as the most reprehensible: the gun-running and bomb targeting, or the fact that the promised money had not been forthcoming.

The year 1977 was characterised by the usual bombings and shootings, an increase in the number of SAS men sent to the province, an increase in unemployment, and the failure of another attempt by Loyalists to stage a power strike. This began on 3 May, but despite the support of Paisley, who joined farmers in road-blocking in his constituency of Ballymena, Co. Antrim, the strike was a failure.

1978 saw one of the worst atrocities of the entire period. A function at La Mon House Hotel at Comber, Co. Down was firebombed by the Provisional IRA, and failure to allow for vandalised phone boxes meant that delayed warning calls resulted in the place not being cleared when the bombs went off. Twelve young people died in the conflagration and twenty-three were injured. This was also the year when the Dirty Protest (described in Chapter Nine), which led to the hunger strikes at Long Kesh prison, began to make news. On 1 August Cardinal O'Fiaich issued a statement to the papers saying that the prisoners were living in inhuman conditions, worse than the slums of Calcutta.

The rising tension in the community and the lack of political progress caused the SDLP executive, which the previous year had resisted a similar motion, to vote at its annual conference on 4 November for a British withdrawal. But far from withdrawing, the House of Commons on 28 November passed a motion by a majority of 7 to 1 for increasing the parliamentary representation from the North to Westminster by five seats. By this act of artificial insemination, Callaghan increased the progeny of the mother of parliaments, but, as we have seen, lost power the following year.

When it was announced in July that the Pope intended to visit Ireland the following September, both Ian Paisley and the Orange Order issued statements warning the Pontiff to keep out of the North. Paisley said on 21 July: '. . . this visit is not on – full stop. The pope is anti-Christ, the man of sin in the Church. Pope Benedict blessed the 1916 rebels . . . from that has flowed the IRA.'[4] It was a good example of Paisley's technique, a combination of Maria Monk-like bigotry and historical inaccuracy. Pope Benedict had in fact been trying to dissuade the rebels from staging the rising when an emissary, Count Plunkett, startled him by informing him that he was in Rome as a matter of courtesy to inform His Holiness that a rebellion was being planned in Dublin, but that the Pontiff had no cause for alarm, the rebels were not communists![5] John Paul II received a greater inducement to stay away from Northern Ireland on 27 August, when the Provisional IRA set off bomb explosions at Warrenpoint in Co. Down which claimed eighteen soldiers' lives. On the same day Lord Mountbatten, his fourteen-year-old grandson, a crew member and a friend, the Dowager Lady Brabourne, all died as a result of an explosion in Mountbatten's fishing boat at Mullaghmore in Co. Sligo, with consequences for Northern Ireland's security policy which are discussed in Chapter 10.

As we will see later, the Pope's visit to Ireland also had other more significant and far-reaching consequences but these did not appear at the time. The

Provisionals rejected his appeal at Drogheda on 29 September: 'On my knees I beg of you to turn away from the paths of violence.' A statement issued to the press by the Provisionals on 2 October said that the British would not withdraw unless force continued to be used. The statement said however that: '... upon victory, the Catholic Church would have no difficulty in recognising us'.[6] The year ended with five soldiers being killed by IRA bombs on 16 December.

1980 was marked by the growth in importance of the H Block issue. In pursuit of their demands for political status, the prisoners began a hunger strike in October after a period during which warders were shot and Loyalist assassination squads murdered people who took part in organising H Block demonstrations (see Chapter 9). However, it appeared, wrongly, that the situation had been defused on 18 December, and the strike was called off.

The first month of 1981 saw an attempt on the lives of Bernadette McAliskey (née Devlin) and her husband at Coalisland, Co. Tyrone. Both were seriously wounded. Five days later, on 21 January, the IRA shot dead two prominent Unionist politicians, Sir Norman Stronge and his son James. On 1 March Bobby Sands went on hunger strike in the H Blocks. On 9 April he was elected as the MP for Fermanagh/South Tyrone where a by-election had been caused by the death of Frank Maguire. His election was greeted with jubilation by the Republicans and outrage by the Loyalists. Fierce rioting broke out in Belfast, Lurgan, Cookstown and Derry as a result. In Derry, after almost a week of rioting, two teenagers were killed by an army Land Rover.

The hunger strikes caused increasing US interest in the situation. President Reagan mirrored this on 28 April when he said, while declaring that the US would not take an interventionist position, that he was nevertheless 'deeply concerned at the tragic situation'.[7] A few days later, on 5 May, Bobby Sands died and there was rioting not only across the province but in Dublin. By this stage ten prisoners had joined the hunger strike. One of these, Francis Hughes, died on 12 May and there was further fierce rioting. Both Sands' and Hughes' funerals attracted attendances of the order of 100,000. On 15 May, Senator Edward Kennedy said: 'Unfeeling inflexibility will achieve nothing but more deaths.'[8] But Margaret Thatcher refused to budge. Four days later five British soldiers were blown up in Co. Armagh by a landmine.

It took one of the biggest police operations ever seen in Dublin to save the British Embassy when, on 18 July, an H Block march attempting to pass the embassy ended in one of the most ferocious riots of the period. Four days earlier, the Irish Government had appealed, without result, to America to intervene with Britain over the hunger strike.

The hunger strike ended on 3 October, and three days later James Prior announced that the prisoners would be allowed to wear their own clothes. The IRA riposted by setting off a nail bomb outside Chelsea Barracks in London. A woman was killed and twenty-three soldiers and seventeen civilians were injured.

1982 saw a growth in approaches to America by Dublin to bring pressure to bear on Britain to further Irish unity by consent. As we have seen, the Falklands War further exacerbated Dublin–London tensions. Bombings and shootings continued, the most notable of these being two attacks in London on 20 July in which eleven soldiers were killed and fifty-one people injured. The bombs, one at the Knightsbridge Barracks and the other at the Regent's Park bandstand, also killed a number of horses, a fact which elicited more outrage from the British tabloids than did the deaths of the soldiers. The worst single atrocity of the year occurred on 6 December when the INLA bombed a pub, the Dropping Well in Ballykelly, Co. Derry, which was frequented by security personnel. Eleven soldiers and six civilians died in the atrocity.

1983 could be described under many headings, continuing violence, of course, being one of them. For example, in July the marching season's tensions were heightened by the IRA blowing up four UDR members with a landmine, the biggest single loss that the regiment had suffered. It was also a year characterised by the increased use of supergrasses – that is, informers who were promised immunity and a new start in life in return for giving evidence against IRA and Loyalist paramilitaries (see Chapter 10). But the most significant happening of the year was the emergence of Gerry Adams and Sinn Fein on to the parliamentary stage.

Adams and Hume were the only two Nationalists to win seats in the Westminster election of 9 June. Fifteen Unionists were returned to Westminster but Gerry Fitt was not. His increasing isolation from his own constituents from the time of the hunger strikes resulted in his coming in third after the SDLP candidate Joe Hendron.

The Provisionals received a huge morale boost on 25 September, when thirty-eight of their top men broke out of Long Kesh. It was the biggest jail break in British prison history. Nineteen managed to remain at liberty. An even more significant incident occurred on 13 November. The northerners took over the leadership of Provisional Sinn Fein, Gerry Adams being elected president. Adams, Joe Austin, Martin McGuinness, Jim Gibney, Tom Hartley and Danny Morrison were among the emerging figures who replaced the southern-based leadership of Ruairi O'Bradaigh and Daithi O'Conaill.

By contrast with the increasing professionalism of PSF, the disorganised state of another Republican movement, the Irish National Liberation Army, was seen a week later when an unauthorised attack by members of the INLA killed worshippers at a Pentecostal service in Darkley, Co. Armagh. The year ended with a gun battle in Co. Leitrim in which the Irish Army and police force eventually rescued Don Tidey, the English head of an Irish supermarket chain, who had been kidnapped by the Provisionals. An Irish soldier and a Garda cadet were killed in crossfire. It was not clear that the Provisionals had in fact fired the fatal shots but the incident added greatly to Dublin's already high political blood pressure. The following day, the Provisionals added to outrage in London by detonating a car bomb outside Harrods which killed five people and injured eighty more.

1984, the year when, as described earlier, Margaret Thatcher rejected the findings of the New Ireland Forum, thus involving herself in controversy with the Irish Government, began with the Iron Lady also clashing with the Irish church leadership. Thatcher had pointedly visited a UDR base in Armagh on a Christmas Eve trip to the north. A number of its occupants were at the time facing charges relating to the shooting of Catholics. On 15 January, Cardinal O'Fiaich made the public statement on RTE in which he described the visit as 'disgusting' (see Chapter 9). In the same broadcast he said of Sinn Fein membership that: 'If a person is convinced that he is joining for these reasons [Sinn Fein's community activities] and that his positive reasons outweigh any interpretation that may be given his membership as condoning support for violence and crime, he may be morally justified.' This led to O'Fiaich being labelled 'the Sinn Fein Cardinal'[9] and disowned in Dublin. The anti-Republican Dublin coalition government was aghast and issued its own statement, on the 16th, saying that it could not identify with the Cardinal's remarks.

In March the Provisionals shot dead the assistant governor of Long Kesh prison, and a week later, on 14 March, Gerry Adams was shot and wounded in Belfast by what was alleged to be a UFF hit squad (see Chapter 10). Also in March, St Patrick's Day, the 17th, was marked by a notable first in north–south relations: Dominic McGlinchey, the INLA leader whose activities are described in Chapter 10, became the first political offender of the Troubles to be extradited from the south to the north.

In the same month, the continuous allegations of a shoot-to-kill policy on the part of the security forces in Northern Ireland were given a new lease of life during the trial of an RUC constable, John Robinson, for murder. Robinson stated that he had been ordered by his superiors to tell lies. His statements were apparently well founded, because on 4 April the British Government apologised to the Irish Government for RUC undercover actions which had taken place in the Republic the previous year.

The Provisional IRA themselves staged a shoot-to-kill operation a few days later (8 April) when, in an attempt to kill a magistrate, Tom Travers, as he left Mass in Belfast, they succeeded only in wounding him but shooting his daughter, Mary, dead. Unionists afterwards pointed out that at the time Travers was trying a case in which Gerry Adams was charged with obstruction.

The continuing interest of American politicians in things Irish was underlined on 25 May when both houses of Congress unanimously backed the New Ireland Forum report. But the difference in approach by the Democrats and the Republicans was underlined during a visit made by President Reagan to the Republic a few days later. In a joint address to the Dail and Senate on 4 June, he too praised the New Ireland Forum report but went on to say that current US policy was not to interfere in Irish matters.

On 12 July, however, the Orange Order demonstrated that they did not share the US Congress's opinion, and there were many resolutions passed from Orange platforms condemning the NIF report. Two further noteworthy evidences of American interest in the Irish situation occurred in this year too. In one, Martin Galvin, the Noraid leader, suddenly received nationwide coverage on American network TV. He had been banned by the British from appearing in the UK and when the RUC moved in to arrest him at a west Belfast rally, on 14 August, a riot broke out, during which a civilian, Sean Downes, was struck in the chest by a plastic bullet and died. His death was shown on prime-time American TV. After the screening, James Prior said that the ban on Galvin was 'a bad mistake'. Prior obviously felt that his entire Irish interlude was something of a mistake because he retired from the fray on 10 September, being succeeded as Secretary of State for Northern Ireland by Douglas Hurd.

The second major evidence of American interest came on 28 September when a joint British–Irish security force operation resulted in the seizure of seven tons of arms and ammunition from the trawler *Marita Ann*. They had been ferried from Boston aboard the SS *Valhalla* and transhipped to the *Marita Ann* off the Kerry coast. However, a fortnight later, on 12 October, the IRA demonstrated that they had other sources of explosive when they detonated the bomb in the Grand Hotel, Brighton, which came within an ace of killing Margaret Thatcher and several members of her cabinet.

1985 began with a chink of light showing through the gloom. On 1 February John Hume accepted an invitation to begin talks with the Provisionals. This flew in the face of Garret FitzGerald's anti-IRA stance, and on the 3rd he issued a statement saying that such a meeting could be used by the IRA for propaganda purposes. However, Haughey backed the idea of dialogue. Douglas Hurd opposed it, saying that it would give credibility to the Provisionals. British pressure to deny this credibility resulted in the State Department refusing Gerry Adams a visa to visit the US to address congressmen. The British, notoriously sensitive to American influence on the Irish situation, followed up this denial by arranging to have Margaret Thatcher make an address to Congress on 20 February during which she appealed to Americans not to support Irish Northern Aid (NORAID), an Irish-American support organisation.

The slight hopes that had been entertained following the commencement of dialogue between the Provisionals and Hume were snuffed out a few days later, on 23 February, when Hume broke off his conversations with the Provisionals because the IRA attempted to video the discussions. On the same day, three Provisionals were shot dead by British soldiers in Strabane, and the following day the Provisionals riposted with a mortar attack on an RUC barracks in Newry which killed nine people.

On 2 September Tom King succeeded Douglas Hurd as Northern Ireland Secretary of State. King, a staunch Unionist, thus became a signatory (with Thatcher, Garret FitzGerald, and the Republic's Foreign Minister, Peter Barry) of the Anglo-Irish Agreement at Hillsborough, Co. Down, on 15 November. As a result, King was subsequently attacked by Unionists on a visit to City Hall, Belfast. One Loyalist councillor, George Seawright, was later jailed for nine months for his part in the attack.

1986 was marked by intense Loyalist indignation at the Anglo-Irish Agreement. Protests of all sorts took place, including the petrol-bombing of the homes of RUC officers. On 3 March a Unionist 'Day of Action' shut down the province's shops, offices and factories. As a result of this display of 'loyalism' the British Government was forced to send extra troops to the Six Counties to help the RUC withstand the onslaughts on the forces of the Crown to which the protestors were claiming to be loyal. On 2 May the RUC Chief Constable Sir John Hermon stated that fifty RUC and seventy-nine Catholic families had been firebombed in the month of April. Scores of RUC officers were injured. Unionist assembly members attempted to smash down defences around Stormont Castle to break up meetings of the Anglo-Irish governmental conference. There were continuous Loyalist strikes and protests of all sorts, including an invasion of the Republic. Peter Robinson of the Democratic Unionist Party heightened the temperatures of the marching season by leading some 500 Loyalists on an after-dark descent on the Monaghan town of Clontibret, two miles inside the Republic's border, on 7 August. The raid, which terrorised the villagers, won Robinson some favourable publicity in DUP circles, particularly after it generated some Belfast-style rioting and petrol-bombing in Dundalk when his case came to trial on 15 August.

1985 also saw the controversial Stalker affair. John Stalker, the Deputy Chief Constable of the Greater Manchester area, was eventually cleared of allegations of misconduct on 22 August after he had become the victim of obstruction and a whispering campaign in his attempts to investigate allegations of a shoot-to-kill policy on the part of the RUC. (This case will be discussed at greater length in Chapter Ten.)

1987 was a turbulent year during which Garret FitzGerald resigned as Fine Gael leader (on 11 March). He was succeeded by Alan Dukes. On St Patrick's Day Reagan acknowledged the importance of the Irish-American vote by authorising the first tranche ($50m) of a $150m American grant to further the work of the Anglo-Irish Agreement by helping Six County employment projects.

The Provisionals also had their own methods of generating international interest in the Irish situation. They set off a bomb at an officers' club at a joint Army/RAF base in Rheindalen, West Germany, in which thirty-one people – most of them neither army nor RAF, but German nationals – were injured. The reason for this attack was that the British were using the base to spy on Irish nationals working in Germany. A month later, on 25 April, the Provisionals blew up Lord Justice Maurice Gibson and his wife Cecily with a car bomb at Killeen, Co. Down (see Chapter 10). Gibson thus became the fifth member of the Northern Ireland judiciary to be killed by the IRA.

On 8 May, the IRA suffered one of its worst reverses of the entire campaign when an active service unit was wiped out by the SAS at Loughgall, Co. Armagh. Some of the IRA's top operatives, including the unit's leader, James Lynagh, were killed in this operation, five in combat and three who were ordered to lie on the roadway after arrest and were then executed.

The 5th of September encapsulated the disaffection of both the Orange and the Green traditions. In Belfast the Unionist leaders James Molyneaux and Ian Paisley were summonsed for holding illegal marches to protest against the Anglo-Irish Agreement, and in Winchester three citizens of the Republic were charged with conspiracy to murder Tom King. They were released the following year. During a press conference which he gave on proposals to restrict the right of accused persons to remain silent, King made remarks which were deemed to have a bearing on their case. Another, potentially more grisly, sense of appropriateness could have been adduced the following 1 November (All Saints' Day) when 150 tons of arms and explosives were seized off the French coast aboard the *Eksund* en route to the IRA from Libya. Then on 8 November the IRA detonated a bomb during the Remembrance Day ceremony at Enniskillen which killed eleven and badly injured sixty-three others.

A combination of the *Eksund* discovery and the Enniskillen blast prompted an extraordinary security response both in the Republic and in the Six Counties. It became known that a number of other successful arms shipments had been made from Libya to the Provisionals, and on 23 November the country was ransacked by the security forces in an unsuccessful attempt to discover the dumps. Evidence of careful preparations was uncovered in the form of huge underground bunkers in different parts of the country, but no arms were found. Some forty Provisional supporters were arrested in the course of the search operation, both north and south of the border. But the year concluded with grim demonstrations of the IRA's ability to continue its operations. A bomb went off outside the Belfast home of another judge, Donal Murray, on 17 December, without injuring him; but five days later the prominent UDA leader John McMichael was not so lucky. He was blown up by an IRA car bomb (see Chapter 10).

John Hume resumed his dialogue with Gerry Adams on 11 January 1988. This potential for improved relationships was, however, somewhat overshadowed on 25 January by the announcement by Sir Patrick Mayhew, then the Attorney-General, that eleven RUC officers who had been investigated by John Stalker, and by his successor, Colin Sampson, Chief Constable of the West Yorkshire force, would not be prosecuted. Mayhew cited reasons 'of national security' for his decision. Dublin protested and on 9 February the European Parliament asked Britain to reconsider the decision. Bowing to the pressure, King announced that there would be disciplinary inquiries within the RUC as a result of the Stalker/Sampson investigation. March saw an extension of the shoot-to-kill policy to Gibraltar. Three IRA members were shot dead by the SAS without being given a chance to surrender. Sixty British Labour MPs signed a statement condemning the shootings as 'capital punishment without trial'. (These killings and a set of horrific incidents which they triggered are discussed in Chapter 10.)

The IRA demonstrated that neither Gibraltar nor Loughall had crippled the organisation, by killing six soldiers in a bomb blast in Lisburn on 15 June as they were being taken in a bus on what was described as a 'fun run'. A few days later, on the 23rd, the Provisionals shot down a helicopter at Crossmaglen. Another Provisional bombing went very badly wrong on 23 July when an explosion intended to kill a judge at the border instead killed three innocent civilians, Robert and Maureen Hanna and their son David. On 20 August the Provisionals killed eight British soldiers in a bomb attack on a bus at Ballygawley, Co. Tyrone.

Apart from the inevitable fall-out from such incidents in Dublin–London relations, there was more friction between the Republic and the UK throughout 1988 over another continuing bone of contention – extradition. This chiefly centred on the Father Ryan case. The Irish refused to extradite Ryan, who had been flown back to his native country from Belgium, where he had been held in custody. Thatcher criticised both Belgium and the Republic of Ireland in a statement on 30

November, even though her law officers admitted that there were errors in the Ryan extradition warrant. There was a major row in the Commons over the issue on 1 December, and three days later the Irish Attorney-General issued a statement which set out twenty new questions on the Ryan warrant. The controversy created an increase in Haughey's popularity so that an opinion poll recorded a 62 per cent majority of public support for his handling of the affair, which Thatcher, on the 14th, had described as an 'insult to the British people'.

The year ended with a message from the Provisionals on 30 December warning British politicians and members of the Royal Family that they were now legitimate targets.

1989 opened with a set of contrasting events which helped to illustrate the difficulties confronting those who attempt to reach across the sectarian divide. On 7 January, a member of the SDLP, Ms Mary McSorley, who had devoted her life to promoting tourism in Northern Ireland – not the most rewarding of fields – was awarded an MBE. The party disowned her as a result. A week after this snub to the British connection, the leader of the SDLP, John Hume, invited the Unionists to talk with Nationalists and with the Irish Government in an effort to perhaps transcend the continuing Unionist difficulties with the Anglo-Irish Agreement. The offer was not taken up but at the end of the month, on 29 January, Gerry Adams told the Sinn Fein Ard Fheis that 'the IRA had to be careful and careful again to avoid civilian casualties'. Adams at least appreciated what 'mistakes' like the deaths of the Hannas were doing to the IRA's public image.

The Hannas were only three of the seventeen civilians who had been killed by such mistakes in 1987–8. But Adams' most significant statement came on 5 March when he clearly indicated a preference for a political as opposed to a military role for the Republicans. He said that he sought a 'non-armed political movement to work for self-determination' in Ireland as a whole. That a 'non-armed' movement was not on the agenda of some wings of Unionism at least was illustrated the following month when on 22 April three Ulster Resistance members, a South African diplomat and an arms dealer were detained by police in Paris. Ulster Resistance was a Loyalist paramilitary movement with whose foundation both Ian Paisley and Peter Robinson were associated.

Later in the year, on the twentieth anniversary of the arrival of British troops, the IRA displayed a more familiar attitude on its part to the question of armed struggle by detonating a bomb at the Royal Marines School of Music at Deal in Kent which killed ten bandsmen.

However, the new Northern Ireland Secretary, Peter Brooke, who had succeeded Tom King on 24 July (King moved to Defence), stated publicly on 3 November that the Provisional IRA could not be defeated militarily and said that for his part he would not rule out talks with Sinn Fein if the violence were to end. The SDLP followed up Brooke's statement the next day during its annual conference, calling on the Unionists to talk to Dublin and on the IRA to lay down its guns. Significantly, in the middle of the month (16 November), Provisional Sinn Fein launched a document entitled 'Scenario for Peace' which stated that as the Nationalists were the ones who sought unity there was an onus on the established parties to launch an international campaign to bring about this end. The word 'peace' was beginning to pop up with greater regularity amidst the horrors.

On a constitutional level, 1990 was the year in which the phrase 'talks about talks' frequently cropped up in newspaper comment. But the idea that Unionists would talk to Dublin or that Sinn Fein could be spoken to without a ceasefire were sufficiently anathema to render these approaches nugatory. The shadow of the Anglo-Irish Agreement hung over all Unionist thinking. That of older established arguments in the Six Counties did so also.

Whereas Paisley and his colleague, William McCrea, scenting there might be change in the wind, mounted a campaign to ensure that there would be 'hands off the UDR', the IRA continued to declare the organisation a legitimate target. Four UDR men were blown up by a landmine at Downpatrick on 9 April. Issues like the Stevens inquiry (see Chapter 10) into the matters which neither Stalker or Sampson had been able to get to the bottom of continued to outrage Nationalists.

The possibility of a break in the talks logjam opened up on 11 May when, after a meeting between Peter Brooke and a group of Unionist leaders, it was announced that, though the Anglo-Irish Agreement would not be suspended, there would be a moratorium on meetings of the Anglo-Irish Intergovernmental Conference. However, Unionist conditions on when these talks should begin – not until after there had been substantial progress on devolution – made both Dublin and the SDLP go cold on the proposal, and on 5 July, during a debate on the renewal of direct rule, Brooke was forced to inform the House of Commons that he was unable to report any schedule for talks.

The IRA didn't require one. On 24 July, in Armagh, a 1,000lb bomb triggered by a command wire not only killed three RUC men but claimed the life of a nun, Sister Catherine Dunne, into the bargain. At the end of the month, on 30 July, the IRA also killed Ian Gow, the Sussex MP, with a car bomb outside his home. Two IRA men were shot dead at Loughgall on 9 October. And on the 24th of the month the IRA retaliated by killing five soldiers near Derry and another soldier and a civilian near Newry, in 'human bomb' attacks in which the drivers were strapped into cars and forced to drive to their targets.

The following day, the Anglo-Irish Intergovernmental Conference met in London and again failed to find any formula for talks between London, Dublin and Belfast. But on 9 November, Brooke made a significant statement. Speaking to his constituency party in Britain he said that the UK had 'no selfish, economic or strategic interest in Northern Ireland and was prepared to accept unification by consent'.

The idea of consent was taken up on behalf of Fine Gael by John Bruton on 20 November. Bruton had just succeeded Alan Dukes as leader of the party. He accepted that there could be changes in Articles 2 and 3 of the Republic's constitution to include the principle of consent. However, within days, Paisley, at least temporarily, scuttled the idea, telling the DUP annual conference on 24 November that he rejected the idea of power-sharing or any place for Dublin at talks.

An event then occurred which was to have far-reaching consequences in helping to overrule Paisley's objections in historic fashion three years later. On 27 November, John Major replaced Margaret Thatcher as leader of the Conservative Party. Major consistently took a more flexible approach to things Irish than had his predecessor, although the new approach can hardly have been encouraged by an old approach on the part of the Provisional IRA.

On 7 February 1991 the IRA launched three mortars at Downing Street from a parked van, causing a cabinet meeting on the Gulf War to be abandoned hurriedly. The government buildings were subsequently reinforced. While this unpromising commencement to Major's reign did not bode well for the future, two less-publicised events which had occurred a couple of days earlier (on 29 January) were possibly a better guide to the future.

In one, Tom Hartley of Sinn Fein announced publicly that Provisional Sinn Fein would no longer comment on the activities of the IRA – not a disowning of violence, but a disassociation. And by coincidence, on the same day Rhonda Paisley, Ian Paisley's daughter, called for a ban on the UDA. New thinking was making its presence felt.

It seemed that this new thinking might bear substantial fruit when on 25 March the DUP, the UUP, the Alliance and the SDLP all agreed on a formula for talks. The omens began to look distinctly promising when the Loyalist paramilitaries announced (on 22 April) that they would declare a ceasefire for the duration of the talks. The principle behind the talks was that they would be three-stranded: one strand London and Dublin; one internally in the Six County area; and the third between north and south. There then ensued a delay while a chairman was sought for the north–south strand. On 15 June it was announced that Sir Ninian Stephen, a former governor-general of Australia and an Australian high court judge, had agreed to act as independent chairman.

Helped by the spin doctors in London, Dublin and the NIO, the media had been filled with hopeful speculation as to what these talks might yield. There was considerable dismay when on 3 July they yielded precisely nothing. Brooke announced that the talks had ended because the Unionists were not willing to continue discussions beyond 9 July, and in those circumstances the SDLP refused to make specific proposals. The Loyalist paramilitaries responded by ending their ceasefire from midnight on 4 July. Their first targets were Provisional Sinn Fein election workers. One, Patrick Shanahan, was shot dead on 11 August, another, Bernard O'Hagan, on the 16th. More than a dozen such activists were subsequently fatally targeted. The Provisional IRA's riposte included a bomb attack on 2 November on Musgrave Park Military Hospital in Belfast in which two soldiers died and eighteen were injured.

1992 began badly. A Provisional bomb devastated Belfast city centre on 4 January and further damage was caused by another bomb the following day. A briefcase bomb containing 5lb of explosive went off a few hundred yards from Downing Street on the 10th of the month, doing little harm but demonstrating the Provisionals' ability to strike almost at will. The worst atrocity of the month, indeed of the year, occurred on 17 January, when the IRA blew up a bus containing Protestant workmen at Teebane Crossroads, near Cookstown, Co. Tyrone, killing eight workers who had been engaged in construction work for the security forces. Peter Brooke was a collateral casualty of this tragedy. He appeared later that day on RTE's *Late Late Show*, and when pressed by the show's compère, Gay Byrne, yielded to his urgings to sing a song, 'My Darling Clementine'. This outraged the Unionists, and the unfortunate Brooke, who was recognised as having made a contribution to moving the peace process forward, subsequently joined Clementine in the foaming brine of the Anglo–Irish relationship, being replaced as Secretary of State for Northern Ireland, as we shall see, later in the year.

A tit-for-tat slaughter of Catholics for Teebane occurred on 5 February when five Catholics were murdered by a Loyalist who opened up on the customers of a bookie's shop on the Ormeau Road in Belfast. In Dublin, Albert Reynolds was elected leader of Fianna Fail on 6 February and shortly afterwards met John Major, with whom he had struck up a good personal relationship from their days as ministers of finance together in the EEC.

The IRA blew the heart out of the commercial centre of Lurgan, Co. Armagh, on 5 March with a 1,000lb bomb, and on the same day caused further damage to Belfast city centre with another explosion. With an election looming in England, the political parties of Northern Ireland agreed to meet at Stormont on 9 March.

This was the year which saw the most far-reaching commitment ever given by an American politician to Irish-Americans (see Chapter 12). Presidential candidate Bill Clinton committed himself if elected to reversing the ban on Gerry Adams, appointing a peace envoy and greatly stepping up the level of American involvement in the Northern Ireland situation. However, this commitment achieved relatively little publicity at the time.

Attention focused instead on a happening later in that month, on 10 April. The Conservatives won the general election and Gerry Adams became a casualty of tactical voting in West Belfast, where Loyalists deliberately voted against the Unionist candidate and for Joe Hendron of the SDLP in order to defeat the Sinn Fein president. The post-election reshuffle also cost Peter Brooke his services to Northern Ireland. He was replaced by Sir Patrick Mayhew.

The deadlocked talks began again in June, but by September it was obvious that they were not going to get anywhere, and at a meeting on 25 September John Major and Albert Reynolds agreed to set a time limit on the talks. Relying on their own relationship, they began a Dublin–London dialogue in the absence of the Unionists. Intransigence had helped to bring about the Unionists' own worst nightmare – the prospect of a deal between Dublin and London over the heads of the Belfast politicians. As we shall see in Chapter 12, the new approach was to yield significant dividends.

An outsider would have been forgiven for being sceptical of the prospects of any such progress taking place. On 21 August twenty-one-year-old Hugh McKibben achieved the melancholy distinction of becoming the 3,000th victim of the Troubles, a casualty of the internal feuding in the INLA (see Chapter 10). In addition, 113 people were killed in Britain, 110 in the Republic and ten in Europe.[10]

It was a period marked also by enormous bombings. Belfast was badly hit by two bombs in Bedford Street on 2 August. In September, the Northern Ireland Forensic

Science Laboratories were devastated by a 2,000lb IRA bomb which damaged 700 homes and injured several people. On 21 October, the main street of Bangor in Co. Down was blitzed, as was the heart of Coleraine on 13 November. And Belfast's central shopping area was again attacked on 1 December. The first member of the Royal Irish Rangers (into which the UDR had been subsumed) to be killed by the Provisionals was shot on 20 October. No matter what the uniform of the security forces, they were the enemy in any shape or guise.

The Protestant paramilitaries stepped up their campaign also, threatening the 'entire Republican' community in a statement on 6 November. By this they apparently meant not only Sinn Fein personnel, but members of the SDLP, of the Republic's political parties and of Nationalist sporting organisations such as the Gaelic Athletic Association. The new expertise which the Protestant paramilitaries had been demonstrating for some time in the targeting of PSF personnel had been starkly illustrated shortly beforehand. On 16 October a lone UVF gunman coolly walked into a student pub near Queen's University and shot dead a law student, Sheena Campbell, who had been a Provisonal Sinn Fein by-election candidate. The year would end with the UDA threatening (on 31 December) that it would step up its campaign 'to a ferocity never imagined'. In 1992 the Loyalists outkilled the Provisionals by 39 to 36. This was the first time such a thing had happened since the early seventies when the Provisionals started to become a tightly organised force. Moreover, 1993 would hold in store IRA operations such as the Warrington bombing of 20 March, which killed two little boys (thereby sparking off another major peace movement, Peace Initiative '93, on the lines of the 1976 Peace People), and the 24 April Bishopsgate bombing in London's financial district, which caused several hundred millions of pounds' worth of damage.

Nevertheless, the 'peace process era' was well under way, and despite many denials and accusations, the British Government was changing its stance. On 16 December, Sir Patrick Mayhew made a significant speech at Coleraine. In the course of it he said that troops could be taken off the streets, and Sinn Fein included in talks, if the violence ended. Paisley reacted sharply, saying that Mayhew had made 'a U-turn and is putting out Dublin propaganda. His whole speech, in tone and content, is weighted heavily in favour of republicanism.'[11]

Paisley's interpretation of Mayhew's words was overstated. But his political antennae had picked up a correct signal. As we shall see in Chapter 12, the British were engaged in covert contacts with Sinn Fein. But before reaching that more hopeful stage in our story we must now turn, in our next chapters, to a more detailed examination of the bloody wasteland that had first to be traversed.

NINE

THE GREENING OF THE IRA

What I understand by 'philosopher': a terrible explosive in the presence of which everything is in danger.

Nietzsche

THE STORY OF the IRA from the collapse of the Whitelaw talks is one of evolution from a rather hobbledehoy movement, fuelled by a schoolboy enthusiasm as much as anything else, and unlimited recruitment, into one of the most tightly focused, disciplined and ruthless guerrilla movements the world has seen. This is how the Provisionals' HQ in Derry's Bogside no-go area appeared to me in 1972 before Operation Motorman shut it down:

> . . . It was more like a youth hostel than a terrorist headquarters. The place was filled with young boys and girls, and Martin McGuinness, the blond, six-foot leader of the IRA in the city, at the time was himself only twenty-one. There was laughter and chat in the headquarters as though those who came and went were going on mountaineering excursions instead of setting out to kill someone or blow up something. The house was full of boxes of clothes either for use in disguise or to be passed out to needy people in the area, while other cartons contained fuses, ammunition, and some weapons. In the kitchen chattering girls sat around a fire and made tea for anyone who wanted it . . .
>
> McGuinness wore a scapular that his mother had given him around his neck and went regularly to Mass: 'It really puts it up to the priest if he has been giving out about you from the pulpit to see you going up there to Communion.'[1]

The often horrible catalogue of events listed in the previous chapter serves to demonstrate both the other face of the 'youth hostel' activities, and how, from the 'rape of the Falls' to the declaration of the 1994 ceasefire, the IRA continued to be the motor force of the Northern Ireland situation. The Provisionals were able to maintain this strength of continuity for two principal reasons: one, the IRA's own reorganisation; the other, the manner in which policies directed against the movement created not a weakening effect, but a tremendous accession of strength.

The first factor, the IRA's reorganisation, became public knowledge on 2 December 1977 when its then chief of staff, Seamus Twomey, was captured and documents found on him revealed what the IRA had in mind.[2] Although few people realised it, either at the time or subsequently, the IRA's blueprint was a quite extraordinary example of how history repeats itself. One of the most significant things that Michael Collins did in the post-1916 reorganisation of the Volunteers, who subsequently became the IRA, was to restructure the existing set-up while at the same time attempting to present a philosophy to the recruits. In the first two issues of the Volunteer paper, *An tOglach*, he wrote:

> . . . we have to place before ourselves a definite aim and then make arrangements to achieve it. Let us accept the words of a great Prussian – adapted by Ruskin – 'I desire for my own country to secure that her soldiers should be her tutors and the captains of her armies – captains also of her mind.'

Collins stated that what he had in mind called for a

> complete organisation for the Company, for the Battalion and for the Brigade. It ensures the recognition by Headquarters of smaller units than the Company in special districts . . . lays down the manner of electing officers . . . discipline and courts martial . . . Forget the Company of the regular army. We are not establishing or attempting to establish a regular force on the lines of . . . standing armies. If we undertake any such thing we shall fall.[3]

It is unlikely that the originators of the scheme unearthed by Twomey's capture studied Collins closely. They were northerners, and at that stage writing about him still tended to promote the view promulgated by those who supported de Valera, that he had sold out the north by agreeing to partition.[4] Obviously, like Collins, who was influenced in his time by the South African farmers' guerrilla tactics against the British, they took note of what lessons there were to be learned from contemporary guerrilla movements. But like Collins there was something almost genetic in the young northerners' approach to warfare. As in his case, they were responding instinctively to the duress of the circumstances.

Their formula combined the Collins approach of both a new type of military organisation, in which they too would 'Forget the Company', and the advocacy of a new philosophy. The Provisionals also intended to become 'captains of the mind'. Militarily, their response to the pressures being exerted on the movement was the creation of a cell system. Speaking on the BBC's *Panorama* programme[5] one of Britain's foremost counterinsurgency experts, General James Glover, who as we shall see shortly knows more than most of his countrymen about the IRA, said that the cells were 'based on the communist system'. In fact the cell system pre-dates the devotees of Marxist-Leninist doctrine. It was in reality a reversion to the methods favoured by Continental secret societies in the 1840s. Irish refugees from the failed Young Ireland upheaval of 1848 came into contact with these groupings during their exile in Paris. The original Irish Republican Brotherhood, or Fenian movement, founded (by a Protestant, James Stephens) on St Patrick's Day 1858, modelled itself on these conspiratorial exemplars. In time, Michael Collins would become president of the IRB.

The cells advocated by the Provisionals over a hundred years after the formation of the IRB, and fifty years after Collins' death, also replaced, as Collins had suggested, the old brigade and battalion structures. The names of those generally credited with furthering the new departures are Gerry Adams, Ivor Bell, Brendan Hughes and Martin McGuinness. Outside the ranks of these younger men, who gained an ascendancy in the Republican world from the seventies onwards, there were some older figures who helped to refine some of their other ideas. These bore fruit in the *Green Book*, which we will shortly discuss. The Republican community operates very much as a clan. Men and women each have their roles. The elders are consulted when occasion warrants. Since the middle seventies the Adams-McGuinness faction have encouraged incessant discussion. Ideas and new policies are dissected and teased out to the nth degree before being accepted or rejected. Adams in particular is mentioned as being keen to encourage internal debate, as a means of strengthening both understanding and the resolution to carry through whatever course is finally decided upon. In the Republican University of Long Kesh, he and his comrades demonstrated that, whatever their formal education, they fully understood the significance of the fact that the word education stems from the Latin *educare*, meaning to draw out. They ended the decade very different people from the young men who had been flown to Cheyne Walk to meet William Whitelaw. They had been hammered out on the anvil of circumstances.

Put simply, a cell, or active service unit (ASU), generally, but not inevitably, consisted of four people, of whom only one, the leader, was in contact with higher authority. Thus, operating on the need-to-know principle, security leaks were cut down and effectiveness was increased. The 'Staff Report' found on Twomey stated:

> The three day and seven day detention orders are breaking volunteers and it is the Republican Army's fault for not indoctrinating volunteers with a psychological strength to resist interrogation. Coupled with this factor which is contributing to our defeat, we are burdened with an inefficient infrastructure of commands, brigades, battalions and companies.
>
> This old system with which the Brits and Branch are familiar has to be changed. We recommend reorganisation and remotivation, the building of a new Irish Republican Army. We emphasise a return to secrecy and strict discipline. Army men must be in total command of all sections of the movement . . . anti-interrogation lectures must be given in conjunction with indoctrination lectures. The ideal outcome should be that no volunteer should be charged unless caught redhanded . . . we must gear ourselves towards Long-term Armed Struggle based on putting unknown men and new recruits into a new structure. This new structure shall be a cell system.
>
> Ideally a cell should consist of four people. Rural areas should be treated as separate cases to that of city and town brigade/command areas. For this reason our proposals will affect mainly city and town areas where the majority of our operations are carried out and where the biggest proportion of our support lies anyway . . . From now on all new recruits are to be passed into a cell structure.

Interestingly, the new IRA blueprint also envisaged a greater role for women. It stated: 'Women and girls have greater roles to play as military activists and as leaders in sections of civil administration, in propaganda and publicity.' Later, when the movement developed a political wing, women were given an enhanced status. There was positive discrimination on a gender basis, and women held important positions in the party's ruling body, the Ard Comhairle. When the declaration of the 1994 ceasefire ultimately led to Sinn Fein taking part in talks at Stormont Castle, it was noticeable that the negotiating teams always included one or more woman.

The document made the significant point that a political wing must be developed:

> Sinn Fein should come under Army organisers at all levels. Sinn Fein should employ fulltime organisers in big Republican areas. Sinn Fein should be radicalised (under Army direction) and should agitate around social and economic issues which attack the welfare of the people. Sinn Fein should be directed to infiltrate other organisations to win support for and sympathy to the Movement. Sinn Fein should be re-educated and have a big role to play in publicity and propaganda departments.

That paragraph says all that is required by way of answer to the frequently asked question, what is the relationship of Sinn Fein to the IRA?

Along with this mechanical change in operation, the IRA also developed a philosophical text: the *Green Book*, which set forth the history, aims and methodology of the movement for the benefit of new recruits. Like the cell system, its detail was worked out in the prisons. The 'Sandhurst of Terror', as Long Kesh became known in British circles, was a not inappropriate sobriquet.

The *Green Book* set out to give the recruit a firm ideological grounding. In the first lecture contained in the work a recruit learned that:

> Commitment to the Republican Movement is the firm belief that its struggle both militarily and politically is morally justified. That war is morally justified and that the Army is the direct representative of the 1918 Dail Eireann Parliament, and that as such they are the legal and lawful government of the Irish Republic, which has the moral right to pass laws for, and to claim jurisdiction over the territory, airspace, mineral resources, means of production, distribution and exchange and all of its people regardless of creed and loyalty.

Thus, a recruit is informed:

> All volunteers are and must feel morally justified in carrying out the dictates of the legal government, they as the Army are the legal and lawful Army of the Irish Republic which has been forced underground by overwhelming force. The Army as an organisation claims and expects your total allegiance without reservation. It enters into every aspect of your life. It invades the privacy of your home life, it fragments your family and friends. In other words claims your total allegiance. All potential volunteers must realise that the threat of capture and of long jail sentences are a very real danger and a shadow which hangs over every volunteer. Many in the past joined the Army out of romantic notions, or sheer adventure, but when captured and jailed they had afterthoughts about their allegiance to the Army. They realised at too late a stage that they had no real interest in being volunteers. This caused splits and dissension inside prison and divided families and neighbours outside.

The recruit is enjoined clearly that:

> Before any potential volunteer decides to join the Irish Republican Army he should understand fully and clearly the issues involved. He should not join the Army because of emotionalism, sensationalism or adventurism. He should examine fully his own motives, knowing the dangers involved, and knowing that he will find no romance within the Movement. Again he should examine his political motives bearing in mind that the Army are intent on creating a socialist republic.

And, most starkly of all, the recruit is told:

> Volunteers are expected to wage a military war of liberation against a numerically superior force. This involves the use of arms and explosives. Firstly the use of arms. When volunteers are trained in the use of arms, they must fully understand that guns are dangerous, and their main purpose is to take human life, in other words to kill people and volunteers are trained to kill people. It is not an easy thing to take up a gun and go out to kill some person without strong convictions or justification . . . convictions which are strong enough to give him [the volunteer] the confidence to kill someone without hesitation and without regret. The same can be said about a bombing campaign. Again all people wishing to join the Army must fully realise that when life is being taken, that very well could mean their own. If you go out to shoot soldiers or police you must fully realise that they can shoot you.
>
> Life in an underground army is extremely harsh and hard, cruel and disillusioning at times. So before any person decides to join the Army he should think seriously about the whole thing.

By way of making a recruit think 'seriously' before joining the IRA, a section on interrogation was included in the *Green Book*. This warned would-be recruits that on arrest they could expect physical torture, psychological torture and humiliation, all aimed at breaking down their resistance and getting confessions or information from them.

The volunteers were warned that from the moment of arrest, their natural feelings of anxiety and failure at having allowed themselves to be caught would be exploited and that physical torture 'in the form of beatings, kickings, punching and twisting of limbs . . . even burning from cigarette ends are all part of what one may expect'. The psychological torture would include as a matter of course threats to 'his family, his friends and himself e.g. threats of assassination and threats to castrate him'.

Under 'humiliation' the volunteers were warned to expect to be stripped of their clothes and to hear remarks passed about their sexual organs. Volunteers were warned to expect periods of interrogation lasting for two hours at a time, sometimes ending with them being confronted by a real or faked confession from some associate. They were told that a normal ploy at this stage, if the volunteer refused to comply, was for interrogators to leave the cells, promising to be back shortly to break every bone in the recruit's body: 'This process can continue for seven days without a break, the minimum of sleep is allowed and if they deem it necessary no sleep would be allowed. Lack of sleep causes the prisoners to become confused.'

One of the *Green Book*'s key passages is:

> Before we go on the offensive politically or militarily we take the greatest defensive precautions possible to ensure success, e.g. we do not advocate a United Ireland without being able to justify our right to such a state as opposed to partition; we do not employ revolutionary violence as our means without being able to illustrate that we have no recourse to any other means . . . we do not mount an operation without first having ensured that we have taken the necessary defensive precautions of accurate intelligence, security, that weapons are in proper working order with proper ammunition and that the volunteers

know how to handle interrogations in the event of their capture etc. . . . and of course that the operation itself enhances rather than alienates our supporters.[6]

The points about resisting interrogation and alienating support merit comment. Taking the last first: the IRA on occasion have enlarged their list of 'legitimate targets' at will and sometimes with disastrous effects. They have indulged in kidnappings to raise funds; forced informers to drive proxy bombs to targets, where the bombs blew up killing both bomber and victims; shot contractors who carried out work on barracks for 'helping the enemy war machine'; and enforced order in ghetto districts by dropping concrete blocks on the limbs of alleged criminals. All this, of course, in addition to judges, policemen, soldiers, members of the UDR, innocent victims caught in crossfire, and so on. Even the IRA would not claim that most of these actions 'enhanced' anything. The fact that the movement has survived these actions of its own, rather than the onslaughts of its enemy, probably says more for the strength of its support than any claim that has ever appeared in *An Phoblacht*.

In attempting to assess how well the Provisionals' preparations enabled IRA members to withstand interrogation and pursue these activities, including awful, bloody blunders like Enniskillen and the overall attrition of a guerrilla's life, one could simply point to the sheer continuity of the movement. But a more enlightening assessment comes from a British general charged with confronting the IRA, General J. M. Glover, an intelligence expert. At a time when the cell system and *Green Book* techniques were only just beginning to make their effects felt, Glover drew up a paper on the likely future of the IRA: *Northern Ireland: Future Terrorist Trends*. It was a top-secret document, completed on 2 November 1978, reviewing the IRA's progress to that date and its likely activities to the end of 1983. It was captured in the mail by the Provisionals and, after study in IRA intelligence, published in the *Republican News*, the IRA newspaper.[7] Not surprisingly, after being at the receiving end of this practical display of the IRA's 'future trends', General Glover, Commander of Land Forces in Northern Ireland, reorganised British Army intelligence operations in the province. It was he who, during 1980, set up one of the most secret of the army's undercover operations, the Force Research Unit or FRU (see Chapter 10), which handles what are known in intelligence jargon as 'human sources' or sometimes, depending on their worth, 'national assets'. In other words, spies and informers.

Glover said frankly: 'Even if the present system of government is maintained the current muted support for the forces of law and order will remain delicately balanced and susceptible to any controversial government decision or security force action.' The accuracy of this assessment can be judged from both the hunger strike issue, described below, and any one of a number of incidents cited in Chapter 9. Glover made a number of other highly charged and courageous assessments in his paper. For example, though he avoided stating flatly that the Provos would continue to exist in the vacuum created by London's policies, or lack of them, he made his point by saying: 'The Provisionals' campaign of violence is likely to continue while the British remain in Northern Ireland . . . We see little prospect of political development of a kind which would seriously undermine the Provisionals' position.'

Glover came in for considerable criticism, both for his judgement and, in particular, for the following:

> Our evidence of the calibre of rank and file terrorists does not support the view that they are merely mindless hooligans drawn from the unemployed and unemployable. PIRA now trains and uses members with some care. The active service units (ASUs) are for the most part manned by terrorists tempered by up to 10 years of operational experience.

The General was correct in the foregoing assessment and in a number of others, particularly that dealing with the IRA's ability to withstand being, as he put it, 'hard hit by security force attrition':

> Trend and calibre: The mature terrorists, including for instance the leading bomb makers, are usually sufficiently cunning to avoid arrest. They are continually learning from their mistakes and developing their expertise. We can therefore expect to see increased professionalism and a greater exploitation of modern technology for terrorist purposes. PIRA's organisationn is now such that a small number of activists can maintain a disproportionate level of violence . . . there is a substantial pool of young Fianna aspirants, nurtured in a climate of violence, eagerly seeking promotion to full gun carrying terrorist status and there is a steady release from the prisons of embittered and dedicated terrorists. Thus, though PIRA may be hard hit by security force attrition from time to time, they will probably continue to have the manpower they need to maintain violence during the next five years.
>
> Leadership: PIRA is essentially a working class organisation based in the ghetto areas of the cities and in the poorer rural areas. Thus if members of the middleclass and graduates become more deeply involved they have to forfeit their lifestyle. Many are also deterred by the Provisionals' muddled political thinking. Nevertheless there is a strata of intelligent, astute and experienced terrorists who provide the backbone of the organisation. Although there are only a few of these high grade terrorists, there is always the possibility that a new charismatic leader may emerge who would transform PIRA again.
>
> Technical expertise: PIRA has an adequate supply of members who are skilled in the production of explosive devices. They have the tools and equipment and have the use of small workshops and laboratories.

Another of Glover's assessments which proved accurate was:

> Although the Provisionals have lost much of the spontaneous backing they enjoyed early in the campaign, there is no sign of any equivalent upsurge in support for the security forces. There are still areas within the province, both rural and urban, where the terrorists can base themselves with little risk of betrayal and can count on active support in emergencies. The fear of a possible return to Protestant rule and oppression will underpin this kind of support for the Provisionals for many years to come. Loyalist action could quickly awaken it to a much more volatile level.

The most famous of the 'areas within the province' referred to by Glover was Crossmaglen in South Armagh. This self-contained market town in the shadow of Sliabh Gullion Mountain had been a Catholic and Gaelic stronghold for centuries.

In earlier periods of hostilities against the English South Armagh had acquired a well-deserved reputation for ferocious resistance to the Crown. This was revived by the Fourth Northern Division of the IRA in the pre-partition war. However, a U-shaped loop from a cartographer's pen enclosed it within the Six Counties' territory as the area was being partitioned. It was a decision the British Army and the RUC must have cursed a thousand times. Prior to the troubles, the district, which is crisscrossed by tiny roads fringed with high ditches, was known only as a smuggler's paradise. The terrain and its proximity to the border made it a classic example of what Lord Gowrie, then Minister of State at the Northern Ireland Office, had in mind when he said: 'The Border is an economic nonsense, anyone with initiative can laugh all the way to the bank.'[8]

The laughing stopped when the army and the RUC moved in and started roughing up the inhabitants. This was partly because 'Cross', as it is known, had a reputation for being a Nationalist stronghold, which led the RUC Special Branch to make the same sort of assumptions that had led to the out-of-date internment lists being prepared. Partly also because it was suspected that the smuggling expertise might be devoted to 'the cause'. It was, but not because the people of Cross had originally intended it that way. Initially the locals wanted to keep clear of the troubles because it was feared the consequences would bring police attention to their smuggling trade. However, perceptions were altered by the internment era with its rough-handed searches, planting of weapons in houses, where they could be 'discovered' in subsequent visits, and abrasive encounters at checkpoints.

The turning point came when a Crossmaglen resident was shot by the army on the Falls Road because his car backfired. His companion was badly beaten up. From then on, Crossmaglen became a no-man's-land to the security forces. The army post in the town could only be serviced by helicopter. One of the IRA's folk heroes is Michael McVerry, who was killed in a raid on Keady RUC barracks in 1973. He was the first to exploit the terrain by staging ambushes, being chased by army vehicles, guns blazing like something out of a film, until his knowledge of the district enabled him to shake off his pursuers. In between inveighing against their tormentors in 'bandit country', as the security forces' spin doctors christened South Armagh, Unionist apologists changed the argument sometimes to say that it was the security provided by the Republic which made South Armagh so dangerous.

South Armagh is the IRA's safe haven. It is provided by the fathers and mothers, sons and brothers, uncles and aunts of the volunteers. So deep is the clan tradition that even the writ of the IRA leadership sometimes has to contend with the authority of the local chieftains. The phrase 'Tell Them Nothing' hangs invisible and omnipresent over the fields of South Armagh.

Glover's report was attacked in decision-taking circles in both Dublin and London; in London because of the unwelcome admission that the Provos were not mindless terrorists, mindless criminals, at a time when the entire thrust of British policy (as we shall see in Chapter 9) was directed towards criminalising the IRA in the public mind. Glover, concerned merely with the facts of the situation, not the politics, in fact included a balance sheet in his report to indicate the scale of IRA finances. This gave completely the opposite impression: IRA volunteers were risking their lives for 'pay' of only £20 a week.

Glover's estimate of the Provisional IRA's annual income and expenditure probably underestimated the movement's income from bank robberies and donations, particularly from Irish-American sympathisers. For example, in the year he attempted the exercise (1978), the Provisionals had already netted £1m by mid-June through an application of their particular philosophy of banking – based on withdrawals only. The General defined the Provisionals' other main illegal source of income as 'protection payments from shops and businesses and fraud involving dole money and "lost" pension books'. He reckoned this brought in about £250,000, but thought the figure likely to decline 'in the face of RUC countermeasures'. He reckoned that 'incompetence and dishonesty' had been the hallmarks of the Provisionals' business activities, with the possible exception of the Black Taxis, whose operations he thought the police would also inhibit. At the time of writing, seventeen years later, the Black Taxis still offer the cheapest and most efficient taxi service in Belfast.

However, from my own knowledge I can say that the General was accurate in his assessment of what the IRA was paying its members as of June 1978 – £20 a week. He said:

> We estimate that some 250 people would draw this and perhaps 60 would get £40 per week ... Apart from arms expenditure the Provisionals have to bear the cost of their prison welfare work including payment to prisoners' dependants, travel and transport costs and propaganda expenses, especially the Republican newspapers whose sale does not cover their cost.

The balance sheet guesstimate was as follows:

Theft in Ireland	£550,000
Racketeering	£250,000
Overseas Contributions	£120,000
Green Cross (Prisoners welfare fund) UK & Eire	£30,000
Total	£950,000

Expenditure, under all the headings covered above, pay, prisoners, etc. – was reckoned to be £780,000, leaving a balance of £170,000 for arms purchases. All these figures would have to be revised upward, in line both with inflation and with the growth in efficiency of IRA fund-raising in the US and amongst its supporters in Ireland by way of socials, raffles, dances, bingo, even poitin-making! The constant black propaganda about drug-trafficking may be discounted. But, unless the peace process takes deep root, I would certainly not advise any aspirant builder to open up in west, or for that matter east, Belfast. Between material going missing, and collectors being only too omnipresent, bankruptcy for all but government contracts was, and to a degree still is, a constant hazard. However, this said, it has to be pointed out that the IRA in Collins' time also partly financed itself by a system of levies, which, despite some abuses, were generally paid willingly enough. The same sort of system existed in the Glover period. While there was some extortion, most of the contributions to the IRA were voluntary. What Glover's figures do indicate is that the Provisionals have been remarkably successful in running a cut-price revolution, for all the talk of godfathers and racketeering. The House of Commons was informed on 28 April 1994 by Michael Ancram, the Minister for Political Affairs and Education, that the cost to the British taxpayer of running the Six Counties was three billion, eight hundred million pounds, and this did not include the cost of the army.

Along with the foregoing there was of course the equally uncomfortable acknowledgement by Glover that the IRA could not be militarily defeated. Nor did either the RUC or the army welcome the publication of the fact that there were areas in the Six Counties wherein the Provisionals could operate with relative impunity. The Republic for its part was somewhat underwhelmed by the fact of Glover's including in his report the statement that the 'south provides a safe mounting post for cross-border operations and safe training areas'.

Having said that the Republic provided a safe transit area for the IRA's guns and ammunition, explosives and operations of all sorts, Glover went on to claim that 'terrorists can live there without fear of extradition for crimes committed in the North. In short the Republic provides many of the facilities of a classic safe haven so essential to any successful terrorist movement. And it will probably continue to do so for the foreseeable future.'

Ironically as Glover was writing this in 1978, the IRA were moving towards becoming a solidly northern-based organisation, cutting away much of the southern apparatus to which Glover and his colleagues mistakenly attached such importance. The British military appreciation of the IRA's origins and strengths was flawed in other respects too. But it is valuable for an understanding of how, through the period under review, there was frequent tension between Dublin and London over extradition. London either could not or would not accept Dublin's difficulties in this regard, and regarded objections over issues such as inaccurately prepared warrants as hair-splitting. When the law got in the way the British, as we shall see, simply changed the law.

The Glover Report states flatly that:

Republican sentiment and the IRA tradition emanates from the South. Although the Fianna Fail government are resolutely opposed to the use of force, its long term aims are, as Mr Lynch himself admits, similar to those of the Provisionals. Any successor to Lynch in the ruling party will probably follow at least as Republican a line of policy. Fine Gael though traditionally less Republican is also now committed to a roughly similar line. We have no reason to suspect that PIRA obtains active support from government sources or that it will do so in the future, but the judiciary has often been lenient and the Gardai, though co-operating with the RUC more than in the past, is still rather less than wholehearted in its pursuit of terrorists ... We believe that the Republic will continue to act as a haven for terrorists.

One could probably argue that the Glover thesis proceeds from the fact that the

1916 rebellion was staged in Dublin not Belfast, but apart from the fact that it overlooks the broader sweep of Irish history, it is and was centrally deficient in the human factor. The British Army simply did not, and do not, understand the psychology of the IRA. The military men persisted in attempting to apply to Ireland the lessons of their colonial experience in other countries. What they should have done was to apply to the Irish situation the lessons learned in Ireland over the centuries. A sentence in the Glover Report dealing with the effects of growing up under unionism in an area like Ballymurphy, where the basin of vinegar was always to hand to ward off the worst effects of CS gas, would have been more enlightening for its insight into the sources of recruitment to, and the sustainment of, the IRA campaign than the animadversions on the Irish judicial system.

In fact the IRA, whose principal thinker at this period, far from looking on the south with favour, once told me that he regarded 'a garda as a British soldier in another uniform', had moved towards their own recognition of the realities of the northern struggle, i.e. that it *was* a northern struggle, based in Northern Ireland, conducted by northerners. For the IRA was reorganised in the autumn and winter of 1976, with the Northern Command holding its first meeting in the November, almost two years to the day before Glover completed his report.

The Northern Command soon had an impact on IRA operations. In addition to the cell system, ASUs were set up which operated partly on a target of opportunity basis, and partly on predetermined planning, striking across the entire rural area of the Six Counties. Martin McGuinness first took over the Northern Command and subsequently, on Seamus Twomey's arrest, became chief of staff, being succeeded in 1979 by Gerry Adams.

The younger McGuinness was frequently referred to as 'The Cool Clean Hero'. Red-haired, slim and tall, wearing a tweed jacket, an Aran sweater and a friendly smile, he caught the imagination of the younger Derry Nationalists. A devout Catholic, I have known him to be denounced from the pulpit and applauded by the congregation. His principal relaxations are his family and fishing. He is also an extremely tough, hard-minded military and political thinker. The northern security forces never succeeded in recapturing him following his release after a short sentence from the Curragh. During the period of his leadership the Provisionals managed to bomb, and rebomb, economic targets in Derry without causing any loss of civilian life, though there were numerous casualties amongst the security forces. It was this selectivity that ensured that the women of Derry never marched on the Provisionals as they had done with the Officials, to demand that they call off their campaign.

Other younger stars in the Republican firmament who were moving upward at this period included Joe Austin, Jim Gibney, Mitchell McLaughlin, Tom Hartley, and Danny Morrison, who specialised in publicity, becoming editor of the *Republican News* and transforming it into an effective, well-laid-out, hard-hitting propaganda organ. The *Republican News* soon had more influence on Republicans than the Dublin-based *An Phoblacht*, which was more responsive to the O'Bradaigh–O'Conaill faction. One of the *Republican News*'s most popular features was a column written from Long Kesh by 'Brownie', Gerry Adams.

These changes were furthered by two developments which were initiated from outside the ranks of the Provisionals and which, for a time, appeared to spell disaster for the movement. The developments, which will be described shortly, may be summarised as the truce route and the H Block route. These intertwined, culminating in the hunger strikes of the 1980–1 period. The strikes elevated Sinn Fein to a plane of influence which led to the party becoming a major player – at times, in fact, the most significant one – in the Anglo-Irish drama.

The first of the two processes, the truce route, may be said to have begun at Feakle, Co. Clare, on 10 December 1974. A courageous group of Protestant clergymen braved the wrath of not only Paisley and his ilk, but even moderate members of their congregations, to meet a Provisional delegation. My information is that while the motives of the clergymen were of the highest, those of the British were somewhat lower. There would appear to have been an effort to use the churchmen to inveigle the Provisionals into a damaging situation. I have been informed that the churchmen were encouraged in their Feakle approach by the Northern Ireland Office, under the tutelage of Sir Frank Cooper. Cooper, a mandarin's mandarin, was effectively the head of the Northern Ireland civil service. He was regarded by many people as the man who actually ran Northern Ireland while Merlyn Rees was there.

The clergy were Dr Arthur Butler, the Church of Ireland Bishop of Conor; Dr Jack Weir, the clerk of the Presbyterian Assembly; Revd Ralph Baxter, Secretary, and Revd William Arlow, Assistant Secretary to the Irish Council of Churches; Revd Eric Gallagher, former president of the Methodist Church in Ireland; Dr Harry Morton, Secretary of the British Council of Churches; Right Revd Arthur MacArthur, Moderator of the United Reform Church in England; and Stanley Worrall, a former headmaster of Methodist College, Belfast. The Provisionals were Ruairi O'Bradaigh, Daithi O'Conaill, Maire Drumm, Seamus Twomey, Kevin Mallon and Seamus Loughran.

The clergymen wanted to talk peace. To their surprise and gratification they found that the Provisionals apparently wanted to do so also. Dr Butler later said: 'We were all most impressed with their attitude, with their fair-mindedness, and we were so pleased to find that they were talking seriously and deeply and with great conviction and had listened very carefully to what we had to say.'[9] However, the Dublin Government was not at all pleased. There had been virtually no contact between London and Dublin since the collapse of the power-sharing executive earlier in the year. Dublin, set in a rigid law-and-order mode, regarded talking to the Provisionals as something akin to deliberately spreading a life-threatening infection. Even before the Sunningdale experiment collapsed, members of the Government had reacted with fury to an earlier British overture to the Provos.

Feakle was in fact the fourth attempt at peace talks which the Provisionals had taken part in. That involving Whitelaw we have already discussed. The first of the other three was the unveiling of the Eire Nua (New Ireland) proposals on 5 September 1971. In return for British acceptance of this idea, and one or two other small matters such as ending internment, abolishing Stormont and leaving the country, the Provisionals were prepared to declare an immediate halt to violence.

Of course the Eire Nua concept of setting up a group of regional parliaments in each of the four provinces would have meant a diminution not only of Belfast's power, but also of Dublin's. This fact, which the Provisionals never had to confront because London ignored their plan anyhow, would probably have killed the initiative even without Loyalist opposition.

The second peace initiative of the decade involved Harold Wilson. Through the intermediacy of the Dublin Labour politician John O'Connell, he met a group of Provisional leaders at O'Connell's house on 13 March 1972, while on a visit to Dublin ostensibly to make governmental contacts and appear on a TV programme.

To prepare the atmosphere the IRA had declared a seventy-two-hour ceasefire. This, in Sean MacStiofain's words, was to 'demonstrate that the IRA was under effective control and discipline'.[10] Socially they were under more control also than Wilson had bargained for. He apparently had expected them to he hard-drinking, hard-swearing toughs. He accordingly peppered his language with oaths and was considerably taken aback to find that few of his hearers drank and none of them swore. Quite politely they informed him of their demands, which included a withdrawal of British troops to barracks (in preparation for ultimate withdrawal), the abolition of Stormont, and a declaration by Britain that she had no right to interfere in Irish affairs. Not surprisingly, Merlyn Rees, whom Wilson had brought along in his capacity as Northern Ireland spokesman, subsequently wrote in his memoirs: 'There was no sign of compromise.'[11]

There was none on the part of Dublin either. As Wilson was meeting the Provos, Stan Orme was presiding over a British Embassy reception for Irish Labour Party figures. At the conclusion of his meeting Wilson rang Orme to inform him of what he had been doing. The thunderstruck Orme thought it best to inform his guests before the media did. They were aghast. Orme has said that: 'Conor Cruise O'Brien did his nut and they all walked out.'[12] Now, at Feakle in 1974, the fourth peace overture of the period, O'Brien was a cabinet minister. Not surprisingly, the meeting was broken up by a tip-off that the Irish Special Branch were on their way.

However, Feakle afforded the churchmen the opportunity of giving the IRA a policy document.[13] It was aimed at eliciting a ceasefire from the Provisionals based on the acceptance of the following five points which had been cleared with the British Goverment:

1. The Government stated it had no political or territorial interests in Ireland beyond its obligations to the Northern Ireland citizens.
2. The Government's prime concern was the achievement of peace and the promotion of such understanding between the various sections of Northern Ireland as would guarantee to all its people a full participation in the life of the community, whatever be the relationship of Northern Ireland to the EEC, United Kingdom or the Republic.
3. Contingent on the maintenance of a declared ceasefire and effective policing, the Government would relieve the army as quickly as possible of its internal duties.
4. Until agreement about the future government of Northern Ireland had been

freely negotiated and guaranteed, armed forces would be retained in Northern Ireland.

5. The Government recognised the right of all those who had political aims to pursue them through the democratic process.

The IRA's reply to these points was as follows:

1. Until the Government clearly stated that it had no claim to sovereignty in any part of Ireland, the statement was meaningless. 'We accept that economic commitments must be honoured.'

2. 'A noble wish with which we concur but we believe can only be realised in the full community of the people of Ireland.'

3. The IRA had no difficulty in maintaining community peace, if a bilateral truce were agreed between the army and the IRA. On this point it stated that discussions with Loyalist groups in maintaining the peace would be welcomed.

4. The IRA said that if a declaration of intention to withdraw were made, the IRA would accept that there should be a limited army presence during the negotiation period pending an agreed settlement.

5. The IRA stated that it 'is meaningless to talk of democratic processes while . . . 2,000 political prisoners are in jail'.

The jail question was one which was shortly to burst on to the public consciousness in particularly shattering fashion. At the time, in the flurry of controversy occasioned by the mere fact of the churchmen's talking to the IRA, public attention was diverted to the issue of the rights and wrongs of having such discourse. However, on 20 December, the IRA declared that a temporary ceasefire would hold from 22 December until January 1975. This public declaration fuelled speculation that a British declaration of intent to withdraw from Northern Ireland was imminent. Merlyn Rees has stated, in a letter to the London *Times* in July 1983, that the proposal was considered by the Cabinet but that there was no agreement on it. But, despite the obvious discrepancies between the churchmen's document and that of the Provisionals, there was sufficient common ground for the truce to be extended on 2 January (to the 17th) as a result of talks between the Provisionals and NIO civil servants.

On 17 January the ceasefire apparently ended. Ten days later there were four bomb explosions in London and one in Manchester which injured nineteen people. However, the talks got back on the rails and later Ruairi O'Bradaigh would write (in the *Irish Times* of 30 April 1992):

Resulting from Feakle a unilateral truce by the Irish Republican Army was declared and observed on December 22nd 1974 until January 16th 1975. Following the expiration of this and renewed army activity by both British forces and the IRA, talks were entered into – at the request of the British – for three weeks and the outcome was a bilateral truce on written terms on February 10th with monitoring mechanisms in place.

The 'written terms' to which O'Bradaigh referred consisted of the following:

1. The release of a hundred detainees within two weeks.
2. The phasing-out of internment within a specific period.
3. The effective withdrawal of the army to barracks, meaning 3,000 to 4,000 troops returning to Britain within six months.
4. An end to the system of arrests and screening and large-scale searches in Catholic areas.
5. The establishment of incident centres manned by Sinn Fein members and connected with an incident room at Stormont to monitor the ceasefire.
6. Provision for army-to-army discussions at local level.
7. The ending of military checkpoints and roadblocks at the edge of Catholic areas.
8. Immunity from arrest for specific persons.
9. Firearms licences for specific persons.
10. No immediate attempts to introduce the RUC and UDR into Catholic areas.
11. A form of ceasefire agreement to be drawn up by the British.
12. Further talks to take place between IRA leaders and senior British representatives.[14]

While there is little doubt that the IRA leaders of the period (O'Bradaigh, O'Conaill, etc.) believed these terms to be genuine, there is considerable reason to doubt whether or not the British were ever sincere about delivering. Possibly MI6 favoured a political solution, but certainly MI5 and the army did not. However, the publication of the foregoing touched off an angry debate in Dublin and Belfast. Dublin was horrified at the prospect of negotiation taking place with the Provisionals, and Loyalist paramilitaries stepped up the assassination campaign against Catholics. The moderate SDLP party was dismayed to find that its Sinn Fein rivals had been given power bases, the incident centres, from which to influence local opinion.

The so-called incident centres did rapidly become advice centres and sources of political propaganda for Sinn Fein. The security forces also adopted a low profile in Catholic areas and a blind eye was turned when leading Provisionals were sighted. But this last provision was certainly not observed by the Dublin authorities, who made a particular point of hunting down Daithi O'Conaill. He was captured and jailed in July of 1975.

Ruairi O'Bradaigh gave three reasons for the failure of the truce (*Irish Times*, 30 April 1992). These were the increase in the activities of the Loyalist death squads; the fact that Dublin indicated to London that a British withdrawal must not be contemplated; and the capture of O'Conaill. All these reasons are valid in themselves. The Dublin Government was increasingly suspicious of London's intentions. Dublin moreover was deeply disturbed by the kidnapping of a Dutch industrialist by what were suspected to be Republican elements. The industrialist, Dr Tiede Herrema, was eventually released unharmed after a seventeen-day siege at a house at Monasterevin, Co. Kildare, on 6 November 1975. And the Loyalist death squads did claim an unprecedented toll. The 'truce' was in reality one of the most bloodstained periods in the history of the troubles. Two hundred and forty-seven people were killed in 1975 alone. On 22 September 1975, the IRA devastated towns all across the Six Counties with a series of bomb blasts. The UVF took a hand in the game on 2 October by killing twelve innocent Catholics. On top of that there was a renewal of vicious feuding between the Provisional IRA and the Officials. Hostilities also broke out between the two major Loyalist paramilitary groupings, the UDA and the UVF. (The violence and feuding will be discussed in more detail in Chapter 10.) The sectarian killing reached its nadir in January 1976 when after five Catholics were murdered on the 4th, the IRA was involved the following day in the slaughter of twelve Protestants. The 'truce' had been effectively over for months, but the incident centre experiment could be said to have been officially disowned on 18 March 1976, when the army closed the Falls Road centre.

All these things played a part in the revolt of the younger Republicans who took over from O'Bradaigh and O'Conaill. Adams in particular could see clearly that, apart from the lack of military, moral or political justification, the course of events was heading towards disaster. Special Category status was clearly under threat and the atrocities of the period were giving the British sufficient propaganda to justify its removal. On top of all the incidents which have been and will be described, the IRA degenerated into pub bombings at this stage. In response to the Miami Showband atrocity, the IRA staged one of their own the following month. A bomb planted in the Bayardo bar on the Shankill Road killed five Protestants.

But, apart from the violence and the reasons stated by O'Bradaigh, there is evidence to suggest that the truce, on the British part, was seen largely as a tactical ploy. Readers might care to re-examine point 3 of the churchmen's proposals when they have had an opportunity to study the implications of 'police primacy' discussed in Chapter 10. The bait of withdrawing the army in return for 'effective policing' does appear to contain a barb. Policing to the British did not merely mean consigning the army to barracks and, ultimately, boat, and replacing the soldiers with bobbies on the beat. It involved armed, native-born counterinsurgents, who under the 'Ulsterisation' policy also to be shortly discussed would remove the burden of the war against the IRA from the army. Over the years other pieces of evidence point so strongly to a hidden agenda on the part of the British negotiators that the British themselves came to be eager to distance themselves from the 'truce' episode.

In 1993, when British officials were again talking to the IRA, the Provisionals' negotiators were assured that the nineties talks would not be a repetition of those of the seventies. A letter from Merlyn Rees to Harold Wilson was quoted by the British side. In the letter, Rees said that the purpose of the talks had been to con the IRA: 'we set out to con them and we succeeded'.[15]

I also know that Daithi O'Conaill cited an example of British goodwill which was highly dubious. He had asked for a public sign that the British meant what they said privately about cracking down on the Unionists. He was told that one would be forthcoming, that the British Government intended not to nationalise the Belfast shipyards, as was being done in the UK. The 'mainland' British were in fact hoping that the separate and highly favourable terms provided for the Belfast yards would make nationalisation unnecessary. However, nationalisation was duly announced by Stan Orme on 26 March 1975. But the background was not as O'Conaill had been led to suppose. An incident involving Sir Frank Cooper had occurred several months earlier.

Approaching 6.30 p.m. on a normal Monday in the Northern Ireland Office, the two top executives of Harland and Wolff unexpectedly appeared in Cooper's office. They had a disturbing message. If money were not forthcoming immediately, the yards could not pay the following Friday's wages. Cooper was aghast, not least because one of the executives concerned, a Dane, had been hired at a princely salary to prevent just such an eventuality occurring. This incident was the genesis of the government takeover. It finally brought to a head the feelings of dismay in Whitehall at the way money seemed doomed to pour into a black hole where Harland and Wolff was concerned.[16] (After a period of nationalisation and further losses, it was announced, on 28 June 1988, that the yard was to be privatised. A management buyout ensued the following December.)

But more tangible evidences of a hidden agenda were available to the Republicans. This was the period when three policies which were vitally to affect the Six County security policy and the situation in the jails were put into effect. The setting-up of the Diplock courts has already been adverted to. Diplock's Report was presented to and accepted by the House of Commons on 20 December 1972.[17] In it, he made a distinction between detention and internment. The report stated:

> The only hope of restoring the efficiency of criminal courts of law in Northern Ireland is to deal with terrorist crimes by using an extra-judicial process to deprive of their ability to operate in Northern Ireland those terrorists whose activities result in the intimidation of witnesses. With an easily penetrable border to the south and west the only way of doing this is to put them in detention . . . It does not mean imprisonment at the arbitrary dictat of the executive government which is to many people a common connotation of the term internment. We use it to describe depriving a man of his liberty as a result of an investigation of the facts which inculpate the detainee by an impartial person or tribunal by making use of procedure, which, however fair to him, is inappropriate to a court of law because it does not comply with Article 6 of the European Convention.

Diplock defined the types of 'scheduled offences' which would be dealt with by the juryless courts which he set up – murder, grievous bodily harm, explosive charges, possession of arms – and stated that where these offences were concerned a 'confession made by the accused' should be admissible as evidence unless it was obtained by torture or inhuman or degrading treatment. Diplock decreed that:

> A signed written statement made to anyone charged with investigating a scheduled offence should be admissible if the person who made it cannot be produced in court for specific reasons and the statement contains material which would have been admissible if that person had been present in court to give oral evidence.

The provision about the admissibility of confessions was so liberally availed of that over 80 per cent of those convicted in the Diplock courts were detained as a result of confessions, which despite the proviso made as to torture were certainly extricated by sometimes very brutal methods. But obtained they were, with the result that prison populations shot up from around 700 at the start of the troubles to over 3,000 in the period under review. In order to make it appear that the IRA was simply a criminal organisation, and to allay Unionist and Tory backbench anger at the prisoner-of-war status enjoyed by Special Category prisoners, the British throughout the 1975–6 period also began developing what became known as the 'criminalisation policy'.

This was paralleled by the 'Ulsterisation' and 'normalisation' approaches. Under Ulsterisation, security was progressively handed over to the RUC and Ulster Defence Regiment in a Six County version of what the Americans used to refer to during the Vietnam War as 'Vietnamisation': in other words, letting the natives do the fighting. Normalisation was intended to return the province to a normal way of life as soon as possible. This entailed making it look normal also. One result of this policy was that practically as soon as the echoes of an IRA bomb blast died away, builders were at work repairing the damage. Abnormality thus set in, because the amount of building, at government expense, drew the attention of gangsters to the potential for extortion. The plethora of leisure centres, cultural events, road-building, and other forms of imparting an air of 'normalcy' to the Six Counties all, in their way, provided rich pickings, be these legal or otherwise.

'Criminalisation' meant what it said: that the Provisionals were henceforth to be regarded and treated as common criminals. Central to the operation of this strategy was the Gardiner Report.[18] The author of the report, Lord Gardiner, a former Lord Chancellor, considered 'in the context of civil liberties and human rights measures to deal with terrorism in Northern Ireland'. By this time there were some 1,119 Special Category prisoners and a further 535 detainees. The Gardiner Report condemned the granting of Special Category status, saying:

> Although recognising the pressures on those responsible at the time, we have come to the conclusion that the introduction of Special Category status was a serious mistake . . . it should be made absolutely clear that Special Category prisoners can expect no amnesty and will have to serve their sentences . . . We recommend that the earliest practicable opportunity should be taken to end the Special Category.

Gardiner objected to the fact that under the existing circumstances Special Category prisoners were

> . . . allowed to wear their own clothes and are not required to work. They receive more frequent visitors than other prisoners and are allowed food parcels and can spend their own money in the prison canteen. They have segregation in compounds according to the paramilitary organisation to which they claim allegiance . . .

Gardiner recommended that the way to deal with this problem was to build more conventional prisons in Northern Ireland along the normal cellular lines. It was as a result of his report that the H Blocks were constructed in the Long Kesh complex which as a result of the new policy was renamed the Maze Prison. Six days after the report was published, Merlyn Rees announced in the House of Commons that the new prisons were to be built. There thus arose a situation in which the British were conducting a Janus-faced set of talks: one, ostensibly at least, aimed at holding a

222

truce and conferring a certain political status on Sinn Fein by conceding the incident centres; the other, which began secretly with the prisoners' leaders, aimed at doing away with Special Category status and identifying the IRA as criminals.

The H Blocks were built during the talks period, so there was ample tangible evidence before the IRA leadership's eyes of what was planned. However, all sorts of baits were offered to distract the IRA's gaze from what was taking place. For example, a house in Rosemary Street, in downtown Belfast, was proposed to both the IRA and Loyalist paramilitaries as a sort of HQ for terrorists where they could all meet (and be bugged) under the one roof. At first sight the idea appears ludicrous, but I suppose one must take it in conjunction with the fact that at the time everyone in Belfast appeared to be aware that the British secret service, MI6, was housed in Laneside, a large house overlooking Belfast Lough. The scheme progressed to a point whereby, despite the fact that sectarian assassination was rampant at the time, the four paramilitary organisations entered into an agreement that they would not attack any of their rivals in the vicinity of the Rosemary Street premises. In the event the terrorist HQ idea collapsed because the IRA, mistrusting British involvement in the scheme, ultimately vetoed the so-called 'welfare centre'.

As part of this negotiation process, the prisoners' leader, David Morley, was shown a copy of a speech which Merlyn Rees was to deliver in the House of Commons on Thursday 25 March 1976. Morley had been warned beforehand that it would contain some strong language and that it would have a bearing on the Special Category issue. He was allowed to make some changes in the script before Rees actually delivered the speech, a remarkable circumstance in itself. One wonders what the Unionists and Tory backbenchers would have said had they known that an Irish 'felon' had been given the right to alter a speech made in the House of Commons by the Secretary of State for Northern Ireland!

However, neither Morley nor the IRA had any power to alter the substance of the speech, a decision to remove Special Category status. Days after Rees spoke, the IRA handed over a document to the prison authorities stating that negotiations were being broken off. This document said: 'We are prepared to die for the right to retain political status. Those who try to take it away must be fully prepared to pay the same price.'[19]

At the time this seemed like a piece of braggadocio, but both the IRA and the British were serious about their respective policies. Prison Officer Cassidy was one of the warders subsequently shot (on 16 April 1979). He was attending a wedding at the time. As he emerged from the church with his three-year-old daughter he was shot in the body. He fell to the ground, squirming, his screaming child standing over him. Another gunman pushed through the crowd and shot him in the head. With the ending of Special Category status and the closing of the incident centres, the British also stepped up their campaign against the IRA. The combined effect of the new policies is reckoned to have cut the active service life of an average IRA volunteer to around three months in the 1975–6 period.

Rees was succeeded by Roy Mason in August 1976. He pursued a hard-line policy with vigour. He launched an advertising campaign, 'Seven years is enough', and spoke about 'squeezing the IRA like toothpaste'.[20] The IRA countered this with a slogan campaign of their own: 'Seven hundred years is too much' appeared on many a Belfast gable wall. What did not appear in public was the fact that a new form of warfare had broken out in the Six County prison system.

Special Category status had been abolished from 1 March 1976. From that day on, no further prisoners were admitted to the compounds, which retained their prisoner-of-war status. New prisoners were expected to serve their sentences in the H Blocks and to wear prison uniform and conform to prison discipline. However, on 14 September 1976, four days after Mason arrived in the province, Kieran Nugent, a young IRA volunteer who had been sentenced for hijacking a van, proceeded to make history. He informed the prison authorities that if they wanted him to wear the prison uniform, 'they would have to nail the clothes to my back'. This defiance caused Nugent to become the first of the 'blanket men'.

As a punishment, all furniture was removed from his cell and he remained from 7.30 a.m. until 8.30 p.m. each day on a concrete floor with no mattress, bed or reading material. His diet was also adversely affected, and, as he would not wear the uniform, his only clothing became a blanket. As other prisoners began to follow Nugent's example, a general 'no-wash' protest spread amongst the prisoners. They wore their prison clothes to accept visits only, but at other times had only a towel to cover themselves. When they went to the showers they had to use this towel, so they asked for a second. When this was refused they also refused to wash, on the grounds that they should not be forced into nakedness. The sole item of furniture in their cells was a chamber pot. It was shortly to assume a degree of significance in the situation.

The prison routine was 'food in – slops out'. A trolley would come around with food for the prisoners, followed by another trolley for their slops. The prisoners claimed that the warders only half-emptied the pots and sometimes up-ended them on the floors. From this 'the Dirty Protest' evolved.

The prisoners began throwing their solids out of the windows of the cells, and the warders started throwing them back in again. Later, the prisoners began disposing of their faeces by smearing them on the walls. By 1980 there were some 400 protesters 'on the blanket' in both the Long Kesh complex and the women's prison in Armagh jail. The protest received curiously little publicity for some years, until Cardinal O'Fiaich visited the prison and on 1 August 1978 issued a lengthy statement detailing what he had seen. It included the following:

> Having spent the whole of Sunday in the prison I was shocked by the inhuman conditions prevailing in H Blocks 3, 4 and 5 where over 300 prisoners are incarcerated. One would hardly allow an animal to remain in such conditions let alone a human being. The nearest approach to it that I have seen was the spectacle of hundreds of homeless people living in sewer pipes in the slums of Calcutta. The stench and filth in some of the cells, with the remains of rotten food and human excreta scattered around the walls, was almost unbearable. In two of them I was unable to speak for fear of vomiting.
>
> The prisoners' cells are without beds, chairs or tables. They sleep on mattresses on the floor and in some cases I noticed that these were quite wet. They have no covering except a towel or blanket, no books, newspapers or reading material except the Bible (even religious magazines have been banned since my last visit), no pens or writing materials, no TV or

radio, no hobbies or handicrafts, no exercise or recreation. They are locked in their cells for almost the whole of every day and some of them have been in this condition for more than a year and a half.

The statement also included the point that these prisoners had been treated by special courts in a very special way. Their convictions were secured by methods which by the time of the Cardinal's visit had aroused the condemnation of Amnesty International.[21] But having been put into prison in a very special way, a deeply burning resentment was created by the taking away of their special category. Another factor which added to the tensions in the prison was the fact that while the prisoners were Nationalists and Catholics, the warders were Protestants and Loyalists.

However, neither the Cardinal's protest nor increasing pressures from Dublin brought any change in the official position, which was defined by an NIO statement as follows:

These criminals are totally responsible for the situation in which they find themselves. It is they who have been smearing excreta on the walls and pouring urine through cell doors. It is they who by their actions are denying themselves the excellent modern facilities of the prison . . . Each and every prisoner has been tried under the judicial system established in Northern Ireland by parliament. Those found guilty, of the due process of law, if they are sent to prison by the courts, serve their sentence for what they are – convicted criminals. They are not political prisoners. More than 80 have been convicted of murder or attempted murder and more than 80 of explosives offences.[22]

This view was shared by leading Protestant churchmen. The Presbyterian governing committee condemned the Cardinal's statement and the *Church of Ireland Gazette* said he had left 'the rest of us in little doubt about where his loyalties lay'.

The prisoners stayed in these conditions for a further two years. I described a visit I paid to the prison in 1980, two years after the Cardinal's statement, as follows:

I was allowed to pick the two cells I wished to visit at random after a tour of the prison led by the Governor. The Governor placed no barriers in my inspection save warning the two occupants of the first cell I came to that there was to be no conversation. . . . as if to underline this, two enormous warders, either of whom would dwarf me (and I am not a small man), entered the cell and stood behind the cell's occupants. They were aged 21 and 22, as I afterwards learned, serving ten and twelve years respectively. When the cell door opened they both looked frightened. They looked anxiously at us for a moment. They were pallid and naked except for a blanket draped over their shoulders. They stood silently, fear hardening into defiance, I felt, as we looked at the cell.

It was covered in excrement almost to the ceiling and all four walls. In one corner there was a pile of rotting, blue-moulded food and excrement and the two boys had evidently been using bits of their foam rubber mattresses to add to the decor as we entered. There wasn't much of a smell but the light was dim and the atmosphere profoundly disturbing and depressing. I felt helpless and angry as I stood and looked at these appalling and disgraceful conditions, prevented by bureaucracy and by history from talking to two of my fellow human beings who had brought themselves and been brought to this condition of self-abnegation.

I couldn't speak for a few minutes after visiting the cell and had to compose myself before entering a cell which the well known Republican, Martin Meehan, was occupying. Meehan was attempting to bring some variant into the monotony of his days by drawing palm trees on his cell walls with his own excreta using pieces of foam rubber mattress. By the time I met him I had recovered sufficiently to disregard the rules about no conversation and at least had regained my composure to the extent of shaking hands with him and exchanging the normal greetings. But for several days afterwards the memory of the cells abided with me and I would have said that the visit to Long Kesh was one of the worst and most shocking experiences of my life had I not subsequently paid a visit to the women's prison in Armagh.

Here the cells were gloomier, because the prison was an old one and the effect of seeing young women caked in grime through not having washed for several months added to the appalling conditions in their cells. In addition to smearing urine and faeces on the walls they disposed of their menstrual fluid in this way also.[23]

How some mass epidemic did not break out I could never understand. It was commonplace for the prisoners to wake up in the morning with their eyes, ears, mouths and anuses filled with tiny white maggots. Seeing these conditions later helped me to understand what it was that led Mairead Farrell, whom I interviewed during the Armagh visit as the leader of the protesting women, to go on the mission to Gibraltar which led to her death at the hands of the SAS in 1988 (see Chapter 10). But of more long-term significance politically, experiencing those conditions even fleetingly and as a non-participant did help one gain an insight into how so much of of the Nationalist population of Northern Ireland later came to support Sinn Fein.

The bulk of the prison population were not only drawn from the smaller section of the community, but were also drawn from a subdivision of it, i.e. the Catholic ghetto districts in the urban areas, and some rural heartland areas also. Therefore the impact of the Dirty Protest was concentrated and magnified.

This was true of the Troubles' effect generally. The deaths, the shootings, the beatings, the jailings, daily and weekly, gave a new meaning to Yeats' line about 'great hatred little room'. The prisons came to be the focus of that intensity of feeling. There is a strip of roadway in the Andersonstown district of Belfast, between Shaw's Road and Stewartstown Park, which is about the same length as the road I live on in Dublin. Thirty-five of the families living along the Andersonstown road have someone in jail at the time of writing. At times of crisis the number went even higher. No family in that district has been untouched by the Troubles in some way.

As the Dirty Protest continued, the atmosphere in the Catholic areas gradually sharpened into one of widespread defiance coupled with fear. At the time of writing, Patrick McGeown is a leading member of Sinn Fein. In 1980 he was in Long Kesh. I interviewed his wife, Pauline, about the situation. She had none of the knee-jerk propaganda one meets with amongst some Republican supporters. Indeed, she was prepared to talk about issues arising from jail, and the protest, that other women at the time would never mention to a journalist. The Valley of Squinting Windows syndrome of the ghetto pertained: 'They watch every move you make when they know your husband is away in the Kesh. The gossip is terrible,' she said. She was able to articulate the attitude of the families of the men on the Dirty Protest while at the same time expressing her reservations about the use of violence. Describing how Pat came to be in the situation he was in at the time, she said:

> He was always interested in politics and he used to talk to me about what he read. The trouble is he was too bright. When they sweep the areas, they lift the brains. They know he has got a political mind, that he reads a lot and could see ahead, therefore he is a threat. Talking is not enough to change the system. You must take action. What type, though, is another matter. I wonder does it have to be violence but you can't walk away from it. We are all in a prison here. If you try to run away you are only running away from yourself.
>
> You don't leave H Block behind you. I worry about Pat's mental condition. I think he is deteriorating but I know he will stick it out. I am afraid hunger striking is only around the corner. They can't give up the protest, it is part of them. They would lose their spirit, lose their soul. By failing to resist and admitting the criminal status, they would admit that the whole cause is criminal. It goes back to the moment you were born. Pat was 10 when he was on the barricades.

Pauline was right: the hunger strike was just around the corner. Hunger-striking is the obverse side of the IRA's medal of infliction: endurance. It is a practice which has its roots deep in Irish history and is found also in Hindu tradition. Both the earlier Celts and the Hindus used self-immolation by starvation as a means of discrediting someone who had done them wrong. An unpaid poet or tradesman would starve himself to death, if necessary, outside the home of an uncaring patron, achieving satisfaction either through their wrong being rectified or through death sullying forever the reputation of the wrongdoer.

The period of the hunger strikes could be taken as epitomising the cultural and religious differences between the Irish and the English. The Irish demonstrated both their defiant natures and their sense of identity in a manner which gave a new definition to the term 'back to basics'. For example, throughout the Dirty Protest, the prisoners continued to hold Irish classes. They tapped out a word on the central-heating pipes and then inscribed it on to the walls of their cells in their own excrement, sometimes using the crucifixes on their rosary beads as stylos. Throughout the strikes and protests the prisoners communicated with the outside world in a variety of ways, all basic but efficient. It was quite commonplace for a prisoner to receive a communication from the outside world in the morning, reply to it in an early afternoon visit, and possibly receive another message in response before the end of the day. Men secreted coms (messages written on cigarette papers) in their anuses, behind their testicles or in their foreskins. Women did likewise in their vaginas, sanitary towels, under their breasts or in their hair. One prisoner is alleged to have transported some forty coms in his foreskin. Another told me of a colleague who secreted a pen, a comb and a lighter in his anus.[24]

The British fought with order, rule book, discipline, their propaganda conveying a sense of disdain at this bizarre and repellent behaviour in the surroundings of one of the most modern prisons in Europe. Insofar as physical facilities were concerned, the H Blocks were indeed models of cellular confinement. They took their name from the cluster of individual H-shaped blocks which formed the prison.

The cells were of the most modern design known to penology. But it was demonstrated literally in Long Kesh, not for the first time in Irish history, that prison bars and walls do not a prison make.

The most famous hunger-striker in Irish Republican history, up to the time of the building of the H Blocks was Terence McSwiney, the Lord Mayor of Cork, who died, after seventy-four days, during the Anglo-Irish war of 1919–21. McSwiney became the inspiration for W. B. Yeats' play, *The King's Threshold*, in which Seanchan, a poet, starves himself to death. During World War II, de Valera had allowed IRA men to die on hunger strike rather than concede them the right of political status. Hunger-striking was not a feature of the 1956–62 IRA campaign but it reappeared significantly with Billy McKee's fast in 1972 which led to the truce and the concession of Special Category status in the first place, and to the flying of Adams and company to meet Whitelaw.

Sean MacStiofain, the then chief of staff, who had been arrested in the Republic, subsequently lost face within the movement as the result of coming off a hunger strike in 1973 after fifty-seven days. But by 1980, two hunger-strikers had gone the full way down the agonisingly slow path that leads to a starvation death. The first hunger-strike fatality of the contemporary troubles was Michael Gaughan, who died in Parkhurst Prison on 3 June 1974, the sixty-fifth day of his strike, and was buried in his native Mayo. His partner on the strike, Frank Stagg, lived and later went on strike again, dying in Wakefield prison on 12 February 1976.

Stagg's death precipitated a bizarre incident involving the Government of the Republic. The IRA had intended to stage a military funeral for Stagg and bury him alongside Gaughan. But the Government had the plane carrying the coffin diverted to Shannon, where Special Branch detectives ensured that the body was buried without Republican ceremony, and under a layer of concrete to prevent re-internment. However, six months after the fuss had died down, Stagg was dug up under cover of darkness and reburied, with the blessing of a priest, alongside his friend.

Both men had died for the same cause, the right to be transferred to Ireland to complete their sentences. The two Price sisters, Dolours and Marian, were more successful. After more than 200 days on strike, during which they were force-fed, they were repatriated to Armagh jail. However, the publicity surrounding the force-feeding process caused the then Home Secretary, Roy Jenkins, to decide that from then on (June 1974) any prisoner who went on hunger strike would not be force-fed. The process is a fairly brutal one involving the clamping of a metal device around the mouth and the insertion of a tube into the patient's stomach. If, as sometimes happens, the tube enters the windpipe, the patient can die.

Jenkins' decision was to make Sinn Fein a powerful political party in Ireland. The IRA did not welcome hunger strikes. They created an emotional focus which detracted from a military campaign, and there was always the risk of an adverse effect if the strike failed, as it had in the case of MacStiofain. However, a current of opinion built up in the H Blocks in favour of a strike. One prisoner, Martin Meehan, despairing of effecting change in his position through drawing faecal palm trees, went on an unauthorised strike which lasted for sixty-five days before he was cajoled off it by the intervention of Cardinal O'Fiaich.

The IRA leadership attempted to control the prison issue by backing the National H Block/Armagh Committee, which involved not only Sinn Fein, but a number of civil liberties groups. This became active throughout the month of October 1979. Its most prominent member was Bernadette McAliskey, the former Bernadette Devlin, who was one of the six members of the committee to be shot in highly controversial circumstances. McAliskey and her husband were two of the lucky ones; the other five H Block Committee leaders died. The committee did, however, generate a good deal of publicity on behalf of the prisoners' demands, which could be summarised as follows:

1. The right to wear their own clothes.
2. The right to abstain from penal labour.
3. The right to free association. (This at the time meant, not moving from their cells, but freedom of association within their own prison area, i.e. in a cell block.)
4. The right to recreational and educational facilities in conjunction with the prison authorities.
5. Restoration of remission. (The Dirty Protest meant that this concession had been withdrawn.)

Cardinal O'Fiaich, and a number of bishops, backed the Five Demands, as they became known, and throughout 1980 the Cardinal held a series of meetings with the Secretary of State, Humphrey Atkins, but to no avail. Apart from relying on the publicity work of the H Block Committee, the IRA broadened its campaign to include warders. Eighteen of them, and the wife of one, were murdered before the movement was prevailed upon to stop the killings in the unrealised hope that this would give Cardinal O'Fiaich's efforts a better chance of success.

Two events which occurred in 1980 brought the matter to a head. One was the Meehan strike, the other the threat of a hunger strike in Wales. Gwynfor Evans, the president of Plaid Cymru, the Welsh Nationalist Party, announced that he would start a hunger strike to the death on 6 October unless the Government honoured its manifesto pledge to give Wales a Welsh-language station on the proposed new television channel. On 17 September William Whitelaw announced that Wales was to get its service. So far as the Long Kesh prisoners were concerned, this decision, coming on top of the example set by Meehan, was the turning point.

Brendan Hughes, the prisoners' leader, sent out word that the IRA leadership was out of touch with the intensity of feeling in the prison; that the National H Block Committee had proved ineffectual, as had the Cardinal and others. The only thing that would resolve the crisis one way or the other was a hunger strike. Adams and the other newer figures in the Republican leadership were opposed to a strike, not least because of what might happen if it failed. 'Break the lads in prison, and you break the lads outside' is an old IRA maxim. Also, a prison defeat creates a knock-on effect on families and supporters outside the jails.

Far from urging on a hunger strike for publicity purposes, the outside leaders at first tried to prevent one occurring. Danny Morrison, who accompanied me on a visit to the H Blocks during the height of the crisis, remarked wonderingly to me that: 'The IRA were very slow to see the potential of the situation.' But the sheer weight of the prison population, abnormally swollen by the 'conveyor belt system', meant that those inside the prisons now constituted too large a proportion of the IRA as a whole to be ignored. The Army Council agreed to back a strike. Sinn Fein announced on 10 October that a strike would commence seventeen days later. It was led by Hughes himself, who went on the protest with six other prisoners. The total of seven was chosen because there had been seven signatories to the proclamation issued by the rebels during Easter 1916. Moreover, the strikers came from all of the Six Counties.

Before his capture, Hughes had been charged with devising a new 'cover' apparatus for the IRA and had hit on the idea of setting up a series of businesses. It was based on the oft-proved thesis that security forces never suspect a man in a pinstriped suit of being a terrorist. He took on the name and identity of a dead man, Arthur McAllister, dyed his hair and grew a moustache. He posed as a toy salesman, kept a diary of 'business appointments' and went out each morning to call on shops from a house in Belfast's Knockbreda area. To complete his disguise he had a seemingly equally 'yuppie' wife, an IRA woman. He rented premises in exclusive parts of Belfast, like the Malone Road, with a view to both storing arms and explosives and installing IRA operators from the ghetto areas.

Hughes had also drawn up maps and plans against a 'doomsday situation' in case of all-out sectarian war. When he was captured, on 10 May 1974, the army suppressed the contingency nature of the plans, both for general propaganda reasons and in particular for Harold Wilson's benefit. The idea, which for a time succeeded, was to make it appear that the IRA was preparing an onslaught on Protestants. This both helped to heighten the tension during the Loyalists' strike and provided an argument why the army should not engage the Loyalists while such a threat existed from the IRA.

I visited Hughes in Long Kesh when he had been on strike for a month, the purpose of the visit being to attempt to evaluate for Charles Haughey whether the strike was rooted in a real jail problem or was merely an IRA publicity stunt. Given Hughes' reputation, I had expected to find a cross between James Bond and Al Capone, but instead found only an unobtrusive, middle-sized man, who talked about the strike as though it were happening to someone else. His hands were slightly clammier than normal, and despite his nickname, 'Dark', because of his complexion, he seemed pale. But though he told me he had lost twenty pounds, there was nothing in his speech or movements to show he had not eaten for more than thirty days. He had walked from his cell to meet me. His only problem, he said, was that he woke up drenched in sweat. Apart from the presence of warders in the visiting room we might have been in a hospital anteroom chatting about fasting. Danny Morrison added the only touch of drama to the occasion by passing him a com under the noses of the guards.

The strike lasted until 18 December. The intervening period was one of remarkable intensity. On the one hand, there was the public drama of the hunger strike itself. On the other, there was a secret but intensive high-level negotiation between London and Dublin. Haughey was increasingly anxious that destabilisation might occur in the Republic as well as the north if the hunger strike persisted to the death. There was considerable evidence in the conversation of the Sinn Fein activists of the period that the word 'destabilisation' had a high place in their vocabularies. All the ground of prison defiance and resistance had been gone over many times in the histories of both the Republic and the Six Counties.

The most recent chapter in the Republic's prison history had ended in a compromise only three years before, in 1977. It had defused one of the worst threats to the stability of the Republic in the history of the troubles. The IRA regards jail either as another battlefield or as 'the Republican university' wherein one may either fight on or obtain a higher education, not all of it of an academic nature. As they regard themselves as prisoners of war, not criminals, they will inevitably come into conflict with prison regulations if a spirit of compromise does not prevail.

After a particularly vicious spell of rioting and conflict in Portlaoise jail under the Fine Gael–Labour coalition government which fell in 1977, the incoming Fianna Fail administration moved along the compromise route and the situation in Portlaoise returned to normality. Inside the jail the Republican prisoners achieved *de facto* political status. They wore their own clothes, communicated with the authorities through their own elected officers, and were segregated from other prisoners into their own groupings – Provisionals, Officials, INLA, and 'mavericks', who had either never belonged to any of the three or had been expelled from them. But in all other respects the prisoners conformed to prison discipline and served out their sentences in a peaceful atmosphere.

During the period of tension there were attempts on the Governor's life, a number of explosions, escapes, and attempted escapes during which a garda and a prisoner lost their lives. Outside the jail there was continuous and increasingly angry agitation on the prisoners' behalf. Inside the perimeter walls, the normal army presence was greatly increased, as was the number of warders. I once counted sixteen warders on duty on each landing of the prison. This was in addition to a heavy warder presence at every strategic door, gate or assembly place in the jail. Sixteen warders per shift represents a total of something in excess of three times that many per week. So the financial cost of trouble in prisons is something to be avoided if at all possible. Then, in the light of Irish history, a factor which continually has to be weighed in the balance between law and order is the question of how much potential for destabilisation, through the arousal of public sympathy, is contained in any given prison protest.

The answer, in the six north-eastern Irish counties in the early 1980s, could be summed up in one word – enormous. However, Thatcher was in no mood for a Portlaoise solution. Reports on episodes like Airey Neave's death and Warrenpoint figured larger in her reading list than did *The King's Threshold*. She summed up the British position on 20 November:

Let me make one point about the hunger strike in the Maze Prison. I want this to be utterly clear. There can be no political justification for murder or any other crime. The government

231

will never concede political status to the hunger strikers or to any others convicted of criminal offences in the Province.[25]

The dispute escalated sharply throughout December, with three of the women prisoners in Armagh joining the strike on the 3rd of the month and twenty-three of the men in Long Kesh joining on the 15th. It could in fact have been resolved very simply by one concession – on clothing. Of my own knowledge I know that the IRA would have accepted a face-saving formula whereby they were allowed to wear even tracksuits and runners supplied by their families, for a portion of their day, as a symbol that they were not 'criminalised'.

But a Portlaoise-type compromise solution was not to be had. There were serious riots in Armagh, Belfast and Derry. However, the Government continued to be unyielding. On 10 December, Humphrey Atkins again took a hard line. Speaking in the House of Commons, he said:

> The protest movement within the prisons, from which the hunger strike stems, is one important arm in the strategy of the Provisional IRA. Its struggle to destroy law and order and overthrow democratic institutions in Northern Ireland does not stop at the prison gates; it is continued through other means inside. The Protest is designed to contribute to its objective of securing political legitimacy for a movement whose only weapon is violence. It is also part of a wider attempt to discredit the measures which the government have been compelled to introduce to protect society from terrorism.[26]

The strike ended on 18 December 1980 in a burst of prison poker, which the authorities at first believed they had won. One of the prisoners, Sean McKenna, whose eyesight was failing, a sure sign that death was near, also showed signs of psychological deterioration, sometimes defiant, at others wanting to come off the strike. To my knowledge, the British authorities repeatedly told Dublin that there was no need to worry about destabilisation: the strike would collapse because of McKenna. Then, to heighten the pressure on the remaining strikers, on 18 December McKenna was unexpectedly switched from Long Kesh to Musgrave Military Hospital outside Belfast. There was a secondary purpose to this move.

Apart from removing McKenna from his colleagues' purview, thereby creating uncertainty as to whether he had died or was about to die, it also set the scene for the introduction of a document from the Foreign Office to the prison. This was conveyed by a priest, a Redemptorist, who had been in touch with the prisoners, the British, and Haughey. He was so generally trusted that he was given an Irish name: *an Sagairt Mait*, the Good Priest. When the document's approach was made known to Hughes he was faced with a dilemma. He had been prevented from keeping in touch with McKenna's condition but he knew he could not last long. Hughes was in a bad way himself, as were his other five comrades. The fact that the document was on the way might mean that McKenna was dying uselessly, for concessions which had in fact been granted. Hughes called off the strike. But the concessions had not been granted. When the thirty-four-page document arrived it spoke in vague diplomatic terms of the possibilities of movement once the strike ended.

Knowing nothing of what had happened, the nation heaved a sigh of relief. Haughey summed up the situation by issuing a statement which said: 'A potentially dangerous and tragic situation has fortunately been averted and all who have contributed to the ending of the strike deserve the gratitude of the Irish people.' Few had worked harder to prevent the strike reaching the point of tragedy than two Redemptorist priests, Fr Alec Reid, whom we shall meet later in our story, and *an Sagairt Mait*, Fr Brendan Meagher. Fr Meagher was not deceived by the seemingly happy ending to the affair. He called at my house for what should have been a celebratory drink on Christmas Day but became instead a worried speculation as to what might lie ahead.

Inside the prison it soon became apparent that the prisoners had been outmanoeuvred. A confusing situation arose which basically still revolved around whether or not the prisoners could wear their own clothing. There were all sorts of compromise formulae floating about: that their own clothes would be delivered by their relatives and simultaneously they would be issued with 'prison-style' clothing which they would wear for part of the day, using their own clothes at other times, and so on. All this was contingent on good behaviour, the ending of the Dirty Protest, and on its being clearly seen that the Governor's writ ran in the jail.

Mrs Thatcher was still not in a mood to countenance any compromise. By the middle of January the conflicting versions of what the ending of the strike meant were out in the open. From the outset, Bobby Sands, who had succeeded Hughes as the prisoners' leader, had been clear that the strike had ended in defeat. He wanted to go on strike himself, immediately. He was restrained by the outside leadership, who felt that the public would not support a strike so soon on the heels of what had happened. Nevertheless, within the jail, preparations went on. Sands took names from volunteers who wished to go on strike, and communications went out from the jail, all over the world, seeking information on hunger strikes. Palestinians proved to be a fertile source of information, not only on hunger strikes, but on thirst strikes also.

Inside the prison, morale amongst the Republican prisoners was falling by the hour. Their cells were still filthy, but their Dirty Protest was going nowhere. They were getting increasingly abrasive treatment from the warders. Sands feared for a collapse of the prisoners' organisation within the jail. In response to a communication from the Army Council, counselling against a strike and warning that the military campaign could not be suspended for its duration on this occasion, he sent out the following:

> We have listened carefully to what you have said . . . we do not deny your or criticise your extreme cautiousness. But, however distressing it may be, we regret that our decision to hunger strike remains the same and we re-confirm this decision now with the same vigour and determination. We fully accept and in full knowledge of what it 'may' entail, the right of the army to carry on unlimited operations in pursuance of the Liberation struggle and without handicap or hindrance. We accept the tragic consequences that most certainly await us and the overshadowing fact that death may not secure a principled settlement . . . We realise the struggle outside must also continue. We hope that you accept that the struggle in H Blocks, being part of the overall struggle, must go on in unison.[27]

The outside leadership reluctantly conceded that a strike was inevitable, and it was decided that Sands would begin it, followed at intervals by other prisoners, including INLA prisoners. On 5 February 1981, a statement was issued to the press by Sinn Fein on behalf of the prisoners, announcing the decision. It said: 'Our last hunger strikers were morally blackmailed . . . Where is the peace in the prisons, which like a promise, was held before dying men's eyes?'

There was to be no peace. The references in the communications between Sands and the IRA Army Council to the continuation of the campaign help to explain why. The continuing violence, heightened and intensified because of the strike, made the summer of 1981 into one of the bloodiest periods of the troubles. In all, some sixty-one people died during the protest. Thirty-four of them were civilians. Seven of these, including two girls aged eleven and fourteen, died from injuries inflicted by plastic bullets. The IRA killed fifteen members of the RUC, eight soldiers, and seven members of the UDR. In one incident, at Camlough, Co. Armagh, the home of a hunger-striker, Raymond McCreesh, an IRA bomb killed five soldiers in a single explosion. As has been said before, the IRA's coin is two-sided: on one side is imprinted endurance, on the other infliction. The summer of 1981 illustrated both sides as rarely seen either before or since.

Bobby Sands came to epitomise the type of young Catholic who got caught up in the troubles. He was twenty-seven at the commencement of the strike. He was born in Rathcoole in northern Belfast, a Protestant district. At an early age his family were intimidated out of their home. In their second house, the young Bobby survived both a knife attack and several incidents in which the Sands' residence was surrounded by chanting Protestants. Finally, after a Protestant 'welfare worker' – she was in fact a UDA activist – had been seen indicating the house to a young Protestant couple, a dustbin came through the window one night. It was an indication that the welfare officer had found new tenants for the Sands' home. The family then moved to Twinbrook, a Catholic district in west Belfast, in June 1972. Here Sands was apprenticed to a coach-building firm; here, too, he joined the IRA. He got married, but his marriage did not survive his arrest, as part of a team that had bombed a furnishing company at Dunmurray. I understand that he only joined the unit by accident, volunteering when he discovered that one member had not turned up. Those were the pre-cell days of the IRA, when there was a wasteful use of manpower. It was not uncommon for ten or twelve operatives to be sent out on a job which could easily have been carried out by two, or even one.

Sands' impulsive offer to join an operation in which he had not originally been included, but for which he received a fourteen-year sentence, helped to change Irish history. He was feisty, argumentative and showed considerable potential, as both a poet and a prose writer, his considerable output being set in a revolutionary mould, reflecting both his surroundings and his taste in reading material: Fanon, Guevara, Jackson, Torres. He is remembered amongst other things for having had a prodigious memory. In the prisons, 'talking books' are a feature of the entertainment. Sands memorised Leon Uris' mammoth *Trinity* and was able to pass it on to his cell mates in instalments each evening. Fr Meagher described him as a 'human dynamo'.

On 1 March 1981, chosen because it was the fifth anniversary of the ending of

Special Category status, Bobby Sands went on hunger strike. To focus attention on his protest, the rest of the prisoners called off the Dirty Protest.

Sands died at 1.17 on the morning of Tuesday 5 May. On the previous Friday, Don Concannon, Labour's spokesman on Northern Ireland, had visited him in Long Kesh. Concannon had been the minister of state who presided over the withdrawal of Special Category status. His message for Sands was that Labour was supporting the Government over the strike. He gave a press conference afterwards at which he said that he did not want Sands to misunderstand Labour's position.

Sands' condition was described by Owen Carron, his election agent, who saw him for the last time later that day:

> He found Sands in no shape to talk. He was lying on the waterbed, his left eye was black and closed, the right eye nearly closed and his mouth twisted as if he had suffered a stroke. He had no feelings in his legs and could only whisper. Every now and then he started dry retching. He managed to ask Carron if there was any change. The Fermanagh man said no, there was no change. Sands said: 'Well, that's it.' He told Carron: 'Keep my Ma in mind.' Carron bent over the bed, hugged him and kissed him.[28]

Later still that evening, Lord Carrington, the Foreign Secretary, said on independent radio: 'Do not tell me the IRA represent people in Northern Ireland. They have no status, they are not accepted by anyone.' Carrington was quite wrong. By that time the IRA represented quite a number of people in Northern Ireland, or at least Sands did. A death which had preceded Sands' – that of Frank Maguire, the independent MP for South Tyrone – had changed the Northern Ireland political scene dramatically, creating a necessity for a by-election. Still pursuing the traditional abstention policy, Sinn Fein saw no opportunity in an electoral contest and it was generally assumed that Maguire's brother, Noel, would stand for and probably win the seat. Then Bernadette McAliskey took a hand. Although still suffering from her wounds (sustained as recently as 16 January), she announced her candidacy, saying that she would only stand down in favour of an H Block candidate. This suggestion was taken up by a prominent Sinn Fein member in Belfast, Jim Gibney, who succeeded in persuading his colleagues to nominate Sands. In the vortex of emotion generated by the hunger strike, the SDLP withdrew Austin Currie's nomination and with less than ten minutes remaining on the closing day for nominations (29 March), Noel Maguire also withdrew. His last-minute decision made it impossible for Currie to re-enter the race, and the stage was set for an historic campaign.

Sands won the seat on 9 April, beating Harry West. By then he had been on strike for forty days and had lost nearly thirty pounds. The British reaction was to produce on 12 June an amendment to the Representation of the People Act prohibiting prisoners from standing for Parliament. But the reaction for Sinn Fein was far more significant. Gerry Adams analysed the significance of the 1981 Fermanagh by-election as follows:

> It was educational for us. We learned about presiding officers, impersonation officers, how to campaign. It was exhilarating. Sometimes we would come into a little town with the

Catholics coralled away up at the top as usual, the loyalists living along the main street with the businesses and so on. We would have the tricolour flying, the music blaring – and the Catholics up on the top of the hill would come out to us as though we were the relief cavalry.[29]

Sometimes the cavalry had to fight its way through Indian territory being ambushed by posses of hostile Loyalists. But in the fervour of the moment, with a candidate wasting away in a cell by the hour, against a background of Irish history, Sinn Fein won the seat.

And, after Sands died, they won it again, on 20 August, when Owen Carron stood as 'An Anti-H Block Proxy Political Prisoner'. By now the fevered atmosphere generated by the hunger strike had completely converted Sinn Fein to ending the abstention policy. In the Republic, in an election held on 11 June, two H Block prisoners, Kieran Doherty and Paddy Agnew, had both been elected to the Dail. Their victories, and the erosion of the Fianna Fail vote because of the strikes, returned a Fine Gael–Labour minority coalition government in place of Fianna Fail.

Following Carron's victory, Sinn Fein decided that henceforth it would not merely campaign on H Block tickets but would act as a normal political party to take on the SDLP full-frontally. Gerry Fitt, who had opposed the hunger strike vehemently, was to be targeted in West Belfast by Gerry Adams.

In all, ten hunger-strikers died between May and August 1981, seven Provisionals and three from INLA. The long-drawn-out agony of the 'Ten Men Dead', as they became generally known, had something of the same effect on Six County nationalism as did the long-drawn-out executions of the 1916 leaders on the twenty-six counties. The Ten Men Dead were:

Bobby Sands, 27, after sixty-six days, on 5 May; Francis Hughes, 25, after fifty-nine days, on 12 May; Raymond McCreesh, 24, after sixty-one days, on 21 May; Patsy O'Hara, 23, the leader of the INLA men, after sixty-one days, also on 21 May; Joe McDonnell, 30, after forty-six days, on 8 July; Martin Hurson, 27, after forty-six days, on 13 July; Kevin Lynch, 25, INLA, after seventy-one days, on 1 August; Kieran Doherty, 25, after seventy-three days, on 2 August; Thomas McElwee, 23, after sixty-five days, on 8 August; Michael Devine, 23, INLA, after sixty-six days, on 30 August.

The circumstances and the impacts of their deaths varied. Kieran Doherty, for example, who had been elected as a TD in an election held in the Republic in June, created a particular reaction south of the border, as well as north. All ten were young men and their ordeal occasioned a high degree of emotional stress and suffering, both for them and for their families. As the skeletal figures passed away into the pantheon of Irish history, sometimes being followed to their graves by as many as 100,000 people, the stories of how they had endured, and how they died, spread around not only the Six Counties and Ireland, but throughout the world.

The last hunger-striker to die was Michael Devine, a member of the INLA and a convinced socialist. David Beresford described his final hours as follows:

Father Pat Buckley took Mass in the hospital and went in to see Mickey, who had been too ill to make it. There was an awful smell – almost cancerous of the eating away of flesh mainly from his mouth, but so pervasive that his whole body seemed to be breathing it. Mickey confessed that he was scared, afraid to die. Buckley asked him why he was afraid – he was a free agent; if he was not happy he did not have to do it. Mickey said he felt it was the right thing to do but he was still scared. His eyes were wet and Buckley, taking out a handkerchief to mop his cheeks, could feel the tears in his own eyes. Mickey asked if he could take his confession. Buckley put an arm around him and listened. Red Mickey was finding comfort in the ancient faith.[30]

Ironically, the turning point in the strike probably came when Pauline McGeown authorised taking Patrick off the strike after he lapsed into unconsciousness on the day Devine died. McGeown, who had had reservations about the strike, had been fasting for forty-two days.

Although Mrs Thatcher won the battle of the hunger strikes, she lost the war. The victory was to prove a pyrrhic one not only for her policy but for the cause of unionism. Against the accusations of racketeering, drugs-dealing and godfathering, the IRA could now make the irrefutable point: the Mafia don't starve themselves to death for an ideal.

Throughout the strike the Iron Lady remained impervious both to international gestures of solidarity with the strikers and to high-level appeals for compromise. The Pope showed his concern by sending his secretary, the then Monsignor John Magee, to entreat with Sands to end his protest, while at the same time senior Irish church figures asked Thatcher to be flexible. However, she turned down approaches from Cardinal O'Fiaich, Bishop Daly of Derry, and the Irish Commission of Justice and Peace, a body representing the Irish hierarchy. Airey Neave's death had stiffened an already inflexible character.

In the Indian parliament, the opposition party observed a minute's silence on Bobby Sands' death. In New York Union Jacks were pulled down and burned. In Le Mans a street was named after Sands. In Cuba Fidel Castro said: 'The Irish patriots are in the process of writing one of the most heroic pages in human history.'[31] In Paris, the French Foreign Minister, Claude Cheysson, spoke publicly of the 'supreme sacrifice' which the hunger-strikers had made, going on to state that their courage demanded respect. The French Government also offered the Dublin Government two gestures of solidarity which Dublin declined. One was to boycott the British royal wedding, the other that President Mitterrand attend Bobby Sands' funeral.

In April Mrs Thatcher had publicly turned down a request from three Irish MEPs – Neil Blaney, John O'Connell and Sile de Valera, who had all visited Sands – to meet the British Government to discuss the situation. She said, speaking in Saudi Arabia on 20 April 1981: 'It is not my habit or custom to meet MPs of a foreign country about a citizen of the United Kingdom.' As we shall see, the following year the British put something of a coach and four through the 'United Kingdom' argument. But while the strike continued, Thatcher, and her mouthpiece Humphrey Atkins, maintained a relentlessly hostile line to the prisoners' demands. While still in Saudi Arabia Thatcher stated (on 21 April): 'We are not prepared to consider Special Category status for certain groups of people serving sentences for crime. Crime is crime, is crime. It is not political.' And she greeted Sands' death with a statement in the Commons: 'Mr Sands was a convicted criminal. He chose to take his own life. It was a choice that his organisation did not allow to many of its victims.'[32] Her words provided a potent recruiting slogan for the young men and women amongst the 100,000-strong cortège which followed Bobby Sands to the grave two days later in Belfast.

An important turning-point was reached on 13 September when Humphrey Atkins was replaced as Secretary of State by James Prior. Throughout the strike, Atkins, 'Humph the bumf', as the Republicans called him, had been regarded as something of a puppet's glove, the hand in which was Margaret Thatcher. Prior did not want to go to Northern Ireland, and indeed threatened to resign, but Thatcher insisted. When he eventually got to Belfast the strike was nearing its end and he was able to inject some of the 'Portlaoise spirit' into the situation. Sinn Fein was under pressure to use its influence to end the protest. The Dungannon priest Fr Denis Faul was becoming increasingly effective in his efforts to persuade the families of the strikers to use their influence to end the strike. As a consequence he was nicknamed 'Denis the Menace' and some IRA men took to walking out of his Mass. But he allowed this to disturb him as little as did the hostility of the security forces to his dossiers on their misbehaviour.

The end came on 3 October. The five strikers still fasting were ordered off and the following statement was sent out from the H Blocks on behalf of the Republican prisoners:

> Mounting pressure and cleric-inspired demoralisation led to interventions and five strikers have been taken off their fast. We accept that it is a physical and psychological impossibility to recommence a hunger strike after intervention [by the families]. A considerable majority of the present hunger strikers' families have indicated that they will intervene and under these circumstances, we feel that the hunger strike must for tactical reasons be suspended.[33]

Three days later the beginnings of the 'Portlaoise solution' began to be put into effect. Prior announced that prisoners would be allowed to wear their own clothes. Subsequently all the prisoners' demands were conceded, to a point where at the time of writing they have been issued with the keys of their own cells and are free to come and go within their wings at any hour of the day or night as they wish, watching videos, reading or playing chess.

Outside the prison walls these gains were paralleled and magnified, in political terms. Scenting the wind, Sinn Fein's director of publicity, Danny Morrison, speaking at the party's Ard Fheis on 31 October 1981, announced that the party would contest elections and argued in favour of this step by saying: 'Who here really believes we can win the war through the ballot box? But will anyone here object, if, with a ballot paper in one hand and the armalite in the other, we take power in Ireland?' Using this formula, Sinn Fein pressed on into the electoral arena, although to balance the sentiments of the old anti-abstentionist thinkers in the party, at the next Ard Fheis, on 29 October 1982, the following resolution was passed: 'Candidates in national and local elections must be unambivalent in support of the armed struggle.'

The armalite and ballot box strategy worked, in the north. In the south, the hunger strike peak of emotion was never again achieved. By 1987 Sinn Fein's share of the poll fell to only 2 per cent. In the north it took some 10 per cent of the vote in the assembly election which it contested in October 1982, and in the June 1983 Westminster election won 43 per cent of the Nationalist vote (13.4 per cent of all the Northern Ireland vote). The most important aspect of this upsurge was the defeat of Gerry Fitt by Gerry Adams. Fitt, who had strongly opposed the hunger strikers' demands, had left his own party and was becoming increasingly estranged from his constituents. On 10 November 1980, he had declared his opposition to concessions for the Blanket Men, saying:

I have to tell the House that I bitterly regret having made those representations [the concession of Special Category status in 1972]. At that time there were 80 Republican prisoners and 40 Loyalist prisoners. I believed that because of the special circumstances at that time, the granting of political special category status would end the strife. I was terribly wrong . . . the government should make it clear to those engaged in the hunger strike that they will not obtain political status. By telling the truth, and telling it in such a way that it cannot be misunderstood, it is possible that the men on hunger strike will realise the error of their ways and bring the strike to an end . . . The government must show their resolution and not allow themselves to be blackmailed by people giving support to the hunger strike . . .[34]

Then, opposing the moving of a writ for the by-election caused by Sands' death, proposed by the Welsh Nationalist MP Daifydd Thomas, Fitt said:

Have you taken into account, Mr Speaker, that the emaciated, dead or dying body of an IRA hunger striker is a more lethal weapon than an armalite rifle in the arms of the men of violence? By accepting the motion now, the house may be condemning hunger strikers and others to death.[35]

Fitt became increasingly unpopular in West Belfast, to the extent that he had once to eject protestors from his home by drawing a revolver. On 3 July 1983, his house was virtually burned down. Demonstrators broke in, piled his furniture in the back yard, burned it and then set fire to the house. It was the final act in a drama of political evolution which had seen Fitt enter parliamentary politics as a Republican Socialist. He was to leave Belfast politics as a member of the House of Lords. Nineteen days after the burning of his home, it was announced that he had been offered and accepted a life peerage. What was not announced was the fact that Margaret Thatcher had herself nominated him. Fitt had originally been proposed on Michael's Foot's list. However, Thatcher was so impressed with his stand during both the hunger strike and the period of the Falklands War, when he also supported her against the Dublin Government, that she told Foot that he could have another peer for his list and included Fitt's name in her own.[36]

If Fitt's elevation to the peerage may be taken as symbolising the Tories' attitude towards its supporters in the hunger strike, that towards its opponents at Westminster had been exemplified the previous December. Ken Livingstone, the Labour MP, had invited Adams and Morrison, then newly elected assembly members, to London to explain their policies. Both were banned from the UK mainland under the Prevention of Terrorism Act. Mrs Thatcher was silent on the position of citizens of the UK on this occasion. The exclusion order did nothing to check the rise of the northern Sinn Fein leaders. At the November 1983 Ard Fheis Ruairi O'Bradaigh and Daithi O'Conaill had stood down as president and vice-president of the organisation. Their stated policy reason was that the party was now contesting elections. Adams became president and the party moved to build on its hunger-strike-gained election expertise to set up advice centres throughout the north and to broaden its electoral base, to the extent that by 1991 the party was the second largest on Belfast City Council.

In 1992 Adams suffered a personal reverse when he was defeated by the SDLP's Joe Hendron. Tactical voting on the part of Loyalists in support of Hendron rather than a Unionist candidate ensured Adams' ousting in electoral terms, but it did nothing to stem his rising popularity. Ironically, by 15 November 1985 even Mrs Thatcher had come to obliquely concede that Sinn Fein had become a power in the land. She had been forced to agree to the Anglo-Irish Agreement, a concealed effort to shore up the SDLP against the Sinn Fein tide.

TEN

LEGAL WEAPONRY

The law should be used as just another weapon in the Government's arsenal, and in this case it becomes little more than a propaganda cover for the disposal of unwanted members of the public. For this to happen efficiently, the activities of the legal services have to be tied into the war effort in as discreet a way as possible.

Frank Kitson, *Low Intensity Operations*

St Andrew's Hotel,
Exchequer St.
Dublin

Dear———
    Have duly reported and found things is [*sic*] a fearful mess but think will be able to make a good show, [*sic*] Have been given a free hand to carry on and everyone has been very charming. Re our little stunt I see no prospects until I have got things on a firmer basis but still hope and believe there are possabilities [*sic*]. As I intend to put in for my allowances for February should be awfully grateful if you would kindly tell me the War Office rates for Ration, Servant, Lodging Fuel and Light and shall I send them to you for signature or put them [indecipherable]?[1]

The foregoing was written by a junior British officer, known as 'Captain X.Z.', on 2 March 1920. Almost seventy-five years later, in the course of researching this book, I asked a very senior one if, during the period of his counterinsurgency work in Northern Ireland, he and his men had studied the career of Michael Collins. He replied that he could not recall Collins' name ever being mentioned. I found this curious for two reasons. First, it appeared odd that, engaged in the same type of struggle against Collins' successors which Collins had waged earlier in the century, the British Army in Ireland still apparently preferred to ignore the brutal lessons taught by the Irish founder of modern urban guerrilla warfare in favour of relying on techniques developed by Frank Kitson against unfortunate members of the Mau Mau in far-off Kenya.[2] In the same way that he had used former Mau Mau activists to attack their erstwhile comrades, Kitson, then a brigadier, attempted to use ex-IRA members or supporters, known as 'freds', to confront serving Provos. Whatever success this scheme may have had in Kenya, it seems to have achieved very little in Ireland.[3] Kitson, because his was the first name to be associated with army intelligence, and because he wrote books, has achieved a paradoxical notoriety for being the IRA's *bête noire*, although his service in Northern Ireland appears to have been confined to the years 1970–2.

The second reason I was surprised at the senior officer's reply to my question was that in fact the army were still using the sort of tactics hinted at in the 1920 letter. The officer's 'free hand' to carry out his 'little stunt' required him to live under an assumed name and occupation at a civilian address, from which he and his comrades in British intelligence would sally forth, generally under the cover of darkness, to carry out unattributable assassinations against Sinn Fein targets. The letter was intercepted by Collins, who, on Bloody Sunday 1920, wiped out the leading members of the 'little stunt' operation. In shooting a driver for the 'Four Square Laundry', and carrying out an attack on an army-run massage parlour in Belfast on the same day, 2 October 1972, the IRA drew public attention to the existence of the Military Reconnaissance Force attached to the 39th Infantry Brigade. The MRF was formed by Frank Kitson during his tour of duty in Northern Ireland, as commander of the brigade. Its stated objective was 'surveillance', but amongst the 'surveillance' activities which can be attributed to it was a tendency towards shooting at Catholics from passing cars.[4]

One significantly maladroitly timed shooting, for which two MRF members were actually subsequently charged with (but acquitted of) attempted murder, took place on the day after the June 1972 IRA truce began, following the Cheyne Walk talks. This, as has been pointed out, could have wrecked the peace talks, which MI6 were keen to further and had indeed taken an active part in setting up.[5] Like the Foreign Office, MI6 'believed neither that the Labour Party represented the Parliamentary end of a subversive wedge, nor that the IRA was some rough equivalent of the Malay Communist Party . . . the Provisional Irish Republican Army was a political organisation which could be outwitted, not merely a terrorist organisation which must be destroyed.'[6] However, the fatal flaw which emerged in British policy towards Ireland over the next twenty years was that the issue was seen largely as being merely one of eradicating or containing terrorism. Initially, some elements in the British Establishment, with a memory of the help given by the Six Counties during World War II, provided Unionist politicians with sensitive intelligence information. Merlyn Rees, who constantly tries to play down the attacks on him from within the British Establishment during his period as Secretary of State for Northern Ireland, was stunned when Kevin McNamara revealed to him at an off-the-record Oral History seminar that the hard-line Bill Craig received information from MI5. Craig, MacNamara said, had told him 'specifically he got things from the British Government'[7] – and then pleaded the Official Secrets Act to protect his sources. All Rees could muster in reply was a bemused: 'Well, blow it!'[8]

After the ending of the 1972 truce the Foreign Office and the hard-liners in the security forces rivalrous to MI6 gained the ascendancy. One result of this was a smear campaign, largely orchestrated by elements in the security forces and the NIO targeting both Wilson and Rees, by 'expanding the category of "the enemy" to include Westminster politicians'.[9] In his memoirs Rees makes light of suggestions that his relationships with the army were something less than ideal. He stresses the good relationships he enjoyed with the GOC, Sir Frank King. But he does concede that tensions between the army and the RUC had led to 'serious army criticism of my office'.[10] However, the record of the period shows that there was a good deal more involved in the army's attitude to Rees than the rivalry between it and the RUC. The army were opposed to Rees' policy of phasing out detention. Figures were concocted and issued to journalists at a briefing in Lisburn in July 1974 'proving' that more than half of all released detainees returned to terrorism within months. The army also said that a recent upsurge in violence was caused by the release of some sixty-five internees that year. The fact that the violence might have had something to do with the Loyalist workers' strike, which had just brought down a historic effort to resolve the conflict, was not mentioned. Three years later, in March 1977, both the *Sunday Times* (on the 13th) and the *Irish Times* (on the 21st) carried reports saying that the true figure for internee recidivism was 20 per cent.

Moreover, the year after the Lisburn briefing, General King publicly criticised Rees' political leadership. He told a meeting of the St John's Ambulance Brigade in Nottingham that the IRA would have been beaten in a matter of months were it not for political interference from Whitehall. Afterwards it was suggested that it was not merely the St John's Ambulance Brigade that brought the General to Nottingham – it was also the town in which one Maurice Tugwell was stationed. Tugwell was a former head of Information Policy in the Six Counties. Nottingham is not exactly the focal point of the information highway; nevertheless, as Robert Fisk wrote afterwards, King's comments reached the papers 'with extraordinary speed'.[11]

To follow the details of this campaign by British security force personnel against their own elected leaders would be fascinating, but outside the scope of this book. Suffice it to say that the MRF was but one of a myriad of similar operations created with a similar objective: to gain, and act on, intelligence in such a way as to destroy the IRA by fair means or foul. To paraphrase the 1920 letter: things were still 'a fearful mess'. For example, though I have already described the effect of internment in 1971, I think that, in the context of intelligence-gathering, the following is worth reproducing:

> The next fortnight saw a huge batch of wholesale arrests in Dublin. Big internment camps were started for Sinn Fein prisoners at Ballykinlar, in the North, and at the Curragh. Whole neighbourhoods in the city were 'combed out', street by street, and practically house by house, and every young man against whom there was a shadow of suspicion was sent to an internment camp. Under the circumstances it was amazing to see how little damage was done to the Volunteers by these manoeuvres. Most of the Dublin fighting men were already taking the precautions of not sleeping at their homes, and so evaded capture.[12]

That was written by a colleague of Michael Collins, Piaras Beaslai, about an internment round-up which took place fifty years before that of 1971, but with remarkably similar, ineffectual, results. From certain British points of view, the problem was the same. William Craig informed Kevin McNamara that 'the information he had from MI5, which he had got as Minister for Home Affairs, said that the civil rights movement was riddled with IRA'.[13] How was the problem to be combated? Much the same formula was evolved in the post-1971 years as had been arrived at in earlier times. The army were used to the extent that public opinion would allow, and then reined back, generally after a bout of bad publicity, in favour of a police-based operation. In both the Collins and Provisional phase of hostilities the war between the British and Irish forces was not a matter of pitched battles between uniformed soldiers, but a contest, often a fearful one, between two sets (on the British side a multiplicity of sets) of secret services.

The British Army was visible – uniforms and armoured vehicles abounded on the streets in both sets of conflicts – but it had a limited practical value in operational terms and some decided drawbacks in the all-important propaganda war. Sinn Fein, for example, were able to make particularly good use of the SAS's activities in the Republicans' PR campaign. As one authority has stated: 'The Regiment's acronym became associated with every mysterious happening. It acquired a mystique equal to that of the hated and feared Black and Tans.'[14] And, one might add, not without good reason. The activities of the SAS will be described later (see p. 288). Here it is sufficient to note that one result of this malign mystique was that the chant of 'the primacy of the police' became so irresistible that the concept of a 'police war' was dusted off and refurbished. The British were again portrayed, just as in Collins' time, as dealing not with politically motivated violence but with Mafia-style 'godfathers' and 'racketeers'; in short, the doctrine of criminalisation was adopted as an arm of security policy. Along with this there went, as we have seen, a bending of the legal code to produce the 'conveyor belt' system. When even this did not produce the required results, the 'supergrass' system was introduced. Paid informers signed whatever statements the police required in order to obtain convictions. Censorship was employed, as was the hotly debated, frequently denied, policy of 'the enemy of my enemy is my friend'. In other words, whether officially or no, intelligence, and sometimes weapons and training, were placed at the disposal of Loyalist paramilitaries so that people targeted by the security forces were eliminated without any smoking guns being left around.

In a strange way, perhaps deriving from the nature of the conflict, perhaps from something deeper in the nature of man, the various forces in the field tended to react to the duress of the circumstances in similar fashion. Both the British/Unionist security forces and those of the Republicans and the Loyalists were riven by rivalries which must have detracted from their respective abilities to pursue their stated objectives. On the British side the divisions were caused by two major factors: cultural differences and interservice rivalry. So far as we know, unlike the feuds in the Loyalist and Republican ranks, these did not lead to actual blood-letting, but the bureaucratic infighting appears to have been ferocious. The British and Unionist security personnel impacted on each other with the same abrasion that characterised the arrival of British civil servants amongst their Stormont counterparts. And from the outset there were difficulties between the heads of the army and the RUC. For example, I found that, unprompted, senior military personnel voiced criticisms of Sir Arthur Young's view of his role as RUC Chief Constable.

Subsequently, morale problems within the badly shaken RUC, unwillingness to share information, and rows over who was in control, the army or the RUC, contributed to the tensions. From the time of the Ulsterisation, normalisation and criminalisation policy formulations in the mid-seventies it had become obvious that, if the conflict was to be Vietnamised and the natives were to do the fighting, then the much-talked-about 'primacy of the police' would have to become a reality. The policy was officially instituted in 1976. But if one had to point to a watershed date as a result of which the police actually wrested real power from the army I would select 27 August 1979.

This was the day of the slaughters at Warrenpoint and Mullaghmore which wiped out, amongst others, eighteen paratroopers and Lord Mountbatten. Lieutenant-General Timothy Creasey, the GOC, attempted to use Margaret Thatcher's visit to the Six Counties in the wake of Warrenpoint to lobby her to restore military primacy. Thatcher in fact had visited the province as a result of the *crise de moral* which Warrenpoint engendered. General Creasey, known as 'the Bull' in military circles, 'freaked out', according to one report.[15] His position was exactly the same as that of Field Marshal Sir Henry Wilson during the Collins era. Then too the thought was that the terrorists could be defeated by the army if only the politicians showed the necessary will to declare all-out war on the IRA.[16] Wilson ultimately ended up advising the new Six County Government on the formation of the RUC, and was later shot on Michael Collins' instructions. Creasey was luckier than Wilson in escaping a like fate, but he lost the war over police supremacy. Mrs Thatcher turned to the force Wilson had established, rather than the one Creasey commanded, to deal with the situation. She accepted the arguments of Kenneth Newman, the head of the RUC, who asked her for an extra 1,000 men. An all-out war as advocated by Creasey was not a political or a PR option. Newman got his extra police.

However, there was much bad blood as a result between the army and the RUC, to say nothing of the various undercover units. On the suggestion of Frank Cooper, the Iron Lady prised the former head of MI6, Maurice Oldfield, out of his retirement at All Souls College, Oxford, in October 1979, to act as a peacemaker. Oldfield, who had earlier experience of Northern Ireland, was given the official title of Security Co-ordinator. He is said to have had a soothing effect during his brief interlude in Ireland, but he died the following year. As we will see later, he was allowed neither to die nor rest in peace. Ruffled feathers were also smoothed by the departures of both Creasey and Newman within the same period. The redoubtable Jack Hermon succeeded Newman, who became Commandant of the Police Staff College and later Commissioner of the Metropolitan Police. Creasey was succeeded by Lieutenant-General Richard Lawson of the Royal Tank Regiment. Whether General Lawson's experience of armoured warfare was reckoned to have fitted him more for the situation in the streets of Belfast or for that obtaining between the rival security forces was not stated. Although the policy was to generate much controversy as to whose finger was actually on the trigger, the police's or the army's, it did have positive advantages from the British point of view, cutting down army casualties and, politically, making it easier to extract from

245

Dublin Gardai co-operation with the RUC than would have been the case with the army. Personalities apart, a principal source of friction between the army and the RUC was intelligence-gathering. Colin Wallace, who was involved in army intelligence himself at the time, once wrote that:

> To understand fully the complexities . . . that existed in Northern Ireland . . . one would need to have a detailed knowledge of conflicts and rivalries that plagued the Intelligence community at the time. The 1973/4 period was particularly critical because it was, in my opinion, a watershed in the battle for supremacy between MI5 and the SIS (MI6). In UK the problems associated with the increase in international terrorism, the miners' strike, the 3-day week, alleged increases in power and influence by Left Wing activists all had a profound effect on the roles of these two services. In Northern Ireland the chief intelligence post was given to an MI5 officer . . . much to the chagrin of the SIS . . . There was a strong difference of opinion between MI5 and the SIS over who should have overall responsibility for the Irish problem – particularly in the case of operations in the Republic. To make matters worse, the two services regarded Army Intelligence as amateurs and the RUC Special Branch as totally unreliable.

Normally the SIS (Secret Intelligence Service, also known as MI6) served abroad, and MI5 at home, but the difficulties about defining whether the Six Counties were part of the 'UK mainland' or the 'UK overseas' had resulted in MI6 taking over, or rather being given the turf, after the 1971 internment fiasco. Heath overcame the objections of Sir Maurice Oldfield that MI6 should not become involved. Oldfield's preference was for political-type activity. He favoured the planting of long-term informers and ordered MI6 to desist from the use of assassination as a tool worldwide. It was not until the period described by Wallace that MI5 won the battle, having begun to 'invade' the province from the time in 1972 when the IRA started to extend its bombing campaign to the 'UK mainland'. The outcome of these rivalries in Ireland, according to two experts, Dorrill and Ramsay, corroborates Wallace's opinion:

> By 1973, the British state [the 'state' referred to is the powerful underworld linkage of the intelligence community and the security forces] had introduced into Ireland its standard counter-insurgency kit, developed in the Empire in the post-war era. The Army undercover units, Army intelligence, IRD (Information Research Department), MI5 and MI6 – and the RUC, RUC Special Branch and the Ulster Defence Regiment – were all jostling each other in this tiny patch, deployed against an enemy whose 'territory' consisted of a handful of housing estates and a strip along the Border with the Republic.[17]

Two points should be noted here. First, the IRA's strength was, and is, somewhat greater than the foregoing would suggest. For example, in parts of Tyrone, which does not lie along the border, an IRA man on the run would probably be safer than he would in the Republic. Secondly, the area we are talking about is relatively tiny – the entire Six Counties is only the size of Yorkshire, which must say something about the efficiency of the British military effort in Northern Ireland. Nevertheless, Dorrill and Ramsay's description of the security forces' overlapping is accurate enough. The authoritative Mark Urban has noted: '. . . distrust and rivalry between the Army and RUC was to plague the whole anti-terrorist campaign'.[18] The body which was supposed to eliminate these differences was the Northern Ireland Security Policy Committee.

Two major new players joined this committee in 1976: Roy Mason, who succeeded Merlyn Rees as Secretary of State for Northern Ireland; and Kenneth Newman, the Chief Constable of the RUC. The latter faced a rather different police landscape from that which had confronted Sir Arthur Young. From 1976 on, the RUC began to develop 'a variety of specialist surveillance and firearms units of its own'.[19] Mason, the key figure on the committee, was security-oriented, remembered in Belfast as being uninterested in political activity and in favour of economic expenditure on the area, combined with a tough policy towards the IRA. This was summed up by his resonant declaration that he intended to squeeze the IRA 'like a tube of toothpaste'.[20] The year after Mason arrived he was joined on the security committee by two army commanders who shared his outlook towards the IRA. They were the GOC, General Creasey, and Major-General Richard Trant, Commander Land Forces (CLF). This high-powered quartet, together with another forceful personality, Jack Hermon, combined on the NISPC to step up the level of covert operations in the province.

In military terms these operations probably did attain a degree of success. One can only speculate as to what the IRA's reorganisation and regrouping in the cell system/*Green Book* era would have achieved without the NISPC's operations. However, this type of underground warfare, conducted in what was portrayed as a west European democracy, was doomed inevitably to attract publicity, criticism and controversy. As a British general who conducted counterinsurgency operations put it to me: 'It gets dirty when you get down to that level.' The level the general was referring to may be thought of as the Deniable Zone. For several years it was denied that 'dirty tricks' were an integral part of security policy. The notion that there could be collusion between the security forces and Loyalist paramilitaries was scoffed at. So too were Nationalist claims that the RUC and the army were operating a shoot-to-kill policy in which targeted IRA men, and sometimes innocent people who were mistaken for IRA men, were summarily 'taken out' by the forces of law and order.

Throughout the seventies and eighties these and related claims of security force brutality were well documented by a group of priests, acting either separately or together. These were Fr Brian Brady, Fr Denis Faul and Fr Raymond Murray. Between them they produced a flood of pamphlets and dossiers on human rights abuses by the security forces – and sometimes, particularly in the case of Fr Faul, by the IRA. No student of the troubles can overlook their courageous, exhaustive, and exhausting, work. Fr Brady for example was a pioneer in the field of job equality. His ideas were taken up by Nationalist politicians and eventually led to the setting-up of the Fair Employment Agency. He furthered Fr Sean McManus' idea of the MacBride Principles, governing American investment in the Six Counties. Sean MacBride agreed to lend his name to the scheme after a visit from Brady. Though often denied and resisted, sometimes by their own conservative, episcopal superiors, the claims of ill-treatment by the three priests gradually forced their way on to the agendas of the Department of Foreign Affairs in Dublin, civil rights agencies such as Amnesty International and the Association for Legal Justice, and, probably most tellingly, Irish-American activists.

The shoot-to-kill incidents generally tended to occur as a result of the mounting of stake-outs or checkpoints. After the fusillades died away it would be alleged that the dead had opened fire when challenged to put up their hands, or perhaps had driven past the checkpoints, firing at the security personnel, or somesuch. In any event, only insiders realised that the deaths resulting from these sanguinary encounters usually included prominent IRA activists such as a local OC, or a much-wanted sniper or bomber. Usually, but not inevitably. To give but one example: sixteen-year-old John Boyle, shot dead in broad daylight by the SAS on 11 July 1978, had nothing whatever to do with the IRA. He had entered a graveyard out of curiosity to examine an arms cache which his family had reported finding to the police. Although he then went on to acquit the soldiers involved Mr Justice Lowry found, on 4 July 1979, that after the teenager's death the soldiers had emptied the contents of the bag containing the guns on to the ground to make it appear that the lad had been shot moving the cache. The judge said:

> The Army and Soldier A [in such cases it is common practice to refer to soldiers by letters of the alphabet only, so as to protect their identities] and the patrol gravely mishandled the operation because they shot an innocent boy who, whether he was holding a gun or no, had no capacity to harm them.[21]

Cornelius Boyle, the boy's father, told friends[22] afterwards that he felt the police had let him down. They should have warned him that a stake-out was mounted after he reported the cache. Had they done so he said his son would still be alive. But speaking about the army he said: 'I have little to say about the army. They have not deviated one inch from the path ever trod by their predecessors in Ireland.' It was a sentiment many Nationalists would have echoed. However, in shoot-to-kill cases, outsiders, particularly Unionist and Tory outsiders, tended to share the views of another prominent Northern Ireland judge, Lord Justice Gibson. Acquitting three RUC officers of murder, Gibson commended them for having brought three men, shot dead at a roadblock, to 'the final court of justice'.[23]

The most significant figures involved in publicising the 'dirty tricks' and 'shoot-to-kill' policies are two former army operatives, Colin Wallace and Fred Holroyd, and three senior British detectives, John Stalker, Colin Sampson and John Stevens. All, undeniably, spoke from a position of having inside experience of how the system worked. I will therefore confine discussion of the policies to matters concerning them and exclude allegations emanating from Nationalist circles. I am also excluding the examination of Loyalist claims, of which there are many. These range from well-known UDA figures like the former soldier, Albert Wallace Baker – from whom Fr Faul took lengthy and disturbing statements concerning army involvement in unacknowledged deaths – to contacts of my own who, over the years, have given examples of collusion between some branches of the security forces. Baker, who was sentenced to life imprisonment in 1973 for a series of robberies, mutilations and murders, was allowed to serve his sentence in England. Here, in addition to being interviewed by Fr Faul, he gave a tape-recorded interview[24] to the Labour MP, Ken Livingstone, in the course of which he said that RUC weapons were given to the UDA 'on higher authority'. He gave details of an assassination carried out 'with police guns and machine-guns – Sterling sub-machine guns'. Apart from such dramatic statements concerning the illegal disposal of material to known killers, I have been supplied with lesser details, which nevertheless indicate Loyalist paramilitary collusion with the security forces. For example, I was given the name of a military installation where one notorious UDA figure, reckoned to have notched up some thirty murders, could be seen regularly filling up his car with free petrol. Such small anecdotes can speak volumes.

All of the five security figures mentioned above were in their turn involved in events which created massive publicity. All must have endured a greater or lesser degree of frustration as a result of their work in Northern Ireland; certainly the three detectives did. Initially, at least, the authorities failed to act on the findings of Sampson and Stevens. Holroyd, Stalker and Wallace all suffered severe reverses in their careers. Wallace actually served a prison term for manslaughter on what he avers was a trumped-up charge.

This is how his saga began. In the early stages of the Troubles the Foreign Office sent to Northern Ireland a team of psychological warfare experts who had worked in other colonial trouble spots.[25] They were members of the Information Research Department (IRD). One of their number, Hugh Mooney, was seconded to the army to set up a psychological warfare unit. It carried out what was known in Brigadier Kitson's terminology as 'information policy', operating from Army HQ in Lisburn under the guise of the Army Press Office. Colin Wallace was officially described as the Senior Information Officer (Psychological Operations), Army HQ. He was a member of the Northern Ireland Information Co-ordinating Committee. At various times he posed as a member of the UDR and as a barrister involved in the Bloody Sunday Tribunal set up under Lord Widgery. In plain language, information policy, from 1971 onwards, meant engaging in professional lying. Wallace was one of its principal exponents. But, unlike those around him in the IRD world, he was an Ulsterman. This fact may have had a bearing on what befell him.

Until his career fell apart, Wallace had been a highly successful operator. For example, he was so successful in planting propaganda on one journalist, who figured large in the Belfast media circus, that the man's life was threatened by the IRA. He had published a story concocted by Wallace describing IRA 'embezzle-ment'. Wallace had to secrete the journalist in Butlin's Bognor Regis holiday camp until the fuss died down. He became internationally known through his dealings with the hordes of correspondents who swarmed into Belfast as the Troubles gathered momentum. Wallace later described information policy as containing, apart from normal press briefing, the following function:

> Information policy . . . was seen as a counter-propaganda organisation dealing in white information. It did have a . . . totally undeniable role in which black operations popularly known as dirty tricks were used. Being the only unit of its kind in the province, the Information Policy undertook other assignments for other agencies such as the Northern Ireland Office, the RUC, etc . . .[26]

Some of the 'other assignments' included preparing a bogus speech for Merlyn Rees in which he inveighed against the savagery of the IRA internees who had deliberately burned police dogs to death when they burned their huts at Long Kesh. In fact the only dogs ever killed in the conflict were shot by army snipers in the Ballymurphy area of Belfast because their barking betrayed the presence of army patrols. The Rees speech was concocted with an eye to the British dog-loving public. Other planted stories included 'eyewitness' accounts of IRA units raping girls at gunpoint. Some were said to have been made pregnant. Wallace, a cool, self-controlled individual who relaxed by doing parachute jumps, was dismissed for allegedly passing a classified document to Robert Fisk, then the *Times* correspondent in Belfast. At the time of writing he was working on what he described as 'management consultancy, engaged in the selection and training of graduates'.[27] Fisk in fact never saw the document which the authorities claimed Wallace attempted to leak to him.[28] He was in London, making arrangements in connection with a transfer to the foreign desk which had been agreed some time earlier. He had just been named Journalist of the Year and intended to round this out by writing two major stories: one a series on the fact that the army were running undercover death squads; the other that there was a 'black propaganda' unit operating out of Lisburn.

I have known and admired Fisk and his work for more than twenty-five years; Wallace I only met as a result of my researches for this book. He was obviously conspiracy-minded, but he impressed me as a sane, rational individual. The following account is based on what Wallace told me.

Towards the end of 1974, Lisburn became aware that both sets of paramilitaries, Loyalist and Republican, had been giving indications to journalists of the existence of collusion with death squads. At this stage there was a lot of leaking to journalists; partly because of the RUC/army rivalry. But partly also because of a general unhappiness amongst some of the more morally conscious in both police and army. I have known journalists to receive unsolicited information of a highly sensitive nature from officers who had decided that their reporting made them trustworthy. One reporter, stopped at what appeared to be a routine army checkpoint, suddenly found himself being handed a classified document and told: 'You know we're being pulled out.' In another incident an unidentified RUC Special Branch man pulled alongside a prominent journalist and began reading to him from a diary specific examples of army misbehaviour. Apparently the RUC man was angered by some of the army shootings which had taken place shortly before.

Fisk's investigations into 'dirty tricks' and the use of black propaganda were potentially fissionable in this uncertain climate. It was decided that, if leaks had reached such proportions that there was a prospect of the Journalist of the Year writing in the London *Times* about things which had even been kept from the ears of the Secretary of State for Northern Ireland, Merlyn Rees, then special measures were called for. The army's civilian PR head, Peter Broderick, had already tried to report Fisk to *The Times* as a 'hostile reporter'.[29] According to Wallace it was decided to deal with the affair by staging what was described as a 'study day' on psychological warfare.

The study day, held in mid-January 1975, was supposed to be under the auspices of General Peter Leng, then Commander Land Forces. It was attended by various branches of the security forces, including the RUC. It was said at the time that the RUC would be most likely to leak details of what transpired. Wallace did not attend the study day, but he wrote the script for it. The picture of psychological warfare which was to emerge from the carefully crafted seminar was bland, and dealt mainly with the use of information. There was no indication that the army went in for disinformation, black propaganda or dirty tricks, nothing sinister. Wallace's understanding of the operation was that, being conducted with apparent secrecy, it would give the desired impression of what the army press section was doing when leaked to the media. Wallace later talked to Fisk about the sanitised version of information policy and promised to deliver the script to him. He says he cleared this with his superiors.

At the time the study day was held, Wallace, like Fisk, was also preparing to leave Belfast. He had been posted to Preston, to serve at Army HQ, North West, and had thrown a farewell party. On the day he was leaving, he drove first to the docks to place his belongings aboard a ship for Liverpool. He realised he was being followed, and thinking his shadowers were terrorists pulled into an army installation, Tyrone House, on the Malone Road, to phone Lisburn, but when he came out the car had disappeared. He says he then carried on to Hillsborough, to push the envelope containing the script through Fisk's letter box. Outside the house was a post office van containing what Wallace now believes to have been members of MI5. He took up his Preston posting early in February and was visited soon afterwards by a sergeant and an inspector from the RUC investigating the Fisk incident.

Wallace says now that he thinks the entire study day operation was a 'sting' aimed at himself. He says he had earlier fallen out with his superiors over other dirty tricks he disapproved of, principally the Kincora House scandal and the 'Clockwork Orange' operation. Clockwork Orange involved stratagems such as falsifying 'IRA records' to show misappropriation of funds, involvement with communism and other pieces of disinformation. He says that this falsification involved producing bogus Sinn Fein Ard Fheis resolutions, also designed to show a pro-communist slant, and that these efforts were not confined to the Republicans. The Orange paramilitaries were subject to the same treatment. For example, the Tara organisation was used to fabricate links between the UVF and communism. He alleges that the dirty tricks went even further afield, linking both Stan Orme and Merlyn Rees with left-wing groups through the operations of the Housing Executive, and involving the forging of CIA identity cards.

The RUC told Fisk that a neighbour of his had seen a document while in his house. Fisk did not believe this story and refused to accompany three RUC officers, and instead asked the officers to read back the notes which they were making of the interview so that he could tape them![30] They were understandably nonplussed, as readers will deduce for themselves when they come to read about Castlereagh (see p. 274): this was not how RUC men from Castlereagh interrogation centre were accustomed to conducting their interviews. Fisk added to their confusion by asking them to show him the document. They could only show him its heading, marked

'Confidential'. The police left after Fisk agreed to go to Castlereagh in his own time.

Instead he packed his files and notes and headed south. Across the border he phoned his boss, Charles Douglas-Home, the editor of *The Times*, to say that something strange was happening. He then booked into Jury's Hotel, Dublin. What he did not do was phone the British Embassy. The next evening, however, he received a visit from Michael Daly, who described himself as First Secretary of the British Embassy but who was thought by the Irish security authorities of the time to be an MI6 agent. Fisk was later to be informed by an Irish diplomat that Daly had raised eyebrows by abruptly departing from an official dinner shortly beforehand. He certainly caused Fisk to raise his when he explained his mission.

Daly said that he had reason to believe that Fisk was 'in possession of documents the property of Her Majesty's Government'.[31] Obviously there was panic at a high level that Fisk had got his hands on something more explosive than a document dealing with the study day. It is quite possible that Wallace did push such a report through Fisk's door, but that someone else retrieved it and substituted something stronger.

At all events I have been told that the document which the police were worried about dealt with Kincora. Daly wanted Fisk to take him to his room, but instead Fisk threatened to call the police to have Daly charged with threatening behaviour. Daly left, and Fisk informed the Irish diplomatic service what had happened. His safety in the Republic was guaranteed and he stayed on in Dublin for another two weeks. During this time his editor approached Merlyn Rees, who said the affair was 'a police matter'. Fisk himself got word to the RUC, threatening that if they had set up the document's 'discovery', then this would amount to a conspiracy to commit breaking and entering.

As he had also publicised Daly's approaches in the *Times*, the pressures bore fruit. A mysterious invitation to tea with the RUC Chief Constable was pushed under his hotel bedroom door. Fisk checked that the invitation was real and drove to Belfast. The tea passed off swimmingly. Nothing was said about what had gone before and Fisk was granted the privilege of spending a night on tour with the RUC's Special Patrol Group. Douglas-Home suggested that it would be a good idea for Fisk to stay on in Belfast for a couple of months before taking up his new posting so that it could not be said that he had been pulled out of Belfast as a result of the affair.

During this time Fisk managed to get his hands on a parachute officer's report on another house Fisk had occupied, 'complete with furnishings and wallpaper but that was about all'.[32] He also spoke to the person who was supposed to have gone into his house, who confirmed that the RUC had made the approach to go into the house to 'discover' the Wallace document. Fisk's assessment of the affair was that it was an army/RUC 'sting' designed to nobble both himself and Wallace under the Official Secrets Act. This would have rendered Wallace liable to prosecution and prevented Fisk from writing about what had happened. Both men could then have been easily smeared by the information policy operators at Lisburn and there would have been plenty of time to unearth, or plant, whatever other classified documents had allegedly gone missing.

Fisk later had the satisfaction of revealing some highly sensitive information concerning information policy, including the fact that the dirty tricks brigade at Lisburn had been forging journalists' press passes. Fisk also established that a committee, known as the Information Co-ordinating Committee, had been set up at Stormont, under Michael Cudlipp, which had decided, amongst other things, to use details about 'the personal lives of extremist leaders' to discredit them in the eyes of their supporters.[33] One of the dossiers described by Fisk consisted of information about Americans alleged to be supporters of the IRA. The dossier gave their names, home telephone numbers and addresses. It also contained titillating information such as the fact that one of those named had '40 adulteries during a three month period'. It was the army's decision to generate details about the personal lives of not only 'extremist leaders' but also politicians and community leaders that led to setting up the rent-a-boy ring, drawn from boys' homes in the Six Counties, and to the Kincora scandal described below.

Wallace's subsequent career can be traced through the world's headlines, and a mountain of filmed interviews.[34] In September of 1980, while he was working as Chief Information Officer to Arun District Council in Sussex, he was charged with the manslaughter of Jonathan Lewis, a Brighton antique dealer. Wallace had been having an affair with his wife, Jane. The Duke of Norfolk, a former army intelligence officer with the Ministry of Defence, offered to give bail for him. Wallace's wife, Eileen, was the Duke's secretary. The following March Wallace received a ten-year sentence. Readers can learn more of the story from Paul Foot's book, *Who Framed Colin Wallace*.[35] It should preferably be read in conjunction with that of the former British intelligence operative Peter Wright, *Spycatcher*,[36] whose publication Margaret Thatcher tried to prevent. Between the two books there emerges a picture of skulduggery and partly out-of-control intelligence agencies operating in an England in decline. A combination of the old-boy network and the power of the British security establishment, both of which have strong links to the media, facilitated the spread of disinformation about anything they wished to target, including their own Labour government, with a view to keeping themselves in business.

A principal smear was that the Comintern had Wilson and his cabinet in their pay. Speaking of the period between the two elections of 1974, Marcia Falkender, Wilson's much-discussed secretary, said with feeling: 'It is difficult to write about those few months without inviting a charge of paranoia.'[37]

Robert Fisk, who covered the situation on the ground in the Six Counties, recalled that it was

a time when naval officers allegedly booed Wilson on a visit to a Royal Navy vessel and when Charles Douglas-Home, the then Home Editor of *The Times* . . . was able to suggest in *The Times*, in all seriousness, that British officers might in some circumstances consider mutinying against the Labour government (I even think that it was the same period that Cecil King asked Mountbatten if he'd like to run the country . . .).[38]

253

When I asked him how it felt to serve such a sentence in the circumstances, Wallace replied laconically: 'They were seven long years.'[39] Their length, however, has not made him any the less inclined to fight his case. He is suing the Attorney-General and still defends startling claims about the shoot-to-kill policy in the Six Counties such as those contained in a letter he wrote in 1986 to the Labour MP, Peter Archer:

> During the first six months of 1975 thirty-five Roman Catholics were assassinated in Ulster. The majority of these were killed by members of the security forces or loyalist paramilitary groups such as the UVF, UFF, PAF, UDA, etc., working as agents of the security services and supplied with weapons by the security forces.[40]

In conversation with me, Wallace went even further than this, giving chapter and verse of how, to protect a particularly nasty piece of collusion, the authorities connived at the murder of an RUC sergeant who had begun to pursue the case. Wallace named the man whom he said had carried out the murder, a notorious UDA hit man in the Lurgan–Portadown area. The unsavoury affair involved another RUC death, that of an inspector who was driven to commit suicide. 'The RUC is not clean,' said Wallace musingly.

The case of Fred Holroyd has also received enormous publicity. Ironically enough a major TV exposé of his case, by Duncan Campbell and Christopher Hird in a *Diverse Reports* programme, was screened on Channel Four on the evening (2 May 1984) of the publication of the North of Ireland Forum Report in Dublin.[41] The juxtaposition provided a classic illustration of the contrast between real life – and death – in the Deniable Zone and the talking-shop activities of politicians, largely carried on for the benefit of the optics.

In 1974–5, Holroyd was a captain in military intelligence on undercover attachment to the RUC Special Branch unit in Portadown. He also worked closely with the HQ of the army's 3rd Brigade which was responsible for the Republican stronghold of South Armagh and carried out assignments for MI6, who had a unit at Army HQ in Lisburn known as 'the political secretariat'. He was thus in a cockpit position to know exactly how the war was being waged. One of those who saw how in turn Holroyd waged his part of that war, RUC Assistant Chief Constable Charles Rogers, described him as '. . . a man of unquestionable loyalty, outstanding courage with a devotion to duty that one looks for but rarely finds today'.[42] It was said that he had a success record against terrorists that 'had not been equalled before or since' his period of service.[43]

That service came to an end in 1975, apparently as a result of the MI6 war with MI5. The SIS chief in the Six Counties at the time, Craig Smellie, was also transferred in 1975 (to Athens, to take over its station there). Holroyd's downfall may have occurred because Smellie asked him to brief him on his activities without telling his superiors. Holroyd did tell his boss and found himself the piggy in the middle in the resultant crossfire. He was peremptorily transferred from his post in the Six Counties on the grounds that he needed psychiatric treatment which could only be supplied in a British hospital. He resigned his commission in 1976 and joined the Rhodesian Army.

Subsequently he became increasingly bitter at his treatment, and at the pressures which he felt were brought to bear on employers who might otherwise have given him jobs commensurate with his previous status. During 1994–5 when I had knowledge of his circumstances he was working as a £3-an-hour security guard. He showed me army-issue utensils and items such as coffee, tea, and packet soups supplied by friends at the nearby paratroop base. Only this sort of help, he said, had enabled him to survive on his return to England from Rhodesia. Amongst the disclosures which he felt driven to make on the Channel Four programme as a result of his experiences were: that Loyalist killers were deliberately allowed to go unpunished; that British forces carried out kidnappings, snatching wanted men from the Republic; that sometimes the security forces deliberately allowed operations which they had foreknowledge of to go ahead so as to discredit the IRA, thereby putting civilian lives at risk; that similarly, instead of capturing weaponry and explosives found in IRA dumps, they would sabotage the material so that it would booby-trap its owners; that the security forces carried out acts of intimidation, such as sending threatening letters containing bullets to civil rights activists; and that they carried out bank raids and conducted illegal break-ins.

I can certainly testify to the truth of some of these charges. For example, I know that Sean McKenna, the hunger-striker whose condition caused the calling-off of the first big IRA hunger strike, was kidnapped at Christmas 1980 by the SAS from the Republic and brought across the border, thus fetching up in H-Blocks. The existence of a shoot-to-kill policy, sometimes involving Loyalist paramilitaries, will, I think, hardly be disputed after reading this chapter, nor indeed can one doubt that acts of intimidation and activities such as bank robberies also took place in view of what happened during the H Block protest and the Littlejohn saga, for example. Where dirty tricks are concerned, there are those who might demur at entering in this category one of Holroyd's ruses concerning a Catholic woman informant in Lurgan. In effect he reversed the IRA's 'honey-trap' enticement of sometimes using women to lure unsuspecting soldiers not to bed but to the tomb. In return for information, he had the woman's sexual needs attended to at regular intervals by soldiers who added a new dimension to the term 'volunteering for service'.

But there can be no dispute about including in the dirty tricks category the deliberate derailing of a train in a Catholic area of Portadown, after the army and the RUC were informed that it contained an IRA bomb.[44] The bomb failed to go off, thus frustrating the hope that it might have killed Catholics and thus discredited the IRA.

Holroyd was also telling the truth when he cited as a dirty trick the case of Eugene McQuaid, who was blown up while 'doing a turn', ferrying an IRA rocket on his motorbike. The explosion was not accidental. Having learned of the rocket's existence in a dump south of the border, the British Army, instead of tipping off the Gardai, crossed the border secretly and doctored the explosives so that they became highly volatile. Thus, on the morning of 5 October 1974, as he drove along the busy main road to the bustling, predominantly Catholic town of Newry, McQuaid in fact constituted a serious danger to himself and to the public. The bomb went off, blowing him to pieces, after he had executed a sudden U-turn on spotting an army checkpoint, which he could just as easily have destroyed. By chance I drove past about ten minutes after the explosion. Pieces of McQuaid's body were being covered with sheets and there were dozens of armed soldiers on the road and in the fields around, all obviously in a high state of alert. Not the place to pull up. But rounding the first corner after the scene, about two hundred yards away, I saw an RUC man and slowed to ask him what had happened. Had there been an explosion? He looked at me hard and then, speaking with a distinctly hostile air, made a response which symbolises the entire official policy towards dirty tricks. 'Explosion, what explosion? I didn't see anything, didn't hear anything. I mind my own business . . .'

Obviously officialdom was also keen to discredit Holroyd and Wallace's claims. A major effort in this direction appeared, surprisingly, or perhaps cleverly enough, in the London *Independent*. The paper's Northern Ireland correspondent, David McKitterick, came into possession, or was fed, information which caused him to write a lengthy piece challenging some of the Holroyd/Wallace evidence.[45] In particular he disputed a claim by Holroyd that he had heard from Captain Robert Nairac's own lips a boast that this famous (or, if one is a Republican, infamous) young officer had crossed the border to kill a prominent IRA man called John Francis Green. Holroyd claimed that Nairac had given him a polaroid picture which he had taken of Green after he had killed him. Green's death was one of the reasons the 1975 IRA ceasefire finally ended. MI6 had helped to engineer the truce; MI5 wanted it broken down.

Wallace complained to the Press Council that the *Independent* articles had contained inaccuracies about him. His complaint was upheld. Later, in 1990, the Calcutt Inquiry, set up under David Calcutt QC, found that Wallace had been unjustly dismissed, and said that his appeal against being fired had been rejected after the Ministry of Defence had contacted the appeal board. Calcutt recommended that Wallace receive compensation. Holroyd too received a small gesture of atonement, indicating that his departure from the army was not what was claimed. The 'mental stability' allegation was expunged from his record. Another indication that the pair could have been the victims of disinformation came from Archie Hamilton, Minister for the Armed Forces, in reply to a parliamentary question, when he announced the setting-up of the Calcutt Inquiry. He said:

> It has not since the mid-1970s been the policy to disseminate disinformation in Northern Ireland in ways designed to denigrate individuals and/or organisations for propaganda purposes.[46]

Decoded, that means the Government was at least admitting there was a disinformation policy in operation at the material time. But it also marked a further effort to convince public opinion that the dirty tricks campaign had been an aberration which had now concluded. Information was leaked to the *Sunday Times* and the *Guardian* in 1977 which led the *Guardian* to conclude: '. . . the so-called "dirty tricks" department seems to have all but ceased operations in 1975. There is little evidence of organised skulduggery after that.'[47]

There was in fact a great deal of 'organised skulduggery after that'. In saying this, I am not attempting to evaluate the claims of Holroyd and Wallace. I am concerned to show two things: first, the nature of the war in Northern Ireland; secondly the fact that despite efforts to discredit both men, the policies they spoke of continued in operation after their departure from Northern Ireland, right up to the ending of hostilities in 1994. Let us for a moment allow for the possibility that either, or both, men could be malicious, misinformed or simply mistaken. Are we to believe that then, after Holroyd and Wallace's service in the Six Counties had long ended, successive teams of detectives, led by experienced, respected English policemen, were also wrong and malicious? I think not. Certainly, whatever evil was going on in Northern Ireland in the world of counterinsurgency, it worked a powerful alchemy. Michael Bettaney, the MI5 officer who was involved in counterinsurgency at Stormont from 1976 to 1978, went to jail in 1984 for twenty-three years for passing secrets to the Russians. His rethinking of his attitude to his government was stated by the *Guardian* to have been caused by his Belfast duties. The paper said: 'The experience set off an emotional and intellectual earthquake in him and he began to have serious doubts about the British role in Northern Ireland.'[48]

Before discussing the activities of the policemen concerned, an attitude of distrust towards the north's courts system, widely prevalent in the security forces, has to be borne in mind. The army, realising that the Diplock courts, in the absence of juries, were unlikely to convict soldiers accused of killing a civilian 'in the line of duty', saw little virtue in disclosing soldiers' identities by having them arraigned before such courts in the first place. Both the army and the RUC tended to regard the presence of lawyers in court as a source of aid and comfort to terrorists. Mark Urban, a former soldier and defence correspondent for the *Independent* for three years, found that:

> . . . officers regard many of the lawyers representing suspects or the families of people shot dead by the Army as unofficial agents of the IRA. They suggest, for example, that a lawyer may agree to pass a message from a terrorist to his commander, or might use cross-examination of a security force witness in an attempt to probe whether an operation has resulted from a leak within the IRA.[49]

He quotes a 'senior officer' as saying: 'If you go into underground warfare, you know that you will never fully be able to explain that side of life.' Nor that side of death, it might be added. For it was these attitudes that cost the life of one of the most prominent lawyers in the Six Counties, the Nationalist solicitor, Pat Finucane. Finucane was having his evening meal with his wife and children on 12 February 1989 when Loyalist gunmen called at his Belfast home and shot him dead. Other Nationalist lawyers have received death threats.

Another area of legal procedure where the army's views on due process demonstrably brought about change is that of coroners' verdicts. Urban quotes Frank Kitson's attitude to the law in a counterinsurgency situation:

> Everything done by a government and its agents must be legal. But this does not mean that

the government must work within exactly the same set of laws during an insurgency which existed beforehand.[50]

This sentiment falls squarely within the grand tradition of British justice in Ireland. The law should not be broken, merely changed. And changed it duly was in 1980. Up to that year security force shootings, including those of the SAS and of RUC undercover squads, were subject to normal inquest proceedings. Then the Conservatives directed that coroners' rules be amended so that open verdicts could not be recorded. This meant that a coroner could no longer indicate that it was not the deceased who was responsible for his or her death. Instead coroners were restricted to 'findings' saying when, where and how the person had died. The change helped to increase the controversy over (and the number of) shoot-to-kill incidents. The Armagh coroner, Mr Gerard Curran, resigned (on 22 August 1984), telling the media that he was doing so because of 'grave irregularities' in RUC files dealing with the deaths of two INLA members, described below.

These deaths formed part of a cycle of seven killings in November and December of 1982 which moved the debate on the shoot-to-kill policy on to a new plane. Although individual responsibilities were not fixed, and the policy was continued by other elements in the security forces, notably the SAS, the ill-fated Stalker Inquiry did establish that history was repeating itself in Ireland.

In reply to the success of Michael Collins' unit, 'The Squad', in wiping out informers and intelligence agents, the British formed not only 'Captain X.Z.'-type army units, but RIC death squads also. In Dublin the principal police assassination team was led by Head Constable Igoe.[51] In Belfast, the doings of Inspectors Harrison and Nixon of the (then newly formed) RUC are still remembered with horror by Catholics, acclaim in certain Loyalist circles.[52] The incidents which established that latter-day Igoes and Nixons were again active were as follows.

On 11 November 1982, an RUC death squad shot dead three unarmed men at Tullygally, near Lurgan, Co. Armagh. They were Eugene Toman, Sean Burns and Gervaise McKerr. On the 24th of the month the same death squad shot another two youths, again near Lurgan, at a hayshed in Ballyneery Road North. One, a seventeen-year-old, Michael Justin Tighe, died; the other, nineteen-year-old Martin McCauley, was badly injured but recovered. Neither was armed. On 12 December another member of the squad shot two men dead 'at a roadblock'. The dead were Seamus Grew and Roddy Carroll of the INLA; again, neither was armed.

The foregoing formed the core of the ill-fated Stalker investigation. Because of a mounting tide of adverse publicity, London was forced to concede an inquiry. John Stalker, one of the rising stars of the British police firmament – at the time Deputy Chief Constable of the Greater Manchester area – was asked, in May 1984, to head an investigation into the allegations of the existence of a shoot-to-kill policy. Too late, Stalker discovered that by accepting the invitation he had destroyed his police career. His enquiries and those of his team were resented and resisted by, amongst others, Jack Hermon, the then Chief Constable of the RUC, and he was eventually forced into resigning from the profession which he had both loved and adorned.[53] Said Stalker: 'There undoubtedly developed a strongly hostile feeling towards us at middle and senior levels of the RUC Special Branch.'[54] The doings of the NISPC were not for the prying eyes of an idealistic Manchester cop. 'Remember, Mr Stalker, you are in a jungle now' were Hermon's parting words to Stalker after their first meeting.[55] On that occasion Hermon also surprised Stalker by handing him Stalker's mother's family tree, sketched on the back of a flattened cigarette package – the tree, containing the names of relations Stalker had never previously heard of, showed that she was a Catholic ... However, though his official inquiry was aborted, Stalker's efforts, and the court cases resulting from some of the shootings, chiefly those of Grew and Carroll, did establish some undeniable facts about the shoot-to-kill policy.

These included the fact that there was a linking factor in the first two fatal shootings listed above. The three dead men, Toman, Burns and McKerr, and the wounded McCauley had all been named by an informer as having being implicated in the blowing-up of three RUC men at Kinnego, near Lurgan, on 27 October 1982. As there was no other evidence against them they were never interrogated but, as Stalker says, they 'were shot by police within the next six weeks'.[56] The hayshed in which McCauley was wounded and his companion, Michael Tighe, was shot dead was the same one in which the Kinnego explosives had been stored. At McCauley's trial the police admitted that they had told lies about having seen a gunman enter the hayshed. They had, they said, reiterated a story laid down for them by their seniors.

Moreover, the old inter-service rivalry factor reasserted itself. It transpired that, unknown to the RUC, MI5 had planted an electronic bug in the shed which had recorded the true sequence of events. However, Stalker was not allowed access to this crucial piece of evidence. Hermon at first refused to hand over the tape, and finally told him that it had been destroyed.

During his trial for the murder of Seamus Grew, of which he was acquitted (no one was charged with Carroll's death), Constable John Robinson also stated that he had been instructed by his superiors to tell lies about the incident. It later transpired that Grew and Carroll had not been shot because of a chance roadblock, but as a result of a lengthy surveillance operation, which had involved entering the Republic, not so much to follow the two dead men as to get a line on their leader, Dominic McGlinchey, the head of the illegal Republican group, the Irish National Liberation Army (see p 277).[57] But again the deadly Keystone Cops nature of the RUC–army rivalry played a malign role in the affair.

The cover story statement put out by the RUC after the shootings of Grew and Carroll said that they had been shot after crashing a roadblock and injuring a policeman. Stalker felt that he might have been able to prove that, to bolster this story, an RUC constable was made to roll in mud so as to make it appear he had been hit by a car.[58] In fact Grew and Carroll had avoided police surveillance because of yet another cock-up between the army and the RUC. There was a crash involving an undercover army car and a police car in which a policeman suffered a broken leg. The police later claimed that the policeman's broken leg was caused by Grew and Carroll crashing the checkpoint. (The case could have been worse: in another RUC/army incident, trigger-happy RUC men shot two British soldiers dead.)[59]

The RUC inspector who had trailed them in the Republic seeing the crash realised that his quarry had slipped by unnoticed in the confusion. He stopped to pick up Constable Robinson, who was a member of E4A, the RUC undercover death squad which was trained by the SAS, and followed the two escaping INLA men. At Mullacreavie Park, a Catholic area of Armagh, the inspector pulled ahead of Grew and Carroll, causing them to stop. Robinson shot both men dead, emptying and reloading his revolver. Stalker comments:

> The Special Branch Inspector, who had had the opportunity to see everything and knew the truth, drove off, and his evidence was kept secret from the CID investigating the deaths and from the Director of Public Prosecutions and courts. Records were altered to hide the use of undercover cars in that part of Northern Ireland.[60]

In fact there was another witness who 'knew the truth'. There was a second policeman involved in the shooting. He fired a number of rounds from a .223 Ruger rifle into the car. As Michael O'Connell has commented: 'It is a fact that the last moments of Seamus Grew and Roderick Carroll were witnessed not only by the man who killed them both, but also by another eyewitness who could have supported his version of events but did not do so.'[61]

John Stalker ceased to be a policeman on 13 March 1987, and the following month the IRA concluded this particular vignette of justice, Northern Ireland-style, with a car bomb which sent Mr Justice Gibson and his wife to 'the final court of justice'. Of course the sort of incident investigated by Stalker did not end there. His inquiry was wound up, the NISPC was not. The policy-makers in Whitehall and Stormont continued in their old ways with some new variations.

As the Stalker affair had aroused not only national, but international criticism, particularly in America, a token effort was made to appease public opinion by apparently continuing his efforts to investigate the shoot-to-kill policy. Another English policeman, Colin Sampson, Chief Constable of West Yorkshire, was appointed. In 1988 Sampson recommended to the Director of Public Prosecutions, Sir Barry Shaw, that eleven members of the RUC be charged in connection with the six killings in Armagh in November and December of 1982. The DPP agreed, but the Attorney-General, Sir Patrick Mayhew, ruled that while there was prima-facie evidence of attempts to pervert the course of justice, there would be no prosecutions on the grounds of 'national security'.[62]

However, the following year, 1989, the savage immorality of the 'enemy of my enemy is my friend' policy burst upon the public consciousness once more in such a way as to force yet another official inquiry. This time the investigating team of British detectives was headed by John Stevens, the Deputy Chief Constable of Cambridgeshire. Their work was to establish the most revealing insight into how British intelligence operated in the Six Counties which the public had yet been afforded. In fact the public were not given the full story. Part of what follows is based on court proceedings, but some of the information given below has not hitherto been published and was supplied to me privately in the course of my researches.

The inquiry was prompted by the killing of Loughlin Maginn, on 25 August 1989. He was shot by the UDA as he sat in his home watching television. The UDA announced that he had been a Provo, but his family claimed, correctly, that he had been the innocent victim of a sectarian assassination. Stung, the UDA attempted to prove their case by publishing a leaked, top-secret security file. It was but the first of a flood of such documents which the UDA unleashed. All had clearly been supplied either by sources within the RUC or by one of the various British intelligence agencies milling around in the north's murky underworld. Some in fact came from the army. The documents massively reinforced the claims of Catholic spokesmen who averred that the RUC were supplying information to Loyalist paramilitaries to enable them to kill Catholics. Dublin, understanding full well the implications of this disclosure, communicated its extreme displeasure to London, using the growing leverage provided by the intergovernment conference set up by the Anglo-Irish Agreement. But the UDA proceeded to rub salt into the wounds by circulating still more files and photographs to the media. Pictures of alleged IRA men given to the UDA by the army, the RUC and British intelligence were openly displayed in Loyalist Belfast.

Examination of the RUC's files by the Stevens team led them to Brian Nelson, the UDA's chief intelligence officer, who was also working for General Glover's brainchild, the Force Research Unit, then headed by a 'Colonel J.'. The Force Research Unit, apart from being an intelligence-gathering agency, is another example of the intelligence community's tendency to bureaucratic overlap. The unit owes its existence to the belief within the army's upper echelons that it is better at the spying business than either the RUC Special Branch or MI5. Lord Carver has stated openly in his memoirs that he would have preferred a 'total integration of police and military intelligence'.[63] But he felt that the RUC had lost the will to carry out rigorous interrogations. Independent army intelligence-gathering, however, became necessary because of '. . . the inefficiency of the RUC Special Branch, its reluctance to burn its fingers again, and the suspicion, more than once proved, that some of its members had close links with Protestant extremists'.[64]

Day after day Nelson had sat in the UDA headquarters collating intelligence material on a computer, controlled by the UDA leader, John McMichael. Everything that he put on to that computer was available to the security forces. I know this from a source of my own, a former member of the UDA and of the UDR, who was at the time working for the RUC Special Branch.[65] He also worked with Nelson, and his reports too went on to the computer. One of the operations of which he placed a report on the computer was the result of his surveillance, south of the border, of the Irish Foreign Minister, Peter Barry, whom the UDA were planning to murder at the time in retaliation for the Anglo-Irish Agreement.

Apart from the 'official' UDA computer, Nelson also used a personal computer in his house to build files. Rarely can paramilitary activities have been so well documented. But his card-indexing system of Catholic and Loyalist suspects was hidden by the army to prevent the Stevens team from scanning its contents. The fact that named Catholics were being targeted for death had not led to security forces acting to save their lives. Using what in the circumstances might be termed restrained language, Mark Urban has stated: '. . . it is clear that attempts to exploit this intelligence to ambush loyalists have rarely if ever been made'.[66]

In a mini re-enactment of the Larne gun-running, the army allowed weapons from South Africa to be landed on the Co. Down coast in January 1988. In the three years prior to the landing the UDA are reckoned to have killed some three people only. However, after the weapons arrived the Loyalist death squads appear to have acquired not only material, but a mysterious expertise as well. Their training, their efficiency as killers, their ability to withstand police interrogation, all seemed to suddenly improve to a point where, prior to the IRA and Loyalist ceasefires of 1994, the Loyalist paramilitaries were claiming more victims than were the Provisional IRA. In the five years to January 1993 the Loyalist death squads succeeded in killing 160 people, using the South African weaponry. Amongst those who died were thirteen Sinn Fein members, including some councillors, the Catholic solicitor, Patrick Finucane, and the bystanders whom Loyalist gunman Michael Stone shot down in Belfast's Milltown Cemetery as they were attending the funerals of the IRA trio who died in the SAS's extension to Gibraltar in March 1988 of the shoot-to-kill policy.

Was this another facet of 'Ulsterisation'? Had someone adapted to the nineties a deadly version of Frank Kitson's 1970s doctrine of making the Catholics glad to 'vomit out the IRA'? As the Loyalist campaign was still in full swing when I began researching this book, I took the opportunity presented by the necessary interviews with several British decision-takers to get their views on the matter. One distinguished gentleman blandly summed up the general reaction: 'The Catholics have been handing it out to the Loyalists and now the Loyalists are handing it out to the Catholics.' No one could offer any assistance, however, on the question of who might have assisted in the handing-out process. Certainly the presence at UDA headquarters of Nelson, the most celebrated though far from being the only British agent in the ranks of the Loyalist paramilitaries, was not caused by a simple desire for revenge on Catholics. Nelson in fact wanted a more specific focus on known IRA men than the random assassination of innocent Catholics which the UDA were carrying out with the army's connivance. In the course of their investigations the Stevens team were told by British officers that the UDA was used as surrogate killers.

Nelson, a former Loyalist paramilitary, who had earlier links with the FRU, had left Belfast and gone to work in Germany, but in 1986 it appears that all the British intelligence agencies' purse strings were untied, and he returned to the Six Counties after an attractive offer from 'Colonel J.'. The customary bout of inter-agency infighting ensued between the FRU and MI5, which had also been given more money and wanted to spend some of it on Nelson, whose pre-departure reputation still shone brightly in the murky undercover Loyalist paramilitary world. 'Colonel J.' won out and Nelson operated unscathed until Maginn's death put Stevens on his trail. It was decided to arrest him and two other members of the UDA against whom evidence of collusion with MI5 in the deaths of Catholics had been accumulated.

However, the first arrest date, 8 January 1990, was leaked, and there were press enquiries. The arrests were postponed for three days. On the night before they were to take place, fire broke out on the third floor of the Police Authority headquarters at

Seapark, Carrickfergus, near Belfast. The fire destroyed much of the Stevens team's hard-garnered evidence. During the conflagration, which appears to have reached a remarkable intensity between 10 p.m., when the offices were locked, and 11.05, when some returning members of the team discovered the blaze, a number of peculiar phenomena were discovered.

Two sets of alarms and the phone system failed to alert the fire brigade or RUC Headquarters. Despite all this, Stevens went ahead with his plan to arrest Nelson, but discovered that he had fled to England some hours before the fire started. The peculiarities of the affair did not end there. In order to get some of the files sought, the team had also to exert extreme pressure on the army even to get Nelson back to Ireland for questioning.

The opening of the Nelson can of worms caused enormous tensions between the various intelligence-gathering agencies. On 20 January 1992, two days before his trial began, no less a personage than John Major unexpectedly flew into the Six Counties for conversations with members of the NISPC and other interested parties in the security world. I have been informed that the Nelson case was discussed during the Major visit, and was probably the principal reason for it. It has been suggested that the manner in which the Crown handled the prosecution indicates that high-level influences were brought to bear. Nelson was sentenced to ten years' imprisonment on 22 January. He pleaded guilty to five charges of conspiracy to murder and to fifteen other offences, after a bout of plea-bargaining had led to two charges of murder being dropped.

Later that year, on 8 June, a BBC *Panorama* programme claimed that Nelson had been involved in ten murders or murder plots carried out by the UDA with the knowledge of the army. *Panorama* said that he had also targeted sixteen other people who were subsequently killed or had attempts made on their lives. The programme also revealed that army intelligence had failed to pass on to the RUC information about certain planned attacks. However, by pleading guilty Nelson ensured that no FRU personnel were called upon to explain their involvement with him. I am reliably informed that had this been done, documents uncovered by the Stevens team would have proven FRU involvement in many more murders and woundings than came out in court. The documents concerned were the notes taken for the record in FRU debriefings.

'Colonel J.' gave evidence as to Nelson's worth and character, claiming that his activities had saved many lives. The Colonel's estimates as to how many have, I understand, subsequently been revised downward drastically by police investigators – to some 2 per cent of what he claimed. However, one result of this testimony was that the sentencing judge described Nelson as a man who had 'shown the greatest courage'. Understandably, he was allowed to serve his sentence in England where, within two years, he had qualified for compassionate Christmas leave. The then Secretary of State, Tom King, also showed a degree of compassion towards Nelson by writing a letter to the court on his behalf. Readers, remembering the composition of the Northern Ireland Security Policy Committee, may decide for themselves why King should have written such a letter in the light of 'Colonel J.'s' evidence. Having told the court that he conducted regular high-level briefings, at which Nelson's information was passed on, the Colonel explained to the court the sort of level he had in mind: 'The Secretary of State for Northern Ireland might also be interested in such information.'[67]

What the Nelson case really illustrates of course is not so much the equal-parts-brutality-and-inefficiency nature of British intelligence operations in the Six Counties as the vacuum created by the absence of a coherent British political policy. It was a vacuum in which the power of the British security establishment exerted an undue and unhelpful influence. The inevitable coda to the affair was that 'Colonel J.', and some of Nelson's handlers, were interrogated under caution and files were sent to the DPP. He in turn contacted the Attorney-General, Sir Patrick Mayhew, who once again decided not to prosecute. Evidently Sir Patrick agreed with Tom King, who said:

> There is only one 'shoot to kill' policy – that carried out by the IRA. They shoot anybody, shoot first and often. That's the 'shoot to kill' policy. The Army and the security forces operate under the rule of law and I have the greatest confidence in the way they conduct their operations.

Not surprisingly, perhaps, Sir Patrick eventually became a successor of Tom King's as Secretary of State for Northern Ireland. Equally unsurprisingly, Nationalists generally continue to regard the police with intense suspicion. Prior to the ceasefires of 1994 it took an escort of, on average, between eight and sixteen soldiers to guarantee the safety of a two-man RUC foot patrol on a west Belfast street. Even after the ceasefire those memories, and what gave rise to them, will not go away. Thus is a great injustice perpetuated on many decent members of the RUC who are not involved in undercover squads and who want nothing more than to be allowed get on with their lives as ordinary policemen. However, the sort of thing outlined above allowed them to be shot at by the IRA as 'legitimate targets', with the (at least tacit) approval of large sections of the Nationalist community. The fact that what might be termed 'rule-of-law-England' could produce policemen like Stalker and Stevens, and wish to see their efforts succeed, was completely lost in the bloody wash of life as it was lived, and lost, in the Catholic ghettos.

There are some people in the legal and security establishment who are not prepared to see the Nelson affair die uninvestigated. Their influence, and that of Dublin, resulted in an effort being made to kick-start the Stevens inquiry back into life. In August 1993 Hermon's successor as RUC Chief Constable, Sir Hugh Annesley, who was born in Dublin, and a new Northern Ireland DPP, Sir Alasdair Fraser, formally invited Stevens to reopen his investigations. He did so, and the papers were sent to the DPP the following January. I understand that they squarely implicate four named members of the RUC as being involved in sectarian killings. However, on 13 May 1995 it was officially announced that there would be no prosecutions. The DPP was taking no action. Most Nationalists would agree with Seamus Mallon's comment: 'Fundamental issues of collusion that put people in danger and led to loss of lives have been swept under the carpet.'[68] But such comments were made following the hushing-up of other inquiries, to no avail. By way of a coda to the Stevens affair, in the same week a judge upheld a governmental gagging order preventing John Stalker from giving evidence on matters affecting 'national security' in a case involving a businessman's successful civil action against Manchester police.

Prior to the fate of the Stevens Inquiry being made known, greater control over undercover operations had been promised, and a new Deputy Chief Constable of the RUC, Blair Wallace, was tasked with directing operations. Of course, under the doctrine of 'police primacy' the RUC should have been fully conversant with and in control of such operations all along. The 1994 Defence White Paper states clearly that the RUC Chief Constable is ultimately responsible for the control of all security operations in the Six Counties. However, what White Papers, circulated at Westminster for the benefit of mere MPs, say and what the British security establishment decides are two separate matters. In the event, along with the Blair Wallace appointment, the RUC were also given some security toys to keep them happy, including a new spotter plane. The best that one can say of this sorry chapter of events is that hopefully the IRA ceasefires will mean that they have nothing to spot.

Readers will not of course need reminding of the nature and extent of the calendar of events I outlined in Chapter Eight. On the Irish, as on the British, side of the abrasion there were reprehensibilities of a high (or low) order. The IRA acts as judge, jury and executioner when it wishes. To take but one set of circumstances, the provision, or the securing, of information was the key element in the underground war between the two secret services. The journalist John Ware has truly (see next chapter) said that 'good advanced intelligence can do more to save a life than all the 20,000 soldiers and armed police on the streets in the province today'.

But Ware also points out that:

> vital though this undercover war is, it has become a very Dirty War. There have been too many unexplained killings, too many examples of collusion between Loyalist paramilitaries and rogue members of the security forces, too many stories of unjustifiable pressure applied on young men and women to become 'informers' against the paramilitaries – for which the penalty in Northern Ireland is usually hideous torture and death.

I don't know how 'rogue' the security personnel involved in the Dirty War are, and how much in reality they are obeying the orders of their superiors. One thing is certain; because of the centrality of the intelligence factor some sixty people, including a number of women, have been shot by the Provisionals as informers. On what evidence, and under what circumstances, we can generally only guess. I have been told of yet another parallel with Collins' time. There is said to be a Provisional IRA unit, like his 'Squad' which dealt with informers, in the South Armagh area set up to interrogate and execute informers. Fr Denis Faul has been quoted as saying he knew of premises used by the IRA for interrogations in which electrodes and other vicious methods of extracting information were used.[69] Certainly it is generally accepted that Robert Nairac, the British intelligence officer whom the Provisionals captured on a spying mission in the Three Steps Inn, a pub in South Armagh, on 14

May 1977, was brutally tortured before being killed. His body has never been found.

Nairac was something of a latter-day Lawrence of Arabia. The son of a Catholic father and a Protestant mother, he was educated at the leading English Catholic public school, Ampleforth, and at Oxford. An all-round athlete, he became a boxing blue and joined the Grenadier Guards while still at university. Much of his knowledge of Irish ballads, and Irish culture generally, stemmed from his boyhood friendship with Lord Michael Killanin's sons. He used to holiday at their home in the Irish-speaking district of Spiddal in Connemara. This background, combined with an almost uncanny ear for dialect, enabled him to pass himself off in IRA districts of Northern Ireland under a variety of aliases, gathering information for the SAS, until his luck ran out.

Another different, but similarly notorious, case in IRA circles also does something to illustrate both how the IRA's system of justice sometimes worked and how British intelligence apparently took advantage of its workings.

In 1974, Vincent Heatherington, aged eighteen, and Myles McGrogan, nineteen, were both remanded to Crumlin Road jail, Belfast, on charges relating to the shooting of two policemen in the city that May. They opted for, and were accepted into, the Provisional area, A Wing. As standard pattern dictates, the two teenagers were debriefed as to the circumstances of their capture so that the IRA could find out what slip-up had occurred, or whether an informer might be at work. When the results of the debriefing were analysed on the outside it was realised that the pair were not involved in the policemen's deaths. Nor were they in the IRA. Inside the jail, the intensity of Heatherington's interrogation was stepped up. He admitted that he had been working for the RUC under duress, but that he had done little else beyond infiltrating himself into the prison. Then, under extreme pressure, at the point in such procedures at which the victim either demonstrates convincingly that he has told all he knows, or breaks down and reveals his real secrets, Heatherington apparently broke down. He told his tormentors that he had been suborned into working for the RUC Special Branch. Two officers had attempted to make him fire on a football crowd. When he failed to pull the trigger they took the gun from him and, indicating that they were wearing gloves, warned him that the only fingerprints on the weapon were his own. It would be used to commit a murder and he would be blamed.

Amongst the activities which he said that he and McGrogan subsequently carried out on Special Branch instructions were the bombing of a Catholic pub, and several armed robberies. All were seemingly aimed at discrediting the IRA. Some of his other disclosures were even more alarming. Further interrogation elicited details of not only IRA, but Loyalist informers. Heatherington revealed that he had been trained at venues in Dublin and England by British-accented specialists in various undercover skills, including anti-interrogation techniques. During his sojourns at these places, money, sex and alcohol was also made available, he said. As these disclosures were being made, in what at the time seemed an unconnected incident a prisoner attacked a warder. Later it was remarked that this prisoner was not a Republican and should not have been in A Wing. However, the A Wing prisoners were locked in their cells as a result of the attack. When they were reopened McGrogan and Heatherington were found to have been transferred elsewhere. At the subsequent court hearings into the policemen's deaths in March 1975, they were acquitted of all charges.

However, in the North's prisons, and particularly in Long Kesh, their revelations, in particular Heatherington's, caused consternation. Something like a witch-hunt occurred. There was more brutal interrogation by IRA prisoners of colleagues either directly implicated or brought under suspicion by the A Wing revelations. A Long Kesh governor told me that piano wire and electric current were among the torture devices used. As a result men admitted to crimes they could not have committed.

The story now moves on two levels. On one, a dreadful spate of killings occurred because of the 'evidence' produced by the interrogations. Some prominent Belfast Republicans died as a result of a two-year campaign to root out informers. Heatherington and McGrogan were among those killed. The second level, however, takes us deep into the Deniable Zone. There is a thesis that the whole Heatherington/McGrogan saga was a British intelligence 'sting'.[70] Heatherington did not crack under pressure, but was programmed to start releasing tainted information into the IRA's intelligence stream, at a point where his seemingly desperate condition would give his disclosures credibility.

At the time there was an increasingly bitter debate within the ranks of the IRA. On one side was a 'Young Turk' element, which later rallied to Gerry Adams' leadership. On the other were older men, who at the time were conducting truce negotiations with the British. The older men felt that a withdrawal was imminent. The younger element thought the whole thing was a ruse, that a long war was inevitable, and that the emphasis on physical force would have to be broadened to include political activity. The older faction got their truce in February 1975. It nearly destroyed the IRA, which was both penetrated by British intelligence and weakened by becoming involved in sectarian warfare with the Loyalists, who were inflamed by the rumours that the truce was in fact a prelude to withdrawal. Thus the pressures of both sets of paramilitaries were deflected from the British. The policy of *divide et impera* at its best. A Provisional spokesman has been quoted as saying:

We were had. We knew we had fallen for it. It was very much in the mould of the MRF operations, clever, well planned and brilliantly executed. The IRA knew and found it difficult to admit that British military intelligence was brilliant. They almost destroyed us. They created paranoia in the ranks and left us severely damaged.[71]

One can certainly argue that all's fair in love and war and that the Provisionals' fire had to be met with fire. No one can excuse IRA atrocities such as the Enniskillen bombing of November 1987, which killed eleven innocent civilians and injured sixty-three more; the wiping-out of the entire Hanna family, all Protestants, in July 1988, by a bomb-blast; the planting of a bomb in a Shankill Road fish shop in October 1993, which killed ten shoppers and one of the bombers and injured scores of other people. But there is another side to the coin. The British, after all, had one power denied to the IRA, the UDA, the Unionists, the SDLP and the Dublin

Government: the power of initiative. In the event, they chose to exert this, not with a view to seeking a political solution, but with an eye on the Unionist MPs' effect on the parliamentary balance at Westminster. From the fall of the power-sharing executive of 1974 until the IRA ceasefire of 1994, Britain presided over a political vacuum that spawned a violent degeneracy not seen elsewhere in western Europe since the ending of World War II.

Readers will be able to judge the truth of this assertion in the brief glimpse afforded by this chapter of some of what occurred as a result. Hence the diseased clarity of vision that produced the Heatherington 'sting'. I should also point out that it is a demonstrable fact that the 'turning' of young ghetto-dwellers like Heatherington by the sort of methods used by the RUC detectives to get his fingerprints was a widespread practice. The fate meted out to these young 'touts' was a commonplace one, on both sides of the religious divide. Life in the Deniable Zone for this sort of player, be they voluntary or involuntary, did indeed tend to be nasty, short and brutish. Whitehall's moralistic condemnations of 'the men of violence', delivered behind a façade of pinstripe and plummy accents, are probably best summed up by the unknown Dublin wit who described the formulation of 'Ulster' policy as follows: when you ring the office of the Secretary of State for Northern Ireland, you are greeted by an answerphone message, spoken in an Oxbridge accent, which tells you to: 'speak after the high moral tone . . .'

Sometimes the lack of imagination, and lack of commitment, on the northern issue by Dublin governments facilitated this approach, but it never excused it. At all times London held the power of initiative. Its dubious exercise of that initiative in Ireland does not appear to have been confined to the northern part of the country. Dublin's wariness on the northern issue was not always dictated solely by questions of commitment, or lack of it, to ancestral Irish Nationalist goals. During the twenty-five years of hostilities in the Six Counties some very stark warnings occurred as to what could happen in the Republic also. In 1972, the year of Bloody Sunday, and of the consequent burning of the British Embassy in Dublin, MI6 was still in a powerful position in the Irish intelligence-gathering world. At that time, despite the fact that the Official IRA had declared a ceasefire the previous May, the SIS still saw the Officials as presenting the greatest threat to the status quo in the Six Counties.

Amongst other counter measures the agency (MI6) recruited two British agents, the brothers Keith and Kenneth Littlejohn, to penetrate the Official IRA. As part of their brief the brothers apparently felt free to rob banks throughout the greater part of 1972. This eventually led to Kenneth receiving twenty years' imprisonment, and Keith fifteen, in the Special Criminal Court, Dublin, on 3 August 1973.[72] In his defence Kenneth Littlejohn used the same argument advanced years later on behalf of Brian Nelson, claiming that his actions had saved the lives of many people.[73] Whatever debate there may be on that point, it is incontrovertible that the Littlejohns' presence in the dock came about as a result of Dublin pressure on London to have them extradited. However, the extradition proceedings were held in camera for 'reasons of national security'. The case was tried before Lord Widgery, who also presided over the Bloody Sunday Inquiry. The in camera decision meant that the Littlejohns failed in their two stated objectives: first, to make public the role of several distinguished English people, including Lord Carrington, in both their recruitment and their subsequent activities in Ireland; secondly, to give details of what Kenneth, a former paratrooper, claimed were specific instructions from the SIS to carry out not only bank robberies, but assassinations. The Dublin court case dealt only with matters arising from the Grafton Street robbery and could not be used by the Littlejohns as a pulpit from which to publicise other facets of their activities. Much of what Kenneth had to say only came to light after he broke out of Mountjoy jail on 11 March 1974 and began giving press conferences on the Continent. But these were not as well publicised in England as they were in Ireland. His criminal record also served to detract from his credibility, so that the Littlejohn affair became largely forgotten about in the UK.

But, whether connected or not, as mentioned earlier a happening in Dublin serves to keep the Littlejohns' memory alive in Ireland. On the evening of 1 December 1972, I was working at my desk in the *Irish Press* offices in Burgh Quay, Dublin, when suddenly a bomb went off just across the river. A second explosion followed, the two blasts between them killing two and injuring 127 more. At the time the Dail was debating the introduction of a new anti-IRA law which London was keen on seeing passed. The Offences Against the State (Amendment) Bill proposed to make it possible to secure a conviction in the Republic if a garda superintendent swore that he believed an accused to be a member of the IRA. The Fine Gael party was unhappy with the Bill and there was every indication that it would fail. However, when word of the explosions reached the Dail Fine Gael abstained and the Bill sailed through by 69 votes to 22.

But though the Fianna Fail Government had won a victory it was not prepared to accept it at any price. On 19 December the Gardai arrested a John Wyman in the act of receiving documents from Garda Special Branch Sergeant Patrick Crinion. Wyman was the MI6 handler who ran the Littlejohns and other British agents in the Republic. However, a deal was struck between Dublin and London: as soon as the extradition of the two Littlejohns was agreed, Crinion and Wyman were put on a plane to the UK. But Jack Lynch did publicly indicate the feelings of the Cabinet on the Dublin bombings by saying that there was a 'suspicion' in Dublin that the bombs were the work of British intelligence.[74] It was after this episode that MI6's wings were clipped and MI5 gained its ascendancy in Irish spying.

Britain may fairly claim to be one of the world's more advanced democracies. But even the most benign tree in the forest kills others in its shade. The 1972 Dublin bombings perfectly illustrate the problems 'backyardism' presents for small countries in the lee of big ones, whether they lie across the Irish Sea or in Latin America. The Lynch administration was caught between the Scylla of curbing subversion and the Charybdis of being seen to do nothing about a most curiously opportune bombing of its capital city. What protest could it make that would be in any way effective in London without at the same time inflaming Irish public opinion and thus giving aid and comfort to the IRA? There was suspicion in plenty amongst Irish intelligence and political circles, but where was the proof? The Provisional IRA solved its part of the problem in its own way on 21 July 1976 by blowing up the then British Ambassador to the Republic, Christopher Ewart-Biggs. He, it was alleged, had been an MI6 agent.

Dublin was to be again faced with the problems of the December 1972 bombings in greater, more ghastly, form two years later. The worst single day of the troubles occurred on 17 May 1974 when no-warning car bombings claimed thirty-five lives in Dublin and Monaghan. This was the period when the Loyalist strikers were in the process of destroying the power-sharing executive in the Six Counties. Initially, public opinion in the south assumed vaguely that the bombs were in some way connected with the strike. But shortly afterwards one began to hear other suspicions voiced. I was told by people I trust in both Special Branch and military intelligence that they suspected that the explosions were the work of Loyalist paramilitaries from Portadown who had been trained and led by British intelligence agents. The agents were said to have actually provided the bombs.

Various motives were suggested: on the Loyalists' part a desire to bring home to Dublin the horror of no-warning car bombing, which had become a feature of Belfast life; on the intelligence side a wish to impress upon Dublin what could happen if there was not better co-operation against the IRA, combined with the laying of a marker warning that it would not pay the Republic to be too zealous in pressing London to stand up to the strikers and uphold the Sunningdale agreement. All that can be said about this with certainty is that the Merlyn Rees–army approach did cause a coolness in Dublin–London relations which lasted throughout most of 1974 and well into 1975. Also, the Dublin Government, a coalition between Fine Gael and Labour which included the rabidly anti-Nationalist Dr Conor Cruise O'Brien, was particularly tough on the IRA, adopting extremely strict policies in the areas of censorship, jail conditions and police behaviour. All of these, particularly the activities of a 'heavy gang' in the Gardai, eventually combined to rouse public opinion to a point where the 'gang' became a factor in the Government's eventual downfall in 1977. But in 1974, in the absence of really hard evidence, such a government was a priori disinclined to be seen to raise the matter too publicly with London, lest the affair redound to the credit of the IRA. And hard evidence was not forthcoming – the RUC refused to co-operate with the Gardai in furthering enquiries in the Six Counties. Dublin does not appear to have pressed very strongly for co-operation. My information is that a file compiled by Irish Military Intelligence and the Garda Special Branch which was forwarded to the Government contained material which went some significant way towards establishing British complicity in the bombings. The matter lay fallow for several years, during which the names of those said to be responsible for the bombings gradually came to be generally known in informed circles.

Fred Holroyd attempted without success to widen the circle in 1987. On 6 December of that year the *Sunday World* published a written statement from him. For fear of libel the paper suppressed the names he supplied, but printed his allegations. He said flatly that a Sergeant X of the RUC Special Branch controlled a number of key activists in the UDA/UVF. He gave details of Loyalist paramilitary operations planned by Captain Nairac when on secondment to the SAS. He also said that the weapons used in the Miami Showband atrocity (see p. 192) had come from a cache whose presence he had disclosed to Sergeant X. Holroyd said: 'On one occasion while on duty with Sergt. X during a surveillance operation, he confided in me that the Portadown UDA/UVF were responsible for the car bombs that detonated in Dublin.'

By 1993 the political climate had altered somewhat. There was another coalition in power in Dublin, again depending on Labour support, but a different style of Labour Party to that of the Cruise O'Brien era. Its leader, the Foreign Minister Dick Spring, had placed Northern Ireland at the top of his agenda, and later in the year the new taoiseach, Albert Reynolds, achieved a historic breakthrough on the north by securing from John Major, with the aid of White House pressure, the Downing Street Declaration (see Chapter 12). It became known that official Dublin co-operation was being extended to Yorkshire TV in the making of a documentary on the bombing of Dublin in 1974 for the *First Tuesday* series.

When the programme was screened, on 6 July 1993, it contained material supplied by garda and Irish military intelligence sources, and interviews with former officers in both services. This was a notable departure from traditional Irish security information policy, and clearly required prior official clearance. The material, coupled with the testimony of former British intelligence agents who also appeared on the programme, included the names of the Loyalists whom I had previously been told were implicated in the bombing. By then those mentioned were all dead, most of them either killed in Loyalist feuds or by the IRA. The programme also included the names of two dead British officers who were alleged to have prepared the bombs: Julian (also sometimes known as Tony) Ball, who died in a car crash in Oman in 1988; and Robert Nairac, killed by the IRA in 1977. At the time of the bombings, Ball and Nairac were a captain and a lieutenant respectively in an intelligence unit based at Castledillon House near Co. Armagh, known as the 'Fourth Field Survey Troop'.

The contributions made by the British agents who appeared on the programme included statements that the UVF, at the time of the bombings, was controlled by British intelligence and that the Loyalist paramilitary organisation did not have the expertise necessary to make the bombs used. Albert Reynolds ordered an inquiry into the programme's allegations, but at the time of writing this appears destined for the fate of other inquiries, such as the one led by Stevens in the north, although the reasons for the south's lack of progress are somewhat different: Reynolds being ousted, yet another Fine Gael–Labour coalition taking power, and the overall delicacy of Dublin–London relations because of the tough secret negotiations which followed the ceasefires.

The list of dirty tricks employed by the security forces neither began nor ended with the shoot-to-kill policy, or the other matters discussed above. The use of torture and of highly paid informers, supergrasses, who gave whatever evidence the police required, was also a feature of the conflict. Again, as in the case of the shoot-to-kill policy, I will largely confine discussion of the torture question to information emanating from official reports. The first of these we have already encountered: the Compton Report, the result of the inquiry set up under Sir Richard Compton[75] in November 1971 into the practices which accompanied the internment swoop of the previous August. The Compton Inquiry suffered from the disability that, with but one exception, all of the detainees involved refused to give evidence on two grounds: first that the inquiry was not held in public; secondly, that there was no opportunity to cross-examine official witnesses. But even so, its efforts to sanitise what had happened – finding that there had been ill-treatment, but not brutality – aroused such widespread criticism that the Government was forced to set up another inquiry almost immediately.

This time the investigating committee was headed by Lord Parker of Waddington. It issued a majority and a minority report on 31 January 1972. The majority report, by Lord Parker and John-Boyd Carpenter, found that the methods used were illegal under UK domestic law, but not immoral. Lord Gardiner, however, dissented and issued the minority report saying that the techniques investigated were not morally justifiable. Public opinion agreed with him. The Prime Minister, Ted Heath, was forced to make a declaration in Parliament (on 2 March 1972) that:

> The Government, having reviewed the whole matter with great care and with reference to any future operations, have decided that the techniques . . . will not be used in future as an aid to interrogation.

But Heath's promise came too late to defuse the controversy. Moved by the furore surrounding the issuing of Compton's report in November, the Irish Government had acted the following December[76] to bring 'the torture case', as it was known in Ireland, to Strasbourg. The case chuntered around the labyrinth of the European Commission and Court procedures for several years, before judgement was delivered on 18 January 1978. By a majority of 16 to 1, the judges of the European Court of Human Rights found '. . . that the use of the five techniques in August and October 1971 constituted a practice of inhuman and degrading treatment, which practice was in breach of Article 3'.[77]

Article 3 of the Convention on Human Rights states that no one shall be subjected to torture or to inhuman or degrading treatment or punishment. However, having found that the use of the 'five techniques' was in breach of Article 3, the court then proceeded to find that 'they did not constitute a practice of torture within the meaning of the Article'. The court had visited Greece during the hearing of a Greek torture case to interview witnesses. However, in the Irish case the British had argued that attempts to interview witnesses would jeopardise their lives. Accordingly the judges did not visit Northern Ireland. The result was that not only were witnesses not examined, neither were the barracks wherein the five techniques had been employed (Girwood, Hollywood and Palace). But even the finding concerning the techniques not constituting a practice of torture did not satisfy Sir Gerald Fitzmaurice, the one judge who opposed. His findings have abided with me through the years. He had this to say:

> According to my idea of the correct handling of languages and concepts to call the treatment involved by the use of the five techniques 'inhuman' is excessive and distorting, unless the term is being employed loosely and merely figuratively . . .

He then went on to give examples of figurative speech:

> One hears it said, 'I call that inhuman', the reference being to the fact that there is no dining-car on the train. 'It's degrading for the poor man', one hears with reference to an employee who is being given all the unpleasant jobs. 'It's absolute torture to me' and what the speaker means is having to sit through a boring lecture or sermon. There is a lesson to be learned here on the potential danger of hyperbole.[78]

Unfortunately Patrick Shivers and some of the other 'hooded men' on whose behalf the torture case was begun did not have very much time to study Sir Gerald's warnings on the dangers of hyperbole. As indicated earlier, they began dying shortly afterwards as a result of their experiences.

Two other reports dealing with torture which were issued shortly after the Court of Human Rights decision have to be considered jointly as they deal with the police interrogation methods which developed in the wake of the setting-up of the Diplock courts. One was an Amnesty International finding, published in June 1978 following the visit of an Amnesty team to Northern Ireland. The other was the result of the Bennett Commission, published in March 1979, which, at least in part, owed its origin to the Amnesty report. In his introduction to the report which led to the establishment of the courts that bore his name into Irish folk memory, alongside such terms as 'packed jury', Lord Diplock said:

> We would not condone practices such as those which are described in the Compton Report (Cmnd. 4823) and the Parker Report (Cmnd. 4901) as having been used in the crisis resulting from the simultaneous internment of hundreds of suspects in August 1971. The use of any methods of this kind has been prohibited for many months past. As already mentioned they are, in any event, now regarded as counter-productive. Certainly the official instructions to the RUC and the army are strict. So are the precautions taken to see that they are strictly observed. There is stationed on permanent call at the centre where suspects are questioned by the police an army medical officer who is not attached to any of the operational units stationed in Northern Ireland, but is sent out on a rota from England for a period of four to six weeks. He conducts a thorough medical examination of each suspect on arrival in the absence of the police and similar examination at the conclusion of the questioning. He informs the suspect that if he wishes he will be allowed to see the doctor at any time while he is at the centre. The possibility of ill-treatment which injures the suspect physically or mentally going undetected is remote.[79]

'Remote' is an apt description of the extent of the contact between Lord Diplock's observations and reality. He also admitted in his foreword that he had made his findings on the basis of two visits of two days each to Northern Ireland. During these visits he recorded the fact that he had met 'members of the security forces on the ground'. The rest of the seven weeks taken to produce his report were spent in London. Rarely can any seven-week stint have impacted so strongly on what is normally understood by the phrase 'due process'. Six years after Diplock penned the foregoing, the *Sunday Times* reported as follows:

> Researches undertaken by the Law Department of Queen's University, Belfast, showed that ninety-four per cent of the cases brought before the Diplock Courts resulted in conviction.

Between seventy per cent and ninety per cent of the convictions are based wholly or mainly on admissions of guilt (self-incriminating statements) made to the police during interrogation.[80]

Before the *Sunday Times* report appeared, the thirty solicitors who most commonly worked in the Diplock courts had written to Roy Mason stating that:

... ill-treatment of suspects by police officers, with the object of obtaining confessions, is now common practice, and that this most often, but not always, takes place at Castlereagh RUC station and other police stations throughout Northern Ireland.[81]

Sir Kenneth Newman had been responding to such charges with the bizarre allegation that prisoners 'were injuring themselves as part of an IRA propaganda campaign against the police'.[82] However, mounting public unease at what was happening in Six County police barracks led to the Amnesty report, which was sent to Roy Mason on 2 May 1978. It had become common practice to use beatings and threats to extract confessions. Heath's declaration forswearing the use of the five techniques did not prevent men having their testicles kicked, beaten and squeezed; women being threatened with rape; threats that if a suspect did not talk, his family would be harmed; and, shades of Heatherington and McGrogan, the interrogation of minors without the presence of their guardians or parents. Under the Special Powers Act it was virtually impossible for a suspect to see a solicitor while in police custody, against the wishes of his, or her, interrogators.

Naturally the system created a burning sense of injustice in the Nationalist community against whom it was mainly, if not exclusively, directed. The 94 per cent conviction rate obtained by the 'conveyor belt' system explains both the high prisoner population, and the sense of outrage amongst the population that led to the outbreak of the hunger strikes. The Amnesty report found that: 'maltreatment of suspected terrorists by the RUC has taken place with sufficient frequency to warrant the establishment of a public inquiry to investigate it'.[83]

Readers will recall Lord Diplock's references to the efficacy of the presence of an army medical personage in preventing such abuses. Several police doctors complained about what was going on. But when one of them, Dr Robert Irwin, went on television after the publication of the Amnesty report to describe what was happening at Castlereagh, where he was the police surgeon, he became the victim of a smear campaign orchestrated by the Northern Ireland Office. The campaign made a mockery of Hamilton's assurance to the House of Commons that 'dirty tricks' had been brought to an end by that date. The fact that Dr Irwin's wife had been raped was put about so as to make it appear that he was in some way unhinged by the experience and bitter against the RUC.

The Irwin controversy helped to bring to light a number of other facts concerning the police and Sir Kenneth Newman. It was revealed that the Northern Ireland Police Authority had a number of meetings with him to discuss the doctor's complaints, at which they warned him that, having hired him, they could also fire him. Newman, however, added a new dimension to the term the 'primacy of the police' by quoting the Northern Ireland Police Act to prove that though they could hire him – they could not fire him! Newman had strong backing in his stand. Because of the Ulsterisation policy the British were keen to support the Chief Constable. We have seen how Margaret Thatcher adopted his advice over that of General Creasey. Moreover, I have been told that as part of her 'hands-on' approach to the war against the IRA, she kept in touch with the Chief Constable by phone. Then, on 16 March 1979, the report of the inquiry called for by Amnesty was published. It was conducted by Judge Harry Bennett, QC, who found that: '. . . examination of medical evidence reveals cases in which injuries, whatever their precise cause, were not self-inflicted'.[84]

This finding destroyed the RUC stock response, that prisoners were deliberately injuring themselves, either to discredit the force, or to gain compensation. Bennett made a number of recommendations. These included improved access to solicitors for defendants and the supervision of police interrogations. These reforms made it difficult for the RUC to obtain confessions by their previous methods and led instead to the reliance on supergrasses. On the UK 'mainland' the police already had a tradition of using supergrasses, criminals who had turned Queen's evidence to put away accomplices. In return they received a variety of rewards, ranging from reduced sentences to large cash payments and a new life abroad. The system was adapted for use in Northern Ireland. As in England, the supergrasses received inducements to tell what they knew about their former comrades. But, as the Diplock courts accepted uncorroborated evidence, the procedure was amplified so that the RUC also programmed the supergrass witnesses to tell the courts anything the police wished them to say.

The first supergrass was Stephen McWilliams whose appearance in court during March 1980 caused the jailing of four IRA men. Twelve more followed in September of that year on the word of supergrass James Kennedy. By March 1983 some 300 suspects were behind bars on the word of supergrasses. But there were limits to what even the Northern Ireland judicial system would tolerate. Also in March, Mr Justice Higgins threw out charges against forty-two Loyalists based on the word of one William 'Budgie' Allen. Allen, said Judge Higgins, was a 'liar'.[85] Liar or no, three years later, on 11 May 1986, Allen was granted the Royal Prerogative of Mercy by the then Secretary of State, Tom King. In 1984 a report by Lord Gifford said that the supergrass system was 'not justice', it led to the 'telling of lies' and the programming by the RUC of witnesses to 'concoct and rehearse statements'.[86] Nevertheless, for a time the supergrass phenomena – or, in the malodorous euphemism used by Sir John Hermon in the RUC's Annual Report for 1985, the 'converted terrorist process' – posed a serious threat to the IRA. In the report Sir John claimed that in parts of Belfast, 'terrorist murders dropped by 73% and all terrorist crimes by 61%'. These results were achieved because, as two authorities have written, apart from avoiding prison:

potential supergrasses were offered the prospect of a new life and identity in the country of their choice, private education for their children, a healthy pension for life – like supplementary benefit only far more – and even elocution lessons to neutralise their Belfast accents.[87]

This description of how one set about creating a born-again terrorist is accurate insofar as it goes. What it leaves out is the cost. In 1985, the then Northern Ireland Secretary, Douglas Hurd, said that over the previous seven years it had cost £1.5m in 'direct expenditure'.[88] This expenditure covered such items as paying for information, pocket money, and finding living accommodation and jobs abroad. But Hurd was only referring to eight of the twenty-seven supergrasses who had given information by that time. Nor did his figures refer to the cost of the RUC men who had rehearsed the supergrasses. These rehearsals often took place out of the country in expensive hotels. And in addition there was the cost of guarding the informers, and frequently their relatives. The expense and difficulty of securing the supergrasses was such that in 1986 a newly built prison at Maghaberry, costing £40m, held only four prisoners, all supergrasses.

At that date there were reckoned to be twenty living under assumed names in Britain. No other country had proved willing to take them. By way of underlining the increasing futility of the supergrass experiment, the appeals of eighteen men jailed on the word of supergrass Christopher Black were upheld the same year (in July 1986). But it was the IRA, not distaste on the part of lawyers for the supergrasses, that really ended their effectiveness.

Initially the Provos were seriously worried by the supergrasses, who at long last appeared to be destroying the IRA's hitherto successful safeguards against informers. These safeguards were not relaxed, but two additional tactics were introduced. Lawyers sympathetic to the Provisionals devised a method of turning the damaging effect of the use of uncorroborated evidence against their enemies. For so long as the only evidence against suspects was uncorroborated, then its retraction meant the end of the prosecution's case. It was therefore conveyed to supergrasses, via their families, that if they retracted their evidence no harm would come to them. To underline this promise the IRA also announced an amnesty for informers (in 1982). Sometimes pressures such as kidnapping of relatives were brought to bear on the families concerned. The tactics worked: one by one the supergrasses began retracting their evidence and the system virtually collapsed.

Stephen Greer, a legal expert, writing in the *Law Quarterly Review* at a time when the supergrass experiment was demonstrably failing to secure the results claimed for it by its apologists, said that the system might ultimately do as much harm to respect for law and order as had the introduction of internment.[89] I disagree with that assessment. By 1986, after seventeen years which had seen not only internment but the Falls Road curfew, the shoot-to-kill policy, dirty tricks, and all the other 'little stunts', there was no respect left for the supergrass system to damage. That fact constitutes the bedrock of the IRA's support.

It is a support which the Republicans themselves have often done a great deal to erode, even to the extent of alienating sympathisers by vicious feuding in which they kill each other. I have already adverted to the feud between the Official and Provisional wings of the IRA (see Chapter Four). This broke out again briefly in October 1975, and claimed about a dozen deaths and some fifty other casualties. Mediation by two priests, Fr Alec Reid, and Fr Des Wilson, eventually restored a peace which more or less held throughout the subsequent hostilities. However, within the ranks of the Officials, personality clashes had already created another, internal, feud, which continued throught the year. The vicious Irish National Liberation Army (INLA) and its political wing, the Irish Republican Socialist Party (IRSP), had been formed on 8 December 1974 in a Co. Dublin hotel.[90] The split cost the lives of leaders on both sides. Hugh Ferguson, a prominent member of the IRSP, was murdered in February. Billy McMillen, the Belfast Official IRA leader, was gunned down in April by a sixteen-year-old, Gerard Steenson, whose subsequent career, which ended in a hail of bullets twelve years later, earned him the nickname Dr Death.

Bernadette McAliskey, who, with Seamus Costello, formerly of the Official IRA, had founded the IRSP, left within a year of the foundation because of the militarism. Costello, who, independently of McAliskey, had also founded the INLA, was assassinated in 1977. However, the movement still had sufficient killing strength to murder Airey Neave in March of the following year. His public utterances had marked him out as an enemy of Irish nationalism, particularly of a militant nature. He was not in favour of power-sharing and had made encouraging noises about the death penalty, internment, and an increased use of the SAS. He was also expected to get his wish to be sent to Ireland to replace Roy Mason when, as appeared inevitable, the Tories won the general election scheduled for April 1979. Moreover, the movement had an informant who averred that Neave had a private agenda. He intended to institute a rightist 'backlash' in England, using Margaret Thatcher, whose rise he had masterminded, as a front.[91] Accordingly, on 30 March 1978, an INLA unit killed him with a bomb, activated by a mercury tilt switch, which was placed in his car at the Palace of Westminster car park.

Though the INLA carried on a war against the British Army, as one would expect of a militant Irish Republican organisation, it also indulged in sectarian murder, racketeering and torture. Its quotient of idealism, which did lead three of its members to die on hunger strike during 1981, was vitiated by its failure to develop either military discipline or a political wing. The three INLA members who died on hunger strike were Patsy O'Hara, Michael Devine and Kevin Lynch – 30 per cent of the 'Ten Men Dead' who had such a crucially significant effect on the electoral fortunes of Provisional Sinn Fein. The Official IRA made little impact in the Six Counties, but achieved some success in the Republic. Elements in OIRA first evolved into Sinn Fein, the Workers' Party, subsequently mutated into the Workers' Party and, then after a split, into the Democratic Left, which in 1994 became part of a 'rainbow coalition government' in the Republic.

During the hunger strike period the INLA succeeded in attracting more recruits than did the Provisionals in parts of Belfast, particularly in the Markets district. Here the INLA operated quite openly, wearing distinctive military-style clothes and making little effort to hide either guns or identities. There is a suspicion that a certain blind eye may have been turned to the organisation's growth in this early phase. British intelligence was not unaware of the benefits which could accrue from the growth of a movement that might draw off strength from the Provisionals. INLA's path, however, led relentlessly to the depths. In 1982 Dominic McGlinchey became the movement's leader and for a time the best-known Republican leader in Ireland. Some of the worst atrocities of the entire troubles took place under him.

Like many another young man in the Nationalist community his fearsome career began through an encounter with the security forces. He had been taking part in some local civil rights marches, but was not a member of the IRA, when he was picked up at the age of seventeen in the internment swoops of August 1971. For five days he was subjected to some of the brutal interrogation methods which landed Britain before the European Court of Human Rights. But on emerging from Long Kesh, McGlinchey had recourse not to courts but to the Provos. He became one of the Provisionals' most-wanted men, a legendary figure in his native South Derry. He was captured by the Gardai in 1977 and served a five-year sentence for possession of weapons and the hijacking of a garda car. But, although he had been one of the Provisionals' most-admired figures, he appears to have fallen out with the Provisional leadership while serving his sentence in Portlaoise jail. On his release in February 1982 he joined the INLA.

The subsequent history of the movement is appalling. On 6 December 1982 the INLA bombed the Droppin' Well Inn at Ballykelly, which was frequented by British servicemen. A no-warning explosion killed eleven soldiers and six civilians, four of them girls. The Grew and Carroll shooting referred to earlier occurred a few days later. The RUC mounted the operation thinking that the men would be driving McGlinchey back to the Six Counties from the Republic. A year later another awful slaughter followed, the 'Darkley massacre', an attack on a religious service. Ostensibly this was the work of an organisation known as the Catholic Reaction Force. The CRF was in fact a cover name for an INLA group: the Deniable Zone was not completely confined to the British side of the conflict. Shortly before Darkley there had been a number of sectarian killings of Catholics in that part of South Armagh. Some members of the UDR were boasting openly that they had carried them out. In revenge, a relative of one of the dead took part in the CRF attack on Darkley Pentecostal Mission Hall. Using INLA weapons the murderers sprayed a gospel service with bullets on 21 November 1983, killing three church elders and wounding several of the congregation.

From November to the following March, when he was finally arrested after a shoot-out, McGlinchey became the most wanted man in Ireland, becoming known as 'Mad Dog' to the tabloids. Paradoxically, he also contrived to inject something of a Robin Hood element into this image by adding a new definition to the term 'peeler', a sobriquet referring back to the police force initially formed by Sir Robert Peel in the nineteenth century. McGlinchey updated it on a number of occasions by holding up gardai and forcing them to peel off their uniforms. After his capture he made legal history by becoming the first Republican to be extradited to the Six Counties to face a murder charge, that of Ms Hester McMullen, a sixty-seven-year-old postmistress, accidentally shot dead during one of McGlinchey's many armed robberies. He was freed on appeal by Lord Justice Gibson, the judge who entered (and departed) our story earlier for taking a somewhat less lenient view of terrorists. Gibson said that McGlinchey's fingerprints, found in the car used for the killing, could have been placed there after the murder.

McGlinchey was re-extradited to the Republic on 11 October 1985 and subsequently imprisoned in Portlaoise on charges relating to the shoot-out in which he was captured. On 1 February 1987 his wife, Mary, was bathing their two young sons, Dominic and Declan, at their home in Dundalk when two men wearing balaclavas burst into the house and shot her dead in front of the screaming children. My information is that she was killed in revenge for the murder of the brother of her assailants. Mary McGlinchey is known to have taken an active role in her husband's operations, and is said to have been involved in some of his killings. McGlinchey asked me to visit him in Portlaoise some months after her death – why, I was never quite sure. He seemed anxious to talk about commonplaces as much as about anything related to his former life. He seemed to have an idea who it was who had killed his wife, but expressed no bitterness. He denied involvement in the Darkley massacre, but admitted to an involvement in the Droppin' Well atrocity. All he seemed to want to do when he got out of jail was look after his two children. Short, slight, balding, he seemed tired, reduced by his past and by prison, and in no way threatening or a 'mad dog'. My impression was shared by the governor of the prison and by every member of the staff who came in contact with him.

However, there may have been a darker side to McGlinchey, even at that stage. Prior to his imprisonment he had run the INLA in dictatorial and ruthless fashion. He had been responsible for literally scores of deaths, while in both that organisation and the Provisional IRA. Many of these were by his own hand. He conducted interrogations with the aid of instruments such as a red-hot poker. But on his release in March 1993 he appeared to be chiefly concerned with making good his promise to devote time and care to his children. He was taking them to a birthday party for his son Dominic, in June 1993, near Ardee in Co. Louth, when an attempt was made on his life. Describing it afterwards, McGlinchey said that a machine gun and a pistol were used by two men who spoke with 'English accents'.[92] He was categoric in his assertions that the men were British agents. This claim, however, has to be questioned. A second, successful, attempt was made on him the following February. He was shot down on a Drogheda footpath, dying in front of his son Dominic on 10 February 1994. It subsequently became generally accepted, by both police and former associates, that he had been murdered by revenge-seeking ex-colleagues. McGlinchey, it was said, had intended both to extract revenge for his wife's murder and to resume his role of gang leader.

By the time of his death the INLA was splintered and weakened, from both its own internal dissensions and a crackdown by the Provisionals. McGlinchey would have had a choice of a number of splinter groups, all murderously feuding with each other, as a vehicle for reasserting his authority. The various components of the INLA had degenerated into drug-dealing, something which had always been anathema to the Provos, and racketeering of all kinds. Torture was commonly used. A member of one INLA splinter group, the Irish Revolutionary Brigade, boasted of using a bolt-cutter to lop off a man's fingers before he murdered him because he 'wanted to give him a hard death'. An autopsy revealed that he had forced another of his victims to eat his own fingers before killing him. The leader of this wing, Dessie O'Hare, who became nationally known as the 'Border Fox', is now in

Portlaoise jail following a notorious kidnapping in 1987. A prominent Dublin dentist, John O'Grady, was captured by his gang and his fingertips were hacked off with a hammer and chisel for inclusion with a ransom note.

A 'peace conference' arranged between representatives of the INLA leadership of the time and its main rival faction, the Irish People's Liberation Organisation, turned out to be in effect a Chicago gangster-style 'set-up'. When the four INLA men arrived at the Rosnaree Hotel in January 1987, they were gunned down by hit men aligned with, and possibly led by, Gerard Steenson, by then better known as 'Dr Death'. Two of the INLA men, Ta Power and John 'Big Man' O'Reilly, died; the other two recovered from their wounds. After the murders, both the Steenson and the O'Reilly wings issued statements to the media, each claiming that the other side had been acting as British agents. Again, in the circumstances, one would have to question such allegations.

However, an incident later in the year does raise valid questions about police/army activity, or lack of it. In March Steenson made another murderous attempt on his rivals. This time he and a henchman badly wounded the McQuillan brothers in their home in New Barnsley, Belfast. The shooting took place in the small hours of the morning, a matter of yards from an RUC barracks. But according to Kevin McQuillan, who was badly injured in the attack, it took two hours and several phone calls appealing for assistance before either police or army crossed the road to investigate.[93]

A little later there occurred an event which gives a degree of substance to allegations of undercover security force involvement in the INLA/IPLO feuding. Steenson had only a few days to live after the McQuillan incident. On the night of 14 March, not long after midnight, he and a companion, Anthony McCarthy, drove into Springfield Avenue, Belfast. Behind them a member of a waiting gang closed the security gate into Springfield Road. McCarthy and Steenson were trapped. Their lives ended in a fusillade of bullets. According to some authorities the man who closed the gate was one Alexander Lynch.[94] It is known that Lynch was at the time an RUC agent.[95] As the feuding died away the RUC advised him to join the Provisionals. He did so, but came under suspicion and was captured and interrogated by the Provisionals. On 7 January 1990, the second day of his interrogation, the house he was being held in was surrounded by an army patrol. Amongst those arrested, and later sentenced, was Provisional Sinn Fein's leading publicist, Danny Morrison.

The fact that Lynch was regarded as being of sufficient importance to engage the attention of a figure of Morrison's stature would seem to indicate that another Heatherington and McGrogan-style 'sting' had come to a successful conclusion. Obviously the security forces would have had a vested interest in the sort of mayhem involved in the foregoing. It weakened republicanism generally. Specifically it resulted in several activities that assisted in the godfathers-and-racketeers image of the IRA which the NIO spin doctors were keen to foster.

While also continuing to kill police, soldiers and UDR personnel as opportunity offered, the divided INLA indulged in fratricidal murder of its former comrades, drug-dealing, extortion, robbery, heavy drinking, and sexual promiscuity. The

Provisionals finally took a hand in the action on Halloween night, 31 October 1992. A prominent IPLO leader, Sammy Ward, was shot dead and a wave of kneecappings and warnings to leave the country literally crippled the organisation. It was disbanded, and several former members of both the IPLO and the INLA subsequently became professional criminals, both north and south of the border. The INLA still exists, but very much in the shadow of the Provisionals. Whatever co-operation there is between the two movements lies deep in the Deniable Zone.

I do not wish to burden the reader with a further catalogue of horrors, but when discussing dirty tricks one must advert to the Loyalists also, however briefly. Here two sets of occurrences have to be noted: first, that the Republican feuding was replicated amongst Loyalist paramilitaries; secondly, that, despite the nature of some of the appalling events catalogued in the foregoing pages, it is probably true to say that if one had to pick out the worst single set of atrocities of the entire troubled era, then that grisly accolade should go to the activities of the Loyalist group known as the Shankill Butchers.

Taking the feuds and splits first, it can be fairly stated that these were both numerous and ferocious. The first hard-core killing machine to emerge from the ranks of the Loyalists was the Ulster Volunteer Force which, as we have seen, committed the first murders of the period in 1966: three years before the turning-point Derry civil rights march of October 1968; four years before the Provisionals were formed; and five before the Provos killed Gunner Curtis, the first British soldier to die in the Troubles. Even after the emergence of the numerically superior UDA, whose growth has already been noted, and with which it sometimes came into brutal conflict, the UVF remained a tightly organised, dedicated and deadly force. Outside Belfast the UVF founded and controlled other front organisations in rural areas, notably the Protestant Action Force and the Protestant Action Group. These were responsible for scores of murders, particularly in the notorious 'murder triangle' area of Dungannon, Moy and Portadown.

Several other smaller Loyalist paramilitary organisations came into being over the years, but did not show either the cohesion or the staying power of the UVF. These included the Shankill Defence Association, founded by John McKeague, which took a leading part in the attempts to burn out Catholics during 1969. The Red Hand Commando was another McKeague creation, set up after he had fallen out with the SDA in 1972. The RHC and the SDA were both aligned with the UVF. The Orange Volunteers was also founded in 1972, amongst members of the Orange Order. Tara, one of the earliest anti-Catholic groupings of the troubles, was formed in 1966 by William McGrath of Kincora ill-fame. Another early anti-Catholic creation was the Ulster Protestant Volunteers, which, as we have seen, supported Paisleyite agitation in the years leading up to the August 1969 riotings and burnings. Like McKeague's organisations the UPV's membership overlapped with that of the UVF. There were also a number of organisations which derived from the disbanded B-Specials. The Ulster Service Corps was the largest of these and was chiefly active in rural areas throughout the seventies. In Belfast, the Woodvale Defence Association became subsumed into the UDA, which also ran a youth wing, the Young Militants. The YM had a sinister history, being used for a time in the seventies by the UDA as a front organisation to carry out several murders. The Young Citizen Volunteers stands in the same relationship to the UVF as does the Fianna to the IRA: a military scouting movement which acts as a youthful recruiting agency.

The sheer multiplicity of all these organisations made rivalries inevitable, chiefly in Belfast where numbers, and opportunities for racketeering, were greatest. McKeague's organisations, for example, frequently came into conflict with the UVF. A petrol bomb meant for him caused the death of his mother. He was eventually shot on 29 January 1982, apparently not by the UVF, but by the INLA, who phoned newspapers to claim his killing. However, the McKeague/UVF feuding was but a skirmish to the war which broke out between the UDA and the UVF. There had been trouble between the two groups during the Loyalist strike of 1974, but this was as nothing to what happened in 1975. Trouble first broke out on the night of 30 March in Belfast, when the UDA shot up the homes of a number of UVF men. There was more shooting the following night and counterattacks by the UVF over the next week. Bombs as well as guns were used. Two UDA leaders were seized and murdered. Their bodies were not found until October when their discovery, near Islandmagee in Co. Antrim, led to the jailing of thirty-one UVF men.

The UVF created such carnage in that month that the organisation was proscribed on 3 October. The previous day a series of UVF attacks had killed twelve people, three of them women, and injured forty-six others. Were British intelligence agents behind the UVF's self-destructive activities? Professor Steve Bruce says that there was a '... constant "stirring" by the security forces, who used such black propaganda vehicles as the fictitious Ulster Citizens' Army to exacerbate the always considerable tensions within the UVF'. Evidence is always difficult to come by in these matters, as the Stalker and Stevens affairs demonstrate.

The UDA, though highly threatening to outsiders, appeared to be able (or was directed) to control its inner tensions better than the UVF. After the upheavals of the Tommy Herron era passed, the leader of the UDA, Andy Tyrie, remained in office until he was forced out in 1987, a long sit in such a hot seat. His departure followed a sanguinary sequence of events which will shortly be described. These events contributed to the low esteem in which the UDA was increasingly held. And not merely by the Nationalist spokesmen who incessantly, but unavailingly, called for the organisation to be banned. As we have seen, even Rhonda Paisley joined the chorus. Nevertheless, in September of that year the Secretary of State, Peter Brooke, was still stoutly denying that British intelligence was directing its operations,[96] even though by then of course the Nelson affair was well known. Brooke's denials were rather undercut a few days later by a *Dispatches* programme shown on Channel 4 on 2 October which gave very chilling indications of collusion between an 'inner circle' within the RUC, the UDR, and the UDA. The RUC reacted with fury, placing newspaper ads, north and south of the border, carrying Sir Hugh Annesley's denials of the programme's charges. But the ads were not placed until 2 August 1992. On 31 July Channel Four and the programme's makers, Box Productions, had been fined £75,000 in London's High Court, under the

Prevention of Terrorism Act, for refusing to name their sources. The programme had been prompted by the increasing ferocity and expertise of the UDA's onslaught on Catholics, not merely in Belfast, but elsewhere in the province.

A string of some thirty-eight sectarian assassinations seems to have led Sir Patrick Mayhew to ban the UDA on 10 August 1992. It would appear the organisation had finally become too much of an embarrassment, even for the men running the Northern Ireland Security Policy Committee. Sir Hugh Annesley, the head of the RUC, was quoted as saying of the UDA that: 'the team that are coming through are more aggressive. I think they are prepared to match some of the atrocities the PIRA have committed.'[97] But the ban was not accompanied by any discernible affirmative action. In the succeeding five months the combined total of UDA men charged with membership was – one! And even he was held less for being a UDA member than because of a murder charge. The ban may equally have been a cosmetic move designed to bait Sinn Fein into talks. Unionists claimed that it was angled to attract the SDLP leaders into talks with the NIO and should have been extended to Sinn Fein as well. The UDA itself authorised a newspaper interview in which its spokesman threw more light on Sir Hugh Annesley's description of the 'team' that were 'coming through'. The UDA man said that the security forces had directed the organisation for the past sixteen years and that the ban had been introduced because 'they couldn't direct us any more'.[98]

One has to be just as careful in assessing this claim as in considering the counter-assertion that the British had nothing to do with the UDA's policies. For example, it was quite clearly the British who put down a movement in Scotland to aid the UDA. In June 1979 eleven members of the Scottish UDA – there is of course an ancient tradition of Orangeism in Scotland – were given long sentences for aiding the UDA in Northern Ireland in arms procurement. The leader of the group, James Hamilton, got fifteen years. The truth as to where lies the real balance of control and inspiration in the ranks of the Loyalist paramilitaries must obviously be, to some degree, a matter of speculation. Probably the best way to assess the issue is to view it in terms of two agendas which sometimes had a shared objective.

First, that of the security forces, which obviously had a vested interest (a) in knowing what what was going on in the world of paramilitarism, be it Republican or Loyalist, and (b) turning that knowledge to advantage, wherever and whenever possible. Second, that of the Loyalists themselves. Loyalist paramilitary motivation has always retained something of the visceral, anti-Catholic, anti-Republican response that first gave it a rebirth at the start of the Troubles in 1966. That rebirth was a direct reply to the celebration of the fiftieth anniversary of the 1916 rising. Other reasons for becoming a Loyalist paramilitary presented themselves as the Troubles wore on: revenge for IRA atrocities; fear that a 'doomsday' situation was approaching in which 'Ulster' would be thrust out of the Union and placed at the mercy of the IRA; a sincerely held belief that it was a man's duty to defend his heritage from a ruthless enemy; encouragement from Loyalist women for their menfolk to show the courage to 'do what the IRA is doing'. This last was sometimes a more powerful factor in recruitment, particularly in the early stages of the UDA's growth, than is always acknowledged. *Per contra*, it was a growing abhorrence of killing amongst the women of the Loyalist community that played an important part in bringing about the Loyalist ceasefire in 1994. Two other less defensible and more widespread causes of Loyalist paramilitary activity were the encouragement and advice given surreptitiously by some Loyalist politicians, and racketeering.

The bloody deeds with whose description I will conclude this brief outline of Loyalist paramilitary activity concern the first and last reasons given above for joining the UDA, the UVF or one of the organisations in the penumbra: hatred and racketeering. Lenny Murphy was impelled by both motivations. He operated out of two well-known Shankill Road UVF drinking dens, the Lawnbrook Club and the Brown Bear Bar. From the patrons of these establishment he put together a gang which became known as the Shankill Butchers. Court proceedings and the researches of Martin Dillon[99] have established that not only did the Butchers murder their victims, they tortured them savagely as well. The IRA's bombing atrocities of Bloody Friday, 21 July 1972, would appear to have been the pretext for Murphy's first venture into ritualistic murder. In revenge a Catholic, Francis Arthurs, was kidnapped, taken to the Lawnbrook Club and systematically beaten to a pulp by a UVF group, including Murphy, until he was finally shot dead.

Murphy subsequently participated in a number of other murders before being taken into custody for the murder of one Edward Parvis in January 1973. Thomas Madden, whom he helped to kill before being apprehended for the Parvis murder, died a particularly terrible death. He was suspended from the roof of a garage, stripped, and slowly stabbed one hundred and forty-seven times. While on remand in Crumlin Road jail, Murphy stole cyanide and administered it to the man who had accompanied him on the Parvis killing, Mervyn Connor. Before doing so he forced Connor to write a confession saying that he was the one who had killed Parvis.

With Connor dead there was no evidence against Murphy and he was released from jail in 1975 after a brief sentence imposed for attempting to escape while on remand. When he emerged from prison he formed a gang from the Brown Bear clientele which proceeded to murder Catholics using the methods described in Madden's case. In addition to knives, axes were also used. As part of a litany of beatings, shootings, robberies and extortions, the gang also took part in the UDA/UVF feud, shooting a number of UDA men. Murphy was again jailed, on a firearms charge, in 1976 and was not released until 1982. In his absence his gang continued their slaughters until they were rounded up in May 1977.

On 20 February 1979, eleven of the gang were convicted of 112 offences, which included nineteen murders, and were given a total of forty-two life sentences. It is said that their capture resulted from the testimony of one of their victims, Gerrard McLaverty. On 10 May 1977, McLaverty was beaten and stabbed and left for dead, but recovered and was able to identify his assailants when taken around the Shankill in a police car. This may well have been what happened, but it is also a fact that by that time the authorities' attitude to the Loyalists had changed markedly from that of 1974. Another Loyalist strike took place that month, but this time the authorities faced it down. Roy Mason took a more hands-on approach than had Rees in the negotiation with workers and security chiefs. Paisley was amongst those arrested and charged with obstruction. In the event the power workers did not support the strike, which collapsed on 13 May.

Unquestionably the unfortunate McLaverty did survive and did identify his assailants from a police car. But what were the RUC and all the intelligence forces doing in the months while the Shankill Butchers were operating more or less openly out of well-known paramilitary drinking haunts? As Martin Dillon has pointed out:

> . . . it is clear that many policemen compromised their neutrality by continuing to frequent and socialise in premises controlled by the paramilitaries. In the Shankill area the UDA often killed people in illegal drinking clubs and were not concerned about leaving traces of the victim's blood on the floor or walls . . . The police knew such places were being used for murder . . . I uncovered evidence that as late as 1975 policemen in the Shankill were drinking in pubs which were the haunts of UDA and UVF units . . .[100]

In addition to having the opportunity of drinking in clubs and pubs frequented by criminals and used for crimes, the RUC possessed what would appear to be another invaluable aid to successful detection: most RUC members were drawn from the Loyalist community and had sources of intelligence and insight which they were denied in the case of the largely Catholic IRA. One would have thought this circumstance should have simplified the task of preventing the spate of Loyalist murder. It is a matter of speculation as to whether the changed attitudes of the authorities to Loyalists in 1977 had anything to do with the Butchers being put away. Dillon is certainly correct in his assertion that Shankill drinking clubs were well known as murder sites, or, in the gallows humour of Belfast, 'romper rooms', after a popular TV programme. Albert Baker, mentioned earlier, received his life imprisonment sentence for his part in crimes such as the following:

> Baker struck McCartan repeatedly on the back with a wooden pickshaft until it broke in two . . . Baker produced a dagger and stabbed McCartan twice through the palm of his left hand and once through the palm of his right hand . . . someone suggested 'cutting the balls off him'. Baker ran the knife up his left buttock, opening up a long shallow incision. They tied a rope round one hand and another round his ankles, held him by the ankles and dropped him on the concrete floor on his head . . .[101]

The unfortunate McCartan was finally bundled into a car, 'frogmarched' to a piece of waste ground, hooded and shot. But the circumstances of his death were revealed, not through detection, but because Baker, a deserter from the British Army, walked into an English police station and gave himself up. Nor was Murphy's career terminated by the police. On his release from jail in 1982 he resumed both his killing and his racketeering. This brought him into conflict with a leading Loyalist gangster, and UDA leader, Jimmy Craig. Craig secretly passed information about Murphy's movements to the Provisionals. On 16 November 1982, Murphy had just stopped his car outside his girlfriend's Belfast home when a van pulled up in front of the car. Two gunmen jumped out and shot him twenty-six times.

The deputy leader of the UDA, John McMichael, had been becoming increasingly disturbed by both Craig's racketeering activities and his contacts with Republicans. He ordered Craig to break off his contacts with Republicans and apparently initiated an inquiry into both the circumstances of Murphy's death and those of other Loyalist paramilitaries. McMichael's movements were conveyed to the Provisionals, who planted a bomb under his car on 22 December 1987.

Sir John Hermon's handling of a question at a press conference, a week after McMichael's death, gave rise to speculation that it was someone in the UDA who had helped to set up McMichael. Hermon said:

> The murder of John McMichael, whoever committed it, or whoever orchestrated it regardless of who may have committed it, was designed to cause grievous dissension and disruption and to eliminate a threat to whosoever that threat may have existed. I would not wish to take it further than that. But think of my words very carefully.

The RUC and, it appears, MI5, were also keeping Craig under surveillance and after McMichael's death a video film taken during this surveillance was leaked to the UDA. It showed Craig in a pub with a prominent Provisional. On 15 October 1988, Craig was shot dead in a Belfast pub. Earlier that year, on 11 March, following the discovery of a bomb under his car four days previously, Andy Tyrie lost a vote of confidence in the UDA inner council. McMichael had been his ally on this council. He prudently resigned his chairmanship of the UDA and the younger, 'more aggressive' elements mentioned by Sir Hugh Annesley subsequently took over the running of the movement. One of the complaints against Tyrie was that he had not been 'militant' enough.

While interviewing him once he mentioned to me that the IRA's no-warning car bombings were 'maddening' the Loyalist people. As a result, demands for tit-for-tat sectarian assassinations were mounting. I mentioned this to Daithi O'Conaill, the IRA leader who is said to have first advocated the use of car bombs. O'Conaill authorised me to tell Tyrie that the car bombing would stop in the expectation that assassinations would follow suit. Both cessations duly occurred and lasted for some time. Tyrie also figured in another creditable incident in UDA history. Early in his reign there was yet another demand from the ranks for an intensification of sectarian killing. Tyrie called a meeting and threw down a revolver and a list of names and addresses of known IRA men, telling his audience that whoever wished could pick up the gun and the list with his blessing. No one did. Both incidents tell us something about the character of Loyalism. Certainly it contains a strong revenge-seeking element, but it also contains a continuing questioning element which seeks to advance politically, outside the ranks of the established political groupings.

Glen Barr, at the time both a leading member of the UDA and of Craig's Vanguard Party, inaugurated a long-running debate on 'Ulster Nationalism' in a widely reported speech to the assembly at Stormont on 25 October 1973. He said:

> I have no intention of remaining a British citizen at any price . . . Ulstermen have got more pride than to accept a white paper that has been thrown across the Irish Sea at them . . . An Ulsterman's first allegiance must be the state of Ulster. True Ulstermen must reject

anything which in any way indicates that Ulster is going to be put into a United Ireland. True Ulstermen must therefore reject the Constitution Act. Let it be put on record that I stand here as an Ulster Nationalist.

In 1978 Tyrie, Barr and another former prominent UDA leader, Harry Chicken, co-operated in setting up a group called the New Ulster Political Research Group. This came into being during January, and by July of that year Tyrie could be heard making statements to the effect that the UDA 'would no longer be the willing tool of any aspiring or ready-made politician'.[102] Another notable effect of the new thinking was the fact that the number of Loyalist paramilitary killings dropped to a mere eight in 1978.

The NUPRG experiment attracted a good deal of media attention. Barr and Chicken were advocates of a negotiated independence for Ulster. I remember once sharing a speaking occasion with Barr[103] at which he summed up his and Chicken's thesis about Northern Irish people having a distinctive identity. He said they were: '... not second-class Englishmen but first-class Ulstermen'. Barr and Chicken visited the US amongst other countries, and were impressed by the US Constitution. They published a policy document (in 1979), 'Beyond the Religious Divide', which embodied their American experiences. The new policy envisaged a bill of rights to protect civil and religious liberties, and a president, nominated from outside the political parties. The president in turn would have chosen an executive from the worlds of academia, the professions and the trade unions. The activities of the executive were to have been overseen by a committee system drawn from elected representatives. Unfortunately, this type of thinking became stifled within the UDA by internal jealousies and the more traditional preoccupations with killing Catholics and racketeering. Barr and Chicken resigned from the UDA and John McMichael became the movement's political guru.

Given McMichael's reputation as a hard man there was a surprised welcome when he too showed signs of trying to reach a political accommodation with the minority, if not to the same extent as either Barr or Chicken. He was behind a document, 'Common Sense', which the UDA unveiled on 29 January 1987. This proposed a constitutional conference, including Sinn Fein, with a view to creating a devolved assembly wherein a coalition government would operate on the basis of party strengths. However, McMichael was dead by the end of the year and in a very real sense common sense did not prevail. Nevertheless, the UDA's 'political interludes' do indicate that, given responsible leadership, Loyalist paramilitaries can answer to that leadership rather than to the urgings of the insensate, or the shadow intelligence figure.

The Special Air Services (SAS) regiment, with a headquarters in Hereford, and another in London, in the Duke of York Barracks on the King's Road, was founded in Egypt during 1941. It was designed to carry out sabotage and intelligence operations behind enemy lines. These generally fell squarely within the Deniable Zone. For example, it was agreed to send the SAS to Oman in 1958 (where the regiment has since served on and off in aid of the Sultan's forces), 'provided all possible steps were taken to avoid publicity. We should maintain ... it was intended to assist in the training of the Sultan's own forces.'[104] Even membership of the SAS is deniable, since many of its members are assigned from other regiments. For example, in discussing allegations of dirty tricks by Holroyd involving Robert Nairac, Mark Urban writes:

> Lt. Nairac was never in the SAS; although he died later in Northern Ireland, his name was not inscribed on the clock tower at the regiment's camp in Hereford where all SAS men who fall in action are listed.[105]

Nairac was, in fact, on assignment from the Grenadier Guards at the time of his death. Members of the SAS have a high level of fitness and train to be impervious to pain, both by direct physical maltreatment and by procedures such as carrying out 'a 45-mile endurance march to be completed in 24 hours while carrying a 50lb bergen rucksack'.[106] The regiment is also expert in the infliction of pain. It was the SAS who conducted the 'deep interrogation' of the 'hooded men' at Ballykelly Barracks in 1971 after internment. They are also suspected of involvement in the training and running of the undercover 'pseudo-gangs', the Dublin and other cross-border bombings, and a number of assassinations south of the border. The SAS is acknowledged to have shot eleven people as a result of stake-outs in 1977–8 alone. SAS men's training is aimed at enabling its members to live for days in the open, on spartan rations, in dugouts, defecating into plastic receptacles while waiting for a suspect to show up.

The veil of secrecy over the SAS's operations was lifted to a degree in 1976. Harold Wilson announced on 7 January that units of the force were to be sent into South Armagh. Opinions differ as to why the announcement was made. Some say it was because the IRA had previously succeeded in killing, or blowing up, forty-nine soldiers in the area. Others point to a bout of horrific sectarian warfare over the previous six months. This reached a peak with the shooting of eleven Protestant workmen by the 'South Armagh Republican Action Force', an organisation lying very much within the Deniable Zone, along the lines of the Catholic Reaction Force mentioned earlier. The slaughter came in retaliation for the killing of five Catholics by Protestants a few days earlier. Later, on 7 March 1978, Roy Mason announced that every army unit in the Six Counties was to have its own undercover SAS support group. The intensification of the Ulsterisation policy also meant more work for the SAS in training UDR and RUC squads and in planning undercover operations. SAS men were deployed in plain clothes on the streets. Humphrey Atkins in fact spoke publicly on two occasions in 1979[107] of the existence of a 'Secret Army'.

The SAS's involvement in the shoot-to-kill policy is thought to have accounted for thirty-one deaths between 1981 and 1989, including 'spectaculars' such as the Loughgall and Gibraltar shootings. The regiment is also thought to have trained UDA squads in collaboration with John McMichael. It is believed that McMichael provided men while the SAS supplied the training and intelligence to enable a number of killings to take place during the H Block agitation. Though at the time these appeared to have been linked solely to the H Block issue, a connection has subsequently been alleged with 'operation RANC', a series of revenge killings following the murder of Airey Neave by an INLA car bomb in March 1979.[108]

British intelligence is said to have masterminded the plot, which claimed the lives of the H Block activists John Turnley, Miriam Daly and Ronald Bunting and very nearly claimed that of Bernadette McAliskey and her husband. Ronald Bunting had taken a remarkably different path from that of his father, Major Ronald Bunting, Paisley's one-time henchman. Bunting Junior was an active member of the INLA. The others, however, were engaged only in constitutional political activity.

This particular spate of killings would appear to have ended following some very strong private representations by the Dublin Government. All I can say on the matter is that I know from my own sources that the representations were made. In the case of Turnley, a Protestant civil libertarian, it was stated in court, by one of the four-man UDA team sentenced to life imprisonment on 10 March 1982 for the murder, that the killing was committed at the instigation of the SAS. The UDA man, Robert McConnell, who named the SAS men he said he had worked with, said that they had given him weapons and discussed the activities not only of Turnley but also of Daly, Bunting and McAliskey. An RUC officer admitted at the trial that notes of an interview with McConnell's brother Eric, also sentenced to life imprisonment, had been destroyed because they contained 'sensitive information'.

The McAliskey attempt paralleled one on Gerry Adams' life in a number of ways. In the McAliskeys' case the assailants were captured after they had carried out the shooting and were preparing to drive off. Their captors were a group of paratroopers who had been on a stake-out nearby. It was never explained why paratroopers were involved, as the Argyll and Sutherland Highlanders were stationed locally. Nor, of course, was it made clear why the paratroopers did not appear until after the shootings had taken place. When they did show up, the soldiers said they could not summon aid as their radio was not working and the McAliskeys' phone lines had been cut. They left to find the Argylls, who arrived twenty minutes later and rendered the medical aid that saved the couple's lives.

In Adams' case, the shooting occurred on 14 March 1984, during the lunchtime adjournment of a case he was involved in at Belfast Magistrates' Court. He told me afterwards that he had been expecting something to happen that day. 'All my sixth senses were working. I had a presentiment.' He and three companions were wounded by three UDA men. The UDA men were captured immediately afterwards by what were described as an off-duty UDR man and two members of 'the Royal Military Police', who happened to be driving by in plain clothes and an unmarked car. While the authorities have denied SAS involvement, Adams has always maintained that the shooting was an SAS/intelligence operation and that the UDA men were set up. As in the McAliskey case there were no smoking guns found on military personnel. In fact, men with army connections were made to appear as saviours in both cases. John McMichael, the UDA leader who had helped to plan the attempt on Adams, was, as we have seen, subsequently killed by the IRA. One of the soldiers involved in capturing Adams' assailants lost both his legs in an IRA bomb attack five years later.

In the incidents at Loughgall and Gibraltar there is no dispute about SAS involvement. In the former, which occurred on 8 May 1987, the SAS were lying in wait for a top IRA ASU which had arrived in the village to blow up what they thought was an untended RUC station. The ASU drove into an ambush, not an arrest. All eight were killed, three after surrendering. A passenger in a passing car was also shot dead. It was the biggest single loss for the IRA since 1921, when twelve volunteers had been killed in an engagement at Clonmult, Co. Cork.

The IRA may have been planning a revenge 'spectacular' in Gibraltar for Loughall and for a number of other incidents which had occurred prior to 6 March 1988. It is believed that the planned target was a band and changing of the guard ceremony involving the Royal Anglian Regiment at Ince's Hall, Main Street, Gibraltar. The bomb was found across the Spanish border in Marbella two days later after the SAS had cut down the IRA scouting party without warning. The British Government had been aware of the IRA group's activities for some months, an earlier visit to Spain by the group having come to the attention of British intelligence the previous November (1987). An SAS team was flown to the Rock on 2 March 1988, and whatever action it took, I cannot believe that it did so without official authorization. Three people – Mairead Farrell, Danny McCann and Sean Savage – were shot dead. All were unarmed. Savage was a nephew of Billy McKee, the former Belfast IRA Commander. Farrell had been the leader of the dirty protest in Armagh Jail. I had last seen her coated in filth in a dingy cell lined with faeces and menstrual fluid. McCann, who by the time of his death had become a top IRA operator, was from Clonard. He had been twelve years old the day the mobs invaded his district . . .

Apart, however, from illustrating aspects of the northern struggle, such as the continuing importance of the Clonard area, Gibraltar has a deeper significance. In the last analysis an army, or a part of an army, such as the SAS, is only a tool, an instrument of policy. If the tool is misused its actions can have a knock-on emotional and, ultimately, political effect, particularly in a complex situation like Northern Ireland. What the SAS could get away with safely in Oman might have unforeseen results close to home. This is what happened over Gibraltar. As the victims were being buried in Belfast on 16 March 1988, a Loyalist gunman, Michael Stone, made a gun and grenade attack on the mourners, killing three of them. While one of the victims, Kevin Brady, was being buried three days later in an atmosphere of extraordinary tension, two British corporals in plain clothes drove into the funeral, apparently unaware of what was going on. The soldiers, Robert Howes and Derek Wood, were dragged from their vehicle by a mob, beaten, stripped and then shot. For me the photograph of Fr Alec Reid, who had vainly tried to save the men, praying over one of the bodies subsequently became one of the most searing images of the entire Troubles.

But the harmful effects of Gibraltar did not end with the soldiers' deaths. The Amnesty International Report for 1992 cited the trial of seven men charged in connection with their deaths in support of Amnesty's contention that the United Kingdom's behaviour in Northern Ireland had made it into one of the worst human rights violators in Europe. The report pointed out that the courts '. . . drew adverse inferences against defendants for having remained silent during police questioning or at trial'. The case is bracketed in many Nationalists' minds with the miscarriages of justice in the Birmingham Six and Maguire family cases.

One could go on and fill many books with accounts of other forms of 'dirty tricks'. I know of one case involving an English woman journalist and a prominent Northern Irish Nationalist politician who were filmed by an RUC undercover unit *in flagrante*. It took intercession by a taoiseach with the British Government to prevent the videotape being used for blackmail purposes. Other incidents, like the disgraceful saga of Kincora, the boys' home in east Belfast which MI5 used as a source of male prostitution, are at least partly known. Colin Wallace was one of the first to allege that MI5 and the army were not only fully conversant with what was happening there but encouraged it.[109] He says that his complaints were ignored because Kincora was in fact an MI5 blackmail operation, designed to give the agency a hold over certain prominent people.[110]

Kincora was run by William McGrath, a member of Ian Paisley's Free Presbyterian Church, who also ran the Loyalist paramilitary group Tara, a specifically anti-Catholic, as opposed to merely anti-Republican, organisation. Several of Tara's members were also in the UVF, one of the more deadly of the Loyalist paramilitary groupings. Apart from abusing the boys himself, McGrath hired them out to stag clubs.

This may have been the cause of his undoing. My understanding is that two of the boys, whom he had sent to a stag club in Scotland, made a pact that they would commit suicide. While one subsequently drowned himself, the other did not, but his information set in train an RUC investigation which was aborted by British intelligence. Eventually, as a result of public disquiet, largely fuelled by some first-class investigative journalism by the *Irish Times* and the *Irish Independent*, yet another police inquiry was held, under the aegis of a British policeman, Sir George Terry, formerly Chief Constable of Sussex. His report was made public on 24 October 1983. It proved inconclusive. Sir George said he could find no evidence that civil servants, RUC or military intelligence were involved in a homosexual ring or that they had conspired to withhold evidence.

That is probably true. Such evidence would be extremely difficult to find. Kincora was one of the most deniable of the Deniable Zone scandals. McGrath received only a two-year sentence for his Kincora crimes. His Tara activities drew no penalty whatever. Martin Dillon, one of the most exhaustive researchers in the Deniable Zone, is not alone in his assertion that McGrath was shielded in order to protect the identity of well-known homosexuals within the British military intelligence community. The disclosures could also have damaged others in high places in British public life. Dillon bears out some of Colin Wallace's allegations about Kincora:

> [McGrath] had been working for British Intelligence . . . He also monitored the life of his fellow loyalists, but his other life included the provision of boys for homosexual colleagues within the British Intelligence community in Northern Ireland and for several leading members of the British Establishment who visited Belfast regularly . . . In 1979 a Military Intelligence liaison officer sabotaged RUC attempts to trace the history of McGrath and his British intelligence connection.[111]

Not only were the RUC sabotaged. Of my own knowledge I can state that a UDA leader who interrogated McGrath in jail was subsequently murdered, and that journalists who tried to follow up the story were intimidated. I know some Kincora-watching journalists who smiled grimly on 23 April 1987. On that date, following disclosures by the journalist Chapman Pincher, Margaret Thatcher felt compelled to reveal in the House of Commons that the former head of MI6, Sir Maurice Oldfield, was a homosexual who had lost his positive vetting clearance. She said that Sir Maurice had admitted to being a homosexual, but denied that this had ever led to security being compromised. After Thatcher's declaration, former colleagues of Oldfield's in MI6 denied indignantly that he had ever been a homosexual. He had had some fleeting sexual experimentation as a student, but nothing subsquently. However, information supplied from Belfast to London which found its way to Pincher and later to Thatcher alleged that Oldfield's Special Branch guards had observed him partaking of Kincora's facilities. The unfortunate Oldfield, whose term in the Six Counties was cut short by stomach cancer, had to contend with both his illness and these allegations in the last days of his life. By the time Thatcher made her revelations, Oldfield had been dead for six years. But it would appear that, even beyond the grave, the war between the intelligence services continued. Colin Wallace has been quoted as saying that the reason for the allegations about Sir Maurice was that:

> Oldfield had a Mr Clean approach in Northern Ireland, particularly against assassination plots and the dirty tricks war. There was a remarkable campaign of character assassination directed against Oldfield which could only have been co-ordinated by people who actually had very detailed inside information . . . MI5 wanted him removed from Ulster because he would never have sanctioned the E4A-type activities [E4A is the RUC undercover death squad, referred to on p. 258]. It was no secret to anyone who knew Maurice Oldfield that he was totally opposed to assassination. MI5 saw him as a threat to their activities in Ireland.[112]

As to the myriad forms which the intelligence war takes on this side of the Styx, one can only speculate. Were there, for example, attempts to poison John Hume and Gerry Adams? Adams suffers from hepatitis-like symptoms from time to time. He also has some kidney problems, dating from a bout of interrogation in Castlereagh when he was kicked unconscious and drenched in cold water. Was more than cold water used while he was unconscious? John Hume certainly does not rule out the possibility. Since the mid-eighties he has had periodic bouts of ill-health which may or may not be traceable to a certain SDLP fund-raising dance. On the crowded dance floor Hume suddenly 'felt a jag' in his thigh. He started feeling unwell shortly afterwards. Later he discovered a circular inflamed blotch on the affected limb. In London shortly afterwards he began to feel progressively worse. Chris Patten, then a Northern Ireland Office minister, arranged for him to be admitted to a London hospital, where he received treatment. The blotch subsided but Hume never subsequently enjoyed quite the same robust health he had previously. We discussed the incident in Jury's Hotel, Dublin, on a bright May day in 1994 before the IRA ceasefire was announced.[113]

Our interview was delayed while John talked to a detective. Outside the hotel window a Garda squad car circled the grounds. He had just been warned that 'the

Loyalists were going to try to get him in the Republic – to make a point'. The threat was obviously both explicable and real. But I remember thinking at the time (and still do) that it was curious that the Loyalist paramilitaries would have chosen that moment to make such a point. They could have shot him ten times over in his native Derry, or in Belfast. John Hume is one of the most visible, and therefore vulnerable, public figures in Northern Ireland. I have known his car to break down in the middle of the night on lonely roads where he had to wait for almost an hour before getting a lift. He has had innumerable death threats. In times of controversy, the Provisionals have been known to fire on his home. All that has kept him alive has been the understanding between the Republicans and the Loyalists that if anything happened to a leader such as himself or Adams, then leading Loyalist politicians would be 'taken out' in retaliation. But at the time we spoke there was a good deal of outrage in the Tory press, amongst Conservatives, and, of course, in Unionist circles about talks which Hume had been conducting with Adams. Hume, 'St John', the revered leader of constitutional nationalism, was perceived as giving aid and comfort to the process of respectabilising Sinn Fein. Yet, as has been demonstrated since the ceasefire, it was obvious that if Sinn Fein were brought in from the cold, the Loyalist paramilitaries would automatically follow and reap any benefits in the way of amnesties, etc. which might ensue. Why shoot a man who was helping to bring this about?

Whatever attitude one may take to all of the foregoing, it must be acknowledged that the episodes, described and surmised, unquestionably point towards a very dirty form of warfare all round. The first essential, therefore, if this form of 1920s, secret service, colonial-style 'dirty tricks' war was to succeed in a west European democracy was the muzzling of the media.

ELEVEN

THE MEDIA WAR

There is a question to be answered one day as to how far the BBC – and Fleet St too – was responsible for not informing the rest of the country of the conduct of public affairs in Northern Ireland in the fifties and sixties.

Alasdair Milne, *The Memoirs of a British Broadcaster*

THE MEDIA, PARTICULARLY the electronic media, was, and still is, one of the most important theatres of operations in the dirty tricks war. It is also the phase of the struggle which illustrates most clearly how the Unionists, who amount to only some 2 per cent of the United Kingdom's population, managed to exert a sometimes decisive influence on what the other 98 per cent got to know about the conflict. As with many other aspects of the troubles – the Loyalist workers' strike of 1974, the hunger strikes, or the IRA's development – the media war has generated a substantial body of work. I would particularly direct readers to Liz Curtis' book, *Ireland, the Propaganda War*,[1] and to a collection of contributions of various sorts edited by Paul Madden, *The British Media and Ireland: Truth, the First Casualty*.[2] Within the parameters of this book, however, discussion of the role of the media, or more accurately the pressures to which it was subjected as a result of the northern conflict, from the early 1970s to the present day, must of necessity be indicative rather than exhaustive.

Having reported on the Anglo-Irish situation for over thirty years, I am inclined to compare the effects of both Irish and British coverage on public opinion to looking across the Irish Sea through a telescope with a cap on. To begin with, it is a given of the situation that the Irish media makes almost no impact on the United Kingdom. Conversely, although at the time of writing some six out of ten papers bought in the Republic are British, and the electronic coverage of the BBC, Sky and ITV is increasingly available, UK reportage on the Six Counties, or on Anglo-Irish relationships, is often automatically discounted by the Irish, almost at a subconscious level, as being just that: a UK view, meaning a propagandist one.

In one sense this is unfair to the work of many great journalists and programme controllers who have covered the conflict for the British printed and electronic media. Mary Holland, Robert Fisk, Robert Kee, Keith Kyle, Jonathan Dimbleby, Peter Taylor, John Ware, John Whale, Simon Winchester, Harold Evans, Roger Bolton, Jon Snow, Jeremy Isaacs and his successor as head of Channel 4, Michael Grade, for example, have all showed both professionalism and courage in their attempts to make what happened in Northern Ireland explicable to British audiences. Indeed, reporters and camera crews on the ground have frequently had to show courage above and beyond the normal call of duty because of the passions which make reporting Northern Ireland such a hazardous affair.

I regard their efforts as particularly creditable in light of the fact that not only have they been operating against a backdrop in which the IRA were both sending coffins back to England and bombing British cities into the bargain, they have also been acting, and continue to act, under severe legal constraints. As we shall see, ingrained political attitudes probably constitute as great an obstacle to the dissemination of information about Ireland as anything else. The United Kingdom is an area where authority, deference, and secrecy have traditionally flourished. British society is such that accent is commonly used both as a means of control and as an indication of social superiority.

Harold Evans, who as editor of the *Sunday Times* fought, and won, landmark battles for press freedom, on issues such as the right to publish the Crossman diaries, and informing the public as to the extent of the damage caused to unborn children by the drug Thalidomide, has written:

> The freedom of the press is commonly discussed in relation to government and law. These external restraints are important. I spent a considerable amount of my career as an editor in finding ways round them. In 1974 in the Granada Guildhall lectures, frustrated by laws of contempt and confidence, I characterised the British press as 'half free', by comparison with the press of the United States. The comparison remains, in my judgement, substantially as valid today as then.[3]

If Evans were writing the foregoing, not in 1983, but at the time this is being written (1995), he would have to change the last phrase to read 'more valid today than then'. His book makes two things clear. Firstly, that his campaigns were made possible by the financial and professional support of his proprietor, Roy Thompson. Secondly, that the extension of Rupert Murdoch's control over the British newspaper industry brought a virtual closure to the Evans school of journalism. It partly reopened with the foundation of *The Independent*, but how long those doors will stay open must remain a matter of speculation. What Evans' book does not touch on is the manner in which the Irish situation, as regards both electronic and press media, was used to make it questionable whether the British media deserves to be regarded as even 'half free'.

John Ware of the BBC, who has covered Ireland for both print and television, began an important paper he wrote on the difficulties of reporting on Ireland with the following:

> Secrecy, said the late Richard Crossman, is *the* British disease; and it's my belief that this disease has taken such firm roots here because we revere and defer to authority so much . . . A proper cure for this secrecy disease remains as elusive as ever. So deeply embedded is it in British culture that, as the journalist and historian Peter Hennessy puts it, secrecy is built into the very calcium of the policy makers' bones. One by-product is being economical with the truth. We have seen this elevated to an art form – Westland, *Spycatcher*, Matrix Churchill – and now this past week – Ireland.[4]

Ware was writing a few days after both Sir Patrick Mayhew and John Major were proved to have been lying as 'in confident, precise, well-modulated tones', they gave the House of Commons 'categorical denials of contacts with the IRA'.[5] Lying, and being condescending, about Ireland, is a well-established practice amongst British politicians. The statutory instruments which both assist them in so doing, and prevent journalists from exposing them, can be described with some precision.

Publication gags include the right to injunct publication. This was used for example by the Thatcher administration to stop the British public reading the *Spycatcher* memoirs. There is also the Public Interest Immunity certificate. This instrument allows a minister to prevent information from being disclosed during a trial, 'in the public interest'. As we know from the Matrix Churchill trial, concern for 'the public interest' led to four ministers signing such certificates to prevent the public learning that the Government was involved in armaments trade with Iraq. Only the action of a conscientious judge prevented the PII certificates from wrongfully sending defendants to jail.

The 1981 Contempt of Court Act can force a journalist to declare his source if the court finds disclosure to be 'in the interests of justice or national security or for the prevention of disorder or crime'. That formula might just as well include the words 'or in the interests of Uncle Tom Cobleigh and all'. Then, as we shall see shortly in one of the many campaigns waged against BBC programmes in the period under review, the Prevention of Terrorism Act is an all-powerful weapon. No public interest defence against turning informer is permitted under the Act. Finally, to copper-fasten the position of the state against leaks from civil servants, politicians or others in state employ, there is the 1989 Official Secrets Act. Section 2 of the OSA specifically removes any possibility of pleading the public interest as a defence for a state employee, say, telling someone like myself how the shoot-to-kill policy worked.

There is a saying, attributed to G. K. Chesterton, concerning Bernard Shaw, to the effect that the man in the street is fundamentally ignorant and fundamentally correct. Chesterton said that Bernard Shaw did not believe in God, did not eat meat, and did write plays. The man in the street probably had not seen the plays, but he was aware of their existence. In the same way the Irish public came to realise that, though they could not see the hidden hands controlling the British information faucet, someone was manipulating the flow.

The major turning points at which the taps were tightened can be documented.[6] The BBC had always walked on eggshells in Belfast. Alasdair Milne has recorded:

> ... our colleagues in Belfast were more sensitive about the Stormont Government than was common BBC practice with governments at Westminster. Indeed, Andrew Stewart, who was controller there after the war, told me that he had almost been treated as an unofficial member of the Northern Ireland Cabinet.

But from the time of the Tories' accession to power in 1970, the BBC began to run scared of Westminster also. All items on Northern Ireland had to be cleared in advance with the formidable Northern Ireland BBC Controller, Waldo Maguire, who was regarded by broadcasters with something of the awe accorded by his pupils to the Revd James Leigh Joynes, the legendary Etonian flogging tutor.[7] On top of this, interviews with members of the IRA had to be cleared at director-general level. The introduction of internment in 1971 heightened the Tories' conviction that militaristic policies on the streets of Belfast or Derry necessitated a media back-up in London.

The biggest and most successful spin doctor coup on the part of the Tories was the handling of the fall-out from Bloody Sunday. Concurrent with the setting-up of the Widgery Tribunal, allegedly to throw light on what had happened on Bloody Sunday, the Downing Street press office spread darkness over the media. First journalists were warned that the contempt of court laws meant that any anticipation of the tribunal's findings would be a contempt. This was accepted unchallenged by the media, which agreed with the position as stated by the *Sunday Times*: 'The law is that until the Chief Justice completes his inquiry, nobody may offer to the British public a consecutive account of the events in Derry last weekend.'[8] This warning aborted efforts at investigative journalism in general and in particular three major investigations which had been undertaken by the *Observer*, the *Sunday Times* and Thames TV. It is now known that all, or indeed any, of these would have fatally undermined the official version of the shootings.

Then, on the eve of the Widgery Report's scheduled publication, 19 April 1972, the spin doctors got in a pre-emptive strike. Ministry of Defence spokespersons phoned the defence correspondents of the national newspapers, giving highly selective versions of the document's contents. No concern for contempt accompanied the uncritical printing of these leaks. The overriding attitude of the press on the morning of 19 April may be accurately gauged from the *Daily Express*' finding: 'Widgery blames IRA and clears Army'. The MOD continued to manage the news after the report's release, by holding a press conference to which only defence correspondents were invited. This excluded journalists such as Simon Winchester, who, unlike the defence correspondents, had actually witnessed the shootings and was in a position to ask awkward questions.

As a result, the following day's coverage again went the army's way. The *Daily Mail*'s editorial of 20 April may be taken as summing up the general reaction:

> Against cynical propagandists the British Government replies with judicial truth. It is like trying to exterminate a nest of vipers with Queensberry rules. Even so, over the past $2\frac{1}{2}$ years of mounting terrorism, the record shows – and it is a record which now includes Lord Widgery's report – that our troops are doing an impossible job impossibly well.

This tide of chauvinism swept over the handful of dissentients, such as Simon Winchester, who wrote in the *Guardian* that the report was 'a profound disappointment'. By the time Winchester's book appeared, the army version – that they had only fired at snipers and nail-bombers – was so firmly entrenched that even passages like the following could not demolish the myth:

> A soldier below me suddenly turned my way. He pointed his rifle up and there were two sharp jerks of his arm. 'Christ, he's firing at us!' I yelled to a young boy who was watching

the scene. We dropped on to the road and stayed as still as we could for a minute . . . we had indeed been the target of the paratroopers down below.[9]

Widgery was so uncritical of the army's claims that he accepted that four nail bombs were found in the pockets of one of the Derry victims, Gerald Donaghy. Yet two doctors, one of them a British medical officer, an army captain, gave evidence to the tribunal that they had separately examined Donaghy thoroughly, adjusting and opening his jeans and jacket, without seeing any signs of bombs. As Michael O'Connell would write, years later, the Donaghy case at least presented '. . . an opportunity for Lord Widgery to demonstrate that he was conducting an inquiry which was impartial and independent . . . He failed to do so.'[10]

Fleet Street also failed to demonstrate either impartiality or independence. Indeed, like the colleague mentioned by Simon Winchester in his book, some journalists thought Bloody Sunday 'a jolly good show'.[11]

As the troubles escalated, the BBC became a prime target. One Conservative backbencher wrote openly to the *Daily Telegraph* stating: 'No national army can in the 1970s sustain its morale without the support of home television and radio.'[12] He was echoing the views of the Defence Secretary, Lord Carrington, who had written to the BBC chairman, Lord Hill, a little earlier, not merely castigating the BBC for its reportage of army behaviour but demanding an end to it, on the grounds that it was 'unfairly loaded to suggest improper behaviour by British troops'.[13] One of the many instances of 'loaded ' reporting cited by Carrington concerned the shooting dead of a Catholic priest, Fr Hugh Mullan, the day after internment was introduced. Carrington objected to the fact that the presenter of BBC Radio's *World at One* programme had ended an eyewitness account of the shooting with the words: 'An eyewitness putting the blame fairly and squarely on the British Army.'

Fr Mullan had in fact been shot dead by a British soldier as he administered the last rites to a dying man. But Carrington's onslaught elicited from the BBC a public apology for making 'an error of judgement'.[14] Subsequent BBC policy followed that cringing mind set. So did that of the commercial TV network, headed by the Independent Television Authority (ITA). Lord Aylestone, chairman of the ITA, once said: 'Britain is at war with the IRA in Ulster and the IRA will get no more coverage than the Nazis would have done in the last war.'[15] In Ulster itself the ITV counterpart to Waldo Maguire, 'Brum' Henderson, saw to it that the Maguire approach applied to Ulster Televison (UTV) also. Sometimes programmes were banned, sight unseen, merely because they dealt with the Troubles.[16] There was a particular burst of Tory outrage at the publicity which followed the *Sunday Times* confirmation (on 17 October 1971) that the army had been using torture in the wake of internment.

The furore was a classic example of the capped telescope syndrome. Such reports had been commonplace in the Irish media for months,[17] but it was only when they crossed the Irish Sea to appear in a British publication that they drew a reaction – a very hostile reaction. The representatives of the officer and gentleman class on the Conservative backbenches arose in wrath. After all, this was how the army had traditionally operated, in Aden, Cyprus, Kenya, Malaya and other places.

Why should it now have to contend with carping criticism merely because it was dealing with wogs from the bog?

Eighty Conservative backbenchers saw Reginald Maudling, the Home Secretary, on 15 November to advocate 'patriotic censorship'.[18] Amongst them was Lieutenant-Colonel 'Mad Mitch' Mitchell, who had gained some notoriety in the tabloid press because of his conduct in the Aden conflict. He apparently felt that this background fitted him to analyse the BBC's coverage on Ireland as 'subsidised subversion'.[19] He said that the BBC was 'contributing towards IRA objectives by undermining the will of the home population to fight in Ulster'. Maudling acted on the complaints of the Mitchellites with a decisiveness he did not show in any other area of his Irish policy. He immediately sent for the chairmen of both the BBC and the ITA. Next day, in the House of Commons, the Minister for Posts and Communications, Christopher Chataway, summed up the policy enjoined on, and accepted by, both gentlemen.

Radio and television were not required to be impartial as between the IRA and the Stormont Government. They were not required to be impartial as between the army and the IRA. The IRA and the army were definitely not to be regarded as being on the same moral plane.

In both BBC and ITV, 'impartial' came to be translated as 'balanced'. On the grounds that they were not 'balanced', programmes and programme ideas fell like autumn leaves before the self-censors. Brian Faulkner led a charge that almost knocked out a huge *Tribunal* programme that the BBC put out in January of 1972. Lords Caradon and Devlin and Sir John Foster presided for hours over an investigation into various proposed solutions to the conflict in a manner which was generally held to have been 'responsible to the point of dullness'.[20] Afterwards, calls to the BBC were five to one in favour, though before the programme there had been a phone campaign which ran ten to one against.[21] On the morning of its showing the *Belfast Newsletter*'s headline on the story was: 'The Full United Kingdom is Now in Peril!' But, despite peril, as the BBC's official historian Asa Briggs chronicles, the programme only went out because one independent-minded Unionist, Jack Maginnis, MP, defied Faulkner and agreed to appear.[22] This not only had the effect of getting around the 'balance' rule, but also caused Paisley to abandon his earlier refusal to appear!

Anything that could be represented as 'anti-army' was rejected. In a famous unsigned article in the *New Statesman*, Jonathan Dimbleby described the results:

> The censorship and restrictions now imposed on reporters and editors make it practically impossible for them to ask the question 'Why?' Why do the Catholics now laugh openly when a British soldier is shot down and killed, when a year ago they would offer the army cups of tea? Why do the Catholics refuse to condemn the bombings and the shootings? Why do they still succour the IRA?
>
> What influence today does the Civil Rights Movement have? Or the SDLP? The answers to such questions are fundamental to understanding the problem, crucial to any judgement of British policy, yet they cannot be asked by BBC employees.[23]

In practice the creed of 'balance' operated so that Unionists, British Government and army spokespersons could appear on air saying what they wished, without any contrasting view being sought. But, as Dimbleby pointed out:

> ... in the case of members of the SDLP, the government and the opposition of the Irish Republic, all critics of the British army, the government, or of Stormont policy, the rule is strictly applied.

Apart from the obvious imbalance thus created, a further bias was added by the logistical difficulties involved. A programme maker only had to find one spokesperson if the Establishment were approached. But getting someone from the ranks of the critics involved at best the hassle of producing a second counter-balancing voice; at worst, discovering that if one did find an SDLP, or more particularly a Republican 'talking head', the broadcasting equivalent of Paisley's countermarch tactic would be brought into play. The item involving the critic could be rerouted into oblivion, if the Establishment declined to provide 'balance'. The latitude extended to the Unionist point of view rebounded badly against the Labour Government during the Loyalist workers' strike of 1974.

The autonomy created in BBC Northern Ireland both before and during the Waldo Maguire era resulted in a situation summed up by Merlyn Rees in his memoirs as follows:

> I had no doubt that the UWC [Ulster Workers Council] had been helped all along by the BBC's treatment of the strike as an industrial dispute and not a political stoppage. Individual members of the UWC had become overnight the stars of television and radio. Complaints had poured in from Brian Faulkner and the Executive members in particular, and from the SDLP and minority population in general. Stan Orme considered that the BBC acted as 'quislings', and I later learned that the Irish government had also reacted strongly to the BBC's policy, thought that is perhaps understandable given its own policy of 'control' of RTE.[24]

Rees' list of complainants has two significant omissions, given the record of the two bodies concerned in spin-doctoring throughout the conflict. Neither the army nor the RUC found fault with the BBC on this occasion. The indulgent coverage of the strike gave audiences no indication that both the army and police were heavily criticised by the SDLP, and by Dublin ministers (privately), for their pro-Loyalist attitudes and failure to take down illegal road blocks. In a nutshell, the army, and significant elements within the RUC, were anti-Government during the strike, and like-minded figures in the BBC stunted the public's awareness of this.

All of this contributed towards creating a general climate of public ignorance about what was happening in Ireland which persists to this day. Nothing remotely resembling the anti-Vietnam war movement in America emerged. So far as pressuring MPs was concerned, such Irish lobbies as did build up in the UK (for example the Troops Out movement) never got significantly beyond the sort of interest group stage described by James Callaghan in the seminar earlier. The ignorance levels were topped up systematically to a point where what might fairly be described as statutory controls were exerted on the media.

A policy of news management was espoused by both Conservatives and Labour.

Four years after the happenings described above, another major assault on the media was unleashed under Labour. The Gardiner Report treated the media as an essential component of the 'criminalisation' policy. In order to make a success of army tactics, and both the abolition of Special Category status and the accelerated prison-building programme (the H Blocks) which it recommended, the report made important suggestions concerning the media. These merit quotation at some length:

> The view has been expressed to us that the news media must bear a degree of responsibility for the encouragement of terrorist activity in Northern Ireland. Interviews with terrorist leaders on television and radio and the practice of some newspapers in accepting advertisements from paramilitary groups may provide propaganda platforms for those whose aim is the violent overthrow of lawful government.
>
> There is a tendency, which exists elsewhere, towards sensational reporting of shooting and bombing incidents which lends a spurious glamour both to the activities themselves and to the perpetrators.

The next sentence is particularly significant:

> In addition there are ill-founded and false allegations against the security forces.

The report went on:

> There can be no question of introducing censorship in a free society in time of peace. But this does not mean that nothing can be done. We recommend that it be made a summary offence for editors, printers and publishers of newspapers to publish anything which purports to be an advertisement for or on behalf of an illegal organisation or part of it.
>
> The authority of the Press Council extends to all newspapers and magazines within the United Kingdom, including Northern Ireland. Although it possesses only the powers to censure a publication, newspapers are, in fact, highly sensitive to such action by their peers. It also has the authority to consider general policies about publication with the public interest in mind; it has, for instance, issued a general caveat against newspapers printing and paying for the memoirs of criminals. In the present situation we suggest that the Press Council should closely examine the reconciliation of the reporting of terrorist activities with the public interest.

Since at all times the prime target in the government communication onslaught was the electronic media, the concluding paragraph is of particular interest:

> Finally, the Governors of the British Broadcasting Corporation and the Independent Broadcasting Authority should re-examine the guidance they give to programme controllers or companies about contact with terrorist organisations and the reporting of their views and activities.

Few people endorsed that recommendation with more fervour than Roy Mason, a Secretary of State for Northern Ireland who will long be remembered for the vigour with which he pursued a security policy in general and the Gardiner findings in particular. Journalists still speak wonderingly of the off-the-record briefings he gave, *circa* September 1976, soon after arriving in the province. The *Irish Press* was informed at the time that he wanted to introduce a special Six County D-Notice system which would prohibit all mention of paramilitary activities, or statements, in either the electronic or the print media. At what became known as 'The Second Battle of Culloden', in the Culloden Hotel, Belfast, he gave an explicit illustration of how thorough he thought this censorship should be.

Asked did he mean that if the IRA assassinated him the following day the fact should not be reported, he replied: 'That is exactly what I mean.' The occasion of the Second Battle of Culloden was in fact an off-the-record dinner given by the Governor-General of the BBC, Sir Michael Swann, on 4 November 1976. It was attended not only by several chieftains of the BBC, but by leaders of Six County society who included the heads of the army, judiciary and RUC. What transpired became public knowledge the following January via the inevitable press leaks.[25] Apparently, before the dinner began, Mason had been nettled by what he considered to be a piece of *lèse-majesté* on the part of the BBC Northern Ireland's *Spotlight* programme, a profile of himself. Mason had refused to take part, apparently thinking that the 'balance' factor would mean that his refusal would effectively kill the programme.

But the *Spotlight* team, being Ulstermen, were made of sterner stuff. They not only put out the programme, but worse, concluded it with a contribution from Anthony Howard, then editor of the *New Statesman*, which made it clear that Mason was far from being Howard's favourite politician. All this boiled up when Sir Michael Swann somewhat incautiously asked Mason what he thought of the BBC's coverage. Alasdair Milne records that Mason availed himself of the opportunity to come at the BBC luminaries 'like an Exocet'.[26] According to *The Observer*, Mason said, amongst other things, that he was involved in decisions about the BBC's charter and income which was something those present should ponder.[27] The BBC's coverage was 'quite appalling', providing a 'daily platform for the IRA'. Mason was assisted in his advance on the ramparts of the BBC by heavy supporting fire from the representatives of the army and the judiciary, Major General David Young and Sir Robert Lowry, the Chief Justice.

Readers will be able to gauge for themselves the effect of the Carrington/Mason-type approach in the representative list of aborted and still-born programmes given below. But first may I be permitted to jump forward in time to indicate how the fall-out from the Second Battle of Culloden influenced the coverage of yet a Third Battle of Culloden, which occurred nearly twenty years later, as I was writing this book. This Third Battle also provides a classic example of the capped telescope syndrome. On Thursday 13 April 1995, almost eight months into the IRA ceasefire, I was in London, having, appropriately enough, gone there to address a group of media moguls on the inadequacy of the British approach to the Irish situation.

I awoke to hear a profoundly depressing item on the BBC news concerning the peace process. Sir Patrick Mayhew was excluding Sinn Fein from a series of bilateral talks, involving all the interested political parties, due to commence after Easter. This report was repeated in succeeding bulletins and corroborated by the *Guardian*. Understandably, Martin McGuinness of Sinn Fein was quoted by the BBC as being 'bitterly disappointed'. Other reports revealed that Mayhew had been speaking at a Belfast dinner in the presence of John Bruton, the Republic's new taoiseach. This had profound implications: Bruton, the leader of Fine Gael, was widely perceived as having strong pro-Unionist leanings. I knew that reservations about him existed in some SDLP and Sinn Fein circles. Nevertheless, his initial resolute espousal of the peace process since taking office a few weeks earlier had helped to allay fears that he would seek once again to isolate Sinn Fein from mainstream Irish political life. But now it appeared that a new Dublin–London axis might indeed be emerging.

The prospect of Sinn Fein's being able to keep the IRA onside in such an eventuality would be remote. The outlook for the peace process appeared bleak, not only to me, but to others. An English publishing friend and a minicab driver volunteered their opinions on what they had heard on the news. The publisher said he thought the news 'awful' and 'profoundly depressing'. The minicab driver was from Belfast. He had grown up never knowing peace and had emigrated to London. His parents had just come over for an Easter holiday and, prior to hearing the news, he had been finding their stories of life in a peaceful Six Counties amazing and delightfully unfamiliar.

The only crumb of comfort we derived from the 4 p.m. BBC news on the car radio as we drove to Heathrow was an IRA statement to the effect that there was no plan to end the ceasefire. My plane took off for Dublin at 5.30 p.m. Only then could I lay hands on an Irish newspaper. On page one of the *Irish Times* I discovered what had really happened. Mayhew's original script had indeed included a passage which indicated an apparent British intention to 'separate Sinn Fein from involvement in the peace process'.[28] Far from agreeing to this, however, Bruton had expressed 'concern', and a major confrontation ensued. As a result, Mayhew's script was changed so that what he actually said was:

> I hope that our intensive and ongoing communications with Sinn Fein will shortly make it possible to add them to the numbers [of participants].

Mayhew did not make the change easily or willingly, as the *Irish Times* report made clear:

> ... the Northern Secretary's announcement that Sinn Fein could be engaged in bilateral talks only came after an intensive 40-minute meeting with the Taoiseach, Mr Bruton, in the Culloden Hotel outside Belfast, earlier in the evening, when the Taoiseach succeeded in having the references to the talks process changed.

Thus, as a result of Bruton's 'intensive' initiative – and, as I later discovered, sustained effort on the part of a senior Irish diplomat, Sean O'hUiginn – the peace process remained intact. But not a word of either the threat to it, or Dublin's part in averting it, had appeared in the British media. The original Mayhew script, aimed at Conservative back bench opinion, was carried unrevised. One could understand early editions of newspapers, or bulletins broadcast immediately after the speech, carrying the first Mayhew script, but I find it hard to understand how no member of either the BBC's staff, or any other station that I tuned into so worriedly that day in

London, picked up on the fact that such an important piece of disinformation was being broadcast.

This incident occurred when London was allegedly engaged on a shared quest for peace with all parties concerned. One can imagine the spirit which prevailed while the killing was in progress. Peter Taylor once wrote:

> When it comes to Northern Ireland the presssure is constant. It consists of not just the standard letters of protest from Government and opposition to the IBA and the offending contracting company, but personal meetings between the Chairman of the Authority and the Secretary of State and Chief Constable of the RUC.
>
> These discussions are confidential, but their results gradually filter down though the broadcasting structures suggesting that more 'responsible' coverage would be welcome (there is little talk of censorship, Government and broadcasting authorities are usually far too adept and experienced to fall into that trap).[29]

Taylor's reference to 'the offending contracting company' should be noted. At the time of writing (1978) he was working as a reporter for Thames TV. Seven years later, in 1988, Thames made what was probably the single most controversial programme of the entire period, Roger Bolton's *Death on the Rock*, about the Gibraltar shooting. The programme showed beyond all doubt that either the British or the Spanish authorities could easily have arrested the unarmed IRA trio without the slightest difficulty. Instead it had been decided to set up an ambush and use the SAS to gun them down. The fury of the Tories in general, and Margaret Thatcher in particular, exceeded even that of 'Mad' Mitchell nineteen years earlier.

In his book, Roger Bolton has described in detail both how the storm broke and how Thames and the ITA stood firm against efforts to block the programme. These included a well-publicised intervention by the Foreign Secretary, Sir Geoffrey Howe, on 28 April 1988. The catchphrase widely used by the Tories at the time was 'trial by television'. Having failed to stop the message, the Government attempted to try the messengers on charges of having transmitted 'damaging inaccuracies'.[30] The methodology chosen for this was one which had already served the purposes of successive British governments where Northern Ireland was concerned: a government inquiry was set up to investigate the programme's claims, under the chairmanship of Lord Windlesham.

Windlesham, however, departed from the tradition established by Compton, Diplock, Widgery and Gardiner. To the Government's annoyance, on 26 January 1989 he reported that the programme had been generally accurate. Thatcher rejected this finding and said that criticisms of the programme had been justified. Two years later, in 1991, the franchises of the independent television companies came up for renewal. Thames's licence was not renewed.

British governmental media policy had its roots in the Westminster convention of leaving the Unionists to run their own affairs. Then, as Britain became more and more involved, the British attitude altered to seeing the media as an arm of security policy. The Kitsonian term 'information policy' springs readily to mind as one examines the lengthy list of banned or censored TV programmes which resulted.[31] It covers documentaries, dramas and current affairs. Before giving some indication

Above left: Mourners pray beside a blood-stained banner in the aftermath of Bloody Sunday, January 1972, in which paratroopers shot dead thirteen anti-internment marchers.

Above right: Man against the inferno, street scene, Belfast 1972.

A body is taken from the wreckage in Talbot Street, Dublin, one of the blast sites at which no-warning car-bombs claimed thirty lives in the Republic on 17 May 1974, the worst single death toll of the entire Troubles.

Left: The differing approaches of the British press to coverage of the Irish Troubles is exemplified by this montage of Fleet Street papers following the IRA bomb explosion which claimed the life of Mountbatten on 27 August 1979.

Below left: Carcases of horses from the Household Cavalry, which were killed in an IRA explosion near the bandstand at Regent's Park, London, in which three people were killed in July 1982.

Right: The aftermath of the IRA bomb attack on the Grand Hotel, Brighton in October 1984, in which Prime Minister Margaret Thatcher had a narrow escape, four people were killed, and several injured.

Below: The devastated City of London on 24 April 1993, after two IRA bombs ripped through the financial centre, causing enormous damage.

Right: Bodies lie in the street after the Remembrance Day bomb at the Cenotaph at Enniskillen in November 1987.

Below: The IRA bomb in the Shankill Road in October 1993, which killed ten people.

Above: July, 1983, Gerry Fitt, the former leader of the SDLP, stands amidst the ruins of his burned out home in Belfast.

The inferno caused by the Le Mon House Hotel bombing at Castlereagh on the outskirts of Belfast. Blazing petrol was sprayed over diners and there were twelve deaths and many burns.

Fr Alec Reid gives the last rites to one of the two British Army corporals, stripped and killed during a funeral in Belfast in March 1988.

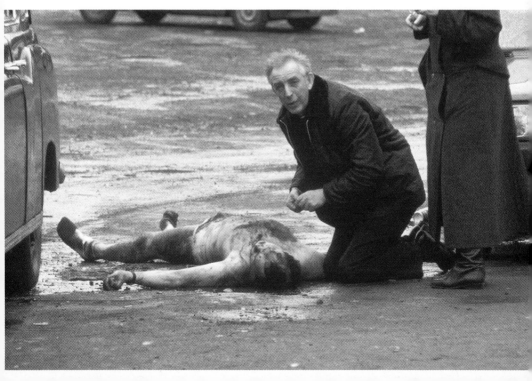

Above: Provisional leaders give a press conference in Belfast. From left: Martin McGuinness, Daithi O'Conaill, Sean MacStiofain and Seamus Twomey.

Right: Joe Cahill, a veteran Provisional leader.

Far right: The young Martin McGuinness.

Below: Two leading members of Sinn Fein, Gerry Adams, President, and Jim Gibney, carry the coffin of Thomas Begley, the IRA man who was blown up in a bomb blast in a fish shop in the Shankill Road, Belfast in October 1993 which cost ten lives.

Right: Former President of Sinn Fein, Ruairi O'Bradaigh, pictured in 1970.

Right: Albert Reynolds and John Major shake hands outside No. 10 Downing Street after the two Prime Ministers had concluded the Downing Street Agreement of 15 December 1993.

Below: 22 November 1993, the anniversary of the Dallas slaying of her brother, President Kennedy, US Ambassador to Ireland, Jean Kennedy-Smith, poses in Government Buildings, Dublin, with Albert Reynolds and Senator Gordon Wilson, whose daughter Maria was one of the eleven Enniskillen bomb victims in 1987. Senator Wilson himself died in 1995 of a heart attack.

Below: The brokers of the Loyalist cease-fire which was announced on 13 October 1994. From left, Johnny White, Davy Adams, Jim McDonald, Gusty Spence, David Ervine, William Smith and Gary McMichael.

Right: Editor and Columnist. Publisher and editor of the New York *Irish Voice*, peace-broker Niall O'Dowd, pictured at the paper with Gerry Adams, who writes a column for the *Voice*.

Left: For the first time in the history of the Six County Statelet, a Sinn Fein delegation was received at Stormont Castle, Belfast, on 9 December 1994. The delegation consisted of (left to right): Sean MacManus, Siobhan O'Hanlon, Martin McGuinness, Lucilita Breathnacht and Gerry Kelly. Symbolically, perhaps, the chamber in which the discussions were held was subsequently damaged by a fire which appears to have been caused by spontaneous combustion in the wiring system.

Below: Watched by the Republic's Foreign Minister and Deputy Prime Minister, Dick Spring, President Clinton greets Secretary of State for Northern Ireland, Sir Patrick Mayhew, at the Washington Investment in Northern Ireland Conference, held in May, 1995.

of what programmes were banned I should reinforce the point, illustrated by the treatment of Robert Fisk that individual journalists were also targeted.

For example, Bernard Falk spent four days in jail during May 1971 because he would not identify Leo Martin, of the IRA, as the man whom he had interviewed for a *Twenty-Four Hours* programme. Robert McKay was held for almost a day in Glasgow under the PTA in March 1979. Charges brought against him included failing to properly complete his landing card. These were subsequently dropped. At the time of his detention McKay was returning from Belfast where he had researched an article on a new army intelligence computer. The article was temporarily confiscated, but later ran, uncensored, in *Time Out*. Another celebrated arrestee was Pierre Salinger, President Kennedy's former press secretary. He was held for a half a day at Castlereagh interrogation centre a few months after the McKay case. He had come to Belfast to make a film for ABC TV on the IRA, in the wake of the Mountbatten assassination. While he was held, the RUC screened the contents of his videotape for their own purposes.

Another constant hazard for journalists was the technique described by Anne McHardy as consisting of offering London-based editors 'lunch and warnings that Belfast reporters were becoming too partial on the wrong side'.[32] Many examples of this approach could be cited, because the editors involved subsequently tipped off their reporters as to what had happened. But what about the cases where doubt was sown without the reporter, or programme maker, ever being made aware of the fact? How many resignations or transfers did the practice lead to?

As far back as 1956 Alasdair Milne found that 'all hell had broken loose'[33] after the BBC had run an item on the IRA, by way of explaining why the organisation had just blown up one of the BBC's transmitters. After 'much telephoning between the BBC and Stormont Castle', Lord Brookeborough appeared on *Panorama* to 'put the record straight'. In 1959 Brookeborough again strong-armed the BBC, this time forcing the Corporation to allow him to prevent various programmes dealing with his statelet from being shown. The first was a BBC screening of the second of two interviews conducted in the US by the American broadcaster Ed Murrow for his *See it Now* show with the Irish actress Siobhan McKenna. Brookeborough successfully intervened to have the second programme dropped. In the first, the actress had referred to IRA men, whom de Valera had interned in the Republic, as 'young idealists'.

The second series had the melancholy distinction of becoming the first of many BBC-made programmes to be axed. It had been conceived as an eight-part series of ten-minute reports conducted by Alan Whicker for *Tonight*.

The first programme dealt with the innocuous subject of betting shops. But it included a reference to the fact that the Six Counties had armed police, and showed a police revolver in close-up. As Whicker wrote afterwards: 'The Ulster sky then fell on *Tonight*, and on me.' There was uproar for weeks afterwards, resulting in the succeeding programmes being dropped at Brookeborough's behest. Whicker's judgement was: 'For the first time the new-look BBC TV service kowtowed to silly sound and fury. It was not a glorious moment for the Corporation.' Nor was it to be an isolated one.

The arrival of the Tories in power in June 1970 was marked the following month by a notable 'first' in censorship terms. For the first time BBC Northern Ireland 'opted out' of screening a BBC programme made on 'the UK mainland'. Hitherto BBC policy had been to treat both areas as identical for broadcasting purposes. The target chosen to make the distinction was the BBC's prestigious current affairs programme, *Panorama*. Interviews with the relatives of six people killed in Belfast were deemed 'inflammatory'. *Panorama* and current affairs generally were to feel many more applications of the Leigh Joynes theory of communication. Programmes were not merely 'opted out', but banned altogether.

Waldo Maguire also banned programmes for reasons of internal Unionist politics. For example, in February 1971 he decided that it would not be good for viewers to learn that there was widespread Unionist opposition to the Prime Minister, Major James Chichester-Clark. The BBC's *Twenty-Four Hours* had made a programme indicating that Chichester-Clark could be forced into resignation. The resignation did take place but the programme's screening did not. It was but one of many examples that could be given of the truth of Jonathan Dimbleby's assertion that BBC policy made it impossible for the British public to understand what was happening in the Six Counties. Another occurred later in 1971. The 'balance' argument was used in October to prevent the screening of BBC news footage showing the proceedings at the alternative assembly set up by the SDLP after the party had withdrawn from Stormont following the introduction of internment.

The Independent Television Authority was of course equally circumscribed. An effort by Granada to show how the Republic was being drawn into the troubles was banned a month after the assembly programme. *World in Action*'s 'South of the Border', which included interviews with Sean MacStiofain and Ruairi O'Bradaigh, was described by Lord Aylestone as 'aiding and abetting the enemy'. Many more ITV programmes would go the same route in the years which lay ahead.

The whole period was punctutated by outbursts of uproar over bannings or imposed changes, such as those in the seven-part series *The Irish Way*, directed by Colin Thomas. Thomas resigned in May 1978 over changes ordered by BBC Northern Ireland. Looking back at the coverage of the twenty-five years of conflict it would appear that – apart from the overall consideration of control of the news flow – there were three major concerns in the minds of the censors.

Firstly, a reluctance to allow the screening of material which might tend to arouse support for the Nationalist position, in other words the policies of both the Dublin Government and the SDLP. Secondly, an extreme sensitivity to information which placed the security forces in a bad light (one of the cuts which prompted Thomas's resignation was a shot of a tombstone which read: 'Murdered by British paratroopers on Bloody Sunday'). Thirdly, an abhorrence of anything which depicted the IRA in situations which indicated either the possession of a degree of community support or a human face.

The first concern led, for example, to the banning of *A Sense of Loss*, by Marcel Ophuls, in November 1972. The BBC, according to the *Sunday Times*,[34] found the film 'too pro-Irish'. It consisted of interviews with both sides of the divided northern community, as well as military and political spokespersons. Its real offence apparently was that its overall impact tended to be anti-Unionist. The 'too pro-Irish' argument also led to an invasion by the censors into the field of drama. In 1972 also, both the BBC and the IBA were exercised by plays written by Dominic Behan. Waldo Maguire caused the postponement of one, *Carson Country*, about the origins of the six-county statelet, from May until October, because, it was said, it might have had the effect of 'provoking possible trouble during the marching season'.[35] The IBA asked for an advance viewing of *The Folk Singer*, about a singer's visit to Belfast. The play was passed for screening, in Thames's *Armchair Theatre* series, but went out at 10.30 p.m., not the normal time of 9.30 p.m

Two drama documentaries by Kenneth Griffith were also deemed too 'pro-Irish'. One was about Michael Collins: *Hang out your brightest colours*, banned in 1973.[36] The other, *Curious Journey*, was refused a screening by Harlech in 1980. It consisted both of interviews with Irish veterans of 1916 *et seq.* and of quotations from British statesmen. One of the cuts which Harlech requested, and Griffith refused, was Gladstone's condemnation of the Act of Union.

The touchy subject of the use of torture caused the banning in 1976 of Brian Phelan's play, *Article 5*, which the BBC had commissioned. Phelan did considerable research for the play, including extensive consultation with Amnesty International. The plot centred on the hiring of three mercenaries by an Englishman for service in an unnamed country which involved the use of torture. Its principal offence was the inclusion of a snippet of dialogue citing Northern Ireland as a country where a government used torture.

Another drama, this time based on the Diplock Courts procedures, *The Legion Hall Bombing*, was mauled by the BBC censors in 1978. Originally scheduled for showing in February of that year it was frequently postponed and substantial cuts were ordered. These included the dropping of both the play's epilogue and a proposed studio discussion. It finally went out in August, at 10.25 p.m., instead of the usual time of 9.25 p.m. The changes forced on the programme were of such a nature as to induce both its director, Roland Joffe, and its author, Caryl Churchill, to ask that their names be removed from the credits.

However, drama departments were but a secondary target to the Government's main objective, the current affairs divisions of BBC and ITV. Torture, and the interaction of the three prime concerns of official 'information policy' which I have already listed, lay behind a series of milestone controversies in the history of British broadcasting which occurred between 1977 and 1985. The first of these centred on an interview conducted by Keith Kyle on the *Tonight* programme in March 1977 with Bernard O'Connor, a Catholic school teacher, who had been tortured by the RUC at Castlereagh interrogation centre. Three years later the courts awarded O'Connor £5,000 in compensation for what befell him. But in 1977 Kyle's meticulously researched interview, which was only cleared for transmission after one of the most agonising and exhaustive checking processes in BBC history, unleashed the furies of Conservative, RUC and Unionist wrath to a degree rarely experienced since or before.

Tory backbenchers, led by Airey Neave, savaged first Richard Francis, the

BBC's Northern Ireland controller, for following a different pattern from that established by his redoubtable predecessor, Waldo Maguire, and then the BBC chairman, Sir Michael Swann.[37] Airey Neave delivered a speech with, it is understood, the backing of both Margaret Thatcher and William Whitelaw,[38] in which he said:

> A review of present attitudes to media freedom is needed therefore, to take account of a desperate emergency. Some of the media deny that we are really at war with terrorism. Some of their actions actually stimulate the hardcore terrorist mentality . . . The *Tonight* programme has had the most damaging effects on morale in the RUC. In justifying it on grounds of 'impartiality', the BBC have given the impression they are not really on the side of the civil power in Northern Ireland.[39]

The *Daily Telegraph* joined the cacophony with an interview with an unnamed 'senior officer' who said that because of the programme 'The fear here is that terrorists will seize on this as provocation to kill more policemen.'[40] This line of attack was pressed home by the RUC's federation chairman, Alan Wright, after the Provisionals shot a young policeman in Fermanagh on 14 March. Wright's statement in the following day's press contained the following:

> There can be little doubt in anybody's mind that the BBC has returned a guilty verdict against the Royal Ulster Constabulary. The sentence – a cowardly bullet in the back – has now been carried out by the IRA.

It was against this backdrop that, later in the year, Peter Taylor came up against the problem of giving the Nationalist point of view. He made an effort to report that Nationalists in the Six Counties were considerably underwhelmed by the Queen's Jubilee visit to the area. Taylor showed, accurately, that the visit, contrary to the impression conveyed by the rest of the media, had in fact heightened tensions in a divided community whose reality was far from the impression of tranquil loyalty which the spin doctors were attemping to create. But on 17 August 1977, just two minutes before the *This Week* programme was scheduled to go out, the IBA banned it.

It was, however, shown, with some changes, two weeks after the visit. To ensure that its impact, already considerably lessened through loss of topicality, was further diluted, ITV showed the programme at different times on its various constituent company channels. Taylor was back in the firing line a month later because of another *This Week* programme, which attempted to analyse the Special Category issue. Rightly, as I hope I have explained in Chapter 9, Taylor had divined that the subject was one of great, but little-understood, significance. The film showed prisoners drilling, and wearing paramilitary uniforms. It also included an interview with a prison officer, David Irvine, who came across as a considerable person. But Neave and the Conservatives reacted angrily against what was termed a portrayal of a 'Sandhurst of terror'.[41] Worse, the unfortunate Irvine was shot dead by the Provisionals fifteen days after transmission, as part of the escalating Dirty Protest campaign. *This Week* was blamed for the death. Roy Mason later claimed that Irvine had been murdered 'within forty-eight hours of the programme'.[42] He also said that 'cheque book television is much more dramatic and dangerous than cheque book journalism. It can quickly frighten and more easily incite.'

Nevertheless, Taylor and the *This Week* producer, David Elstein, continued their investigations into the Dirty War. Their programme, *Inhuman and Degrading Treatment*, which went out on 27 October 1977, probed ten documented cases, backed by medical evidence, which had helped to swell the growing tide of complaint against the RUC's interrogation methods. The RUC not only refused to co-operate with the programme, but sought to have it banned. The reaction which this induced in the IBA caused the 'balance' factor to be invoked in a manner which set an unfortunate broadcasting precedent. As the IBA would not allow the programme to be shown without an RUC presence, Elstein and Taylor were finally forced to accept terms set by the RUC's chief constable, Sir Kenneth Newman.

Newman demanded, and got, the right to deliver to the cameras an unchallenged five-minute statement. No questioning was allowed. On top of this Newman issued a statement a few hours before the programme, saying that the RUC were being placed on special alert because 'It is feared that terrorists could use the occasion as an attempt to "justify" attacks against police officers and all members of the RUC have been advised to take every possible precaution as to their safety.' This ignited the intended detonation of outrage. The *Daily Express* described the programme as a 'death sentence by TV'. The *Daily Telegraph* wrote a leader stating that 'If the IBA will not stop this homicidal irresponsibility, the Government must step in.'

The Northern Ireland Office issued a statement saying:

> It is significant that the producers and the reporter of this programme have produced three programmes in quick succession which have concentrated on presenting the blackest possible picture of events in Northern Ireland.
>
> After the last programme on prisons, a prison officer who appeared in the programme was murdered, and last night's programme may well place police officers, who deserve all support, at even further risk. This is not what one expects of responsible commentators.

Mason, Airey Neave and Newman all made protests to the IBA about Thames. The pressures yielded a short-term victory for the censors. Elstein was told to lay off Northern Ireland and to use another reporter. Taylor however was not so easily silenced. Temporarily balked in one field of communication, he eventually counterattacked effectively in another – by writing a successful book on interrogation methods.[43] Meanwhile the widespread use of brutal interrogation methods in the Six Counties forced *This Week* and the torture issue back into the headlines. A year after the rumpus over *Inhuman and Degrading Treatment*, Amnesty International reported in June of 1978 that 'Maltreatment has taken place with sufficient frequency to warrant a public inquiry to investigate it.'

The public inquiry never took place, but a public outcry did. The report was leaked to the *Guardian*, the *Sunday Times* and various politicians before its official publication on 13 June. Mindful of what had gone before, Thames, and *This Week*, played the issue with a very straight bat. A programme was prepared containing a short clip of interviews with some of the Catholic doctors who had treated some of those interrogated. This was to be followed by interviews with Ian Paisley and a

Protestant defender of the RUC. On top of this, 'balance' dictated that a studio discussion would ensue between Enoch Powell, the Unionist John Taylor, and a Nationalist, Patrick Duffy. However, on the day the programme was scheduled for transmission (8 June) the IBA met and banned it, sight unseen.

What followed was literally black comedy. Thames proposed to replace the banned programme with a comedy show. But the company's technicians refused to transmit it, saying the only programme they would put out was the previous year's *Inhuman and Degrading Treatment*! As a result, screens went blank for half an hour in England, and on Ulster Television (UTV). The BBC's *Nationwide* screened portions of the banned programme and their *Tonight* programme also quoted from the Amnesty report. The net effect of the ban was to create a media uproar which did far more to attract attention to the Amnesty report than the original *This Week* programme could ever have hoped to do.

Moreover, the courage shown by the Thames technicians proved contagious and spread to the BBC over what became known as the Carrickmore affair. Carrickmore followed another thunderous row caused by the BBC's transmission of an interview with an INLA spokesman on 5 July of that troubled year of 1979. The interview went out in the same week that the INLA was declared an illegal organisation in Britain and was the last such interview to be conducted. Humphrey Atkins, the Northern Ireland Secretary of State, had tried unsuccessfully to prevent the programme being shown. But there was no particular outcry until Airey Neave's widow wrote to the *Daily Telegraph* complaining that 'the terrorist had been given ample scope to besmirch the memory of my husband'.[44] The *Telegraph* endorsed Mrs Neave's complaint in an editorial which said that the BBC had given a 'forum for murderers'. Thatcher followed up with an onslaught in Parliament which made headlines. She said of the interview: 'I am appalled it was ever transmitted and I believe it reflects gravely on the judgement of the BBC and those responsible.' In fact practically everyone in decision-taking circles in the BBC was responsible, as Roger Bolton, the editor of *Tonight*, which screened the programme, had followed the consultation procedures meticulously, referring the interview upwards, sideways and downwards, so that its content was not merely known, but almost memorised before being shown. Nevertheless Thatcher said that the Attorney-General, Sir Michael Havers, was considering whether legal action could be taken. Merlyn Rees supported Thatcher, calling the interview 'a grave error'. The storm petered out to the accompaniment of retreating headlines in the tabloid press such as the *Sun*'s 'Maggie lashes BBC over "appalling" TV interview with Neave terror chief'.[45]

However, the emotional scar tissue left by the INLA affair was rubbed raw anew by the Carrickmore incident in October of that year. This momentous row had its origins in a ten- or twelve-minute clip of film shot in the strongly Republican village of Carrickmore, Co. Tyrone, for the BBC's *Panorama*, but never seen by viewers. In the autumn of 1979 *Panorama* had decided to do a critical investigation of the Provisional IRA to mark the tenth anniversary of the movement's founding. It was cleared through the BBC's decision-taking echelons and discussed in advance with the army, the Northern Ireland Office and the RUC. The security forces indicated a co-operative attitude and one of the BBC's best journalists, Jeremy Paxman, was assigned as reporter for the film, which, it was planned, would include interviews with Ruairi O'Bradaigh, Daithi O'Conaill, and Sean MacStiofain.

On 17 October 1979, the *Panorama* team received a telephone call at their Dublin hotel telling them they would see something of interest if they went to Carrickmore. The anonymous caller was telling the truth. For in the same sense that the Chinese saying, 'May you live in interesting times', is regarded as a curse, Carrickmore proved extremely interesting. The *Panorama* team discovered a hooded IRA unit manning a roadblock and carrying out inspections of driving licences in the name of the Irish Republican Army. The BBC men filmed these proceedings.

As a result, 'a wave of fury swept the Commons'.[46] The fury was caused by two factors, one practical, the other ideological. On practical grounds the incident was extremely embarrassing for the security forces and the NIO. These groups had two settled lines of policy. One, that the situation on the ground was secure. The IRA were being defeated. This was why the publication of the Glover Report, in May of that year, was so unwelcome in some quarters. The second major propaganda claim, by both Unionists and British apologists, was that a root cause of the violence in the Six Counties was the lax security policies of the Republic, which allowed the IRA to strike at will across the border. In fact, as Garret FitzGerald, one of the most committed anti-IRA prime ministers in the history of the Republic, pointed out to the British, only 3 per cent of the total amount of violence committed occurred in the border region.[47]

But in October 1979, the Carrickmore filming, as Mary Holland pointed out in the *New Statesman*, undermined '. . . much of the received wisdom about current security arrangements in Northern Ireland . . . that the border is of crucial importance to the IRA and that their activities get little support from the local community'.[48] Carrickmore is seventeen miles from the border, but only approximately ten from the nearest army base, and, to make matters worse, there was an RUC/UDR barracks only six miles away. The army and RUC reacted to the filming by immediately withdrawing their co-operation. The BBC went into internal convulsions between senior management figures in Belfast and London.

Paxman and his colleagues had made no secret of the incident to their BBC Northern Ireland colleagues. The NIO knew all about it, but the Controller of Northern Ireland, James Hawthorne, was not officially informed until he heard about it from a NIO official at a dinner in London a week later, which naturally made him angry and suspicious. However, the *Panorama* team had acted quite properly. Belfast had been informed in advance of the programme's intended content, though word of this was not apparently passed on to Hawthorne himself. The Carrickmore incident, which had come out of the blue, had not been specifically discussed, because the guidelines which covered BBC activities in Ireland spoke only of the need to get advance permission for interviews. No interviewing had been done at Carrickmore.

But the row ricocheted from BBC boardroom to cabinet room after a paragraph about the incident appeared at the bottom of page eight of the *Financial Times*. Thatcher 'went scatty'.[49] An explanation was demanded from the governors of the BBC. The source of the *Financial Times* paragraph, a sober account of what had transpired in Carrickmore, by an experienced journalist, Ed Moloney, in *Hibernia*, an inconspicuous Dublin opinion journal, was mined by Fleet Street sensation-seekers. It was an occasion when the cap was for once removed from the London media telescope, alas only to be replaced with a distorting, and magnifying, lens. According to the *Evening Standard* the IRA, some 140 strong, had offered to hold the town all night 'as a stunt for the *Panorama* team'.[50] In his book, Roger Bolton, then editor of *Panorama*, describes the pressures that broke over him and his family.

On the day of the *Evening Standard* 'stunt' story the BBC governors reacted to cabinet pressure by issuing a statement which pointed the finger of blame at the *Panorama* team. Carrickmore, said the statement, 'would appear to be a clear breach of standing instructions in relation to filming in Ireland'.[51] The day after the *Evening Standard* story, which was a prototype for others of an even wilder and more inaccurate nature in the next day's *Express, Mail* and *Sun*, the row moved to the Commons floor. James Molyneaux, the Official Unionist leader, said he found the filming 'at least a treasonable activity'.

Thatcher, however, unleashed the real threat. The matter, she said, was one for the police and the Director of Public Prosecutions. Both James Callaghan and Roy Mason agreed with the Prime Minister and criticised both the BBC and *Panorama*. To the accompaniment of a howl for BBC blood from the tabloid press, Scotland Yard's anti-terrorism squad then began an investigation under the Prevention of Terrorism Act. Section 11 of the PTA makes it an offence, punishable by up to five years in prison, not to pass on to the police information which might lead to the capture of terrorists. Using the PTA, Scotland Yard raided the BBC on 13 November 1979 and demanded and got the offending film. It was the first time that either the BBC or ITA had relinquished untransmitted film.

The BBC also used the 'balance' device to ban, at the last moment, a *Spotlight* film on the Carrickmore incident's implications for press freedom. Journalists and politicians had been assembled to discuss the issue, but the BBC declined to furnish a spokesperson. The BBC's campaign of disassociation really went into high gear on 16 November 1979. Following an internal inquiry into the affair the governors issued a statement saying that it was satisfied that there had been no collusion between *Panorama* and the IRA, but there was a sting in the tail. The statement also said that the rule concerning keeping the BBC Northern Ireland Controller fully informed 'was far from fully complied with'. Roger Bolton was sacked as editor of *Panorama*, and John Gau, head of Current Affairs, was reprimanded.

However, the NUJ in both the BBC and ITV rallied to Bolton's support and he was reinstated. The projected *Panorama* programme was never shown and the Battle of Carrickmore effectively resulted in interviews with Republicans coming to a stop for several years. The Director of Public Prosecutions duly carried out his investigation, as directed by Thatcher. He found that there was sufficient evidence to bring a prosecution under Section 11 of the PTA, but the Attorney-General, Sir

Michael Havers, shrank from the potential for a full-scale battle over press freedom which a court case would have precipitated. Instead he put the BBC on notice that the PTA would be invoked if any similar case arose in the future. Writing to the Chairman of the BBC Board of Governors, Sir Michael Swann, Havers said:

> Any interview with a person purporting to represent a terrorist organisation is potentially a source of information of the nature referred to in Section 11 of the Act arising not only from the actual contents of the interview but also any negotiations leading up to and the actual arrangements for it.[52]

The Havers ruling meant in effect that British journalists seeking subsequently to report on the IRA had to be mindful of the fact that failure to disclose any contact they made, of whatever kind, could render them liable to prosecution. When one considers what he went though over Carrickmore, Bolton's subsequent courage in making *Death on the Rock* appears all the more remarkable. For the Tories' visceral response to the broadcasting of matters Republican remained a constant. Nineteen days after the inquest verdict on the Gibraltar shootings (on 19 October 1988, in the House of Commons), the Home Secretary, Douglas Hurd, announced a ban on direct statements by representatives of Sinn Fein, Republican Sinn Fein, and the UDA.[53] This led to the employment of the device of having an actor speak the words of someone like Gerry Adams, while the actual spokesman appeared on the screen, with lips moving silently. Inevitably it was said in Dublin that Sinn Fein could be seen but not Hurd.

Hurd in fact owed his position as Home Secretary to yet another BBC ban, this time on the programme *The Edge of the Union*. Leon Brittan, the then Home Secretary, had written to the BBC governors, asking the corporation, on security grounds, not to show a scheduled programme in the BBC series *Real Lives*, on 30 July 1985. In the letter Brittan quoted Margaret Thatcher's celebrated phrase about 'starving the terrorists of the oxygen of publicity on which they depend'.[54] The real lives which the programme intended to portray were those of the DUP's Gregory Campbell and, the cause of the uproar, Provisional Sinn Fein's Martin McGuinness.

But after receiving Brittan's letter, the BBC governors saw the programme and decided to ban it because '. . . it was a lousy programme . . . It made them out to be nice guys, bouncing babies on their knees.'[55] Alasdair Milne, the BBC's Director-General, was on holiday in Helsinki when the row broke out and did not see the film until he had travelled back to London. He thought it should have been shown. The NUJ again flexed its muscles, staging a strike on 7 August which, amongst other results, had the effect of putting the BBC World Service off the air for the first time. In Belfast, striking journalists played and replayed a video of *Real Lives* outside the BBC offices, and at one stage the Controller of BBC Northern Ireland, James Hawthorne, threatened to resign. Ultimately the programme was shown with a few minor changes. But the affair left some very bad blood between the BBC's board of governors and its management.

Brittan's handling of the affair was widely criticised and in a reshuffle the following month (on 3 September) he lost his post as Home Secretary. Hurd was transferred from the NIO to succeed him and Tom King became Secretary of State for Northern Ireland. Appropriately enough King is remembered for following in Hurd's censoring footsteps. The day after the ban on Sinn Fein/UDA voices was introduced, King laid a draft order in council before Parliament (on 20 October 1988) which had the effect of curtailing defendants' right to remain silent. The Tories wished to have Republicans heard in the dock if not on the box.

The foregoing list of bannings and suppressions played a major part both in supporting the capped telescope syndrome and, by their curtailment of debate, in prolonging the war. But they are, I repeat, merely a sample of well-known examples of what took place. Some public indication of the extent of censorship was given in September of 1994, when, to mark the twenty-fifth anniversary of the troops' arrival in Northern Ireland, the BBC permitted Peter Taylor to present a series of films which had earlier been banned. These both included frank admissions of the use of torture against wounded IRA men and, *per contra*, gave an indication of the horrors inflicted by the IRA bombing campaign. But much more remains to be told. I will conclude this glimpse of the difficulties placed in the way of the British public's gaining an understanding of what happened in Ireland via television by citing a few examples of which I have personal knowledge.

The BBC's *Panorama* of 22 November 1982 came a month after Gerry Adams had topped the poll in the Assembly election. Liz Curtis is absolutely correct when she says that the *Panorama* reporter Fred Emery 'showed little interest in explaining why Adams had topped the poll in West Belfast. Instead, his overriding concern was to undermine Adams' new status and to establish that Adams was a member of the IRA.'[56] This attitude was made clear to me during a lengthy filming session for the programme in my own home. I was interviewed because of my book on the IRA, which rendered me an 'authority' within the programme's terms of reference. My living room has been the scene of many a TV, radio and newspaper interview. But the *Panorama* interview was one of the longest I can remember; a number of reels were used. The presence of a large crew and the heat from the very bright lighting made the room stuffy. Emery's repetitive questioning, which revealed his bias but little else, did nothing to assuage my growing irritation. Finally he asked me a question about Adams' real standing in the community. Did he have authority? At the time I had been following the serialisation of James Clavell's Japanese opus, *Shogun*, on TV, and this prompted me to answer rather waspishly, 'Of course, he's the Shogun.'

Triumphantly Emery replied to the effect that the term 'Shogun' had a military connotation. That brief exchange, deployed in such a way as to indicate that I supported the programme's thesis – namely that Adams had a 'spurious legitimacy' and had merely adopted 'the guise of community politician' – was the only snippet used from the huge expenditure of film. Why so many people should have voted for Adams was never explained. In fairness to the BBC men, I should point out that they were far from being alone in their attitude. It was shared for example by the Irish Prime Minister, Garret FitzGerald. He noted in his autobiography that he felt it necessary to give Thatcher 'some feel for the scale of the intimidation and personation by the IRA and Sinn Fein at the recent election'.[57]

He also stated that he decided (in 1982) to 'give priority to heading off the growth of support for the IRA in NI'.[58]

A further example concerns a BBC *Timewatch* programme which intended to show how the Troubles developed in the sixties, culminating in the introduction of internment. It was researched by Martin Dillon in 1992 and the transcripts amount to an impressive contribution to the history of the time. Every section of opinion of any consequence was approached. Historians, Republicans, Unionists, civil rights leaders, SDLP founders, southern politicians, the lot. The project was one which could only have been funded by an organisation such as the BBC. The mass of interview transcripts is larger than the manuscript of an average-sized book. From the interviews a picture emerges of how Unionist sins of commission and British ones of omission combined to ignite the powder keg.

Evidently this picture was displeasing to influential eyes. A row developed over the programme, Dillon resigned and the interviews were never screened. *Timewatch* did put out a programme entitled *The Sparks that Lit the Bonfire*, on 27 January 1993. But it was not based on the Dillon interviews. It consisted of an attempt to prove that the Provisional IRA had been formed by Fianna Fail in 1970!

I have given some indication of how the British national newspapers reacted to the Irish situation at various moments of crisis. As with the electronic media, the subject merits a study in its own right. British national newspaper coverage of Ireland, what there is of it, is governed by more complex considerations than either simple anti-Irish prejudice, or a spirit of 'Our Army Right or Wrong'. Instances of these attitudes can certainly be given, and it is true that British papers have largely failed to cover the Dirty War, for example, thus assisting in its prolongation. But they have also failed to adequately cover a great many developments in the UK. As far back as 1978 Raymond Williams wrote:

> What is fundamentally wrong with most of the British press . . . is that it is cast in profoundly residual forms: politically, geographically and technically . . . there are extremely important political and economic interests whose future is tied up with the maintenance of these residual forms . . . the faults of the residual forms are easily seen; the in-built and increasing bias . . . the propagation of a falsely centralised and falsely personalised version of the nature of political and industrial life; the cultural polarisation within an actual cultural diversification; the dominance of the mixed corporations; the dominance of 'London' (meaning a small class sector in London, near the centre of political and economic power) . . . [59]

That judgement remains true today for Ireland (or for that matter Scotland or Wales), although the intervening seventeen years have seen the growth of other 'dominances', those of Rupert Murdoch, Wapping and the introduction of new technology to the publishing world as a whole. The 'London' dominance of which Williams wrote is largely the influence of a section of the Conservative Party, still unable to acknowledge that the empire has gone and that Europe, and in particular Germany, has arrived. These people have consistently shown themselves to be as indifferent towards the feelings of the ordinary people of the UK as they have been towards those of the Irish. Myopia, and cost, have played as important a role in how

British newspapers covered Ireland as have Establishment spin doctors. The latter merely had to manipulate existing attitudes, not create them.

For example, for the first decade or so of the Troubles, most serious Irish newspaper readers, if asked which was the most important British paper where Ireland was concerned, would almost certainly have replied, 'The *Sunday Times*,' with the *Guardian* coming second, some way down the field, and favourable mention also being given to Mary Holland's articles in the *Observer*. The ratings were based on the Insight team's and John Whale's coverage not only of controversial topics such as torture, or army behaviour, but of the actual hows and whys of the way the tragedy erupted. Such research resulted in the compilation of one of the best books to emerge from the Troubles, a study of the conflict's origins by the Insight team.[60]

I always found Harold Evans, the crusading editor responsible for this output, to be more interested in Ireland than anyone else in Fleet Street. But one would be sadly disappointed if one turned to his memoirs in the expectation of finding that the *Sunday Times* coverage of Ireland represented a priority on his part.[61] A study of the index will direct one to the fact that Sean MacBride, the former Chief of Staff of the IRA, who won both the Nobel and Lenin peace prizes, was the inspiration for the successful legal battle fought on thalidomide, but to little else of Irish interest beyond the revelation that it was John Whale who was constantly 'pressing' for political initiatives.[62] The Insight book is mentioned in the bibliography only. While Evans edited *The Times*, the paper's editorial policy appears to have evolved from a clash of opinions between two leader writers rather than from any burning conviction on his part.[63]

It would appear, therefore that even under Evans, the Irish situation was far from being a burning issue with the *Sunday Times*. After Murdoch's arrival and Evans' departure, the paper's Dublin approval ratings slipped badly. But, ironically, at the time of writing the *Sunday Times* is once again concentrating on Irish coverage, though less out of a sense of commitment than a desire to achieve 'dominance' in the lucrative Irish market. The nature of the coverage is, however, a far cry from the Evans era. While matters cultural or sporting may be read on their merits, things political give the impression of having been vetted by either MI5 or C13 (the RUC's counterinsurgency unit).

Largely because of its stance as the *Manchester Guardian*, under C. P. Scott, during the 1916–21 period, most Dublin readers would have expected the *Guardian* to be a sympathetic voice raised on the Catholic and Nationalist side after the Troubles broke out. But this was far from being the case. I gained an insight into at least part of the reason during one of the most abrasive radio encounters to occur during the early days of the Troubles. The clash was between myself and John Cole, who later became the well-loved political correspondent of the BBC. I remember a little Englishman, who for some reason was in the studio with us, saying afterwards: 'I was terrified. There I was, alone, with these two great big Irishmen going for each other. I thought I'd be killed!'

In fact the difference between John and me lay in the fact that whereas I argued as a Nationalist, he considered himself British and adumbrated the principles of his

Belfast, Unionist and Protestant background. I often thought subsequently that that little Englishman symbolised the perplexity of the average British man, or woman, in the street as he tried to make sense of the media coverage of what was happening in Ireland. Cole took his attitudes with him to the *Guardian*, where he became an editorial executive. He is believed to have written the *Guardian*'s leader after Bloody Sunday which conveyed a very different impression from that of the paper's eyewitness reporter Simon Winchester. It said:

> The march was illegal. Warning had been given of the danger implicit in continuing with it. Even so, the deaths stun the mind and must fill all reasonable people with horror. As yet it is too soon to be sure of what happened. The army has an intolerably difficult time in Ireland. At times it is bound to act firmly, even severely. Whether individual soldiers misjudged their situation yesterday, or were themselves too directly threatened, cannot be known. The presence of snipers in the late stages of the march must have added a murderous dimension. It is a terrible warning to everyone involved.

John O'Callaghan, a reporter with the *Guardian*, who had become increasingly disaffected by the paper's line, resigned. He talked with me at the time about joining the *Irish Press*, but eventually took a post with RTE as London correspondent. In an interview with the *Irish Press*, prior to which he had made a three-week tour of Northern Ireland in January 1972 to investigate how the Nationalist population were faring, he said: 'I found the Catholic minority have had a far worse battering than ever appears in any English papers.'[64] He felt that if the *Guardian*, 'with its tradition of opposition towards every kind of state or institutionalised violence', were seen to be backing the army, the result would be that the army would feel that 'nobody is looking or going to question them at all'.

Years later, long after Dublin criticism of the *Guardian* had ceased, I asked Peter Preston, then the paper's editor, how he felt about the *Guardian*'s Irish coverage and its impact on British public opinion. He regarded the Cole/O'Callaghan controversy as relatively unimportant. 'Just a row between a Nationalist Father of the Chapel and a Unionist deputy editor.'[65] He felt that 'liberal England expects to be confused over Ireland, soldiering onwards and backwards after twenty-five years'. He had experienced no pressure from the army, nor had any D-notices fallen on him over Ireland. He regarded Ireland as the most important domestic issue for the UK, but saw coverage as a duty rather than a circulation-builder: 'There's no pay-off at the news stands.'

The lack of interest, or pressure, amongst the highly politically aware *Guardian* readers which Preston indicates also gives one an insight into the lack of pressure on MPs to act over Ireland. In addition, it helps to explain of course how the small but tightly focused group of Unionist MPs can exert the influence they do at Westminster. Another celebrated liberal bastion which became subject to controversy over its Irish coverage was the *Observer*. This time the author of the pressure was an Irishman, Dr Conor Cruise O'Brien. After his removal from Irish political life in 1977, he became editor-in-chief of the *Observer*.

His opening salvo at his erstwhile political opponents in Fianna Fail was a signed editorial describing a call by the Taoiseach, Jack Lynch, for a British withdrawal from the Six Counties as 'poisoned rhetoric'.[66] He followed this up with an attack on Mary Holland, his paper's principal source of information on Ireland. Holland had won the Journalist of the Year award in 1970 for her reportage. However, O'Brien took exception to a piece she had written in the *Observer* colour supplement about a Republican woman in Derry, Mary Nelis, who had two sons in prison for IRA activities.[67] He ordered part of the issue pulped, and had changes made in the remainder. He also wrote to Holland, objecting to her portrayal of Nelis and her family, saying:

> Since Irish Republicanism – especially the killing strain of it – has a very high propensity to run in families, and since the mother is most often the carrier, I incline to the view that a mother whose sons behave in this way has had something to do with what they believe and how they behave.[68]

Readers might be forgiven for commenting that Bloody Sunday and the entire history of Derry might also have had something to do with the Nelises's beliefs. However, O'Brien went on to say that he was 'personally ashamed' that Holland's piece should have appeared because he felt it would be of 'considerable assistance' to the H-Block campaign. He conceded that Holland had been acting from 'honourable' motives but continued:

> I also think however that it is a serious weakness in your coverage of Irish affairs that you are a very poor judge of Irish Catholics. That gifted and active community includes some of the most expert conmen and conwomen in the world and I believe you have been conned.

By the time that was written Holland had been covering Northern Ireland for fourteen years. A time span which one would have assumed had given her an adequate opportunity to assess the character of Catholics. Nevertheless her contract with the *Observer* was subsequently terminated.[69]

For the rest of the London press, I would advise that one use the term 'London' as Raymond Williams did. But that said, it must be acknowledged in fairness that there is no glaring bias in contemporary Irish coverage. In fact that of the *Daily Telegraph* is greatly improved since the current editor, Max Hastings, took over from the Thatchers' friend, William Deedes. The *Times, Independent* and *Financial Times* all make an intelligent effort to cover Ireland within the constraints of a sub-regnum Wapping press. As with the electronic media, I have to state as a matter of demonstrable fact that with the passage of time, British journalists as a class have tried to cover the Irish situation both sympathetically and intelligently.

Where the tabloid press is concerned, let me say merely that, as with Aids and cancer, I hope that some day a cure will be found. Xenophobic and strident, the tabloids may not have seriously damaged the course of Anglo-Irish relations. But certainly, whatever influence publications such as the *Sun* have had on their readers, it has not been helpful. However in all honesty it has to be said that the British tabloids have very little influence in Ireland. The flood of stories from the army and RUC spin doctors centring on either the gallantry of the security forces or the drug-dealing and racketeering activities of the IRA make little impact in Ireland. The irony is that because rather than in spite of their 'royals and rubbish' formula, and in particular because of their sports, sex, and TV coverage, British tabloids represent the growth end of the Irish Republic's newspaper market. Some six out of ten of all newspapers sold in the Twenty-Six Counties are British, most of them tabloid. This penetration was part of the reason for a series of meetings between the Irish Government and leaders of the newspaper industry in the early summer of 1995. These may or may not yield some communal defence against the Murdochs and the Conrad Blacks. But for the moment the spin doctors can advance on Dublin unchecked, behind the fig leaf of Page Three.

As with the UK, the main target of the Government censors in the Irish Republic was the national broadcasting service, Radio Telefis Eireann (RTE). It began gently enough. I remember being called, along with other editors and the Director-General of RTE, to Government Buildings in Merrion Street, Dublin, one morning to hear 'suggestions' from the Taoiseach, Jack Lynch, as to how coverage of IRA activities could be toned down. Mildly, Lynch said he felt that some of the TV interviews with Republican spokespersons only just stopped short of inviting them to produce their weapons for the cameras. Where the newspapers were concerned he thought that it would be 'helpful' if we did not 'glamorise' the IRA in reports of their activities. For example, not to record that the IRA had pulled off a daring raid. Simply to say a raid had taken place.

But as the British cracked down on their own media, they also intensified pressure on Dublin to do likewise. The pressure told; following a few squabbles with RTE over IRA interviews in the months after the Lynch meeting, the Irish Government acted. Again the rapidly deteriorating security situation – post-internment – was the determining factor. On 1 October 1971, the Minister for Posts and Telegraphs, Gerry Collins, issued a directive to RTE, under Section 31 of the Broadcasting Act, to

> refrain from broadcasting any matter . . . that could be calculated to promote the aims or activities of any organisation which engages in, promotes, encourages or advocates the attaining of any particular objective by violent means.

The ban was strictly enforced but inevitably, as in the case of the BBC, some interviews which displeased the Government slipped through the censor's net. Accordingly, a year after the issuing of the Section 31 directive, the government adroitly cast the net afresh so that it enmeshed both an IRA leader and a broadcaster, and, subsequently, the entire RTE Authority, the equivalent of the BBC's board of governors. Obviously phones had been tapped, because, in the early hours of 19 November 1971, as he drove away from the home of an RTE journalist, Kevin O'Kelly, detectives were waiting to arrest Sean MacStiofain, then the Provisionals' Chief of Staff. O'Kelly was also arrested, but refused to identify MacStiofain in court as the man he had interviewed. On 25 November 1972 O'Kelly was sentenced to three months' imprisonment for contempt. On appeal this sentence was commuted to a £250 fine.

However, there was no appeal for the Authority, which was sacked the day before the O'Kelly court case. A new Authority was appointed and, speaking in terms of which 'Mad' Mitchell would have approved, Collins told the Dail that he had acted as he did to save life by preventing RTE from becoming a recruiting ground for the IRA.[70] To further this aim the new Authority issued fresh guidelines for the implementation of Section 31. Interviews with either Official or Provisional IRA members were banned. Their political colleagues in either wing of Sinn Fein could only be filmed or recorded after reference upwards. 'The strictest care' was enjoined upon broadcasters in following the directive, which also contained a threat of retribution against anyone who attempted to disregard it.

Curiously, in the light of what was to come, one of the strongest critics of the Government's performance was Conor Cruise O'Brien. Speaking in the Dail, he attacked what he termed the 'sinister' Section 31 directive in these terms:

> I do not think the Irish public would like to see RTE brought into line and being made the object of what the National Socialists used to call Gleichschaltung, co-ordination, being brought into line with the party, and being made transmission systems for the party's ideology . . . in any modern democracy the autonomy of radio and television is as vital as the freedom of the press.[71]

But when a change of government occurred on 2 March 1973, as a result of which O'Brien succeeded Collins as Minister for Posts and Telegraphs, the outcome was one of the greatest U-turns in Irish politics. The Fine Gael/Labour coalition implemented such a rough-handed security and information policy that O'Brien came to stand out in the history of the period as the leader of the ensuing assault on 'the autonomy of radio and television' and the 'vital' freedom of the press. It is probably true to say that the political eclipse which overcame him in 1977 came about as a result of the role he adopted and the publicity which arose from the ensuing clash with myself and the *Irish Press*.

Before describing the row it is necessary to say something about the climate which obtained at the time. Although it is sometimes difficult to believe it in the enlightened days of the nineties, given the state's benignity towards the arts, Ireland has an even worse history of censorship than England. Its efforts at literary censorship had made the country an international laughing stock until these began to be relaxed in the sixties. In 1973 the Emergency Powers acts of the Second World War years were still on the statute books. Section 30 of the Offences Against the State Act, 1939, gave the Gardai the right to hold anyone for twenty-four hours. This in effect meant forty-eight hours; all that was needed to double the holding period was the signature of a Garda chief superintendent.

From the outset the coalition espoused a tough security policy. A part of it was directed against public opinion. Within a few months of taking office the coalition had prosecuted all the national newspapers, including the fortnightly *Hibernia*, on contempt of court charges arising out of the reportage of the treatment of IRA suspects. The *Irish Press* was the only one to win its case. It is said that when the power-sharing executive fell in the summer of 1974 Cosgrave said to O'Brien: 'The Protestants have won – isn't that it.'[72] From then on Dublin's only policy was one of security, to contain the problem on the far side of the border. In October of that year Dublin dinner tables buzzed with reports of a public row between O'Brien and Desmond Fisher, the head of RTE's current affairs section, at a Galway hotel.

It proved to be the Republic's version of Mason's Battle of Culloden. O'Brien was incensed at the fact that the wall of censorship which he was attempting to build between the Republic and happenings in the Six Counties had been breached by the broadcasting by RTE of clips from a film made by an independent London company. The film, *Behind the Wire*, was shown on RTE's current affairs programme, *Seven Days*. In it, internees described the sort of treatment for which O'Brien's government was at that stage pursuing Britain through the European courts.

Nevertheless, a few days after the row, changes occurred in the RTE current affairs division. The programme's producer, Eoghan Harris, was removed from *Seven Days*. In the words of two writers who were describing one of the massive miscarriages of justice of the period:

> An atmosphere of moral righteousness was being created. The intricate and sometimes savage results of the disintegration of the Northern state were reduced to who supported the provos and who opposed them . . . The parameters of political debate were systematically narrowed. Conor Cruise O'Brien was nominally Minister for Posts and Telegraphs but in practice was devoting most of his considerable talents to influencing such debate as existed on the North . . .
>
> He was concerned that nobody should appear on RTE who might 'glamorise' the IRA, went from there to anyone who might 'promote the aims and activities' of the IRA, and from there to an outright ban on the appearance of anyone from Sinn Fein, using Section 31 of the broadcasting Act.[73]

The ban referred to was clearly worked out in tandem with the British. Not only did it prohibit all interviews, or reports of interviews, with IRA groupings, it specifically provided for the banning of all organisations proscribed in the north. The northern statelet's disintegration, as I have indicated elsewhere, had indeed brought 'savage results'. But none of the foregoing did anything to alleviate those evil consequences. On the contrary, as in England, censorship resulted in a limiting of the debate which ensured that for decades no sense of urgency built up in political circles demanding a solution.

On the contrary the climate of fear and pressure on the police had produced a 400 per cent increase in the numbers held under Section 30 of the Offences Against the State Act between 1973, when the coalition took office, and 1976, when my controversy with O'Brien arose. It had also led to the inculcation of the same spirit amongst the Irish Gardai that produced, for example, the Birmingham Six case in England. It emerged that, using Section 30, a garda 'heavy gang' was going about the country extracting statements by the same sort of methods which the RUC used in Castlereagh.[74] This disclosure, by the *Irish Times*, was used adroitly by the MoD and NIO spin doctors to turn British media attention from unfavourable news from Strasbourg about the predicted verdict against Britain in the torture case, and on to the doings of the Irish police force.

Yet another *Panorama* programme bit the dust as a result. A film on the background to both the Strasbourg case and the origins of the northern conflict was scrapped. Instead a short item on the *Irish Times* disclosures was screened (on 14 February 1976). This featured an interview with the then senator Mary Robinson, the only coalition representative with the courage to appear, who did what she could to explain the differences in the nature and extent of what was occurring north and south. Extraordinarily, just as it was an O'Connor who brought the Castlereagh maltreatment to light, another O'Connor, Thomas O'Connor, was the cause of the 'heavy gang's' existence being discovered. He jumped from the second-floor window of Cahir Garda station and suffered injuries which included a broken nose and pelvis, and severe lacerations. O'Connor, who was not charged with any crime, said he jumped to avoid the ill-treatment to which he was being subjected.

Police brutality was particularly alleged in connection with the Sallins train robbery on the night of 30 March 1976. Huge round-ups took place, resulting in several dozen arrests. It is said that confessions were extracted by physical and psychological torture and that, as a result, innocent men were sent to jail. One of these, Nicky Kelly, was rearrested after he had returned from the US in 1980. Although he had skipped bail, he believed he was safe, because the Court of Criminal Appeal had freed his remaining two co-defendants.[75] However, he served four years before being released in 1984. As this book was written he was finally awarded damages against the state amounting to some three-quarters of a million pounds. The atmosphere both in the police and towards the media during the O'Brien era may be summed up by an incident involving the respected police journal, the *Garda Review*, which my father was instrumental in founding, at the inception of the force, back in 1922.[76] The June 1976 issue carried an editorial critical both of government policy towards the Gardai and of the Garda commissioner, Edmund Garvey. Garvey had the editorial referred to the Director of Public Prosecutions, in an unsuccessful attempt to have the editorial board charged with subversion and incitement to violence.

It is perhaps not to be wondered at, therefore, that Garret FitzGerald should quote in his memoirs the admiring reaction of a Unionist to such policies. The OUP man felicitated FitzGerald on the Republic's 'will to win' and sighed sadly: 'If only the British had the same.'[77] However, the basic inefficiency of this 'will to win' approach – which of course also nearly made of Portlaoise jail another H Block – was fatally underlined by its failure to protect the new British Ambassador, Christopher Ewart-Biggs. A few days after his appointment he met with Garda officers to discuss his security. He raised with them, according to his diary, the possibility of an attack on his car. 'It hasn't happened yet,' he was told.[78] Nine days later it did happen and he was killed by a Provisional IRA bomb a few hundred yards from his official residence.

Enraged and embarrassed in equal proportions, the coalition set about bringing in a new battery of laws to proclaim a fresh state of emergency. Changes to the Emergency Powers Act and the Criminal Law Act were to include: longer sentences; longer periods of detention, from forty-eight hours to seven days; the introduction of virtual police powers for the army; and a proposal that anybody encouraging or supporting the IRA could be charged. Initially the significance of this last provision escaped most people's notice, including my own.

But on 3 September 1976, Bud Nossiter, of the *Washington Post*, interviewed Cruise O'Brien as to how he envisaged the new legislation being implemented. O'Brien responded by pulling open a drawer in his desk filled with letters to the editor of the *Irish Press*. Many of these either disagreed with some aspect of government policy, were about the Portlaoise or Six County situation, or expressed a Nationalist viewpoint. Nossiter, coming from the paper that uncovered Watergate, was understandably appalled. Did O'Brien intend to take action against people whose crime was to write letters to the newspapers? Not the writers, the editor, was O'Brien's reaction.

Nossiter, who had intended to drive straight to the airport, detoured to the *Irish Press* to warn me that I had better look out for myself. I did – by reprinting Nossiter's *Washington Post* article, a full page of the offending letters, and opening editorial war on O'Brien in the leader column. A lively debate on press freedom ensued, in which Fianna Fail, ever noted for its concern for editorial integrity, joined vigorously! The then President, Cearbhall O'Dalaigh, a Fianna Fail nominee and a former Irish language editor of the *Irish Press*, was also a distinguished lawyer. Apart from being a former Irish Attorney-General and Chief Justice, he had also been a judge of the European Court. During his time in Europe he made it a practice to send me material on any proposed changes in European law which might affect the press. The publicity firestorm which I unleashed caused the coalition to drop the proposals to extend Section 31-type powers to the newspapers. Nevertheless the controversy continued to escalate. Three weeks after the O'Brien disclosures, on 24 September 1976, O'Dalaigh was sufficiently worried about the general drift of affairs to send the Emergency Powers Bill to the Supreme Court to test whether it was 'repugnant to the Constitution' before he signed it into law.

This caused annoyance in coalition circles which was given vent to publicly in unusual circumstances the following month (on 18 October) by the Minister for Defence, Patrick Donegan. Speaking in the convivial atmosphere which prevailed following the opening of a new canteen at Columb Barracks in Mullingar, he said, in the hearing of journalists from the national papers, that O'Dalaigh was a 'thundering disgrace' for his 'amazing decision' to refer the bill to the Supreme Court. As the officers whom Donegan was addressing had received their commissions from the President these comments were widely regarded as being extremely improper. A governmental apology was issued, but Donegan did not resign and the coalition resisted a Fianna Fail Dail motion aimed at having him sacked.

As a result O'Dalaigh himself resigned on 22 October, to establish both his own integrity and the unassailable nature of the presidential office. All of the foregoing matters may have been recalled by O'Brien and the other main protagonist of the offending legislation, Patrick Cooney, the Minister for Justice, the following year during the general election campaign of June 1977. Both lost their seats. However, the broadcasting ban remained in place until after Sinn Fein came in from the cold following the outbreak of peace in August 1994.

Insofar as the impact of the Irish print media on north–south relations is concerned, a land-based version of the capped telescope syndrome may be said to apply. While the *Irish Times* probably does have some importance in decision-taking circles in Northern Ireland, the rest of the Republic's papers have little political impact north of the border. The northern daily papers are scarcely read at all in the south, and in the north sectarian differences apply to newspaper choice. Generally speaking, Catholics take the *Irish News*, Protestants the *Newsletter*. The *Belfast Telegraph*, an evening paper, is immensely successful, commercially speaking, in reaching across the divide, but politically has declined in influence from the early days of the Troubles, when it was edited by Jack Sayers.

To sum up, then, it may be said that throughout the conflict the media was more often a cause of heat than light. Only since the ceasefire, when conditions eased somewhat for broadcasters, has the electronic media become something of a formative, as opposed to a reflective, influence, principally through the medium of studio discussions and vox pop reports. These have tended to have the effect of showing that, while ancestral beliefs remain strong, the people (on both sides of the Irish Sea) are more open to accommodation and change than are the politicians, particularly on the Unionist side.

TWELVE

HOW THE PEACE WAS MADE—
AND THREATENED

Some seeds fell by the wayside . . . Some fell upon stony places . . . But others fell upon good ground and brought forth fruit, some an hundredfold. Who hath ears to hear, let him hear . . .

Matthew 13: 4–9

THERE IS AN old IRA saying that the darkest place is under the light. It was given a historic validation on 29 September 1979 when, in full media glare, and in the presence of 250,000 people, Pope John Paul II sowed the seeds of the IRA ceasefire of fifteen years later, even though no one, not even the IRA, was aware of the fact. The Pope was speaking at Drogheda, some twenty miles from the border. It had been expected that he would visit the Six Counties, which, in a very real sense, was one of the last places in the world where Catholics were still dying for their faith. As Fr Desmond Wilson wrote: 'It was their very allegiance to the Pope that made them unacceptable.'[1] Paisley had fiercely opposed the idea of such a visit, but it appeared likely that it would go ahead nevertheless until the Warrenpoint slaughter occurred. It was then cancelled despite the criticism of people like Fr Wilson, who thought it 'an utter disgrace that the Pope would not even take the risk of a 15-minute helicopter ride across the Border to Armagh'. The Vatican feared less for the Pope's safety than that Paisleyite opportunism would feed on the reaction to create unseemly incidents which, if flashed around the world, would mar the extraordinary images of welcome which the papal visit was (correctly) expected to generate.[2]

Against that background, before an audience of 250,000 people, the Pope appealed for an end to violence in the following terms:

> . . . do not believe in violence; do not support violence. It is not the Christian way. It is not the way of the Catholic Church. Believe in peace and forgiveness and love; for they are of Christ. On my knees I beg you to turn away from the paths of violence and return to the ways of peace. You may claim to seek justice. I too believe in justice and seek justice. But violence only delays the day of justice. Violence destroys the work of justice . . . do not follow any leaders who train you in the ways of inflicting death.
>
> Those who resort to violence always claim that only violence brings change. You must know that there is a political peaceful way to justice.[3]

325

Predictably, these sentiments were rejected by the IRA a few days later. Their statement, which adverted to Bloody Sunday, internment and the torture which accompanied it, saying that their campaign was in the traditions of the earlier war against the Black and Tans, claimed that: 'This action was totally in keeping with the traditional Christian teaching on the right to resist oppression. Sinn Fein would welcome clarification as to whether this teaching on the right to resort to legitimate revolt and the right to engage in a just war had been changed.'

However the papal speech, which it is generally believed was written by the then Bishop of Down and Conor, Dr Cathal Daly, contained more subtleties than a mere condemnation of violence, *simpliciter*. The text also said:

> To all who bear political responsibility for the affairs of Ireland, I want to speak with the same urgency and intensity with which I have spoken of the men of violence. Do not cause or condone conditions which give excuse or pretext for violence. Those who resort to violence always claim that only violence brings about change. They claim that political action cannot achieve justice. You politicians must prove them wrong. You must show them that there is a peaceful, political way to justice. You must show that peace achieves the work of justice.

In the wash of controversy that followed the IRA's rejection of the Pope's appeal, these remarks were generally lost sight of. How much weight he intended should be placed on them in the first place is a matter of conjecture. But it is ironically true that initially, albeit unintentionally, Dr Daly himself aided in their obscuring. He was at the time regarded as the cerebral voice of the Irish hierarchy. An authoritarian, conservative, but kindly figure, he was deeply affected by the continuing trauma afflicting his people, and over the next few years spoke out strongly against violence in the cadences of Drogheda. Eventually, in 1983, after a particularly strong denunciation, Gerry Adams took up the cudgels with the Bishop and challenged him to

> . . . outline the hierarchy's attitude to the injustices of partition. I challenged him to give us his views on British occupation; on the methods of pacification and repression deployed by the British government in our country. I called on him to stop condemning the IRA and to apply himself instead to developing solutions to the problems which faced us.[5]

As Adams has said, 'a public debate of sorts' went on between the two men for the rest of the year. It was a debate in which the Bishop rarely replied directly to Adams.[6] Moreover, as with the papal/IRA exchange, the significance of Adams' remarks about the Bishop applying himself to 'developing solutions' was largely lost in controversy over the on-going campaign. But between them these questions contain the germ of what later became known as 'the pan–Nationalist front' idea and that about the responsibility for developing an alternative strategy, other than violence, to solve the Irish problem. In February 1983, an open letter addressed to the hierarchy by a number of well-known priests added to the Republican–Daly controversy. Amongst those who signed the letter were Fr Desmond Wilson, Fr Daniel Berrigan, S. J. and Fr Brian McCreesh, whose brother, Raymond, had been one of the H-Block prisoners who fasted to death. The letter said:

If a political system has been created by force and maintained by force then leaders within the Christian community have a responsibility not only to speak against but actively resist such a system. Surely this is the primary violence in our country that must be confronted. The Second Vatican Council gives a direct mandate to Bishops to confront injustice and tyranny even if this means taking a public stand against the authority of the Church.

Adams challenged Dr Daly on an oblique reply which the Bishop made to this and other salvoes the following month. Adams criticised a defence which the Bishop had made of aspects of the Stormont regime which he said had 'had notable successes and achievements to its credit'. He then went on to attack a statement by Daly that Unionists were justified in: '. . . believing in the right and duty under law to defend these political institutions against the threat of armed uprising'. Having reminded the Bishop that 'no Unionist politician has ever been prosecuted "under law" for their "shoot-to-kill" speeches', Adams went on:

I would remind the Bishop that the six-county state itself was established under threat of armed uprising by Unionists and has been maintained to the present day by a system of legal and extra-legal violence directed against the nationalist people, the victims of this violent Unionist state.

One man saw the possibilities of hopeful movement in what he was saying. In effect, what was occurring was a dialogue, containing the seeds of a new approach, between the political leadership of the militant Republicans, and the Irish Roman Catholic Church, on the basis of a speech which, whoever was the author, had been delivered by the Pope himself. One observer who understood the significance of this was the Redemptorist priest, Fr Alec Reid, a member of the Clonard community.

Since the 1969 burnings, the Clonard men had consistently sought to heal the wounds of Belfast. They were, and are, respected by the Loyalist paramilitaries as well as by the various wings of militant Republicanism. For over twenty years, whenever a feud flared, one could expect to find first Alec Reid, and then, when he joined the community, some years later, Gerry Reynolds, engaged in either trying to broker a truce or comfort the bereaved. Whatever one may think about the response of the official church to the challenge, and about the scandal of the spectacle of Christians at war, the attitude of the monks who make up the Clonard community has been in the highest traditions of those who went before them in Carolingian times. Years later, when after many heartbreaks their work had borne fruit, John Hume, a figure of both nobility and centrality to the peace process, would say of the Clonard men, and a Presbyterian clergyman whom we shall encounter later in our narrative:

As everybody now knows, the patience, skill and determination shown by clergy such as Fr Alec Reid CSSR, Rev Roy Magee, Fr Gerry Reynolds, CSSR and others as well in their work of reconciliation, has been nothing less than indispensable in bringing about the peace we now enjoy. I can say that without them the present hopeful situation would not and could not have come about.[7]

Fr Reid had been my guide and interlocutor in researching my book *On the Blanket*. We had both hoped that such a book would have the effect of helping to avoid a hunger strike by bringing enough publicity to bear on the H Block situation to encourage a solution, perhaps along Portlaoise lines. Apart from the fact that we failed, I found the task a draining experience. The horror of the faeces-smeared cells, the anguish of the families involved, faced with the prospect of the situation being worsened by a mass hunger strike, were bad enough. But there was also the tension of the ghetto areas. The fear of sectarian killings. Of a bomb, or gunfire, suddenly exploding. Of the wrecking midnight descent by troops. Of robbery, or rape perpetrated by some of the hordes of 'hoods' who flourished in the abnormality of the times. Of bereavement: one woman I interviewed, a widow, had one son 'on the blanket', and another had been shot dead by the IRA. Many of those I spoke to had lost a husband, a son, or a daughter in the Troubles. The emotional experience was such that, following the publication of the book in the summer of 1980, I did not write anything of consequence for another seven years.

But Fr Reid continued, in that ever-heightening atmosphere throughout the crisis of both the 1980 and 1981 hunger strikes. In addition to wearing, fruitless negotiations with British politicians and NIO officials, his pressures were added to by his other pastoral work. This involved breaking the news of a tragedy to a family, or ferrying distraught wives or parents around casualty departments, police barracks and sometimes morgues, in search of a loved one reported 'lifted', injured or killed. Everyone came to him with their troubles. Inevitably his health gave way. I remember visiting him in a hospital in Drogheda on a fine summer's day. He was lying on a made-up bed, fully dressed, his arms folded peacefully, apparently looking at the ceiling. He was in fact quite blind. Loss of sight was one of the multiple stress-induced ailments which had afflicted him.

By coincidence, two other unexpected visitors also showed up: Gerry Adams and his wife, Colette. That friendship was to have lasting and beneficial results. But at the time no one could have expected to see Alec Reid play a significant role in anything, ever again. Although, he was, as usual, courteous, and concerned with everyone's welfare except his own, the man appeared exhausted, a burned-out case. His superiors sent him to Italy to recuperate at a Redemptorist monastery. Gradually he recovered, and returned to Ireland, first to Redemptorist foundations in the Republic under strict instructions to take things easy. However, by the time of the Adams–Daly exchange he was back in Belfast, moved to attempt once again to knit up the ravelled sleeve of peacemaking.

During his efforts he was particularly cast down by yet another death, the killing by the IRA of a UDR man in South Armagh. But he persevered, deciding in effect to explore the possibility of having the resources of the Church deployed in conflict resolution, using Adams' call for dialogue as a starting point. In order to be able to state authoritatively, albeit unofficially and off the record, what the Sinn Fein thinking was, he and a colleague saw Adams and a representative group of the Sinn Fein leadership. At this meeting it was stated that Sinn Fein would:

1) Welcome the involvement of the Church, as one of the principal parties involved, in a

process of dialogue. Without this there was no hope of persuading the IRA to end its campaign.

2) It was pointed out that, whereas in the public mind the lasting deposit of the Pope's speech had been his condemnation of violence, he had also spoken of the responsibilities on decision-takers to ensure that injustices were resolved so that the conditions for violence would be removed.

3)Therefore the only way to persuade the IRA to end its campaign was to demonstrate to them the existence not only of an alternative, peaceful strategy, but also of a coalition of forces sufficiently powerful as to make this achievement a credible possibility.

Next, to ensure that the Sinn Fein peace initiative was theologically well grounded, Reid contacted another Redemptorist, the respected theologian Sean O'Riordain, to ask him what he thought of the morality of Adams' call on Daly. O'Riordain took the view that politics was an activity aimed at the good of the people, all the people, Protestant and Catholic, Nationalist and Unionist, and that therefore the Church, Adams, and everyone else should question and answer each other.

O'Riordain in particular singled out the validity of the two questions which Adams had addressed to Daly: 'You call on Republicans to renounce violence and join in the peaceful struggle for the rights of Nationalists. What peaceful struggle?' and '. . . those who express moral condemnation of the tactic of armed struggle have a responsibility to spell out an alternative course by which Irish independence can be secured'. To this Adams had added: 'I, for one, would be pleased to consider such an alternative.' He went on: 'I know that many of my constituents, who are also lay people in your diocese, would be equally anxious to have such a strategy – that is an alternative to the armed struggle – outlined for them.'

O'Riordain thought it right and reasonable that, for the good of the people, the Church should become involved in helping to develop a strategy which would result in an end to violence. Many in influential places in the Church thought otherwise, however. Adams had made a written submission to the hierarchy, but as he says himself, it proved to be 'another vain attempt to get a positive engagement on the issues I had put to Bishop Daly'.[8] During the 1983 Westminster election in which he defeated Gerry Fitt, Adams and the other Sinn Fein candidates had to surmount considerable Church opposition to the idea of Catholics voting for an organisation which supported violence. It was fortunate that at this juncture the See of Armagh was occupied by Cardinal Tomas O'Fiaich. Although the fact of being a cardinal did not give O'Fiaich authority over the other bishops, his influential moral position made him an invaluable ally in the peace process.

O'Fiaich both encouraged Reid's efforts and agreed to meet Adams privately. The radical Belfast priest, Fr Desmond Wilson, joined in the discussions. The Republican leadership was moving steadily towards a new political vision based on three concepts.

One, that as part of the 'alternative method', there should be a shared approach to the problem by all the Nationalist parties, north and south. This concept, as we shall see, was later to be broadened to include the Nationalist-minded of the Irish diaspora, particularly in America.

Two, that whatever new Ireland might emerge from such an approach, it did not necessarily have to conform to the preferred Republican option of a thirty-two-county socialist republic, provided that it was a) democratic and b) worked out free of British dictation. The Government of Ireland Act would have to be abrogated.

Three, that if and when a position was achieved wherein the Nationalists and the Unionists sat down to negotiate the new political institutions which such a new Ireland presupposed, providing a) and b) operated so that a form of genuine self-determination was possible, then Sinn Fein would accept any democratic decisions arrived at.

What all this added up to was something very different from the traditional Republican approach of 'Brits out' and then on to a thirty-two-county republic. Adams and his colleagues were evolving away from the gun, and towards a political approach based on self-determination, for both Nationalists and Unionists. In a word, the Republicans were beginning to sue for peace. It was a turning point which demanded, and received, not only enormous moral and physical courage from Adams and his friends, but also political skills of an unusually high order.

The relationship between Sinn Fein and the IRA is intricate in the extreme. While taken together they form the principal components of the Republican movement, there are obvious overlaps, and the basic comity of a shared objective exists. Nevertheless, the two wings remain two separate organisations with separate leaderships. Putting point 3 of the Sinn Fein policy outlined above in another way, if the armalite were to be laid down, the alternative of the ballot box would demonstrably require a real chance of succeeding. It was not merely a matter of attempting to get Sinn Fein to disown force. If that approach had been followed Sinn Fein would probably have split and disintegrated, and the IRA would have continued without a political arm – and very likely without Adams and those around him also. Enough has been said in earlier chapters about Republican splits to make it unnecessary for me to labour this point further.

However, Adams, Martin McGuinness, Paddy Doherty, Jim Gibney, Tom Hartley, Danny Morrison, Mitchel McLoughlin and the other Sinn Fein leaders successfully initiated and carried through a process of dialogue within the movement, which, as we have seen earlier, resulted in their taking firm control of Sinn Fein, even to the extent of dropping the abstention policy, without any bloodshed. The culmination of the internal debate that had been taking place within the movement for some five years since the Adams–Daly exchange bore fruit in 1987, with the publication of the Sinn Fein discussion paper, 'Scenario for Peace'.

Adams has described this document as marking:

> . . . the public launch of our developing peace strategy. We called for an end to British rule, and argued that an enduring peace would only come about as a result of a process which won the support of a wide representation of Irish, British and international opinion. Such a peace process would have to contain the necessary mechanics of a settlement; the framework, timescale and the dynamic necessary to bring about an inclusive, negotiated and democratic settlement.[9]

But by 1987 the 'dynamic' had proved slow in coming and would prove slower. The process of making Sinn Fein respectable proceeded at such a pace from the

IRA ceasefire in the summer of 1994 to the time of writing (the following summer) that it is necessary to remind readers of the extent to which the Republicans were regarded as pariahs during the mid-eighties. The effects of the various broadcasting bans described earlier, the attempts to 'cleanse the culture' of Nationalist infections, all had their effect. The seventy-fifth anniversary of the 1916 rising was scarcely celebrated in the Republic lest it stir ancient emotions. As Gerry Adams remarked, the southern establishment was '. . . afraid of all the skeletons in the cupboards of the state, afraid that if it scratches a Terence McSwiney, up jumps a Bobby Sands'.[10] But above all there was the revulsion at the violence for which the Republicans were regarded as carrying the major share of blame. I doubt whether the Republicans, preoccupied with their external pressures and internal dialogue, fully appreciated the depth of feeling in the south on this issue. As late as June 1993 the fact that President Mary Robinson proposed to shake hands with Adams, in his capacity as a local representative, during a visit to West Belfast became a *cause célèbre,* drawing official displeasure from London,[11] and stirring controversy in Dublin.

In these circumstances, therefore, the effort to sell the idea of the 'alternative strategy' to parties outside Sinn Fein proved difficult in the extreme. To begin with, almost by definition, the centre with the greatest power of initiative, London, was correctly assessed, for the moment at least, as being not merely beyond influencing, but hostile. Where the Unionists were concerned it was recognised that the people, as opposed to the politicians, would be capable of and willing to make a more imaginative response than 'Ulster says No'. Nevertheless, this was the cry which attracted Loyalist support in the run-up to, and the aftermath of, the signing of the 1985 Anglo-Irish Agreement. The general climate of betrayal and rage in the Unionist family rendered the prospects for dialogue virtually *non est.*

This meant that realistically, apart from working to win over church and internal Sinn Fein support, the main focus had to be on the SDLP and on Dublin. But by 1986 neither source of potential support had proved fruitful. Fr Reid had been disappointed in his efforts to involve the SDLP in talks with its arch-rival, Sinn Fein. Fr Desmond Wilson, whose cousin, John Wilson, was a Fianna Fail front-bencher, had not succeeded in interesting Haughey in the 'alternative strategy'. There was no question of approaching Fine Gael, the second biggest party in the Republic. At the time the FitzGerald administration was thought to be in discussion with the British about the possibility of introducing internment north and south. Yet it was essential that Dublin be involved. The influence of any Dublin government, with its diplomatic and political clout, is central to any discussion on Northern Ireland. When a taoiseach decides to utilise that influence in a positive way, the results can be spectacular, as Albert Reynolds was to demonstrate so forcefully in the years 1993–4. Above all, Dublin's wishes are of major significance in America. If Washington is to be moved to take up positions supportive of Nationalism, which may displease London, it is essential that any peace process has the backing of the Dublin government of the day. The White House will not take action against the wishes of both sovereign governments involved in the Anglo-Irish problem.

In 1986 Charles J. Haughey was not in government, but it was a reasonable assumption that he soon would be. Moreover, his party, although far from the wild and swirling days of the Arms Trial, was still the most Nationalist on the island, after Sinn Fein itself. Adams therefore made another effort to enter into dialogue with Haughey. Fr Reid contacted me and asked me if I would help to bring this about. Through my researches into the IRA I had some inkling of what was going on within Sinn Fein. I had come to know many of the Republican leaders over the years, and was well aware, the use of force notwithstanding, that figures like O'Bradaigh, O'Conaill, and now Adams, McGuinness and the rest of the northern leadership were men of calibre and integrity. Having observed how he bore himself during the racking days of the hunger strike, I regarded Adams in particular as a considerable person.

I had no uncertainties therefore about attempting to convince Haughey of his bona fides. Accordingly, at the beginning of October 1986 Haughey agreed to meet me for lunch in the Berkeley Hotel, Dublin. Ironically we sat at the same table from which he had jumped up in anger, leaving me sitting by myself, not long beforehand, because I had criticised his attitude to the Anglo-Irish Agreement. However, there was no anger this time. Knowing that politically Haughey believed in a philosophy of describing not only his geese as swans, but his ducks also, if he thought this would be acceptable to his hearers, I began by pitching the tent of expectation as far up on the mountain of possibility as I could.

I told him that there was a real possibility that developments currently taking place within the Republican movement could lead to his being instrumental in bringing about both peace and a united Ireland. Haughey's response was: 'Phew. That's a glittering prize if it could be had!' I then suggested that he should meet first Fr Reid and then Gerry Adams, and/or make some public supportive statement. The paramilitary world sets great store by tangible gestures of commitment. Haughey was fully aware, through his intelligence sources, of Adams' importance in the Republican firmament: 'He's the Boss,' he said simply. But, though the 'glittering prize' continued to shimmer distantly behind the clouds of uncertainties, he fought shy of meeting Adams.

At one stage his reasoning was based on a speech Adams made attacking Fianna Fail. 'He says he wants to meet me, and now this! It doesn't add up.' At another juncture, he argued that the time was not opportune. Sometimes I wondered if his motivation went much beyond wishing to ensure that the basic 5% Republican vote in the Republic came Fianna Fail's way. But this was probably unjust. More likely, Haughey was simply still weighed down by his ideological baggage from the Arms Trial days. He was extremely courteous and supportive of Fr Reid, both continuing to hold meetings with him personally, and ensuring that the priest became a regular and welcome visitor to the office of his principal adviser on Northern Ireland, Dr Martin Mansergh. Thus an invaluable line of communication between Sinn Fein and successive Dublin governments was established and maintained. The line continued both when Haughey became Taoiseach in February of 1987, and subsequently, when he was deposed, by Albert Reynolds in 1992. Despite the fact that Reynolds had ousted him, Haughey made a point, within a week of Reynolds' taking power, of giving him a full briefing on how the peace process had developed to that stage. By then, with the help of John Hume, drafting had begun, on the basis of an idea suggested by Fr Reid, of a Joint Declaration by Dublin and London of the principles which should govern a peace settlement. Haughey had also raised the possibility of a new initiative with John Major.

In January of 1988 Fr Reid wrote to Sinn Fein asking if the party would meet formally with the SDLP, 'to explore whether there could be agreement on overall nationalist political policy strategy for justice and peace'.[12] He abandoned his efforts to interest other SDLP sources and addressed a similar appeal to John Hume. Beginning in 1982 (the year of the Adams–Daly exchange) Sinn Fein had made common cause with two of the Six Counties' small parties, the Irish Independent Party and the People's Democracy, and attempted to set up a dialogue with the SDLP. The SDLP had, however, always rejected these advances. Now, very courageously, Hume agreed to meet Adams. They held a lengthy meeting on 11 January 1988. They subsequently agreed to set up a series of talks, involving delegations from both parties. On the SDLP side, Hume, Seamus Mallon, Sean Farren and Austin Currie. On that of Sinn Fein, Adams, Tom Hartley, Danny Morrison and Mitchel McLaughlin. It was agreed that they would not have a 'military agenda'.

The Hume–Adams meeting aroused great controversy. It was condemned by the Secretary of State, Tom King, Paisley and Molyneaux. Paisley called for Unionist unity in the face of this 'new alliance'. Molyneaux claimed that the talks were 'a fatal step for democracy', coming so close to a 'breakthrough' in the Unionist talks which were then being conducted with the British Government, and which he averred might have led to talks with the SDLP. Press reaction was not favourable either. The *Newsletter* headline said: 'Unionists blame Hume – SF talks slammed'. The *Belfast Telegraph* thought the talks a 'serious mistake'. The prospect of the talks bringing Sinn Fein in from the cold inaugurated an era when, from being the subject of near-universal media adulation, Hume became the object of sustained criticism in some sections of the press, notably the Dublin *Sunday Independent*.

Hume had once broken off negotiations with a wing of the Republican movement. During 1985 he had agreed to secret talks with the IRA, but ended these when he discovered that the IRA intended to videotape the proceedings. But throughout 1987 he did not allow that memory to come between him and the prospect of peace, however nebulous. He frequently had to defend his position, but never deviated, once saying that he did not give 'two balls of roasted snow' for his critics' views. It was an unusual and unwelcome position for Hume to be in. For twenty years he had been the most respected political figure to emerge from the Troubles. Now, by agreeing to talk with his younger rival, he had in effect agreed to take part in a bruising contest for the hearts and minds of the North's Nationalists. (Hume was then 50, Adams 39.) Adams would later describe the January 1988 meeting as marking 'the beginning of the most significant discussions in formulating a new peace initiative in the North of Ireland'.[13] One of the most important aspects of the Hume–Adams contact was the understanding that built up between the two men. Later this would give Hume in particular the certitude he needed both to withstand criticism of the talks process, and subsequently to forcefully argue for its fruits with both Dublin and London. His influence on Albert Reynolds' thinking at a formative stage during the latter's taking of office had a direct bearing on the securing of peace.

Peace did not come easily. The 'discussions' between Sinn Fein and SDLP delegations began in the New Year of 1988 and continued until the autumn. The last meeting was held on 30 August 1988. During this time several papers were exchanged between the two sides and much constructive thinking followed. The basic positions of the two sides were as follows:

Hume argued that the Anglo-Irish Agreement had made violence redundant. On the basis of his Westminster soundings, he advanced the opinion that Britain, through the Agreement, was sending a powerful signal that she was adopting a neutral position in matters Irish. He told Adams that London no longer had any interest in Ireland and that her only concern was to foster agreement amongst the inhabitants of the island of Ireland.

Hume was mistrustful of the Sinn Fein demand that Britain should make a declaration of intent to withdraw. He argued that a declaration to withdraw was in effect the same thing as a decision to withdraw:

> The political vacuum is immediately created . . . This route is the route of maximum risk and it is a risk which we believe no one has the right to take unless they do so with the full authority of the Irish people . . . we would have a Cyprus/Lebanon style formula for permanent division and bloodshed. What would the 12,000 armed members of the RUC do? What would the 8,000 armed members of the UDR do? . . . Is the risk involved in such a policy not an awesome one and likely to ensure that the peace and unity of Ireland will never come?

Hume, whose preferred option was all-party dialogue, sought, in the event of Unionists refusing to parley, to engage Sinn Fein with 'the Irish Government and other nationalist participants in preparing a peaceful and comprehensive approach to achieving agreement on self-determination in Ireland'.

He asked if Sinn Fein endorsed the right of the Irish people to self-determination, which meant in practice 'agreement of both the unionist and nationalist traditions in Ireland'. He sought to get from Sinn Fein a recognition of the fact that the Irish people were 'deeply divided on the question of how to exercise self-determination'.

Adams refused to accept that Britain was 'neutral' and argued that her 'presence distorts the political landscape'. In return the SDLP refused to adopt his belief that the way for Britain to demonstrate her neutrality lay in her '. . . adopting a policy of ending the Union and then actively seeking agreement among the people who share the island of Ireland on how this can be accomplished'.[14]

Sinn Fein's bottom line in the talks was the achievement of a common approach with the SDLP on the issue of self-determination, so that this would in turn be taken up by the other Irish Nationalist parties and made the subject of a diplomatic offensive from Dublin. Apart from the fact that the talks initiated a closer understanding between Hume and Adams, which prompted them to continue their dialogue in private after the discussions ended, they also yielded two important points of agreement between the parties. They were contained in the communiqué which Sinn Fein issued after the talks had ended:

> Our discussions with the SDLP elicited the shared political view that the Irish people as a whole have the right to national self-determination and that the Irish people should be defined as those people domiciled on the island of Ireland. In that context it is accepted that an internal settlement is no solution.[15]

The foregoing formed the basis of the positions which continued to be argued between Hume and Adams over the next five years. The criticisms of the talks, mentioned earlier, continued, and indeed intensified in right-wing circles, particularly amongst Fine Gael and the Unionists. The latter said publicly that they would refuse to talk to the SDLP so long as the party remained in contact with Sinn Fein. Privately the Unionists did in fact meet with SDLP representatives at secret talks held in Duisburg, West Germany, on 14–15 October 1988. These were attended by Fr Reid, and by representatives of the Alliance Party (Gordon Mawhinney), the SDLP (Austin Currie), the UUP (Jack Allen), and the DUP (Peter Robinson). Any chance these talks might have had of surmounting the difficulties posed for Unionists by the Anglo-Irish Agreement faded when the BBC broadcast a report (on 1 February 1989) of their existence, despite the fact that a newspaper poll showed 63% in favour of the talks.[16]

Although he had sanctioned the attendance at the talks of his deputy, Peter Robinson, Paisley's public posture at the time may be gleaned from his performance at a meeting of the European Parliament addressed by the Pope, three days before Duisburg. He was removed from the assembly chamber during the Pope's speech for holding up a placard saying: 'John Paul II Antichrist' and shouting: 'I renounce you as Antichrist.' I remember speculating privately to myself as to the likely apoplectic reaction had the old ranter been made aware of the fact that at the time moves were afoot to bring about a settlement whose origins lay in one of the Pope's speeches.

But there was very little else about to laugh at. The peace process went slowly as, apart from those indicated, people outside the ranks of Sinn Fein proved wary about getting involved. Cardinal O'Fiaich was anxious to see a meeting between Adams and Haughey, even going to the extent of suggesting Maynooth College as a venue. The extensive grounds of the college, its many buildings, exits and entrances, made this major seminary and university an ideal site for a secret meeting, but Haughey refused. The most he was prepared to sanction by way of contact with Sinn Fein was a meeting by two of his senior politicians. From time to time I would ask Fr Reid how things were going, and, keen GAA follower that he is, he would indicate progress, or lack of it, by the Holy Spirit's position on the field of play. When things were going well He was at full forward. If He were in the backs the opposite was the case.

An event which occurred in 1990 made me wonder if the Holy Spirit was even supporting the team any longer, never mind playing. As, apart from Hume, no major Establishment figure had been prepared to risk meeting with Adams publicly, Cardinal Tomas O'Fiaich decided that he would have to make the breakthrough himself. The meeting would have been a major step in the mainstreaming of Sinn Fein, and would have accelerated the peace process considerably. But before the meeting could take place, the Cardinal died unexpectedly, of a heart attack, on 8 May, while on a visit to Lourdes. Ironically, such was the atmosphere of the time, the mere fact that Adams and McGuinness attended his funeral mass created controversy. The attendance also included President Hillery, Charles Haughey, the RUC Chief Constable, Sir Hugh Annesley and, a man who was to play an honourable and constructive role in furthering the peace process, the Secretary of State, Peter Brooke.

Brooke, an example of that unique phenomenon, the caring wing of the Conservative party,[17] had Irish connections. Connections which at first sight would not have suggested an impulse to reach out to Nationalist Ireland. His branch of the Brooke family was related to that of Lord Brookeborough. Possibly by way of counterbalance, he also took pleasure in telling Irish people that his ancestor, the eighteenth-century poet, Charlotte Brooke, was the first person to use the term Fenian in the English language.[18] However, even before coming to Ireland, Brooke had displayed signs of wishing to diminish, rather than increase, the ties that bound the British Conservative and Unionist party to Ulster. As Conservative Party Chairman (1987–9) he had opposed moves to have the Conservatives organise in the Six Counties. He lost that battle, and when he came to Ulster in 1989, to succeed Tom King, he found the local Conservatives arrayed against him. The array was not a very large one, as the Tories never struck deep roots in the Six Counties, but they did attempt to obstruct what might be termed his overground efforts to find a path to peace.

Brooke was trying to increase the amount of devolution in the area, as provided for in the Anglo-Irish Agreement. The Ulster Conservatives, however, favoured the Canute approach of seeking closer integration with the 'UK mainland'. As we have seen earlier, Brooke, in his overground capacity, laboured from 1989 until 1991 in a morass of 'talks about talks'. There yielded the concept of the 'three-stranded talks': those between Dublin and London, between Belfast and Dublin, and between most of the northern parties. Sinn Fein were excluded, but the two major Unionist groupings took part, as did the Alliance Party and the SDLP. The talks brought teams of southern politicians north and some Unionists south. Molyneaux led a delegation to Dublin, but Paisley refused his invitation. Where all this would have led to ultimately had Brooke's rendering of 'Clementine' on *The Late Late Show* not abruptly lowered his political tam ratings with the Unionists must remain a matter of conjecture. But it was obviously an interesting process of considerable potential.

This potential would have been very considerably heightened had Brooke's underground activities borne the fruits he intended. For, while the talks about talks and the three-stranded approach continued, Brooke also sanctioned secret contacts with Sinn Fein. He would appear to have proceeded from a variety of motives.

Firstly there were the continuing psychological shock waves within the Conservatives stemming from the Brighton bombing. Alan Clark has recorded his reaction to the explosion in the following terms:

> But what a coup for the Paddys. The whole thing has a smell of the Tet Offensive.[19] If they had just had the wit to press their advantage, a couple of chaps with guns in the crowd, they could have got the whole Government as they blearily emerged – and the assassins could in all probability have made their getaway unpunished.[20]

Although I cannot state that I have found any evidence that Clark's attitude towards the 'Paddys'' failure to maximise their sanguinary opportunities was widely shared by his Tory colleagues, his 'Tet Offensive' reaction certainly was and to a degree still is. The Brighton bombing had a galvanic effect on Conservative thinking which did not cease with the signing of the Anglo-Irish Agreement. On top of this, the new thinking in the ranks of Sinn Fein, which Brooke's contact with John Hume helped him to evaluate, was increasingly evident to anyone with their political wits about them. Apart from intelligence reports, and the availability of documents published by Sinn Fein such as 'A Scenario for Peace', the Sinn Fein leaders' speeches were sounding a new note. On 5 March of the year Brooke arrived in the province (1989), for example, Gerry Adams said that his objective was a 'non-armed political movement' to work for self-determination in Ireland.[21] 'Non-armed' was an interesting concept on the lips of the leader of the political wing of the Irish physical force movement.

Brooke choose the occasion of his first hundred days in the Six Counties (3 November 1989) to make some interesting, and widely reported, noises of his own. Subsequently, most of the attention, and controversy, which these aroused centred on evidences of 'Tet' thinking which he gave, although the conflict analogy which he drew was centred on Cyprus rather than Vietnam. He admitted that the IRA could be contained militarily, but not defeated. He said that the Government would be 'flexible and imaginative' if the IRA renounced violence. Using Cyprus as an example, he commented that he would not say 'never' to talks with Sinn Fein should the violence end.

These remarks aroused such wrath amongst Conservatives, the Labour Party and the Unionists that he was forced to back-pedal over the next few days. In the wake of charges that he was encouraging terrorism he apologised for using the Cyprus analogy. However, I found, in the context of what happened subsequently, that a leading Sinn Feiner, Jim Gibney, was inclined to treat as really significant another, rather Delphic, utterance of Brooke's which most people overlooked.[22] The Secretary of State showed himself mindful of the fact that Sinn Fein was striking up newer airs by declaring an interest in 'what they were saying behind the mountains'. In October of 1990, Brooke took steps to investigate matters *ultra montane*.[23]

Despite the official cannonading about 'no talking to terrorists' the British have always had methods of talking to Sinn Fein. This was demonstrated at the time of the Whitelaw talks, the talks which continued in the 1970s under Merlyn Rees, and again during the hunger strikes to which they led. The 'line', as it is known, was reactivated in October of 1990 by the British. A top civil servant, who was on the point of retiring, met with Martin McGuinness.[24] By way of impressing on Sinn Fein that Brooke meant business the British subsequently sent the Republicans an advance copy of a speech which Brooke intended to deliver at his constituency on 9 November. This speech, afterwards known as 'The Whitbread Speech', was entitled 'The British Presence'. It contained the celebrated statement that Britain had no 'selfish strategic or economic interest' in Northern Ireland and was prepared to accept a united Ireland by consent.

It was not the first time that Republicans had been given sight of a Secretary of State's speech before he delivered it. I remember the then prisoners' leader, David Morley, telling me how he was sent a copy in Long Kesh of Merlyn Rees' speech in which he announced the removal of Special Category status. Adams and McGuinness, who had come to ascendancy through the British–Republican talks of those years, were not overimpressed by this latest re-run of an old ploy aimed at investing negotiations with importance – and perhaps distracting from their real objective. However, time had moved on from Morley's days, and the British were now more in earnest than they had been. The IRA's strength, as evidenced by Brighton, and other episodes, including the mortaring of Downing Street on 7 February 1991, the ending of the Cold War, and the sheer cost of maintaining the British presence in Northern Ireland, were all signs of the ineluctable dialectic of history.

In April of 1991, by way of underlining their sincerity (and this fact should perhaps be noted in the context of the debate over the nature and extent of British involvement with Loyalist paramilitary death squads), the British also forwarded to Sinn Fein one other detail. The Republicans were advised that, in order to create a good atmosphere for the three-stranded talks, the Loyalists were about to declare a moratorium on shooting Catholics. On 22 April the Combined Loyalist Command, as the overall Loyalist paramilitary grouping was known, duly announced a ceasefire. This ceasefire, which applied to the UDA, UVF and the Red Hand Commando, stayed more or less intact except for an incident where a Sinn Fein councillor, Eddie Fullerton, was shot dead in the Republic, on 25 May, by the UFF at his home in Buncrana, Co. Donegal. The moratorium lasted until 4 July of that year when Catholics again became fair game. By January of 1993 the Loyalists' hit list had expanded to cover what was known as a 'pan-Nationalist front'. Apart from the provisional IRA itself this included members of the GAA, the SDLP, Sinn Fein, and the Dublin Government.[25]

The contacts between Sinn Fein and the British Government were authorised at the highest level from London. In June 1991, the official designated to talk to the Sinn Fein representatives produced a letter of authorisation signed by Peter Brooke. The talks continued after Brooke's departure. The British took pains to inform Sinn Fein that Brooke's successor, Sir Patrick Mayhew, was 'fully on board'. But that apart from Mayhew, and the Cabinet Secretary . . . no one in the Government, apart from John Major himself, and Douglas Hurd, knew of the talks' existence. The Republicans were kept fully briefed on the progress of the three-stranded talks' progress, or lack of it, and were informed that the British did not expect them to succeed.

For their part, the Republicans took care to ensure that the 'non-armed' strategy continued and that the British were made aware of it in the most public and significant way possible. The annual commemoration ceremonies at Wolfe Tone's grave in Bodenstown, Co. Kildare, are an annual high-water mark of affirmation of Republican beliefs. A Bodenstown address is a key indicator of Republican thinking. Jim Gibney delivered the 1992 Bodenstown oration on 2 June. In it he gave the clearest possible indication of the Republicans' intention to sue for peace. After quoting a Protestant who had said, at a Sinn Fein seminar, that Republican appeals to Protestants 'could not be heard above the deadly sound of gunfire', Gibney asked his audience if Republicans:

> had been deafened by 'the deadly sound of their own gunfire?' . . . trapped inside a complex web of struggle from which they can't or don't emerge, hostages to an immediate past because of all the pain, suffering and commitment to past views expressed, trenchantly, which in time solidify into unyielding principles?

He then went on to state that:

> . . . The answers are to be found in the evolutionary changes that have taken place in republican thinking over the last ten years. These cover many issues, the most pressing one being the need for peace in our country. We know and accept that the British government's departure must be preceded by a sustained period of peace and will arise out of negotiations. We know and accept that such negotiations will involve the different shades of Irish nationalism, and Irish unionism engaging the British government either together or separately to secure an all-embracing and durable peace process.[26]

The importance of Gibney's speech was underlined by its being made the lead story in the following edition of *An Phoblacht*, under the heading 'Determined to achieve peace'. To anyone familiar with the Republican world it was obvious that major changes were afoot. On the British side the custom of sending Sinn Fein advance copies of the contents of forthcoming important speeches by the Secretary of State continued. One of these texts, concerning a speech which was later delivered in Coleraine by Sir Patrick Mayhew, on 16 December, was forwarded to Sinn Fein on 26 October. It confirmed what Brooke had said in his Whitbread speech about including Sinn Fein in talks if violence ceased, and gave an indication that in such an eventuality army activity would be scaled down. It also contained the following:

> Successive Governments have stressed that any new structures for the Government of Northern Ireland must be acceptable to both major traditions. A return to the old Stormont political system would not meet this and other publicly stated criteria. The British Government also recognises the need for any new North/South arrangement adequately to cater for and express both traditions.

When he delivered the speech Sir Patrick gave a boost to a Nationalist method of expressing their tradition – a ban on having street names in Irish was removed. He also repeated that, if violence ceased, Sinn Fein could be included in talks and troops withdrawn from the streets. The Unionists reacted with outrage. Paisley said that Mayhew had 'taken leave of his senses' and, while accusing him of doing a U-turn and putting out Dublin propaganda, also said that the 'whole speech, in tone and content, is weighted heavily in favour of Republicanism'.[27] At this stage the Tory Party strategists were increasingly preoccupied with the gathering storm over Europe. The whips became alarmed that Mayhew's speech might be a bridge too far. If the Euro-sceptics, many of whom were Unionist-inclined anyhow, decided to add Ireland to their grievances a bad situation would be made infinitely worse.

These worries were conveyed to Sinn Fein by the British. On 2 March 1993 Mayhew made a speech designed to calm ruffled Unionist feathers. He said:

> The reality is that if Northern Ireland's position as part of the United Kingdom is ever going to change it will only be by the will of a majority of its people . . . We are not indifferent; we are not neutral in our resolve to protect the people of Northern Ireland from terrorist violence. We are not neutral in defending the right of Northern Ireland people to democratic self-determination.

The Unionists were not impressed. The following day's *Belfast Telegraph* carried comments from the three main Unionist parties which showed that the Ulster Unionist Party believed that John Hume had a veto over progress in the province. Paisley accused Mayhew of being happy to push the North out of the union 'as soon as there is a majority of just one in favour'. John Alderdice, for the Alliance Party, summed up the Unionist position accurately when he said: 'There is considerable unhappiness about the relatively rudderless approach by the Government.' There would have been a great deal more unhappiness if the Unionists had known that six days before Mayhew delivered his speech the British Government had agreed to hold substantive talks with Sinn Fein.

On 26 February 1993, the British representative had told Sinn Fein that two to three weeks of private talks were envisaged at a neutral venue. Sweden, Denmark, Scotland or the Isle of Man were suggested. If, during that time, the violence had ceased, even without a public announcement of the fact, the British believed that they could convince Sinn Fein that armed struggle was no longer necessary. On 19 March, the British sent Sinn Fein a position paper which contained their basis for entering into talks. Paragraph seven said:

> The British Government does not have, and will not adopt, any prior objective of 'ending of partition'. The British Government cannot enter a talks process, or expect others to do so, with the purpose of achieving a pre-determined outcome, whether the 'ending of partition' or anything else. It has accepted that the eventual outcome of such a process could be a united Ireland, but this can only be on the basis of the consent of the people of Northern Ireland . . . unless the people of Northern Ireland come to express such a view, the British Government will continue to uphold the union . . .

A few days later, on 23 March, the British Government official charged with contacting Sinn Fein held a meeting with the party's representative at which he somewhat undermined the force of this declaration. He said that Martin

McGuinness' speech to the Sinn Fein Ard Fheis the previous month had triggered action. In this speech McGuinness had referred to the fact of there being a new government in Dublin and also to the rumours about a possible resumption of the Brooke/Mayhew talks on the basis of separate talks being held with all of the parties involved. McGuinness said that this situation 'actually provides both the British and Dublin governments with an opportunity to bring Sinn Fein into the peace process'. He argued that 'If both governments have the courage of their private convictions they should now finally meet with Sinn Fein.'

There was evidence of new thinking in the McGuinness address. It did not call for a British withdrawal. In fact it could have been taken as indicating that Sinn Fein was moving towards compromise. McGuinness said:

> We would approach any serious talks accepting that we haven't got all the answers but we most certainly believe we have some of them . . . we are quite prepared to be open and flexible to serious proposals which can lead to realistic agreement . . .

He also spoke of the need for

> . . . new and radical thinking to the predicament Unionists find themselves in. The plight of Unionists is requiring particular consideration to guarantee and protect their interests which will be needed to resolve the conflict.

The British contact explained that the British Government realised that no solution which did not involve Sinn Fein could work. Nor could a settlement be envisaged which did not include all of the people, north and south. The official said that this solution would have to be one that '. . . won't frighten Unionists. The final solution is union. It is going to happen anyway. The historical train – Europe – determines that. We are committed to Europe. Unionists will have to change . . . The island will be as one.' These sentiments were of course not merely different from those which Mayhew was addressing to the Unionists, they were not what a large number of Conservative MPs were saying about Europe either.

However, on 10 May, after much further toing and froing between the two sides during the months of March and April, Sinn Fein informed the British that the IRA had agreed to a two-week ceasefire to allow the talks to begin. Sinn Fein's position paper for the commencement of negotiations said:

> The route to peace in Ireland is to be found in the restoration to the Irish people of our right to national self-determination – in the free exercise of this right without any impediment of any kind. British sovereignty over the Six Counties, as with all Ireland before partition, is the inherent cause of political instability and conflict. This must be addressed within the democratic context of the exercise of the right to national self-determination . . . We believe that the wish of the majority of the Irish people is for Irish unity. We believe that an adherence to democratic principles makes Irish unity inevitable.

Sinn Fein also shared the British confidence in Europe as a means to secure unity:

> The emerging political and economic imperatives both within Ireland and within the

broader context of greater European political union support the logic of Irish unity . . . the British Government should play a crucial and constructive role in persuading the Unionist community to reach an accommodation with the rest of the Irish people.

On 10 April, Adams and Hume recommenced their meetings, confirming this fact with a public statement, issued on 24 April, in response to media enquiries. It said:

Everyone has a solemn duty to change the political climate away from conflict and towards a process of national reconciliation which sees the peaceful accommodation of the differences between the people of Britain and Ireland and the people of Ireland themselves . . . we accept that an internal settlement is not a solution because it obviously does not deal with all the relationships at the heart of the problem. We accept that the Irish people as a whole have a right to national self-determination. This is a view shared by a majority of the people on this island, though not by all its people.

On the face of it, all this powerful thrust towards a settlement, at both public and private level, would appear to have inevitably borne results, as indeed ultimately they did. But despite the offer of an IRA ceasefire on 10 May 1993, one did not come about until August of the following year. For the issue of Europe and the crucial vote on the Social Chapter of the Maastricht Treaty in the House of Commons in July 1993 now fell across the path of the Irish peace process. On 17 May, when the plans for the Sinn Fein talks were put to John Major, he decided not to proceed without consulting the Home Secretary, Kenneth Clarke. The following day Clarke advised that, with Maastricht looming, the hour was not propitious for talks with Sinn Fein. Amongst other IRA actions of the time, the Warrington bombing had occurred in March, the Bishopsgate bombing in London in April. Effectively the underground moves towards peace stalled at this point.

Patrick Mayhew's energies turned to persuading the Unionists to come onside for the Social Chapter vote. Previously, all the Unionist MPs. with the exception of Sir James Kilfedder, had voted against the ratification of Maastricht. Now, however, Mayhew's efforts paid off, and Molyneaux and his followers broke ranks with Paisley to support the Government on the Social Chapter issue. On 23 July Major denied in the House of Commons that there had been any deal with Molyneaux. But there was a wave of speculation that the Ulster Unionists had been promised a House of Commons Select Committee on Northern Ireland in return for their support. In Dublin on 27 July the Taoiseach, Albert Reynolds, warned that a Select Committee could undermine the Anglo-Irish Agreement. The Tories continued to deny the existence of a deal with the Unionists on the basis of such a committee for several months, until the Select Committee was formally announced in the House of Commons on 17 December.

By then, the committee question had become a relatively minor one, almost drowned in the tidal wave of publicity that broke over the related issues of the Hume–Adams talks; the revelation shortly beforehand that the British had been in contact with Sinn Fein, despite all the denials; and the announcement of the Downing Street Declaration on 15 December. But before discussing these matters we must turn to another powerful outside influence that helped to bring the

Downing Street Declaration about – the Irish-American dimension and its influence on the White House.

The 'Irish-American lobby' does not exist in a formal sense, with offices in Washington and branches throughout the country. Rather it is a reservoir of uncoordinated strength, which at moments of excitation in the Anglo-Irish relationship exists to be tapped on behalf of the Irish. When this is done properly the results can be dramatic. One of the best assessments on record concerns an episode in which it was not properly used, during that other great convulsion of the century involving Ireland and England, the Black and Tan war. De Valera was responsible for the dropping of a pro-Nationalist plank from the Republican Party's presidential programme, at the Republican Party Convention in Chicago during 1920. He had objected to it because it had been inserted at the behest of his Irish-American rival, Judge Cohalan, instead of a proposal which de Valera himself had drafted.

The pro-British Republicans gladly used the disagreement as an excuse for having no Irish plank in their platform. Commenting on the wrangle and its outcome, the British Ambassador of the day, Sir Auckland Geddes, made an assessment of Irish-American political clout which is as valid for our day as it was for his:

> The incident illustrates in an interesting manner the immense influence Irishmen can exert on American politicians if they proceed wisely; and how ready American politicians are to withdraw themselves from that influence if they can find some colourable pretext for doing so.[28]

As we shall see, Irishmen did not always 'proceed wisely' as they sought to influence American policy during the Troubles. The sleeping giant of Irish-American opinion was stirred into increasing life from the era of the hunger strikes onward, with an active flexing of the muscles occurring from the time William Clinton entered the presidential race.

Irish-American influence was very much a self-starting phenomenon. Since the ending of the Black and Tan war, Dublin policy-makers had proved curiously negligent of this potentially mighty asset, even where vital national interests unrelated to Northern Ireland were concerned. A story involving Tip O'Neill illustrates the point perfectly. O'Neill, one of the most powerful men in the world when the Speaker of the House (1977–86), used to say of the 1965 Immigration Act, which restricted the Irish, as it did others, from entering the States: 'I was waiting for a call from the Irish Embassy. I could have walked on to the floor of the House at any time and got the Irish exempted in five minutes. But the call never came.'

There were two reasons for the call not coming. On the question of emigration, Dublin hesitated to do anything because there was a belief abroad in the optimistic sixties that the problem would soon disappear. However, even if the sixties had not been buoyant economically, Dublin would have balked at doing anything which might be taken as not only encouraging, but even acknowledging emigration, the callous safety valve which made the containment of the Republic's economic

problems possible. The treatment of her emigrants by successive Irish governments has been a story of continuing neglect since the establishment of the state. On
the other hand Ireland had simply given up in the American popularity stakes.
Firstly, Frank Aiken, the long-time Irish foreign minister in both the fifties and
sixties, had been highly unpopular with the Roosevelt administration because of
his activities in support of Ireland's neutrality during World War II. Secondly, in
the sixties, Aiken devoted most of Ireland's diplomatic activity to the UN,
spending several months at a time in New York. The other great focus of Irish
diplomatic activity, prior to the outbreak of the Troubles, was on gaining entry to
the EEC.

Consequently Irish-American political ties were neglected to a point where, after
Bloody Sunday, Dr Hillery, Aiken's successor, found an unsympathetic reception
for Dublin's views in Washington. The British had completely taken over the high
ground. This failure to cultivate the Irish-American wing of the Irish diaspora
appears all the more remarkable when one considers the numbers involved (some
43 million Americans give their ethnic origin as Irish at census time) and the near-
papal welcome accorded to President Kennedy when he visited the land of his
ancestors in 1963. It was generally accepted in Dublin after the visit that, had he not
been assassinated, Kennedy would have given priority to the Irish issue. As a
senator he had sponsored several resolutions on Ireland and the welcome he
received there made a deep impression on him.

After his death, his youngest brother, Teddy, became the major standard-bearer
on Ireland. On 20 October 1971, he annoyed the British, and sent shivers down
cabinet spines in Dublin, by calling on the US Congress to support the withdrawal
of British troops from Ireland and the encouragement of a united Ireland. Jack
Lynch said that Kennedy did not know what he was talking about. Kennedy's
nephew Joe, who succeeded to Tip O'Neill's seat in Massachusetts, would also
take a strong pro-Nationalist position, and Teddy's sister Jean, who became the
American Ambassador to Ireland in 1993, would combine with Teddy to play a
pivotal role in the peace process. However, Irish-American strength was at such a
low ebb at the onset of the Troubles that this seemed inconceivable at the time. The
comparison between the Jewish lobby for the state of Israel and that of the Irish-
Americans for Ireland was pathetic.

There had been heavy emigration from Ireland in the fifties but the North had not
been an issue then. Accordingly no strain of radicalism crossed the Atlantic until
within a matter of months after the August 1969 burnings, when first Joe Cahill,
then Daithi O'Conaill and later Sean Keenan, another prominent Republican from
Derry, visited America. These visits resulted in the foundation of Irish Northern
Aid (NORAID) by a group of old Irish-American IRA supporters of whom the
most prominent was Mike Flannery, then in his eighties. NORAID assisted the
relatives of IRA volunteers, either on the run or in jail. Both London and Dublin
accused NORAID of being simply a front to raise money to buy guns and
explosives, but while some of its members unquestionably collected money for
such purposes, in the main the organisation did what it said it was doing and sent

clothes and money to alleviate Republican distress. This did of course indirectly help the Republicans' war effort as it freed money for other purposes.

Constitutional Irish Nationalists failed to create an organisation similar to NORAID. In the absence of any lead from Dublin the Irish in America had largely devoted their energies to the Church, or organisations like the Ancient Order of Hibernians (AOH), or to their careers and politics. Dublin's early efforts to influence American policy-makers were bedevilled, not only by indifference and the effects of British influence, but by a replication of the splits and divisions which had produced the Arms Trial saga back in Ireland. So much of the Irish diplomatic effort went into saying 'don't support the IRA' that it was sometimes very difficult for people to know what they were meant to support. This was not a new phenomenon in Irish-American affairs. The basic issue at stake – who controls the Irish in America, the Irish at home or the Irish in the US? – had been used by de Valera in 1920 in a bruising controversy to advance Dublin's claims (i.e. his own) which had ultimately led to a damaging split.

One man who was clear about what he wanted was John Hume, who made it a policy to get prominent Irish-American politicians, rather than Irish-American organisations, interested in the Northern situation. He succeeded so well that Ted Kennedy came to describe him as: '. . . one of the finest and most creative political leaders of our generation'.[29] But for several years the debate vitiated Irish lobbyists' efforts in Washington and helped to give the British a free rein in the execution of draconian security policies in Belfast. In the early seventies, yet another Redemptorist priest enters our story, Fr Sean McManus, a North of Ireland Nationalist. One of his brothers, Patrick, had been a prominent Republican who was killed during the 1950s IRA campaign. Another, Frank, became a Nationalist Unity MP for Fermanagh South Tyrone. A gifted lobbyist, McManus founded an organisation called the Irish National Caucus and proceeded to enlist the support of organisations such as the AOH and, most notably, a New York Italian congressman, Mario Biaggi, who had become interested in the Irish situation after Bloody Sunday. Biaggi eventually managed to organise an Ad Hoc Committee of congressmen and senators which at one stage claimed some 125 members. In 1979 he succeeded in getting Congress to halt the sale of weapons to the RUC because of that force's abuse of human rights.

The early aims of the Caucus were to secure hearings on Northern Ireland which would be open to all interested parties, including Republicans. Following Bloody Sunday, the leading New York Democrat, Hugh Carey, had been instrumental in getting a hearing before a subcommittee of the House Foreign Affairs Committee in the spring of 1972, but this had expressly excluded the Republicans. Visa restrictions forbade the entry of IRA or Sinn Fein spokesmen to the USA. McManus wanted these lifted. In the event McManus' most clear-cut success in the visa area lay in persuading a friendly congressman, Hamilton Fish, to go to Ireland with a colleague, Congressman Joshua Eilberg, on a fact-finding mission. The congressmen discovered that the State Department did not object to Loyalist paramilitary spokesmen visiting the US, because, in the words of the American consul in Belfast, Charles Stout, the UDA: 'did not try to overthrow the government in Northern Ireland, or kill police'.[30] As a result, from 1980 onwards the Loyalists also came under interdict.

Later goals would be widened to include a promotion of the MacBride principles. Dublin did not look with favour on either these ambitions or the Caucus tendency to praise IRA leaders like Ruairi O'Bradaigh and Daithi O'Conaill as latter-day Jeffersons and George Washingtons. Biaggi joined McManus on Dublin's hit list when the congressman gave a press conference in Dublin on 30 April 1975, in the company of a leading Caucus figure, Frederick Burns O'Brien. The attendance at the press conference included O'Bradaigh and Joe Cahill. Biaggi praised both the Caucus goals and the IRA, which he said had 'focused attention on the Six Counties'. But it was McManus who really created the red alert of the period in the Irish Department of Foreign Affairs, where Garret FitzGerald was at the time the minister.

In the week prior to Carter's election as president in 1975, the Caucus succeeded in eliciting from him a set of major commitments. Carter, who had made human rights a major plank in his platform, called for an international commission in Northern Ireland. He also said that America should play a more active part in helping to resolve the Irish conflict, and stated that the Democratic Party was committed to Irish unity. These of course were perfectly valid goals for an Irish government to have pursued. But, piqued at being upstaged by what was wrongly perceived as the pro-IRA McManus securing the ear of the President of the United States, Dublin at first called for 'clarification' of Carter's remarks. Then, reassured that Carter was not contemplating membership of the Provisional IRA, Dublin at last launched a coherent campaign to gain some influential ears of its own.

The depth of the previous neglect of the American dimension to the Anglo-Irish relationship by the Irish can be measured by the speed with which the campaign brought results. With the assistance of John Hume, the Irish Embassy in Washington assembled 'The Big Four': Tip O'Neill, Edward Kennedy, Hugh Carey and Patrick Moynihan. This formidable quartet, who became known as the Four Horsemen, were seen by Dublin primarily as 'a club with which to beat NORAID and Caucus supporters'.[31] Within a few months of Carter's inauguration, on St Patrick's Day 1977, the Big Four issued a statement which appealed to

> ... all those organisations engaged in violence to renounce their campaigns of death and destruction ... We appeal as well to our fellow Americans to embrace the goal of peace and to renounce any action that promotes the current violence or provides support or encouragement for organisations engaged in violence.

As most Irish-Americans, not merely the NORAID and Caucus elements against whom this was directed, regarded British policy as the prime cause of the northern troubles, the absence of any similar salvo directed towards London aroused great bitterness. But this leniency was not reciprocated by Whitehall, which throughout the spring and summer of 1977 used its influence on the Anglophile State Department to either block or de-nature a statement of support for the Dublin/ SDLP position which the Big Four, led by Speaker O'Neill, were seeking from the

Carter administration. As Sean Donlon, one of the Irish diplomats concerned with the Carter initiative, later wrote:

> We reckoned without the British influence and the skills of British diplomacy in exploiting to the full the special relationship between London and Washington. It took six months of patient and at times painful and bruising Irish diplomatic activity to overcome the many obstacles created by the British and to nudge the Carter administration into its new position ... The episode also starkly illustrated a problem which Irish diplomats in the US have to deal with regularly; not only are they inevitably in confrontation with IRA supporters, but they are sometimes also in confrontation with the British, even when there are important shared objectives.[32]

Some Irish diplomats worsened the problem for themselves by seeing IRA fellow-travellers where there were only Irish Nationalists anxious to do what they saw fit for their native country, free of the dictation of diplomats. For the Carter initiative, when it came on 30 August 1977, marked a breakthrough. In guarded language, the presidential statement abandoned the principle of not getting involved in the Irish situation, which hitherto had been regarded as a British sphere of influence. It said:

> I ask all Americans to refrain from supporting, with financial or other aid, organisations whose involvement direct, or indirect, in this violence delays the day when the people of Northern Ireland can live and work together in harmony ... We support the establishment of a form of Government in Northern Ireland which will command widespread acceptance throughout both parts of the community ... In the event of such a settlement the United States Government would be prepared to join with others to see how additional job-creating investment could be encouraged to the benefit of all the people of Northern Ireland.

Nine years later, during March 1986, in the wake of the Anglo-Irish Agreement, which Irish-American pressure helped to bring about, O'Neill and Kennedy used Carter's statement on investment to wrest from President Reagan a generous financial underpinning of the AIA, some $250 million in all.[33] The Biaggi/McManus forces were still powerful enough to ensure that a rider was added to the aid bill. This committed Reagan and his successors each year to assure Congress that the human rights position in the Six Counties was satisfactory, before that year's tranche of money was paid over. The rider also gave a boost to the MacBride Principles campaign on fair employment, which the McManus forces also espoused. However, Carter's coded suggestion about power-sharing, a form of government that would 'command widespread acceptance' in the Six Counties, fell on stony ground in London. Callaghan was preparing to do his deal with the Unionists which increased rather than diminished their influence on his administration. But it was not only in London that the plight of the Northern Ireland minority fell victim to political football. Dublin took a hand in the game also. And Dublin's influence has to be reckoned amongst the forces which allowed the British to use the methods which led to the Stalker/Stevens scandals.

For, having failed in 1976 to interest the State Department in the use of torture by the authorities in Northern Ireland – the Department did not even refer to Northern Ireland in its overview of the world human rights situation that year – the Caucus turned to Biaggi who, in 1977, enlisted ninety-three members of his Ad Hoc Committee in a drive to hold Congressional hearings on the issue. However, Dublin successfully lobbied O'Neill to intervene to prevent the hearings being held. As one expert has written:

> ... as far as the Irish government and its diplomatic mission were concerned, open hearings dealing with these allegations would have played into the hands of the IRA and its American supporters. To the Irish authorities it was more important that the IRA be given no opportunity to enhance its credibility than that the British be criticised for their violation of human rights.[34]

When Sean Donlon was appointed Irish Ambassador to Washington he continued vigorously to espouse a similar policy. On one occasion he wrote to Congressman Hamilton Fish about Fr Raymond Murray, who had succeeded in interesting the congressman in the miscarriage of justice involved in the case of the Birmingham Six. In support, Donlon quoted a Loyalist politician who had depicted Murray as undermining the work of the security forces. After the Carter triumph, Donlon and Michael Lillis, who had been active in the campaign to set up the Four Horsemen, persuaded the then Taoiseach, Jack Lynch, to write a letter to Biaggi attacking him for giving support to the IRA. The letter was subsequently circulated to the members of Biaggi's Ad Hoc Committee.

This caused such division in Irish-American circles that Lillis, and Jack Thornton, the editor of the New York *Irish Echo*, once got into a scuffle at a reception. Lillis had been criticising the *Irish Echo* for not following the embassy line. As Jack Holland has noted, in what Donlon himself is quoted on the cover as calling a 'very well researched book', some Irish-Americans found Donlon's behaviour 'obsessive'.[35] After Haughey became Taoiseach in 1979 he attempted to shift Donlon, but this was resisted by, amongst others, Kennedy and O'Neill. Thus, against the wishes of his Prime Minister, Donlon stayed on in Washington. When FitzGerald replaced Haughey, Donlon became Secretary of the Department of Foreign Affairs.

During this time, Haughey made a speech in New York (on 1 March 1985), in which he said:

> There has been a major failure of communication in recent decades. Conflicting and confusing signals have been coming from Ireland to the Irish in America. There has been no clear message on policy; no specifically enunciated national objective behind which all right-thinking Americans could rally and to which they could give their unambiguous up-front support. More often than not the official message was negative, condemnatory and critical ... Americans who wished only to offer genuine support and encouragement were met with suspicion, rebuff and disapproval ...

My observation of the time bore out this analysis. Dublin's strategy was based on a twin-track approach of attempting to sideline the IRA, while at the same time following Hume's example in targeting mainstream American political figures in an effort to get them to influence British policy. Dublin could, and did, point to a number of successes in the pursuit of these goals: the Carter initiative; the smooth switching of points from Carter to Reagan when the Republicans took office. This was particularly facilitated by Donlon's cultivation of William Clarke, Reagan's National Security Advisor, who became a frequent visitor to Dublin and ensured that, despite the President's admiration for Thatcher, Reagan, on occasions during the truce of the Anglo-Irish Agreement, conveyed the Irish view to the Iron Lady. Important Republican figures such as Reagan, James Baker and Ed Meese joined Edward Kennedy and Tip O'Neill at Irish Embassy functions. I once attended a St Patrick's Day event hosted by Donlon, at which my luncheon companions included Reagan, O'Neill, Teddy Kennedy and Laurence Eagleburger, not hitherto a name associated with the wearing of the Green.

However, outside this golden circle, the Irish of the worlds of the county associations, the Gaelic League, Irish dancing and Gaelic football, to whom Biaggi and the Caucus appealed, felt excluded and spoke of the 'tyranny' of the Irish consular circuit. The efforts by the small but able and energetic Irish diplomatic mission were felt throughout the Irish-American community. Subtle sanctions were applied. Invitations to consular functions were withheld, access to Irish newspapers at consulates was denied, organisers of speaking engagements at which the speaker did not appeal to the embassy circuit were called in for de-briefing sessions at which the official line would be made clear. The extent to which the attempt to, as it were, extend Section 31 of the Broadcasting Act to America was carried may be gauged from an episode involving the Irish Forum of San Francisco in 1984.

The Forum existed to provide a platform for airing the Irish issue in California. Speakers at it have included James Prior, Bishop Pike, Sile de Valera, Peter Robinson and myself. But when the founder, Pat Goggin, led a delegation to Ireland in 1984, a planned visit to the Taoiseach, Garret FitzGerald, was cancelled because during the northern leg of the Forum's tour the Americans had met Sinn Fein spokesmen. This kind of approach led many prominent Irish-Americans to go their own way. For example, Paul O'Dwyer, the veteran civil rights activist, got a group of like-minded lawyers together and founded the Brehon Law Society to take up cases involving Irish, or Irish-Americans, who, because of the Troubles, had come into conflict with American laws.

Accordingly, and not altogether surprisingly, when Haughey's return to power appeared imminent in 1987, Donlon resigned his post and went into business. By then the divisions between the consular circuit and a wide swathe of Irish-American opinion had been added to by divisions between Biaggi and McManus over the Anglo-Irish Agreement, which Biaggi supported and McManus did not. In 1987 also, Biaggi was fined and sentenced to jail on corruption charges alleging the taking of kickbacks to secure defence contracts. But there was yet another problem affecting the Irish in America which required urgent attention that year, attention that it did not always receive from the Irish Government. The problem, which was to have a significant effect on Northern Ireland, was that of the plight of the vast number of illegal Irish immigrants in the US.

This is how the situation appeared to me in 1987:

There is one problem on which every shade of Irish-American opinion could co-operate . . .
Since the 1965 Emigration Act, the Irish have increasingly come shoaling into the States on
tourist visas and then stayed on illegally to work. They can be met in the traditional Irish
centres in New York, Boston, Chicago and San Francisco, working in bars and building
sites – some with MAs and PhDs but without social security, job security, or residential
security. They are at risk if they come home for a funeral or a wedding, because their tourist
visa may not be renewed in Dublin, and they are continually subject to employer
exploitation . . . If the young Irish could be allowed to work at the jobs for which they are
qualified, rather than work illegally as waiters and so on, it would be an obvious plus for the
American economy . . .[36]

In fact by 1987 a notable turnaround on the issue had begun, though its effects had
not had time to show. This was spearheaded by a young Irish electrical engineer
from Cork, Sean Minihan, who was the prime mover behind the Irish Immigration
Reform Movement. The IIRM had enlisted a powerful ally in the Boston
congressman Brian Donnelly, who in 1986 had succeeded in getting a bill passed,
increasing the number of visas available to the Irish. The fight continued until 1991
when, with the help of Senator Ted Kennedy, a bill sponsored by another
Democrat, Congressman Bruce Morrison of Connecticut, reached the statute
books. The effect of the two bills taken together was both to regularise the position
of the existing Irish illegals and to make an increased number of visas available.
The IIRM campaign marked a watershed for tens of thousands of young Irish who
could now live legal, normal, open lives.

One of those involved was Niall O'Dowd, a former teacher from Ireland, who
had worked in Irish-American journalism in San Francisco for five years before
coming in 1985 to New York, where he and Patrica Harty founded *Irish America
Magazine*, a glossy, up-market journal devoted to Irish and Irish-American
concerns. Two years later he founded the weekly newspaper, *The Irish Voice*.
O'Dowd had been an interested participant in the IIR campaign. He had noted the
nature of both the campaign and the campaigners. The latter were younger, more
radical and better educated than their older and more conservatively Catholic
predecessors who had arrived in America in the fifties and before. They brought
their Irish education and training to bear on the American system. They sought co-
operation, not confrontation. The older county associations, the Kilkenny men, the
Tipperary men and so on, gave them support and encouragement. Their descent on
Washington won them both results and friendships.

Instead of being assailed by conflicting voices, and finding themselves caught in
crossfire between the Irish Government and the Irish-American organisations,
congressmen and senators found themselves being approached on a straight-
forward emigration issue (emigration was not then the thorny topic it later became).
I remember Congressional staff at the time saying that the young Irish lobbyists
were the most efficient and easy to deal with of their experience. A change of
government in Dublin, and a realisation of the value of what the IIRM were doing,
helped to calm the Irish-American scene also. O'Dowd, who had first become
convinced of the need to do something about the northern issue during the hunger
strikes, decided to attempt to canalise the dynamism of the newer immigrants into
helping to resolve an old controversy.

With the help of revered figures in the Irish-American community, such as Morrison, a former classmate of Bill Clinton, Ray Flynn, the Mayor of Boston, and Paul O'Dwyer and his son Brian, also a lawyer, O'Dowd began work on setting up a new organisation, Americans for a New Irish Agenda (ANIA). He found an ally in an unlikely setting, the Irish Consulate in Boston, where Brendan Scannell was the Consul. Scannell subsequently moved to Washington to become effectively the number two man in the Embassy. His advice and support were important factors in the success of the ANIA. Through *Irish America Magazine*, O'Dowd had attracted the attention of important businessmen. People who, as he says himself, 'were always interested in their Irish roots, but had never really found a vehicle for them'. Prominent amongst these were Bill Flynn, chairman of a multi-billion-dollar insurance corporation, and Chuck Feeney, the billionaire founder of the duty-free shops familiar to every air traveller, who had taken part in the emigrant campaign. Flynn would later invite both Gerry Adams and Loyalist paramilitary leaders to New York. He once paid for a group of the Loyalists to travel to America at his expense, putting them up in Fitzpatrick's Hotel, a mecca for Irish visitors from both north and south.

The ANIA had a number of policy objectives, the most important of which were the appointment of a peace envoy to Northern Ireland, the furtherance of the MacBride Principles, securing a visa for Gerry Adams and, last but not least, bringing American influence to bear in nudging the British towards a settlement process. As the 1992 presidential campaign loomed up, the ANIA leadership carefully studied the list of Democractic contenders and decided to target Clinton. O'Dowd met Clinton and was pleasantly surprised at his knowledge of and sympathy with the Irish situation, as part of his world overview of how America should react to the ending of the Cold War. Others, including John Hume and Albert Reynolds, have told me the same thing. Seemingly Clinton became interested in Ireland through being at Oxford when the civil rights campaign started, and he was aware of what had befallen the peaceful protest movement.

Clinton told the ANIA delegation, at the Sheraton Hotel on 5 April 1992, that:

> I think sometimes that we are too reluctant to engage ourselves in a positive way because of our long-standing special relationship with Great Britain and also because it seemed such a thorny problem.
>
> But I have a very strong feeling that, in the aftermath of the Cold War, we need a governing rationale for our engagement in the world – not just in Northern Ireland, with our European allies – but around the world. I think the United States is now in a position to think clearly about positive change, and about support for freedom and democracy and human rights as well as economic opportunities around the world.

The Americans for a New Irish Agenda decided to back Clinton and became 'The Irish-Americans for Clinton-Gore'. Ray Flynn became co-chairman of the Clinton campaign, Feeney a major contributor to Clinton's campaign fund, and O'Dowd used his publication enthusiastically to endorse the Arkansas Governor. Clinton later said of O'Dowd and his friends: 'Those Irish know how to thank people.'

The Clinton aide who liaised with the ANIA was Nancy Soderberg, who had handled Irish issues for Ted Kennedy. After the election she was appointed Staff Director of the National Security Council, which in effect made her the number three person in the NSC. Subsequently the ANIA would deal with the NSC, rather than with the State Department, which was regarded as being so Anglophile that one Irish-American described the personnel there as 'Brits with American accents'. Immediately after the election, O'Dowd and some of his group met the Clinton transition team at Little Rock to discuss what was and was not available. In terms of political clout and sophistication The Irish-Americans for Clinton-Gore were light years away from the simplicities of the 'Brits out' NORAIDers.

They were concerned to make it as easy as possible for Clinton to deliver on his promises, being aware of the depth and complexity of the relationship between the US and Britain. However, they decided that granting a visa to Adams and cajoling the British into some sort of peace process were both feasible objectives. The question of peace talks was in the air at that point as the Hume–Adams contacts had been revealed. O'Dowd was in touch with Adams, who writes a column for *The Irish Voice*, and also with Kieran Staunton, an old friend of both himself and Adams, who was also one of Sinn Fein's principal activists in America. He was not aware of what was happening in the Hume–Adams talks, nor of the contact between Sinn Fein and the British. In fact, probably the only people fully aware of who was saying what, when, and to whom were Gerry Adams and a small circle in the Sinn Fein and IRA leadership. Such people believe strongly in keeping their lions in separate cages, and there was no loose talking.

However, O'Dowd and Bruce Morrison put together a delegation of Irish-Americans for the Clinton-Gore team and made arrangements for a visit to Ireland in September 1993. This was to prove an important event. Before leaving America, O'Dowd was in a position to inform the Clinton administration that there would be an IRA ceasefire to mark their visit. The delegation in turn brought with them a letter from Clinton which criticised aspects of the northern statelet, such as the 2:5 unemployment ratio against Catholics, and the 'wanton use of lethal force' by the security forces. Significantly, the letter warned against 'further collusion' between these forces and the Loyalist paramilitaries. In Ireland the Irish-Americans met all the key players, the Taoiseach, the Deputy Prime Minister, the Unionists, Sir Patrick Mayhew, and the leadership of Sinn Fein. During the meeting with the Republicans the IRA did call a seven-day ceasefire and it was made clear that Sinn Fein regarded the visa for Adams as a key issue. The ceasefire and the concentration on the visa issue were a clear signal to the delegation of the importance Sinn Fein placed on the American dimension. O'Dowd and company decided to make the granting of the visa their number one priority.

At this stage two new and vital figures have to be introduced. The first is Albert Reynolds, who succeeded Haughey as Taoiseach in February 1992. Haughey was forced to resign when revelations about a phone tapping scandal caused his coalition partners, the small Progressive Democrats Party, to threaten to withdraw from partnership in government with Fianna Fail unless Haughey went. The other pivotal figure is Jean Kennedy Smith, whose nomination as American Ambassador to Ireland was announced by President Clinton on St Patrick's Day 1993. Behind her stood her brother, Senator Ted Kennedy, the man who, after President Clinton himself, had most influence over Irish policy in America. The alignment of forces on the side of Irish nationalism had suddenly achieved a coherence and an influence which was unparalleled in historical terms. Not even in Parnell's time, when, in what was known as the New Departure, the Fenians, the Land League and the forces of constitutionalism joined together under his leadership, had such a powerful coalition been forged. The strength of the American connection, coupled with Reynolds' emergence on the scene, had added a new dimension to the Irish question.

Niall O'Dowd assessed Reynolds' contribution as follows:

> Albert Reynolds made the greatest personal contribution of anyone. I think everyone else in this issue is peripheral. If the Irish Prime Minister is not going to go for the Golden Glove, no one else can reach for it. Everything that we did he enhanced. I will always remember the first meeting with him in September '93. He shut the door, threw all his aides out and he talked to us for two hours solid. Everything he said in that meeting he delivered on. It was extremely impressive for us to see him being this straightforward and being this committed.
>
> For many years Irish-Americans had a lot of lip service from people who should have known better and I think Reynolds probably more than anyone else deserves the number one slot for his dynamic approach to the issue.[37]

Reynolds' 'dynamic approach'[38] on the northern situation surprised most people who had studied his career. He had seemed the archetypal Fianna Fail business-man-turned-politician. He had built up a fortune operating dance halls and manufacturing dog food and, before becoming Taoiseach at the age of sixty, his political priorities appeared to be indicated by the ministerial portfolios he had held, those dealing with industry and finance. However, his very business contacts had given him both an interest and an insight into the northern problem. His native county of Longford is nearer the border, both geographically and psychologically, than Dublin, and partition was consistently a live topic in his area. Moreover his business frequently brought him into contact with Unionists several times a day.

He was aware that, despite the shrill obduracy of Unionist politicians' rhetoric, ordinary Protestant businessmen and their families, with no vested interest in intransigence, were prepared to be more reasonable.[39] A countryman with a countryman's relaxations, the affable Reynolds regularly attended greyhound and horse races with such people, and had no difficulty in relating to them. Also, his shrewd political antennae had been picking up the different sounds emanating from the various Sinn Fein statements about 'self-determination'. A family man himself, he decided that 'these lads are getting to the age where their kids are coming up and they'd like to see a bit of peace'. Accordingly, on taking office he surprised his aides by declaring: 'Gentlemen, my priority as Taoiseach will be Northern Ireland. If that means my taoiseachship will be of short duration, well so be it.' His taoiseachship was to be of short duration, but not because of Northern Ireland. However, before he vacated his office, Albert Reynolds was to go a good way towards achieving his priority.

The Clonard connection and a long talk with John Hume in his first few days in the taoiseach's chair confirmed him in his view that the current northern scene offered what he terms 'possibilities'. Hume was able to give him a first-hand evaluation of Adams and of Republican thinking, the calibre of its leadership, its willingness and more importantly its ability to deliver. Hume's assessment of the situation was an essential factor in Reynolds' thinking. After talking to Hume, Reynolds saw clearly that trying to make peace in Ireland without talking to the IRA was like trying to make peace in Vietnam without talking to the Vietcong. This of course involved talking to Loyalist paramilitaries also. He decided that the time had come to recognise the reality that the way to stop the violence was to bring both sets of paramilitaries into the mainstream of political life.

An important consideration in the overall situation was Reynolds' relationship with John Major. The two had become friendly on the European circuit, in their respective capacities as finance ministers. Both were self-made men, streetwise politicians with an innate sense of decency. One of the ironies of their situation was that, uniquely in the Anglo-Irish relationship, the English Prime Minister was not in the same position of strength as his Irish counterpart. Throughout the peace process, and indeed up to the time of his re-election as Tory leader, the London leader has been in a weaker position than the Dublin one domestically. Reynolds began by sacking eight of the twelve members of the existing Fianna Fail cabinet when he took over and was completely in control of his party. Major, having inherited a Conservative Party fissured over Europe, had to soldier on with a complement of what he himself on a famous occasion termed 'bastards'. The 'bastards', the right wing of the party, who regard Europe, the Irish, the unions, as part of the sub-species who conned them out of an empire that most of them will still not fully acknowledge has disappeared, would prove a retarding factor in the days that lay ahead.

Initially, at their first prime ministerial meeting, on 26 February 1992, Reynolds found that Major was not really interested in the Irish situation. He had not been to Ireland until 1990 and had never read the Government of Ireland Act. It is a curious anomaly of British politics that the one continuing life-and-death issue of a quarter-century's duration did not and does not figure in MPs' postbags. Even though Major himself had begun his premiership by narrowly missing death from an IRA rocket, he had no sense of the Irish issue being a priority. Reynolds set out to both engage his attention and increase his friendship. Three steps which Reynolds undertook to further these aims deserve particular mention. The first was aimed at settling Major's doubts about what Reynolds told him about the new thinking in the IRA and the ability of Adams and the others to deliver. Was there any tangible evidence that the IRA had any intention of stopping the violence?

From his increasing contact with the Republicans, Reynolds had learned of an important development involving the IRA on the continent, specifically in Germany. The German authorities had made plans for a massive clampdown on the IRA units which were targeting British service personnel and British military installations in Germany, sometimes with disastrous results for innocent civilians. The plan envisaged a deployment of all the ruthless Teutonic efficiency which had demolished the Baader-Meinhof gang. But a group of German clergy intervened and succeeded in negotiating a cessation of the campaign. Reynolds was able to inform Major that the attacks on his soldiers were to stop. At that stage Major had heard nothing of this from his own intelligence people. He was duly impressed when enquiries revealed that Reynolds was right.

The second step concerned the peace envoy idea for which the Irish-Americans had secured President Clinton's backing. This proposal had always been regarded by Unionists with anger and suspicion. The peace envoy was envisaged as being in reality a Nationalist emissary, blessed by the White House in his efforts to undermine them. The British, for their part, were so enraged at the prospect of intrusion on their turf that, on the day Clinton was installed as President, Whitehall briefed journalists in London that the dropping of the peace envoy idea would be the Conservatives' first demand on the new administration.

Reynolds reckoned that if he secured a staying of Clinton's hand on the envoy appointment his gains in Major's confidence would outweigh the losses in his popularity with Irish-Americans. Accordingly he put it to Clinton (on St Patrick's Day 1993) that it would assist his 'big picture approach', as he termed it, if the envoy proposal were put on the back burner. Clinton accepted Reynolds' suggestion, although he did point out to him that the Irish-Americans had been helpful to him in his campaign and that he would come under pressure to honour his promise. Major, however, was suitably impressed at Reynolds' gesture, and, as matters unfolded, O'Dowd and company ultimately wound up in Belfast being their own peace envoys. Reynolds' other major contribution was to 'deliver' for Major at the EC Summit at Edinburgh, which was staged during the British presidency. Major was reluctant to contemplate the budgetary increases which European enlargement implied for the structural and convergence funds. But Reynolds helped to soothe his doubts with an account of a meeting which he had had earlier with the man who was in effect the real paymaster of Europe, Germany's Chancellor, Helmut Kohl. Kohl was in fact envisaging an even greater expansion than occurred, and was prepared for the consequential expense. Behind the scenes Reynolds also conducted an extensive lobbying operation on behalf of the enlargement with other European countries, the Dutch in particular. Major backed the enlargement at Edinburgh and the British presidency ended on a far more positive note than had seemed possible during the earlier, unhappy summit at Birmingham. All these things helped to bring Major aboard the Irish peace train.

The train had a very small crew. Major and Reynolds met either *tête-à-tête*, or with a limited circle of civil servants and advisors. Initially Reynolds brought with him only Dermot Nally, the former Secretary to the Government, whom he enticed back from retirement. Nally was the Old Man of the Mountains so far as the Irish Civil Service was concerned, his youthful, fit physique making it difficult to believe that he had served under a total of six Irish prime ministers. However, anyone who faced him across a table soon discovered that in that lengthy period Nally had forgotten nothing and learned much. At the first Major–Reynolds meeting Major quickly noted his calibre, and as he and Reynolds got further into the discussion on the Six Counties he pointed to Nally and said, 'No pencils, please!' Subsequently Nally was joined by Sean O'hUiginn, the head of the Anglo-Irish Desk at Foreign Affairs.

O'hUiginn, a diplomat's diplomat, who enjoys displaying his skills as either arabist or francophile, has the reputation amongst his colleagues of having a fondness for 'talking in spiritual terms'. His spirituality is inclined to evaporate at the conference table, where his pinstripes show a tendency to end in a sharp point. The third member of the Reynolds team, Martin Mansergh, is something of an exotic in the smoke-filled backrooms of Fianna Fail. The party's head of research and northern expert, he floats rather grandly above the grime of day-to-day politicking. A surprised BBC reporter, who had just met him for the first time, described him as sounding 'just like an upper-class Brit'. Mansergh, a son of the distinguished British public servant and historian, Nicholas Mansergh, is in fact devoutly Republican in sentiment, and a political analyst of laser-beamed acuity. He is also a Protestant, a fact which Reynolds made use of to impress James Molyneaux.

Another Irish civil servant who should be mentioned is Noel Dorr. Dorr, who was the Irish representative at the UN charged with executing Haughey's Falklands policy, subsequently drew the short straw and became the Irish Ambassador to London! The experience stood him in good stead in the 1992–4 era of the Anglo-Irish relationship, during which he was the Secretary of the Department of Foreign Affairs. As the Department could also call on figures such as Brendan Scannell (back in Dublin to take charge of the administration of the Ireland Fund set up under Reagan at the time of the Anglo-Irish Agreement) and David Donoghue (one of the brighter stars of the rising school of younger diplomats, who served under O'hUiginn at the Anglo-Irish desk), the Irish at official, as well as political level, at this moment in Anglo-Irish relationships, were able to field an unusually strong team.

The strength was added to rather than diminished by an incident towards the end of 1992 which at first sight bade fair to remove Reynolds from the scene altogether. Concurrent with the events of the peace process described so far, another, very Irish drama was being played out. The great Irish saga of legend and epic poetry is known as the *Tain Bo Cuailagne* (the Cattle Spoil of Cooley), a war which broke out between the men of Ulster and those of the west over a bull. Now, in contemporary times, as events of great moment were again taking place in the affairs of Ulster, another, costly, comic-opera version of the Spoilation of the Tain was also taking place. The main beneficiaries of this were lawyers who represented witnesses before a tribunal set up to investigate allegations of fraud in the Irish beef industry. Ultimately the tribunal would cost £35 million in direct costs, and at the time of writing the mandarins in Brussels were preparing to fine the Irish Government, i.e. the tax-payers, something in excess of £100 million arising out of the various allegations of evasion and skulduggery which, no pun intended, formed the meat of the tribunal's investigations.

All the tribunal itself resulted in was a burst of well-publicised activity without movement. There was some quite sharp criticism of individuals and of the industry in the report.[40] Albert Reynolds and the Government Press Secretary, Sean Duignan, pulled off a public relations stroke of monumental proportions by getting out a version of it to the media in advance of official publication, which put

Reynolds in a relatively good light. As one political commentator described the Reynolds/Duignan version: 'There were a number of extracts quoted, then a few dots, then a few more extracts. What was not pointed out was that the few full stops covered about thirty-seven missing pages of criticism!'[41] This piece of spin-doctoring so soured relationships between Reynolds and his coalition partner, Dick Spring, that it was a contributory factor in Spring's subsequently pulling out of coalition with Fianna Fail.

But no criminal blame attached to any individual. No one went to jail. The barrister who represented the chief beef baron involved later became the Attorney-General. The chairman of the tribunal was appointed Chief Justice. However, in the course of his evidence Reynolds appeared to cast doubts on the honesty of one of the architects of the tribunal, Desmond O'Malley, the leader of the Progressive Democrats. During his term as minister in a previous cabinet, O'Malley had stopped the granting of government export credits for insurance to companies sending beef to unstable areas, such as the Middle East, because of his disquiet at practices within the industry. Now, at the material time, he was a minister in the coalition partnership with Albert Reynolds and Fianna Fail.

His party was in fact a Fianna Fail Adam's rib. O'Malley, having tried unsuccessfully to lead a revolt within the party against Haughey, had eventually been expelled from Fianna Fail (in 1984) for taking issue with Haughey on the latter's assertion that unity was the solution to the Irish problem. He founded the Progressive Democrats in 1985 and in 1992 succeeded in forcing Haughey's resignation as Taoiseach, after Haughey had had to bring the Progressive Democrats into coalition in 1989. Again in coalition with Fianna Fail under Albert Reynolds, this time in July 1992, O'Malley went before the beef tribunal to say that he found some of Reynolds' actions as Minister for Industry and Commerce 'grossly unwise, reckless and foolish'.

Reynolds hit back two months later when his turn came before the tribunal. He said that he found O'Malley's remarks 'reckless, irresponsible and dishonest'. O'Malley pressed for a withdrawal, and when this was not forthcoming, withdrew from government.

The result was a general election on 25 November 1992. Reynolds and Fianna Fail were badly mauled. Fianna Fail lost nine seats (falling to sixty-eight) and dropped to 30 per cent of the vote, the lowest total recorded since 1927.

Throughout all this period Reynolds kept his nerve where the north was concerned. He continued in contact with Major, who remained supportive of the peace initiative, although he did once drop a fly at Reynolds by asking him if he thought he would be still around when the time came to conclude a deal. Reynolds brushed this off with an airy 'Of course!'

And around he was. Some hard bargaining with the main beneficiary of the election, Dick Spring, the leader of the Labour Party, which practically doubled its representation, to thirty-three seats, resulted in Reynolds emerging once again as Taoiseach, this time at the head of a Fianna Fail/Labour coalition. Thus, although his representation had fallen, Reynolds, with over 100 seats (in a Dail of 166 members), was leading a stronger government than ever when the Irish-American delegation showed up in his office in September 1993.

Spring too proved himself committed to a resolution of the northern conflict. As Labour Party leader he had shaped Labour Party policy so that by the time of the 1992 general election the party was effectively calling for a review of Articles Two and Three. In his first major speech after he and Reynolds hammered out the coalition arrangement, in which he became Foreign Minister and Deputy Taoiseach, he said that the Government would be prepared to change the articles and put any agreement which eventuated from any new dialogue to the people by way of referendum. He went on:

> Our besetting failure on the nationalist side has been a persistent tendency to underestimate the depth and strength of the Unionist identity. We are perhaps only now coming to terms with the full dimensions of this reality. We have amends to make for this failure, no less than others for theirs. Our two traditions cannot become frozen in a kind of sullen stalemate which allows terrorism to proliferate.[42]

However, after a summer spent working without result against the 'depth and strength' of Unionist and Tory back-bench obduracy, these liberal sentiments sounded less frequently. By July he was engaged with both elements on two fronts. In Brussels, as part of his bargaining position to secure a huge aid package for the Republic from the EU (roughly £8 billion), he was held responsible for delaying £2.5 billion for the UK. In the north he was execrated by Unionists when, on 8 July, pointedly on the morning of an Irish Inter-Governmental Conference, he suggested that the two governments should agree above their heads. (John Hume had been driven to the same conclusion earlier in the year.) He proposed that Dublin should come to agreement and submit it to the people by way of referendum. Later that month he criticised the Tory–Unionist deal over Maastricht, and in his subsequent public utterances continued to push the idea that governments should act independently in the face of any Unionist boycott of talks.

To some degree, Spring had come up against the reality of Six Counties politics. There has to be an element of coercion in any NI settlement, in this sense: progress will only come by London and Dublin working constructively together, and not by the decision-takers, with the power of initiative, merely sitting back waiting for a far-distant day when the birth rate will do the politicians' work for them. No gross step can or should be contemplated, such as forcing the Unionists either out of the union or into a united Ireland. Such would be a recipe for civil war. But in September–December 1993 – as at the time of writing, and as it will remain in the future – a basic 'Canute' factor in Unionist political philosophy had to be by-passed. If this had not happened, both Anglo-Irish relations and those within the Six Counties between Nationalists and Unionists could not proceed on a normal, organic basis of democratic development. Without such by-passing there would have been no peace process.

The following are the positions of the two largest Unionist parties, as they themselves spelled them out in the period under review. First the Ulster Unionist Party:

Union with Great Britain is a union in the hearts and minds of the Unionist People and something which we cannot change even if we wanted to. This feeling of Britishness is so deeply engrained as to be almost genetically encoded . . . for Unionists their basic political heritage is their Britishness. Failure to recognise this is a fundamental and enduring mistake of Irish nationalism . . .

While the rest of the Irish people choose a Gaelic, nationalist and independent Ireland, Unionists show a clear preference for continued membership of a modern, pluralist and liberal democracy . . . Britishness in its best form seeks to manifest a tolerance and respect for different cultures: pluralistic and exhibiting a common decency, it does not seek to interfere with the faith, creed or aspiration of any group . . .

Unionists have the right to say *yes* to a 32-county state but they also have the right to say *no*. The so-called guarantee to Unionists by Westminster is simply an acceptance of reality . . . to countenance an independent 32-county Irish Republic is for Unionists, by definition, impossible.[43]

The Democratic Unionist Party position was spelled out by Ian Paisley, who attacked Dublin because it:

poses the problem in terms of the very existence of Northern Ireland and not as a problem of governing Northern Ireland within the United Kingdom.[44]

On Articles 2 and 3 Paisley said:

There can be no peace between Northern Ireland and the Irish Republic until this illegal, criminal and immoral claim is given up. Unilaterally made, it must be unilaterally withdrawn. Dublin must recognise Ulster's right to self-determination. It must be prepared to spell out Northern Ireland's status as an integral part of the UK both *de facto* and *de jure* . . . Let me make it perfectly clear that these talks are not and cannot be about any re-negotiation of the union.

While Nationalist assent to these propositions would understandably not be forthcoming, they do not nevertheless add up to an unreasonable political position. The 'Canute factor' emerges subsequently in the DUP submission:

Continuous bleating that communities cannot express their identities and aspirations and that institutions must be created to allow 'accommodation' has led to such folly as the Anglo-Irish Agreement . . . The truth is that as political philosophies, Ulster Unionism and Irish nationalism are irreconcilable. Unionists cannot have their cake and let the Irish Republic eat it. The Irish Republic received its share of the cake in 1921–22 and confirmed its acceptance, legally, formally and internationally, in 1925.

Thus Paisley continued, after twenty-five years of bloodshed, to deny the validity of the Nationalist identity and attempted to put the clock back to the settlements of the 1920s, as though the era of the Anglo-Irish Agreement had never dawned. Paisley was still trying to take down the tricolour in the window, just as he had been attempting to do when he provoked Belfast's first riots of the sixties.

But while Paisley and his ilk continue to try to turn the clock backwards, there are signs that the Troubles have brought both attitudinal and statistical changes. While these are, unfortunately, not all benign, they have to be borne in mind while attempting to analyse the environment in which the search for peace took place. Firstly, insofar as the Official Unionists' definition of their Britishness is concerned, it would be fair to say that for most of the conflict the Republican response would have been to simply point out the reality of how the Unionists, in power, chose to exercise it: not with reference to British standards of justice and fair play, but in the worst traditions of Orangeism's bigotry and discrimination against Catholics. From failing to accept that Nationalists had any grievances, they then moved blandly on to a position where these, 'if they ever existed', were now 'resolved'.

However, speaking on 5 May 1995, at a significant occasion, the fourteenth anniversary commemoration of Francis Hughes' death on hunger strike and the seventy-ninth anniversary of James Connolly's execution, Jim Gibney struck a more accommodating note:

> . . . we must reassess our historical attitude to those almost one million people who are of British origin and have lived on this island for several hundred years. They have carried their sense of Britishness with them during this time and while at one level it was a source of conflict at another level they have contributed to what constitutes the Irish nation today . . . nationalists must rediscover those positive aspects of Britishness of a sizeable section of the Irish people. The same is true of those who display Britishness. They too must examine their past and rediscover their Irishness . . .

Obviously it would be in the Unionists' interests to actively engage with this kind of thinking. But there is still a hankering after the old days, a refusal to recognise that a basic component of Unionism is gone for ever – supremacy. A second problem for Unionism is the unacknowledged fact that, for all their talk of British heritage, a majority of the British on the 'UK mainland' would cheerfully vote them out of the Union if they ever got the opportunity do so by way of referendum.

At a premier of Frank McGuinness' play, *Observe the Sons of Ulster marching Towards the Somme*, in Dublin, I met the wife of then British Ambassador and asked her what she thought of this depiction of 'her fellow countrymen'. She replied instinctively, with horror: 'Them! I've nothing to do with them. That tribe.' But in a very real sense that 'tribe' had died in their thousands at the Somme for what many of their descendants still believed she represented. The feeling of loss, and of near betrayal, which Sir Kenneth Bloomfield spoke of after Stormont fell is deeply felt in the Unionist community. There is a saying amongst the Unionist community which also relates to the Somme carnage: 'We were lions led by donkeys.'

Protestants have an increasing sense of grievance. 'The Catholics get everything' is a common sentiment. A Protestant community leader in Derry spoke for his co-religionists across the province when he told the Opsahl Commission: 'The central government believes resources must be invested in the DLP to stop Sinn Fein. Britain throws all the money at the Catholics.'[45] But, instead of being encouraged by their leaders to do as the Catholics have done, agitate for a fairer share of the cake, the Protestants tend to react by moving out. In Derry at the time of writing there are in effect two Derrys, the Catholic area to the west of the Foyle

River which is very definitely Derry, and the Protestant Waterside across the river which is equally definitively Londonderry.

The community leader explained why the Protestants had fled: 'In a situation of a Catholic majority, Protestants move away. Protestants are happier and safer when they feel they are in a majority.'[46] That mind set has led to a Protestant migration to the east, which has left the Catholics with almost 60 per cent of the statelet's land mass. And the migration does not stop at the seashore. The middle class, whose children should be providing the Protestant élite of the future, are increasingly sending their children to be educated in English universities and, *ipso facto*, to mainland English society. The result is that the Catholic enrolment at Queen's University, Belfast, is nearing the 65 per cent mark.

Meanwhile, on the ground in working-class areas, as Protestants move out or lose heart, as many have done since the Anglo-Irish Agreement, great swathes of Protestant heartland become an educational desert. For example, the Church of Ireland Bishop Dr Samuel Poyntz has said that 'only 4% passed the Eleven-Plus in 1987. Only ten children passed in 1988 . . . There's only one secondary school for the whole area, while in the Falls there are plenty. The Shankill is not getting educated, but the Catholics have a good set-up.'[47]

Nothing in the core values expressed above by the two major Unionist parties is even remotely tailored to addressing the reality of the education vacuum. There is a leadership deficit on the Unionist and Loyalist side. Under the old Stormont regime Protestants were encouraged by the system, dominated by the landowner and the industrialist, not to protest, even when their conditions were as bad as those of the Catholics. Protest was equated with disloyalty. As a result the Protestants lack cohesion. Sectarian violence on the part of young Protestant paramilitaries, whether assisted by a hidden British hand or not, was a logical outcome of growing frustration before the ceasefires. The young braves saw a diminishing Protestant community and a Catholic community in the ascendant, growing in confidence and economic and political expertise. The territorial imperative prescribed only one answer to the situation. Its results may be charted in Catholic graveyards.

Ironically the Republicans appear to be more keenly aware than are the Unionist politicians of the problems posed for the future by the existence of a disaffected lumpenproletariat. A Sinn Fein activist surprised me by remarking that: 'When things settle down a little and we can be seen talking to each other, we'll show them how it's done, electioneering, campaigning, using the system, that sort of thing. We'll train them.' At first sight those remarks might appear arrogant. But the Opsahl Commission was told, some three years before the Sinn Feiner made his comments:

> The Catholic political future is vibrant, active, with a dynamic civil society – they have, for example, a profusion of community groups. The Protestant community, by comparison, is apolitical. Outside the public life of the churches, civil society barely exists.[48]

But while Catholics have made great strides psychologically and politically, they have made far fewer gains economically than the Protestants generally imagine. The European Parliament's Committee on Social Affairs, Employment and the

Working Environment[49] tabled a report on 18 March 1994, stating that although anti-discrimination legislation of a 'high order' had been introduced, the legislation 'over the last 20 years has not brought about any substantial improvement in the employment of Northern Irish Catholics'. The *Directory of Discrimination*[50] has stated that Catholic unemployment is 'steadily increasing', with knock-on effects for the future and an even greater potential for disaster than exists in the demoralised Protestant community:

> 52% of schoolchildren aged fifteen years or under in Northern Ireland are of Catholic origin. Throughout the coming decade, young Catholics will be flooding on to the employment market in a ratio of 5:1 of their co-religionists currently in employment; while the ratio of young Protestants will be 2:1.[51]

I mentioned earlier the percentage of Catholic students attending Queen's University, roughly 65 per cent. The *Directory of Discrimination* avers that academic staff in 1991 was 90.7 per cent Protestant and 'other', to only 9.3 per cent Catholic. A Catholic solicitor working in the field told me that there are discrimination claims in excess of £5 million outstanding against the universities. The *Directory* also cited damning statistics in the higher reaches of industry and the financial institutions. For example, in the building societies, regional managers based in Northern Ireland were 100 per cent Protestant, and managers and senior staff 92 per cent Protestant. Three major banks, the Northern, Trustee Savings, and Ulster, recorded managerial percentages of 92, 94 and 93 respectively. One could go on, but the message is unmistakable: whilst change has brought uncertainty and population movement to the Protestant community, the Six Counties overall has enormous economic problems. Catholics can, and do, achieve success in private business and the professions, but a good deal of institutional discrimination remains to be tackled. This is why, despite the resistance of those who argue that they can lead to disinvestment, the MacBride Principles have gained a wide measure of Catholic support. Only a sustained period of peace, new inward investment and, even more important, new forward thinking will solve the north's deep-rooted economic problems.

For all their seemingly rational rhetoric, there is little evidence of this occurring in the ranks of the major Unionist parties. The Opsahl Report concludes with this devastatingly appropriate cautionary tale:

> Clifford Smyth, formerly of the DUP, appeared to argue a Unionist case that he described as 'fair, rational and moderate'. He even said that Protestants 'might accept a united Ireland some day'. Yet a month later, Dr Smyth organised a conference at Orange House where his first speaker, Michael de Semlyn, railed that not only was the Pope the anti-Christ and that all Catholics were 'lost on a road paved with idolatry and superstition', but that after the fall of communism, the Vatican was poised to take over the world through the evil machinations of the Maastricht treaty. Asked how he felt about the speech, Dr Smyth said he was well pleased.

The writer of the report[52] summed up accurately: 'Students who perform nicely for teacher will often get up to mischief when they are allowed out to play.'

Obviously, therefore, if London and Dublin are ever going to move ahead, they will, in some degree, have to do this without Unionist agreement. John Hume in fact advocated such a course on 29 March 1993, when the three-stranded approach was breaking down in the face of Unionist obduracy. He suggested that the British and Irish governments should get around the Unionists' refusal to return to talks by agreeing on proposals and then submitting these to the people, north and south of the border, by way of referendum.

At the time, however, this brought a torrent of abuse upon his head from the Unionist parties, the British, and some of the parties in the Republic; and a studied rejection from the Dublin Government, which said that the only way to get the situation moving was by all-party round-table talks.[53] Here Reynolds was masking his hand somewhat, as he was in fact attempting to reach a solution through agreement with London. Using the Fr Reid/Martin Mansergh channel he had been in touch with the Republicans, and was constantly in contact with John Major. As Mansergh has noted, he 'picked up the threads of the proposed initiative [begun under Haughey], and pushed it with vigour'.[54] Between April 1992 and June 1993 Reynolds masterminded what he called a 'formula for peace'.

This had to bear in mind both what the traffic would bear in London and the 'Brits out' aims of Sinn Fein. There were problems between Reynolds' office and Sinn Fein over the timescale for agreement and the definition of what was meant by the term 'self-determination'. Did it apply to all Ireland, or just to the Six Counties? In addition Sinn Fein were determined to cast London in the role of a persuader to convince the Unionists of the wisdom of a united Ireland. The likelihood of achieving this goal may be assessed by reference to the mind set of the Unionists as set out already above. But above all there was the problem of a democratic, western European government, bound by international agreements to respect existing boundaries, trying to enforce Sinn Fein's interpretation of 'consent' on the Unionists. Under the terms of the Anglo-Irish Agreement this simply could not be done. What was voted on in the south could not be made binding in the north. The Republic had always given a *de facto* recognition to the Six Counties, and in real terms the Anglo-Irish Agreement, for all the Unionist wrath it elicited, had converted this into virtual *de jure* recognition.

However, Martin Mansergh claims that 'the initial draft went to the outer limits of what was acceptable'.[55] It was submitted to the British in June 1993:

> ... not without much soul-searching on the Republican side, the draft was handed over to the British Government by the Taoiseach. To say that they handled it with kid gloves would be something of an understatement. They were prepared to discuss but not negotiate it, and on several occasions in the autumn of 1993 many of them would have preferred to sideline it.[56]

As I have already explained, there were parallel sets of talks continuing at this time between the Irish-Americans and the Republicans, between the Republicans and the British, and between John Hume and Gerry Adams. The attacks on Hume which these had generated in March were as nothing to the wrath which broke around his head in September when, on the 25th, he and Adams issued another statement stating that they were forwarding a report on their discussions to Dublin on which, they said, '. . . a process can be designed to lead to agreement among the divided people of this island, which will provide a solid basis for peace'.[57] The statement said that the two were suspending their talks pending consideration of their report.

Hume was under tremendous pressure from his party, who felt that he was giving legitimacy to their enemy, Sinn Fein, by engaging in dialogue with Adams. There was a feeling that he was not keeping the party sufficiently well informed about his activities. The deputy leader of the party, Seamus Mallon, in particular, expressed reservations about the talks, as did the West Belfast MP Dr Hendron, who stood to lose his seat to Adams if and when a Westminster election was called. As Loyalist fears mounted amidst talk of deals and sell-outs, the UFF placed bombs at the homes of four SDLP councillors. Up to now Hume had set the agenda for Dublin where Northern Ireland was concerned. It was a very personal and fundamentally decent approach. He was the one intellectual politician thrown up by constitutional nationalism in Northern Ireland. If Dublin had to deal with the north, against its will, then John Hume's formula for so dealing was the way to do it: reform within the system; no interference with the rights of property and the middle class; a divided people must resolve their differences within the parameters of the Six Counties. Now, however, other times and other men had crept up on him.

Hume's evolution from opposition towards recognition of the authenticity and strength of the Republican current was something of an embarrassment for Reynolds. He had to recognise the reality behind the Republican taunt: 'St John'. There had been times during the Troubles when Hume, with his mastery of the media and his debating skills, could have stood for any party in any constituency in the Republic, and been elected. On the other hand, Dublin's long period of sheltering behind the fig leaf of the SDLP's 'respectability' on the smelly subject of the north had now to be faced up to. Reynolds was in the process of making respectable the Great Unwashed, Sinn Fein, at the same time as Hume was undertaking this very exercise for his own puposes.

Suffering from the strain of his talks and the criticism they engendered, Hume now compounded Dublin's dilemma. Having joined in the Hume–Adams statement, and announced that proposals were on the way to the Dublin Government, he then took off for America on a previously arranged trade mission. He did not make a formal report on his discussion with Adams to Reynolds and Dick Spring until 7 October 1993. He told the Irish Government leaders that he and Adams had agreed that these proposals would form the basis of a peace initiative. Adams corroborated this in a speech the same day. Subsequently, John Major told Hume (on 1 November) that the Hume–Adams initiative was 'not the way to proceed'. Meanwhile, Adams and Sinn Fein reaped an enormous media harvest and Loyalist fears literally grew to murderous proportions at the presumed prospect of a 'pan-Nationalist front' becoming a reality.

All this proved to be too much for Major and Reynolds. It was one thing for Reynolds to attempt to bring Sinn Fein in from the cold, it was another to expect a Tory prime minister to convince his back-benchers of the worth of settlement proposals bearing Gerry Adams' fingerprints. And of course, the most significant point of all, Adams' concept of self-determination applied to the whole country, not merely the Six Counties. To Sinn Fein, restricting self-determination to that area of the country alone meant that effectively the word 'consent' translated as 'veto'. Accordingly, at an EU summit in Brussels on 29 October, Major and Reynolds agreed to put some space between themselves and the Hume–Adams initiative while proceeding towards a Joint Declaration along the lines suggested by the Reynolds 'peace formula'.

The Reynolds–Major Brussels communiqué said:

> The Taoiseach gave the Prime Minister an account of the outcome of the Hume/Adams dialogue in the light of the Irish Government's own assessment of these and other related matters. They acknowledge John Hume's courageous and imaginative efforts. The Prime Minister and Taoiseach agreed that any initiative can only be taken by the two Governments, and there could be no question of their adopting or endorsing the report of the dialogue which was recently given to the Taoiseach ... They agreed that the two Governments must continue to work together in their own terms on a framework for peace ...
>
> There could be no secret agreements or understandings between governments and organisations supporting violence as a price for its cessation.[58]

Hume was informed on 2 November that the Irish Government would prefer it if he would 'stand back' while the two governments moved on 'to another plane'. The strain of the whole affair told on him and he was admitted to hospital suffering from exhaustion on 8 November. Reynolds acquiesced in this, in effect, hanging out Hume to dry, '... on the firm understanding that the Draft Declaration would be pursued'.[59] As we shall see, however, the British did not keep their side of the bargain. One of the toughest bouts of behind-the-scenes diplomacy since those that occurred during the fraught days of Irish neutrality in World War II now lay ahead.

But, before the scenes, what also lay ahead was an even bigger detonation of publicity than accompanied the Hume–Adams affair. The British–Sinn Fein talks became public knowledge. Sufficient speculation about the talks' existence had crept into the media for Sinn Fein to have communicated with the British in July and August criticising leaks, which were ascribed to RUC and NIO sources, and questioning British commitment to the talks. On 5 November 1993, in response to a communication from Sinn Fein, the British virtually closed off the talks avenue. A message to Sinn Fein quoted the passage from the Brussels communiqué quoted above and stated:

> It is the public and consistent position of the British Government that any dialogue could only follow a permanent end to violent activity.[60]

This statement of course has to be evaluated in the light of the fact that the British had been conducting 'dialogue' with Sinn Fein for the previous three years. But it also marked a point at which figures in the British intelligence community apparently decided that the time was ripe to expose the talks. The Belfast journalist Eamon Mallie first broke the story on 8 November. The subsequent burst of outraged denials are a classic example of why the words of British politicians have come to be treated with extreme reserve in Dublin. Sir Patrick Mayhew kicked off by telling the BBC's breakfast-time TV (on 16 November):

> There has been no negotiating with Sinn Fein, no official, as I see, is alleged to have been talking to Sinn Fein on behalf of the British Government.

Asked if there had been contact with Sinn Fein or the IRA by people who could be regarded as emissaries or representatives of the Government, Mayhew answered: 'No, there hasn't.'

Later, when reporters followed up on these remarks, Mayhew stated categorically: 'There have been no negotiations with Sinn Fein . . .'[61] This denial was repeated later in the day by a spokesperson from the Prime Minister's office who said there had been no 'protracted contract and dialogue with Sinn Fein'. On the 19th Mayhew told reporters in Derry: 'Nobody has been authorised to talk or negotiate on behalf of the British Government with Sinn Fein or any other terrorist organisation.' But it was John Major who selected the largest banana skin to step on. On the 20th he not only told the House of Commons that he would not countenance talks with Sinn Fein, he added that the prospect of talks with Gerry Adams would 'turn my stomach'.

Alas, the Deniable Zone was no longer deniable. For while the lies poured forth, an official in the NIO had already given a copy of a British communiqué to Sinn Fein to the DUP MP, Willie McCrea. He passed it to the *Observer* on 17 November. The paper ultimately sent it to the British Government on 26 November and asked for comment. At that the Government realised the jig was up and sent for Molyneaux to assure him that no sell-out was intended. He issued a coded statement later on the 26th, advising his followers not be alarmed at information which they would receive over the weekend.

The information came out the next day. Mayhew attempted to pre-empt the *Observer* story by issuing a statement admitting contact with Sinn Fein. However, he tried to put a spin on the admission by claiming (wrongly) that the contact had been in response to a message from Martin McGuinness asking for help in ending the war. On Monday the 29th he attempted to cover his tracks by lodging documents in the Library and Vote Office at Westminster which claimed to be a complete record of what had gone on. Sinn Fein had no difficulty in proving that the contact had extended for some four times the length claimed by Mayhew. On 2 December, Gerry Adams released the correspondence exchanged between the two sides, saying that the behaviour of the British Government had been 'despicable, devious and damnable'. Mayhew was forced to admit that there were 'inaccuracies' in his account and to concede that he had been contemplating resignation, a factor which was to have a marked bearing on what was about to happen.

For, startling as all this was, it was as nothing to the drama that was taking place concurrently behind closed doors as Reynolds struggled to force Major to uphold his Brussels promise to produce a Joint Declaration with him on a peace formula. Martin Mansergh, who was with Reynolds every step of the way, has said:

> . . . there were an extraordinary series of diplomatic crises behind the scenes. The

Taoiseach resisted enormous pressure to drop the initiative, making it clear that he would try to proceed with it in some shape or form, if necessary recast it as a purely Irish initiative, regardless of whether he had the British government with him or not, and of course in those circumstances he would not be prepared to cover for them in America or elsewhere.

Mansergh's emollient use of language does not give a sense of the intensity of the atmosphere that prevailed at some of the meetings, both at the level of officials and between the two prime ministers. I asked Reynolds if it was true that at one encounter he called Major an 'eejit' (the Irish version of idiot). He replied, 'I couldn't say that I didn't. It could have happened. It was tough going there for a while.'

It was extremely tough going. But then it always is. I have given indications earlier of the sort of problems that Dublin administrations habitually encounter with London: Mrs Thatcher's 'out, out, out' to the Forum Report; Sean Donlon's wonder at the fact that Irish diplomats in America often engaged in controversy with their own countrymen because of what were presumed to be shared Anglo-Irish objectives, but found themselves when the crunch came hindered rather than helped by their British counterparts. Brendan O'Brien, in his book, *The Long War*, writes of the encounters between Dublin and London during the three-strand process which immediately preceded the Reynolds–Major saga:

> . . . conflict between the nationalist side and the Unionist might have been expected. But the head-to-head antagonism between the two governments was more surprising. It showed up an extraordinary lack of trust and understanding, even after seven years of working closely through the Anglo-Irish Agreement.[62]

It might appear 'extraordinary' to the outsider, and O'Brien, RTE's senior television current affairs reporter, is hardly an outsider, but it is not unusual. The antagonism of some of the British participants during the period under review was such that on two occasions representations were made to Albert Reynolds that O'hUiginn was hostile and unhelpful, and should be removed. On both occasions Reynolds forcefully supported O'hUiginn, whom he regarded, correctly, as one of the stars of his team. In terms of policy, as opposed to personalities, as far as the Irish Government was concerned, the Anglo-Irish Agreement should be built on until a final resolution of the Irish problem was achieved. To London it was the outer limit of a process of eroding British sovereignty in Ireland that had been going on since the treaty of 1921. Now was the time to halt that process and get rid of Articles Two and Three. And as Reynolds and Major wrestled, the British had another preoccupation, the deal (the existence of which Mayhew also continually denied) struck with the Unionists over Maastricht. To ideology and prejudice there was therefore added political exigency.

Being only too well aware of all this, my reaction, when I first read the Downing Street Declaration in New York, after it ultimately appeared on 15 December 1993, was to turn to Niall O'Dowd and say incredulously: 'Jesus Christ, Niall, there's IRA language in a document issuing from Downing Street!' What neither O'Dowd nor I realised at the time was that the Declaration also contained UDA and UVF language. This is how it got there.

Reynolds was concerned to reach any element within the Unionist communion which he felt would be open to his argument that he was not trying to impose a solution on the Six Counties along the lines of joint authority. What he sought was peace, as an end in itself. There was no point in trying to convince Paisley, but Molyneaux was a different matter, as was the Alliance Party. Reynolds saw to it that Dr John Alderdice was briefed throughout the negotiations. Reynolds' channel to Molyneaux was Archbishop Robert Eames, the Church of Ireland Primate of All Ireland, who was known to have a good relationship with the Ulster Unionist Party leader. The Taoiseach showed the Archbishop a draft of the proposed Declaration. Dr Eames' verdict was that it would be received in the north as being tilted towards the Nationalist community. The Archbishop then proved to be a co-operative and benign influence on the peace process. He agreed to take the draft away 'for consideration' – code for talking it over with James Molyneaux.

Subsequently, as a result of this 'consideration', Dr Eames' hand was to be seen in paragraphs three to six of the Downing Street Declaration, those dealing with the creation of a greater understanding between north and south. The Archbishop also briefed Downing Street on the extent of the desire for peace amongst the Unionist community, provided that this did not entail a sell-out on principles. Evidence of a yearning for peace was not easy to come by, as at this stage the Loyalist paramilitaries' response to the fears of 'a pan-Nationalist front' was taking the form of assassinating Catholics practically every day. The Provisional IRA, in a botched attempt at killing the leaders held to be responsible for the slaughter, detonated a bomb in a fish shop in the Shankill Road, which on 23 October claimed ten innocent lives and injured fifty-eight people.

The controversy over this atrocity was heightened when Gerry Adams helped carry the coffin of an IRA bomber, Thomas Begley, who died in the attack. Before the month ended, Protestant gunmen had killed twelve people in response, seven of them in a gun attack on a bar in Greysteel, Co. Derry. Overall, the violence during that October, 1993, was the worst for seventeen years. It was against this background that, while still maintaining his contact with the Official Unionists and the Republicans, Reynolds also reached out to the Loyalist paramilitaries. This time his intermediary was a Presbyterian clergyman, the Revd Roy Magee, who had the trust of respected figures in the Loyalist paramilitary world. Their input was sought and it too figured later in the drafting of the Downing Street Declaration.

Reynolds spoke highly of the role played by the Revd Magee and by para-military leaders like David Irvine and Gusty Spence: 'They were the people who brought about the silence of the Loyalist guns.' Speaking to them in turn, it was evident that they also developed a high regard for Reynolds, a microcosm one hopes of an ultimate macro-understanding on the island. In fact, although the Republicans resisted aspects of the Declaration, it would be true to say that, of the parties involved in the behind-the-scenes negotiations, the major stumbling blocks in the talks process were provided by the British, and not by John Major.

Plump, plummy, pinstriped Sir Patrick Mayhew had become so wrong-footed over the denials and controversy which had existed since early summer, first over getting the Unionists onside over Maastricht, and then because of the discovery of the contact with Sinn Fein, that he proved extremely unhelpful during the negotiations. Like Brooke before him, Mayhew had Irish connections. His mother was a Roche, the family name of the lords of Fermoy, but his Cork ancestry did not give him any Brooke-like empathy for the situation. It was known in Dublin before he was appointed that he was keen to be sent to the north, and a degree of polite diplomatic dismay was registered. Mayhew, as Attorney-General, had been involved in a number of cases which had raised Nationalist hackles. The British had failed to observe proper legal procedures during the Fr Ryan extradition case, which led to Mayhew's opposite number, John Murray, refusing to extradite the priest to London on terrorist charges in 1988.

Mayhew's fury at this decision was conveyed to Dublin, which however showed itself to be more concerned with some of Mayhew's own decisions, in that same year. He refused a Dublin suggestion that in Northern Ireland's non-jury courts three judges should sit, and, most controversial of all, there was his role in the 1982 Armagh 'shoot-to-kill' cases. As we have seen, he accepted that there was a prima-facie case against eleven members of the RUC but refused to prosecute on grounds of 'national security'. However, through his influence with John Major (he gave Major his first big political break, appointing him his PPS while Mayhew was Minister of State at the Home Office, 1981–3), Mayhew duly arrived in Belfast.

In the final days prior to the signing of the Downing Street Declaration, Mayhew's natural predilection for the Conservative and Unionist alliance had been heightened by the storm he had just passed through. His relationship with Major had been a not inconsiderable factor in his remaining in office. Nevertheless, his position, and his membership of the cabinet sub-committee dealing with Northern Ireland, made him a key figure.

It is said that when Reynolds set out to lobby the sub-committee, Kenneth Clarke, the Chancellor of the Exchequer, although doubtful that anything could be achieved, pledged himself 'not to stand in the way'.[63] Another Treasury figure, however, Michael Portillo, was simply considered by Reynolds to be 'out'. Douglas Hurd, Foreign Secretary, was analysed as being 'supportive' and Mayhew 'dubious'.

The dubiety was confirmed to Dublin's very great lack of satisfaction when, in what Reynolds had hoped were to be the final stages of the Declaration saga, Mayhew unfurled a new document of his own. So far as Dublin was concerned, this bade fair to restore the old Stormont, restrict the Republic's input into the situation, and put the clock back unacceptably. The Irish team's response to Mayhew's performance was summed up for me by one participant, who said: 'Why didn't Major send us over a good one of his own, instead of a West Cork Brit?' Reynolds refused to give the document any consideration whatsoever. He would not countenance its being regarded as having even been put on the table.

'It was rough,' he says, 'tables were thumped, pencils were broken, but I wouldn't give in. I always reckoned that they wouldn't give me a deal in Dublin anyhow. They could never bring themselves to do that. It would have to be in London.' On 2 December, Reynolds issued a statement saying that a series of meetings was a more sensible approach to Northern Ireland. As he was meeting

John Major in Dublin Castle the following day, in what had widely been forecast as an Anglo-Irish summit which would produce historic results, the statement was a clear signal to the British that he was not going to be lightly coerced into agreeing to anything. The situation grew to such a pitch of intensity that two of his leading officials, Dorr and O'hUiginn, came to him and urged him to settle, lest a historic opportunity be lost.

But Reynolds still held out. 'No,' he said, 'I'll get a better deal in London.' And get it he did. The Downing Street Declaration was signed in London on 15 December 1993, albeit after a further bout of ferocious negotiation and a Reynolds-inspired phone call to John Major from President Clinton urging him 'to go the extra mile for peace'. Reading the Declaration, one would find it hard to understand what all the fuss was about. Yet Reynolds describes it as the 'potentially most important statement of principle for seventy years'. Major, in the contrary way of Anglo-Irish relationships, set out to prove its importance in the opposite fashion, by announcing the next day the Select Committee conceded to the Unionists for their support over Maastricht; and by devoting most of his House of Commons speech on the Declaration to a reassurance to the Unionists of what was not in it. A few days later, on 21 December, he visited the north to sound the same reassuring air.

The Declaration described the achievement of peace in Northern Ireland as 'the most urgent and important issue' facing the two governments. It made a

solemn commitment to promote co-operation at all levels on the basis of the fundamental principles, undertakings, obligations under international agreements, to which they have jointly committed themselves, and the guarantees which each government has given and now reaffirms, including Northern Ireland's statutory constitutional guarantee. It is their aim to foster agreement and reconciliation, leading to a new political framework founded on consent and encompassing arrangements within Northern Ireland, for the whole island, and between these islands.

The British pledged themselves to uphold

the democratic wish of a greater number of the people of Northern Ireland on the issue of whether they prefer to support the union or a sovereign united Ireland . . . the British Government . . . have no selfish strategic or economic interest in Northern Ireland. Their primary interest is to see peace, stability and reconciliation established by agreement . . . they will work together with the Irish Government to achieve such an agreement, which will embrace the totality of relationships. The role of the British Government will be to encourage, facilitate and enable the achievement of such agreement over a period through a process of dialogue and co-operation . . . The British Government agree that it is for the people of the island of Ireland alone, by agreement between the two parts respectively, to exercise their right of self-determination on the basis of consent, freely and concurrently given, North and South, to bring about a united Ireland, if that is their wish . . .

For his part Reynolds accepted that

the democratic right of self-determination by the people of Ireland as a whole must be achieved and exercised with and subject to the agreement and consent of a majority of the people of Northern Ireland and must, consistent with justice and equity, respect the democratic dignity and the civil rights and religious liberties of both communities . . .

Reynolds also promised:

in the event of an overall settlement, the Irish Government will, as part of a balanced constitutional accommodation, put forward and support proposals for change in the Irish Constitution which would fully represent the principle of consent in Northern Ireland.

The Declaration was greeted with a very wide measure of welcome. Only the DUP and Sinn Fein sounded notes of dissent from their different perspectives. Paisley greeted the Declaration by telling Major that he had 'sold Ulster to buy off the fiendish Republican scum'. He then began a series of 'Save Ulster' meetings. On the Ulster Unionist Party side, the Reynolds approach to Dr Eames resulted in James Molyneaux playing the role of the dog in the Sherlock Holmes story: he did not bark. He sought clarification on a number of points, stating a preference for an eighty-five-seat Assembly in the north, with formal links to the Republic, though not of an executive nature.

Overall, as the document was digested on both sides of the Irish Sea, it soon became apparent that those who opposed the Declaration, including Sinn Fein, were in danger of being isolated. Right to the last moment, Sinn Fein urged Reynolds not to sign; the principle of consent was, as they saw it, couched in such a way as to enshrine the Unionist veto. This reserve on Sinn Fein's part was a cause of the long wrangle that developed on the issue of 'clarification' along the road to the IRA ceasefire, which still lay some nine months away. But before the resolution of that issue, another major battle arose over the granting of a visa for Gerry Adams to visit the US. The winning of this fight involved Jean Kennedy Smith.

Her first two major embassy functions of 1993 struck the grace notes which were to predominate during her ambassadorship. The first was the annual Fourth of July garden party. Apart from the glitterati of Ireland, the attendance also included a large contingent of disadvantaged young people, many of them in wheelchairs, for whom a band and a special marquee were provided. Some days later she gave a private dinner, attended by members of the Cabinet. Albert Reynolds delivered a speech in which he said: 'Tonight we do not say welcome to Ireland, Madam Ambassador. We say welcome home to a friend.' Listening to him, I was struck by the thought that while, to an outsider, his address would have sounded schmaltzy in the extreme, nevertheless for a Kennedy, ambassador or no, coming to Ireland was indeed coming home.

The ambassador's residence is opposite Aras an Uachtarain, the residence of the President of Ireland. It used to be the home of the British viceroys who once ruled the country. During the visit of President Kennedy to Ireland in 1963, I had stood beside him as he planted a sapling in the garden of the Aras, in the shade of a gigantic oak which Queen Victoria had planted. Victoria's visit had taken place during the potato famine which had driven Kennedy's ancestor from tiny Dunganstown in Co. Wexford to America, and the Kennedy dynasty. One would have had to be utterly deficient in a sense of history not to have felt the significance of that little tree-planting ceremony – or not to have experienced an eerie sensation at the symbolism of the fact that the sapling later died. Was it killed by the shade of Victoria's oak, or did a wind blow from Dallas?

And so, imbued with a sense of race and place, and motivated by the humanitarian concerns that led her to have the disadvantaged young people at her first party, Jean Kennedy Smith set out to earn her welcome. She had come through a bad few years before arriving in Dublin, nursing her husband through his last illness, and sitting through her son Will's protracted trial in Florida. But now, she was no longer just one of the Kennedy girls. She was somebody in a position of consequence and she was going to show that she merited it. As the violence was continuing, she could not contact Sinn Fein, and so I arranged a lunch for her at my house with Fr Reid. A practising Catholic, she was obviously impressed when he opened by saying, 'I'm only interested in stopping the violence. I feel the Church should get involved. Even as we're talking here at this moment, there's probably someone being killed.' Visibly moved, she kept repeating 'awful, awful', as he described the horrors of the situation and the difficulties facing Hume and in particular Adams and the peace party in the Republican movement. She was subsequently criticised for being too pro-Green in her activities, but her next move accurately reflects her concerns throughout: she wanted to meet a representative group of northern Protestants. This was arranged, through the Clonard network, and she later kept in touch with those she met on this occasion and built on their contacts. She also developed a particular rapport with Albert Reynolds, and personal friendships with many of the various officials and members of the coalition dealing with the north.

From the time of the September visit by the Morrison/O'Dowd group, the issue of the Adams visa had been steadily pursued. In New York, Bill Flynn, in his capacity as chairman of the prestigious Committee on American Foreign Policy, issued an invitation to Adams to address a conference hosted by the Committee in New York on 1 February 1994. In Dublin, Brendan Scannell is credited with the suggestion that Adams should apply for the visa from Dublin this time. He had already been turned down when he went through Belfast. Mayor Dinkins of New York had invited Adams to come to New York in November to explain the peace process. But the British supplied Clinton with material which he described as 'credible evidence' that Adams was involved 'at the highest level in devising IRA strategy'. The President turned down the visa application, to the great annoyance of the ANIA, which made it very clear to the White House that 'those Irish' knew how to convey displeasure as well as gratitude. Reynolds was of course supportive of the visit. Had he opposed it there would have no point in applying.

Ted Kennedy took a hand. He came to Dublin with his wife Vicky, to see in the New Year with Jean, and to make his own soundings on the visa question. I have never since ceased to marvel at his endurance. After landing, he drove first to the US residency for a shower, and then straight out to my house for lunch with Jean. Anyone who can face my cooking, sleepless, after an Atlantic crossing, deserves admiration. We had a Homeric interlude. In dark moments later, when the peace process appeared to be floundering, I used to comfort myself with the thought that if the visa question could survive that lunch, it could survive anything. The message I gave the Senator was basically the same that he received in more orthodox fashion from decision-taking Dublin.

I felt that it would benefit Adams personally in his efforts to convince the IRA that the American card was the one to play. If it were handled properly, there would be no need for violence. The 'non-armed' approach would receive enormous help. Having just concluded a coast-to-coast book tour of the States, I was quite certain that it would have a double-edged impact. On the one hand it would push Ireland up the American, and hence the British, agenda, and on the other it would be of educational benefit to the Republicans themselves. Adams would discover a huge well-spring of pro-Irish, as opposed to pro-IRA good will. A sentiment compounded of an instinct for freedom, for peace, an end to violence and an ancient quarrel, and the sensation of doing something for their own ethnic origins. The canalisation of all this into the peace process could only do good. A refusal of the visa would do corresponding harm, fuelling the arguments of those who thought physical force the only course. At this stage, slogans such as 'Gerry Adams is a collaborator' had been known to appear on some West Belfast gable walls.

Ted Kennedy went back to America, convinced that he should support the visa campaign. Niall O'Dowd summed up the importance of this as follows:

> He had tremendous influence with President Clinton on this issue. In fact we knew for a long time that the system would only move as far as Kennedy wanted it to move. We had done the ground work. We had taken full page ads in the *New York Times*. We arranged the invitations to the conference Bill Flynn was hosting, but Senator Kennedy went to bat for us, and basically, single-handedly delivered the President on the issue . . .
>
> When we went through that visa battle we faced the Justice Department, the CIA, the FBI, the State Department, the British government. 'This man is a terrorist. This is insane, Mr President. You can't do this.' It went right to the President's desk to be signed, and that overturned a 50-year hegemony over Irish policy in this country that the British government had exercised through the State Department.

Actually, Clinton did more than that. He also set a precedent, for which he was heavily criticised in some quarters, by allowing the Sinn Fein leader into the US without first being subjected to the so-called Arafat test – a renunciation of violence. Adams actually only got a forty-eight-hour visa, but he reckons that the impact his visit made and the events it set in train moved the peace process forward by about a year. His visit to New York (beginning on 31 January 1994) produced one of the largest, if not the largest, harvests of media attention ever recorded in a two-day spell. Emerging from a wilderness of obscurity and broadcasting bans into a blaze of mainstream publicity Adams dominated every major media outlet, from the front page of the *New York Times* to *The Larry King Show*. Hitherto, and not without reason, publicity had tended to be evaluated on the basis of the equation: one horse dead in London equals ten Paddys in Ireland. Even the dullest IRA volunteer could see the benefit of this new development.

After the sparks from the media bonfire died down, most of the subsequent action took place behind closed doors, between February and 31 August 1994. Under the terms of the Downing Street Declaration a liaison committee, consisting of officials from each side, was set up to consider how the principles enshrined in the Declaration could be made the basis for a framework document which would, as the title suggests, form a framework within which all-party negotiations would take place on the creation of a peaceful, new-look Ireland. So as not to inflame the Unionists' detestation of the Anglo-Irish Agreement, this was envisaged as taking the form less of joint sovereignty than joint management. Reynolds had received assurances from John Major that he envisaged a redrafting of the 1920 Government of Ireland Act, and he for his part directed that new drafts of Articles Two and Three of the Irish Constitution be prepared.

I have seen some of these drafts, and certain minutes of the proceedings of the liaison committee's proposals, and there is no doubt that in the spring and summer of 1994 any reasonable person would have concluded that, despite their differing starting points and whether one spoke of joint authority or joint management, Dublin and London had a joint approach. Nevertheless, at a different level, I was getting different signals. I was researching this book, and consequently was in and out of the Houses of Parliament and the offices of London decision-takers involved in the Irish question over the previous quarter-century. I found plenty of good will, but no belief that the Downing Street Declaration was much more than an optical exercise. 'Oh, there's plenty of time,' said a former prime minister, adding: 'Another generation or two.' The Downing Street Declaration was seen merely as a collection of pious aspirations which, in the real world, would not be allowed to disturb the status quo.

All the commitment and enthusiasm seemed to lie in Ireland. Though this said, the principal British civil servants engaged in the talks, Sir John Chilcott, Permanent Secretary of the Department of Defence, and effectively head of the NIO, and his deputy, Quentin Thomas, were both regarded in Dublin as doing what they could to move the process forward within the limits of their both being conscientious British civil servants. Sinn Fein were visibly edging into the spotlight: there was the Adams handshake with Mary Robinson, the growing American dimension symbolised by the visa triumph, and Reynolds' relaxation of the broadcasting ban, so that Sinn Fein spokespersons such as Adams and Martin McGuinness could be heard and seen over the airwaves in pre-recorded interviews.

Above all, the principles enshrined in Downing Street were weighted heavily in favour of Nationalists. Whatever hedgings accompanied the statement, the Unionists were being told from Downing Street by both London and Dublin that the British had no interest in staying in Ireland. The Republican phrase 'self-determination' was sounding ominously throughout the document, for all the talk of 'consent', and Irish unity was openly spoken of. Yet for all that, Sinn Fein had fallen far short of wresting a declaration of intent to withdraw. 'Self-determination' clearly did not mean self-determination for the whole island. And Britain was not joining the ranks of the persuaders for Irish unity. The political leadership of Sinn Fein could see the pluses, but the minuses were evident too, particularly to the fighters, men and women, in the IRA. Was it for this that twenty-five years of bloodshed had been endured? Adams and company were hoping to create an alliance between Fianna Fail, Sinn Fein and the SDLP, which, with American support, would present a united front to the British. But Reynolds fought shy of this, not wishing either to give substance to the much-talked-of 'pan-Nationalist front' or to get too close to Sinn Fein. The Sinn Feiners were convinced that Britain did not have a bottom line, and could be pushed in their direction. It was obvious that British policy-makers did not form a monolith. Sometimes a dovish wing of the Conservative Party appeared to be in the ascendant, sometimes the hawks flew high. At other times MI5, or perhaps the NIO or the RUC, called the tune.

But one thing Adams and his friends were determined on: 'There'll be no splits.' One was told this constantly. Whether the movement opted for peace or war, it would do so unitedly. The amount of deliberation and consultation that went on within Sinn Fein in the years and months before the ceasefire was truly remarkable. Fr Reid sometimes caught the Belfast train to Dublin, returned to Belfast, went back to Dublin, and caught the last train back to Belfast, all in the one day. Before any decision was taken, every communication was scrutinised word by word by politicians who had learned their trade the hard way in the 'Republican university', jail and street confrontation. In turn each decision was prefaced by an exhaustive bout of consultation before being translated into action. Albert Reynolds' people developed a marked respect for Martin McGuinness in particular. Reynolds himself regards him as a highly significant figure in the whole process.

While the British Government went slowly, because of the Unionist pact and because of its own back-benchers, Sinn Fein was concerned neither to go so slowly as to become isolated by public opinion in the wake of the huge welcome which the Downing Street Declaration received, nor so fast as to cause divisions in the ranks. Adams' ploy to achieve both conflicting goals was to greet the Declaration on the day after publication by seeking 'clarification' of various points. John Major refused to do this, publicly in a statement from Downing Street on 22 December and privately when pressed by John Hume at a fairly tense meeting in Downing Street on 14 January. Ultimately Reynolds, having been in private contact, took the public step on 31 March of calling on Sinn Fein to say what it was they wished clarified. Subsequently both the British and Sinn Fein agreed that he would become the conduit through which flowed both the questions from Sinn Fein and the answers from the British. The answers were finally given to Sinn Fein on 19 May 1994.

Before passing them on, Reynolds rang an incredulous Bill Clinton to tell him that he had both the questions and the answers in his hand. Clinton was impressed: 'The questions *and* the answers, boy, that's what politics are all about!' Clinton had been distinctly unimpressed two months earlier when the IRA mortared Heathrow Airport on three successive days. Dummy rockets had been used and no one was injured. But while the incident was seen by the IRA as a valuable morale booster, it was not so received in the White House. Attacks of any sort on a civilian airport were regarded as being a very poor return for the by-passing of the Arafat test. Correspondingly, a three-day ceasefire which the IRA called at Easter (which in fact extended for ten days), following the mortaring, was regarded as a completely inadequate response to the Declaration. It was an example of the kind of dilemma which the Republicans would henceforth face now that Sinn Fein was becoming respectable. Hitherto their strength had been linked to the extent of their violence. After the Adams visa saga, violence would only serve to alienate those who fought to bring Sinn Fein in from the cold. In mainstream America, the world of the Ted Kennedys, the Bill Flynns and the Chuck Feeneys, 'terrorism' was the contemporary equivalent of what the term 'communism' had represented during the Cold War.

However, behind the scenes, the IRA Army Council had voted in secret not to reject the Downing Street document. This allowed the peace process to go forward within the movement. Externally, the media of western Europe, America and further afield focused on the Sinn Fein Special Conference at Letterkenny, Co. Donegal, on 24 July 1994, which it was popularly assumed would be the occasion of a ceasefire declaration. It was not to be: though Adams and his colleagues might be thought of as doves, favouring a ceasefire, there were still some hawks to be hooded. There was a not inconsiderable element within the Republican ranks which feared that if a ceasefire were declared, the British would simply accept its benefits and make no move towards meeting Sinn Fein goals. (A melancholy prediction which, as we shall see, British policy in 1995 went far towards validating.) Their fears were added to when, in the run-up to Letterkenny, a source close to negotiations between Sinn Fein and Dublin leaked to the *Daily Mail* the fact that a ceasefire was being contemplated.

The leak temporarily froze the ceasefire announcement. Adams spoke in coded terms about the failure of the Declaration to 'deal adequately with some of the core issues' (in other words, to adopt the Sinn Fein agenda). He said Sinn Fein intended to pursue the Hume–Adams initiative. The media responded to this with a howl of outrage and disappointment. However, there was activity behind the apparent lack of movement. O'Dowd had made something like a dozen visits to Ireland in the previous eighteen months. Shortly after Letterkenny, word reached him in New York that the Sinn Fein leadership would like to see his group in Belfast towards the end of August. Reynolds and Dick Spring also wanted to see them at Government Buildings when they landed in Dublin. It was obvious that something was afoot, but, speaking of the Reynolds meeting, O'Dowd recalled:

> We could not read that meeting as well as we had read previous meetings. The delegation were fairly split down the middle as to what exactly was going on. We were briefed to ask the Sinn Feiners straightforward, simple questions, and to get straightforward, simple answers. No stuff about 'being engaged in a peace process' and so on. Just: 'Is there going to be a ceasefire, and when?!' Afterwards I polled our group as to what they thought was going to happen. They were split down the middle. Everything was going to happen. Nothing was going to happen.

O'Dowd remembered how he felt going into the historic meeting with the Sinn Fein leadership:

> I was always impressed with their honesty. Always impressed with their directness. Always impressed that whatever they said, they delivered on. And there were times when it had been very tough. We were really speaking a different language coming from here [New York] in trying to understand where they were coming from.

These were men (and women) who had lived in a situation for 25 years where every day could be their last. They were coming from a place where, whatever demonisation had occurred, they had survived everything. They had survived the second most powerful army in the world throwing everything at them. They had survived total indifference and disdain from Dublin. They had survived large sections of their support being eaten away by the SDLP. They had survived death squads and punishment shootings. Everything . . .

They were people whom you knew had experienced something, something very deep and a truly revolutionary thing. Their camaraderie was impressive. Of course there were times when you became aware that they were also dangerous people . . .

Going into the meeting, in the Whiterock Leisure Centre, O'Dowd did not know whether to expect to see the camaraderie facet of Sinn Fein or the danger signals. The group had been asked to prepare a paper. One expectation of the form the encounter would take was that it would be discussion on this document. There had been considerable communication back and forth across the Atlantic about the nature of any ceasefire. 'Offensive posture' and 'defensive posture' had been discussed. There had been lengthy argument as to what constituted 'defensive posture'. O'Dowd summed up the Irish-Americans' position on these issues:

We had basically said: 'You are going to get all the blame and none of the credit unless you just do it clean.' So we went in expecting to hear something about defensive posture.

Instead the meeting opened with Gerry Adams announcing that there was to be a complete cessation of military operations. O'Dowd said: 'We were delighted. There was a huge sigh of relief around the table. It was a classic example of the way Adams does things. You go in expecting one meeting and you end up having another one. It is very clever. Very, very clever.'

Then something not so clever happened. There was a last-minute hitch, caused not by Sinn Fein, but by the British. The Irish-Americans came out of the leisure centre biting their lips so as to give nothing away to the huge media corps which was waiting outside.

For the Sinn Fein activists in America, the NORAID supporters, had yet to be briefed. The public announcement of the ceasefire had to be delayed until this was done. Part of the Irish-American scene is extremely radical. The famine tradition, the Fenians, the defeated Republicans of the Irish civil war period, those who emigrated because of unemployment in the fifties, or fled the contemporary Troubles, they all combine to produce a strain of thinking which worries that any tendency towards the ballot box, and away from the Armalite, is heading for a sell-out. If the ceasefire was to work it was essential that when this element first learned of its existence, they did so from the lips of someone they trusted. Joe Cahill, the man who had set up NORAID in the first place, was the one man that the representatives of the physical force tradition in America would be certain to listen to.

However, the attempt to send him to America almost foundered on the rocks of British opposition to the Americans granting him a visa. Albert Reynolds was furious. He knew that a historic moment was being put in jeopardy, but there was nothing he could do. Everyone had gone on holiday, on both sides of the Atlantic.

Nancy Soderberg could not be found, Jean Kennedy Smith had left Dublin for the South of France. But, with a sense of obligation to the peace process for which she will long be remembered in the annals of Irish diplomacy, she broke off her holiday as soon as she heard of the Cahill crisis. As Reynolds said to me: 'Would you even know where to find another ambassador, never mind have them come back off their holidays?'

Kennedy Smith was in fact spending her holiday with the former Conservative Chief Whip, Michael Jopling, and his wife. Jopling, relaxing by a swimming pool, was at first perplexed by the blizzard of phone calls from Dublin that suddenly swept through his holiday home. After his house guest had abruptly departed, one last call came through to the swimming pool. 'Who *is* this?' inquired the outraged Jopling. 'This is the Irish Taoiseach, Albert Reynolds,' was the reply, the first indication Jopling had had of what was going on. Back in Dublin the Jean Machine went to work to good effect. Even a Washington on holiday listens to a Kennedy. But not attentively enough to satisfy Irish pride. Reynolds was outraged when at one stage he discovered that, while Jean Kennedy Smith was largely successful in extracting a visa from Foggy Bottom, at British insistence it would be subject to conditions which would limit Cahill's freedom of manoeuvre. A sulphurous phone call to the American Embassy ensued, on the lines of: 'This is a sovereign republic. I, as Taoiseach of the Sovereign Republic of Ireland, will not allow adjectival conditions to be attached to a visa issued to an Irish passport holder at the behest of the adjectival British Government!' Kennedy Smith returned to the drawing board.

It was a long night. Every hour, on the hour, Fr Reid phoned the Reynolds residence. Still no word. Eventually the centre of gravity in the dispute moved to the office of the American Attorney-General. Under the law as it stood Cahill's record meant the visa could not be granted as required. The only person who could grant the visa was President Clinton himself. Jean Kennedy Smith got back on the phone. At five o'clock in the morning, Irish time, as the shape of the deer could dimly be seen through the great windows opening to the east of the residence of the American Ambassador to Ireland, word arrived from the White House.

Cahill was to present himself at the American Embassy in Ballsbridge, where he would be granted his visa without conditions. And so Joseph Cahill of Belfast, once sentenced to hang in the year of Our Lord 1942, took off from Dublin Airport a few hours later. Before he landed in the US a triumphant Albert Reynolds had been on the phone to read the full text of the IRA ceasefire announcement to John Major and William Jefferson Clinton. The next day, 31 August 1994, at 11.25 a.m., RTE broadcast a tape given anonymously to a reporter a little earlier. It contained the following:

> Recognising the potential of the current situation and in order to enhance the democratic peace process and underline our definitive commitment to its success, the leadership of *Oglaigh na hEireann* have decided that as of midnight, Wednesday 31 August, there will be a complete cessation of military operations. All our units have been instructed accordingly.

The statement was greeted with understandable euphoria by the Irish everywhere. Champagne corks popped from West Belfast to the West Coast of America.

Paraphrasing Danny Morrison's famous remark about the Armalite and the ballot box, Gerry Adams appeared before the cameras in Belfast with, as he pointed out, 'a bottle of champagne in one hand and a bunch of flowers in the other hand'. Speaking in Irish, he said: '*Is e seo rud tabhachtach, agus is e sin an fhirinne.*' (The literal meaning is: 'This is something important and this is the truth.' But *an fhirinne* means more than 'the truth'; it also conveys both 'honour' and 'genuineness'.

Buying time until the Loyalists worked out their own response to the ceasefire, David Irvine, an emerging figure in the Combined Loyalist Command, where the UVF were concerned, sent his cohorts out along Sandy Row and the Shankill Road, putting up slogans which graciously accepted the IRA's 'unconditional surrender'! Thus, the Orange was able to celebrate the coming of peace without seeming to be upstaged by the Green. As the *Irish Times* said in the editorial which, for the first time in living memory, it carried on page one, 'There must be a welcome';[64] but it also identified two key areas of worry, the absence of the word 'permanent' and 'the fears which rack the unionist community' that they had been sold out. As the leader said:

> The conviction runs deep that only a secret deal could have brought about yesterday's declaration. Addressing that reaction, and other attendant suspicions, must be the main task now facing those who would make the peace process complete.[65]

The conviction ran so deep that, prior to the ceasefire announcement, Dr Eames had taken the precaution of securing from John Major permission to make known the fact that there had been 'no underhand dealing to bring this about on the part of the British government'. In fact a cynic, and there were many in Dublin, could have concluded that there was a better prima-facie case of a deal being done over the timing of the ceasefire announcement between Reynolds and the IRA. A special three-day emergency debate on the beef tribunal had to be interrupted for statements on the ceasefire! The reports of its subsequent proceedings were completely lost in those describing the reactions to the ceasefire. The truth is there was no deal, as subsequent British policy made all too clear.

Reynolds attempted to make the peace process work. He knew that for it to succeed two things were essential: momentum and reconciliation. He moved swiftly to do what he could on both fronts. Spring was dispatched on a round of briefing visits to world leaders from Bonn to Washington. Reynolds himself formally received both Hume and Adams in a historic meeting at Government Buildings on 6 September, and the three posed for photographs, shaking hands together. They issued a highly significant statement, saying: 'We reiterate that we cannot resolve this problem without the participation and agreement of the Unionist people.' Reynolds also announced that a Forum for Peace and Reconciliation (foreshadowed in paragraph eleven of the Downing Street Declaration) would be set up in Dublin Castle on 28 October. It was envisaged that this would be attended by parliamentarians and interested persons representing every shade of involved opinion, including Sinn Fein. The release of a number of Republican prisoners was also put in train and, as a symbolic gesture, the State of

Emergency, which had technically continued to exist since the days of World War II, was officially lifted.

But the response of the British was far less enabling. Unpublicised relaxations of the regime in the H blocks took place. But publicly there was a refusal to accept that the ceasefire was genuine. The first statement from John Major said that he was greatly encouraged, but '. . . we need to be clear that this is indeed intended to be a permanent renunciation of violence, that is to say for good'. Later that day Molyneaux emerged from an hour-long meeting with the British Prime Minister to say that Major could not accept the IRA ceasefire announcement because it did not meet the criteria set by the Downing Street Declaration. Subsequent speeches by Major and Mayhew revealed the difficulty of balancing a welcome for the ceasefire with the attitudes of Tory back-benchers and Unionists. The word 'permanent' rang out across the airwaves incessantly. Dublin learned subsequently that British intelligence reports were unhelpful in this regard, tending to give a pessimistic interpretation of events, in marked contrast to what the Irish were telling London.

For ideological reasons the statement was grounded in the language used to announce the previous great Republican ceasefire of the century, that which ended the Irish civil war in 1923. Then de Valera and Frank Aiken had instructed the IRA to cease fire and dump arms. The 1994 statement had announced a 'complete cessation of military operations' and a 'definitive commitment' to the 'democratic peace process'. Martin McGuinness underscored the commitment in interviews given after the announcement in which he stressed that 'the ceasefire will hold in all circumstances'.

The group possibly best placed to assess the sincerity of the commitment to peace, the Loyalist paramilitaries, accepted the Republicans' bona fides on 13 October 1994, after an extensive process of consultation, including consultation with Dublin. The man who had been one of the first to become involved in the conflict, the Loyalists' folk hero, Gusty Spence, was also the man chosen to bring it to a close. He read the ceasefire declaration, a document which also contained some surprisingly noble-sounding sentiments:

> After a widespread consultative process initiated by representations from the Ulster Democratic and Progressive Unionist Parties [fringe Unionist parties representing the UDA and the UVF] and having received confirmation and guarantees in relation to Northern Ireland's constitutional position within the United Kingdom, as well as other assurances, and in the belief that the democratically expressed wishes of the greater number of people in Northern Ireland will be respected and upheld, the CLMC will universally cease all operational hostilities from 12 midnight, on Thursday, October 13th, 1994.

After praising the Loyalist fighters, in and out of prison, pledging continued support to their families, and warning that if the IRA resumed their campaign, violence would recommence, the statement went on to say, at Gusty Spence's insistence:

> In all sincerity we offer the loved ones of all innocent victims over the past twenty-five years abject and true remorse. No words of ours will compensate for the intolerable suffering they have undergone during the conflict.

380

Let us firmly resolve to respect our differing views of freedom, culture and aspiration and never again permit our political circumstances to degenerate into bloody warfare.

We are on the threshold of a new and exciting beginning with our battles in future being political battles, fought on the side of honesty, decency and democracy against the negativity of mistrust, misunderstanding and malevolence so that together we can bring forth a wholesome society in which our children and their children will know the meaning of true peace.

However, the British continued to move as though motivated by the 'negativity of mistrust'. Statement after statement stressed the need for Sinn Fein to guarantee that the peace was 'permanent'. No meeting with Sinn Fein, even at official level, took place until a 'decontamination' period of approximately three months was considered to have elapsed in early December. They initially boycotted the Forum for Peace and Reconciliation when it first opened. To the time of writing the Conservative back-bench Committee on Northern Ireland, chaired by Andrew Hunter, has still not visited the Forum, although the Bow Group has, as has the Inter-Parliamentary group, which has Tory representation, led by the liberal Peter Temple-Morris. But no gesture on the release of prisoners was even contemplated. And the only positive gestures towards the ceasefire, after a lapse of several weeks, consisted of a lifting of the exclusion order barring Gerry Adams from entering the 'UK mainland'; a diminution of army patrols during daylight hours and the reopening of some border roads. This last only took place at John Major's insistence after the NIO and the army had proposed to spin out the road-opening process for a number of years. And the gesture was considerably diminished in Nationalist eyes by the decision to go ahead with the building of huge, permanent forts at Crossmaglen and Newtownhamilton.

Some have sought to explain this behaviour on the grounds of caution concerning the reactions of the main Unionist parties. Paisley and two of his henchmen (Peter Robinson and William McCrea) were angrily ordered out of Downing Street by John Major after the ceasefire for refusing to accept his word that no deal had been done with the IRA. The three then locked themselves in a lavatory to compose a press statement before leaving Downing Street, causing themselves to be nicknamed the 'Pee Musketeers'. In fact events would appear to prove Martin Mansergh correct when he averred that: 'The only deal was the one laid out in paragraph ten of the Downing Street Declaration.'[66] This paragraph says:

The British and Irish Governments reiterate that the achievement of peace must involve a permanent end to the use of, or support of, paramilitary violence. They confirm that, in these circumstances, democratically mandated parties which establish a commitment to exclusively peaceful methods and which have shown that they abide by the democratic process are free to join in dialogue in due course between the governments and the political parties on the way ahead.

Certainly, far from indicating the existence of a 'deal', British behaviour, publicly towards Adams, and privately towards Dublin, was more indicative of a rearguard action in the field than shared co-operation in a peace process. Paragraph ten was systematically flouted. Contacts of mine, Irish officials engaged in trying to negotiate the long-gestating framework document, spoke of 'emotional' meetings, at which a 'bitter and mistrustful' spirit prevailed. Once, after I had speculated to a member of the Coalition Cabinet as to what had become of the spirit of generosity which we had been given to understand would prevail if the violence were stopped, the minister burst out: 'Generosity! The Brits don't know the meaning of the fucking term!'

The attitude towards Adams became manifest at the time of his second visit to the US in 1994. After the usual British-inspired resistance from the State Department, he secured a longer visa, covering the first two weeks of October. This meant he could travel and address meetings, but the real target of his visit was the White House. To be received there, possibly by a high official, or perhaps by the Vice-President, Al Gore, who had met with Unionist representatives, would be a boost for the peace process in Republican circles. Of course, not to be made welcome to Pennsylvania Avenue would be correspondingly damaging. However, the O'Dowd lobby had no reason to suppose that this would happen. They were dumbfounded and angered therefore to discover, as the Adams trip began, that the White House was off limits. In order to soothe feathers ruffled by the granting of the visa, the National Security Council had bowed to British pressure to keep Adams off the Rose Lawn. Says O'Dowd:

> It was the first really clear red flag signal that we had got, telling us that the Brits were not serious about the process.

His analysis of the situation was that a re-run of the Curragh Mutiny/1974 situations was occurring. A weak and vacillating British prime minister was responding to pressures from the military establishment and to figures who, for reasons of either pride or pocket, had a vested interest in seeing the violence continue. At all events Major personally phoned Clinton twice to implore him not to allow Adams to be received at the White House. The Irish-Americans, however, had an equally vested interest in seeing that the visit went ahead. It fell to O'Dowd to conduct the negotiations which led to a compromise being worked out. Adams could not talk directly to the White House at the time – it was still within the 'decontamination' period and the Loyalist ceasefire had not yet been declared. In his own inimitable way O'Dowd described how as a result he had

> the distinct pleasure, one Sunday afternoon, of having hours on the phone, not only with Soderberg but also Tony Lake [head of the National Security Council], trying to come up with a compromise which would allow this visit to go forward. Because if at that point Adams had been shunned in America it would have been very, very serious. Very serious for him.

An Irish solution to an Irish problem was eventually arrived at. Adams was not received at the White House, but neither was he shunned. O'Dowd explains:

> We eventually came up with a compromise which was that Vice-President Gore would call Adams. This was to give him the same status as Unionists in terms of contact with the Vice-

President. It was set up in a beautifully symmetrical way – when he was at the home of Ethel Kennedy [Robert Kennedy's widow]. Without the Kennedys there wouldn't be peace. And I think the people who want to rub the Kennedys' noses in it have no understanding or comprehension.

The people of Massachusetts made that clear when they elected five of them – and Patrick, Ted's son, is still to come!

Earlier in the year, in February, Ethel Kennedy had also demonstrated her interest in the Irish situation in a very personal way. Her son-in-law, Paul Hill, who is married to her daughter, Courtney, was one of the wrongfully convicted Guildford Four. He had been released in 1989 after serving fifteen years, but his life had been on hold since then because there was also a conviction alleging involvement in the murder of a British soldier dating back to the time of his conviction. Ethel, her son Joe, a congressman, and a phalanx of Kennedy relations descended on Belfast for the hearing of Hill's appeal, staying in a guest house run by the Redemptorists! Whether the Kennedy clan's presence had anything to do with the result I cannot say, but Hill was acquitted.

Foiled in their attempts to have Adams snubbed by the White House, the British had to be content with a minor bout of spoiling. Although in Ireland, or the UK, Unionists would not appear on television with Sinn Fein spokesmen, the official Unionist MP, Ken Maginnis, a former B-Special, was flown to New York to appear on *The Larry King Show* in opposition to Adams (on 4 October) and to star at a reception hosted by the British Consulate. Far from improving, London's dealings with Sinn Fein continued to be conducted at that level of petulance until, in March the following year, they spilled over to affect the London–Washington relationship also. Adams had returned to America in December where, on the 6th, he was received at the White House by Tony Lake. This time his mission was to get official US sanction to openly collect funds for Sinn Fein, subject to the customary laws and accountancy practices governing such political fund-raising in America.

As this clearly committed Sinn Fein more to the normal democratic political process, and away from the subterranean gathering of money for arms, or other purposes associated with the Irish physical force tradition, it was regarded in both Dublin and Washington as a move towards the light. Not so in London. Again the fund-raising proposal was fought like a rearguard action in the field. Bracketed with it was the prospect of Adams being an honoured guest at a gala White House function, hosted by the Clintons, which was planned for St Patrick's Day, 17 March 1995.

Possibly the British had taken heart from the huge gains made by their traditional allies, the Republicans, in the mid-term elections. The Republicans were now in a majority on Capitol Hill. However, there was still a Democrat in the White House. Moreover Clinton was becoming acutely conscious of two things. First, the fact that Ireland was his major, in fact his only, foreign policy success. Secondly, that the Irish-American lobby was growing in strength. For once he had a white ethnic group on his side! Adams' repeated visits were having the effect of involving more and more people of Irish background in the Irish issue. The consciousness of being Irish was being heightened. O'Dowd was impressed by this phenomenon:

The thing I noticed most during Adams' second visit was the crowds that turned out. There were a lot of faces who hadn't been around for a long time. One guy summed it up for me in Hartford, Connecticut. He said: 'You know, it's great to celebrate a victory. It's great to come out after 25 years of Bloody Sunday and the Guildford Four and Birmingham Six, and finally have something that's put the British on the back foot.' And that's how it was seen here.

As St Patrick's Day neared, and the pressures built up over the the linked issues of the Sinn Fein fund-raising and Adams' presence at the White House gala, Senator Chris Dodds and the President of the United States of America found it convenient to play a round of golf. Dodds, a close friend of Ted Kennedy, had been the chairman of the Senate Foreign Relations Committee before the Republican clean sweep. Now he was national chairman of the Democratic Party. As such, one of his principal responsibilities was to ensure that his golfing companion was returned as president in the 1996 election. Dodds, who is also the owner of a cottage in Roundstone in Connemara, to which he makes periodic visits 'to catch up on his reading', as he described it to me, was more than ordinarily conscious of the importance of the Irish-American factor. At the seventeenth hole he enquired whether the President had 'made up his mind on that Adams thing yet'. The President had not, but subsequent events bear the interpretation that between the seventeenth and the eighteenth holes he inspiration sought, and inspiration found. As matters turned out, not only was Gerry Adams at the White House on St Patrick's Day, but so also were the Loyalist paramilitary leaders.

But first, another Clinton initiative should be mentioned. The peace envoy, as we have seen, did not materialise, but an economic envoy did, on 2 December 1994. It was a tangible example of Clinton's oft-repeated statement that he intended to be a friend to Ireland, not merely on St Patrick's Day, but every day of the year.[67] Two months before making the appointment, Clinton had set up an inter-departmental committee under Nancy Soderberg to examine what economic initiatives were feasible in Northern Ireland and along the border counties. This was an initiative long recommended in Washington by John Hume. With Clinton's backing a team was assembled consisting of officials from USAID, the Treasury, the Departments of State and Trade and the Office of Budget Management.

On the basis of their report Clinton appointed one of Washington's most respected figures, Senator George Mitchell, the former senate majority leader, as Special Advisor to the President and Secretary of State for economic initiatives in Ireland. Clinton said: '. . . at this historic and hopeful moment, it is essential to create more economic opportunity in a region whose prospects have been so blighted by bloodshed. There must be a peace dividend in Ireland for the peace to succeed. Peace and prosperity depend on one another.[68] He backed these words by increasing the International Fund for Ireland's allocation from $20 million to $30 million over the next two years. But the major single item in his package was the announcement of an investment conference on Ireland of unparalleled scope and prestige, to be held under the auspices of the White House in 1995.

Clinton also sent the Secretary of State for Commerce, Ron Brown, to another investment conference, which John Major was hosting in Belfast in the first week of December. This was marred by arguments over a refusal on the part of the British to extend to Sinn Fein the same parity of esteem extended to the other guests. For example Sinn Fein were not invited to the dinner which Major hosted to mark the conference. Adams, who was in America and in touch with the White House at the time, pointed out to Tony Lake the folly of discriminating against Sinn Fein at a gathering whose stated aim was to put an end to discrimination. The Americans let it be known to the British that they might not attend the conference if Sinn Fein were not put on the same footing as the other invitees, and the squabble was resolved.

The row threw an ominous shadow over another historic conference held in Belfast around the same time. On Friday 9 December, Martin McGuinness led a Sinn Fein delegation to Stormont, to meet openly with officials. Unlike Albert Reynolds' full-frontal performance in Dublin with John Hume and Gerry Adams, there were no politicians present. Sinn Fein was not mainstreamed but tributarised. It was a milestone event and the publicity surrounding it obscured the significance of the British niggling over the economic conference. Subsequently, when the chamber where the meeting took place burned down, it was averred that the blaze was caused, not by a wiring fault, but by the sparks generated by Carson's statue in the grounds revolving on its plinth.

But both Belfast meetings were in their turn completely overshadowed by even more dramatic events taking plce in Dublin: the fall of Albert Reynolds as Taoiseach. This was one of the most shambolic occurrences in Irish political history. A tale to be told, not by a historian, but by a dark humorist of the school of Swift or Flann O'Brien. The proximate cause of Reynolds' departure was a paedophile priest. On 6 October 1994, the Belfast TV programme, *Counterpoint*, broadcast allegations that Dublin was delaying the extradition of a Norbetine priest, a Fr Smith, from the Republic to the Six Counties where he was wanted on child sex abuse charges.

By November 1994, allegations were being made in the Dail that the Attorney-General's office was responsible for the delays. Nevertheless Reynolds decided to press ahead with a decision to appoint the Attorney-General, Harry Whelehan, as President of the High Court. The decision was taken in Government Buildings, Dublin, on the afternoon of 11 November. At the same time, on another floor of the same building, Martin Mansergh was co-chairing a meeting of the liaison committee with Sir John Chilcott, on the question of achieving a balanced constitutional understanding between Dublin and London, involving changes in the Government of Ireland Act and Articles Two and Three. Alas, balanced understanding proved to be required somewhere nearer to home – between the coalition partners. It was not forthcoming.

Eoghan Fitzsimmons, who succeeded Whelehan, made two damaging revelations almost immediately after being appointed. The first, that this was not the first time there had been delays in processing an extradition request of this type involving a priest. The second, that Reynolds had known this when appointing Whelan to the High Court. On the 16th Dick Spring announced to the Dail that he and his party were withdrawing from the coalition. Reynolds continued in office as an interim taoiseach, being succeeded as leader of Fianna Fail by Bertie Ahern on 19 November. Ahern and Spring had almost completed negotiations on the formation of another government when a fresh crisis broke.

On 5 December, the *Irish Times* reported that Reynolds had not only known of earlier delays in the Attorney-General's office, he had in fact attempted to dissuade Whelehan from going forward with the High Court position, on the grounds that if he did so Reynolds might be forced to resign with harmful consequences to the peace process. However, Whelehan had insisted on being given the job, refusing even to delay his swearing-in, and Reynolds, having failed to get him to withdraw, then sent him into the Dail to defend his credentials for the post. Spring decided that, because Fianna Fail ministers had known of the discussions with Whelehan, he could not enter coalition with them. He broke off his negotiations with Ahern, Whelehan resigned his judgeship, and the country was plunged into a sea of confusion and gossip.

We need not concern ourselves with the various rumours and questions which arose. The effect on the peace process is our main concern. Sir Patrick Mayhew was quickly off the mark with a statement that the instability would have the effect of delaying the drafting of the framework document.[69]

And indeed initially it appeared that Reynolds' departure would not merely cause delay, but derailment. So much so that rumours have since surfaced in both Dublin and Washington, where the Irish-Americans have sources of information in both the CIA and the FBI, that the Smith affair had been masterminded by British intelligence as a 'sting' to get rid of Reynolds, who had become the dread of sections of Whitehall (and NIO) officialdom through his evident influence over Major. It became known that, during the time that the Six Counties authorities were seeking the priest's extradition, he paid at least four documented visits to the north with the knowledge of the RUC. Yet no effort was made to apprehend him.

Nowhere was Reynolds's departure greeted with more dismay than amongst Irish-Americans. Their champion, the man who had successfully reached for the golden glove, had suddenly been hurled from his pedestal. I happened to be in New York in a pub one night during the drama with three of those most affected, Niall O'Dowd, Kieran Staunton and Sean Mackin. Mackin was one of the principal figures whom Joe Cahill was anxious to brief on the ceasefire. Like Staunton, Mackin is a man of considerable energy and intelligence. The pair would have been wealthy men if they applied the time to their working careers which they devoted to their cause. Mackin was in the pub, killing time until a club which needed attention to its plumbing would close, so that he and his companion could work for the rest of the night. Staunton was the barman.

They talked casually about their efforts, mentioning a recent successful dinner for businessmen they had organised in Omaha, Nebraska, and how already some of the new Republican intake on Capitol Hill had proved responsive to their lobbying. O'Dowd was on the 'phone to Dublin and Belfast. Every so often he would come back to the bar to deliver a progress report. With each new piece of information Staunton would pour himself another cup of tea and groan: 'John Bruton as Taoiseach. Well we can't blame the Brits this time.' Finally, as Mackin finished describing how a prominent Republican Senator and a number of Congressmen had promised support in the past few days, Staunton banged down his cup and exploded, 'Businessmen! Congressmen! Senators! And I'm a fucking barman and you're a fucking plumber! We must be doing something wrong. John Bruton for Taoiseach!'

Bruton, the leader of Fine Gael, who is widely liked on all sides of the political divide for his fundamental decency, is also suspected in some Nationalist circles of a pro-Unionist stance. Even by the standards of the right-wing Fine Gael party, his attitudes are regarded as unusual. A Conservative MP who had dealings with him remarked wonderingly to me: 'You know, he's a bigger bloody Unionist than I am.!' Bruton did become Taoiseach, cobbling together a 'rainbow coalition' with both Spring's Labour Party and the small Democratic Left party. He then appointed Sean Donlon, already mentioned in this chapter, as his adviser on Northern Ireland. This appointment was not received with joy in the ranks of Irish-American activists. Initially, Bruton was opposed to Sinn Fein collecting in the US. However, once he became convinced of the worth of the initiative, he supported it wholeheartedly. And in fairness to Bruton it must be said that he addressed the peace process with as much dedication as one could have wished. It was just that stylistically something seemed to have gone from the scene. Tongues wagged knowingly in political circles during April 1995, when it became known that, in response to an unexpected question at a Fine Gael function[70] in Cork, he had burst out in exasperation at this 'fucking peace process'. It was taken as a true indication of his regard for an issue that was taking up time he would have preferred to devote to other concerns. Reynolds, on the other hand, both had an empathy for the problem and rated it as his top priority. He had called me to his office one afternoon shortly before the ceasefire, and I put an extra coin in the meter, purely as a precaution against there being a delay before he could see me for the expected fifteen- or twenty-minute discussion.

In fact the meeting turned out exactly as O'Dowd described his encounter with the American delegation. Aides with bulging files were banished whenever they appeared in his office. Countless cups of tea were drunk, as Reynolds, clearly totally preoccupied with the Northern situation, teased out every possible permutation and combination of events, or, as he described it in his favourite phrase, tried to 'call it'. He showed the light-hearted interest and enthusiasm of a man trying to guess the outcome of a horse race or a business deal. Yet the stakes were extremely high and the position serious. He had written to Sinn Fein delivering what was in effect an ultimatum. He had said that if 'for whatever reason' the party could not show tangible progress towards a cessation of violence, then he would have to re-consider his policy. When I emerged, so much time had elapsed, in excess of two hours, that the traffic wardens had gone off duty.

For all the undoubted sincerity of his well-meaning approach, Bruton just was not naturally enthused by the Northern issue to the same degree as Reynolds. Nor did he have the same working relationship with Major, although he consistently went out of his way to praise the English Prime Minister. Reynolds however could ring up Major and consult with his opposite number as to whether the climate was right at the moment to advance some aspect of policy or other. If Major was in difficulties, the two men were able to come to an agreement on timing and nuance. But when Bruton raised with Major, at a Paris EU meeting, the unwisdom of Major's bowing to pressure to release the paratrooper Private Lee Clegg, who had been jailed for the murder of a Belfast joy-rider, while Republican prison releases had still not begun, he was, in the words of his critics, publicly 'slapped down'.[71] Major said that this was a matter for the British only to decide, and decide it they did. Given the state of Major's back benches he could have said nothing else, but it is a safe speculation that had Reynolds still been in office, the Clegg matter would have been raised without public consequences.

There was one permutation that nobody on the Irish negotiating team had 'called' at the time of his becoming Taoiseach. As one Irish diplomat described it bemusedly: 'We factored in every possible eventuality except the possibility that the British would espouse the Unionist position.' Cynics might have observed that given the history of Anglo-Irish relationships, that should have been regarded as the first possibility. But in the euphoria that surrounded the Downing Street Declaration, this had seemed unthinkable. However, as 1995 wore on it became more and more evident that this was what was happening.

One can point to the date on which the rot began to spread: 6 December 1994, appropriately enough the same day that it was made known to the Dail that Harry Whelehan had refused to resign, even though he had been informed that this would mean that Reynolds would have to go, thus jeopardising the peace process. In the House of Commons the Ulster Unionist Party MPs joined with Labour and Tory party rebels to defeat the Conservatives 319 to 311 over a proposal to increase VAT on fuel bills. Thus with Reynolds gone, there was both a heightened doubt about John Major's continuation in office, and a clear indication of the strength of the Unionists' influence in either increasing or resolving said doubts. The importance of the vote was initially obscured by what seemed a major step forward in the peace process, the publication by the two Governments of the Framework Document on 22 February 1995.

Its stated aim was to 'assist discussion and negotiation involving the Northern Ireland parties.'[72] It built on both the three-strand process and the Downing St Declaration in adopting a number of 'guiding principles':

The principle of self-determination, as set out in the Joint Declaration.

That the consent of the governed is an essential ingredient for stability in any political arrangement.

That agreement must be pursued and established by exclusively democratic, peaceful means, without resort to violence or coercion.

That any new political arrangements must be based on full respect for, and protection and expression of, the rights and identities of both traditions in Ireland and even-handedly afford both communities in Northern Ireland parity of esteem and treatment, including equality of opportunity and advantage.

The Framework Document envisaged far-reaching changes, in existing structures involving the two islands, in relationships within the two parts of Ireland and within the North. The new North-South institutions were envisaged as having executive functions of 'clear identity and purpose, to enable representatives of democratic institutions, north and south, to enter into new, co-operative and constructive relationships'. And the East-West structures clearly gave Dublin a role in the 'operation of the new arrangements'. There was to be a new parliamentary forum and new working arrangements between the northern and southern civil services. The Document also spoke of a 'balanced accommodation' on constitutional issues involving an 'agreed new approach to the traditional constitutional doctrines on both sides'.

Far reaching proposals indeed. However documents propose and men dispose. The Unionists were not disposed to talk to Dublin and the British increasingly showed themselves unwilling to encourage them to do so. Meanwhile the British also showed themselves increasingly unwilling to talk to Sinn Fein. The Stormont talks at official level achieved very little and the British only sanctioned a meeting between McGuinness and Michael Ancram, Minister for Political Affairs, after Adams had been formally received at the White House, in the teeth of British disapproval, in March 1995. Even then the talks were described by the British as being merely 'exploratory'. Mayhew only agreed to meet Adams in a hotel room in Washington the following May, at the commencement of the economic conference initiated by President Clinton, because otherwise the conference would have been dominated by media efforts to picture the two men together, rather than by the theme of investment opportunities in Ireland. Full scale all-party talks, including Sinn Fein, to give effect to the Framework Document remained a remote possibility. Whatever inclination there may have been in Whitehall to attempt risking Unionist wrath, at least to the extent of starting such talks without Paisley's party, evaporated as Major's position in the House of Commons steadily weakened.

The stated argument against involving Sinn Fein in talks was 'de-commissioning'. Netted down, this meant that the British wanted the IRA to give up its arms and explosives before talking to Sinn Fein. Two points should be noted concerning this demand. One, it is in clear breach of the commitment given in Article 10 of the Downing St Declaration quoted above, about the admission of democratically elected parties to talks, 'once they proved that they intended to abide by the democratic process'. Secondly it was never mentioned either in the talks that went on between the British and Sinn Fein in 1992–3, nor in those involving the British and Albert Reynolds. But it began to be heard with increasing frequency after the Unionists' anti-Tory vote on the VAT issue.

Had, say, either McGuinness or Adams attempted any such thing, they would not only have seriously jeopardised their own safety, but that of the peace process also. As Adams said, even a symbolic gesture of de-commissioning IRA weapons in advance of talks would 'symbolise an IRA surrender'.[73] He accused Britain of 'attempting to gain by stealth what it could not achieve in 25 years of military conflict'. The Sinn Fein position is that 'de-commissioning' should take place as a result of an all-party agreement on a total demilitarisation of the Six Counties.

At the time of writing there were 130,000 legally held weapons in Loyalist hands.[74] In addition to these there were the countless thousands that either fell off, or did not get put on, lorries, at times such as the abolition of the B-Specials and the UDR, and those smuggled into the country by British intelligence with the help of Brian Nelson. Each of the 32,000 security force members also carries a personal weapon, apart from those they have access to. The combined British Army/RUC presence means that in 1994/5 there was one security force person to every 3.7 Catholic males between the age of sixteen and forty-four. In addition there are the 1,000 MI5 personnel whom the MI5 Director, Stella Rimington, estimates[75] are engaged in combatting the IRA. The omnipresent security presence was such that, in an area the size of Yorkshire, there were 135 fixed military installations. Even Nationalists who oppose the IRA's use of force are made uneasy by these statistics at the prospect of Republican guns being handed in while Loyalist ones and the former death squads, remain at large.

However, the sheer numbers of counter-insurgency personnel involved give the military a strong say in what happens to them in any 'de-commissioning' talks. Where the RUC are concerned, to reduce the force to the policing levels obtaining in the Republic would entail a reduction of 12,000 members of the force. From 16,000 to 4,000 to arrive at the Republic's ratio of 1 Garda: 400 civilians. Where the Army is concerned, the North of Ireland has been an invaluable experimental training ground for weapons systems, anti-riot techniques and counter-insurgency, which has resulted in lucrative sales and contracts. For example Russia and the Baltic Republics were among the countries that had arrangements with the Ministry of Defence for training with the SAS and Parachute regiments in these skills at the time of writing.

Knowing the complexity of the issue, and understanding the passions involved, the Republic's leaders have opposed the use of the de-commissioning ploy to stall talks. While broadcasting a strong appeal[76] against hanging up on the 'de-commissioning' question, Albert Reynolds recalled how both his own party, Fianna Fail, and the Democratic Left had both emerged from the physical force tradition – but by dumping their arms, not surrendering them – and so were able to carry their followers with them into the parliamentary arena. He also referred pointedly to the need for an agreed police force, which could command the support of both communities, emerging from 'de-commissioning' talks. Dick Spring went even further. He said 'If we take the attitude that nothing with happen unless there is a surrender or de-commissioning of arms, then I think that is a formula for disaster.'

Spring was speaking in Washington on 1 March 1995, at a particularly highly charged moment: The eve of the opening of a serious fissure in the much vaunted Special Relationship between London and Washington over the Irish issue. At the time Spring spoke, it appeared that the British had won a significant victory. Patrick Mayhew had successfully lobbied Washington not to allow Sinn Fein to collect funds in the US and not to invite Gerry Adams to the White House for the Clintons' gala on St Patrick's Day. However his hardline approach and domineering manner had offended a key figure in the Clinton administration: Vice-President Al Gore, who had hitherto been unfavourably disposed towards the idea of Sinn Fein being allowed to collect funds. By contrast, Spring, visiting Washington during the same period, had made an excellent impression, and he was strongly in favour of Sinn Fein being allowed to collect. So far as decision-taking Dublin is concerned, the more dividends the peace process can be made to show for the Republicans, the less likely is a return to war.

It was at this juncture that, on Tuesday, 7 March 1995, Chris Dodd and Bill Clinton played their historic game of golf. Clinton did not immediately reveal his hand. Washington had already tilted towards London, following Mayhew's visit. The CIA, The State Department, The Justice Department, and, surprisingly, even the National Security Council had all come out against fund-raising permission being granted. However at a White election stratagy meeting after the golf game attended by Gore and his chief of staff, Jack Quinn, Dodd returned to the charge. This time he found to his surprise that he was strongly backed by both Gore and Quinn. After Mayhew's visit Gore had re-thought his position. Still Clinton said nothing.

At this stage Republican Congressmen Peter King, who had just returned from attending the Sinn Fein Ard Fheis, unexpectedly received a 'phone call from the President. He had called the White House as a matter of courtesy to pass on any observations which might be thought useful concerning his visit. To his surprise his call was returned not by a member of the President's staff but by Clinton himself. Afterwards King told Niall O'Dowd: 'It was amazing to me. Here was the President reaching out to me, someone from the opposite party, and he just talked my ear off on Ireland. Although he never revealed his hand I had a feeling he was making the right decision.' In the meantime Jean Kennedy Smith, in O'Dowd's words, had 'kept up a relentless stream of pressure from Ireland on the key congressional and White House figures.'

To ensure that King's feeling about Clinton's making the right decision came through, Dodds enlisted Ted Kennedy's aid for one last push. The Senator 'phoned Clinton and urged him to follow his own instincts – and trust the people who had advised him correctly on the Adams visa issue and the subsequent ceasefires. It worked: a surprised Tony Lake and Nancy Soderberg were called into the Oval Office and told, in the words of the Framework Document, that a little 'balanced constitutional arrangement' was needed. In other words they were to negotiate a mechanism with Sinn Fein whereby, in return for a statement moving the de-commissioning issue forward, permission to fund-raise in the USA would be granted. Niall O'Dowd acted as an intermediary between Adams and the NSC. A Sinn Fein statement was duly cobbled together which showed flexibility on the de-commissioning issue. It then began to appear, to the Irish lobby at least, that the British agreed to begin talks at ministerial level provided that Sinn Fein agreed to discuss de-commissioning, as part of those talks.

St Patrick's Day in the White House was a night to remember. The roof almost lifted off to the sound of the cheers that greeted John Hume, when he broke off singing 'The Town That I Loved So Well' to say: 'come up here Gerry and join in.' As the applause for the Hume and Adams duet died away, Bruce Morrison turned to Niall O'Dowd and asked: 'Do you think the State Department will get the message now?' It was truly a night in which Irish eyes were smiling. Nuns and priests,

Loyalist paramilitary leaders, Cardinals and diplomats, the great and the good of America seemed to be saying that peace in Ireland was assured. Travelling around the country at that time I found that a glow had spread through the Irish community. However, after the party, the hang-over. The Irish-Americans had not anticipated the virulence of the British reaction to the reversal on the fund-raising decision and the extending of the invitation to the White House to Gerry Adams. John Major was so furious that for a whole week he refused to accept a 'phone call from Clinton. It was a moment unparalleled in recent Anglo-American relationships.

And it was not an isolated fit of pique. Nearly three months later, on 14 June, the *Irish Times* Washington correspondent, Conor O'Clery, reported that London was making difficulties about a visit by Clinton to Belfast which he had planned to make in November and December 1995, as part of a visit to both Ireland and England. O'Clery reported that the British had told the White House that there were 'scheduling problems' over the dates proposed. London had earlier turned down Clinton's suggestion that he should come in August. O'Clery quoted a White House spokesman as saying pointedly of Clinton: '. . . we have played a helpful role in nurturing that process and he [Clinton] intends to continue to do so. Availability to travel is one aspect of that.'

Clinton had intended to announce his Irish visit during the course of a most significant demonstration of American good will to the peace process, the White House Economic Summit on Ireland which opened at the Sheraton Hotel, Washington, on 25 May. According to the *Irish Times* it: '. . . represented the most significant engagement by the United States in the affairs of any European country since President Truman's Marshall Plan after the Second World War, which helped put Western Europe back on its feet.' President Clinton presided over the three-day conference, which was also attended by Vice-President Al Gore, the Commerce Secretary Ron Brown, the Secretary of State, Warren Christopher and of course Senator George Mitchell. The object of the conference was to bring to the attention of American business leaders the opportunities for American investment both in the Six Counties and in the counties of the Republic which lie along the border: Louth, Cavan, Monaghan Sligo, Leitrim, and Donegal.

This all-Ireland approach did not please Whitehall, which privately let it be known that there were objections to the idea of Ireland being considered as one unit. And the NIO was concerned lest the Republic gain the lion's share of the hoped-for investment, because the Republic's incentives for attracting industry are better than those of the UK, which of course apply in the Six Counties. Nevertheless, for three days corporate America was treated to a hymn to the virtues of Ireland, orchestrated by the White House. The fourteen-hundred-strong attendance included of some of America's biggest businessmen and -women. Nothing on the same scale had ever occurred in the USA before. The Irish trade agencies say that the effect is likely to be incalculable and that the event 'surpassed all expectations'.[77] The American administration has thrown its weight behind an effort to revitalise the economy of Ireland.

In the course of an elegant and often humorous appeal for peace and prosperity in

Ireland, and after pointing out the contribution which Ulster Protestants had made to America, including forming part of his own ancestry, Clinton said[78]:

> I urge American businessmen and all others to consider investing in Northern Ireland and the Border counties. The opportunities are excellent. The workforce is well educated and well motivated. The productivity levels are high. The unit labour costs are low. The labour relations are good. The infrastructure, the communications, the access to the European market are fine.

Coming from the President of the United States, this was a remarkable endorsement of a country and its people. But it was another part of Clinton's speech, a reference to the sombre back-drop to the conference and the vexed question of de-commissioning, which was at the heart of a dispiriting controversy that blights the Peace Process as this book goes to the press. The President also said:

> I call on all those who continue to employ violence to end the punishment beatings and the intimidation. And to take the next step and begin to discuss serious de-commissioning of weapons. Paramilitaries on both sides must get rid of their bombs and guns and the spectre of violence that has haunted Ireland must be banished once and for all . . .
>
> Many innocents disappeared during the Troubles. Others were banished from their homes. Today there are families that have still not had the chance to grieve in peace, to visit the homes of their loved ones, to re-unite after years of separation. It is time to allow families to be whole again.[79]

There can be nothing but agreement and approval for the second paragraph above. Gerry Adams was amongst those seen to applaud when President Clinton read it out. The statement describes some of the tragic detritus of war: victims of the Troubles, banished from their homes by the IRA, or in the case of the 'disappearances' (perhaps twelve in all), people whom the IRA shot for some reason but without announcing the fact, because the deceased, who lie in unmarked graves, were members of families whom the Republicans either respected or were beholden to. However the President's first appeal, dealing with de-commissioning, generated serious tensions for the Irish-Americans and for Sinn Fein, as was no doubt intended by those who pressed for the inclusion of such a reference in the President's speech in the first place – the British.

Anxious to get the British back on side, after the St Patrick's Day affair, because of Bosnia and other considerations, the National Security Council had become progressively more responsive to London's urgings. Downing Street, for its part, had adapted to the American tactic of making a figure such as Nancy Soderberg at the NSC, rather than some State Department diplomat, the principal conduit of Irish policy to and from the White House, by working through channels other than the Foreign Office. Rod Liney became a key figure in London's strategy. Liney, once officially described as a secretary to John Major, came to be regarded by those in Dublin, Belfast and Washington who saw him in operation as deploying political rather than secretarial weaponry, and fairly heavy weaponry at that. President Clinton's de-commissioning reference, which did not of itself constitute a requirement that Sinn Fein agree to dispose of its arms before being admitted to all-party talks, nevertheless came to be represented as such in Washington. The bombing of the FBI building in Oklahoma by a right-wing fanatic using home-made explosives similar to those used by the IRA, which occurred while the controversy was at its height, added to Clinton's pressures.

Sufficient heat was generated from London to make it seem not only reasonable but essential to expect capitulation on the de-commissioning issue by Sinn Fein, for having gone out on a limb for the Irish. As a result the London *Times* was able to report (on 6 July 1995) that Gerry Adams had been told by the White House that it was: 'time for him to deliver on the issue of de-commissioning the IRA's arsenal'. Days before the story appeared, Adams had in fact been presented not with one, but with two documents containing what *The Times* correctly termed 'strongly worded demarches'. To underline the seriousness of the White House approach, the Sinn Fein leader had been given one by Jean Kennedy Smith, the other by the American Ambassador in London, Admiral Crowe.

But Adams had been made an offer he could not accept. Three weeks after the *Times* story appeared (on 27 July 1995) he wrote a strongly worded commentary on the de-commissioning issue in *An Phoblacht/Republican News* in which he said that a review of the peace process, 'even from the most neutral perspective', would find that:

> the Unionist parties had not engaged at all and indeed that their leaderships are highly suspicious and hostile to the process ... From an Irish Nationalist or Republican perspective the judgement would be much more damning. The British Government would be seen to have been minimalistic, begrudging and provocatively negative in its approach.

He was even more forthright on the de-commissioning issue:

> The British Government and others may be miscalculating the IRA's position on de-commissioning or the Sinn Fein leadership's room for manoeuvre on this issue. If this is so they do so with the benefit of having heard at first hand from Sinn Fein that the IRA will not de-commission or surrender its weapons to anyone as a precondition for all-party talks. This is no room for manoeuvre ... If a surrender of weapons had been imposed as a pre-condition to peace negotiations prior to the cessation there would have been no IRA ceasefire.

Adams' article appeared at a low point. Although some small rays of sunlight had begun to break through the clouds of gloom over-shadowing the peace process, even the most sanguine observers now realised that, putting de-commissioning apart, if the IRA could have foreseen the minimalist British response there would have been no ceasefire announcement on 31 August 1994. More important, it was seen to be highly unlikely that, if London continued to do as it was doing, the peace would hold much beyond 31 August 1995. Responding to the widespread worry in the Republican community at the lack of progress, Adams had spoken publicly of 'a crisis building up' in the course of a radio interview in mid-June[80]. He said there was no question of IRA 'de-commissioning' in advance of talks, and warned that there was a possibility of a return to violence unless 'progress' occurred in the peace process. By 'progress' Adams meant that Sinn Fein should be treated like other political parties and admitted to talks as had been promised in the Downing Street Declaration.

Martin McGuinness underlined the danger during his key-note Bodenstown address delivered the day after Adams made his assessment.[81] He said that Britain intended to wreck the peace process by making use of the 'de-commissioning' ploy, and made it clear to journalists after his speech that he was 'quite fearful' about the prospect of violence resuming as a result of British stalling tactics. Nevertheless, while ruling out unilateral de-commissioning, he said:

> However, it is equally obvious and inevitable that there must be and will be a universal de-commissioning of arms, British and Irish, once an all-encompassing political discussion and framework is agreed upon.[82]

Following McGuinness's Bodenstown speech, Bruton attempted to cool the situation by denying that there was a crisis in the peace process, referring to the continuing behind-the-scenes Dublin–London contacts as grounds for optimism. However, despite his words, as the *Irish Independent* pointed out in an editorial comment the next day (2 June 1995), the situation was obviously 'precarious'. It stayed precarious, and Bruton's various attempts to be reassuring in the succeeding weeks, in the face of the self-evident facts, had one unwelcome result in some Republican circles: A body of opinion built up that the British were succeeding in their efforts to drive a wedge between Dublin and Sinn Fein. This did not happen; despite his stylistic differences with Reynolds, Bruton remained equally committed to the peace process, and Adams and he established a working relationship.

Nevertheless no movement occurred, and with the anniversary of the ceasefire looming up in August, pressures on the Sinn Fein leadership were clearly building from those within the IRA who felt that this ceasefire was doomed to go the way of all earlier cessations, and was merely being used by the British as a ploy to split the movement. The Dublin Government conveyed these fears to London, but to no avail. In fact in places like East Tyrone, where, as in South Armagh and elsewhere, opposition to the ceasefire amongst Republicans was known to be strong, the security forces harrassed young men, as though peace had never come. Also, as if to stoke up the fires, members of the RIR (formally UDR) were quietly told to resume carrying their personal weapons in the anticipation of what Unionist spokesmen began referring to as a 'rolling return' to violence: in other words a planned, gradual return to full-scale hostilities throughout the Six Counties. On what intelligence those reports are based one can only speculate, because the consensus in Republican circles concerning a possible resumption of violence (and this is manifestly not desired by the overwhelming majority of the leadership) is that if the ceasefire does break down, the war would be resumed not in Ireland, but in Britain.

However around Portadown, some of the Loyalist paramilitary leaders who had been most prominent in the Catholic assassination campaign, but who had kept a low profile since the ceasefires, became highly visible once again. Contacts of mine spoke of feeling in the Loyalist paramilitary world running 'at 1974 levels'. Whether this meant that there was a sense that Loyalism should be mobilised, lest there be a 'sell-out' to Republicanism, or that some hidden intelligence hand was at work, I cannot say. But whatever orchestration was taking place, it was obviously no rehearsal of a hymn to peace. This fact was disturbingly underlined by the detention of a group of Loyalists in Glasgow at the end of July on arms procurement charges. One of them, Lindsay Robb, had been conducting negotiations with Stormont ministers on behalf of the Loyalist paramilitaries (the UVF).

Placing the most charitable interpretation possible on the course of events, it would appear that John Major's Irish policy was at best affected by the drift and paralysis engendered by his problems within the Conservative Party, and at worst by a calculated attempt to influence his more atavistic supporters by acting in a manner designed to appease them, particularly over the treatment of prisoners. The issue of prisoners generally, as we saw during the hunger-strike saga, is one of the most sensitive aspects of the entire conflict. But the position of Irish prisoners in British jails is particularly fraught. Apart from normal tensions, there were other problems: the existence of widespread prejudice in the British prison system against 'Irish terrorists', which even innocents like the Birmingham Six or the Guildford Four encountered; the difficulties experienced by relatives in finding the money and opportunity to travel to England to see prisoners, who are frequently switched from one jail to another at very short notice; the particularly harsh sentences imposed on the 'UK mainland', as compared even to the Six Counties with their Diplock Courts. At the time of writing, one prisoner, Paul Norney, had served twenty-one years without review, for a life sentence imposed when he was seventeen years old. But beyond these factors there is an unacknowledged policy of using the Republican prisoners in British jails as hostages or bargaining counters in underground negotiations with the Republicans.

I remember Daithi O'Conaill in a matter-of-fact way telling me how during one such series of talks the IRA had offered to: 'stop knocking off off-duty UDR personnel, if the Brits would ease up on our lads in British jails.' For the record, neither cessation occurred. 'It gets dirty down there . . .' One would have thought that the ceasefire would have led to an improvement in the attitude towards the Irish prisoners, but as the Fianna Fail spokesperson on Foreign Affairs, Ray Burke, pointed out, these prisoners' conditions worsened from the declaration of the ceasefire and a markedly vindictive attitude was displayed towards them by the authorities[83]. Things were getting dirty at the beginning of July in two British jails in particular, Belmarsh and Whitemoor, and a dirty protest by a group of Irish prisoners commenced later in the month at Whitemoor. Any civilised person who heard the British civil rights lawyer Garret Pierce, who defended the Guildford Four, being interviewed about the conditions under which the men were held could not have failed to be appalled.[84] Apart from contending with lack of exercise, and obstacles being placed in the way of their seeing their relatives and lawyers, the men were held in such cramped, unnatural conditions that they faced problems of arthritis and failing eye-sight.

But things were getting dirty in the Conservative Party also. John Major decided that he had no option but to put his premiership on the line and hold a leadership contest, which he duly won early in July. One of the sops which he found it necessary to throw to Cerberus, the Tory right, was the release of the paratrooper, Private Lee Clegg who had become a *cause célèbre* with the tabloid press. The release occurred on the eve of the crucial leadership vote. But more importantly, in the Irish context, it happened just one week before the pinnacle of the 'marching season' on 12 July. Of itself, this was a highly provocative act, coming at a time when Protestant–Catholic relationships are traditionally at their worst in Northern Ireland. However trouble could have been avoided if Clegg's release had been accompanied by a display of similar clemency towards Loyalist and Republican prisoners. In particular the transfer of the Whitemoor and Belmarsh prisoners to jails in Ireland would have been seen as a balancing humanitarian gesture.

No such releases or transfers occurred. Worse, the Tory spokespersons who appeared incessantly before camera and microphone to justify the Clegg decision did so in a manner which came across in Ireland, not merely as an attempt to justify the indefensible, but as a collective manifestation of British post-imperial trauma. In his book, *The State We're In*[85], which appeared, appropriately enough, not long before the Conservative leadership contest and the resultant Clegg release, the distinguished economist Will Hutton summarised some of the effects of sustained Tory rule on Britain, effects which explain, if they do not forgive, London's Irish policy as follows:

> . . . politicians seem incapable of reaching out beyond their own tribal loyalties . . . There is a general sense of fear and beleaguerment . . . Abroad Britain is increasingly isolated. Unwilling to pool sovereignty any further with its European partners or adapt its idiosyncratic institutions to the modern world, it is marginal to the process of constructing a more integrated Europe . . . and continues to spend more on defence than its European allies without any clear strategic idea of what to do with its military hardware. It desperately wants a special alliance with the US, but in the aftermath of the Cold War the Americans have become industrial and trade competitors with Europe . . . The US is increasingly unmoved by its 'special relationship' with a third-class state.[86]

Ireland unfortunately has powerful reasons for being all too moved by its de facto 'special relationship' with Britain. As the Tories used the Clegg affair to mount a horrifying display of the arrogance and remoteness from reality encapsulated in the Hutton critique, Ireland, north and south, was gripped by a sense of anger and injustice. The Tories' stated reasons for Clegg's release were both conflicting and an insult to the intelligence. The release had A: Nothing to do with the leadership crisis and B: Was taken solely on legal grounds. The *Irish Times* accurately summed up most thinking people's sentiments in the Republic when it said that the British Government's attempts to:

> . . . justify the Clegg release on legal grounds has only exacerbated the feelings of anger surrounding the refusal to reconsider the position of Loyalist and Republican prisoners, since the main reason for action has been, in effect, 'The law must follow its course'.[87]

But in the Six Counties reaction spread beyond the editorial columns. The hijacker and the petrol-bomber made a multi-million pound reappearance on the streets. There is no doubt that the Republicans orchestrated and controlled some three days of major destruction, and some lesser acts of hooliganism, during that week of the Conservative leadership battle (3–9 July), before Gerry Adams judged it opportune to make a successful appeal for calm. But had that destruction of property not occurred, there is every likelihood that guns could have come out and there would have been loss of life.

For in the Catholic ghettoes, given the paratroopers' record and the experience of the shoot-to-kill policy and all that had gone before, a very special significance had been attached to the Clegg affair. Just as when one enters the home of a hunter one can see at a glance from the trophies on the wall where his interests lie, so mural culture has traditionally expressed the strident emotions of the Six County streets. Although Tory spokespersons such as Lady Maitland flooded the TV screens to explain that the peace-keeping Clegg's case was different from that of terrorist killers who deliberately went out with their weapons to kill people, TV images of another sort had already seared the minds of Nationalist viewers with disbelief. The huge, crude wall-painting in Clegg's barracks, which no-one had the wit to obliterate before a visit by Neil Kinnock brought the cameras into the mess-room, is one of the best known and oft-repeated clips of the Troubles. It shows a bullet-holed, crashed car, with a bloody, dead joy-rider, hanging from an open door. The sound of bursting petrol bombs was Belfast's answer to that vision and to Lady Maitland's arguments.

Rioting broke out again the following week because of the 12 July parades. This time the Orangemen were the source of the disturbances. In Portadown they clashed with police, demanding to be allowed to march through the Catholic Garvaghy Road area. This was not a 'traditional' march route as the Garvaghy estate was but newly built. Nevertheless Ian Paisley said the right to march through Garvaghy Road was a matter of life or death.[88] A matter of 'Ulster or the Irish Republic, freedom or slavery, light or darkness'. He said of a Jesuit priest, Fr Eamon Stack, who negotiated with the authorities on behalf of the Garvaghy residents, that he had been 'sent by the Pope to Portadown. Anywhere you have a Jesuit you can expect trouble. And there will be trouble.'[89] From the 10th to the 12th there was tension and violence in the town as the police tried to achieve a compromise between the Orangemen and the Nationalists. Plastic baton rounds were fired as the Orangemen tried to break through the cordons keeping them from Garvaghy.

After almost three days of stand-off, a compromise was agreed between the police and negotiators on behalf of the Orange men, who included Paisley and David Trimble, the Ulster Unionist MP, whereby the marchers were allowed to pass through the Catholic area but in silence, without bands and without provocation. Trimble's very public espousal of the Orangemen was apparently related to the leadership struggle which was getting under way in the Unionist party as James Molyneaux prepared to retire. Radio Eireann broadcast bulletins on the Garvaghy confrontation for much of the two nights before the compromise was agreed. Even in the Republic it was a chilling experience to lie in bed listening to the Orangemen, many of them obviously under the influence of drink, beating their drums and howling defiance at the police as they attempted to break into the

Catholic area. What it must have been like for those encircled, particularly with young families, one can only speculate.

Overall the RUC acquitted themselves well at Garvaghy, but there was increased tension between Dublin and London over other actions by the RUC elsewhere. In Belfast the police insisted on routing an Orange march through the Ormeau Road area against the wishes of the local Catholic residents. The Ormeau Road had been the scene of the massacre of five Catholics in a sectarian attack on Graham's bookmakers shop. Previous 12 July marchers had held up five fingers as they passed the shop, and women had danced provocatively outside it. Dublin protested to London that marches should be allowed where they were welcomed, not where they were resented.[90] But the protest did not pacify many Nationalists who bracketed the Ormeau decision with the Clegg affair to make the judgement that, ceasefire or no ceasefire, 'we're right back where we started with civil rights'. This feeling was exacerbated by the decision, apparently sanctioned by Mayhew, to force through further Loyalist marches in the Ormeau Road and in Derry a month later. Inevitably further violence ensued.

Alarmed at the drift of events, Bruton, Spring, Hume and Adams issued a statement on 14 July 1995, directed at London, through the Dublin Government's Information Bureau:

We met today to review the peace process.

We reiterate our total and absolute commitment to democratic and peaceful methods of resolving political problems and our objective of an equitable and lasting agreement that can command the consent and allegiance of all.

The current impasse in the peace process is a cause for concern to all who share that objective. It must be overcome. Accordingly, we are seeking a commencement, as soon as possible, of the inclusive, all-party talks necessary to the achievement of our objective.

The statement was issued on the day the Forum for Peace and Reconciliation ended its deliberations at Dublin Castle for the summer in a 'palpable air of crisis'.[91] A few days afterwards Sinn Fein underlined its frustration at the lack of progress in the peace process by putting into operation a threat which Gerry Adams had made some months earlier. If the peace process were not advanced, then the streets would resound to 'angry voices and marching feet'. In announcing the programme of street protests throughout the North, Adams was tacitly acknowledging that there were tensions within the ranks of Republicanism which demanded an outlet: marching was a better safety valve than bombing. However his announcement put blood-pressures up in Dublin. Adams was summoned to a meeting with the three leaders of the coalition government and urged not to go ahead with the demonstrations. One of the biggest protests had been scheduled for Dublin on 26 August to mark the anniversary of the declaration of the ceasefire.

John Bruton, however, stubbornly refused to accept that there was a crisis, only an 'impasse'. He pointed out that had Garret FitzGerald 'gone on the war path' after Mrs Thatcher had made her 'out, out, out' speech, there would have been no Anglo-Irish Agreement in 1985.

He recalled that FitzGerald 'had kept at it, kept going back'.[92] This was certainly his approach to John Major. He refrained from making public statements on either the Clegg affair, Major's handling of the prisoners issue, or the Orange marches. He placed the same trust in Major's long-term intentions as did Reynolds and, despite the excitations of July, continued to work behind the scenes so that progress could be announced at a summit between himself and the British Prime Minister in Dublin later in the year.

This laudable tenacity deserves a finer interpretation than that placed upon it by at least one Tory spokesman. We have seen how Bruton has been widely perceived as a Unionist. Yet, displaying scant knowledge of Irish politics, Andrew Hunter, the Chairman of the Conservative Back-bench Committee on Northern Ireland, has attributed the failure in communications between Dublin and London to the fact that 'John Bruton is a United Ireland man'.[93] He also said the Irish Government's policy in the peace process was 'simply to dangle a carrot in front of Sinn Fein'. This indication of Tory attitudes is deeply worrying. Despite occupying a relatively lowly position in British domestic politics, Hunter, because of his role, is a figure of some importance in Anglo-Irish relationships. Given such attitudes it is not surprising therefore that by the end of July, in the words of one Government spokesman, 'a measure of despair' had crept into the Irish Government's attitude towards Britain.[94]

The general belief that if Major mastered his right-wing opponents, then progress would follow on Ireland, had not been realised. Indeed his new Cabinet Sub-Committee on Ireland contained some of the most right-wing politicians in Europe. Sir Patrick Mayhew continued as Secretary of State for Northern Ireland. He is regarded in Dublin, at best, as a latter-day version of an old-style Anglo-Irish ascendancy landlord, with supremacist notions of his own as to how the natives should be dealt with. His colleagues on the Sub-Committee include Michael Portillo, Michael Howard, and Lord Cranbourne.

Howard, in charge of prisons, in his capacity as Home Secretary, has been responsible for some of the angriest comments heard in the Dail, in the entire peace process controversy.[95] Dublin regarded a Home Office ban on security grounds on its consulary officials visiting Irish prisoners as being literally a diplomatic insult.[96] In the course of a Dail debate approving a Convention of Human Rights motion on the transfer of sentenced persons, Dick Spring described the prisoners' situation guardedly but firmly: a 'regrettable' matter which 'cannot be helpful in terms of the strengthening of the peace process'. But the Fianna Fail spokesman on Justice, John O'Donoghue, launched a widely publicised personal attack on Howard after the Home Secretary had given a radio interview in which he attempted to justify his refusal to sanction the transfer of Irish prisoners to Ireland. Citing the case of Clegg (who had been returned to a British prison to serve his truncated sentence), O'Donoghue said Howard had been: 'unhelpful, unwise, arrogant and provocative .... No amount of post-colonial imperial ignorance will advance the cause of peace on this island.' O'Donoghue could at least claim that he was in good company in his attack on Howard. At the same time the High Court in London issued a warning that the Home Secretary should either change the rules governing access to prisoners' solicitors or risk contempt of court charges.[97]

That the foregoing should be Britain's apparent response to a peace process which offered the prospect of an end to one of the world's oldest conflicts is of course deeply worrying and disappointing. Clearly John Major's Irish policy has been affected by his having a parliamentary majority of only nine seats when between them the Unionists control thirteen seats. Seen in this light, the 'decommissioning' issue is the contemporary equivalent of the 'Orange card', and we have seen where that led. But is there any other response? Are wise and responsible men secretly working to more noble purposes? Can this chapter of tragedy and prejudice end on a hopeful note? The answer is that it just possibly might. In the run-up to the truce which led to the signing of the Anglo-Irish Treaty of 1921, Lloyd George slept under a framed tract which read: 'There is a path which no fowl knoweth and which the eye of the vulture does not see'. Unknown to his hard-liners he was conducting secret negotiations with Sinn Fein. My own sense of the situation is that something similar may be happening with today's Sinn Fein. There were a number of straws in the wind towards the end of July which pointed in this direction. Probably the most significant of these was a return visit to Ireland on the weekend of the 23rd by the Morrison-O'Dowd delegation.

Again they saw central players in the peace process, including Hume, Adams and Bruton, who flabberghasted the delegates by remarking to Morrison that the fact that he lived 3,000 miles from Ireland necessarily meant that he was somewhat out of touch with the situation. However the Irish-Americans did not allow this and some other unguarded Brutonisms to detract from their mission. They brought with them assurances of continuing commitments from Washington. These are not mere platitudes. Apart from any personal empathy with the Irish, Clinton knows that the Irish peace initiative is his one foreign policy success. The *real politik* of his situation is that a preponderance of white male Americans voted for George Bush at the last presidential election. The Irish-American ethnic group constitutes Clinton's strongest hope of improving on that vote. O'Dowd and company returned to America convinced that Adams was still in firm control of his party, commanding wide support and still determined on peace, but that there is equally undeniably a dangerous groundswell of grass roots anger at the slow rate of progress in the peace process. The Irish-Americans' appreciation was that the British were unlikely to push the situation to a breakdown, at least in advance of Clinton's planned end-of-November visit. If this be true, then time bought can be time well used.

After the Irish-Americans' visit, President Clinton gave an unusual interview to the *Irish Times* Washington correspondent, Conor O'Clery, on 3 August 1995, in which he clearly fired a shot across London's bows on the issue of both talks and prisoners. He said he would welcome movement on both the prisoner and talks issues and, despite the demarches, pointedly did not repeat London's demands for de-commissioning as a pre-condition to talk. In Dublin, Jean Kennedy Smith said she was 'hopeful' that talks would start soon, increasing the speculation that Clinton visualised peace talks beginning in or around the time of his visit.

In addition to these hopeful developments, a few days before the Irish-Americans' visit, Gerry Adams had a secret meeting with Sir Patrick Mayhew in

Derry. Republicans also met with British civil servants in Belfast to discuss the planned economic regeneration of the city. This was followed up after the Americans had left Belfast by a second meeting between Adams and Mayhew, at Stormont. Adams was accompanied by Martin McGuinness. The Republican leaders gave the British a detailed outline of how Sinn Fein saw a solution being found to the talks impasse.

On the day this took place (27 July 1995), it was announced that three prisoners on the dirty protest in Whitemoor were being sent back to the Six Counties to complete their sentences. Rumours that the British are planning to restore the 50% remission of sentence which was withdrawn in 1989 also gained currency. These gestures should not be over-estimated. The Irish government released twelve Republicans from Portlaoise Jail on 29 July, making a total of 32 in all since the ceasefire. At the time of writing, the British, who hold 1,000 prisoners, have not reciprocated by releasing anyone, either Republican, or Loyalist. If a jail protest, like that at Whitemoor, escalated into a hunger strike, the consequences for the peace process would be incalculable, as the Bradford University's Peace Department warned in a report published on 7 August 1995. One of the Whitemoor prisoners who went on the dirty protest, Patrick Kelly, suffered from skin cancer to such an extent that the Irish Government made a public protest about his condition (on 1 August 1995). Jean Kennedy Smith also publicly expressed concern about him on 3 August 1995. He was removed to hospital.

The real political issue is not prisoners but the inclusion of Sinn Fein in all-party talks, which entails a resolution of the de-commissioning issue. However, coming against the arid backdrop described earlier, movement of any sort is welcome. It may be that the proposed Bruton-Major summit will advance the process further. Perhaps the proposed International Commission idea which the British and Irish Governments are examining as a means of breaking the log-jam over de-commissioning will come to fruition. If it does, substantive political talks can start while the de-commissioning issue is dealt with elsewhere. Certainly this is what the vast majority of the Irish – and I believe the English public – wish.

Apart from the saving in human life and the toll of misery exacted by the Troubles, Ireland north and south could blossom if peace finally takes hold. The Republic of Ireland has managed to achieve high levels of inward investment and tourism over a quarter of a century, while at the same time the violence was generating a weight of adverse publicity internationally for Ireland as a whole which could literally be measured by the ton in terms of news-print and TV films. Culturally, almost every form of activity one chooses to examine is undergoing a process of growth and development. In poetry, prose, rock music, film, cuisine and sport, the Republic is playing a role on the international stage out of all proportion to its size. Whilst these achievements have to be kept in proportion and weighed against severe problems such as unemployment, there is one indicator which can be used to assess the economic backdrop: that indispensible entity, 'The Pound in Your Pocket'. Since the decoupling of the Irish punt from the pound sterling in 1969, the punt, which was once quoted at seventy-five pence against the pound sterling, has risen to one hundred and three pence sterling at the time of writing.

How much of this is attributable to the Irish economy rising and the British one falling is a matter of debate. But it is beyond dispute that both countries would benefit immeasurably in terms of life, liberty and human happiness if fetters chaining them to the vicious mythologies of the past were removed. An authoritative survey, The Economic Consequences of Peace in Ireland, has estimated a growth of 32.9% in foreign investment in the Republic.[98] For the North, where inward investment virtually collapsed in the seventies, the figure was 50.5%. Tourism numbers, of which the greatest percentages were expected to be from Great Britain, were estimated to show an average increase of 43.8% in the Republic. As the Six Counties were of course a tourist black spot, the peace dividend is expected to be even higher. Prior to the ceasefire, only one out of ten Continental or US visitors to the Republic spent time in the troubled area. The estimates for an increase in the ECPI survey range from 85% in US tourists to 110% from Germany, 125% from Great Britain and an enormous 158% from the Netherlands. Already the roads north and south of the border are filled with either British-registered cars, southern cars going north or northern cars which have come south.

Against the potential contained in these indicators, the re-emergence of the petrol bombers and the performance at Garvaghy appear to be sheer lunacy. But the peace process is not set in concrete. Though universally welcomed, it can easily be knocked off target. I once asked a Finnish friend of mine to explain how the tiny Finnish Army had managed to mount such an extraordinary performance against the vastly superior Russian Army in the early stages of World War II. 'Snow and vodka', he replied. 'With the snow we could not see how many of them were out there. With the vodka, we didn't care'. Something of the same blind indifference to the odds, and the suffering, that has carried the IRA forward without the aid of either snow or vodka, still has to be reckoned with in assessing the prospects for long-term peace in Ireland. Economic considerations have never weighed with the Republicans, and the average member of the IRA does not expect to share greatly in the prosperity indicated by the statistics I have quoted. If the feeling that they have been conned by declaring a ceasefire gathers strength, then hostilities will recommence. If the British strategists responsible for the delay in pressing ahead with the peace process are calculating on irreparably damaging the movement by engineering a split, then they are badly mistaken. I understand that that contingency has been foreseen and planned for. Should the ceasefire end, for whatever reason, there will be no split. But Sinn Fein, including its present leadership, and the IRA will go over the cliff together. Any future outbreak of violence could be far worse than anything we have seen.

This would be an appalling tragedy, one of the worst lost opportunities in the history of the British-Irish relationship. And it would achieve nothing, save increased death tolls, prison numbers, and the loss of present American benignity to the peace process. When finally, after God knows how many more years, the bombing and the shooting dies away, all the parties would be right back at the point we have now arrived at, although not necessarily with the calibre of leadership now available in Ireland to see through a decent settlement that would respect the traditions of all the people on the island.

As I was finishing this chapter I went for a walk along Killiney beach with a man who has done more than most to bring the present, still hopeful, opportunity within grasp: Fr Alec Reid. In a mood of gloom and anger which I had rarely seen, Fr Alec reckoned that the Holy Spirit, although still on the field, was for the first time in the last-stop position of goal-keeper.

I know Fr Reid will not thank me for adverting to his role in the peace process, but I have done so for two reasons. First, I simply believe that despite his laudable reticence, his efforts deserve recognition. But the other over-riding feeling, which came to me strongly on Killiney beach as I listened to this frail, humble monk, was how much had been achieved by one man, armoured in nothing but goodness and lonely belief. And, correspondingly, how much more could be achieved by the mighty, those with the power of initiative: the Mayhews and the Majors. Ring-fenced by the right though he is, John Major could yet transform the Irish situation and, in so doing, win himself an honoured place, not merely in the history books, but even in the next British general election.

Perhaps his planned participation in a Dublin summit will result in his demonstrating that this is what he intends. It is worth observing that my walk with Fr Reid occurred the day after Mayhew saw Adams secretly in Derry and on the eve of the Morrison-O'Dowd visit.

However, I have also to record that I visited Derry, prior to the Apprentice Boys march on 12 August – the 25th anniversary of the Battle of the Bogside. Once again there was tension in the air over rumours that the Apprentice Boys would once more be allowed to march along Derry's walls, the route which had sparked the riots which first brought the British troops onto the streets of the Six Counties. The authorities had banned the march for the previous fifteen years and there was much speculation in Catholic areas as to whether it would now be allowed to resume at a time when the ceasefire was obviously under pressure.

'This is a defining moment for the RUC and for Unionism,' A Sinn Fein spokesperson told me. 'If they let them march again, on the anniversary of the ceasefire, for the first time in fifteen years, we'll know they're not serious about democracy. That they're not serious about the peace.' As we spoke, news had leaked out that, despite the attitude to Republican prisoners which I have already described, Michael Stone, the perpetrator of the Milltown Cemetery massacre, had been allowed home on a brief compassionate visit, because of a family illness. Stone is such a folk-hero to Loyalists that his denim jacket, worn during the Milltown incident, fetched nearly £1,000 at a Loyalist fund-raising event. His release, albeit a fleeting one, had a Clegg-like effect on Nationalists.

The Apprentice Boys were allowed to march. Martin McGuinness, one of those who led a sit-down to obstruct the parade, was amongst those forcibly removed by the RUC. On the same day (12 August) the RUC batoned protestors in Belfast who unsuccessfully attempted to prevent Apprentice Boys staging yet another march along the Ormeau Road. Plastic baton rounds were fired, one man being shot in the face and seriously wounded. The TV scenes were eerily and disturbingly reminiscent of those which ushered in the Clonard and Bogside riots of a quarter of a century before.

I asked a prominent Sinn Fein Ard Comhairle member, who had been central to the peace-brokering process, for his assessment of the ceasefire's prospects in the light of foregoing. He replied: 'If nothing comes out of the Bruton-Major summit, Gerry Adams and Martin McGuinness would be inviting political assassination if they attempt to argue in favour of continuing with the ceasefire.'

A grim prophecy, but every sounding I have been able to make as the ceasefire anniversary nears indicates that it could be an accurate one, if the British hang up on the de-commissioning issue and do not exercise their power of initiative by calling all-party talks. On the day after the Derry/Ormeau clashes, John Hume, his voice charged with an emotion I have rarely heard, went on TV and radio to appeal for the commencement of talks by mid-September. Obviously he too had been made aware of the dangers of the forces piling up around the Bruton-Major summit.

Perhaps, despite all this, Fr Reid's unshakable faith in a Holy Spirit will yet prove to be justified. As I conclude, I think of him and those who have tried, and are still trying: Gerry Adams, Albert Reynolds, John Hume, Jean Kennedy Smith, Niall O'Dowd, Bruce Morrison, Bill Flynn, John Bruton, Dick Spring and John Major. Their endeavours recall the exhortation of my friend Seamus Heaney:

> History says, Don't hope
> On this side of the grave.
> But then, once in a lifetime
> The longed for tidal wave
> Of justice can rise up,
> And hope and history rhyme.
>
> So hope for a great sea-change
> On the far side of revenge.
> Believe that a further shore
> Is reachable from here.
> Believe in miracles
> And cures and healing wells.[99]

Despite the obstacles, my settled conviction is that peace in Ireland is 'reachable from here'.

EPILOGUE

I AM ALLOWING the optimistic words with which I concluded the first edition of this book to stand, as I prepare to review the events of the months which have passed since they were written. But in doing so I am reminded of the truth of the observation that terror is the basis of optimism. For what really transpired in the interim was not the shared furtherance of a peace process involving London and Dublin, but a period of the most ferocious behind the scenes political in-fighting. The net result was that meetings between British and Irish officials failed to advance the cause of peace against the reality of John Major's dwindling majority at Westminster and his ever-growing reliance on the Ulster Unionists.

So little common ground emerged on the de-commissioning issue that it proved impossible even to hold the September summit meeting which, according to the Republican leader I quoted (on page 405), held such dire possibilities for Martin McGuinness and Gerry Adams. Rather than risk a disastrous outcome the Irish called off the meeting at the last moment.

A discreet Government statement was issued on 5 September 1995 saying:

> The Taoiseach Mr John Bruton TD has suggested the postponement of tomorrow's Anglo-Irish Summit and the British Prime Minister Mr John Major has agreed to this. The purpose for this is to allow some more time to attempt to resolve outstanding differences.

Two days later at a dinner in Dublin Castle, Bruton made a statement which contained two vital elements:

1. The British and Irish Governments were working towards 'agreement on a target date for all-party talks'. Bruton had agreed with Major that these talks were to be conducted on a basis that would 'bring the maximum range of parties to the table'.

2. The context of this agreement was that the Dail, that is Bruton's Government, like its predecessor Fianna Fail now in opposition with the Progressive Democrats, accepted 'that the cessation of violence by the IRA is irreversible'.

406

However these principles proved easier to state than to act upon. Intensive lobbying from Dublin failed to dislodge Major from his Unionist perch. The peace process might be going down, but the Conservative majority certainly was, and this was all that counted. No agreement was reached over the successive months on either the de-commissioning issue or that of all-party talks. Once more the initiative switched to Washington. President Clinton was due to visit Ireland at the end of November. Obviously he could not come if bombs started going off again.

Both the Irish-American lobby and the Dublin diplomatic effort went into overdrive. The Kennedy-Dodds axis, the O'Dowd group, and the National Security Council led by Anthony Lake and Nancy Soderberg ensured that the lines between the White House and London were kept busy. Dermot Gallagher, the Irish Ambassador to Washington, demonstrated an access to, and a personal rapport with, Clinton which became the envy of the Washington Diplomatic Corps. As the end-of-November date for Clinton's visit to Ireland approached, the American efforts intensified. On the morning of 28 November 1995, however, it was not clear that there would be any meeting of minds between Dublin and London. But, behind the scenes, direct intervention by both Lake and Soderberg in visits to the two capitals involved had helped to turn the scale. On the afternoon of 28 November it was announced that a summit meeting would be held later that evening. A hasty dash to London in the Irish Government jet by John Bruton and his officials resulted in the issuing of a Joint Communiqué by the Irish and British Prime Ministers.

It stated that after 'intensive' efforts by both Governments a 'twin-track' process was being launched on both the de-commissioning issue and that of all-party negotiations. Paragraph 2 of the Communiqué stated that the two Governments had the 'firm aim' of achieving this by the end of February 1996. It also announced the setting up of an International Commission under the Chairmanship of the former senate majority leader George Mitchell to 'identify and advise on a suitable and acceptable method for full and verifiable de-commissioning'.

Although British officials briefed journalists that the Communiqué showed that 'Bruton had blinked' it seemed, on the face of it, to contain a breakthrough of the utmost significance. When its terms were conveyed to Clinton, aboard Airforce One as he crossed the Atlantic, he broke open a bottle of champagne to toast Anthony Lake. The images on TV of Clinton's subsequent reception in both Belfast and Dublin spoke for themselves. He received a truly rapturous reception in both cities, his Irish welcome completely overshadowing the publicity accorded to the one-day stop-over in London which preceded his two days in Ireland.

God it seemed was in Heaven, Bill Clinton driving the Peace train, George Mitchell aboard the International Commission, and all would be well with the peace process. Alas, it was not to be. The reasons why British civil servants claimed that Bruton had blinked over the Communiqué began to become obvious. Paragraph 3, dealing with the all-party talks issue, contained an obscure passage which stated that the matters to be considered in the preparatory talks, leading up to the full-blown all-party negotiations '*could* include', not 'would include', an examination of how all those involved could 'properly take account of democratic mandates and principles, including whether and how an elected body could play a part'.

Very few members of the public, and even fewer public representatives associated the foregoing passage with a proposal which David Trimble made shortly after becoming the Ulster Unionist Party leader. Trimble had shown himself concerned, not to develop North-South links, that is between Belfast and Dublin, but East-West ones, between London and Belfast. As part of this approach he suggested a new Assembly for the Six Counties.

A new Assembly dominated by Trimble and his friends, was of course the last thing either Sinn Fein or the SDLP wanted. To them New Assembly translated as Old Stormont, writ small, and with the old Unionist veto on constitutional progress reaffirmed in a new guise. Hume, who was probably the greatest single influence in Bruton's decision to abort the September Anglo-Irish Summit, rather than concede on the de-commissioning issue, was particularly strongly opposed to the Assembly idea. Nationalist distrust of the Assembly idea's provenance deepened following an admission by Dr Conor Cruise O'Brien on RTE television (*Questions and Answers*, 9 December 1995) that the Assembly notion was partly his brain child. He and I appeared together. Recalling that Dr O'Brien was one of the first visitors received by Trimble after his election, I asked him if he had anything to do with the Assembly concept.

O'Brien replied that he had advised Trimble on the kind of Assembly which might be 'acceptable' to Nationalists but that Trimble had not felt himself able to go as far as O'Brien had suggested. The notion of Dr Conor Cruise O'Brien, Unionism's principal intellectual exponent, advising on Nationalists' sensitivities did not receive a warm reception in areas such as the Bogside, Crossmaglen or the Falls Road. But as yet the Assembly idea was a cloud no bigger than a man's hand in the Anglo-Irish skies. The principal focus of attention switched to the Mitchell Commission. The International Body, as it was known, had its first meeting on 15 December 1995 and worked intensively through Christmas and the New Year before issuing its Report on 22 January 1996.

The workings of the Commission impressed everyone who came in contact with its deliberations. From my own experience of making a submission to it I can testify that everyone who made a submission to the body had their contribution carefully studied. There had been some initial suspicions concerning its membership in Nationalist circles. One of the members of the three-man body, the Canadian General John de Chasterlain, was described in newspaper reports as being the son of a former member of MI6. Sinn Fein at least believed that Bruton should have balanced this appointment by getting 'his man' on the Commission. In the event, the third man, Mr Harri Holkari, a former Finnish Prime Minister, proved like Chasterlain himself, to be a model of fair-mindedness and sagacity. Mitchell himself more than vindicated his outstanding reputation both as senate majority leader and as a judge. The expectation grew in Dublin that the Mitchell body would find a way around the de-commissioning impasse.

And to anyone concerned with the situation such a resolution became hourly increasingly more desirable. The spate of punishment beatings throughout the Six Counties was added to by a return of the gun. A group styling itself 'Direct Action Against Drugs' murdered some five Belfast and Derry Catholics accused in wall posters of being drug dealers. While the Provisional IRA disclaimed these killings they are thought to be carried out by Republican ex-prisoners, with para-military experience. Whoever was behind them they certainly vented some pent-up energies on the part of Republican militants, chaffing at the lack of either military activity, or political progress. Although universally condemned by the outside world the killings were welcomed by inhabitants of the districts where the killings occurred. The ravages of the drug trade in Dublin and throughout the Republic generally are well known in Belfast - and to a degree replicated in Loy-alist areas, where some ex-paramilitaries have turned to drug-dealing.

To any thinking person however, the images of grieving widows and children following the coffins along the streets of Belfast once more, especially as some of the processions occurred in the run-up to Christmas, were ominous and dis-turbing. When Mitchell reported on 22 January 1996 he condemned these killings and beatings, terming them 'reprehensible', but judged that the contin-uance of the peace process was the most significant factor in the situation. More importantly he found a formula for ensuring that the de-commissioning argu-ment did not bring the process to an end.

He flatly concluded that de-commissioning in advance of talks was a non-starter. Paragraph 26 stated that 'we have concluded that the paramilitary organ-isations will not decommission any arms prior to all-party negotiations'. But the Report also noted that:

> However the de-commissioning issue is resolved, that alone will not lead directly to all-party negotiations. Much work remains on the many issues involved in the political track. The parties should address those issues with urgency.

To help them do so, and thus take the gun out of Irish politics once and for all Mitchell advocated 'commitment and adherence to fundamental democracy and non-violence'. By an acceptance of the following six principles:

> a. To democratic and exclusively peaceful means of resolving political issues;
>
> b. To the total disarmament of all paramilitary organisations;
>
> c. To agree that such disarmament must be verifiable to the satisfaction of an independent commission;
>
> d. To renounce for themselves, and to oppose any effort by others, to use force or threaten to use force, to influence the course of the outcome of all-party negotiations;
>
> e. To agree to abide by the terms of any agreement reached in all-party negotiations and to resort to democratic and exclusively peaceful methods in trying to alter any aspect of that outcome with which they may disagree;

and

f. To urge that 'punishment' killings and beatings stop and to take effective steps to prevent such actions.

There was momentary euphoria in Dublin, and among Irish-Americans. It appeared that Mitchell had found a way around the de-commissioning road block and that the next step would be all-party talks by the end of February as envisaged in the Downing Street Joint Communiqué of 28 November 1995. The Mitchell press conference to unveil the report was covered live by a multiplicity of radio and TV stations. The consensus of commentators pronouncing on the Senator's performance, and that of his colleagues, was that the light of lasting peace had finally dawned on a far horizon, no matter how agonising the now seemingly inevitable all-party talks might prove to be.

Alas, the euphoria was but momentary. A few hours after the Mitchell conference ended John Major arose in the House of Commons to dash hopes and immeasurably heighten the potential of a return to war. The Mitchell Report, having dealt at length with the de-commissioning process and the practicalities of overseeing it once talks had begun, had then moved on towards the end of the Report to discussing confidence-building gestures. Paragraph 55 (there were 57 substantive paragraphs and five of 'concluding remarks') dealt with policing methods. It recommended that the RUC could 'contribute to the building of trust' by, among other steps, overhauling the use of plastic bullets, recruiting more Catholics into the police force and, significantly, reviewing the situation 'with respect to legally held weapons'.

This last was a clear acknowledgement that part of the Republicans' fear of handing up weapons - and that of much of the larger Nationalist community at the prospect of their so doing - derived from the fact of there being possibly as many as 150,000 legally held weapons in the hands of the Unionists. This circumstance came about through the leniency displayed by both the police and the judiciary towards the existence of Protestant arsenals. However, Major ignored this recommendation, as he did the core Six Principles, itemised above, and seized on the next Paragraph, 56, the Report's penultimate substantive paragraph.

This stated that 'several oral and written submissions raised the idea of an elected body. We note the reference in Paragraph 3 of the Communiqué to 'whether and how an elected body could play a part'. Elections held in accordance with democratic principals express and reflect the popular will. If it were broadly acceptable within an appropriate mandate and within the three strand structure, an elective process could contribute to the building of confidence'.

Ignoring the fact that such an Assembly was, at that stage at least, far from being 'broadly acceptable', Major in effect rejected Mitchell's findings on de-commissioning and opted instead to pursue the question of an elected Assembly. This was to have a 'weighted majority'. The outraged reaction of Nationalist Ireland was spearheaded by John Hume who arose as soon as Major had finished speaking to accuse the British Prime Minister of putting at risk the lives of women and children in Northern Ireland. The initial reaction of Dublin, and the Irish-Americans, was similar. Both John Bruton and Dick Spring insisted that the British and Irish Prime Ministers had committed themselves to a Communiqué promising all-party talks by the end of February and that that agreement between two sovereign Governments must stand.

However, the British immediately launched a clearly well thought out counter-campaign built around the message which the Junior Minister for Northern Ireland, Michael Ancram, was sent to Washington to promulgate: 'Who can be afraid of elections? Who can be afraid of democracy?'

The fact that the Assembly would have no powers and would not address the North-South relationship, or of course, the de-commissioning issue, was conveniently overlooked. As indeed was the fact that the 'weighted majority' principle would hit not alone the Nationalists, but the emerging small Unionist groupings based on the Loyalist paramilitaries, whom the Official Unionist Party and the Paisleyites were equally anxious to stifle at birth. Instead the British and the Unionists argued that such an Assembly would provide a forum for opening all-party talks. So even though the de-commissioning issue was still unresolved the Unionists were prepared to drop their objections to talking to Sinn Fein - but within an Assembly which they would dominate.

In vain did the Nationalists protest that the history of the last twenty-five years had been littered with useless talking-shop Conventions and Assemblies which eventually foundered on the rock of Unionist unwillingness to accommodate the Nationalists (See chapter 6). Britain might be in serious decline but the resources she could still deploy vastly outweighed anything the Irish could produce. Against a handful of brilliant civil servants led by figures like O'hUiginn, O'Donoghue, Scannell, and Dermot Gallagher, the Irish Ambassador to Washington, London had a team of 160 officials fully engaged in the Irish issue. Sinn Fein, and the SDLP had to fight the propaganda war with only a handful of principals and virtually no back-up assistance.

In the weeks which have elapsed between the issuing of the Mitchell Report, and the time of writing, it became clear that Whitehall was ruthlessly deploying its superior muscle both to further the Assembly concept, and vigorously to prosecute, with the aid of the Unionists, a policy of divide and conquer.

True, the Nationalist case did receive some powerful endorsements. On Capitol Hill some seventy Senators and Congressmen wrote to Clinton under the banner of the Ad Hoc Committee on Ireland denouncing the British manoeuvre. Figures like Ted Kennedy and Christopher Dodds swung into action as did Ben Gillman, the Republican Chairman of the prestigious Senate Foreign Relations Committee. His denunciation of Major's Assembly ploy as being nothing more than an attempt to secure Unionists' votes at the expense of the Irish peace process was a significant indication of Washington's bi-partisan approach to the Irish issue. American media reaction was almost universally hostile.

But the most significant reaction came from Clinton himself. After a two-hour luncheon conference between Gerry Adams and Anthony Lake, which Clinton joined, the White House issued a statement (on 1 February 1996) saying that during the lunch:

Mr Lake expressed his gratitude and appreciation to Senator George Mitchell and his colleagues for recommendations to advance the peace process. He found the Report's suggestions on the de-commissioning issue helpful and believes other ideas should be urgently discussed in the political track of the twin-track process.

The President underscored the need for rapid progress to all-party talks. He encouraged all parties to remain committed to the search for peace and determined in its pursuit. Finally, the President discussed his visit to the United Kingdom and Ireland and the overwhelming support of the people to move beyond the violence and hatred of the past.

Decoded, the White House statement was a powerful endorsement of the Mitchell approach - which of course the White House had sponsored - and a rebuke to Major for not 'urgently' discussing 'other ideas' with a view to meeting 'the need for rapid progress to all-party talks'. This statement may in fact have been linked to an imaginative response with which, as we shall see shortly, the Irish David unexpectedly rounded on the British Goliath a little later. But first a word of explanation concerning the mood of the grass-roots Republican supporters is necessary, as this was increasingly becoming an important, and worrying, factor in the situation.

Coming after almost sixteen months of ceasefire and ceaseless diplomatic and political attrition the blow delivered by Major had far-reaching effects on the Nationalist community. To Republican activists, looking at their negotiators growing increasingly drained and stressed from endless participation in apparently fruitless talks, there was one immediate solution: 'The only thing the Brits understand is the bomb and the bullet. We should go back to bombing London.' Outside commentators might point to the fact that in the space of less than three years the Sinn Fein position had rocketed from the horse and buggy stage of international acceptance to that of the space age, wherein Gerry Adams was now a frequent visitor to the White House. But in the ranks of Republican activists one heard comments to the effect that 'nothing had changed'.

Visiting Belfast as this was being written, I found Republican sentiment pre-occupied not with space-age considerations of diplomacy but with grass-roots issues such as the heavy presence of plain clothes security force operatives in Nationalist areas; the lack of progress on reforming the RUC; and, most tellingly in the de-commissioning context, the fact that, while loudly declaring itself in favour of beating swords into ploughshares, the British were in fact building a huge new fortification in the Donegal Road area - the heartland of Republican West Belfast. So far as the average IRA man was concerned every hammer blow struck in the fort's construction was another nail in the coffin of the peace process. Equally obviously however, the Republican leadership was still successfully resisting this ground swell.

At the beginning of February, tensions soared dangerously in the wake of the shooting of the INLA leader, 'Geno' Gallagher in Belfast. Firstly there were rumours that the Provisionals had murdered him because he was threatening to break the ceasefire. Then the RUC attempted to ban a display of paramilitary trappings at his funeral. The situation escalated to a point where the RUC drew batons and were once again seen on TV screens striking down Nationalists. The coffin was carried back into the Gallagher house and the burial was delayed for twenty-fours hours while negotiations on the funeral arrangements took place. Fr Reid played his usual constructive role in helping to broker a compromise between the RUC and the Republicans. The funeral went ahead peacefully with the RUC standing back and a muted display of paramilitarism being mounted by Gallagher's comrades. Sinn Fein successfully countered reports of Provisional involvement in the death, urging a big turn out of mourners and by officially commiserating with the family. And so the situation held.

Inevitably, given the drift and lack of initiative on the part of Whitehall, other strains appeared amongst the Nationalist family as a whole. In the immediate wake of the British reaction only Gerry Adams travelled to Washington; the other party leaders, John Bruton, John Hume, Dick Spring and Pronsias De Rossa remained on the Irish side of the Atlantic. The obvious need to seek outside assistance imposed on Sinn Fein by Major's ploy was indirectly articulated by Senator Mitchell himself when he told David Frost (BBC TV Sunday 4 February 1996) that he feared that the situation held potential for a split in Republican ranks and a return to violence. Although Martin McGuinness, on behalf of the Republicans, immediately denied that there was any likelihood of a split, the reality of the situation is that both Mitchell and McGuinness were correct in their assessments. While a split may not be imminent, continued drift would produce one.

The constricting effect of the disimproving political climate on Sinn Fein's room to manoeuvre was disturbingly well illustrated at the closing of the Forum for Peace and Reconciliation. This is the body which Albert Reynolds set up in the wake of the ceasefires in 1994. It did much valuable work in bringing together various strands of Irish political opinion, despite the fact that neither of the two major Unionist parties attended. But when it came to the publication of the Forum's final report on 2 February 1996 Sinn Fein found that in the circumstances it could not sign up to a core element of the Forum's findings, namely that:

> ...The Democratic right of self-determination by the people of Ireland as a whole must be achieved and exercised with and subject to the agreement and consent of a majority of the people of Northern Ireland...

After all that had happened, Sinn Fein feared that the peace strategy was in danger of, at worst restoring the old Unionist veto, or at best committing the party to accepting the Unionist agenda, not alone in advance of all-party talks but with the very real prospect that such talks were now indefinitely postponed. The Republicans feared that, if the Unionists got their Assembly, they would simply refuse to enter into any further discussions and sit tight on their gains as they had done in the past. As anger, disillusionment, and near despair permeated the ranks of the Republicans, suspicion and distrust multiplied also.

The theory gained ground that Bruton and his officials were veering around to the view that there was no prospect of securing any movement from London prior to an election, which would almost certainly return Labour to power. There-fore, given that Labour would probably prove little better than the Conservatives, there was an inclination towards *sauve qui peut*, a saving of what could be snatched from the collapse of hopes by the acceptance of the Assembly idea.

Even before the débâcle over the Mitchell Report, Sinn Fein had privately been at odds with the Fine Gael approach on the de-commissioning issue. Although a façade of unanimity had been maintained for public consumption, it is said that Gerry Adams wrote a letter to Bruton, while the Mitchell Com-mission was still sitting, saying in effect that speeches made by Bruton himself (in March 1995) suggesting that the IRA might give up weapons in advance of talks, had given the British the excuse to introduce 'Washington Three' to the debate two months later.

Moreover, in so far as the Democratic Left was concerned, Sinn Fein's atti-tude was conditioned by the history of feuding between the Official IRA and the Provisionals. The temperature of relationships between the two groupings may be imagined from the fact that, privately, Gerry Adams is quoted as hav-ing referred acidly to his 'former colleague', Pronsias de Rossa, during heated meetings between the parties at Government Buildings. And, publicly, Democ-ratic Left often gave the impression of singing out of a different hymn book to that used by the other Nationalist parties. For example, during a speech in Belfast (17 January 1996) De Rossa attacked Sinn Fein for not signing up 'unequivocally to the principle of consent' by Unionists. He then went on to praise individual members of the Ulster Unionist Party for 'political courage'. David Trimble he described as possessing 'a sharp political mind'.

This is far from being the view of majority Dublin political opinion. In fact Trimble's personality and utterances are assessed as having a distinctly harmful effect on the efforts of those seeking to restrain rank and file Republicans. Trim-ble, who, readers will recall, described himself as being 'puzzled' as to why Nationalists should have demanded civil rights in the first place, was already distrusted both for his former membership of the hard-line Vanguard movement, and because he came to power through pandering to the supremacist strain of Unionism by his behaviour at Garvaghy. He is assessed privately as possessing the mind, not of a statesman, but of a self-important provincial lawyer, suddenly elevated to a bigger stage than he is capable of performing on constructively. Decision-taking Dublin regarded it as unacceptable gaucherie that when Dick Spring personally rang both his home and his office in an attempt to arrange a meeting he was given no hearing save that of an answering machine. Trimble has also shown an inability to conceal his triumphalism at the extraordinary power which the parliamentary balance at Westminster has thrust into his hands.

He has been known to display arrogance to his own people also. Billy Hutchinson, one of the principal architects of the Loyalist ceasefires, described to a public meeting in Belfast at which he and I were joint speakers, how Trim-ble had informed him that Unionists should leave politics to his superior wisdom. Hutchinson, said Trimble, was 'an un-educated man'. In fact, apart from his cru-cial role in achieving, and maintaining, peace, Hutchinson took a number of degrees, in social studies, while serving a prison sentence. Trimble, and the Unionist hierarchy, fear the rise of Unionist parties, based on former paramilitaries, who can see the folly of fighting to maintain a conservative Unionist party which cares as little for the concerns of the Protestant working class as it does for the Catholic.

Trimble, and his henchman, John Taylor, displayed the workings of the 'sharp political mind' by conducting a number of briefings for journalists, aimed at furthering the divide and conquer strategy. Dick Spring and the Department of Foreign Affairs, were singled out as being the ogres. Sean O'hUiginn, who of course could not reply, had the unusual (and unwelcome) distinction, for a civil servant, of being particularly criticised.

Taylor ultimately brought an unprecedented reaction from Dublin when in an interview with the *Irish Times* (5 February 1996) he attacked Dick Spring for not being as accommodating as the Taoiseach's Department. Spring, said Taylor, was 'the most detested politician' in the Six Counties. He said that the Republic's Deputy Prime Minister was a 'mouth piece for Sinn Fein'. Both Mary Harney of the Progressive Democrats and Bertie Ahern, the leader of Fianna Fail, condemned the Unionists' tactics and pointed out that, though it was a coalition, the Dublin administration was the Government of the Republic. Moreover, as Bertie Ahern said, (6 February 1996) there would have been no Downing Street Declaration, and no ceasefires, had it not been for the Government of Albert Reynolds of which Dick Spring was a member. Spring and the Bruton administration were continuing the policy of those days.

Privately, it is said that Spring's bemused initial reaction at receiving this unexpected endorsement from his political opponents was to wonder whether Unionist onslaught or Fianna Fail support was to be preferred? However, publicly, he and the Irish Government countered the Belfast and London offensive with an audacious initiative. On 8 February 1996 after a meeting of the Anglo-Irish Conference, chaired jointly by Sir Patrick Mayhew and Spring, had earlier in the day made pious commitments towards moving speedily towards all-party talks, a summit meeting, the resolution of difficulties and any other hopeful objective which could be placed on the Anglo-Irish agenda, Spring made an announcement which showed how little real confidence Dublin had in these goals being met.

Spring revealed that Dublin was seeking a Dayton-type conference, on the lines of the two-day meeting during which the Americans brokered the Bosnian peace agreement. The idea was that, that, as in Dayton, a two-day meeting would be held with the parties involved coming together under one roof, but not necessarily in the same rooms while, with the aid of intermediaries, an agreement was hammered out. In such a forum, Assemblies, elections, North-South links and East-West ones, Uncle Tom Cobley and all, could be placed on the agenda and the Anglo-Irish difficulty finally resolved. An Irish version of Dayton would of course of necessity involve outside mediators, i.e. the Americans. Indeed the prospect of Senator Mitchell re-appearing in the guise of the once talked of Peace Envoy began to appear credible.

In the days after Spring unveiled the idea Unionist and Conservative spokespeople took to the airwaves in an attempt to rubbish the idea. The arguments deployed by the British were that the idea was at best 'premature', at worst it involved international agencies in matters which were strictly domestic to the UK. The Unionists were more strident, their comments ranged from 'mischievous', 'malicious', 'crazy' to merely 'unworkable'. Ken Maginnis, the Official Unionist Party spokesperson on Defence, tried combating the idea with sarcasm. In an obvious reference to Sinn Fein he recalled that the Bosnian conference had excluded leaders suspected of war crimes, such as Radovan Karadice and General Maladic. However, Dublin wit speedily riposted that Maginnis need not worry, Sinn Fein had no objection to sitting down with him - despite the fact that he had been a member of the B-Specials and the UDR, both of which had been decommissioned because of behaviour by some of their members which, to Sinn Fein eyes, sometimes amounted to war crimes.

Significantly, Spring and O'hUiginn immediately set off to Washington, where (on 9 February 1996) they were received sympathetically by President Clinton. The suspicion grew in fact that the Dayton idea may have been formulated with American assistance. Certainly Dublin would not have proposed such a step without checking in advance whether Clinton could live with the idea. Off the record briefings confirmed the fact that Washington was comfortable with a Bosnia-type approach. Bosnia was one of Clinton's major diplomatic successes. In an election year, the Dayton resonances chimed readily with his already popular Irish policy which, for example, caused him to be named 'Irish-American of the year' by Niall O'Dowd's Irish-American magazine.

Back in Dublin, John Bruton stoutly defended the Dayton initiative. A fair-minded man, who had gone out of his way to attempt to be accommodating to both Major and the Unionists, he felt betrayed and angered by the Conservative-Unionist response to the Mitchell Report. He pointedly observed that the proposal for elections in advance of talks would fail if the Nationalists boycotted the polls. And he did nothing to quench rumours that Dublin might support such a boycott. It appeared that the Nationalists had regained the initiative in the propaganda war and that the Americans were prepared to take new steps to further the peace process. Certainly the Dayton approach did much to alleviate Sinn Fein fears about undue pro-Unionist tendencies on the part of John Bruton. It also helped the Republican leadership to demonstrate to their more disaffected supporters that the 'alternative strategy' was bringing dividends.

The Dayton formula appeared to offer some light at the end of the tunnel, but that light was well and truly blown out by the shattering sound of an IRA bomb exploding in the Canary Wharf area of London. The unthinkable had occurred. The IRA had ended its ceasefire, it would appear without the knowledge of Adams and the political wing of the Republican movement, Sinn Fein. Although the bomb blast was preceded by a telephone warning accompanied by the IRA's normal identification code, evacuation procedures apparently could not cope fully with the emergency. In the event two people died, over a hundred were injured and the damage bill, according to some estimates, ran as high as 150 million dollars.

The IRA statement foreshadowing this devastation gave the rationale for the blast as follows:

> It is with great reluctance that the leadership of *Oglaigh na hEireann* announces that the complete cessation of military operations will end at 6pm on February 9th, this evening. As we stated on 31 August, 1994, the basis for the cessation was to enhance the democratic peace process and to underline our definitive commitment to its success. We also made it clear that we believed that an opportunity to create a just and lasting settlement had been created.
>
> The cessation presented a historic challenge for everyone and *Oglaigh na hEireann* commends the leadership of Nationalist Ireland at home and abroad. They rose to the challenge.
>
> The British Prime Minister did not. Instead of embracing the peace process the British Government acted in bad faith with Mr Major and the Unionist leaders squandering this unprecedented opportunity to resolve the conflict.
>
> Time and again over the last eighteen months selfish party political and sectional interests in the London Parliament have been placed before the rights of the people of Ireland.
>
> We take this opportunity to reiterate our total commitment to our Republican objectives. The resolution of the conflict in our country demands justice. It demands an inclusive negotiated settlement. This is not possible unless and until the British Government faces up to its responsibilities. The blame for the failure thus far of the Irish peace process lies squarely with John Major and his Government.

Shortly before the explosion Gerry Adams phoned the White House from Ireland to say that he was hearing 'disturbing news'. A few hours later he issued a statement which echoed the IRA's placing of the blame for the situation 'squarely with John Major'. It is too early to say with any certainty whether the Irish peace process will be aborted, or galvanised into fresh life by the London bombing.

For those who opt for the maligned scenario the signs are certainly there. John Bruton responded to the blast by temporarily halting Irish Governmental contact with Sinn Fein, Britain sent an extra five hundred troops back to Northern Ireland, though these were not immediately deployed on the streets, and security in London was greatly stepped up. Almost a week after the bombing (on 15 February) another IRA phoned warning led to a second bomb being discovered in London and defused.

This was followed on 18 February by a premature explosion that destroyed a London bus. One body was discovered in the wreckage. Three days later, the IRA announced that the victim was one of their members, 21-year-old Edward O'Brien, from Gorey, Co. Wexford, who had been living in London for two years.

Senator George Mitchell returned to Ireland on 22 February. In a London stop-over, he declined to comment on the response of John Major to the

Mitchell Report, but agreed on the urgent necessity of all-party negotiations. The senator stated that he shared President Clinton's view that a specific date for all-party talks should be set, as well as a restoration of the ceasefire and a commitment to democracy and non-violence.

Hopes were raised again when a communiqué by the British and Irish Governments announced that ten days of proximity talks were to start on 4 March. Following elections and possibly a referendum, all-party talks would begin on 10 June. However, Sinn Fein remain excluded until the IRA renew their ceasefire, and party leaders were turned away when they arrived at Stormont for the start of the talks, a situation intolerable to Nationalists.

The significant defusing of the situation, if it comes, will hardly be in London. John Major is hopelessly in pawn to the Unionists and the Right Wing Conservative back benchers. In the years following the Downing Street Declaration he has shown no sign of the courage, flair or imagination needed to act on Ireland with a view to history rather than the back benchers. Labour, if it does win the apparently imminent British general election, has given no indication that it has anything to offer on the Irish situation, beyond a possibly more emollient approach on facets of the problem such as the treatment of prisoners. The Unionists have been able to switch their firepower from the de-commissioning and Assembly arguments to that of the renewed bombing to justify their refusal to talk.

Therefore, if the log-jam is to be broken, only President Clinton can do so. He is exposed on the Irish peace issue, having come to Ireland and committed himself to the process. I understand from Washington sources that there is a lively expectation that the National Security Council will be deployed towards pressurising Major into accepting some talks formula, be it along the Dayton lines or any other strategy calculated to initiate negotiations. It is an election year and thus there is an added imperative for the White House to take a pro-active role on the Irish issue. But given the drift and casuistry with which London and the Unionists have handled the opportunity presented by the IRA ceasefire, one has to assess the American potential in terms of hope rather than confidence. The American dream has gone sour with the IRA during seventeen months of wasted opportunity, which must rank in the annals of Anglo-Irish relationships as one of the most wretched chapters in that sorry history. There is still some little room for hope but, as I said at the outset of this epilogue, terror is the basis of optimism.

Tim Pat Coogan
Glenageary, Co. Dublin
8 March 1996

NOTES

Preface

1. Paragraph 10, Joint Declaration between British and Irish Prime Ministers, Downing St, 15 November 1993.

Introduction

1. F. X. Martin, in Art Cosgrave (ed.), *A New History of Ireland*, Vol. II, Oxford, 1987, p. 58.
2. Thomas Cahill, *How the Irish Saved Civilisation*, Hodder & Stoughton, 1995, p. 4.
3. Ludwig Bieler, *Ireland, Harbinger of the Middle Ages*, Oxford University Press, 1963, p. 4.
4. Quoted by Martin, op. cit., p. 57.
5. Houston and Smyth, *Irish Emigration in Canada*, University of Toronto, 1990, and Ulster Historical Foundation, Belfast, p. 19.
6. David Dickson, 'The Other Great Irish Famine', in Cathal Poirteir (ed.), *The Great Irish Famine*, Mercier/RTE, 1995, p. 50.
7. T. A. Jackson, *Ireland Her Own*, Lawrence & Wishart, 1991, p. 217.
8. *American Irish Newsletter*, Political Education Committee of the American Ireland Foundation, New York.
9. On 17 February 1867.
10. *Hansard*, House of Commons, Vol. CCIV, Col. 1053.
11. Quoted in Tim Pat Coogan, *The IRA*, Fontana, 1987, p. 21.

Chapter One

1. Austin Currie, interview with author, 10/3/94.
2. W. Flackes, *Northern Ireland, a Political Directory*, BBC Books, 1983, p. 74.
3. When a group of young Nationalists began to revive the then nearly moribund Brotherhood, or Fenian movement, in 1907, they cloaked their activity under the guise of seemingly innocent discussion groups, known as Dungannon clubs.
4. He and I worked together on the *Irish Press* for a period. His descriptions of

419

northern life are based on some conversations with me, and on interviews with Martin Dillon for *The Last Colony*, Channel Four, 4/7/94.

5. Recommendation of the Irish Committee to the Cabinet on 17/2/19. See Tim Pat Coogan, *Michael Collins*, Arrow, 1991, pp. 333 ff.

6. Steve Bruce, *The Red Hand*, 1992, p. 149.

7. David Bleakley, *Conflict and Consent in Irish Politics*, Mowbray, 1975, p. 53.

8. The seminar, 'The Witness Seminar on British Policy in Northern Ireland 1964–1970', is one of an ongoing series conducted by the Institute of Contemporary British History, founded in 1986. The proceedings are recorded and transcripts provided for the participants to correct or amend for the benefit of posterity. However, certain of my friends decided that the proceedings of the two seminars which the Institute had conducted on Northern Ireland while this book was being researched were worthy of contemporary attention and transcripts were made available to me.

9. By Peter Rose, who read a paper setting the scene for the conference.

10. Ibid.

11. An account of Tallents' activities can be found in Coogan, *Michael Collins*, op. cit., pp. 369 ff.

12. Ibid., p. 371. He changed the term to 'disquieting' in his final draft.

13. James Callaghan, *A House Divided*, Collins, 1973, p. 117.

14. Ibid., p. 1.

15. Ibid.

16. Northern Ireland *Hansard*, Vol. 16, Col. 1091.

17. Andrew Boyd, *Brian Faulkner*, Anvil, 1972, p. 26.

18. The suggestions were made by Brian Maginess, the Attorney-General, and Sir Clarence Graham, chairman of the Standing Committee of the Ulster Council. Under pressure Graham later backed away from the suggestion. It had originated within the ranks of the Unionist Society, an opinion group, and the Young Unionist associations, which are traditionally more liberal than the party leadership. The controversy may be said to have continued on and off from 1959 to 1969 when a Catholic, Louis Boyle, was refused the nomination of the South Down Unionist Association in that year's Stormont election. By then a small number of Catholics had found their way into the Unionist Party, representing those Catholics – their number is difficult to compute – who for various reasons, chiefly economic, were, and are, privately in favour of the Union. However, the subsequent exacerbation of divisions occasioned by the troubles has rendered the issue otiose.

19. Quoted by Boyd, op. cit., p. 36.

20. *Hansard*, North of Ireland Debates, Vol. 16, Col. 1095.

21. Terence O'Neill, *The Autobiography of Terence O'Neill*, Rupert Hart Davis, 1972, pp. 42–3.

22. David Bleakley, op. cit., p. 62.

23. Michael Farrell, *Northern Ireland: The Orange State*, Pluto, 1992, p. 227.

24. *Report of Joint Working Party on the Economy of Northern Ireland*, HMSO, London, October 1962.
25. Estimates vary as to what rate of housing would have been needed to do both. It seems that three times the number provided, some 18,000 per annum, would not be an unreasonable calculation. The statistical picture of housing and social conditions may be examined in further detail in a number of publications. Two in particular are suggested: *General Report, Census of Population, 1961*, HMSO, Belfast, 1965; and *The Hall Report on the Northern Ireland Economy*, HMSO, London, 1962.
26. Roche, Birrell, Hillyard and Murie, *Housing in Northern Ireland*, Centre for Environmental Studies, University Working Papers, London, October 1971.
27. Stormont Senate debates, 8/10/94.
28. *Belfast Newsletter*, 6/3/1961.
29. 'The Town that I Loved so Well'.
30. Quoted in Tim Pat Coogan, *Ireland Since the Rising*, Pall Mall, 1966, p. 318. The chapter 'The North' in this work is based in part on research conducted on the ground into the situation as it was in the Six Counties *circa* the mid-sixties. Much of the information in this book concerning northern conditions at that time is based on that research.
31. These were contained in the *Belfast Regional Survey and Plan*, known as the Matthews Report, published in Belfast in 1961–3.
32. Antrim, Ballymena, Bangor, Carrickfergus, Carnmoney, Larne, Lurgan and Newtownards.
33. Michael Collins was only chairman of a provisional government when he met Sir James Craig early in 1922 in two meetings which proved to be of little value in halting the sectarian killings in Northern Ireland. The meetings and the Craig–Collins Pact which emerged from them are described in Coogan, *Michael Collins*, op. cit., pp. 339 ff.
34. Carter was addressing the Irish Association in Dublin on 19 March 1957. His talk, which was reported in the press of the time, is quoted in Tim Pat Coogan, *De Valera*, Hutchinson, 1993, p. 670.
35. Quoted by Patrick Buckland, *A History of Northern Ireland*, Gill and Macmillan, 1981, p. 152.
36. *The Protestant Telegraph*, 4/1/67.
37. Cooper originally made his observations in a review published in *Hibernia* (2/11/73), part of which was reproduced in Tim Pat Coogan, *The Irish: A Personal View*, Phaidon, 1975, p. 181.
38. *The Protestant Telegraph*, 10/8/68.
39. Ibid., 30/11/66.
40. Ibid., 22/3/69.
41. Hugh McClean, who was one of a three-man group sentenced to life imprisonment in 1966 for the murder of Peter Ward. The other two were Gusty Spence and Robert Williamson.
42. David Boulton, *The UVF*, Gill and Macmillan, 1973, p. 29.
43. *Belfast Newsletter*, 3/10/64. Quoted by Farrell, op. cit., p. 234.

44. Farrell, op. cit., p. 236.
45. Quoted by Farrell, op. cit., p. 236. For the origins of the UVF see also David Boulton, op. cit.
46. *Belfast Newsletter*, 16/3/66.
47. Boyd, op. cit., p. 57.
48. Ibid., p. 58.
49. Ibid., p. 57.
50. Ibid., p. 59.
51. Text in author's possession.
52. *Hansard*, House of Commons, Vol. 728, Cols. 721–2.
53. At the Witness Seminar on British policy.
54. Coogan, *Ireland Since the Rising*, op. cit., p. 317.
55. *Ireland Since the Rising*, 1966, and *The IRA*, 1970.
56. Coogan, *The IRA*, op. cit., p. 328.
57. Ibid., p. 418.
58. The robbery campaign, which was chiefly confined to the Republic, extended between 1967–70, falling into disfavour when, in April 1970, an unarmed garda was shot in Dublin.
59. Mallie and Bishop, *The Provisional IRA*, p. 70.
60. Quoted in Barry White, *John Hume, Statesman of the Troubles*, Blackstaff, 1984, p. 44.
61. The original edition was published in 1973. A new, expanded edition was published in 1993 by Pluto.
62. Eamonn McCann, *War and an Irish Town*, Pluto, 1993, p. 83.
63. O'Neill, op. cit., p. 137.
64. Interview with author, 10/3/94.
65. Ibid.

Chapter Two

1. Boyd, op. cit., p. 23.
2. McCann, op. cit., p. 92.
3. Ibid.
4. Interview with Michael A. Murphy for Ph.D. thesis, 7/6/89. Copy in author's possession.
5. McCann, op. cit., p. 99.
6. O'Neill, op. cit., p. 106.
7. Ibid., p. 102.
8. Ibid., p. 105.
9. White, op. cit., p. 69.
10. The full text of the speech was carried in most of the Irish daily papers and in the *Belfast Telegraph* the next day. It also appears as an appendix in O'Neill's autobiography (op. cit.).
11. For example: apart from obvious figures like Eamonn McCann, Michael Farrell and Bernadette Devlin, the group included Paul Bew and Paul Arthur,

both professors at Queen's University and widely respected as broadcasters and commentators, Michael Wolsey, now a senior journalist with Independent Newspapers, Tom McGurk, a broadcaster and TV script-writer, and Anne Devlin, a playwright and script-writer.

12. Bernadette Devlin, *The Price of My Soul*, André Deutsch, 1969, pp. 139–41.
13. The facts of the police invasion of the Bogside were subsequently confirmed by several sources, including the Cameron Commission. Eyewitnesses interviewed by the author and contemporary writers such as McCann.
14. The Commission is generally referred to as the Cameron Commission after its chairman, a Scottish High Court Judge, Lord Cameron. Its other members were Professor Sir John Biggart and Mr James Joseph Campbell. It sat in private with the assurance that no evidence given to it would be used as a basis for prosecutions.
15. O'Neill, op. cit., pp. 112–13.
16. Terence O'Neill, *The Last Card*, NLI (No. 7), p. 110.
17. Bruce, op. cit., p. 30.
18. Bleakley, op. cit., pp. 40–1.
19. Quoted by Flackes, op. cit., p. 105.
20. Interview with Michael A. Murphy for Ph.D. thesis, 27/7/89. Copy in author's possession.
21. Ibid.
22. Interview with Murphy, 7/6/89, op. cit.
23. Norman St John Stevas likened it to F. E. Smith's legendary maiden speech, and James Callaghan foresaw a place in cabinet for her.
24. *Hansard*, House of Commons, Vol. 782, Cols. 287–8.
25. Ibid.
26. Paddy Devlin, *Straight Left*, Blackstaff Press, 1993, p. 108.
27. The word 'idly' was in Lynch's original script, but was accidently omitted from the teleprompter when he delivered the broadcast.
28. McCann, op. cit., p. 117.
29. Ibid.
30. Ben Pimlott, *Harold Wilson*, HarperCollins, 1992, pp. 548–9.
31. Richard Crossman, *Crossman Papers*, 1975, p. 619.
32. P. Devlin, op. cit., p. 106.
33. Quoted by Bew and Gillespie, *Northern Ireland Chronology, 1968–93*, Gill and Macmillan, 1993, p. 18.
34. White, op. cit., p. 86.
35. Mallie and Bishop, op. cit., p. 111.
36. Crossman, op. cit., p. 620.
37. Ibid.
38. Ibid., p. 623.
39. Ibid., p. 622.
40. Ibid.

Chapter Three

1. Two of the best, both for 'feel' and detail, are contained in Mallie and Bishop, op. cit., and P. Devlin, op. cit.
2. Coogan, *The IRA*, op. cit., pp. 234–5.
3. Because of the unusual circumstances, the sermon was recorded for the Clonard archives. The archivist, Fr O'Donnell, kindly presented me with a copy.
4. According to Mallie and Bishop, op. cit., p. 107: 'Head Constable Rooney decided to baton charge the Catholics, judging them to be the greatest danger to his men.'
5. P. Devlin, op. cit., p. 107.
6. Ibid., p. 106.
7. Callaghan, op. cit., p. 82.
8. Scarman was assisted by two Northern Ireland businessmen, William Marshall, a Protestant, and George Lavery, a Catholic.
9. McCann, op. cit., p. 125.
10. According to White, op. cit., p. 91, he told Hume: 'I can't stand this much longer. I'm fifty-nine.'
11. McCann, op. cit., p. 125.
12. Flackes, op. cit., p. 57.
13. For a description of how these and other parties evolved from the Anglo-Irish war of 1919–21 and the subsequent civil war, see Coogan, *Ireland Since the Rising, The IRA, Michael Collins*, or *De Valera*, all op. cit.
14. P. Devlin, op. cit., pp. 109–11.
15. Mallie and Bishop, op. cit., p. 122.
16. P. Devlin, op. cit., p. 115.
17. Ibid.
18. McCann, op. cit., p. 128.
19. Sean MacStiofain, *Revolutionary in Ireland*, Gordon Cremonesi, 1975, p. 143.
20. In Martin Dillon, *The Dirty War*, Arrow, 1990, xv.
21. Coogan, *De Valera*, op. cit., p. 386.
22. Quoted in Captain James Kelly, *Orders for the Captain*, Kelly Kane, 1971, p. 171.
23. Mallie and Bishop, op. cit., p. 120.
24. J. Bowyer Bell, *The Irish Troubles*, St Martin's Press, 1993, p. 176.
25. Institute of Contemporary British History.
26. P. Devlin, op. cit.
27. Institute of Contemporary British History seminar on Ireland 1970–4.
28. Institute of Contemporary British History conference.
29. In the course of a dinner conversation with Kevin McNamara.
30. Quoted in Tim Pat Coogan, *Disillusioned Decades 1966–87*, Gill and Macmillan, 1987, p. 209.
31. Bowyer Bell, op. cit., p. 186.

Chapter Four

1. Quoted in Coogan, *The Irish: A Personal View*, op. cit., pp. 214–15.
2. P. Devlin, op. cit., p. 147.
3. Bew and Gillespie, op. cit., p. 17.
4. Boyd, op. cit., p. 68.
5. Ibid.
6. Martin Dillon, *The Enemy Within*, Doubleday, 1994, p. 98.
7. The names changed over the years. The cabinet committee that dealt with the Anglo-Irish war period and the introduction of partition was called simply the Cabinet Committee on Ireland. That which negotiated with de Valera in the pre-World War II era was known as the Irish Situation Committee.
8. Dillon, op. cit., p. 96.
9. Devlin, op. cit., p. 153.
10. Ibid.
11. Brian Faulkner, *Memoirs of a Statesman*, Weidenfeld & Nicolson, 1978, pp. 14–15.
12. White, op. cit., p. 112.
13. It was repeated on RTE on 3/11/94.
14. For the Institute of Contemporary History.
15. *Sunday Times*, 17/10/71.
16. On 14 February 1974.
17. Quoted in Coogan, *The Irish: A Personal View*, op. cit., p. 192.
18. Coogan, *The IRA*, op. cit., pp. 546–7.
19. Piaras F. MacLochlainn, *Last Words*, Kilmainham Jail Restoration Society, 1971.
20. Command Paper 4823, HMSO, London, 16/11/71.
21. *Republican News*, Belfast, 11/9/71.
22. Crossman, op. cit., p. 478.
23. *Hansard*, House of Commons, Vol. 826, Col. 1584.
24. Ibid.

Chapter Five

1. Date of interview with Wade, 16/5/94.
2. Martin Dillon, op. cit., p. 106.
3. *The Times*, 1/2/72.
4. *Hansard*, Vol. 830, Cols. 37/et seq.
5. Conor O'Cleary, *Phrases Make History Here*, O'Brien Press, 1986, p. 142.
6. McCann, op. cit., p. 107.
7. Barry White, *John Hume*, Blackstaff, 1984, p. 122.
8. Andrew Boyd, op. cit.
9. *Irish Press*, 25/3/72.
10. Patrick Buckland, *A History of Northern Ireland*, Gill & Macmillan, 1981, p. 163
11. Farrell, op. cit., p. 296.

12. *Irish Times*, 4/9/74.
13. The Scarman Report: Violence and Civil Disturbances in Northern Ireland in 1969, Cmd. 566, HMSO, Belfast, 1972.
14. The Widgery Report: 'Report of the Tribunal appointed to Enquire into the Events of Sunday, 30th of January, 1972, which Led to the Loss of Life in Connection with the Procession in Londonderry on that Day'. HC 220, 1971–72, HMSO, London, 1972.
15. White, op cit., p. 128.
16. Ibid., p. 130.
17. This account is based on the minutes of the meeting kept by the late Myles Shevlin, the recollections of the late Daithi O'Conaill, of Gerry Adams and of Lord Whitelaw, author.
18. William Whitelaw, *The Whitelaw Memoirs*, Aurum Press, 1989, p. 100.
19. Frank Burton, *The Politics of Legitimacy*, Routledge & Kegan Paul, 1978, p. 107.
20. Fathers Faul and Murray, 'Death and a Lie', September 1976, p. 1. National Library of Ireland, FR. 320, pamphlet 98.
21. The Diplock Report: Report of the Commission to consider legal procedures to deal with terrorist activities in Northern Ireland, Cmd. 5185, London, 1972.
22. Farrell, *The Orange State*. op. cit., p. 304.

Chapter Six

1. Robert Fisk, *The Point of No Return: The Strike which broke the British Government*, Andre Deutsch, 1975.
2. *The Future of Northern Ireland*, Discussion Paper, NIO, HMSO, London, 1972.
3. *Northern Ireland Constitutional Proposals*, CMD, 529, London, March 1973.
4. Quoted in Farrell, op. cit., p. 307.
5. Ibid., p. 309.
6. Bew and Gillespie, op. cit., p. 70.
7. *Irish Times*, 20/5/74.
8. Ibid., 22/5/74.
9. Ibid., 26/5/74.
10. White, op. cit., p. 170.
11. Quoted in Fisk, op. cit., p. 223.
12. Quoted in the *Irish Times*, 4/9/74.
13. Interview with Murphy, 27/7/89, op. cit.
14. Interview with author, 21/5/94.
15. *Irish Times*, 16/1/74.
16. Interview with Murphy, 27/7/89, op. cit.

Chapter Seven

1. *Irish Times*, 21/11/81.
2. By the *Irish Press* on the morning of the signing. I had been told of the agreement's contents some days earlier.
3. *Irish Times*, 13/6/74.
4. As recently as 12 December 1994, on RTE's *Pat Kenny Show*, he said that his relations with Mrs Thatcher were always very satisfactory.
5. O'hAnrachain described the incident to me during a series of conversations we held in 1985–6 while I was assisting him with his memoirs. O'hAnrachain, who had served under de Valera, Sean Lemass, and Lynch before Haughey, would have produced an Irish version of Tom Jones' celebrated Whitehall diaries had he lived, but unfortunately he died in 1987 with the task uncompleted.
6. An Irish civil servant who was present at the exchange told me she thumped the table and informed him furiously that he knew very well that there was no question of a united Ireland being involved.
7. *Irish Times*, 22/5/82.
8. Ibid., 26/5/82.

Chapter Eight

1. Mike Mansfield, *Presumed Guilty*, Heinemann, 1993, p. viii.
2. Ibid., p. 234.
3. Ibid., p. 82.
4. *Irish Press*, 23/7/79.
5. Coogan, *De Valera*, op. cit., p. 64.
6. *Irish Times*, 3/8/79.
7. *Irish Press*, 29/4/81.
8. *Irish Times*, 16/5/81.
9. The Revd Eric McComb, speaking at the funeral of a UDR victim of the IRA on 24 January 1984, said: 'We don't need the Sinn Fein Cardinal to be advocating votes for those who are out to murder these men.'
10. Bew and Gillespie, op. cit., pp. 271–2.
11. *Belfast Newsletter*, 17/12/92.

Chapter Nine

1. Coogan, *The Irish: A Personal View*, op. cit., p. 205.
2. The document, 'Staff Report', is quoted from extensively in Coogan, *The IRA*, op. cit., Chapter 26.
3. *An tOglach*, 15/8/18. Collins' 'Notes on Organisation' were subsequently reproduced in Piaras Beaslai, *Michael Collins and the Making of a New Ireland*, Phoenix Publishing Company, 1926, pp. 203 ff.

4. My book on Collins, which appeared at his centenary in 1990, radically altered the prevailing opinion.
5. 30 January 1994.
6. The *Green Book* is extensively quoted in Coogan, *The IRA*, op. cit., Chapters 33 and 34.
7. Copy of original in author's possession.
8. *Belfast Telegraph*, 13/1/82.
9. *Irish Times*, 13/12/74.
10. MacStiofain, op. cit., p. 238.
11. see p. 213 Merlyn Rees' Memoirs
12. Private source.
13. Copy in author's possession.
14. Copy in author's possession.
15. The course of the 1992–3 discussions, and documents involved, including the Rees letter, are described in the final chapter of the 1995 edition of Coogan, *The IRA*, op. cit.
16. Information in author's possession.
17. Tim Pat Coogan, *On the Blanket*, Ward River Press, 1980, pp. 52 ff.
18. The report, published by HMSO, 30 January 1975, was also widely published in the press.
19. Copy in author's possession.
20. Coogan, *On the Blanket*, op. cit., p. 67.
21. The full text of the Cardinal's statement is reproduced in Chapter 13 of Coogan, *On the Blanket*, op. cit., which also contains the objections of Amnesty International and civil liberties groups to what was happening.
22. The full text is given in Coogan, *On the Blanket*, op. cit., Chapter 13.
23. Ibid., p. 207.
24. Joseph Maguire to author, Coogan, *On the Blanket*, op. cit., p. 3.
25. *Hansard*, House of Commons, Vol. 994, Col. 27.
26. Ibid., Vol. 995, Col. 1028.
27. The originals of the H Block communications from Sands and others are preserved in Sinn Fein archives. Some, like this one dated 31/1/81, are reproduced by David Beresford in *Ten Men Dead*, Coogan, Grafton, 1987, p. 54. Sinn Fein hold a vast amount of Sands' writings and it is hoped, if the conditions permit, to reprint these at some future date.
28. Beresford, op. cit., p. 129.
29. Coogan, *Disillusioned Decades*, op. cit., p. 233.
30. Beresford, op. cit., p. 406.
31. Quoted by the *Irish Times*, 19/9/91.
32. *Hansard*, House of Commons, Vol. 4, Col. 17.
33. *Irish Times*, 5/10/81.
34. *Hansard*, House of Commons, Vol. 992, Col. 134.
35. Ibid., Vol. 9, Col. 966.
36. Interview with Murphy, 7/6/89, op. cit.

Chapter Ten

1. Facsimile of British intelligence officer's letter reproduced in Beaslai, op. cit., Vol. II, p. 96.
2. In *The Dirty War*, op. cit., p. 28, Martin Dillon described Kitson thus: 'Frank Kitson at twenty-seven years old was a district intelligence officer who devised techniques for terrorising the terrorists. This involved using "counter-gangs" which could be attributed to the enemy, namely the Mau Mau, in order to discredit them.'
3. There is a voluminous literature on various aspects of the underground war, some of it of dubious value. I would recommend readers to a relatively short reading list for this aspect of the struggle: Bruce, op. cit.; Michael Carver, *Out of Step*, Hutchinson, 1989; Coogan, *The IRA*, op. cit.; Dillon, *The Dirty War*, op. cit.; Dorrill and Ramsay, *Smear*, Grafton, 1991; Mark Urban, *Big Boys' Rules*, Faber & Faber, 1992.
4. Dillon, *The Dirty War*, op. cit., pp. 31 ff., describes the operations of the MRF.
5. Dorrill and Ramsay, op. cit., p. 215.
6. Ibid., p. 217.
7. Copy in author's possession.
8. Ibid.
9. Ibid.
10. Rees, op. cit., p. 302.
11. *Hibernia*, 3/10/75.
12. Beaslai, op. cit., p. 91.
13. McNamara at Oral History conference, London.
14. Urban, op. cit., p. 7.
15. *Irish Times*, 6/10/79.
16. Interviewed by the BBC's *War School* programme after he left Northern Ireland in January 1980, General Creasey said: 'I believe that given the national will, and efficient use of all our resources, both military, police and civil, that are at the disposal of the modern state, terrorism can be defeated and in fact that defeat is inevitable.'
17. Dorrill and Ramsay, op. cit., p. 217.
18. Urban, op. cit., p. 13.
19. Ibid., p. 11
20. Ibid.
21. Quoted by Raymond Murray, *The SAS in Ireland*, Mercier, 1990, p. 229.
22. These included his solicitor and Frs Faul and Murray, who investigated the case.
23. Quoted by John Stalker, *Stalker*, Harrap, 1988, p. 38.
24. Quoted in some detail by Dillon, *The Dirty War*, op. cit., pp. 226 ff.
25. Dorrill and Ramsay, op. cit., p. 216.
26. Dillon, *The Dirty War*, op. cit., p. 197.
27. Interview with author, 24/2/95.
28. The account of what happened is based on a memo supplied to me by Fisk. It

was written by Fisk in Beirut on 11 February 1995.

29. *New Society*, 11/10/73.
30. One officer did read back his notes, and Fisk still has a copy of the tape.
31. Fisk memo to author, op. cit.
32. Ibid.
33. Quoted by Merlyn Rees, op. cit., p. 344. Fisk wrote the article for *The Times*, 22/3/75.
34. A detailed list of newspaper and magazine articles, books, TV and radio programmes is given in Murray, op. cit., p. 467.
35. Paul Foot, *Who Framed Colin Wallace?*, Macmillan, 1989.
36. Peter Wright, with Paul Greengrass, *Spycatcher*, William Heinemann, 1987.
37. Dorrill and Ramsay, op. cit., p. 237.
38. Letter to author, 11/2/95.
39. Interview with author, 4/5/94.
40. Quoted in Urban, op. cit., p. 54.
41. The programme became the basis for a huge amount of coverage in all the major newspapers of Ireland and England. But some of the best writing on the Holroyd case is contained in smaller journals published contemporaneously, notably *Lobster*, *Private Eye* and, in particular, Campbell's own series which accompanied the Channel Four programme, *Victims of the Dirty War*, in the *Statesman*.
42. Quoted by Duncan Campbell in *Statesman*, 4/5/84, first article of series.
43. Ibid.
44. Colin Wallace corroborated this incident to me, unprompted and independently of Holroyd. He named the RUC personnel involved in the decision, recording the comment of one prominent officer that he hoped it would 'teach the Catholics a lesson'.
45. London *Independent*, 2/9/87, articles by David McKitterick and John Ware.
46. Quoted by Urban, op. cit., p. 77.
47. *The Guardian*, 14/3/77.
48. Ibid., 17/4/84.
49. Urban, op. cit., p. 74.
50. Ibid.
51. Coogan, *Michael Collins*, op. cit., 182–3.
52. Ibid., pp. 355–6.
53. The details of how the Stalker Inquiry came to be first set up and then aborted have been exhaustively discussed in the media (both print and electronic) of the English-speaking world, but the best account is Stalker's own indispensable work (op. cit.).
54. Ibid., p. 34.
55. Ibid., p. 30.
56. Ibid., p. 50.
57. Ibid., p. 52.
58. Ibid., p. 54.
59. The dead men were Corporal Michael Francis Herbert and Corporal Michael John Cotton. They were shot on 20 March 1970, at Mowhan, South Armagh.

60. Stalker, op. cit., p. 53.
61. Michael O'Connell, *Truth, the First Casualty*, Riverstone, 1993, p. 222.
62. Flackes, op. cit.
63. Quoted by Urban, op. cit., p. 22.
64. Ibid.
65. I have described this person's activities at length in *The IRA*, op. cit.
66. Urban, op. cit., p. 217.
67. Coogan, *The IRA*, op. cit., p. 453.
68. *The Sunday Times*, 14/5/95.
69. Dillon, *The Dirty War*, op. cit., p. 378.
70. Martin Dillon makes a convincing case for this argument in a closely researched chapter ('The Sting', pp. 58–92) in *The Dirty War*, op. cit.
71. Ibid., p. 84.
72. The sentence was related to the robbery of the Allied Irish Bank in Dublin's Grafton Street on 12 October 1972. During the robbery the raiders addressed each other by military titles, 'Sergeant', 'Corporal' and so on, and forced the manager to assist them by kidnapping his wife, sister-in-law and children.
73. Dillon, *The Dirty War*, op. cit., p. 110.
74. Ibid.
75. The other members of the inquiry were Edgar Fay, QC, Recorder of Plymouth, and Dr Ronald Gibson, former chairman of the BMA Council.
76. quoted in T.P. Coogan *The IRA* p. 439, HarperCollins, London, 1995.
77. The findings were carried extensively in the major Irish and English newspapers. See also Coogan, *The IRA*, op. cit., pp. 333 ff., and Coogan, *On the Blanket*, op. cit., pp. 132 ff.
78. Quoted in Coogan, *The IRA*, op. cit., pp. 333–4.
79. Quoted in Coogan, *On the Blanket*, op. cit., p. 137.
80. *The Sunday Times*, 23/10/77.
81. Coogan, *On the Blanket*, op. cit., p. 138.
82. Coogan, *The IRA*, op. cit., p. 334.
83. Coogan, *On the Blanket*, op. cit., p. 139.
84. Ibid., p. 138.
85. Ibid., p. 394.
86. Ibid.
87. Mallie and Bishop, op. cit., p. 408. The authors deal comprehensively with the supergrass issue on pp. 393–410. See also Coogan, *On the Blanket*, op. cit., pp. 393–5.
88. Quoted by Coogan, *On the Blanket*, op. cit., p. 393.
89. Stephen C. Greer, 'Supergrasses and the Legal System', *Law Quarterly Review*, April 1986.
90. Some aspects of the INLA, its leadership and feuding are dealt with in Coogan, *The IRA*, op. cit. But for a full-length book on the subject readers are recommended to Jack Holland and Henry McDonald, *Deadly Divisions*, Torc, 1994.
91. Holland and McDonald, op. cit., p. 138.

92. Coogan, *The IRA*, op. cit., p. 411.

93. *Irish News*, 10/3/87.

94. Holland and McDonald, op. cit., p. 297.

95. This became public knowledge at his trial on 29 October 1991.

96. Flackes, op. cit., p. 331.

97. *Fortnight* magazine, September 1992.

98. *Sunday Press*, 16/8/92.

99. Principally in Martin Dillon, *The Shankill Butchers: A case study in mass murder*, Hutchinson, 1989.

100. Dillon, *The Dirty War*, op. cit., p. 253.

101. Ibid., p. 260.

102. Flackes, op. cit., p. 330.

103. In the unlikely surroundings of the Franciscan friary at Gormanstown, Co. Meath, at which we were both invited to usher in the New Year of 1980 by giving our prognostications for the coming decade. Both of us being threatened with optimism, we were proved wrong.

104. Foreign Office Papers, quoted by Murray, op. cit., p. 14.

105. Urban, op. cit., p. 40.

106. Ibid., p. 6.

107. On 3 December, while addressing the Newry and Mourne District Council, and on 30 October, while addressing an audience of Belfast businessmen.

108. Murray, op. cit., p. 259.

109. Urban, op. cit., pp. 56–7.

110. Dillon, *The Dirty War*, op. cit., p. 200.

111. Martin Dillon, *Stone Cold*, Arrow, 1992, p. 136.

112. Murray, op. cit., p. 258.

113. John Hume, interview with author, 14/5/94.

Chapter 11

1. Liz Curtis, *Ireland, the Propaganda War*, Pluto, 1984.

2. Paul Madden, ed., *The British Media and Ireland: Truth, the First Casualty*, Information on Ireland, 1979.

3. Harold Evans, *Good Times, Bad Times*, Coronet, 1984, p. 25.

4. John Ware, *Secrecy, the Right to Truth and Peace in Northern Ireland*, December 1993. Ware, who is frequently in demand as a lecturer, wrote the paper for this purpose, and kindly gave me a copy.

5. Ibid.

6. Readers seeking such documentation can be recommended to Curtis, op.cit.

7. Lower Master of Eton, 1878–87.

8. *The Sunday Times*, 6/2/72.

9. Simon Winchester, *Holy Terror*, Faber & Faber, 1974, p. 200.

10. O'Connell, op. cit., p. 37.

11. Winchester, op. cit., p. 20.

12. Evelyn King, MP, *Daily Telegraph*, 24/8/71.

13. Ibid., 20/8/71.
14. *The Guardian*, 20/8/71.
15. Curtis, op. cit., p. 10.
16. This happened (in November 1971) in the case of Granada's *South of the Border* programme, which sought to illustrate how the Troubles affected the Republic, despite the fact that the board of Granada had voted unanimously to show the programme.
17. As early as ten days after internment (19/8/71), the *Donegal Democrat* carried eight pages of detailed reports from both eyewitnesses and victims of maltreatment. The paper's page one headline read: 'Warning: don't read this if you have a weak stomach.'
18. *The Times*, 16/11/71.
19. *Financial Times*, 17/11/71.
20. Alasdair Milne, *The Memoirs of a British Broadcaster*, p. 101.
21. Asa Briggs, *Governing the BBC*, p. 230.
22. Ibid., p. 229.
23. *New Statesman*, 31/12/71.
24. Rees, op. cit., p. 74.
25. The *Daily Mail* on 6/1/77, the *Irish Times* the following day and *The Observer* on the 23rd.
26. Milne op. cit., p. 102.
27. Ibid.
28. *Irish Times*, 13/4/95.
29. Peter Taylor, 'Thames Television', *Index on Censorship*, Vol. 7, no. 6, 1978.
30. Bew and Gillespie, op. cit., p. 214.
31. The work of both Curtis and Madden provides such lists.
32. *The Guardian*, 23/2/80.
33. Milne, op. cit., p. 98.
34. *The Sunday Times*, 5/11/72.
35. *Evening Standard*, 11/5/72.
36. It was finally shown by the BBC in 1994.
37. At a private meeting in the House of Commons on 7 March 1977, which was reported on by the *Irish Times* of 10 March.
38. Curtis, op. cit., p. 55.
39. *The Sunday Times*, 14/3/77.
40. *The Daily Telegraph*, 4/3/77.
41. Coogan, *On the Blanket*, op. cit., p. 147.
42. *The Times*, 26/11/77.
43. Peter Taylor, *Beating the Terrorists*, Penguin, 1980.
44. *The Daily Telegraph*, 11/7/79.
45. *The Sun*, 13/7/79.
46. *Daily Express*, 9/11/79.
47. Garret FitzGerald, *All in a Life*, Gill and Macmillan, 1991, p. 279.
48. *New Statesman*, 16/11/79.

49. Vincent Hanna, quoted on p. 73 of the minutes of the ADM of the NUJ, April 1980.
50. *Evening Standard*, 9/11/79.
51. *The Guardian*, 9/11/79.
52. *The Times*, 2/8/80.
53. *Hansard*, Vol. 138, Col. 893.
54. Milne, op. cit., p. 140.
55. Quoted by Milne, op. cit.
56. Curtis, op. cit., p. 184.
57. FitzGerald, op. cit. p. 472.
58. Ibid., p. 462.
59. Charles Curran (ed.), *The British Press, a Manifesto*, Macmillan Press Ltd, 1978, p. 28.
60. *The Sunday Times* Insight team, *Ulster*, Andre Deutsch and Penguin, 1972.
61. Evans, op. cit.
62. Ibid., p. 284.
63. Ibid., p. 293.
64. *Irish Press*, 5/2/72.
65. Interview with author, 5/5/94.
66. *The Observer*, 17/1/78.
67. *Observer* colour supplement, 1/10/78.
68. Curtis, op. cit., pp. 192–3.
69. As the shadow of O'Brien lessened over the *Observer* – he ceased to be editor-in-chief in 1981 and became a consultant editor – Holland's by-line reappeared in the paper.
70. The affair is described by Paul O'Higgins in 'The Irish TV Sackings', *Index on Censorship*, 1/1973.
71. 23 November 1972.

Chapter 12

1. *Cork Examiner*, 17/9/79.
2. Over one million people attended the centrepiece of the visit, an open-air Mass, celebrated by the Pope, in Phoenix Park, Dublin.
3. The Pope's speech was carried in full in the following day's national papers. Later in 1979 a complete collection of all his speeches in Ireland (he made an average of three to four a day) was published in Dublin by Veritas Publications.
4. The statement was released at a press conference conducted by O'Conaill, O'Bradaigh and other prominent Republicans in Dublin on 2/10/79. It was subsequently widely publicised in the national press.
5. Gerry Adams, *Free Ireland, Towards a Lasting Peace*, Brandon, Dingle, 1995, p. 193.
6. Ibid.

7. *Link-Up*, p. 19, December 1995. A clerical newsletter published by the Irish hierarchy, edited by Fr Tom Stack, PP.
8. Adams, op. cit., p. 193.
9. Ibid., p. 197.
10. Ibid., p. 159.
11. London advised Dublin against allowing the President to meet Adams, but she not alone persisted in shaking hands with him, on 18 June 1993, but later in Coalisland met local representatives who included Sinn Fein councillors.
12. Unless otherwise attributed, the quotations in the pages dealing with the SDLP–Sinn Fein negotiations are taken from the Sinn Fein publication *Sinn Fein–SDLP, January-September 1989*. The background information to the talks is based on my own knowledge of events.
13. Ibid., p. 197.
14. Ibid., p. 198.
15. Ibid.
16. *Sunday Life*, 19/2/89.
17. Brooke was a principal opponent of Health Minister Virginia Bottomley in the debate that raged through the Tory ranks throughout the spring and summer of 1995 over her efforts to close some of London's famous old hospitals.
18. Revealed by Dr Martin Mansergh, in a lecture to the Royal Irish Academy, Dublin, 22/5/95.
19. An offensive by the Viet Cong in 1970 right across South Vietnam which, though it was eventually repulsed, convinced many observers that the VC were undefeatable. In the course of the onslaught the attackers invaded the American Embassy in Saigon.
20. Alan Clark, *Diaries*, Weidenfeld & Nicolson, 1993, p. 99.
21. Flackes and Elliot, op. cit., p. 49.
22. In conversation with author, 25/5/95.
23. Literally, 'beyond the mountains'. Latin tag to describe aspects of Roman Catholic dogma which are more rigorously applied in other sees, e.g. Ireland, 'beyond the mountains', than they are in Rome itself, within the Roman Hills.
24. The account of the Sinn Fein talks is based on records supplied to me by Sinn Fein. A compilation of these documents, *Setting the Record Straight*, was issued in December 1993 and lodged in the Linenhall Library, Belfast, and the National Library, Dublin. Another, less comprehensive, version of the talks, covering their later stages only, was lodged in the House of Commons Library by Sir Patrick Mayhew. An extensive account of the talks is contained in the final chapter of the May 1995 edition of Coogan, *The IRA*, published by Harper Collins, London.
25. *The Times*, 12/1/93.
26. *An Phoblacht*/Republican News, 25/6/92.
27. *Belfast Newsletter*, 17/12/92.
28. Quoted by Coogan, in *De Valera*, op. cit., p. 181.
29. Quoted by Jack Holland, *The American Connection*, Poolbeg, 1989, p. 125.

30. Ibid., p. 137.
31. Ibid., p. 123.
32. *Irish Times*, 25/1/93.
33. Coogan, *Disillusioned Decades*, op. cit., p. 168.
34. Holland, op. cit., p. 131.
35. Ibid., p. 137.
36. Coogan, *Disillusioned Decades*, op. cit., p. 171.
37. O'Dowd and I were in close contact throughout the period, but for the purposes of this book he formally recorded his recollections and assessments in New York during November 1994.
38. The account of Reynolds' participation in the peace process is based in part on my own observation of his activities, on various conversations with him and on a set of interviews for this book, commencing on 28 May 1995. The quotations are taken from these.
39. Six County attitudes were examined and analysed in depth in The Opsahl Report, Lilliput, 1993. Torkel Opsahl, who died shortly afterwards, was a distinguished Norwegian academic who had attempted to mediate during the Bobby Sands hunger strike. He chaired an inquiry into attitudes in the Six Counties during 1992–3, which found that most people, whatever their religious feelings, thought Sinn Fein should be involved in political talks, although equally a majority felt this could only come about after violence ended.
40. The official report is costly and turgid. More accessible is Fintan O'Toole's *Meanwhile, Back on the Ranch: the Politics of Irish Beef*, Vintage, London, 1995.
41. Tim Ryan speaking on 'Spin Doctors' at the Humbert Summer School, Ballina, 1994. The Beef Tribunal Report was formally released on 2 August 1993. The leakage occurred on 29 July.
42. Delivered to the Irish Association in Dublin, 5/3/93.
43. Paper submitted by the UUP during the three-stranded talks process, on 7 July 1992.
44. Ibid., 6 July 1992, and amplified on succeeding days.
45. Opsahl Inquiry, op. cit., p. 40.
46. Ibid.
47. Ibid.
48. Ibid., p. 44.
49. Rapporteur: Mr. Jaak Vandemeulebroucke.
50. *The Directory of Discrimination* is one of a series of publications linked to the work of Equality, Andersonstown Road, Belfast.
51. Op. cit., p. 3.
52. Lionel Shiver, an American novelist and journalist.
53. *Irish Independent*, 30/3/93.
54. Mansergh lecture.
55. Ibid.
56. Ibid.

57. Quoted in *Setting the Record Straight*, Sinn Fein publication.
58. Copy in author's possession. The communiqué was also printed in the *Irish Times* and *Independent*.
59. Copy in author's possession.
60. Ibid.
61. *Setting the Record Straight*, op. cit.
62. Brendan O'Brien, *The Long War*, O'Brien Press, 1993, p. 247.
63. Private source, author.
64. *Irish Times*, 1/9/94.
65. Ibid.
66. Mansergh lecture.
67. *Irish Times*, 1/9/94.
68. Ibid., 24/5/94.
69. Ibid., 7/12/94.
70. The incident occurred on 21 April 1995, at a meeting of party activists in Cork North-West. Bruton was at first surprised by an unexpected question from a local radio reporter, then, with the microphone switched off and the incident, as he thought, unrecorded, he gave his forthright reply.
71. The term was used by the Fianna Fail Chief Whip, Dermot Ahern, on RTE's *Any Questions* programme on 12/6/95.
72. *A New Framework for Agreement*, published by the Irish Government, printed by Cahill's, Dublin, 1995.
73. 14/12/95.
74. *The Sunday Business Post* carried an in-depth survey of the overall military position of the Six Counties on 6/11/94. The survey was conducted with the aid of Queen's University sociologist, Mike Tomlinson.
75. Ibid.
76. *The News at One*, RTE, 16/6/95.
77. *Irish Voice*, 31/5/95, 4/6/95.
78. *Irish Times*, 26/5/95.
79. Ibid.
80. On Radio Ulster, 17/6/95.
81. *Irish Times, Irish Independent*, 19/6/95.
82. Ibid.
83. In the Dail, and subsequently in a series of TV and print interviews, conducted on the same day, 25/7/95.
84. On RTE's major weekly radio news programme, *This Week*, 23/7/95.
85. *The State We're In*, by Will Hutton, Cape, London, 1995.
86. Hutton, op. cit., pp. 9–10.
87. *Irish Times*, 11/7/95.
88. *Irish Times*, 11/7/95.
89. Ibid.
90. *Irish Times*, 13/7/95.
91. *Irish Times*, 15/7/95.

92. *Irish Times*, 15/7/95.
93. *Sunday Business Post*, 23/7/95.
94. Ibid.
95. Dail debates, 26/7/95.
96. *Sunday Business Post*, 23/7/95.
97. *Guardian*, 27/7/95.
98. *The Economic Consequences of Peace in Ireland*, by Alan Gray, Indecon International Economic Consultants, Dublin, 1995.
99. Seamus Heaney, *The Cure at Troy*, A Version of Sophocles's Philoctetes, Faber, 1990.

List of Organisations

ALLIANCE PARTY Moderate, reformist, Unionist party, set up in April 1970, and attracting middle-class support across sectarian divide.

AMERICAN ANCIENT ORDER OF HIBERNIANS Strongly Nationalist and Roman Catholic grouping which organises annual New York St Patrick's Day parade. Has been involved in controversy because of support by some of its members for the Provisional IRA.

APPRENTICE BOYS OF DERRY Loyalist organisation which annually commemorates the siege of Derry in 1688 which began when apprentice boys shut the gates of Derry in the face of King James' army. It was an Apprentice Boys' march which sparked the riots of August 1968.

ASSOCIATION FOR LEGAL JUSTICE A body set up in 1971 by Nationalist civil libertarians to monitor complaints against the courts and the security forces.

B-SPECIALS A Protestant, state-funded militia which was replaced by the Ulster Defence Regiment following the Hunt Report's recommendation, in 1969, that the force be abolished (see Ulster Special Constabulary).

BLACK AND TANS An organisation of ex-British servicemen, set up in 1920 to augment the regular police force, the Royal Irish Constabulary, during the Anglo-Irish war. The corps was ill-disciplined and, like its counterpart organisation, the Auxiliaries, which was drawn from the ranks of ex-officers, it is remembered for many acts of destruction and death.

CATHOLIC EX-SERVICEMEN'S ASSOCIATION A Nationalist vigilante organisation which was active in the earlier phases of the Troubles.

CENTRAL CITIZENS' DEFENCE COMMITTEE A co-ordinating committee of Nationalist defence organisations set up to repel further Loyalist incursions into Belfast Catholic areas following the burnings of August 1969. It was infiltrated by the IRA, and subsequently taken over by the Catholic clergy.

COMBINED LOYALIST MILITARY COMMAND Umbrella body of Loyalist paramilitaries. Declared Loyalist ceasefire in 1994.

CONSERVATIVE PARTY Formerly known as the Conservative and Unionist party, this right-wing – and frequently ruling – British party, often referred to as the Tory Party, is traditionally associated with opposition to Irish Home Rule movements and the upholding of the Union.

DAIL EIREANN The Irish Parliament, generally referred to as the Dail.

DEMOCRATIC UNIONIST PARTY (DUP) Right-wing, anti-Catholic, Unionist party, formed in 1971 in Six Counties by Revd Ian Paisley.

FIANNA FAIL Largest party in the Republic of Ireland. Centre right, Nationalist party formed from original Sinn Fein Party by Eamon de Valera in 1926.

FINE GAEL Second largest party in the Republic. Formed in 1933 from remnants of Sinn Fein, centrist, and farmers' elements opposed to de Valera in Irish civil war of 1922–3.

GARDA SIOCHANA Unarmed police force of Republic of Ireland.

IRISH LABOUR PARTY Founded in 1912, third largest party in the Republic.

IRISH NATIONAL LIBERATION ARMY (INLA) Established 1975 by breakaway elements from the then Official IRA who had also founded the Irish Republican Socialist Party the previous year (1974).

IRISH PEOPLE'S LIBERATION ORGANISATION (IPLO) Breakaway group from INLA, founded 1976.

IRISH REPUBLICATION ARMY(IRA) . Title given to original Irish Nationalist physical force group which fought the British after the establishment of the first Dail in 1919.

IRISH REPUBLICAN BROTHERHOOD (IRB) The IRB, or the Fenians, as they were termed after the legendary Irish version of the Japanese Samurai, were founded in 1858. The organisation was the inspiration behind the 1916 rebellion and the precursor of the IRA.

LOYALISTS Usually used to mean working-class Unionists.

LOYALIST ASSOCIATION OF WORKERS (LAW) Loyalist workers' grouping centred on shipyards active in Belfast *circa* 1970–74.

NEW ULSTER POLITICAL RESEARCH GROUP Loyalist group which produced the document 'Beyond the Religious Divide', a blueprint for negotiated independence. Served as a think tank for the Ulster Defence Association.

NORTHERN IRELAND CIVIL RIGHTS ASSOCIATION Established in 1967. Spear-headed civil rights protests.

NORTHERN IRELAND LABOUR PARTY Founded in 1924 and collapsed in 1987.

NORAID North American Aid. A US organisation which raises funds for Irish Republican causes.

OFFICIAL IRISH REPUBLICAN ARMY (OIRA) Left-wing IRA group.

OFFICIAL UNIONIST PARTY Protestant anti-power-sharing branch of the Ulster Unionist Party.

ORANGE ORDER Powerful Protestant society, modelled on Freemasons when originally set up in 1795, its colourful annual marches are often a flash-point for Protestant–Catholic clashes.

ORANGE VOLUNTEERS Paramilitary branch of the Orange Order, set up in 1972.

PROGRESSIVE UNIONIST PARTY Formed in 1979. Seen as a political wing of the Ulster Volunteer Force.

PROTESTANT ACTION FORCE Pseudonym of the Ulster Volunteer Force.

PROTESTANT ACTION GROUP Pseudonym of the Ulster Volunteer Force.

PROVISIONAL IRA (ALSO KNOWN AS PROVOS) Militant wing of the IRA which broke away from the OIRA in 1969.

PROTESTANT UNIONIST PARTY The Revd Ian Paisley's first political party, subsumed into DUP.

RED HAND COMMANDO Loyalist paramilitary organisation, founded in 1972.

ROYAL IRISH CONSTABULARY Pre-Partition Irish police force.

ROYAL ULSTER CONSTABULARY Armed Northern Ireland police force.

ROYAL ULSTER CONSTABULARY RESERVES Comprises full- and part-time members and serves as a reserve for the Royal Ulster Constabulary.

SAOR EIRE ACTION GROUP Republican left-wing splinter group.

SHANKILL DEFENCE ASSOCIATION Loyalist vigilante group.

SINN FEIN Originally 'We Ourselves'. Political party and wing of the Provisional Irish Republican Army. Mainly supported by working-class Catholics.

SOCIAL DEMOCRATIC AND LABOUR PARTY (SDLP) Nationalist constitutional party founded in 1970. Believes in the necessity of majority consent for a united Ireland. Its main support comes from the Catholic middle class.

SPECIAL AIR SERVICE (SAS) The special operations force of the British Army against whom most accusations of carrying out a 'shoot to kill' policy are directed by Nationalists.

TARA Founded in 1966 by William McGrath, this anti-Catholic paramilitary organisation was linked to Ulster Volunteer Force.

THIRD FORCE Refers to Ian Paisley's reported efforts to recruit a defensive militia. One such force was Ulster Resistance, formed with the help of Paisley and Peter Robinson, his deputy, in 1986 (see below).

ULSTER ARMY COUNCIL Loyalist paramilitary organisations' talking-shop which folded in 1974.

ULSTER CITIZENS' ARMY Fictitious Loyalist paramilitary organisation invented to generate inter-paramilitary hostility by British Army intelligence.

ULSTER CITIZENS CIVIL LIBERTIES Supported by Ulster Defence Association. Legal representations group.

ULSTER COMMUNITY ACTION GROUP Ulster Defence Association-supported community group association.

ULSTER CONSTITUTION DEFENCE COMMITTEE Organised Revd Ian Paisley's protests in the 1960s against O'Neill.

ULSTER DEFENCE ASSOCIATION Founded in 1971. This is the largest Loyalist paramilitary organisation in Northern Ireland.

ULSTER DEFENCE REGIMENT Formed in 1970 to replace the Ulster Special Constabulary. Subsumed into the Royal Irish Regiment in 1992.

ULSTER FREEDOM FIGHTERS Pseudonym for Ulster Defence Association death squads.

ULSTER PROTESTANT ACTION Unionist ginger group.

ULSTER PROTESTANT VOLUNTEERS A counterpart to Paisley's Ulster Constitution Defence Committee.

UNIONIST PARTY OF NORTHERN IRELAND 'Power-sharing' wing of the Unionist party.

ULSTER RESISTANCE Established in protest over the Anglo-Irish Agreement. Linked to the Ulster Defence Association and the Ulster Volunteer Force. Involved in South African arms deal.

ULSTER SPECIAL CONSTABULARY Established in 1920 as an anti-Irish Republican Army paramilitary force. It was divided into three units at first, 'A'. 'B' and 'C'. Sections 'A' and 'C' subsequently disbanded and unit 'B' remained as a part-time force, replaced in 1970 by the Ulster Defence Regiment.

ULSTER UNIONIST PARTY Largest Unionist party in Northern Ireland. Provided government from Partition to 1972. It has been led by James Molyneaux and is also known as the 'Official' Unionist Party.

UNIONISTS Loyal to the Union and opposed to a thirty-two-county Ireland.

UNITED ULSTER UNIONIST COUNCIL Initially an amalgam of anti-power-sharing Unionist groups comprising the Official Unionist Party, the Democratic Unionist Party and others.

UNITED ULSTER UNIONIST MOVEMENT Established when the United Ulster Unionists Council's coalition of Unionists divided.

ULSTER VANGUARD Unionist grouping, established in 1972 by William Craig.

ULSTER VOLUNTEER FORCE (UVF) Established in 1912 by Edward Carson and James Craig to oppose Irish independence. In 1914 was incorporated as the 36th Ulster Division into the British Army. In 1966 it was the name given to the paramilitary body established by Loyalists in the Shankill Road area. The organisation has since been banned.

ULSTER VOLUNTEER SERVICE CORPS Established in 1973 to succeed the Vanguard Service Corps.

ULSTER WORKERS COUNCIL This succeeded the Loyalist Association of Workers and was involved in organising the strike of 1974.

VANGUARD UNIONIST PROGRESSIVE PARTY The former Ulster Vanguard which became a political party in 1973.

BIBLIOGRAPHY

One of the major sources for this book cannot easily be catalogued: my own experience of living through the period described. As this resource, if resource it is, has been drawn upon copiously, I am tempted to invoke Virgil in seeking the reader's indulgence: *Experto credite* (Trust one who has gone through it!). More importantly, I should point out that where matters of fact are concerned I have sometimes had to make use of conversations with friends and contacts whose positions do not permit of attribution. I am deeply indebted to such people for sharing their insights with me about matters which were always delicate, and sometimes dangerous, and I ask the reader's indulgence for not lifting the veil of secrecy any further. The reading list which I relied upon for my other books (detailed below) may be found in their bibliographies; the selection I made for this work is as follows:

CHRONOLOGIES

Annual Register, Longmans, Harlow.

Keesing's Contemporary Archives, Keesings, London.

Paul Bew and Gordon Gillespie, *Northern Ireland: a Chronology of the Troubles*, Gill and Macmillan, 1993.

Richard Deutsch and Vivien Magowan, *Northern Ireland: a Chronology of Events*, Vols. 1–3 (1968–75), Blackstaff.

W. D. Flackes and Sydney Elliott, *Northern Ireland: a Political Directory, 1968–1993*, Blackstaff, 1994.

NEWSPAPERS AND PAMPHLETS

An Phoblacht/Republican News, Belfast Telegraph, Economist, Fortnight, Guardian, Independent, Irish Independent, Irish News, Irish Press, Irish Times, News Letter, Observer, Sunday Press, Sunday Tribune, Sunday Independent, Sunday Times, New Statesman, Spectator.

Denis Faul and Raymond Murray, series of pamphlets: 'British Army & Special Branch RUC Brutalities', 1972, 'The Hooded Men', 1974, 'The Triangle of Death', 1975, 'The Castlereagh File', 1975, 'SAS Terrorism, The Assassin's Glove', 1976, 'H-Blocks', 1979, 'Hunger Strike', 1980.

The Directory of Discrimination in Northern Ireland, 1991; *The Road from '68*, both Oliver Kearney, Equality, Belfast, 1993.

'Strategy for Peace', Martin McGuinness address to Sinn Fein Ard Fheis, and Gerry Adams, Presidential Address, both 1991; 'Towards a Lasting Peace', 1992; 'The Sinn Fein/SDLP Talks', 1988, and 'The Hume–Adams talks', 1994; 'Setting the Record Straight', account of secret Sinn Fein–British Government dialogue, 1994; 'Reports and Resolutions of Sinn Fein Ard Fheiseanna, 1994–5; Report of Sinn Fein Peace Commission, 1994. All published by Sinn Fein, Parnell Square, Dublin, and Falls Road, Belfast.

REPORTS AND OFFICIAL DOCUMENTS

Amnesty International, UK: *Killings by Security Forces in Northern Ireland* (updated), London, 1990.

Cameron Report into Disturbances in Northern Ireland, Cmnd 532, HMSO, Belfast, 1969.

Hunt Report on Police in Northern Ireland, Cmnd 535, HMSO, Belfast, 1969.

Macrory Report on Local Government in Northern Ireland, Cmnd 546, HMSO, Belfast, 1970.

Report on Reform Programme; A Record of Constructive Change, Cmnd 558, HMSO, Belfast, 1971.

Scarman Report on Northern Violence in 1969, Cmnd 566, HMSO, Belfast, 1971.

Compton Report into Security Force behaviour in August 1971, Cmnd 4823, HMSO, London, 1971.

Parker Report into interrogation procedures of suspected terrorists, Cmnd 4901, HMSO, London, 1972.

Diplock Report of Commission on new legal procedures to deal with suspected terrorists, Cmnd 5185 HMSO, London, 1972.

Widgery Report into Bloody Sunday, January 30th, 1972, HC 220 1971–72, HMSO, London, 1972.

Anglo-Irish Law Enforcement Commission Report, Cmnd 5627, HMSO, London, 1974.

Gardiner Report on Counter-Insurgency Methods (recommended H-Blocks), Cmnd 5847, HMSO, London, 1975.

Bennett Report on RUC Interrogation Methods, Cmnd 7497, HMSO, London, 1979.

European Parliament Report on Discrimination in Northern Ireland, issued by Committee on Social Affairs, Employment and the Working Environment, 18/3/94 (English edition).

Opsahl Report, A Citizens' Inquiry on Northern Ireland, Lilliput, Dublin, 1993.

GOVERNMENTAL BLUEPRINTS FOR SIX COUNTIES

The Future of Northern Ireland, HMSO, London, 1972.

Northern Ireland Constitutional Proposals, HMSO, London, 1973.

The Northern Ireland Constitution, Cmnd 5675, HMSO, London, 1974.

Report of the Northern Ireland Constitutional Convention, HMSO, London, 1974.

Government of Northern Ireland: A Working Paper for a Conference, Cmnd 7763, HMSO, London, 1979.

Government of Northern Ireland, Proposals for Further Discussion, Cmnd 7950, HMSO, London, 1980.

PARLIAMENTARY RECORDS

Dail Debates, Official Reports, Stationery Office, Dublin.

House of Commons Reports, *Hansard*, HMSO, London.

Stormont Debates (end in 1972), HMSO, Belfast.

Northern Ireland Assembly Debates, Official Report, HMSO, Belfast, 1973–4.

INTER-GOVERNMENTAL COMMUNIQUES

Joint Declaration by An Taoiseach, Mr Albert Reynolds, TD and the British Prime Minister, The Rt Hon. John Major, MP, December 15th 1993, Govt Publications, Dublin.

Clarification for Sinn Fein, on above, by NIO through Taoiseach's Office, 17/5/94, Govt Publications, Dublin.

A Framework for Accountable Government in Northern Ireland (Framework Document), 22/2/94, Govt Publications, Dublin.

THESIS AND TRANSCRIPT
Thesis: Doctoral Dissertation of Michael A. Murphy submitted to Loyola University, Chicago, January 1992: Gerry Fitt from Republican Socialist to Peer of the Realm.

Transcripts: Interviews with several participants in Six County affairs during era of civil rights *et seq* conducted by Martin Dillon, 1992.

Fr Egan sermon, August 1969, supplied by Fr Hugh O'Donnell, archivist, Clonard Monastery, Belfast.

Text of Dr Martin Mansergh lecture to Royal Irish Academy 22 May 1995.

SELECT BIBLIOGRAPHY

ADAMS, Gerry: *Falls Memories*; 1982, *Cage 11*, 1990; *The Street*, 1992; *Free Ireland: Towards a Lasting Peace*, 1995, all Brandon, Dingle.

ADAMS, J.: *The Financing of Terror*, Hodder & Stoughton, London, 1988.

ADAMSON, I.: *The Identity of Ulster*, Pretani Press, Belfast, 1982; *The Cruthin, A History of the Ulster Land and People*, Pretani, 1986.

AKENSON, Donald Harmon: *Conor*, McGill-Queen's University Press, Canada, 1994.

ARTHUR, Paul: *Government and Politics of Northern Ireland*, Longman, London, 1980.

BAROID de, Cristoir: *Ballymurphy and the Irish War*, Aisling, Dublin, 1989.

BARRITT, Denis P. and Carter, Charles F.: *The Northern Ireland Problem*, Oxford, 1972.

BEASLAI, Piaras: *Michael Collins and the Making of a New Ireland*, Vols. I and II, Phoenix, Dublin, 1926.

BELL, Geoffrey: *The Protestants of Ulster*, Pluto, London, 1978.

BELL, J. Bowyer: *The Secret Army*, Sphere, London, 1972; *The Gun in Politics*, Transaction Publishers, New Brunswick, 1991; *The Irish Troubles*, St Martin's Press, New York, 1993.

BERESFORD, David: *Ten Men Dead*, Grafton, London, 1987.

BEW, Paul, Gibson, Peter and Patterson, Henry: *The State in Northern Ireland, 1921–72*, Manchester University Press, 1979; Bew and Patterson: *The British State & the Ulster Crisis,* Verso, London, 1985.

BIELER, Ludwig: *Ireland, Harbinger of the Middle Ages*, Oxford University Press, London, 1963.

BISHOP, Patrick and O'Mallie, Eamonn: *The Provisional IRA*, Heinemann, London, 1987.

BOLAND, Kevin: *Up Dev*, Boland, Dublin; *Under Contract With the Enemy*, Mercier, Dublin, 1988.

BOLTON, Roger: *Death On the Rock*, W. H. Allen, London, 1990.

BOULTON, David: *The U.V.F. 1966–73*, Gill and Macmillan, Dublin, 1973.

BOYD, Andrew: *Holy War in Belfast*, Anvil, Tralee, 1969; *The Rise of the Irish Trade Unions*, Anvil, 1985; *Brian Faulkner*, Anvil, 1972. (all p.b.)

BOYLE, Kevin, Hadden, Tom and Hilliard, P.: *Law & State: The Case of Northern Ireland*, Robertson, London, 1975.

BREEN, Richard, with Hannan, Damian, Rottman, David and Whelan, Christopher: *Understanding Contemporary Ireland*, Gill and Macmillan, Dublin, 1990.

BROWN, Terence: *Ireland: a Social and Cultural History, 1982–1985*. Fontana, 1985.

BRUCE, Steve: *The Red Hand*, Oxford University Press, London, 1992; *The Edge of the Union*, OUP, London, 1992.

BUCKLAND, Patrick: *Irish Unionism: One: The Anglo-Irish and the New Ireland, 1885–1922*, 1972; *Irish Unionism: Two: Ulster Unionism and the Origins of Northern Ireland 1886–1922*, 1973; *The Factory of Grievances, James Craig, Lord Craigavon, A history of Northern Ireland*, 1981. All published by Gill and Macmillan, Dublin.

BURTON, Frank: *The Politics of Legitimacy*, Routledge and Kegan Paul, London, 1978.

CAHILL, Thomas: *How the Irish Saved Civilisation*, Hodder & Stoughton, London, 1995.

CAIRNS, Ed: *Caught in Crossfire*, Appletree-Syracuse University Press, Belfast, 1987.

CALLAGHAN, Hugh: *Cruel Fate*, Poolbeg, Dublin.

CALLAGHAN, James: *A House Divided*, Collins, London, 1987.

CAMPBELL, Brian (ed): *Nor Meekly Serve My Time*, Beyond The Pale Publications, Belfast, 1994.

CHUBB, Basil: *The Politics of the Irish Constitution*, IPA, Dublin, 1991.

CLARK, Alan, *Diaries*, Weidenfeld & Nicolson, London, 1993.

COLLINS, Peter, ed.: *Nationalism & Unionism*, Queen's University, Belfast, 1994.

CONLON, Gerry: *Proved Innocent*, Penguin, 1993.

COOGAN, T. P.: *Ireland Since the Rising*, Pall Mall, London, 1966; *The Irish, A Personal View*, Phaidon, London, 1975; *On the Blanket*, Ward River, Dublin, 1980; *Disillusioned Decades*, Gill and Macmillan, Dublin, 1987; *Michael Collins*, Hutchinson, London; 1990, *De Valera*, Hutchinson, 1993; *The IRA*, Harper Collins, London, 1995.

CROTTY, Raymond: *Ireland in Crisis*, Brandon, Dingle, 1986.

CURRAN, James (ed.): *The British Press: a Manifesto*, Macmillan, London, 1978.

CURTIS, Liz: *Ireland: the Propaganda War*, Pluto, London, 1984.

DANGERFIELD, George: *The Damnable Question*, Constable, London, 1977.

DEVLIN, Bernadette: *The Price of My Soul*, André Deutsch, London, 1969.

DEVLIN, Paddy: *Yes We Have No Bananas*, 1981; *Straight Left*, 1993, both Blackstaff, Belfast.

DILLON, Martin: with Lehane, D.: *Political Murder in Northern Ireland*, Penguin, 1973; with Bradford, R.: *Rogue Warrior of the S.A.S*, Arrow, London, 1989; *The Shankill Butchers*, 1985; *The Dirty War*, 1991; *Stone Cold*, 1993; all Arrow, London; *The Enemy Within*, Transworld, London, 1995.

DUNNE, Derick, and Kerrigan, Gene: *Round Up the Usual Suspects*, Magill, Dublin, 1984.

EDWARDS, R. Dudley: *Ireland in the Age of the Tudors*, Croom Helm, 1977.

ELLIOTT, Marianne: *Partners in Revolution*, Yale University Press, New Haven and London, 1989.

FANNING, Ronan: *Independent Ireland*, Helicon, Dublin, 1983.

FARRELL, Michael: *The Orange State*, Pluto, London, 1992; *Arming the Protestants*, Brandon, Dingle, 1983; *Twenty Years On*, Brandon, 1988.

FAULKNER, Brian: *Memoirs of a Statesman*, Weidenfeld & Nicolson, London, 1978.

FENNELL, Desmond: *Beyond Nationality*, Ward River, Dublin, 1985.

FINLAY, Fergus: *Mary Robinson*, O'Brien, Dublin, 1990.

FISK, Robert: *The Point of No Return*, André Deutsch, London, 1975; *In Time of War*, Deutsch/Brandon, London, Tralee, 1985.

FITZGERALD, Garret: *All in a Life*, Gill and Macmillan, Dublin, 1989.

FITZPATRICK, David: *Revolution*, Trinity History Workshop, Dublin, 1990.

FOOT, Paul: *Who Framed Colin Wallace*, Pan, London, 1980.

GALLAGHER, Eric and Worrall, Stanley: *Christians in Ulster, 1969–80*, OUP, Oxford, 1980.

GRAY, Alan W.: *The Economic Consequences of Peace in Ireland*, Indecon, Dublin, 1995.

GREELEY, Andrew M.: *That Most Distressful Nation*, Quadrangle, Chicago, 1972.

HAMILL, Desmond: *Pig In The Middle: The Army in Northern Ireland, 1969–84*, Methuen, London, 1985.

HARKNESS, David: *Northern Ireland since 1920*, Helicon, Dublin, 1983.

HEZLET, Sir Arthur: *The B-Specials*, Tom Stacey, London, 1972.

HILL, Paul, with Bennett, Ronan: *Stolen Years*, Corgi, London, 1991.

HOLLAND, Jack: *The American Connection*, Poolbeg, Dublin, 1989; with Henry McDonald: *INLA, Deadly Divisions*, Torc, Dublin, 1994.

HOLROYD, Fred and Burbridge, N.: *War Without Honour*, Medium, Hull, 1989.

HOPKINSON, Michael: *Green Against Green: The Irish Civil War*, Gill and Macmillan, Dublin, 1988.

HUSSEY, Gemma: *Ireland Today*, Townhouse, Dublin, 1993.

INSIGHT Team, *Sunday Times*: *Ulster*, Penguin, London, 1972.

IRVINE, Maurice: *Northern Ireland, Faith and Faction*, Routledge, London, 1991.

JACKSON, T.A.: *Ireland Her Own*, Lawrence & Wishart, London, 1991.

JONES, Thomas: *Whitehall Diaries, Vol. III*, OUP, Oxford, 1971.

JOYCE, Joe and Murtagh Peter: *The Boss*, Poolbeg, Dublin, 1983.

KEE, Robert: *Ireland, a History*, Abacus, London, 1993.

KEENA, Colm: *Gerry Adams*, Mercier, Cork and Dublin, 1990.

KELLEY, K. J.: *The Longest War: Northern Ireland and the IRA*, Zed, London, 1988.

KELLY, Henry: *How Stormont Fell*, Gill and Macmillan, Dublin, 1972.

KELLY, James: *Orders for the Captain*, Kelly, Dublin, 1971.

KENNY, Shane: *Go Dance on Somebody Else's Grave*, Kildonore Press, Dublin, 1990.

KEOGH, Dermot and Haltzel, Michael H. (ed.) *Northern Ireland and the Politics of Reconciliation*, Cambridge University Press, London, 1993.

KITSON, Frank: *Gangs and Counter-gangs*, Barrie & Rockliff, London, 1960; *Low Intensity Operations*, Faber, London, 1971.

KOTSONOURIS, Mary: *Retreat from Revolution*, Irish Academic Press, Dublin, 1994.

LAFFAN, Michael: *The Partition of Ireland 1911–1925*, Dublin Historical Association, Dundalgan Press, 1987.

LAWSON, Nigel: *The View from No. 11*, London, Bantam, 1992.

LEE, Joseph: *Ireland, 1912–1985*, Cambridge University Press, 1990; *The Modernisation of Irish Society, 1848–1918*, Gill and Macmillan, Dublin, 1992.

LITTON, Helen: *The Irish Famine*, Wolfhound, Dublin, 1994.

LYONS, F. S. L.: *Ireland Since the Famine*, Charles Scribner's Sons, New York, 1972; Lyons and Hawkins, R. A. J. (ed.) *Ireland Under the Union*, Clarendon Press, Oxford, 1980.

MCCAFFREY, Lawrence, J.: *The Irish Diaspora in America*, Indiana University Press, Bloomington, 1976.

MCCANN, Eamonn: *War and an Irish Town*, Pluto, London, 1993.

MACDONAGH, Oliver: *Ireland, the Union and its aftermath*, George Allen & Unwin, London, 1977.

MCGARRY, John and O'Leary, Brendan: *Explaining Northern Ireland*, Blackwell, Oxford, 1995.

MACLOCHLAINN, Piaras: *Last Words*, Kilmainham Jail Restoration Society, Dublin, 1971.

447

MANSFIELD, Michael: *Presumed Guilty*, Heinemann, London, 1993.

MARRINAN, Patrick: *Paisley, Man of Wrath*, Anvil, Tralee, 1973.

MILLER, David: *Queen's Rebels*, Gill and Macmillan, Dublin, 1978.

MITCHELL, Arthur: *Revolutionary Government in Ireland*, Gill and Macmillan, Dublin, 1995.

MOLONEY, Ed and Pollack, Andy: *Paisley*, Poolbeg, Dublin, 1986.

MOODY, T. W.: *The Ulster Question, 1603–1973*, Mercier, Dublin and Cork, 1974.

MULLIN, Chris: *Error of Judgement: The Truth about the Birmingham Bombings*, Poolbeg, Dublin, 1980.

MURRAY, Raymond: *The SAS in Ireland*, Mercier, Dublin and Cork, 1990.

O'BRIEN, Brendan: *The Long War*, O'Brien Press, Dublin, 1993.

O'BRIEN, Conor and Maire: *Ireland, a Concise History*, Thames & Hudson, London, 1992.

O'BRIEN, Jack: *British Brutality in Ireland*, Mercier, Dublin, 1989.

O'BRIEN, John and Travers, Pauric (ed.): *The Irish Emigrant Experience in Australia*, Poolbeg, Dublin, 1991.

O'CLEARY, Conor: *Phrases Make History Here*, O'Brien, Dublin, 1987.

O'CONNELL, Michael: *Truth, the First Casualty*, Riverstone, Eire, 1993.

O'DAY, Alan (ed.): *A Survey of the Irish in England*, Hambledon Press, London and Roncervete, 1990.

O'FARRELL, Patrick: *England & Ireland Since 1800*, Oxford University Press, 1975.

O'LEARY, Brendan, with Lyne, Tom, Marshall, Jim and Rowthorn, Bob: *Northern Ireland, Sharing Authority*, Institute for Public Policy Research, London, 1993.

OLIVER, John A.: *Working at Stormont*, Institute of Public Administration, Dublin, 1978.

O'MALLEY, Padraig: *The Uncivil Wars*, Blackstaff, Belfast, 1983.

O'NEILL, Terence: *The Autobiography of Terence O'Neill*, Rupert Hart-Davis, London, 1972.

de PAOR, Liam: *Divided Ulster*, Pelican, London, 1977.

PARKER, Tony: *May the Lord in His Mercy be Kind to Belfast*, Cape, London, 1993.

PATTERSON, Henry: *The Politics of Illusion*, Hutchinson, London, 1989.

PHOENIX, Eamon: *Northern Nationalism*, Ulster Historical Foundation, Belfast, 1994.

POIRTEIR, Cathal (ed): *The Great Irish Famine*, RTE/Mercier, Cork and Dublin, 1995.

RAFTER, Kevin: *Neil Blaney, A Soldier of Destiny*, Blackwater Press, Dublin, 1993.

REES, Merlyn: *Northern Ireland, A Personal Perspective*, Methuen, London, 1985.

RICE, Charles: *Divided Ireland*, Tyholland Press, Notre Dame, Indiana.

ROSE, Richard: *Governing Without Consent*, Faber & Faber, London, 1971.

RYAN, Mark: *War & Peace in Ireland*, Pluto, London, 1994.

RYDER, Chris: *The RUC: A Force under Fire*, Octopus, London, 1990; *The Ulster Defence Regiment*, Mandarin, London, 1991.

SHANNON, William, V.: *The American Irish*, Collier Books, New York, 1974.

SHERMAN, Hugh: *Not an Inch*, Faber, London, 1962.

STALKER, John: *Stalker*, Harrap, London, 1988.

STEWART, A. T. Q.: *The Ulster Crisis*, Faber, London, 1967.

TAYLOR, Peter: *Beating the Terrorists*, Penguin, London, 1980.

URBAN, Mark: *Big Boys' Rules*, Faber, London, 1992.

WATT, David (ed): *The Constitution of Northern Ireland*, Heinemann, London, 1981.

WEITZER, Ronald: *Transforming Settler States*, University of California Press, 1990.

WHITE, Barry: *John Hume, Statesman of the Troubles*, Blackstaff, Belfast, 1984.

WHITELAW, William: *Memoirs*, Aurum, London, 1989.

WRIGHT, Peter: *Spycatcher*, Viking, London, 1987.
YOUNGER, Calton: *Ireland's Civil War*, Collins, London, 1979.

INDEX